Dictionary
French – English
English – French

Dictionnaire
Français – Anglais
Anglais – Français

D1022562

Berlitz Publishing
Union, NJ · Munich · Singapore

Contacting the Editors
Every effort has been made to provide accurate information in this publication, but changes are inevitable. The publisher cannot be responsible for any resulting loss, inconvenience or injury. We would appreciate it if readers would call our attention to any errors or outdated information by contacting Berlitz Publishing, 95 Progress Street, Union, NJ 07083, USA. Fax: 1-908-206-1103.
email: comments@berlitzbooks.com

Cover photo © ID Image Direkt CD-ROM GmbH, Germany

Printed in Singapore by Insight Print Services (Pte) Ltd. April 2005

Contents

Table des matières

Preface

In selecting the vocabulary and phrases for this dictionary, the editors have had the traveller's needs foremost in mind. This book will prove a useful companion to casual tourists and business travellers alike who appreciate the reassurance a small and practical dictionary can provide. It offers them—as well as beginners and students—all the basic vocabulary they will encounter and have to use, giving the key words and expressions to allow them to cope in everyday situations.

Like our successful phrase books and travel guides, these dictionaries—created with the help of a computer data bank—are designed to slip into your pocket or purse, and thus have a role as handy companions at all times.

Besides just about everything you normally find in dictionaries, there are these Berlitz bonuses:

- simplified pronunciation after each foreign-word entry, making it easy to read and enunciate words whose spelling may look forbidding

- a unique, practical glossary to simplify reading a foreign restaurant menu and to take the mystery out of complicated dishes and indecipherable names on bills of fare

- useful information on how to tell the time and how to count, on conjugating irregular verbs, commonly seen abbreviations and converting to the metric system, in addition to basic phrases.

While no dictionary of this size can pretend to completeness, we are confident this dictionary will help you get most out of your trip abroad.

Berlitz Publishing

Préface

En choisissant les mots et expressions de ce dictionnaire, nos rédacteurs se sont souciés des besoins essentiels de l'étudiant et du voyageur. Cet ouvrage s'avérera indispensable aux touristes, globe-trotters, hommes ou femmes d'affaires qui apprécient l'appoint qu'apporte un dictionnaire pratique et de format réduit. Il leur offre le vocabulaire qu'ils seront amenés à rencontrer et à utiliser; il leur propose des mots-clés et des expressions leur permettant de faire face aux situations de tous les jours.

A l'instar de nos manuels de conversation et de nos guides de voyage déjà fort appréciés, nos dictionnaires — réalisés grâce à une banque de données sur ordinateur — sont conçus pour se glisser dans une poche ou dans un sac, assumant ainsi leur rôle de compagnons à tout moment.

Ce dictionnaire présente:

- une transcription phonétique facilitant la prononciation de chaque entrée
- un lexique pratique visant à faciliter la lecture du menu dans un restaurant et révélant les mystères de plats jusqu'alors inconnus
- des informations précieuses sur la façon d'exprimer le temps, de compter, sur les verbes irréguliers, sur les abréviations courantes, en plus des expressions usuelles.

Aucun dictionnaire de ce format ne peut prétendre être exhaustif, mais le but principal de cet ouvrage est de permettre à son utilisateur d'affronter avec confiance un voyage à l'étranger.

Berlitz Publishing

French-English

Français-Anglais

Introduction

The dictionary has been designed to take account of your practical needs. Unnecessary linguistic information has been avoided. The entries are listed in alphabetical order, regardless of whether the entry word is printed in a single word, contains an apostrophe, or is in two or more separate words. When an entry is followed by sub-entries such as expressions and locutions, these, too, have been listed in alphabetical order.

Each main-entry word is followed by a phonetic transcription (see Guide to Pronunciation). Following the transcription is the part of speech of the entry word whenever applicable. When an entry word may be used as more than one part of speech, the translations are grouped together after the respective part of speech.

French feminine headwords are shown as follows:

campeur ... *m*, **-euse** *f* camper
descendant... *m*, **-e** *f* descendant
électeur ... *m*, **-trice** *f* voter
citoyen ... *m*, **-ne** *f*

The feminine forms of these headwords are: **campeuse** (pl ~s), **descendante** (pl ~s), **électrice** (pl ~s), **citoyenne** (pl ~s).

The feminine or plural forms of French adjectives have been supplied whenever they diverge from the standard rule for the word-ending in question. Similarly, the plural forms of nouns are given when not in accordance with the rules for the particular word-ending.

Whenever an entry word is repeated in irregular forms, or in subentries, a tilde (~) is used to represent the full entry word.

In irregular feminine and plural forms, a hyphen is used to represent the part of the main-entry word that precedes the relevant word-ending.

An asterisk (*) in front of a verb indicates that the verb is irregular. For details, refer to the lists of irregular verbs.

Abbreviations

adj	adjective	*num*	numeral
adv	adverb	*p*	past tense
Am	American	*pl*	plural
art	article	*plAm*	plural (American)
conj	conjunction	*pp*	past participle
f	feminine	*pr*	present tense
fpl	feminine plural	*pref*	prefix
m	masculine	*prep*	preposition
mpl	masculine plural	*pron*	pronoun
n	noun	*v*	verb
nAm	noun (American)	*vAm*	verb (American)

Guide to Pronunciation

Each main entry in this part of the dictionary is followed by a phonetic transcription which shows you how to pronounce the words. This transcription should be read as if it were English. It is based on Standard British pronunciation, though we have tried to take account of General American pronunciation also. Below, only those letters and symbols are explained which we consider likely to be ambiguous or not immediately understood.

The syllables are separated by hyphens, and stressed syllables are printed in *italics*.

Of course, the sounds of any two languages are never exactly the same, but if you follow carefully our indications, you should be able to pronounce the foreign words in such a way that you'll be understood. To make your task easier, our transcriptions occasionally simplify slightly the sound system of the language while still reflecting the essential sound differences.

Consonants

g	always hard, as in **g**o
ñ	as in Spanish se**ñ**or, or like **ni** in onion
r	pronounced in the back of the mouth
s	always hard, as in **s**o
zh	a soft, voiced **sh**, like **s** in pleasure

The sign (') indicates a so-called aspirate h. It means that no liaison (*les huttes*—lay 'ewt) nor elision (*la hutte*—lah 'ewt) should be made.

Vowels and Diphthongs

aa	long **a**, as in c**a**r
ah	a short version of **aa**; between **a** in c**a**t and **u** in c**u**t
ai	like **ai**r, without any **r**-sound
eh	like **e** in g**e**t
er	as in oth**er**, without any **r**-sound
ew	a "rounded **ee**-sound". Say the vowel sound **ee** (as in s**ee**), and while saying it, round your lips as for **oo** (as in s**oo**n), without moving your tongue; when your lips are in the **oo** position, but your tongue in

the **ee** position, you should be pronouncing the correct sound

igh   as in s**igh**

o   always as in h**o**t (British pronunciation)

ur   as in f**ur**, but with rounded lips and no **r**-sound

1) A bar over a vowel symbol (e.g. $\overline{ew}$) shows that this sound is long.
2) Raised letters (e.g. **oo**[ee], [y]**ur**) should be pronounced only fleetingly.
3) French contains nasal vowels, which we transcribe with a vowel symbol plus **ng** (e.g. **ahng**). This **ng** should *not* be pronounced, and serves solely to indicate nasal quality of the preceding vowel. A nasal vowel is pronounced simultaneously through the mouth and the nose.
4) French vowels (i.e. not diphthongs) are relatively short and pure. Therefore, you should try to read a transcription like **oa** without moving tongue or lips while pronouncing the sound.

à (ah) *prep* to; at, on

abandonner (ah-bahng-do-*nay*) *v* desert

abat-jour (ah-bah-*zhoor*) *m* lampshade

*abattre (ah-*bahtr*) *v* knock down; kill; dishearten

abbaye (ah-bay-*ee*) *f* abbey

abcès (ah-*psay*) *m* abscess

abeille (ah-*bay*) *f* bee

abîme (ah-*beem*) *m* abyss

abîmer (ah-bee-*may*) *v* *spoil

abolir (ah-bo-*leer*) *v* abolish

abondance (ah-bawng-*dahngss*) *f* abundance; plenty

abondant (ah-bawng-*dahng*) *adj* abundant; plentiful

abonné (ah-bo-*nay*) *m* subscriber

abonnement (ah-bon-*mahng*) *m* subscription

abord: d'abord (dah-*bawr*) at first

abordage (ah-bor-*daazh*) *m* collision

aboutir à (ah-boo-*teer*) end at; result in

aboyer (ah-bwah-^{y}*ay*) *v* bark, bay

abréviation (ah-bray-v^{y}ah-s^y*awng*) *f* abbreviation

abri (ah-*bree*) *m* shelter; cover

abricot (ah-bree-*koa*) *m* apricot

abriter (ah-bree-*tay*) *v* shelter

abrupt (ah-*brewpt*) *adj* steep

absence (ah-*psahngss*) *f* absence

absent (ah-*psahng*) *adj* absent

absolu (ah-pso-*lew*) *adj* total, sheer

absolument (ah-pso-lew-*mahng*) *adv* absolutely

absorber (ah-psor-*bay*) *v* absorb

*abstenir (ahp-ster-*neer*): **s'~ de** abstain from

abstraction faite de (ahp-strahk-s^y*awng* feht der) apart from

abstrait (ahp-*stray*) *adj* abstract

absurde (ah-*psewrd*) *adj* absurd; foolish

abus (ah-*bew*) *m* abuse, misuse

académie (ah-kah-day-*mee*) *f* academy; **~ des beaux-arts** art school

accélérateur (ahk-say-lay-rah-*türr*) *m* accelerator

accélérer (ahk-say-lay-*ray*) *v* accelerate

accent (ahk-*sahng*) *m* accent, stress

accepter (ahk-sehp-*tay*) *v* accept

accès (ahk-*say*) *m* access; approach, entrance, admittance

accessible (ahk-say-*seebl*) *adj* accessible; attainable

accessoire (ahk-say-*swaar*) *adj* additional

accessoires (ahk-say-*swaar*) *mpl* accessories *pl*

accident (ahk-see-*dahng*) *m* accident; **~ d'avion** plane crash

accidenté (ahk-see-dahng-*tay*) *adj* hilly; uneven

accidentel (ahk-see-dahng-*tehl*) *adj* accidental

acclamer (ah-klah-*may*) *v* cheer

accommodation (ah-ko-mo-dah-s^y*awng*) *f* accommodation

accompagner (ah-kawng-pah-*ñay*) *v* accompany

accomplir (ah-kawng-*pleer*) *v* accomplish; perform, achieve

accomplissement (ah-kawng-plee-*smahng*) *m* fulfilment, accomplishment

accord (ah-*kawr*) *m* settlement, agreement; approval; **d'accord!** all right!; okay!; ***être d'accord** agree; ***être d'accord avec** approve of

accorder (ah-kor-*day*) *v* grant; tune; **s'accorder avec** match

accoster (ah-ko-*stay*) *v* dock

accoucher (ah-koo-*shay*) *v* have a

baby, be delivered (of, **de**)

accouchement (ah-koosh-*mahng*) *m* childbirth, delivery

accoutumé (ah-koo-tew-*may*) *adj* accustomed

accrocher (ah-kro-shay): **s'~** *hold on

accueil (ah-*kurₑₑ*) *m* reception; welcome

***accueillir** (ah-kur-ʸeer) *v* welcome

accumulateur (ah-kew-mew-lah-*tūrr*) *m* battery

accumuler (ah-kew-mew-*lay*): **s'~** increase

accusation (ah-kew-zah-sʸ*awng*) *f* charge

accuser (ah-kew-*zay*) *v* accuse; charge

achat (ah-*shah*) *m* purchase; **~ à tempérament** hire purchase; ***faire des achats** shop

acheter (ahsh-*tay*) *v* *buy, purchase

acheteur (ahsh-*tūrr*) *m*, **-euse** *f* buyer, purchaser

achever (ahsh-*vay*) *v* finish; complete, accomplish

acide (ah-*seed*) *m* acid

acier (ah-sʸ*ay*) *m* steel; **~ inoxydable** stainless steel

acné (ahk-*nay*) *f* acne

acompte (ah-*kawngt*) *m* down payment; instal(l)ment

à-coup (ah-*koo*) *m* tug

***acquérir** (ah-kay-*reer*) *v* acquire; *buy

acquisition (ah-kee-zee-sʸ*awng*) *f* acquisition, purchase

acquittement (ah-keet-*mahng*) *m* acquittal

acte (ahkt) *m* act, deed

acteur (ahk-*tūrr*) *m* actor

actif (ahk-*teef*) *adj* active

action (ahk-sʸ*awng*) *f* action, deed; share; **actions** stocks and shares

activité (ahk-tee-vee-*tay*) *f* activity; work

actrice (ahk-*treess*) *f* actress

actualité (ahk-twah-lee-*tay*) *f* current events; **actualités** news; newsreel

actuel (ahk-*twehl*) *adj* present; topical

actuellement (ahk-twehl-*mahng*) *adv* nowadays

adapter (ah-dahp-*tay*) *v* adapt; **~ à** suit

addition (ah-dee-sʸ*awng*) *f* addition; bill

additionner (ah-dee-sʸo-*nay*) *v* add

adéquat (ah-day-*kwah*) *adj* adequate; appropriate, proper; sufficient

adhérer à (ah-day-*ray*) join

adieu (ah-*dʸur*) *m* parting

adjectif (ah-jehk-*teef*) *m* adjective

***admettre** (ahd-*mehtr*) *v* acknowledge, admit; **en admettant que** supposing that

administratif (ahd-mee-nee-strah-*teef*) *adj* administrative

administration (ahd-mee-nee-strah-sʸ*awng*) *f* administration

administrer (ahd-mee-nee-*stray*) *v* run; administer

admiration (ahd-mee-rah-sʸ*awng*) *f* admiration

admirer (ahd-mee-*ray*) *v* admire

admission (ahd-mee-sʸ*awng*) *f* admission; entry

adolescent (ah-do-leh-*sahng*) *m* teenager

adopter (ah-dop-*tay*) *v* adopt

adorable (ah-do-*rahbl*) *adj* adorable

adorer (ah-do-*ray*) *v* worship

adoucir (ah-doo-*seer*) *v* soften

adoucisseur d'eau (ah-doo-see-*sūrr* doa) water softener

adresse (ah-*drehss*) *f* address

adresser (ah-dray-*say*) *v* address; **s'adresser à** address

adroit (ah-*drwah*) *adj* skil(l)ful; smart

adulte (ah-*dewlt*) *m/f* adult, grown-up; *adj* adult, grown-up

adversaire (ahd-vehr-*sair*) *m/f* opponent

aération (ah-ay-rah-*s*^{y}*awng*) *f* ventilation

aérer (ah-ay-*ray*) *v* ventilate, air; **aéré** airy

aéroport (ah-ay-ro-*pawr*) *m* airport

affaire (ah-*fair*) *f* business, matter, case; affair, concern; deal; **~ de cœur** affair

affairé (ah-fay-*ray*) *adj* busy

affaires (ah-*fair*) *fpl* business; belongings *pl*; **chiffre d'affaires** turnover; ***faire des ~ avec** *deal with

affamé (ah-fah-*may*) *adj* hungry

affecter (ah-fehk-*tay*) *v* affect

affection (ah-fehk-*s*^{y}*awng*) *f* affection; ailment

affectueux (ah-fehk-*twur*) *adj* affectionate

affiche (ah-*feesh*) *f* placard, poster

affiler (ah-fee-*lay*) *v* sharpen

affilier (ah-fee-*l*^{y}*ay*): **s'~ à** join

affirmatif (ah-feer-mah-*teef*) *adj* affirmative

affirmer (ah-feer-*may*) *v* affirm; state

affliction (ah-fleek-*s*^{y}*awng*) *f* grief

affligé (ah-flee-*zhay*) *adj* sad

affluent (ah-flew-*ahng*) *m* tributary

affranchir (ah-frahng-*sheer*) *v* stamp

affreux (ah-*frur*) *adj* dreadful, frightful

affronter (ah-frawng-*tay*) *v* face

afin de (ah-*fang* der) to, in order to; **afin que** so that

Africain (ah-free-*kang*) *m* African

africain (ah-free-*kang*) *adj* African

Afrique (ah-*freek*) *f* Africa; **~ du Sud** South Africa

after-shave (ahf-terr-*shehv*) *m* aftershave lotion

agacer (ah-gah-*say*) *v* irritate, annoy

âge (aazh) *m* age

âgé (ah-*zhay*) *adj* aged, elderly; **le plus ~** eldest; **plus ~** elder

agence (ah-*zhahngss*) *f* agency

agenda (ah-zhang-*dah*) *m* diary

agenouiller: (ahzh-noo-^{y}*ay*): **s'~** *kneel

agent (ah-*zhahng*) *m* agent; **~ de police** policeman; **~ de voyages** travel agent; **~ immobilier** house agent

agir (ah-*zheer*) *v* act

agitation (ah-zhee-tah-*s*^{y}*awng*) *f* excitement, fuss; disturbance, unrest

agiter (ah-zhee-*tay*) *v* agitate; stir; **agité** restless

agneau (ah-*ñoa*) *m* lamb

agrafe (ah-*grahf*) *f* staple

agrandir (ah-grahng-*deer*) *v* extend; enlarge

agrandissement (ah-grahng-dee-*smahng*) *m* enlargement; extension

agréable (ah-gray-*ahbl*) *adj* pleasing, pleasant, agreeable; enjoyable

agréer (ah-gray-*ay*) *v* accept

agrément (ah-gray-*mahng*) *m* pleasure

agressif (ah-gray-*seef*) *adj* aggressive

agricole (ah-gree-*kol*) *adj* agricultural

agriculteur (ah-gree-kewl-*tūrr*) *m* farmer

agriculture (ah-gree-kewl-*tēwr*) *f* agriculture

aide (ehd) *f* help, assistance, aid; *m/f* helper

aider (ay-*day*) *v* help, aid

aigle (aigl) *m* eagle

aiglefin (ehgl-*fang*) *m* haddock

aigre (aigr) *adj* sour

aigu (ay-*gew*) *adj* (f -guë) acute; sharp; keen

aiguille (ay-*gwee*^{y}) *f* needle; spire; **travail à l'aiguille** needlework

aiguiser (ay-gee-*zay*) *v* sharpen

ail (igh) *m* (pl ails, aulx) garlic

aile (ehl) *f* wing

ailleurs (ah-^{y}*ūrr*) *adv* elsewhere; **d'ailleurs** moreover, besides

aimable (ay-*mahbl*) *adj* kind

aimer (ay-*may*) *v* like, *be fond of,

love; fancy; **aimé** beloved; **~ mieux** prefer

aine (ehn) *f* groin

aîné (ay-*nay*) *adj* elder

ainsi (an̄g-*see*) *adv* so, thus

air (air) *m* air; tune; ***avoir l'air** look

airbag (air-*bahg*) *m* airbag

airelle (ay-*rehl*) *f* blueberry

aisance (eh-*zahn̄gss*) *f* ease

aise (aiz) *f* leisure, ease

aisé (ay-*zay*) *adj* well-to-do

ajournement (ah-zhoor-ner-*mahn̄g*) *m* delay

ajourner (ah-zhoor-*nay*) *v* adjourn, *put off, postpone

ajouter (ah-zhoo-*tay*) *v* add

ajuster (ah-zhew-*stay*) *v* adjust

alarmer (ah-lahr-*may*) *v* alarm

album (ahl-*bom*) *m* album; **~ de collage** scrapbook

alcool (ahl-*kol*) *m* alcohol; **réchaud à ~** spirit stove

alcoolique (ahl-ko-*leek*) *adj* alcoholic

alentours (ah-lahn̄g-*tōōr*) *mpl* surroundings *pl*; vicinity

alerte (ah-*lehrt*) *f* alarm; *adj* smart

Algérie (ahl-zhay-*ree*) *f* Algeria

Algérien (ahl-zhay-*ryan̄g*) *m* Algerian

algérien (ahl-zhay-*ryan̄g*) *adj* Algerian

algue (ahlg) *f* alga; seaweed

alimentation (ah-lee-mahn̄g-tah-*syawn̄g*) *f* nourishment

alimenter (ah-lee-mahn̄g-*tay*) *v* *feed

aliments (ah-lee-*mahn̄g*) *mpl* foodstuffs *pl*; **~ surgelés** frozen food

allaiter (ah-lay-*tay*) *v* nurse

allée (ah-*lay*) *f* avenue

Allemagne (ahl-*mahñ*) *f* Germany

Allemand (ahl-*mahn̄g*) *m*, **-e** *f* German

allemand (ahl-*mahn̄g*) *adj* German

*aller (ah-*lay*) *v* *go; **~ chercher** collect, pick up; **aller et retour** round trip *Am*; **~ prendre** *get; **bien ~** suit; **s'en ~** *go away; depart

allergie (ah-lehr-*zhee*) *f* allergy

alliance (ah-*lyahn̄gss*) *f* alliance; wedding ring

allié (ah-*lyay*) *m* associate; **Alliés** Allies *pl*

allier (ah-*lyay*): **s'~** ally

allocation (ah-lo-kah-*syawn̄g*) *f* allowance

allocution (ah-lo-kew-*syawn̄g*) *f* speech

allonger (ah-lawn̄g-*zhay*) *v* lengthen; dilute

allumage (ah-lew-*maazh*) *m* ignition

allumer (ah-lew-*may*) *v* *light; switch on, turn on

allumette (ah-lew-*meht*) *f* match

allure (ah-*lēwr*) *f* pace

alors (ah-*lawr*) *adv* then

alouette (ah-*lweht*) *f* lark

alphabet (ahl-fah-*bay*) *m* alphabet

alpinisme (ahl-pee-*neezm*) *m* mountaineering

alternatif (ahl-tehr-nah-*teef*) *adj* alternate

alternative (ahl-tehr-nah-*teev*) *f* alternative

altitude (ahl-tee-*tewd*) *f* altitude

aluminium (ah-lew-mee-*nyom*) *m* aluminium

amande (ah-*mahn̄gd*) *f* almond

amant (ah-*mahn̄g*) *m*, **-e** *f* lover

amateur (ah-mah-*tūūr*) *m* amateur

ambassade (ahn̄g-bah-*sahd*) *f* embassy

ambassadeur (ahn̄g-bah-sah-*dūūr*) *m*, **-drice** *f* ambassador

ambiance (ahn̄g-*byahn̄gss*) *f* atmosphere

ambigu (ahn̄g-bee-*gew*) *adj* (f -guë) ambiguous

ambitieux (ahn̄g-bee-*syur*) *adj* ambitious

ambre (ahn̄gbr) *m* amber

ambulance (ahn̄g-bew-*lahn̄gss*) *f*

ambulance

âme (aam) *f* soul

amélioration (ah-may-l^{y}o-rah-s^{y}aw$\overline{ng}$) *f* improvement

améliorer (ah-may-l^{y}o-ray) *v* improve

amende (ah-mah$\overline{ng}$d) *f* fine, penalty

amener (ahm-nay) *v* *bring; lower, *strike

amer (ah-mair) *adj* bitter

Américain (ah-may-ree-ka$\overline{ng}$) *m* American

américain (ah-may-ree-ka$\overline{ng}$) *adj* American

Amérique (ah-may-reek) *f* America; ~ **latine** Latin America

ami (ah-mee) *m* friend

amiante (ah-m^{y}ah$\overline{ng}$t) *m* asbestos

amical (ah-mee-kahl) *adj* friendly

amie (ah-mee) *f* friend

amitié (ah-mee-t^{y}ay) *f* friendship

ammoniaque (ah-mo-n^{y}ahk) *f* ammonia

amnistie (ahm-nee-stee) *f* amnesty

amoncellement (ah-maw$\overline{ng}$-sehl-mah$\overline{ng}$) *m* heap

amont: en ~ (ah$\overline{ng}$-nah-maw$\overline{ng}$) upstream

amorce (ah-mors) *f* bait

amortir (ah-mor-teer) *v* *pay off

amortisseur (ah-mor-tee-surr) *m* shock absorber

amour (ah-moor) *m* love; **mon** ~ sweetheart

amoureux (ah-moo-rur) *adj* in love

ample (ah$\overline{ng}$pl) *adj* detailed; full

ampoule (ah$\overline{ng}$-pool) *f* blister; light bulb; ~ **de flash** flash bulb

amulette (ah-mew-leht) *f* charm

amusant (ah-mew-zah$\overline{ng}$) *adj* funny, entertaining

amuse-gueule (ah-mewz-gurl) *m* appetizer

amusement (ah-mewz-mah$\overline{ng}$) *m* entertainment, amusement

amuser (ah-mew-zay) *v* entertain, amuse

amygdales (ah-mee-dahl) *fpl* tonsils *pl*

amygdalite (ah-mee-dah-leet) *f* tonsillitis

an (ah$\overline{ng}$) *m* year; **par** ~ per annum

analogue (ah-nah-log) *adj* similar

analyse (ah-nah-leez) *f* analysis

analyser (ah-nah-lee-zay) *v* analyse; *break down

analyste (ah-nah-leest) *m* analyst

ananas (ah-nah-nah) *m* pineapple

anarchie (ah-nahr-shee) *f* anarchy

anatomie (ah-nah-to-mee) *f* anatomy

ancêtre (ah$\overline{ng}$-saitr) *m* ancestor

anchois (ah$\overline{ng}$-shwah) *m* anchovy

ancien (ah$\overline{ng}$-s^{y}a$\overline{ng}$) *adj* ancient; former

ancre (ah$\overline{ng}$kr) *f* anchor

âne (aan) *m* donkey

anéantissement (ah-nay-ah$\overline{ng}$-tee-smah$\overline{ng}$) *m* destruction

anémie (ah-nay-mee) *f* anaemia

anesthésie (ah-neh-stay-zee) *f* anaesthesia

anesthésique (ah-neh-stay-zeek) *m* anaesthetic

ange (ah$\overline{ng}$zh) *m* angel

Anglais (ah$\overline{ng}$-glay) *m* Englishman; **les** ~ the English

anglais (ah$\overline{ng}$-glay) *adj* English

Anglaise (ah$\overline{ng}$-glays) *f* Englishwoman

angle (ah$\overline{ng}$gl) *m* angle

Angleterre (ah$\overline{ng}$-gler-tair) *f* England; Britain

angoisse (ah$\overline{ng}$-gwahss) *f* anguish

anguille (ah$\overline{ng}$-geey) *f* eel

animal (ah-nee-mahl) *m* animal; ~ **familier** pet

animateur (ah-nee-mah-tūrr) *m*, **-trice** *f* entertainer

animer (ah-nee-may) *v* enliven; **animé** busy, active, crowded

anneau (ah-*noa*) *m* ring

année (ah-*nay*) *f* year; **~ bissextile** leap year

annexe (ah-*nehks*) *f* annex

annexer (ah-nehk-*say*) *v* annex

anniversaire (ah-nee-vehr-*sair*) *m* anniversary, birthday; jubilee

annonce (ah-*nawngss*) *f* announcement; advertisement; **~ publicitaire** commercial

annoncer (ah-nawng-*say*) *v* announce

annuaire (ah-*nwair*) *m* annual; **~ téléphonique** telephone directory; telephone book *Am*

annuel (ah-*nwehl*) *adj* yearly, annual

annulation (ah-new-lah-*s*ʸ*awng*) *f* cancellation

annuler (ah-new-*lay*) *v* cancel

anonyme (ah-no-*neem*) *adj* anonymous

anorak (ah-no-*rahk*) *m* anorak

antenne (ahng-*tehn*) *f* aerial

antérieur (ahng-tay-r*ʸ*ūʳrr) *adj* prior, previous

antérieurement (ahng-tay-rʸurr-*mahng*) *adv* formerly

antialcoolique (ahng-tee-ahl-ko-*leek*) *m* teetotaller

antibiotique (ahng-tee-bʸo-*teek*) *m* antibiotic

anticiper (ahng-tee-see-*pay*) *v* anticipate

antigel (ahng-tee-*zhehl*) *m* antifreeze

antipathie (ahng-tee-pah-*tee*) *f* dislike, antipathy

antipathique (ahng-tee-pah-*teek*) *adj* nasty; unpleasant

antiquaire (ahng-tee-*kair*) *m/f* antique dealer

antique (ahng-*teek*) *adj* antique, ancient

antiquité (ahng-tee-kee-*tay*) *f* antique; **Antiquité** antiquity; **antiquités** antiquities *pl*

anxiété (ahng-ksʸay-*tay*) *f* anxiety

août (oo) August

***apercevoir** (ah-pehr-ser-*vwaar*) *v* perceive

aperçu (ah-pehr-*sew*) *m* glimpse

apéritif (ah-pay-ree-*teef*) *m* drink, aperitif

apeuré (ah-pur-*ray*) *adj* afraid

apogée (ah-po-*zhay*) *m* height, zenith; peak

***apparaître** (ah-pah-*raitr*) *v* appear

appareil (ah-pah-*ray*) *m* appliance, apparatus, machine; aircraft; **~ à jetons** slot machine; **~ de chauffage** heater; **~ photographique** camera

apparemment (ah-pah-rah-*mahng*) *adv* apparently

apparence (ah-pah-*rahngss*) *f* appearance; semblance; look

apparent (ah-pah-*rahng*) *adj* apparent

apparenté (ah-pah-rahng-*tay*) *adj* related

appartement (ah-pahr-ter-*mahng*) *m* flat; apartment *Am*, suite

***appartenir** (ah-pahr-ter-*neer*) *v* belong

appel (ah-*pehl*) *m* call, cry; appeal; **~ interurbain** trunk-call; **~ téléphonique** telephone call

appeler (ah-*play*) *v* call, cry; **s'appeler** *be called

appendice (ah-pang-*deess*) *m* appendix

appendicite (ah-pang-dee-*seet*) *f* appendicitis

appétissant (ah-pay-tee-*sahng*) *adj* appetizing

appétit (ah-pay-*tee*) *m* appetite

applaudir (ah-ploa-*deer*) *v* clap

applaudissements (ah-ploa-dee-*smahng*) *mpl* applause

application (ah-plee-kah-*s*ʸ*awng*) *f* application; diligence

appliquer (ah-plee-*kay*) *v* apply;

s'appliquer à apply

apporter (ah-por-*tay*) *v* *bring; fetch

appréciation (ah-pray-s^y ah-s^y *awng*) *f* appreciation

apprécier (ah-pray-s^y *ay*) *v* appreciate; judge

*apprendre (ah-*prahngdr*) *v* *learn; *teach; ~ **par cœur** memorize

apprenti (ah-prahn-*tee*) *m*, **-e** *f* apprentice

apprivoiser (ah-pree-vwah-*zay*) *v* tame; **apprivoisé** tame

approbation (ah-pro-bah-s^y *awng*) *f* approval

approche (ah-*prosh*) *f* approach

approcher (ah-pro-*shay*) *v* approach

approprié (ah-pro-pree-*ay*) *adj* appropriate, adequate, convenient; proper, suitable

approuver (ah-proo-*vay*) *v* approve; consent

approvisionner en (ah-pro-vee-z^y o-*nay*) furnish with

approximatif (ah-prok-see-mah-*teef*) *adj* approximate

approximativement (ah-prok-see-mah-teev-*mahng*) *adv* approximately

appuyer (ah-pwee-^y *ay*) *v* press; **s'appuyer** *lean

âpre (aapr) *adj* harsh

après (ah-*pray*) *adv* afterwards; *prep* after; ~ **que** after; **d'après** according to

après-demain (ah-pray-der-*mang*) *adv* the day after tomorrow

après-midi (ah-pray-mee-*dee*) *m/f* afternoon

apte (ahpt) *adj* apt

aptitude (ahp-tee-*tewd*) *f* faculty

aquarelle (ah-kwah-*rehl*) *f* watercolo(u)r

Arabe (ah-*rahb*) *m* Arab

arabe (ah-*rahb*) *adj* Arab

Arabie Séoudite (ah-rah-bee say-oo-*deet*) Saudi Arabia

araignée (ah-ray-*ñay*) *f* spider; **toile d'araignée** spider's web

arbitraire (ahr-bee-*trair*) *adj* arbitrary

arbitre (ahr-*beetr*) *m* umpire

arbre (ahrbr) *m* tree

arbuste (ahr-*bewst*) *m* shrub

arc (ahrk) *m* bow

arcade (ahr-*kahd*) *f* arcade

arc-en-ciel (ahr-kahng-s^y *ehl*) *m* rainbow

arche (ahrsh) *f* arch

archéologie (ahr-kay-o-lo-*zhee*) *f* arch(a)eology

archéologue (ahr-kay-o-*log*) *m/f* arch(a)eologist

archevêque (ahr-sher-*vehk*) *m* archbishop

architecte (ahr-shee-*tehkt*) *m* architect

architecture (ahr-shee-tehk-*tewr*) *f* architecture

archives (ahr-*sheev*) *fpl* archives *pl*

ardoise (ahr-*dwaaz*) *f* slate

arène (ah-*rehn*) *f* bullring

arête (ah-*reht*) *f* ridge; fishbone, bone

argent (ahr-*zhahng*) *m* silver; money; ~ **comptant** cash; ~ **liquide** cash; **en** ~ silver

argenterie (ahr-zhahng-*tree*) *f* silverware

argentin (ahr-zhahng-*tang*) *adj* Argentinian

Argentine (ahr-zhahng-*teen*) *f* Argentina

argile (ahr-*zheel*) *f* clay

argument (ahr-gew-*mahng*) *m* argument

argumenter (ahr-gew-mahng-*tay*) *v* argue

armateur (ahr-mah-*turr*) *m* shipowner

arme (ahrm) *f* weapon, arm

armée (ahr-*may*) *f* army

armer (ahr-*may*) *v* arm

armoire (ahr-*mwaar*) *f* cupboard

armure (ahr-*mewr*) *f* arm(o)ur

arôme (ah-*roam*) *m* aroma

arqué (ahr-*kay*) *adj* arched

arracher (ah-rah-*shay*) *v* extract

arrangement (ah-rahngzh-*mahng*) *m* settlement

arranger (ah-rahng-*zhay*) *v* arrange; settle

arrestation (ah-reh-stah-s^y*awng*) *f* arrest

arrêt (ah-*reh*) *m* stop

arrêter (ah-ray-*tay*) *v* stop; arrest; **s'arrêter** halt; pull up

arriéré (ah-r^yay-*ray*) *adj* overdue

arrière (ah-r^y*air*) *m* rear; **en ~** backwards, back; behind

arrivée (ah-ree-*vay*) *f* coming, arrival

arriver (ah-ree-*vay*) *v* arrive; happen

arrondi (ah-rawng-*dee*) *adj* rounded

arrondissement (ah-rawng-dee-*smahng*) *m* district

art (aar) *m* art; **arts et métiers** arts and crafts

artère (ahr-*tair*) *f* artery; thoroughfare

artichaut (ahr-t^yah-*shoa*) *m* artichoke

article (ahr-*teekl*) *m* article; item; **articles d'épicerie** groceries *pl*; **articles de toilette** toiletry

articulation (ahr-tee-kew-lah-s^y*awng*) *f* joint

artificiel (ahr-tee-fee-s^y*ehl*) *adj* artificial

artisan (ahr-tee-*zahng*) *m* craftsman

artisanat (ahr-tee-zah-*nah*) *m* handicraft

artiste (ahr-*teest*) *m/f* artist

artistique (ahr-tee-*steek*) *adj* artistic

ascenseur (ah-sahng-*surr*) *m* lift; elevator *Am*

ascension (ah-sahng-s^y*awng*) *f* climb; ***faire l'ascension de** ascend

Asiatique (ah-z^yah-*teek*) *m* Asian

asiatique (ah-z^yah-*teek*) *adj* Asian

Asie (ah-*zee*) *f* Asia

asile (ah-*zeel*) *m* asylum

aspect (ah-*spay*) *m* aspect; appearance, look

asperge (ah-*spehrzh*) *f* asparagus

asphalte (ah-*sfahlt*) *m* asphalt

aspirateur (ah-spee-rah-*turr*) *m* vacuum cleaner; **passer l'aspirateur** hoover; vacuum *Am*

aspirer (ah-spee-*ray*) *v* aspire; **~ à** pursue, aim at

aspirine (ah-spee-*reen*) *f* aspirin

assaisonner (ah-say-zo-*nay*) *v* flavour

assassinat (ah-sah-see-*nah*) *m* assassination, murder

assassiner (ah-sah-see-*nay*) *v* murder

assécher (ah-say-*shay*) *v* drain

assemblée (ah-sahng-*blay*) *f* assembly, meeting

assembler (ah-sahng-*blay*) *v* assemble; join

assentiment (ah-sahng-tee-*mahng*) *m* consent

*asseoir (ah-*swaar*) *v*: **s'~** *sit down

assez (ah-*say*) *adv* enough; fairly, pretty, rather, quite

assidu (ah-see-*dew*) *adj* diligent

assiette (ah-s^y*eht*) *f* plate, dish

assigner (ah-see-*ñay*) *v* allot; **~ à** assign to

assistance (ah-see-stahngss) *f* assistance; attendance

assistant (ah-see-*stahng*) *m* assistant

assister (ah-see-*stay*) *v* assist, aid; **~ à** attend, assist at

association (ah-so-s^yah-s^y*awng*) *f* society, club, association

associé (ah-so-s^y*ay*) *m*, **-e** *f* associate, partner

associer (ah-so-s^y*ay*) *v* associate

assoiffé (ah-swah-*fay*) *adj* thirsty

assortiment (ah-sor-tee-*mahng*) *m* assortment

assurance (ah-sew-*rahngss*) *f* insurance; **assurance-vie** *f* life insurance; **assurance-voyages** f travel insurance

assurer (ah-sew-*ray*) v insure, assure; **s'assurer de** ascertain; secure

asthme (ahsm) m asthma

astronomie (ah-stro-no-*mee*) f astronomy

astucieux (ah-stew-s*ʸur*) adj clever

atelier (ah-ter-*l ʸay*) m workshop

athlète (ah-*tleht*) m/f athlete

athlétisme (ah-tlay-*teezm*) m athletics pl

Atlantique (aht-lah*n̄g*-*teek*) adj, n Atlantic

atmosphère (aht-mo-*sfair*) f atmosphere

atomique (ah-to-*meek*) adj atomic

atroce (ah-*tross*) adj horrible

attacher (ah-tah-*shay*) v fasten, attach; tie; **attaché à** attached to

attaque (ah-*tahk*) f fit, attack; hold-up; stroke

attaquer (ah-tah-*kay*) v attack, assault

***atteindre** (ah-*tan̄gdr*) v attain, reach

attendre (ah-*tan̄gdr*) v wait; expect, await; **en attendant** in the meantime

attente (ah-*tan̄gt*) f waiting; expectation

attentif (ah-tah*n̄g*-*teef*) adj attentive, careful

attention (ah-tah*n̄g*-s*ʸawn̄g*) f attention, consideration; notice; ***faire ~** *pay attention, look out; beware; ***faire ~ à** attend to, mind; **prêter ~ à** mind

atterrir (ah-tay-*reer*) v land

attestation (ah-teh-stah-s*ʸawn̄g*) f certificate

attirer (ah-tee-*ray*) v attract

attitude (ah-tee-*tewd*) f attitude; position

attouchement (ah-toosh-*mahn̄g*) m touch

attraction (ah-trahk-s*ʸawn̄g*) f attraction

attrait (ah-*tray*) m attraction; **attraits** charm

attraper (ah-trah-*pay*) v *catch; contract

attribuer à (ah-tree-*bway*) assign to

aube (ōab) f dawn

auberge (oa-*behrzh*) f inn, hostel; roadhouse; roadside restaurant; **~ de jeunesse** youth hostel

aubergine (oa-behr-*zheen*) f eggplant

aucun (oa-*kurn̄g*) adj no; pron none

audace (oa-*dahss*) f nerve

audacieux (oa-dah-s*ʸur*) adj bold

au-dessous (oa-der-*soo*) adv beneath; **~ de** below

au-dessus (oa-der-*sew*) adv over; **~ de** above; over

audible (oa-*deebl*) adj audible

auditeur (oa-dee-*türr*) m, **auditrice** f auditor, listener

augmentation (oag-mahn̄g-tah-s*ʸawn̄g*) f increase, rise; **~ de salaire** rise; raise Am

augmenter (oag-mahn̄g-*tay*) v increase

aujourd'hui (oa-zhoor-*dwee*) adv today

auparavant (oa-pah-rah-*vahn̄g*) adv formerly

auprès de (oa-*pray* der) near

auriculaire (oa-ree-kew-*lair*) m little finger

aurore (oa-*rawr*) f dawn

aussi (oa-*see*) adv too, also; as; **~ bien** as well; **~ bien que** as well as; both … and

aussitôt (oa-see-*toa*) adv at once; **~ que** as soon as

Australie (oa-strah-*lee*) f Australia

australien (oa-strah-*l ʸan̄g*) adj Australian

autant (oa-*tahn̄g*) adv as much

autel (oa-*tehl*) m altar

auteur (oa-*turr*) *m* author

authentique (oa-tahng-*teek*) *adj* authentic, original, genuine

auto (oa-*toa*) *f* automobile

autobus (oa-toa-*bewss*) *m* bus

autocar (oa-toa-*kaar*) *m* coach

auto-école (oa-toa-ay-*kol*) *f* driving school

automatique (oa-toa-mah-*teek*) *adj* automatic

automatisation (oa-toa-mah-tee-zah-*s^yawng*) *f* automation

automne (oa-*ton*) *m* autumn; fall *Am*

automobile (oa-toa-mo-*beel*) *f* motorcar

automobiliste (oa-toa-mo-bee-*leest*) *m/f* motorist

autonome (oa-toa-*nom*) *adj* autonomous; independent

autonomie (oa-to-no-*mee*) *f* self-government

autoradio (oa-toa-rah-*d^yoa*) *m* car radio

autorisation (oa-to-ree-zah-*s^yawng*) *f* authorization; permission

autoriser (oa-to-ree-*zay*) *v* allow; license; ~ **à** allow to

autoritaire (oa-to-ree-*tair*) *adj* authoritarian

autorité (oa-to-ree-*tay*) *f* authority

autoroute (oa-toa-*root*) *f* motorway; highway *Am*

auto-stop (oa-toa-*stop*): *****faire de l'auto-stop** hitchhike

auto-stoppeur (oa-toa-sto-*purr*) *m*, **-euse** *f* hitchhiker

autour (oa-*toor*) *adv* about; around; ~ **de** around, about; round

autre (oatr) *adj* other; different; **entre autres** among other things

autrefois (oa-trer-*fwah*) *adv* formerly

autrement (oa-trer-*mahng*) *adv* otherwise, else

Autriche (oa-*treesh*) *f* Austria

Autrichien (oa-tree-*sh^yang*) *m* Austrian

autrichien (oa-tree-*sh^yang*) *adj* Austrian

autruche (oa-*trewsh*) *f* ostrich

aval: en ~ (ahng-nah-*vahl*) downstream

avalanche (ah-vah-*lahngsh*) *f* avalanche

avaler (ah-vah-*lay*) *v* swallow

avance (ah-*vahngss*) *f* lead; advance; **à l'avance** in advance; **d'avance** before; in advance

avancement (ah-vahng-*smahng*) *m* advance

avancer (ah-vahng-*say*) *v* advance

avant (ah-*vahng*) *prep* before; *adv* before; ~ **que** before; **en ~** forward; ahead, onwards

avantage (ah-vahng-*taazh*) *m* profit, advantage, benefit

avantageux (ah-vahng-tah-*zhur*) *adj* advantageous; cheap

avant-dernier (ah-vahng-dehr-*n^yay*) *adj* last but one

avant-hier (ah-vahng-*t^yair*) *adv* the day before yesterday

avant-saison (ah-vahng-seh-*zawng*) *f* off-peak season

avec (ah-*vehk*) *prep* with

avenir (ah-*vneer*) *m* future

aventure (ah-vahng-*tewr*) *f* adventure

avenue (ah-*vnew*) *f* avenue

averse (ah-*vehrs*) *f* shower; downpour

aversion (ah-vehr-*s^yawng*) *f* aversion, dislike

avertir (ah-vehr-*teer*) *v* warn, caution; notify

avertissement (ah-vehr-tee-*smahng*) *m* warning

aveugle (ah-*vurgl*) *adj* blind

aveugler (ah-vur-*glay*) *v* blind

aviation (ah-v^yah-*s^yawng*) *f* aviation

avion (ah-v^y*awng*) *m* aeroplane; plane,

aircraft; airplane *Am*; ~ **à réaction** jet
avis (ah-*vee*) *m* advice; notice
avocat (ah-vo-*kah*) *m* solicitor, attorney, lawyer, barrister
avoine (ah-*vwahn*) *f* oats *pl*
***avoir** (ah-*vwaar*) *v* *have
avoisinant (ah-vwah-zee-*nahng*) *adj*

neighbo(u)ring
avortement (ah-vort-*mahng*) *m* abortion
avoué (ah-voo-*ay*) *m* solicitor
avouer (ah-voo-*ay*) *v* admit
avril (ah-*vreel*) April

B

babeurre (bah-*burr*) *m* buttermilk
bâbord (bah-*bawr*) *m* port
bac (bahk), **baccalauréat** (bah-kah-loa-ray-*ah*) *m* school-leaving certificate
bactérie (bahk-tay-*ree*) *f* bacterium
bagage (bah-*gaazh*) *m* baggage; luggage; ~ **à main** hand luggage; hand baggage *Am*
bague (bahg) *f* ring; ~ **de fiançailles** engagement ring
baguette (bah-geht) *f* stick, rod; stick of bread; baton; ~ **magique** magic wand
baie (bay) *f* berry; bay, creek
baigner (bay-*ñay*)*v*: **se** ~ bathe
baignoire (bay-*ñwaar*) *f* bath (tub); groundfloor box
bail (bigh) *m* (pl baux) lease
bâiller (bah-*yay*) *v* yawn
bain (bang) *m* bath; ~ **turc** Turkish bath; **bonnet de** ~ bathing cap; **caleçon de** ~ bathing trunks
baiser (bay-*zay*) *m* kiss
baisse (behss) *f* drop, decline
baisser (bay-*say*) *v* lower
bal (bahl) *m* (pl ~s) ball
balai (bah-*lay*) *m* broom
balance (bah-*lahngss*) *f* scales *pl*
balancer (bah-lahng-*say*) *v* *swing; rock

balançoire (bah-lahng-*swaar*) *f* swing; seesaw
balayer (bah-lay-*yay*) *v* *sweep
balbutier (bahl-bew-*s*^y*ay*) *v* falter
balcon (bahl-*kawng*) *m* balcony; circle
baleine (bah-*lehn*) *f* whale
balle (bahl) *f* ball; bullet
ballet (bah-*lay*) *m* ballet
ballon (bah-*lawng*) *m* football, ball; balloon
balustrade (bah-lew-*strahd*) *f* rail
bambin (bahng-*bang*) *m* tot, toddler
bambou (bahng-*boo*) *m* bamboo
banane (bah-*nahn*) *f* banana
banc (bahng) *m* bench; ~ **d'école** desk
bande (bahngd) *f* bunch, gang; tape, strip; **bandes dessinées** comics *pl*
bandit (bahng-*dee*) *m* bandit
banlieue (bahng-l^y*ur*) *f* suburb
bannière (bah-n^y*air*) *f* banner
banque (bahngk) *f* bank
banquet (bahng-*kay*) *m* banquet
baptême (bah-*tehm*) *m* christening, baptism
baptiser (bah-tee-*zay*) *v* christen, baptize
bar (baar) *m* bar
baratiner (bah-rah-tee-*nay*) *v* talk rubbish
barbe (bahrb) *f* beard
baril (bah-*ree*) *m* cask, barrel

bariton (bah-ree-*tawng*) *m* baritone

barman (bahr-*mahn*) *m* barman; bartender

baromètre (bah-ro-*mehtr*) *m* barometer

baroque (bah-*rok*) *adj* baroque

barque (bahrk) *f* boat

barrage (bah-*raazh*) *m* dam

barre (baar) *f* rod, bar, rail; helm; counter

barreau (bah-*roa*) *m* bar

barrière (bah-*r*^y*air*) *f* barrier; fence

bas[1] (bah) *adj* (f ~se) low; **en ~** down; downstairs; **en ~ de** under, below; **vers le ~** downwards, down

bas[2] (bah) *m* stocking; **~ élastiques** support hose

bas-côté (bah-koa-*tay*) *m* aisle

bascule (bah-*skewl*) *f* weighing machine

base (bahz) *f* basis, base

baser (bah-*zay*) *v* base

basilique (bah-zee-*leek*) *f* basilica

baskets (bah-*skeht*) *mpl* tennis shoes, plimsolls *pl*

basse (bahss) *f* bass

bassin (bah-*sang*) *m* pelvis, basin

bataille (bah-*tigh*) *f* battle

bateau (bah-*toa*) *m* boat; **~ à moteur** motor boat; **~ à rames** rowing boat; **~ à vapeur** steamer; **~ à voiles** sailing boat; **bateau-citerne** *m* tanker

bâtiment (bah-tee-*mahng*) *m* building; building trade

bâtir (bah-*teer*) *v* *build; construct

bâton (bah-*tawng*) *m* stick; **bâtons de ski** ski sticks; ski poles *Am*

*battre (bahtr) *v* slap; *beat; shuffle; **se ~** *fight

bavard (bah-*vaar*) *adj* talkative

bavardage (bah-vahr-*daazh*) *m* chat

bavarder (bah-vahr-*day*) *v* chat

beau (boa) *adj* (bel; f belle) beautiful; fair, pretty, lovely, handsome

beaucoup (boa-*koo*) *adv* much; far; **~ de** much; many; **de ~** by far

beau-fils (boa-*feess*) *m* son-in-law

beau-frère (boa-*frair*) *m* brother-in-law

beau-père (boa-*pair*) *m* father-in-law; stepfather

beauté (boa-*tay*) *f* beauty; **produits de ~** cosmetics *pl*

beaux-arts (boa-*zaar*) *mpl* fine arts

beaux-parents (boa-pah-*rahng*) *mpl* parents-in-law

bébé (bay-*bay*) *m* baby

bec (behk) *m* beak; nozzle

bêche (behsh) *f* spade

beige (baizh) *adj* beige

beignet (bay-*ñay*) *m* doughnut

Belge (behlzh) *m* Belgian

belge (behlzh) *adj* Belgian

Belgique (behl-*zheek*) *f* Belgium

belle-fille (behl-*feey*) *f* daughter-in-law

belle-mère (behl-*mair*) *f* mother-in-law; stepmother

belle-sœur (behl-*surr*) *f* sister-in-law

bénédiction (bay-nay-deek-s^y*awng*) *f* blessing

bénéfice (bay-nay-*feess*) *m* profit, benefit

bénéficiaire (bay-nay-fee-s^y*air*) *m/f* payee

bénéficier de (bay-nay-fee-s^y*ay*) profit by

bénir (bay-*neer*) *v* bless

béquille (bay-*keey*) *f* crutch

berceau (behr-*soa*) *m* cradle; **~ de voyage** carrycot

béret (bay-*ray*) *m* beret

berge (behrzh) *f* embankment

berger (behr-*zhay*) *m* shepherd

besogne (ber-*zoñ*) *f* work

besoin (ber-*zwang*) *m* need; want; ***avoir ~ de** need

bétail (bay-*tigh*) *m* cattle *pl*

bête (beht) *f* beast; *adj* silly, dumb; ~ **de proie** beast of prey

bêtise (bay-*teez*) *f* stupidity; blunder; nonsense

béton (bay-*tawng*) *m* concrete

betterave (beh-*traav*) *f* beetroot, beet

beurre (burr) *m* butter

biberon (bee-*brawng*) *m* feeding (*Am* nursing) bottle; tippler

Bible (beebl) *f* bible

bibliothèque (bee-blee-o-*tehk*) *f* library

bicyclette (bee-see-*kleht*) *f* cycle, bicycle

bien (b'ang) *adv* well; **bien!** well!; all right!; ~ **que** though, although; **biens** *mpl* goods *pl*, possessions

bien-être (b'ang-*naitr*) *m* welfare; comfort

bientôt (b'ang-*toa*) *adv* soon; shortly

bienveillance (b'ang-vay-'ahngss) *f* goodwill

bienvenu (b'ang-*vnew*) *adj* welcome

bière (b'air) *f* beer; ale

bifteck (beef-*tehk*) *m* steak

bifurcation (bee-fewr-kah-s'awng) *f* fork, road fork

bifurquer (bee-fewr-*kay*) *v* fork

bigorneau (bee-gor-*noa*) *m* winkle

bigoudi (bee-goo-*dee*) *m* curler

bijou (bee-*zhoo*) *m* (pl ~x) jewel; gem; **bijoux** jewellery, jewelry *Am*

bijoutier (bee-zhoo-t'ay) *m* jewel(l)er

bikini (bee-kee-*nee*) *m* bikini

bilan (bee-*lahng*) *m* balance

bile (beel) *f* gall, bile

bilingue (bee-*langg*) *adj* bilingual

billard (bee-'aar) *m* billiards *pl*

bille (beey) *f* marble

billet (bee-'ay) *m* ticket; ~ **de banque** banknote; ~ **de quai** platform ticket; ~ **gratuit** free ticket

biologie (bee-o-lo-*zhee*) *f* biology

biscotte (bee-*skot*) *f* rusk

biscuit (bee-*skwee*) *m* biscuit; cookie *Am*; cracker *Am*

bistrot (bee-*stroa*) *m* pub

bizarre (bee-*zaar*) *adj* funny, odd, strange

blague (blahg) *f* joke; ~ **à tabac** tobacco pouch

blaireau (bleh-*roa*) *m* shaving brush

blâme (blaam) *m* blame

blâmer (blah-*may*) *v* blame

blanc (blahng) *adj* (f blanche) white; blank

blanchisserie (blahng-shee-*sree*) *f* laundry

blé (blay) *m* corn; wheat; grain

blesser (blay-*say*) *v* injure, *hurt, wound; offend

blessure (blay-*sewr*) *f* wound; injury

bleu (blur) *adj* (pl bleus) blue; *m* bruise

bloc (blok) *m* block

bloc-notes (blok-*not*) *m* pad, writing pad

blond (blawng) *adj* fair

blonde (blawngd) *f* blonde

bloquer (blo-*kay*) *v* block

bobine (bo-*been*) *f* spool; ~ **d'allumage** ignition coil

bœuf (burf) *m* ox; beef

bohémien (bo-ay-m'ang) *m* Bohemian

*boire (bwaar) *v* *drink

bois (bwah) *m* wood; forest; ~ **d'œuvre** timber; **en** ~ wooden

boisé (bwah-*zay*) *adj* wooded

boisson (bwah-*sawng*) *f* drink, beverage; ~ **non alcoolisée** soft drink; **boissons alcoolisées** spirits

boîte (bwaht) *f* box; can, tin; ~ **à ordures** dustbin; trash can *Am*; ~ **à outils** tool kit; ~ **aux lettres** letterbox; mailbox *Am*; ~ **d'allumettes** matchbox; ~ **de couleurs** paintbox; ~ **de nuit** nightclub; ~ **de vitesse**

gearbox

boiter (bwah-*tay*) *v* limp

boiteux (bwah-*tur*) *adj* lame

bol (bol) *m* basin; bowl

Bolivie (bo-lee-*vee*) *f* Bolivia

Bolivien (bo-lee-*v^yang*) *m* Bolivian

bolivien (bo-lee-*v^yang*) *adj* Bolivian

bombarder (bawng-bahr-*day*) *v* bomb

bombe (bawngb) *f* bomb

bon[1] (bawng) *adj* good; enjoyable, nice; kind

bon[2] (bawng) *m* voucher; ~ **de commande** order form

bonbon (bawng-*bawng*) *m* sweet; candy *Am*

bond (bawng) *m* jump

bondé (bawng-*day*) *adj* crowded

bondir (bawng-*deer*) *v* *leap

bonheur (bo-*nurr*) *m* happiness

bonjour! (bawng-*zhoor*) hello!

bonne (bon) *f* maid; housemaid; ~ **d'enfants** nurse

bonne-maman (bon-mah-*mahng*) *f* grandmother

bonnet (bo-*nay*) *m* cap; **gros** ~ bigwig, *Am* big shot

bon-papa (bawng-pah-*pah*) *m* grandfather

bonsoir! (bawng-*swaar*) good evening!

bonté (bawng-*tay*) *f* kindness

bord (bawr) *m* edge; brim, verge, border; **à** ~ aboard; ~ **de la mer** seaside, seashore; ~ **de la rivière** riverside; ~ **de la route** roadside; wayside; ~ **du trottoir** curb

bordel (bor-*dehl*) *m* brothel

borne routière (born roo-*t^yair*) milestone

borné (bor-*nay*) *adj* narrow-minded

bosquet (bo-*skay*) *m* grove

bosse (boss) *f* dent, lump

botanique (bo-tah-*neek*) *f* botany

botte (bot) *f* boot

bottin (bo-*tang*) *m* telephone directory

bouc (book) *m* goat; ~ **émissaire** scapegoat

bouche (boosh) *f* mouth

bouchée (boo-*shay*) *f* bite

boucher[1] (boo-*shay*) *m*, **-ère** *f* butcher

boucher[2] (boo-*shay*) *v* stop up

boucherie (boo-*shree*) *f* butcher's shop

bouchon (boo-*shawng*) *m* cork; stopper

boucle (bookl) *f* buckle; curl; loop; ~ **d'oreille** earring

boucler (boo-*klay*) *v* curl; **bouclé** curly

boudin (boo-*dang*) *m* black pudding, *Am* blood sausage

boue (boo) *f* mud; slush

bouée (boo-*ay*) *f* buoy; ~ **de sauvetage** lifebelt

boueux (boo-*ur*) *adj* muddy

bouger (boo-*zhay*) *v* move; stir

bougie (boo-*zhee*) *f* candle; ~ **d'allumage** sparking plug

***bouillir** (boo-^y*eer*) *v* boil

bouilloire (boo-^y*waar*) *f* kettle

bouillotte (boo-^y*ot*) *f* hot-water bottle

boulanger (boo-lahng-*zhay*) *m*, **boulangère** *f* baker

boulangerie (boo-lahng-*zhree*) *f* bakery

boule (bool) *f* ball

bouleau (boo-*loa*) *m* birch

boulevard (bool-*vaar*) *m* boulevard

bouleversé (bool-vehr-*say*) *adj* upset

boulon (boo-*lawng*) *m* bolt

boulot (boo-*loa*) *m* job

bouquet (boo-*kay*) *m* bunch, bouquet

bouquin (boo-*kang*) *m* book

bourdon (boor-*dawng*) *m* great bell; bumblebee; **faux** ~ drone

bourg (boor) *m* town

bourgeois (boor-*zhwah*) *adj* bourgeois, middle-class

bourgeon (boor-*zhawng*) *m* bud

bourré (boo-*ray*) *adj* chock-full

bourse (boors) *f* purse; **~ des valeurs** stock exchange; **~ d'études** scholarship

boussole (boo-*sol*) *f* compass

bout (boo) *m* end; tip

bouteille (boo-*tay*) *f* bottle

boutique (boo-*teek*) *f* boutique; shop

bouton (boo-*tawng*) *m* button, knob; **~ de col** collar stud; **boutons de manchettes** cuff links *pl*

boutonner (boo-to-*nay*) *v* button

boutonnière (boo-to-*n'air*) *f* buttonhole

bowling (boa-*leeng*) *m* bowling; bowling alley

boxer (bok-*say*) *v* box

bracelet (brah-*slay*) *m* bracelet; bangle; **bracelet-montre** *m* wristwatch; **~ pour montre** watchstrap

braconner (brah-ko-*nay*) *v* poach

braguette (brah-*geht*) *f* fly

branche (brahngsh) *f* branch

brancher (brahng-*shay*) *v* connect; plug in

branchie (brahng-*shee*) *f* gill

branlant (brahng-*lahng*) *adj* unsteady

bras (brah) *m* arm; **bras-dessus brasdessous** arm-in-arm

brasse (brahss) *f* breaststroke; **~ papillon** butterfly stroke

brasser (brah-*say*) *v* brew

brasserie (brah-*sree*) *f* brewery

brave (brahv) *adj* brave, courageous; good

brèche (brehsh) *f* breach; gap

bref (brehf) *adj* (f **brève**) brief

Brésil (bray-*zeel*) *m* Brazil

brésilien (bray-zee-*l'ang*) *adj* Brazilian

bretelles (brer-*tehl*) *fpl* braces *pl*; suspenders *plAm*

breton (brer-*tawng*) *adj* Breton

brevet (brer-*vay*) *m* patent

bricoler (bree-ko-*lay*) do odd jobs; potter

bridge (breej) *m* bridge

brillant (bree-*y'ahng*) *adj* bright; brilliant

briller (bree-*y'ay*) *v* *shine; glow

brin d'herbe (brang dehrb) blade of grass

brindille (brang-*deey*) *f* twig

brioche (bree-*osh*) *f* bun

brique (breek) *f* brick

briquet (bree-*kay*) *m* cigarette lighter, lighter

brise (breez) *f* breeze

briser (bree-*zay*) *v* *break; **brisé** broken

Britannique (bree-tah-*neek*) *m* Briton

britannique (bree-tah-*neek*) *adj* British

broche (brosh) *f* brooch; spit

brochet (bro-*shay*) *m* pike

brochette (bro-*sheht*) *f* skewer; pin

brochure (bro-*shewr*) *f* brochure

brocoli (bro-ko-*lee*) *m* broccoli

broder (bro-*day*) *v* embroider

broderie (bro-*dree*) *f* embroidery

bronchite (brawng-*sheet*) *f* bronchitis

bronze (brawngz) *m* bronze; **en ~** bronze

bronzer (brawng-*zay*) *v* bronze; tan

brosse (bross) *f* brush; **~ à cheveux** hairbrush; **~ à dents** toothbrush; **~ à ongles** nailbrush

brosser (bro-*say*) *v* brush

brouette (broo-*eht*) *f* wheelbarrow

brouillard (broo-*y'aar*) *m* fog, mist

brouiller (broo-*y'ay*) *v* mix; mix up; *sow discord

bruit (brwee) *m* noise

brûler (brew-*lay*) *v* *burn

brûlure (brew-*lewr*) *f* burn; **brûlures d'estomac** heartburn

brume (brewm) f mist; haze

brumeux (brew-*mur*) adj misty; hazy, foggy

brun (bru͞rng) adj brown

brunette (brew-*neht*) f brunette

brusque (brewsk) adj sudden; rude

brut (brewt) adj gross

brutal (brew-*tahl*) adj brutal

bruyant (brwee-*ᵞahng*) adj noisy

bruyère (brwee-*ᵞair*) f heather; moor

bûche (bewsh) f log

bûcher (bew-*shay*) v labo(u)r

budget (bew-*jay*) m budget

buffet (bew-*fay*) m buffet

buisson (bwee-*sawng*) m bush, scrub

bulbe (bewlb) m bulb

bulgare (bewl-*gaar*) adj Bulgarian

Bulgarie (bewl-gah-*ree*) f Bulgaria

bulle (bewl) f bubble

bulletin météorologique (bewl-tang may-tay-o-ro-lo-*zheek*) weather forecast

bureau (bew-*roa*) m office; bureau; desk, agency; ~ **de change** exchange office; ~ **de l'emploi** employment exchange; ~ **de poste** post-office; ~ **de renseignements** information bureau; ~ **des objets trouvés** lost property office; ~ **de tabac** tobacconist's; ~ **de voyages** travel agency; **employé(e) de** ~ clerk; **heures de** ~ business hours

bureaucratie (bew-roa-krah-*see*) f bureaucracy

bus (bewss) m bus

buste (bewst) m bust

but (bew) m purpose, aim; goal

butte (bewt) f mound

C

ça (sah) pron that

cabane (kah-*bahn*) f cabin

cabaret (kah-bah-*ray*) m cabaret

cabine (kah-*been*) f cabin, booth; ~ **de pont** deck cabin; ~ **d'essayage** fitting room; ~ **téléphonique** telephone booth

cabinet (kah-bee-*nay*) m lavatory; cabinet; study; ~ **de consultations** surgery

câble (kahbl) m cable

cacahuète (kah-kah-*weht*) f peanut

cachemire (kahsh-*meer*) m cashmere

cacher (kah-*shay*) v *hide

cachet (kah-*shay*) m stamp; capsule

cactus (kahk-*tewss*) m cactus

cadavre (kah-*daavr*) m corpse

cadeau (kah-*doa*) m present, gift

cadenas (kahd-*nah*) m padlock

cadet (kah-*day*) adj junior

cadre (kaadr) m frame; setting; cadre

café (kah-*fay*) m coffee; café, public house, saloon

caféine (kah-fay-*een*) f caffeine

cafétéria (kah-fay-tay-*ᵞah*) f cafeteria

cafetière (kahf-*tᵞair*) f coffee-pot

cage (kaazh) f cage

cahier (kah-*ᵞay*) m notebook; ~ **de croquis** sketch-book

cahoteux (kah-o-*tur*) adj bumpy

caille (kigh) f quail

caillou (kah-*ᵞoo*) m (pl ~x) pebble

caisse (kehss) f crate; pay desk, cashier Am; ~ **d'épargne** savings bank

caissier (kay-*sᵞay*) m cashier

caissière (keh-*sᵞair*) f cashier

calamité (kah-lah-mee-*tay*) f calamity,

disaster

calcium (kahl-s*y*om) m calcium

calcul (kahl-*kewl*) m calculation; ~ **biliaire** gallstone

calculatrice (kahl-kew-lah-*treess*) f calculator

calculer (kahl-kew-*lay*) v reckon; calculate

caleçon (kahl-*sawng*) m drawers; briefs *pl*, shorts *plAm*, pants *pl*; underpants *plAm*; ~ **de bain** swimmingtrunks

calendrier (kah-lahng-dree-*ay*) m calendar

câliner (kah-lee-*nay*) v cuddle

calmant (kahl-*mahng*) m tranquillizer

calme (kahlm) *adj* calm, quiet

calmer (kahl-*may*) v calm down

calomnie (kah-lom-*nee*) f slander

calorie (kah-lo-*ree*) f calorie

camarade (kah-mah-*rahd*) m/f comrade; ~ **de classe** classmate

cambrioler (kahng-bree-o-*lay*) v burgle

cambrioleur (kahng-bree-o-*lurr*) m, **-euse** f burglar

caméra (kah-may-*rah*) f camera; ~ **vidéo** video camera

camion (kah-m*y*awng) m lorry; truck *Am*; ~ **de livraison** delivery van

camionnette (kah-m*y*o-*neht*) f pick-up van

camomille (kah-mo-*meey*) f camomile

camp (kahng) m camp; ~ **de vacances** holiday camp

campagne (kahng-*pahñ*) f countryside, country; campaign

camper (kahng-*pay*) v camp

campeur (kahng-*purr*) m, **-euse** f camper

camping (kahng-*peeng*) m camping; **terrain de** ~ camping site

Canada (kah-nah-*dah*) m Canada

canadien (kah-nah-*d*y*ang*) *adj* Canadian

canal (kah-*nahl*) m canal; channel

canapé (kah-nah-*pay*) m sofa, couch

canard (kah-*naar*) m duck

canari (kah-nah-*ree*) m canary

cancer (kahng-*sair*) m cancer

candidat (kahng-dee-*dah*) m, **-e** f candidate

candidature (kahng-dee-dah-*tewr*) f application

caniche (kah-*neesh*) m poodle

canif (kah-*neef*) m penknife

caniveau (kah-nee-*voa*) m gutter

canne (kahn) f cane; walking stick; ~ **à pêche** fishing rod

cannelle (kah-*nehl*) f cinnamon

canoë (kah-no-*ay*) m canoe

canon (kah-*nawng*) m gun

canot (kah-*noa*) m canoe; dinghy; ~ **automobile** motorboat

cantine (kahng-*teen*) f canteen

caoutchouc (kah-oo-*choo*) m rubber; ~ **mousse** foam rubber

cap (kahp) m cape; course

capable (kah-*pahbl*) *adj* capable; able; ***être** ~ **de** *be able to

capacité (kah-pah-see-*tay*) f ability; capacity

cape (kahp) f cape

capitaine (kah-pee-*tehn*) m captain

capital (kah-pee-*tahl*) m capital; *adj* capital

capitale (kah-pee-*tahl*) f capital

capitalisme (kah-pee-tah-*leesm*) m capitalism

capitulation (kah-pee-tew-lah-s*y*awng) f capitulation

capot (kah-*poa*) m bonnet; hood *Am*

caprice (kah-*preess*) m fancy; whim

capsule (kah-*psewl*) f capsule

capture (kahp-*tewr*) f capture

capturer (kahp-tew-*ray*) v capture

capuchon (kah-pew-*shawng*) m hood

car[1] (kaar) *conj* for

car[2] (kaar) *m* coach

caractère (kah-rahk-*tair*) *m* character

caractériser (kah-rahk-tay-ree-*zay*) *v* characterize; mark

caractéristique (kah-rahk-tay-ree-*steek*) *f* feature, characteristic, quality; *adj* characteristic, typical

carambolage (kah-rahng-bo-*laazh*) *m* cannon, *Am* carom; collision, crash

caramel (kah-rah-*mehl*) *m* caramel; toffee

caravane (kah-rah-*vahn*) *f* caravan; trailer *Am*

carburateur (kahr-bew-rah-*tūrr*) *m* carburettor

cardigan (kahr-dee-*gahng*) *m* cardigan

cardinal (kahr-dee-*nahl*) *m* cardinal; *adj* cardinal

carence (kah-*rahngss*) *f* shortage; want

cargaison (kahr-gay-*zawng*) *f* cargo

carillon (kah-ree-ʸ*awng*) *m* chimes *pl*

carnaval (kahr-nah-*vahl*) *m* (pl ~s) carnival

carnet (kahr-*nay*) *m* notebook; ~ de chèques chequebook; checkbook *Am*

carotte (kah-*rot*) *f* carrot

carpe (kahrp) *f* carp

carré (kah-*ray*) *m* square; *adj* square

carreau (kah-*roa*) *m* tile; pane; à carreaux chequered

carrefour (kahr-*fōōr*) *m* junction; crossroads

carrière (kah-*rʸair*) *f* career; quarry

carrosse (kah-*ross*) *m* carriage; coach

carrosserie (kah-ro-*sree*) *f* motor body *Am*

cartable (kahr-*tahbl*) *m* satchel

carte (kahrt) *f* card; map; menu; ~ d'abonnement season ticket; ~ de crédit credit card; charge card *Am*; ~

de jeu playing card; ~ des vins wine list; ~ de visite visiting-card; ~ d'identité identity card; ~ marine chart; ~ postale card, picture postcard, postcard; ~ routière road map; ~ verte green card

cartilage (kahr-tee-*laazh*) *m* cartilage

carton (kahr-*tawng*) *m* cardboard; carton; en ~ cardboard

cartouche (kahr-*toosh*) *f* cartridge; carton

cas (kah) *m* case; instance, event; au ~ où in case; ~ d'urgence emergency; en aucun ~ by no means; en ~ de in case of

cascade (kah-*skahd*) *f* waterfall

case (kaaz) *f* section

caserne (kah-*zehrn*) *f* barracks *pl*

casino (kah-zee-*noa*) *m* casino

casque (kahsk) *m* helmet

casquette (kah-*skeht*) *f* cap

casse-croûte (kah-*skroot*) *m* snack

casse-noix (kah-*snwah*) *m* nutcrackers *pl*

casser (kah-*say*) *v* *break; cassé broken

casserole (kah-*srol*) *f* pan

casse-tête (kah-*steht*) *m* puzzle

cassette (kah-*seht*) *f* casket; cassette

cassis (kah-*seess*) *m* blackcurrant

castor (kah-*stawr*) *m* beaver

catacombe (kah-tah-*kawngb*) *f* catacomb

catalogue (kah-tah-*log*) *m* catalogue

catarrhe (kah-*taar*) *m* catarrh

catastrophe (kah-tah-*strof*) *f* calamity, disaster

catégorie (kah-tay-go-*ree*) *f* category; sort

cathédrale (kah-tay-*drahl*) *f* cathedral

catholique (kah-to-*leek*) *adj* catholic; Roman Catholic

cause (kōaz) *f* cause, reason; à ~ de because of; for, on account of

causer (koa-*zay*) *v* cause; chat

causette (koa-*zeht*) *f* chat

caution (koa-*s*ʸ*awng*) *f* bail, security, guarantee; **sujet à ~** untrustworthy

cavalier (kah-vah-*l*ʸ*ay*) *m* horseman; rider

cave (kahv) *f* cellar; wine cellar

caverne (kah-*vehrn*) *f* cavern

caviar (kah-v*ʸaar*) *m* caviar

cavité (kah-vee-*tay*) *f* cavity

ce (ser) *adj* (cet; f cette, pl ces) that; this

ceci (ser-*see*) *pron* this

céder (say-*day*) *v* *give in; indulge

ceinture (sang-*tewr*) *f* belt; **~ de sécurité** safety belt; seat belt

cela (ser-*lah*) *pron* that

célébration (say-lay-brah-*s*ʸ*awng*) *f* celebration

célèbre (say-*lehbr*) *adj* famous

célébrer (say-lay-*bray*) *v* celebrate

célébrité (say-lay-bree-*tay*) *f* fame, celebrity

céleri (sehl-*ree*) *m* celery

célibataire (say-lee-bah-*tair*) *m* bachelor; *adj* single

cellule (seh-*lewl*) *f* cell

celui-là (ser-lwee-*lah*) *pron* (f celle-là, pl ceux-là, celles-là) that

cendre (sah*ng*dr) *f* ash

cendrier (sahng-dree-*ay*) *m* ashtray

censure (sahng-*sewr*) *f* censorship

cent (sah*ng*) *num* hundred; **pour ~** percent

centigrade (sahng-tee-*grahd*) *adj* centigrade

centimètre (sahng-tee-*mehtr*) *m* centimeter *Am*, centimetre

central (sahng-*trahl*) *adj* central; **~ téléphonique** telephone exchange

centrale (sahng-*trahl*) *f* power station

centraliser (sahng-trah-lee-*zay*) *v* centralize

centre (sah*ng*tr) *m* center *Am*, centre;

~ commercial shopping centre; mall; **~ de la ville** town centre; **~ de loisirs** recreation centre

cependant (ser-pahng-*dahng*) *conj* however; but, yet, only

céramique (say-rah-*meek*) *f* ceramics *pl*

cercle (sehrkl) *m* circle, ring; club

céréale (say-ray-*ahl*) *f* grain; corn

cérémonie (say-ray-mo-*nee*) *f* ceremony

cérémonieux (say-ray-mo-n*ʸur*) *adj* formal

cerf (sair) *m* stag, hart

cerise (ser-*reez*) *f* cherry

certain (sehr-*tang*) *adj* certain; **certains** *pron* some

certificat (sehr-tee-fee-*kah*) *m* certificate; **~ médical** health certificate

cerveau (sehr-*voa*) *m* brain

ces (say) *adj* these; those

cesser (say-*say*) *v* cease; discontinue, quit, stop

c'est-à-dire (say-tah-*deer*) *conj* that is (to say), namely

ceux-là (sur-*lah*) *pron* (f celles-là) those

chacun (shah-*kurng*) *pron* everyone; anyone

chagrin (shah-*grang*) *m* sorrow; grief

chaîne (shehn) *f* chain; **~ de montagnes** mountain range

chair (shair) *f* flesh; **~ de poule** goose flesh

chaire (shair) *f* pulpit

chaise (shaiz) *f* chair; **~ longue** deck chair

chalet (shah-*lay*) *m* chalet

chaleur (shah-*lurr*) *f* heat; warmth

chambre (shah*ng*br) *f* room; **~ à air** inner tube; **~ à coucher** bedroom; **~ d'ami** spare room, guest room; **~ d'enfants** nursery; **~ et petit déjeuner**

bed and breakfast; **~ forte** vault

chameau (shah-*moa*) *m* camel

champ (shah$\overline{\text{ng}}$) *m* field; **~ de blé**
cornfield; **~ de courses** racecourse;
sur-le-champ immediately

champagne (shah$\overline{\text{ng}}$-*pahñ*) *m*
champagne

champignon (shah$\overline{\text{ng}}$-pee-*ñaw$\overline{\text{ng}}$*) *m*
mushroom, toadstool

champion (shah$\overline{\text{ng}}$-*p^{y}aw$\overline{\text{ng}}$*) *m*, **-ne** *f*
champion

chance (shah$\overline{\text{ng}}$ss) *f* luck; fortune;
chance

chanceux (shah$\overline{\text{ng}}$-*sur*) *adj* lucky

chandail (shah$\overline{\text{ng}}$-*digh*) *m* jersey,
jumper, sweater

change (shah$\overline{\text{ng}}$zh) *m* change; **bureau
de ~** money exchange

changement (shah$\overline{\text{ng}}$zh-*mah$\overline{\text{ng}}$*) *m*
change; variation, alteration

changer (shah$\overline{\text{ng}}$-*zhay*) *v* vary, change,
alter; exchange, switch; **~ de vitesse**
change gear; **~ en** turn into; **se ~**
change

chanson (shah$\overline{\text{ng}}$-*saw$\overline{\text{ng}}$*) *f* song; **~
populaire** folk song

chant (shah$\overline{\text{ng}}$) *m* song, singing

chantage (shah$\overline{\text{ng}}$-*taazh*) *m* blackmail

chanter (shah$\overline{\text{ng}}$-*tay*) *v* *sing; ***faire ~**
blackmail

chanteur (shah$\overline{\text{ng}}$-*tūrr*) *m*, **-euse** *f*
singer; vocalist

chantier (shah$\overline{\text{ng}}$-*t^{y}ay*) *m* building
site; yard; roadwork, **~ naval** (shah$\overline{\text{ng}}$-
t^{y}ay nah-*vahl*) shipyard

chanvre (shah$\overline{\text{ng}}$vr) *m* hemp

chaos (kah-*oa*) *m* chaos

chaotique (kah-o-*teek*) *adj* chaotic

chapeau (shah-*poa*) *m* hat

chapelain (shah-*pla$\overline{\text{ng}}$*) *m* chaplain

chapelet (shah-*play*) *m* beads *pl*

chapelle (shah-*pehl*) *f* chapel

chapitre (shah-*peetr*) *m* chapter

chaque (shahk) *adj* each; every

charbon (shahr-*baw$\overline{\text{ng}}$*) *m* coal; **~ de
bois** charcoal

charcuterie (shahr-kew-*tree*) *f*
delicatessen; butcher's shop

chardon (shahr-*daw$\overline{\text{ng}}$*) *m* thistle

charge (shahrzh) *f* charge

chargement (shahr-zher-*mah$\overline{\text{ng}}$*) *m*
cargo, load, charge, freight

charger (shahr-*zhay*) *v* charge; load;
chargé de in charge of; **se ~ de** *take
charge of

charité (shah-ree-*tay*) *f* charity

charmant (shahr-*mah$\overline{\text{ng}}$*) *adj* graceful;
glamorous

charme (shahrm) *m* charm, glamour

charmer (shahr-*may*) *v* charm,
enchant

charnière (shahr-*n^{y}air*) *f* hinge

charrette (shah-*reht*) *f* cart

charrue (shah-*rew*) *f* plough

chasse (shahss) *f* chase; hunt

chasser (shah-*say*) *v* chase; hunt

chasseur (shah-*sūrr*) *m* hunter;
bellboy

châssis (shah-*see*) *m* chassis

chaste (shahst) *adj* chaste

chat (shah) *m* cat

château (shah-*toa*) *m* castle

chatouiller (shah-too-*^{y}ay*) *v* tickle

chaud (shoa) *adj* hot; warm

chaudière (shoa-*d^{y}air*) *f* boiler

chauffage (shoa-*faazh*) *m* heating; **~
central** central heating

chauffer (shoa-*fay*) *v* heat; warm

chauffeur (shoa-*fūrr*) *m* chauffeur; **~
de taxi** cab driver

chaussée (shoa-*say*) *f* causeway;
carriageway; roadway *Am*

chaussette (shoa-*seht*) *f* sock

chaussure (shoa-*sēwr*) *f* shoe;
chaussures footwear; **chaussures
de basket** plimsolls *pl*; **chaussures
de gymnastique** gym shoes; sneakers
plAm; **chaussures de ski** ski boots;

chaussures de tennis tennis shoes

chauve (shoav) *adj* bald

chaux (shoa) *f* lime

chef (shehf) *m* chief; manager, boss; chieftain; ~ **cuisinier** chef; ~ **d'Etat** head of state; ~ **d'orchestre** conductor

chef-d'œuvre (sheh-*dūrvr*) *m* masterpiece

chemin (sher-*mang*) *m* lane; **à michemin** halfway; ~ **de fer** railroad *Am*; railway; ~ **du retour** way back

chemineau (sher-mee-*noa*) *m* tramp

cheminée (sher-mee-*nay*) *f* chimney; fireplace; hearth

chemise (sher-*meez*) *f* shirt; vest; ~ **de nuit** nightdress

chemisier (sher-mee-*z*ʸ*ay*) *m* blouse

chêne (shehn) *m* oak

chenil (sher-*nee*) *m* kennel

chèque (shehk) *m* cheque, check *Am*; ~ **de voyage** traveler's check *Am*, traveller's cheque

cher (shair) *adj* dear; expensive

chercher (shehr-*shay*) *v* *seek, search; hunt for, look up, look for; *aller ~ fetch

chère (shair) *f* fare

chéri (shay-*ree*) *m* darling, sweetheart

cheval (sher-*vahl*) *m* horse; ~ **de bois** wooden horse; ~ **de course** racehorse; **cheval-vapeur** *m* horsepower; **monter à ~** *ride

chevalier (sher-vah-*l*ʸ*ay*) *m* knight

chevelu (sher-*vlew*) *adj* hairy

cheveu (sher-*vur*) *m* hair; **coupe de cheveux** haircut

cheville (sher-*veey*) *f* ankle

chèvre (shaivr) *f* goat

chevreau (sher-*vroa*) *m* kid

chevreuil (sher-*vrur*ᵉᵉ) *m* roebuck

chez (shay) *prep* at; to; with; ~ **soi** home

chic (sheek) *adj* (f ~) smart

chichi (shee-*shee*) *m* fuss

chien (shʸ*ang*) *m* dog; ~ **d'aveugle** guide dog

chienne (shʸehn) *f* bitch

chiffon (shee-*fawng*) *m* cloth; rag

chiffre (sheefr) *m* figure; digit, number

Chili (shee-*lee*) *m* Chile

chilien (shee-*l*ʸ*ang*) *adj* Chilean

chimie (shee-*mee*) *f* chemistry

chimique (shee-*meek*) *adj* chemical

Chine (sheen) *f* China

chinois (shee-*nwah*) *adj* Chinese

chirurgien (shee-rewr-*zh*ʸ*ang*) *m* surgeon

chlore (klawr) *m* chlorine

choc (shok) *m* shock

chocolat (sho-ko-*lah*) *m* chocolate

chœur (kūrr) *m* choir

choisir (shwah-*zeer*) *v* *choose; pick, select; **choisi** select

choix (shwah) *m* choice; pick, selection

chômage (shoa-*maazh*) *m* unemployment; **en ~** unemployed

chômeur (shoa-*mūrr*) *m*, **-euse** *f* unemployed worker

chope (shop) *f* mug

choquer (sho-*kay*) *v* shock

chose (shoaz) *f* thing; **quelque ~** something

chou (shoo) *m* (pl ~x) cabbage; **chou-fleur** cauliflower; **choux de Bruxelles** Brussels sprouts *pl*

chouchou (shoo-*shoo*) *m* pet

choucroute (shoo-*kroot*) *f* sauerkraut

chouette (shweht) *f* owl; *adj* fine, splendid

chrétien (kray-*t*ʸ*ang*) *adj* Christian; *m*, **-ne** *f* Christian

chronique (kro-*neek*) *adj* chronic

chronologique (kro-no-lo-*zheek*) *adj* chronological

chuchotement (shew-shot-*mahng*) *m* whisper

chuchoter (shew-sho-*tay*) *v* whisper

chute (shewt) *f* fall

cible (seebl) *f* target; mark

ciboulette (see-boo-*leht*) *f* chives *pl*

cicatrice (see-kah-*treess*) *f* scar

cidre (seedr) *m* cider

ciel (s^yehl) *m* (pl cieux) heaven; sky

cigare (see-*gaar*) *m* cigar

cigarette (see-gah-*reht*) *f* cigarette

cigogne (see-*goñ*) *f* stork

cil (seel) *m* eyelash

ciment (see-*mahng*) *m* cement

cimetière (seem-t^y*air*) *m* graveyard, cemetery, churchyard

cinéma (see-nay-*mah*) *m* cinema; pictures; movie theater *Am*, movies *Am*

cinq (sangk) *num* five

cinquante (sang-*kahngt*) *num* fifty

cinquième (sang-k^y*ehm*) *num* fifth

cintre (sangtr) *m* coat hanger, hanger

cirage (see-*raazh*) *m* shoe polish

circonstance (seer-kawng-*stahngss*) *f* circumstance; condition

circuit (seer-*kwee*) *m* circumference; circuit

circulation (seer-kew-lah-s^y*awng*) *f* circulation; traffic

cire (seer) *f* wax; **musée des figures de ~** waxworks *pl*

cirque (seerk) *m* circus

ciseaux (see-*zoa*) *mpl* scissors *pl*; **~ à ongles** nail scissors *pl*

citation (see-tah-s^y*awng*) *f* quotation

cité (see-*tay*) *f* city

citer (see-*tay*) *v* quote

citoyen (see-twah-^y*ang*) *m*, **-ne** *f* citizen

citoyenneté (see-twah-^yehn-*tay*) *f* citizenship

citron (see-*trawng*) *m* lemon

civil (see-*veel*) *m* civilian; *adj* civilian, civil

civilisation (see-vee-lee-zah-s^y*awng*) *f* civilization

civilisé (see-vee-lee-*zay*) *adj* civilized

civique (see-*veek*) *adj* civic

clair (klair) *adj* clear; plain, light, serene

clairière (kleh-r^y*air*) *f* clearing

claque (klahk) *f* slap; smack, blow; **donner une ~** smack

claquer (klah-*kay*) *v* slam

clarifier (klah-ree-f^y*ay*) *v* clarify

clarté (klahr-*tay*) *f* light, clearness

classe (klahss) *f* class; form; **~ moyenne** middle class; **~ touriste** tourist class

classer (klah-*say*) *v* classify; assort, grade, arrange, sort

classique (klah-*seek*) *adj* classical

clavecin (klahv-*sang*) *m* harpsichord

clavicule (klah-vee-*kewl*) *f* collarbone

clavier (klah-v^y*ay*) *m* keyboard; range

clé (klay) *f* key; wrench; **~ à écrous** spanner, wrench *Am*; **~ de la maison** latchkey

clémence (klay-*mahngss*) *f* mercy; grace

client (klee-*ahng*) *m* client; customer

clientèle (klee-ahng-*tehl*) *f* customers *pl*

clignotant (klee-ño-*tahng*) *m* indicator

climat (klee-*mah*) *m* climate

climatisation (klee-mah-tee-zah-s^y*awng*) *f* air conditioning

climatisé (klee-mah-tee-*zay*) *adj* airconditioned

clinique (klee-*neek*) *f* clinic

cliquer (klee-*kay*) *v* click

cloche (klosh) *f* bell

clocher (klo-*shay*) *m* steeple

cloison (klwah-*zawng*) *f* partition; wall

cloître (klwaatr) *m* cloister

cloque (klok) *f* blister

clos (kloa) *adj* closed; shut

clôture (kloa-*tewr*) *f* fence

clou (kloo) *m* nail

clown (kloon) *m* clown

club (klurb) *m* club; **~ automobile** automobile club; **~ de golf** golfclub

cocaïne (ko-kah-*een*) *f* cocaine

cochon (ko-*shawng*) *m* pig; **~ de lait** piglet; **~ d'Inde** guinea pig

cocktail (kok-*tehl*) *m* cocktail

code (kod) *m* code; **~ postal** zip code *Am*

cœur (kurr) *m* heart; core; **par ~** by heart

coffre (kofr) *m* chest; boot; trunk *Am*; **coffre-fort** safe

cognac (ko-*ñahk*) *m* cognac

cogner (ko-*ñay*) *v* bump; **~ contre** knock against

cohérence (koa-ay-rah*ngss*) *f* coherence

coiffeur (kwah-*furr*) *m* hairdresser; barber

coiffeuse (kwah-*furz*) *f* dressing table

coiffure (kwah-*fewr*) *f* hairdo

coin (kwang) *m* corner

coïncidence (koa-ang-see-dah*ngss*) *f* concurrence

coïncider (koa-ang-see-*day*) *v* coincide

col (kol) *m* collar; mountain pass

coléoptère (ko-lay-op-*tair*) *m* bug

colère (ko-*lair*) *f* anger; temper, passion; **en ~** angry

coléreux (ko-lay-*rur*) *adj* hot-tempered

colis (ko-*lee*) *m* parcel, package

collaboration (ko-lah-borah-s^y awng) *f* cooperation

collant (ko-*lahng*) *adj* sticky; close-fitting, (skin)tight; clinging

collants (ko-*lahng*) *mpl* tights *pl*; panty hose

colle (kol) *f* glue, gum

collectif (ko-lehk-*teef*) *adj* collective

collection (ko-lehk-s^y awng) *f* collection; **~ d'art** art collection

collectionner (ko-lehk-s^y o-*nay*) *v* gather

collectionneur (ko-lehk-s^y o-*nurr*) *m*, **-euse** *f* collector

collège (ko-*laizh*) *m* college

collègue (ko-*lehg*) *m* colleague

coller (ko-*lay*) *v* paste, *stick

collier (ko-*l^y ay*) *m* necklace; collar, beads *pl*

colline (ko-*leen*) *f* hill

collision (ko-lee-z^y awng) *f* collision; crash; **entrer en ~** collide, crash

Colombie (ko-lawng-*bee*) *f* Colombia

colombien (ko-lawng-b^y *ang*) *adj* Colombian

colonel (ko-lo-*nehl*) *m* colonel

colonie (ko-lo-*nee*) *f* colony

colonne (ko-*lon*) *f* column; pillar; **~ de direction** steering column

coloré (ko-lo-*ray*) *adj* colo(u)rful

coma (ko-*mah*) *m* coma

combat (kawng-*bah*) *m* struggle; fight, combat, contest, battle

***combattre** (kawng-*bahtr*) *v* *fight; combat, battle

combien (kawng-b^y *ang*) *adv* how much; how many

combinaison (kawng-bee-nay-z*awng*) *f* combination; slip

combiner (kawng-bee-*nay*) *v* combine

comble (kawngbl) *m* roof; height; *adj* full

combler (kawng-*blay*) *v* fill up; overload

combustible (kawng-bew-*steebl*) *m* fuel

comédie (ko-may-*dee*) *f* comedy; **~ musicale** musical

comédien (ko-may-d^y *ang*) *m*, **-ne** *f* comedian

comestible (ko-meh-*steebl*) *adj* edible

comique (ko-*meek*) *m* comedian; *adj* comic, humorous

comité (ko-mee-*tay*) *m* committee

commandant (ko-mahng-*dahng*) *m* commander; captain

commande (ko-*mahng*d) *f* order; **fait sur ~** made to order

commandement (ko-mahngd-*mahng*) *m* order

commander (ko-mahng-*day*) *v* command; order

comme (kom) *conj* as; like; since; **~ si** as if

commémoration (ko-may-mo-rah-*s^yawng*) *f* commemoration

commencement (ko-mahng-*smahng*) *m* beginning

commencer (ko-mahng-*say*) *v* *begin; commence, start

comment (ko-*mahng*) *adv* how; **n'importe ~** anyhow

commentaire (ko-mahng-*tair*) *m* comment

commenter (ko-mahng-*tay*) *v* comment

commerçant (ko-mehr-*sahng*) *m*, **-e** *f* merchant; trader, shopkeeper

commerce (ko-*mehrs*) *m* commerce; business, trade; **~ de détail** retail trade; *faire du ~** trade

commercial (ko-mehr-*s^yahl*) *adj* commercial

***commettre** (ko-*mehtr*) *v* commit

commission (ko-mee-*s^yawng*) *f* committee, commission; errand, message

commode (ko-*mod*) *f* chest of drawers; bureau *Am*; *adj* convenient, easy, handy

commodité (ko-mo-dee-*tay*) *f* comfort

commotion (ko-moa-*s^yawng*) *f* shock; **~ cérébrale** concussion

commun (ko-*murng*) *adj* common; ordinary

communauté (ko-mew-noa-*tay*) *f* community

communication (ko-mew-nee-kah-*s^yawng*) *f* communication; information; connection; **~ locale** local call; ***mettre en ~** connect

communiqué (ko-mew-nee-*kay*) *m* communiqué

communiquer (ko-mew-nee-*kay*) *v* communicate; inform

communisme (ko-mew-*neesm*) *m* communism

commutateur (ko-mew-tah-*turr*) *m* switch

compact (kawng-*pahkt*) *adj* compact

compact-disc (kawng-*pahkt* deesk) *m* compact disc; **lecteur de ~** compact disc player

compagne (kawng-*pah*-ñe) *f* companion

compagnie (kawng-pah-*ñee*) *f* company; society; **~ de navigation** shipping line

compagnon (kawng-pah-*ñawng*) *m* companion

comparaison (kawng-pah-ray-*zawng*) *f* comparison

comparer (kawng-pah-*ray*) *v* compare

compartiment (kawng-pahr-tee-*mahng*) *m* compartment; **~ fumeurs** smoking compartment

compassion (kawng-pah-*s^yawng*) *f* compassion

compatir (kawng-pah-*teer*) *v* sympathize

compatissant (kawng-pah-tee-*sahng*) *adj* sympathetic

compatriote (kawng-pah-tree-*ot*) *m/f* fellow countryman

compensation (kawng-pahng-sah-*s^yawng*) *f* compensation

compenser (kawng-pahng-*say*) *v* compensate for; *make good

compétence (kawng-pay-*tahngss*) *f*

capacity

compétent (kawng-pay-*tahng*) *adj* qualified; expert

compétition (kawng-pay-tee-s^y*awng*) *f* competition

compiler (kawng-pee-*lay*) *v* compile

complémentaire (kawng-play-mahng-*tair*) *adj* further

complet[1] (kawng-*play*) *adj* (f -plète) whole, complete; total, utter; full up

complet[2] (kawng-*play*) *m* suit

complètement (kawng-pleht-*mahng*) *adv* completely

complexe (kawng-*plehks*) *m* complex; *adj* complex

compliment (kawng-plee-*mahng*) *m* compliment

complimenter (kawng-plee-mahng-*tay*) *v* compliment

compliqué (kawng-plee-*kay*) *adj* complicated

complot (kawng-*ploa*) *m* plot

comportement (kawng-por-ter-*mahng*) *m* behavio(u)r

comporter (kawng-por-*tay*) *v* imply; **se ~** behave

composer (kawng-poa-*zay*) *v* compose

compositeur (kawng-po-zee-*tūrr*) *m*, **-trice** *f* composer

composition (kawng-po-zee-s^y*awng*) *f* composition; essay

composter (kawng-po-*stay*) *v* punch (a ticket)

compote (kawng-*pot*) *f* stewed fruit; **en ~** stewed; to *or* in a pulp

compréhension (kawng-pray-ahng-s^y*awng*) *f* understanding; insight

***comprendre** (kawng-*prahngdr*) *v* *understand; *see; comprise, include, contain

comprimé (kawng-pree-*may*) *m* tablet

compris (kawng-*pree*) *adj* inclusive; **tout ~** all in

compromis (kawng-pro-*mee*) *m* compromise

comptable (kawng-*tahbl*) *m* accountant

compte (kawngt) *m* account; **~ en banque** bank account; **~ rendu** report; minutes; **en fin de ~** at last; **rendre ~ de** account for; **se rendre ~** realize; *see

compter (kawng-*tay*) *v* count; **~ sur** rely on

compteur (kawng-*tūrr*) *m* meter

comptoir (kawng-*twaar*) *m* counter

comte (kawngt) *m* count; earl

comté (kawng-*tay*) *m* county

comtesse (kawng-*tehss*) *f* countess

concéder (kawng-say-*day*) *v* grant

concentration (kawng-sahng-trah-s^y*awng*) *f* concentration

concentrer (kawng-sahng-*tray*) *v* concentrate

concept (kawng-*sehpt*) *m* idea

conception (kawng-seh-ps^y*awng*) *f* conception

concernant (kawng-sehr-*nahng*) *prep* concerning; as regards, about, regarding

concerner (kawng-sehr-*nay*) *v* concern; **en ce qui concerne** as regards, regarding

concert (kawng-*sair*) *m* concert

concession (kawng-seh-s^y*awng*) *f* concession

concessionnaire (kawng-seh-s^{y}o-*nair*) *m* distributor

***concevoir** (kawng-*svwaar*) *v* conceive; devise

concierge (kawng-s^y*ehrzh*) *m/f* concierge; janitor

concis (kawng-*see*) *adj* concise

***conclure** (kawng-*klēwr*) *v* finish; conclude

conclusion (kawng-klew-z^y*awng*) *f* conclusion, end; issue

concombre (kawng-*kawngbr*) *m*
cucumber

concorder (kawng-kor-*day*) *v* agree

*****concourir** (kawng-koo-*reer*) *v*
compete

concours (kawng-*koor*) *m* contest

concret (kawng-*kray*) *adj* (f -crète)
concrete

concurrence (kawng-kew-rahngss) *f*
rivalry

concurrent (kawng-kew-*rahng*) *m*
competitor; rival

condamnation (kawng-dah-nah-
*s*y*awng*) *f* condemnation; sentence

condamné (kawng-dah-*nay*) *m*
convict

condamner (kawng-dah-*nay*) *v*
sentence

condition (kawng-dee-*s*y*awng*) *f*
condition; term

conducteur (kawng-dewk-*türr*) *m*
driver; conductor

*****conduire** (kawng-*dweer*) *v* conduct,
guide; *****drive; carry, *****take; **se ~** act

conduite (kawng-*dweet*) *f* conduct;
lead

confédération (kawng-fay-day-rah-
*s*y*awng*) *f* confederation

conférence (kawng-fay-*rahngss*) *f*
conference; lecture; **~ de presse**
press conference

confesser (kawng-fay-*say*) *v* confess

confession (kawng-feh-*s*y*awng*) *f*
confession

confiance (kawng-*f*y*ahngss*) *f*
confidence; faith, trust; **digne de ~**
reliable, trustworthy; *****faire ~** trust

confiant (kawng-*f*y*ahng*) *adj* confident

confidentiel (kawng-fee-dahng-*s*y*ehl*)
adj confidential

confier (kawng-*f*y*ay*) *v* confide

confirmation (kawng-feer-mah-
*s*y*awng*) *f* confirmation

confirmer (kawng-feer-*may*) *v*
confirm; acknowledge

confiserie (kawng-fee-*zree*) *f*
sweetshop; candy *Am*; candy store
Am

confiseur (kawng-fee-*zürr*) *m*, **-euse** *f*
confectioner

confisquer (kawng-fee-*skay*) *v*
confiscate

confiture (kawng-fee-*tewr*) *f* jam

conflit (kawng-*flee*) *m* conflict

confondre (kawng-*fawngdr*) *v*
confuse; *****mistake

*****être conforme** (aitr kawng-*form*)
correspond

conformément à (kawng-for-may-
mahng) in accordance with,
according to

confort (kawng-*fawr*) *m* comfort

confortable (kawng-*for-tahbl*) *adj*
comfortable; cosy, cozy *Am*

confus (kawng-*few*) *adj* confused;
embarrassed

confusion (kawng-few-*z*y*awng*) *f*
confusion; disorder, muddle

congé (kawng-*zhay*) *m* vacation

congélateur (kawng-zhay-lah-*türr*) *m*
deep-freeze

congelé (kawng-*zhlay*) *adj* frozen

congratuler (kawng-grah-tew-*lay*) *v*
congratulate

congrès (kawng-*gray*) *m* congress

conifère (ko-nee-*fair*) *m* conifer

conjecture (kawng-zhehk-*tewr*) *f*
conjecture, guess

conjoint (kawng-*zhwang*) *adj* joint

conjointement (kawng-zhwangt-
mahng) *adv* jointly

connaissance (ko-nay-*sahngss*) *f*
knowledge; acquaintance

connaisseur (ko-nay-*sürr*) *m*
connoisseur

*****connaître** (ko-*naitr*) *v* *****know; **connu**
well-known

connotation (ko-no-tah-*s*y*awng*) *f*

connotation

conquérant (kawng-kay-*rahng*) *m*
conqueror

*conquérir (kawng-kay-*reer*) *v*
conquer

conquête (kawng-*keht*) *f* conquest

consacrer (kawng-sah-*kray*) *v* devote

conscience (kawng-s^y*ahngss*) *f*
conscience; consciousness

conscient (kawng-s^y*ahng*) *adj*
conscious; aware

conscrit (kawng-*skree*) *m* conscript

conseil (kawng-*say*) *m* advice;
counsel, council; board; **donner des
conseils** advise

conseiller (kawng-say-^y*ay*) *v* advise;
recommend; *m* councillor;
counsellor

consentement (kawng-sahngt-
mahng) *m* consent, approval

*consentir (kawng-sahng-*teer*) *v*
consent, agree

conséquence (kawng-say-*kahngss*) *f*
consequence; result

conséquent: par ~ (pahr kawng-say-
kahng) consequently

conservateur (kawng-sehr-vah-*turr*)
adj conservative

conservation (kawng-sehr-vah-
s^y*awng*) *f* preservation

conservatoire (kawng-sehr-vah-
twaar) *m* music academy

conserver (kawng-sehr-*vay*) *v*
preserve

conserves (kawng-*sehrv*) *fpl* tinned
food, canned food *Am*; ***mettre en
conserve** preserve

considérable (kawng-see-day-*rahbl*)
adj considerable; extensive

considération (kawng-see-day-rah-
s^y*awng*) *f* consideration; respect

considérer (kawng-see-day-*ray*) *v*
consider; **~ comme** regard as

consigne (kawng-*seeñ*) *f* deposit; left

luggage office; checkroom, baggage
check *Am*

consister (kawng-see-*stay*) v: **~ en**
consist of

consoler (kawng-so-*lay*) *v* comfort

consommateur (kawng-so-mah-*turr*)
m consumer

consommation (kawng-so-mah-
s^y*awng*) *f* consumption; drink

consommer (kawng-so-*may*) *v*
consume

conspiration (kawng-spee-rah-
s^y*awng*) *f* plot

conspirer (kawng-spee-*ray*) *v* conspire

constant (kawng-*stahng*) *adj* constant;
even

constater (kawng-stah-*tay*) *v* note,
notice; certify

constipation (kawng-stee-pah-
s^y*awng*) *f* constipation

constituer (kawng-stee-*tway*) *v*
constitute

constitution (kawng-stee-tew-s^y*awng*)
f constitution

construction (kawng-strewk-s^y*awng*) *f*
construction; building

*construire (kawng-*strweer*) *v*
construct

consulat (kawng-sew-*lah*) *m*
consulate

consultation (kawng-sewl-tah-
s^y*awng*) *f* consultation

consulter (kawng-sewl-*tay*) *v* consult

contact (kawng-*tahkt*) *m* contact;
touch

contacter (kawng-tahk-*tay*) *v* contact

contagieux (kawng-tah-zh^y*ur*) *adj*
contagious

conte (kawngt) *m* tale; **~ de fées**
fairytale

contempler (kawng-tahng-*play*) *v*
view

contemporain (kawng-tahng-po-*rang*)
m contemporary; *adj* contemporary

conteneur (kawng̅t-*nŭrr*) *m* container

***contenir** (kawng̅t-*neer*) *v* contain; restrain

content (kawng̅-*tahng̅*) *adj* glad; pleased, happy

contenu (kawng̅t-*new*) *m* contents *pl*

contester (kawng̅-teh-*stay*) *v* dispute

continent (kawng̅-tee-*nahng̅*) *m* continent

continental (kawng̅-tee-nahng̅-*tahl*) *adj* continental

continu (kawng̅-tee-*new*) *adj* continuous

continuel (kawng̅-tee-*nwehl*) *adj* continual; continuous

continuellement (kawng̅-tee-nwehl-*mahng̅*) *adv* all the time, continually

continuer (kawng̅-tee-*nway*) *v* continue; carry on, *keep on, *keep, *go on, *go ahead

contour (kawng̅-*toor*) *m* outline, contour

contourner (kawng̅-toor-*nay*) *v* by-pass

contraceptif (kawng̅-trah-sehp-*teef*) *m* contraceptive

contradictoire (kawng̅-trah-deek-*twaar*) *adj* contradictory

***contraindre** (kawng̅-*trang̅gdr*) *v* compel

contraire (kawng̅-*trair*) *adj* opposite; *m* reverse, contrary; **au ~** on the contrary

contralto (kawng̅-trahl-*toa*) *m* contralto

contraste (kawng̅-*trahst*) *m* contrast

contrat (kawng̅-*trah*) *m* agreement, contract

contravention (kawng̅-trah-vahng̅-*sʸawng̅*) *f* ticket

contre (kawng̅tr) *prep* against; versus

contrecœur: à ~ (ah kawng̅-trer-*kŭrr*) reluctantly

***contredire** (kawng̅-trer-*deer*) *v* contradict

***contrefaire** (kawng̅-trer-*fair*) *v* counterfeit

contrefait (kawng̅-trer-*fay*) *adj* deformed

contremaître (kawng̅-trer-*maitr*) *m* foreman

contribution (kawng̅-tree-bew-*sʸawng̅*) *f* contribution

contrôle (kawng̅-*troal*) *m* control; inspection; **~ des passeports** passport control

contrôler (kawng̅-troa-*lay*) *v* control; check

contrôleur (kawng̅-troa-*lŭrr*) *m* ticket collector

controversé (kawng̅-troa-vehr-*say*) *adj* controversial

contusion (kawng̅-tew-*zʸawng̅*) *f* bruise

contusionner (kawng̅-tew-zʸo-*nay*) *v* bruise

***convaincre** (kawng̅-*vang̅gkr*) *v* convince; persuade

convenable (kawng̅-*vnahbl*) *adj* proper; fit

***convenir** (kawng̅-*vneer*) *v* fit, suit

conversation (kawng̅-vehr-sah-*sʸawng̅*) *f* conversation; discussion, talk

convertir (kawng̅-vehr-*teer*) *v* convert

conviction (kawng̅-veek-*sʸawng̅*) *f* conviction; persuasion

convulsion (kawng̅-vewl-*sʸawng̅*) *f* convulsion

coopérant (koa-o-pay-*rahng̅*) *adj* cooperative

coopératif (koa-o-pay-rah-*teef*) *adj* cooperative

coopération (koa-o-pay-rah-*sʸawng̅*) *f* co-operation

coopérative (koa-o-pay-rah-*teev*) *f* cooperative

coordination (koa-or-dee-nah-

$s^yaw\overline{ng}$) f coordination

coordonner (koa-or-do-*nay*) v coordinate

copain (ko-*pa*$\overline{ng}$) m pal

copie (ko-*pee*) f copy; carbon copy

copier (ko-*p*^{y}*ay*) v copy

copine (ko-*peen*) f pal; girlfriend

coq (kok) m cock; ~ **de bruyère** black grouse

coquelicot (ko-klee-*koa*) m poppy

coquetier (kok-t^y*ay*) m eggcup

coquillage (ko-kee-^{y}*aazh*) m seashell

coquille (ko-*keey*) f shell; ~ **de noix** nutshell

coquin (ko-*ka*$\overline{ng}$) m rascal

corail (ko-*righ*) m (pl coraux) coral

corbeau (kor-*boa*) m raven

corbeille à papier (kor-bay ah pah-*p*^{y}*ay*) wastepaper basket

corde (kord) f rope; cord; string

cordial (kor-*d*^{y}*ahl*) adj hearty, cordial; warm

cordon (kor-*daw*$\overline{ng}$) m cord; string

cordonnier (kor-do-*n*^{y}*ay*) m shoemaker

coriace (ko-*r*^{y}*ahss*) adj tough

corne (korn) f horn

corneille (kor-*nay*) f crow

cornichon (kor-nee-*shaw*$\overline{ng}$) m gherkin; colloquial nitwit

corps (kawr) m body

corpulent (kor-pew-*lah*$\overline{ng}$) adj corpulent; stout

correct (ko-*rehkt*) adj correct; right

correction (ko-rehk-*s*^{y}*aw*$\overline{ng}$) f correction

correspondance (ko-reh-spaw$\overline{ng}$-*dah*$\overline{ng}$*ss*) f correspondence; connection

correspondant (ko-reh-spaw$\overline{ng}$-*dah*$\overline{ng}$) m correspondent

correspondre (ko-reh-*spaw*$\overline{ng}$*dr*) v correspond

corrida (ko-ree-*dah*) f bullfight

corridor (ko-ree-*dawr*) m corridor

corriger (ko-ree-*zhay*) v correct

*****corrompre** (ko-*raw*$\overline{ng}$*pr*) v corrupt; bribe; **corrompu** corrupt

corruption (ko-rew-*ps*^{y}*aw*$\overline{ng}$) f corruption; bribery

corset (kor-*say*) m corset

cortège (kor-*taizh*) m procession

cosmétiques (ko-smay-*teek*) mpl cosmetics pl

costume (ko-*stewm*) m suit; costume; ~ **national** national dress

côte (k$\overline{oa}$t) f coast; rib; chop

côté (koa-*tay*) m side; way; **à ~** next-door; **à ~ de** next to, beside; **de ~** aside, sideways; **de l'autre ~ de** across; **passer à ~** pass by

coteau (ko-*toa*) m hillside

côtelette (ko-*tleht*) f chop, cutlet

coton (ko-*taw*$\overline{ng}$) m cotton; **en ~** cotton

cou (koo) m neck

couche (koosh) f layer; nappy; diaper Am; **fausse ~** miscarriage

coucher (koo-*shay*) v: **se ~** *lie down

couchette (koo-*sheht*) f couchette, bunk

coucou (koo-*koo*) m cuckoo

coude (kood) m elbow

*****coudre** (koodr) v sew

couler (koo-*lay*) v flow, stream

couleur (koo-*lürr*) f colo(u)r; ~ **à l'eau** watercolo(u)r; **de ~** colo(u)red

couloir (koo-*lwaar*) m corridor

coup (koo) m blow; bump, tap, push, knock; ~ **de feu** shot; ~ **d'envoi** kickoff; ~ **de pied** kick; ~ **de poing** punch; ~ **de téléphone** call; **jeter un ~ d'œil à** glance at

coupable (koo-*pahbl*) adj guilty; **déclarer ~** convict

coupe (koop) f cup

coupe-papier (koop-pah-*p*^{y}*ay*) m paper knife, letter opener Am

couper (koo-*pay*) *v* *cut; *cut off

couple (koopl) *m* couple; **~ marié** married couple

coupon (koo-*pawng*) *m* coupon

coupure (koo-*pewr*) *f* cut

cour (koor) *f* court; yard

courage (koo-*raazh*) *m* courage

courageux (koo-rah-*zhur*) *adj* courageous; plucky, brave

couramment (koo-rah-*mahng*) *adv* fluently

courant (koo-*rahng*) *m* current, stream; undercurrent; *adj* frequent, current; **~ alternatif** alternating current; **~ continu** direct current; **~ d'air** draught, draft *Am*; ***mettre au ~** inform

courbatures (koor-bah-*tewr*) *fpl* sore muscles

courbe (koorb) *f* bend, curve; *adj* curved

courbé (koor-*bay*) *adj* curved

courber (koor-*bay*) *v* *bend; bow

courgette (koor-*zheht*) *f* courgette, zucchini *Am*

*courir (koo-*reer*) *v* *run

couronne (koo-*ron*) *f* crown

couronner (koo-ro-*nay*) *v* crown

courrier (koo-*r*ʸ*ay*) *m* mail

courroie (koo-*rwah*) *f* strap; **~ de ventilateur** fan belt

cours (koor) *m* course; lecture; **~ accéléré** crash course; **~ du change** foreign exchange rate

course (koors) *f* race; ride; **~ de chevaux** horserace

court (koor) *adj* short; **~ de tennis** tennis court

court-circuit (koor-seer-*kwee*) *m* short circuit

courtier (koor-*t*ʸ*ay*) *m* broker

courtois (koor-*twah*) *adj* courteous

cousin (koo-*zang*) *m* cousin

cousine (koo-*zeen*) *f* cousin

coussin (koo-*sang*) *m* cushion

coût (koo) *m* cost

couteau (koo-*toa*) *m* knife; **~ de poche** pocketknife

coûter (koo-*tay*) *v* *cost

coûteux (koo-*tur*) *adj* expensive

coutume (koo-*tewm*) *f* custom

couture (koo-*tewr*) *f* seam; **sans ~** seamless

couturière (koo-tew-r*ʸ*air*) *f* dressmaker

couvent (koo-*vahng*) *m* convent; nunnery

couvercle (koo-*vehrkl*) *m* top, lid, cover

couvert (koo-*vair*) *m* cutlery; cover charge; *adj* overcast

couverture (koo-vehr-*tewr*) *f* blanket; cover

*couvrir (koo-*vreer*) *v* cover

crabe (krahb) *m* crab

cracher (krah-*shay*) *v* *spit

crachin (krah-*shang*) *m* drizzle

craie (kray) *f* chalk

*craindre (krangdr) *v* fear, dread

crainte (krangt) *f* fear, dread

cramoisi (krah-mwah-*zee*) *adj* crimson

crampe (krahngp) *f* cramp

crampon (krahng-*pawng*) *m* clamp

cran (krahng) *m* guts

crâne (kraan) *m* skull

crapaud (krah-*poa*) *m* toad

craquement (krahk-*mahng*) *m* crack

craquer (krah-*kay*) *v* crack

cratère (krah-*tair*) *m* crater

cravate (krah-*vaht*) *f* necktie, tie

crawl (kroal) *m* crawl

crayon (kreh-ʸ*awng*) *m* pencil; **~ à bille** Biro; **~ pour les yeux** eyebrow pencil

création (kray-ah-s*ʸ*awng*) *f* creation

créature (kray-ah-*tewr*) *f* creature

crèche (krehsh) *f* nursery

crédit (kray-*dee*) *m* credit

créditer (kray-dee-*tay*) *v* credit

créditeur (kray-dee-*tūrr*) *m* creditor

crédule (kray-*dewl*) *adj* credulous

créer (kray-*ay*) *v* create; design

crème (krehm) *f* cream; *adj* cream; ~ **à raser** shaving cream; ~ **capillaire** hair cream; ~ **de beauté** face cream; skin cream; ~ **de nuit** night cream; ~ **fraîche** crème fraîche; ~ **glacée** ice cream; ~ **hydratante** moisturizing cream

crémeux (kray-*mur*) *adj* creamy

crêpe (krehp) *f* pancake

crépi (kray-*pee*) *m* roughcast

crépuscule (kray-pew-*skewl*) *m* dusk, twilight

cresson (kreh-*sawng*) *m* watercress

creuser (krur-*zay*) *v* *dig

creux (krur) *adj* hollow

crevaison (krer-vay-*zawng*) *f* puncture; flat

crevasse (krer-*vahss*) *f* crack, fissure

crever (krer-*vay*) *v* *burst; die; **crevé** punctured

crevette (krer-*veht*) *f* shrimp; prawn; ~ **rose** prawn

cri (kree) *m* shout, yell, scream, cry; **pousser des cris** shriek

cric (kreek) *m* jack

cricket (kree-*keht*) *m* cricket

crier (kree-*ay*) *v* cry; shout, scream

crime (kreem) *m* crime

criminalité (kree-mee-nah-lee-*tay*) *f* criminality

criminel (kree-mee-*nehl*) *m* criminal; *adj* criminal

crique (kreek) *f* inlet, creek

crise (kreez) *f* crisis; ~ **cardiaque** heart attack

cristal (kree-*stahl*) *m* crystal; **en ~** crystal

critique (kree-*teek*) *f* criticism; review; *m/f* critic; *adj* critical

critiquer (kree-tee-*kay*) *v* criticize

crochet (kro-*shay*) *m* hook; *faire du ~ crochet

crocodile (kro-ko-*deel*) *m* crocodile

croire (krwaar) *v* believe; guess

croisement (krwahz-*mahng*) *m* crossing

croisière (krwah-z^y*air*) *f* cruise

croissance (krwah-*sahngss*) *f* growth

croître (krwaatr) *v* increase

croix (krwah) *f* cross

croque-monsieur (krok-mer-s^y*ur*) *m* toasted ham and cheese sandwich

croustillant (kroo-stee-^{y}*ahng*) *adj* crisp

croûte (kroot) *f* crust

croyable (krwah-^{y}*aabl*) *adj* credible

croyance (krwah-^{y}*ahngss*) *f* belief

cru (krew) *adj* raw

cruche (krewsh) *f* pitcher; jug

crucifier (krew-see-f^y*ay*) *v* crucify

crucifix (krew-see-*fee*) *m* crucifix

crucifixion (krew-see-fee-ks^y*awng*) *f* crucifixion

crudités (krew-dee-*tay*) *fpl* crudités

cruel (krew-*ehl*) *adj* cruel; harsh

crustacé (krew-stah-*say*) *m* shellfish

Cuba (kew-*bah*) *m* Cuba

cubain (kew-*bang*) *adj* Cuban

cube (kewb) *m* cube

*cueillir** (kur-^{y}*eer*) *v* pick

cuillère (kwee-^{y}*air*) *f* spoon; tablespoon; ~ **à thé** teaspoon

cuillerée (kwee-^{y}*er-ray*) *f* spoonful

cuir (kweer) *m* leather; **en ~** leather

*cuire** (kweer) *v* cook; ~ **au four** bake

cuisine (kwee-*zeen*) *f* kitchen

cuisinier (kwee-zee-n^y*ay*) *m* cook

cuisinière (kwee-zee-n^y*air*) *f* cooker; stove; ~ **à gaz** gas cooker

cuisse (kweess) *f* thigh

cuit (kwee) *adj* cooked

cuivre (kweevr) *m* brass, copper

cul-de-sac (kewd-*sahk*) *m* cul-de-sac

culotte (kew-*lot*) *f* panties *pl*; **culottes**

courtes short trousers *pl*

culpabilité (kewl-pah-bee-lee-*tay*) *f* guilt

culte (kewlt) *m* worship

cultiver (kewl-tee-*vay*) *v* cultivate; *grow, raise; **cultivé** cultured

culture (kewl-*tewr*) *f* culture

cupide (kew-*peed*) *adj* greedy

cupidité (kew-pee-dee-*tay*) *f* greed

cure (kewr) *f* cure

cure-dent (kewr-*dahng*) *m* toothpick

cure-pipe (kewr-*peep*) *m* pipe cleaner

curieux (kew-*r*y*ur*) *adj* inquisitive, curious

curiosité (kew-r*y*o-zee-*tay*) *f* curiosity; sight

curry (kur-*ree*) *m* curry

cycle (seekl) *m* cycle

cycliste (see-*kleest*) *m* cyclist

cygne (seeñ) *m* swan

cylindre (see-*langdr*) *m* cylinder; **tête de ~** cylinder head

cystite (see-*steet*) *f* cystitis

D

dactylographier (dahk-tee-loa-grah-*f*y*ay*) *v* type

daltonien (dahl-to-n*y*ang) *adj* colo(u)r-blind

dame (dahm) *f* lady

damier (dah-m*y*ay) *m* check; **à damiers** chequered

Danemark (dahn-*mahrk*) *m* Denmark

danger (dahng-*zhay*) *m* risk, danger

dangereux (dahng-*zhrur*) *adj* dangerous; risky

danois (dah-*nwah*) *adj* Danish

dans (dahng) *prep* into, inside, in, within

danse (dahngss) *f* dance; **~ folklorique** folk dance

danser (dahng-*say*) *v* dance

date (daht) *f* date

datte (daht) *f* date

davantage (dah-vahng-*taazh*) *adv* more

de (der) *prep* of; out of, from, off; about; with

dé (day) *m* thimble

déballer (day-bah-*lay*) *v* unwrap, unpack

débarquer (day-bahr-*kay*) *v* disembark, land

débarrasser (day-bah-rah-*say*) *v*: **se ~ de** *get rid of

débat (day-*bah*) *m* debate; discussion

*débattre (day-*bahtr*) *v* discuss

débit (day-*bee*) *m* debit

déboucher (day-boo-*shay*) *v* uncork

debout (der-*boo*) *adv* standing up, up

déboutonner (day-boo-to-*nay*) *v* unbutton

débrancher (day-brahng-*shay*) *v* disconnect

débrouiller (day-broo-*y*ay): *v*: **se ~ avec** *make do with

début (day-*bew*) *m* start, beginning; **au ~** at first

débutant (day-bew-*tahng*) *m* learner, beginner

débuter (day-bew-*tay*) *v* *begin

décaféiné (day-kah-fay-ee-*nay*) *adj* decaffeinated

décalage (day-kah-*laazh*) *m* shifting; gap, discrepancy

décapsuleur (day-kah-psew-*lurr*) *m* bottle opener

décédé (day-say-*day*) *adj* dead, deceased

décembre (day-*sahngbr*) December

décence (day-*sahngss*) *f* decency

décent (day-*sahng*) *adj* decent

déception (day-seh-*psʸawng*) *f* disap**décerner** (day-sehr-*nay*) *v* award

***décevoir** (day-*svwaar*) *v* disappoint

déchaînement (day-shehn-*mahng*) *m* outbreak

décharger (day-shahr-*zhay*) *v* discharge; unload

déchets (day-*shay*) *mpl* scraps, waste

déchirer (day-shee-*ray*) *v* rip, *tear

déchirure (day-shee-*rewr*) *f* tear

décider (day-see-*day*) *v* decide

décision (day-see-*zʸawng*) *f* decision

déclaration (day-klah-rah-*sʸawng*) *f* declaration, statement

déclarer (day-klah-*ray*) *v* declare, state

décliner (day-klee-*nay*) *v* slope

décollage (day-ko-*laazh*) *m* take-off

décoller (day-ko-*lay*) *v* *take off

décolorer (day-ko-lo-*ray*) *v* fade; bleach

déconcerter (day-kawng-sehr-*tay*) *v* discomfort; confound

décontracté (day-kawng-trahk-*tay*) *adj* easy-going

décoration (day-ko-rah-*sʸawng*) *f* decoration

décorer (day-ko-*ray*) *v* decorate

découper (day-koo-*pay*) *v* carve; *cut up; *cut out

décourager (day-koo-rah-*zhay*) *v* discourage

découverte (day-koo-*vehrt*) *f* discovery

***découvrir** (day-koo-*vreer*) *v* discover; uncover

***décrire** (day-*kreer*) *v* describe

déçu (day-*sew*) *adj* disappointed

dédain (day-*dang*) *m* contempt; scorn

dedans (der-*dahng*) *adv* in; inside

dédier (day-*dʸay*) *v* dedicate

dédommagement (day-do-mahzh-*mahng*) *m* indemnity

***déduire** (day-*dweer*) *v* infer, deduce; deduct

défaillant (day-fah-*ʸahng*) *adj* faint

***défaire** (day-*fair*) *v* *undo

défaite (day-*feht*) *f* defeat

défaut (day-*foa*) *m* fault

défavorable (day-fah-vo-*rahbl*) *adj* unfavo(u)rable

défectueux (day-fehk-*twur*) *adj* faulty, defective

défendre (day-*fahngdr*) *v* defend

défense (day-*fahngss*) *f* defence, defense *Am*; ~ **de doubler** no overtaking; no passing *Am*; ~ **de fumer** no smoking; ~ **d'entrer** no entry

défi (day-*fee*) *m* challenge

défiance (day-*fʸahngss*) *f* mistrust, distrust

déficience (day-fee-*sʸahngss*) *f* deficiency

déficit (day-fee-*seet*) *m* deficit

défier (day-*fʸay*) *v* challenge; defy

définir (day-fee-*neer*) *v* determine, define

définition (day-fee-nee-*sʸawng*) *f* definition

dégât (day-*gah*) *m* waste

dégel (day-*zhehl*) *m* thaw

dégeler (day-*zhlay*) *v* thaw

dégoût (day-*goo*) *m* disgust

dégoûtant (day-goo-*tahng*) *adj* disgusting, revolting

dégoûté (day-goo-*tay*) *adj* fed up with

degré (der-*gray*) *m* degree

déguisement (day-geez-*mahng*) *m* disguise

déguiser (day-gee-*zay*) *v*: **se** ~ disguise

dehors (der-*awr*) *adv* outside, outdoors, out; **en** ~ **de** out of

déjà (day-*zhah*) *adv* already

déjeuner (day-zhur-*nay*) *m* lunch; **petit ~** breakfast

delà: au ~ de (oa der-*lah* der) past, beyond

délabré (day-lah-*bray*) *adj* dilapidated

délai (day-*lay*) *m* time limit; **dans les plus brefs délais** as soon as possible

délégation (day-lay-gah-s*y*aw*n̄g*) *f* delegation

délégué (day-lay-*gay*) *m*, **-e** *f* delegate

délibération (day-lee-bay-rah-s*y*aw*n̄g*) *f* deliberation; discussion

délibérer (day-lee-bay-*ray*) *v* deliberate; **délibéré** deliberate

délicat (day-lee-*kah*) *adj* tender, delicate; gentle; critical

délicatesse (day-lee-kah-*tehss*) *f* delicacy

délice (day-*leess*) *m* delight

délicieux (day-lee-s*y*ur) *adj* delightful, delicious, wonderful, lovely

délinquant (day-la*n̄g*-kah*n̄g*) *m*, **-e** *f* criminal

délivrance (day-lee-*vrah*n̄gss) *f* delivery

délivrer (day-lee-*vray*) *v* deliver

demain (der-*man̄g*) *adv* tomorrow

demande (der-*mahn̄gd*) *f* demand; application, request

demander (der-mahn̄g-*day*) *v* ask, beg; **se ~** wonder

démangeaison (day-mahn̄g-zhay-*zawn̄g*) *f* itching

démanger (day-mahn̄g-*zhay*) *v* itch

démarche (day-*mahrsh*) *f* walk, gait; step, move

déménagement (day-may-nahzh-*mahn̄g*) *m* move

déménager (day-may-nah-*zhay*) *v* move

démence (day-*mahn̄gss*) *f* madness

dément (day-*mahn̄g*) *adj* mad

demeure (der-*mūrr*) *f* home

demeurer (der-mur-*ray*) *v* stay; live

demi (der-*mee*) *adj* half

demi-heure (der-mee-*ūrr*) *f* **une ~** half an hour

demi-pension (der-mee-pahn̄g-s*y*aw*n̄g*) *f* part board

démission (day-mee-s*y*aw*n̄g*) *f* resignation

démissionner (day-mee-s*y*o-*nay*) *v* resign

demi-tour (der-mee-*tōōr*) *m* half-turn, U-turn; **faire demi-tour** turn back

démocratie (day-mo-krah-*see*) *f* democracy

démocratique (day-mo-krah-*teek*) *adj* democratic

démodé (day-mo-*day*) *adj* out of date, old-fashioned

demoiselle (der-mwah-*zehl*) *f* miss

démolir (day-mo-*leer*) *v* demolish

démolition (day-mo-lee-s*y*aw*n̄g*) *f* demolition

démonstration (day-maw*n̄g*-strah-s*y*aw*n̄g*) *f* demonstration

démontrer (day-maw*n̄g*-*tray*) *v* *show, demonstrate, prove

dénier (day-n*y*ay) *v* deny

dénomination (day-no-mee-nah-s*y*aw*n̄g*) *f* denomination

dénouer (day-*nway*) *v* untie

dense (dah*n̄g*ss) *adj* dense

dent (dah*n̄g*) *f* tooth

dentelle (dahn̄g-*tehl*) *f* lace

dentier (dahn̄g-*t*ay) *m* false teeth, denture

dentifrice (dahn̄g-teh-*freess*) *m* toothpaste

dentiste (dahn̄g-*teest*) *m/f* dentist

dénudé (day-new-*day*) *adj* naked

dénutrition (day-new-tree-s*y*aw*n̄g*) *f* malnutrition

déodorant (day-o-do-*rahn̄g*) *m* deodorant

départ (day-*paar*) *m* departure

département (day-pahr-ter-*mahng*) *m* division, department

dépasser (day-pah-*say*) *v* *overtake; pass

dépêcher (day-pay-*shay*): **se ~** hurry

dépendant (day-pahng-*dahng*) *adj* dependent

dépendre de (day-*pahng*dr) depend on

dépense (day-*pahng*ss) *f* expense, expenditure

dépenser (day-pahng-*say*) *v* *spend

dépit: en ~ de (ahng day-*pee* der) in spite of

déplacement (day-plah-*smahng*) *m* moving

déplacer (day-plah-*say*) *v* move

*déplaire (day-*plair*) *v* displease

déplaisant (day-play-*zahng*) *adj* unpleasant

déplier (day-plee-*ay*) *v* unfold

déployer (day-plwah-*y*ay) *v* expand

déposer (day-poa-*zay*) *v* deposit

dépôt (day-*poa*) *m* deposit; warehouse, depot

dépression (day-preh-*s*yawng) *f* depression

déprimer (day-pree-*may*) *v* depress; **déprimé** down; blue; low

depuis (der-*pwee*) *prep* since; *adv* since; **~ que** since

député (day-pew-*tay*) *m/f* deputy; Member of Parliament

déraisonnable (day-ray-zo-*nahbl*) *adj* unreasonable

dérangement (day-rahngzh-*mahng*) *m* trouble; disturbance; **en ~** broken, out of order

déranger (day-rahng-*zhay*) *v* disturb, upset, trouble

déraper (day-rah-*pay*) *v* slip, skid

dermatologue (dehr-mah-to-*log*) *m/f* dermatologist

dernier (dehr-*n*yay) *adj* last; past

dernièrement (dehr-nyehr-*mahng*) *adv* lately

derrière (deh-*r*yair) *prep* after, behind; *m* bottom

dès que (day ker) as soon as

désaccord: *être en ~ (aitr ahng day-zah-*kawr*) disagree

désagréable (day-zah-gray-*ahbl*) *adj* nasty, disagreeable, unpleasant, unkind

désagrément (day-zah-gray-*mahng*) *m* inconvenience

*désapprendre (day-zah-*prahng*dr) *v* unlearn

désapprouver (day-zah-proo-*vay*) *v* disapprove

désastre (day-*zahst*r) *m* disaster

désastreux (day-zah-*strur*) *adj* disastrous

désavantage (day-zah-vahng-*taazh*) *m* disadvantage

descendance (day-sahng-*dahng*ss) *f* origin

descendant (day-sahng-*dahng*) *m*, **-e** *f* descendant

descendre (day-*sahng*dr) *v* descend; *get off

descente (day-*sahng*t) *f* descent

description (day-skree-*ps*yawng) *f* description

désenchanter (day-zahng-shahng-*tay*) *v* disillusion

désert (day-*zair*) *m* desert; *adj* desert

déserter (day-zehr-*tay*) *v* desert

désespérer (day-zeh-spay-*ray*) *v* despair; **désespéré** desperate; hopeless

désespoir (day-zeh-*spwaar*) *m* despair

déshabiller (day-zah-bee-*y*ay) *v*: **se ~** undress

déshonneur (day-zo-*nurr*) *m* disgrace, shame

désigner (day-zee-*ñay*) *v* designate;

appoint

désinfectant (day-zang-fehk-*tahng*) *m* disinfectant

désinfecter (day-zang-fehk-*tay*) *v* disinfect

désintéressé (day-zang-tay-ray-*say*) *adj* unselfish

désir (day-*zeer*) *m* desire, wish

désirable (day-zee-*rahbl*) *adj* desirable

désirer (day-zee-*ray*) *v* want, desire, wish, long for

désireux (day-zee-*rur*) *adj* eager, anxious

désobligeant (day-zo-blee-*zhahng*) *adj* disagreeable

désodorisant (day-zo-do-ree-*zahng*) *m* deodorant

désoler (day-zo-*lay*) *v* grieve; **désolé** sorry

désordonné (day-zor-do-*nay*) *adj* disorderly, untidy

désordre (day-*zordr*) *m* disorder, mess

désormais (day-zawr-*may*) *adv* from now on, henceforth

désosser (day-zo-*say*) *v* bone

dessein (day-*sang*) *m* design

desserrer (day-say-*ray*) *v* loosen

dessert (day-*sair*) *m* dessert, sweet

dessin (day-*sang*) *m* sketch, drawing; pattern; **dessins animés** cartoon

dessiner (day-see-*nay*) *v* sketch, *draw

dessous (der-*soo*) *adv* underneath; **en ~** below; **en ~ de** beneath

dessus (der-*sew*) *m* top; **au-dessus de** on top of; **sens ~ dessous** upside-down

destin (day-*stang*) *m* destiny; fate

destinataire (day-stee-nah-*tair*) *m* addressee

destination (day-stee-nah-s^y*awng*) *f* destination

destiner (day-stee-*nay*) *v* destine

destruction (day-strewk-s^y*awng*) *f* destruction

détachant (day-tah-*shahng*) *m* cleaning fluid, stain remover

détacher (day-tah-*shay*) *v* unfasten, detach

détail (day-*tigh*) *m* detail; **commerce de ~** retail trade

détaillant (day-tah-^y*ahng*) *m*, **-e** *f* retailer

détaillé (day-tah-^y*ay*) *adj* detailed

détailler (day-tah-^y*ay*) *v* retail

détecter (day-tehk-*tay*) *v* detect

détective (day-tehk-*teev*) *m* detective

***déteindre** (day-*tangdr*) *v* fade

détendre (day-*tahngdr*) *v*: **se ~** relax

détente (day-*tahngt*) *f* relaxation

détention (day-tahng-s^y*awng*) *f* detention

détenu (dayt-*new*) *m* prisoner

détergent (day-tehr-*zhahng*) *m* detergent

déterminer (day-tehr-mee-*nay*) *v* determine, define; **déterminé** *adj* definite; resolute

détester (day-teh-*stay*) *v* dislike, hate

détour (day-*toor*) *m* detour

détourner (day-toor-*nay*) *v* divert; hijack

détresse (day-*trehss*) *f* distress; misery

détritus (day-tree-*tewss*) *m* litter, garbage, rubbish

***détruire** (day-*trweer*) *v* destroy, wreck

dette (deht) *f* debt

deuil (dur^{ee}) *m* mourning

deux (dur) *num* two; **les ~** either, both

deuxième (dur-z^y*ehm*) *num* second

deux-pièces (dur-p^y*ehss*) *m* two-piece

dévaluation (day-vah-lwah-s^y*awng*) *f* devaluation

dévaluer (day-vah-*lway*) *v* devalue

devant (der-*vahng*) *prep* in front of, ahead of, before

dévaster (day-vah-*stay*) *v* destroy

développement (day-vlop-*mahng*) *m*
development

développer (day-vlo-*pay*) *v* develop

*devenir (der-*vneer*) *v* *become, *go,
*get

déviation (day-v^yah-s^y*awng*) *f*
diversion, detour

dévier (day-v^y*ay*) *v* deviate

deviner (der-vee-*nay*) *v* guess

devise (der-*veez*) *f* slogan, motto

dévisser (day-vee-*say*) *v* unscrew

devoir (der-*vwaar*) *m* duty

*devoir (der-*vwaar*) *v* *be obliged to,
*be bound to, *have to; need to,
*should, *ought to, *shall; owe

dévorer (day-vo-*ray*) *v* devour

dévouement (day-voo-*mahng*) *m*
devotion

diabète (d^yah-*beht*) *m* diabetes

diabétique (d^yah-bay-*teek*) *m/f*
diabetic

diable (d^yaabl) *m* devil

diagnostic (d^yahg-no-*steek*) *m*
diagnosis

diagnostiquer (d^yahg-no-stee-*kay*) *v*
diagnose

diagonale (d^yah-go-*nahl*) *f* diagonal;
adj diagonal

diagramme (d^yah-*grahm*) *m* graph,
diagram

dialecte (d^yah-*lehkt*) *m* dialect

diamant (d^yah-*mahng*) *m* diamond

diapositive (d^yah-po-zee-*teev*) *f* slide

diarrhée (d^yah-*ray*) *f* diarrh(o)ea

dictée (deek-*tay*) *f* dictation

dicter (deek-*tay*) *v* dictate

dictionnaire (deek-s^yo-*nair*) *m*
dictionary

diesel (d^yay-*zehl*) *m* diesel

dieu (d^yur) *m* god

différence (dee-fay-*rahngss*) *f*
difference, contrast

différent (dee-fay-*rahng*) *adj* different

différer (dee-fay-*ray*) *v* delay; vary,
differ

difficile (dee-fee-*seel*) *adj* difficult,
hard

difficulté (dee-fee-kewl-*tay*) *f*
difficulty

difforme (dee-*form*) *adj* deformed

digérer (dee-zhay-*ray*) *v* digest

digestible (dee-zheh-*steebl*) *adj*
digestible

digestif (dee-zheh-*steef*) *adj, m*
digestive

digestion (dee-zheh-st^y*awng*) *f*
digestion

digne (deeñ) *adj* dignified; **~ de** worthy
of

digue (deeg) *f* dike, dam

diluer (dee-*lway*) *v* dissolve, dilute

dimanche (dee-*mahngsh*) *m* Sunday

dimension (dee-mahng-s^y*awng*) *f* size,
extent

diminuer (dee-mee-*nway*) *v* decrease,
lessen, reduce

diminution (dee-mee-new-s^y*awng*) *f*
decrease

dinde (dangd) *f* turkey

dîner (dee-*nay*) *v* dine, *have dinner;
m dinner

diphtérie (deef-tay-*ree*) *f* diphtheria

diplomate (dee-plo-*maht*) *m* diplomat

diplôme (dee-*plōam*) *m* certificate,
diploma

*dire (deer) *v* *tell, *say

direct (dee-*rehkt*) *adj* direct

directement (dee-rehk-ter-*mahng*)
adv straight away, straight

directeur (dee-rehk-*tūrr*) *m* manager,
director; **~ d'école** headmaster, head
teacher

direction (dee-rehk-s^y*awng*) *f*
management, direction, leadership;
way; **indicateur de ~** indicator,
blinker *Am*

directive (dee-rehk-*teev*) *f* directive

directrice (dee-rehk-*trees*) *f* director; **~**

d'école headmistress, head teacher

dirigeant (dee-ree-*zhahng*) *m*, **-e** *f*
leader, ruler

diriger (dee-ree-*zhay*) *v* direct; head,
conduct, *lead; manage

discerner (dee-sehr-*nay*) *v* distinguish

discipline (dee-see-*pleen*) *f* discipline

discours (dee-*skoor*) *m* speech

discret (dee-*skray*) *adj* (*f* discrète)
discreet, reserved; unobtrusive

discussion (dee-skew-*s^yawng*) *f*
discussion, argument, deliberation;
dispute

discuter (dee-skew-*tay*) *v* discuss,
argue, deliberate

***disjoindre** (deess-zhwangdr) *v*
disconnect

disloqué (dee-slo-*kay*) *adj* dislocated

***disparaître** (dee-spah-*raitr*) *v* vanish,
disappear

disparu (dee-spah-*rew*) *adj* lost; *m*
missing person

dispensaire (dee-spahng-*sair*) *m*
health center *Am*, health centre

dispenser (dee-spahng-*say*) *v* exempt;
~ de discharge of

disperser (dee-spehr-*say*) *v* scatter

disponible (dee-spo-*neebl*) *adj*
available; obtainable; spare

disposé (dee-spoa-*zay*) *adj* inclined,
willing

disposer de (dee-spoa-*zay*) dispose of

dispositif (dee-spoa-zee-*teef*) *m*
apparatus

disposition (dee-spoa-zee-*s^yawng*) *f*
disposal

dispute (dee-*spewt*) *f* argument

disputer (dee-spew-*tay*) *v* argue; **se ~**
dispute, quarrel

disque (deesk) *m* disc; record

dissertation (dee-sehr-tah-*s^yawng*) *f*
essay

dissimuler (dee-see-mew-*lay*) *v* *hide,
conceal

***dissoudre** (dee-*soodr*) *v* dissolve; **se
~** dissolve

dissuader (dee-swah-*day*) *v* dissuade
from

distance (dee-*stahngss*) *f* way,
distance, space

distinct (dee-*stang*) *adj* distinct,
separate

distinction (dee-stangk-*s^yawng*) *f*
distinction, difference

distinguer (dee-stang-*gay*) *v*
distinguish

distraction (dee-strahk-*s^yawng*) *f*
diversion; inadvertence

distrait (dee-*stray*) *adj* absent-minded

distribuer (dee-stree-*bway*) *v*
distribute, *deal

distributeur (dee-stree-bew-*tūrr*) *m*
distributor; **~ de billets** ticket
machine; **~ d'essence** fuel pump
Am; **~ de timbres** stamp machine; **~
automatique** cash dispenser, ATM

distribution (dee-stree-bew-*s^yawng*) *f*
distribution

district (dee-*stree*) *m* district

divers (dee-*vair*) *adj* various, several;
miscellaneous

diversion (dee-vehr-*s^yawng*) *f*
diversion

divertir (dee-vehr-*teer*) *v* entertain,
amuse

divertissant (dee-vehr-tee-*sahng*) *adj*
entertaining

divertissement (dee-vehr-tee-
smahng) *m* pleasure, fun,
entertainment, amusement

divin (dee-*vang*) *adj* divine

diviser (dee-vee-*zay*) *v* divide; **~ en
deux** halve

division (dee-vee-*z^yawng*) *f* division;
department

divorce (dee-*vors*) *m* divorce

divorcer (dee-vor-*say*) *v* divorce

dix (deess) *num* ten

dix-huit (dee-*zweet*) *num* eighteen

dix-huitième (dee-zwee-*t*^y*ehm*) *num* eighteenth

dixième (dee-z^y*ehm*) *num* tenth

dix-neuf (deez-*nurf*) *num* nineteen

dix-neuvième (deez-nur-*v*^y*ehm*) *num* nineteenth

dix-sept (dee-*seht*) *num* seventeen

dix-septième (dee-seh-*t*^y*ehm*) *num* seventeenth

dock (dok) *m* dock

docteur (dok-*tūrr*) *m* doctor

document (do-kew-*mahng*) *m* document, certificate

doigt (dwah) *m* finger

domaine (do-*mehn*) *m* field

dôme (do͞am) *m* dome

domestique (do-meh-*steek*) *adj* domestic; *m/f* domestic, servant

domestiqué (do-meh-stee-*kay*) *adj* tame

domicile (do-mee-*seel*) *m* domicile

domicilié (do-mee-see-*l*^y*ay*) *adj* resident

domination (do-mee-nah-*s*^y*awng*) *f* domination

dominer (do-mee-*nay*) *v* dominate; prevail; **dominant** leading

dommage (do-*maazh*) *m* mischief, damage; **dommage!** what a pity!

don (dawng) *m* faculty, talent; donation, gift

donateur (do-nah-*tūrr*) *m*, **-trice** *f* donor

donation (do-nah-*s*^y*awng*) *f* donation

donc (dawngk) *conj* therefore; so

données (do-*nay*) *fpl* data *pl*

donner (do-*nay*) *v* *give; donate; **étant donné que** given that

dont (dawng) *pron* of which; of whom

doré (do-*ray*) *adj* gilt

*dormir (dor-*meer*) *v* *sleep; **~ trop longtemps** *oversleep

dortoir (dor-*twaar*) *m* dormitory

dos (doa) *m* back

dose (do͞az) *f* dose

dossier (do-s^y*ay*) *m* file, record

douane (dwahn) *f* Customs *pl*; **droit de ~** Customs duty

douanier (dwah-*n*^y*ay*) *m* Customs officer

double (do͞obl) *adj* double

doubler (doo-*blay*) *v* pass *Am*

doublure (doo-*blēwr*) *f* lining

doucement (doos-*mahng*) *adv* gently; softly; smoothly; carefully

douceurs (doo-*sūrr*) *fpl* sweets

douche (doosh) *f* shower

doué (doo-*ay*) *adj* talented, gifted

douleur (doo-*lūrr*) *f* ache, pain; sorrow, grief; **sans ~** painless; **douleurs** labo(u)r

douloureux (doo-loo-*rur*) *adj* painful; distressing

doute (doot) *m* doubt; ***mettre en ~** query; **sans ~** doubtless, probably

douter (doo-*tay*) *v* doubt; **~ de** doubt

douteux (doo-*tur*) *adj* doubtful; unreliable

douve (do͞ov) *f* moat

doux (doo) *adj* (f **douce**) mild; smooth, gentle

douzaine (doo-*zehn*) *f* dozen

douze (do͞oz) *num* twelve

douzième (doo-z^y*ehm*) *num* twelfth

dragon (drah-*gawng*) *m* dragon

drainer (dray-*nay*) *v* drain

dramatique (drah-mah-*teek*) *adj* dramatic

dramaturge (drah-mah-*tewrzh*) *m* dramatist; playwright

drame (drahm) *m* drama

drap (drah) *m* sheet

drapeau (drah-*poa*) *m* flag

dresser (dray-*say*) *v* *draw up; train

drogue (drog) *f* drug

droguerie (dro-*gree*) *f* hardware shop; hardware store *Am*

droit (drwah) *m* right, law, justice; *adj* right, straight; erect, upright; ~ **administratif** administrative law; ~ **civil** civil law; ~ **commercial** commercial law; ~ **de douane** Customs duty; ~ **de stationnement** parking fee; ~ **de vote** right to vote; ~ **d'importation** duty; ~ **pénal** criminal law; **droits** duties *pl*; **tout** ~ straight ahead

droite: de ~ (der drwaht) right-hand

drôle (drōal) *adj* humorous, funny, queer

dû (dew) *adj* (f due; pl dus, dues) due

duc (dewk) *m* duke

duchesse (dew-*shehss*) *f* duchess

dune (dewn) *f* dune

dupe (dewp) *f* victim

duper (dew-*pay*) *v* cheat

dur (dewr) *adj* hard

durable (dew-*rahbl*) *adj* permanent, lasting

durant (dew-*rahng*) *prep* during

durée (dew-*ray*) *f* duration

durer (dew-*ray*) *v* continue, last

duvet (dew-*vay*) *m* down

dynamo (dee-nah-*moa*) *f* dynamo

E

eau (oa) *f* water; ~ **courante** running water; ~ **de mer** sea water; ~ **dentifrice** mouthwash; ~ **de Seltz** soda water; ~ **douce** fresh water; ~ **gazeuse** sparkling mineral water; ~ **glacée** iced water; ~ **minérale** mineral water; ~ **oxygénée** hydrogen peroxide; ~ **potable** drinking water

eau-de-vie (oa-der-*vee*) *f* brandy; spirits

eau-forte (oa-*fort*) *f* etching

ébène (ay-*behn*) *f* ebony

éblouissant (ay-bloo-ee-*sahng*) *adj* glaring

éblouissement (ay-bloo-ee-*smahng*) *m* glare

ébrécher (ay-bray-*shay*) *v* chip

écaille (ay-*kigh*) *f* scale

écarlate (ay-kahr-*laht*) *adj* scarlet

écarter (ay-kahr-*tay*) *v* *spread, part; remove; **écarté** out of the way

ecclésiastique (ay-klay-z^{y}ah-*steek*) *m* clergyman

échafaudage (ay-shah-foa-*daazh*) *m* scaffolding

échange (ay-*shahngzh*) *m* exchange

échanger (ay-shahng-*zhay*) *v* exchange

échantillon (ay-shahng-tee-^{y}*awng*) *m* sample

échappement (ay-shahp-*mahng*) *m* exhaust

échapper (ay-shah-*pay*) *v* escape; **s'échapper** slip

écharde (ay-*shahrd*) *f* splinter

écharpe (ay-*shahrp*) *f* scarf

échec (ay-*shehk*) *m* failure; **échec!** check!; **échecs** chess

échelle (ay-*shehl*) *f* ladder; scale

échiquier (ay-shee-*k^{y}ay*) *m* checkerboard *Am*

écho (ay-*koa*) *m* echo

échoppe (ay-*shop*) *f* booth

échouer (ay-*shway*) *v* fail

éclabousser (ay-klah-boo-*say*) *v* splash

éclair (ay-*klair*) *m* flash; lightning

éclairage (ay-kleh-*raazh*) *m* lighting

éclaircir (ay-klehr-*seer*) *v* clarify

éclaircissement (ay-klehr-see-*smahng*) *m* explanation

éclairer (ay-klay-*ray*) *v* illuminate

éclat (ay-*klah*) *m* glow; glare; chip

éclatant (ay-klah-*tahng*) *adj* bright, gay

éclater (ay-klah-*tay*) *v* *burst

éclipse (ay-*kleeps*) *f* eclipse

éclisse (ay-*kleess*) *f* splint

écluse (ay-*klewz*) *f* sluice, lock

écœurant (ay-kur-*rahng*) *adj* repellent

école (ay-*kol*) *f* school; **~ maternelle** kindergarten; **~ secondaire** secondary school; ***faire l'école buissonnière** play truant

écolier (ay-ko-*lᵉay*) *m* schoolboy

écolière (ay-ko-*lᵉair*) *f* schoolgirl

économe (ay-ko-*nom*) *adj* economical

économie (ay-ko-no-*mee*) *f* economy; **économies** savings *pl*

économique (ay-ko-no-*meek*) *adj* economic

économiser (ay-ko-no-mee-*zay*) *v* economize

économiste (ay-ko-no-*meest*) *m* economist

écorce (ay-*kors*) *f* bark

écossais (ay-ko-*say*) *adj* Scotch; Scottish

Ecosse (ay-*koss*) *f* Scotland

écouler (ay-koo-*lay*): **s'~** flow

écouter (ay-koo-*tay*) *v* listen

écouteur (ay-koo-*turr*) *m* earpiece

écran (ay-*krahng*) *m* screen

écraser (ay-krah-*zay*) *v* mash; overwhelm; **s'écraser** crash

*écrire (ay-*kreer*) *v* *write; **par écrit** in writing, written

écriture (ay-kree-*tewr*) *f* handwriting

écrivain (ay-kree-*vang*) *m*, **-e** *f* writer

écrouler (ay-kroo-*lay*): **s'~** collapse

Ecuadorien (ay-kwah-do-*rᵉang*) *m* Ecuadorian

écume (ay-*kewm*) *f* froth, lather

écureuil (ay-kew-*rurᵉᵉ*) *m* squirrel

eczéma (ehg-zay-*mah*) *m* eczema

édification (ay-dee-fee-kah-*sᵞawng*) *f* construction

édifice (ay-dee-*feess*) *m* construction

édifier (ay-dee-*fᵉay*) *v* construct

éditeur (ay-dee-*turr*) *m* publisher

édition (ay-dee-*sᵞawng*) *f* edition; **~ du matin** morning edition

éditrice (ay-dee-*trees*) *f* publisher

édredon (ay-drer-*dawng*) *m* eiderdown

éducation (ehr-*tsee*-oong) *f* education

éduquer (ay-dew-*kay*) *v* educate

effacer (ay-fah-*say*) *v* wipe out

effectif (ay-fehk-*teef*) *adj* effective

effectivement (ay-fehk-teev-*mahng*) *adv* as a matter of fact

effectuer (ay-fehk-*tway*) *v* effect

effet (ay-*fay*) *m* result; consequence, effect; **en ~** indeed

efficace (ay-fee-*kahss*) *adj* effective; efficient

effilocher (ay-fee-lo-*shay*): **s'~** fray

effondrer (ay-fawng-*dray*): **s'~** collapse

efforcer (ay-for-*say*): **s'~** try hard, endeavour

effort (ay-*fawr*) *m* effort, strain

effrayé (ay-fray-*ᵞay*) *adj* frightened, afraid

effrayer (ay-fray-*ᵞay*) *v* frighten; scare

effronté (ay-frawng-*tay*) *adj* bold; impertinent

égal (ay-*gahl*) *adj* even, level, equal

également (ay-gahl-*mahng*) *adv* as well, likewise, equally, also

égaler (ay-gah-*lay*) *v* equal

égaliser (ay-gah-lee-*zay*) *v* level, equalize

égalité (ay-gah-lee-*tay*) *f* equality

égards (ay-*gaar*) *mpl* consideration

égarer (ay-gah-*ray*) *v* mislay

égayer (ay-gay-*ᵞay*) *v* cheer up

église (ay-*gleez*) *f* chapel, church

égocentrique (ay-go-sahn̄g-*treek*) *adj* self-centred

égoïsme (ay-go-*eesm*) *m* selfishness, ego(t)ism

égoïste (ay-go-*eest*) *adj* ego(t)istic, selfish

égout (ay-*goo*) *m* drain, sewer

égratignure (ay-grah-tee-*ñewr*) *f* graze, scratch

Egypte (ay-*zheept*) *f* Egypt

égyptien (ay-zhee-ps*ʸ*an̄g) *adj* Egyptian

élaborer (ay-lah-bo-*ray*) *v* elaborate

élan (ay-*lahn̄g*) *m* vigour; moose

élargir (ay-lahr-*zheer*) *v* widen

élasticité (ay-lah-stee-see-*tay*) *f* elasticity

élastique (ay-lah-*steek*) *adj* elastic; *m* elastic, rubber band

électeur (ay-lehk-*tūrr*) *m*, **-trice** *f* voter

élection (ay-lehk-s*ʸawn̄g*) *f* election

électricien (ay-lehk-tree-s*ʸan̄g*) *m* electrician

électricité (ay-lehk-tree-see-*tay*) *f* electricity

électrique (ay-lehk-*treek*) *adj* electric

électronique (ay-lehk-tro-*neek*) *adj* electronic

élégance (ay-lay-*gahn̄gss*) *f* elegance

élégant (ay-lay-*gahn̄g*) *adj* smart, elegant

élément (ay-lay-*mahn̄g*) *m* element

élémentaire (ay-lay-mahn̄g-*tair*) *adj* primary

éléphant (ay-lay-*fahn̄g*) *m* elephant

élevage (ehl-*vaazh*) *m* breeding

élévation (ay-lay-vah-s*ʸawn̄g*) *f* rise

élève (ay-*laiv*) *m/f* pupil, scholar

élever (ehl-*vay*) *v* *bring up, rear, raise; *breed

éliminer (ay-lee-mee-*nay*) *v* eliminate

*élire (ay-*leer*) *v* elect

elle (ehl) *pron* she

elle-même (ehl-*mehm*) *pron* herself

éloge (ay-*lozh*) *m* praise

éloigner (ay-lwah-*ñay*) *v* remove; **éloigné** distant, far-away, remote

élucider (ay-lew-see-*day*) *v* elucidate

émail (ay-*migh*) *m* (pl émaux) enamel

émaillé (ay-mah-*ʸay*) *adj* enamelled

émancipation (ay-mahn̄g-see-pah-s*ʸawn̄g*) *f* emancipation

emballage (ahn̄g-bah-*laazh*) *m* packing

emballer (ahn̄g-bah-*lay*) *v* pack up, pack

embargo (ahn̄g-bahr-*goa*) *m* embargo

embarquement (ahn̄g-bahr-ker-*mahn̄g*) *m* embarkation

embarquer (ahn̄g-bahr-*kay*) *v* embark

embarras (ahn̄g-bah-*rah*) *m* fuss

embarrassant (ahn̄g-bah-rah-*sahn̄g*) *adj* awkward, embarrassing; puzzling

embarrasser (ahn̄g-bah-rah-*say*) *v* embarrass

embêtant (ahn̄g-bay-*tahn̄g*) *adj* annoying

emblème (ahn̄g-*blehm*) *m* emblem

embouchure (ahn̄g-boo-*shewr*) *f* mouth

embouteillage (ahn̄g-boo-teh-*ʸaazh*) *m* traffic jam, jam

embrasser (ahn̄g-brah-*say*) *v* kiss

embrayage (ahn̄g-breh-*ʸaazh*) *m* clutch

embrouiller (ahn̄g-broo-*ʸay*) *v* muddle

émeraude (aym-*road*) *f* emerald

émerveiller (ay-mehr-vay-*ʸay*): **s'~** marvel

émetteur (ay-meh-*tūrr*) *m* transmitter

*émettre (ay-*mehtr*) *v* utter; transmit; *broadcast

émeute (ay-*mūrt*) *f* riot

émigrant (ay-mee-*grahn̄g*) *m* emigrant

émigration (ay-mee-grah-s*ʸawn̄g*) *f* emigration

émigrer (ay-mee-*gray*) *v* emigrate

éminent (ay-mee-*nahng*) *adj* outstanding

émission (ay-mee-*s^yawng*) *f* issue; transmission, broadcast

emmagasiner (ahng-mah-gah-zee-*nay*) *v* store

emmener (ahng-mer-*nay*) *v* *take along

émoi (ay-*mwah*) *m* emotion

émotion (ay-moa-*s^yawng*) *f* emotion

émoussé (ay-moo-*say*) *adj* dull, blunt

*émouvoir (ay-moo-*vwaar*) *v* move

empêcher (ahng-pay-*shay*) *v* prevent

empereur (ahng-*prurr*) *m* emperor

empiéter (ahng-p^yay-*tay*) *v* trespass

empire (ahng-*peer*) *m* empire

emploi (ahng-*plwah*) *m* use; job, employment; **solliciter un ~** apply

employé (ahng-plwah-*^yay*) *m*, **-e** *f* employee; **~ de bureau** clerk

employer (ahng-plwah-*^yay*) *v* use; employ

employeur (ahng-plwah-*^yurr*) *m*, **-euse** *f* employer

empoisonner (ahng-pwah-zo-*nay*) *v* poison

emporter (ahng-por-*tay*) *v* *take away

empreinte digitale (ahng-prangt dee-zhee-*tahl*) fingerprint

emprisonnement (ahng-pree-zon-*mahng*) *m* imprisonment

emprisonner (ahng-pree-zo-*nay*) *v* imprison

emprunt (ahng-*prurng*) *m* loan

emprunter (ahng-prurng-*tay*) *v* borrow

en (ahng) *prep* in; by; *pron* of it

encaisser (ahng-kay-*say*) *v* cash

enceinte (ahng-*sangt*) *adj* pregnant

encens (ahng-*sahng*) *m* incense

encercler (ahng-sehr-*klay*) *v* circle, encircle

enchanté (ahng-shahng-*tay*) *adj* enchanted; delightful; **~ de** delighted at, with

enchantement (ahng-shahngt-*mahng*) *m* spell

enchanter (ahng-shahng-*tay*) *v* delight; bewitch

enchanteur (ahng-shahng-*turr*) *adj* (f -teresse) glamorous

enclin (ahng-*klang*) *adj* inclined

encore (ahng-*kawr*) *adv* again; still; yet; **~ que** though; **~ un** another; **~ un peu** some more

encourager (ahng-koo-rah-*zhay*) *v* encourage

encre (ahngkr) *f* ink

encyclopédie (ahng-see-klo-pay-*dee*) *f* encyclop(a)edia

endive (ahng-*deev*) *f* chicory

endommager (ahng-do-mah-*zhay*) *v* damage

endormir (ahng-dor-*meer*) *v* send to sleep; numb; deaden; bore; lull

endormi (ahng-dor-*mee*) *adj* asleep

endosser (ahng-do-*say*) *v* endorse

endroit (ahng-*drwah*) *m* spot

endurer (ahng-dew-*ray*) *v* endure, sustain; *go through

énergie (ay-nehr-*zhee*) *f* energy; power; **~ nucléaire** nuclear energy

énergique (ay-nehr-*zheek*) *adj* energetic

énerver (ay-nehr-*vay*) *v* *get on someone's nerves; **s'énerver** *get excited

enfance (ahng-*fahngss*) *f* childhood

enfant (ahng-*fahng*) *m* child, kid

enfer (ahng-*fair*) *m* hell

enfermer (ahng-fehr-*may*) *v* lock up, *shut in

enfiler (ahng-fee-*lay*) *v* thread

enfin (ahng-*fang*) *adv* at last

enfler (ahng-*flay*) *v* *swell

enflure (ahng-*flewr*) *f* swelling

enfoncer (ahng-fawng-*say*): **s'~** *sink

engagement (ahng-gahzh-*mahng*) *m* engagement

engager (ahng-gah-*zhay*) *v* engage;
s'engager engage

engourdi (ahng-goor-*dee*) *adj* numb

engrais (ahng-*gray*) *m* fertilizer

énigme (ay-*neegm*) *f* mystery, riddle,
puzzle, enigma

enjeu (ahng-*zhur*) *m* stake

enlacement (ahng-lah-*smah*) *m*
embrace

enlever (ahngl-*vay*) *v* remove; *take
away

ennemi (ehn-*mee*) *m*, **-e** *f* enemy

ennui (ahng-*nwee*) *m* annoyance,
trouble; nuisance

ennuyer (ahng-nwee-*^yay*) *v* annoy,
bore

ennuyeux (ahng-nwee-*^yur*) *adj*
annoying; dull, unpleasant, boring

énorme (ay-*norm*) *adj* tremendous,
immense, huge, enormous

enquête (ahng-*keht*) *f* inquiry; enquiry

enquêter (ahng-kay-*tay*) *v* investigate,
enquire

enragé (ahng-rah-*zhay*) *adj* mad

enregistrement (ahngr-zhee-strer-
mahng) *m* recording

enregistrer (ahngr-zhee-*stray*) *v* book;
record

enrhumer (ahng-rew-*may*): **s'~** catch a
cold

enroué (ahng-roo-*ay*) *adj* hoarse

enrouler (ahng-roo-*lay*) *v* *wind

enseignement (ahng-sehñ-*mahng*) *m*
education; teaching

enseigner (ahng-say-*ñay*) *v* *teach

ensemble (ahng-*sahngbl*) *adv*
together; *m* whole

ensoleillé (ahng-so-lay-*^yay*) *adj* sunny

ensorceler (ahng-sor-ser-*lay*) *v*
bewitch

ensuite (ahng-*sweet*) *adv* then,
afterwards

entailler (ahng-tah-*^yay*) *v* carve

entasser (ahng-tah-*say*) *v* pile

entendre (ahng-*tahngdr*) *v* *hear

entente (ahng-*tahngt*) *f* agreement

enterrement (ahng-tehr-*mahng*) *m*
burial

enterrer (ahng-tay-*ray*) *v* bury

enthousiasme (ahng-too-z*^yahsm*) *m*
enthusiasm

enthousiaste (ahng-too-z*^yahst*) *adj*
enthusiastic

entier (ahng-t*^yay*) *adj* whole, complete,
entire

entièrement (ahng-t*^yehr-mahng*) *adv*
wholly, completely, entirely,
altogether

entonnoir (ahng-to-*nwaar*) *m* funnel

entourer (ahng-too-*ray*) *v* encircle;
surround

entracte (ahng-*trahkt*) *m* interval,
intermission

entrailles (ahng-*trigh*) *fpl* entrails, guts

entrain (ahng-*trang*) *m* zest

entraînement (ahng-trehn-*mahng*) *m*
training

entraîner (ahng-tray-*nay*) *v* drill

entraîneur (ahng-treh-*nürr*) *m* coach

entrave (ahng-*traav*) *f* impediment

entraver (ahng-trah-*vay*) *v* impede

entre (ahngtr) *prep* between, among,
amid

entrée (ahng-*tray*) *f* way in, entry,
entrance; appearance; **~ interdite** no
admittance

entrepôt (ahng-trer-*poa*) *m* depository

***entreprendre** (ahng-trer-*prahngdr*) *v*
*undertake

entrepreneur (ahng-trer-prer-*nürr*) *m*,
-euse *f* contractor

entreprise (ahng-trer-*preez*) *f*
enterprise; business, company,
undertaking

entrer (ahng-*tray*) *v* enter, *go in

entre-temps (ahng-trer-*tahng*) *adv*
meanwhile, in the meantime

***entretenir** (ahng-trer-*tneer*) *v*

maintain; support

entretien (ahng-trer-t'*ang*) *m* upkeep, maintenance; conversation

***entrevoir** (ahng-trer-*vwaar*) *v* glimpse

entrevue (ahng-trer-*vew*) *f* interview

envahir (ahng-vah-*eer*) *v* invade

enveloppe (ahng-*vlop*) *f* envelope

envelopper (ahng-vlo-*pay*) *v* wrap

envers (ahng-*vair*) *prep* towards; **à l'envers** inside out

envie (ahng-*vee*) *f* longing, desire; envy; ***avoir ~ de** *feel like; fancy, desire

envier (ahng-*v'ay*) *v* grudge, envy

envieux (ahng-*v'ur*) *adj* envious

environ (ahng-vee-*rawng*) *adv* about

environnant (ahng-vee-ro-*nahng*) *adj* surrounding

environnement (ahng-vee-ron-*mahng*) *m* environment

environs (ahng-vee-*rawng*) *mpl* environment

envisager (ahng-vee-zah-*zhay*) *v* consider

envoyé (ahng-vwah-*'ay*) *m* envoy

***envoyer** (ahng-vwah-*'ay*) *v* *send; dispatch

épais (ay-*pay*) *adj* (f ~se) thick

épaisseur (ay-peh-*surr*) *f* thickness

épaissir (ay-pay-*seer*) *v* thicken

épargner (ay-pahr-*ñay*) *v* save

épaule (ay-*pōal*) *f* shoulder

épave (ay-*paav*) *f* wreck

épée (ay-*pay*) *f* sword

épeler (eh-*play*) *v* *spell

épice (ay-*peess*) *f* spice

épicé (ay-pee-*say*) *adj* spicy, spiced

épicerie (ay-pee-*sree*) *f* grocer's; **~ fine** delicatessen

épicier (ay-pee-*s'ay*) *m*, **-ière** *f* grocer

épidémie (ay-pee-day-*mee*) *f* epidemic

épier (ay-*p'ay*) *v* peep

épilepsie (ay-pee-leh-*psee*) *f* epilepsy

épinards (ay-pee-*naar*) *mpl* spinach

épine (ay-*peen*) *f* thorn; **~ dorsale** backbone, spine

épingle (ay-*panggl*) *f* pin; **~ à cheveux** hairpin; **~ de sûreté** safetypin

épingler (ay-pang-*glay*) *v* pin

épisode (ay-pee-*zod*) *m* episode

éplucher (ay-plew-*shay*) *v* peel; clean; examine closely, sift

éponge (ay-*pawngzh*) *f* sponge

époque (ay-*pok*) *f* period; **de l'époque** contemporary

épouse (ay-*pōoz*) *f* wife

épouser (ay-poo-*zay*) *v* marry

épouvantable (ay-poo-vahng-*tahbl*) *adj* terrible

épouvante (ay-poo-*vahngt*) *f* horror

époux (ay-*poo*) *m* husband

épreuve (ay-*prūrv*) *f* test, experiment; print

éprouver (ay-proo-*vay*) *v* experience; test

épuiser (ay-pwee-*zay*) *v* exhaust; use up; **épuisé** sold out

Equateur (ay-kwah-*tūrr*) *m* Ecuador

équateur (ay-kwah-*tūrr*) *m* equator

équilibre (ay-kee-*leebr*) *m* balance

équipage (ay-kee-*paazh*) *m* crew

équipe (ay-*keep*) *f* shift, team, gang; soccer team

équipement (ay-keep-*mahng*) *m* outfit, gear, equipment

équiper (ay-kee-*pay*) *v* equip

équitable (ay-kee-*tahbl*) *adj* right; reasonable

équitation (ay-kee-tah-*s'awng*) *f* riding

équivalent (ay-kee-vah-*lahng*) *adj* equivalent

équivoque (ay-kee-*vok*) *adj* ambiguous

érable (ay-*rahbl*) *m* maple

érafler (ay-rah-*flay*) *v* scratch

ériger (ay-ree-*zhay*) *v* erect

errer (ay-*ray*) *v* err; wander

erreur (eh-*rūrr*) f error; mistake
erroné (eh-ro-*nay*) adj mistaken
érudit (ay-rew-*dee*) m scholar
éruption (ay-rew-*ps*ᵞ*awng*) f rash
escale (eh-*skahl*) f port of call; stop; call
escalier (eh-skah-*l*ᵞ*ay*) m staircase; stairs pl; ~ **de secours** fire escape; ~ **roulant** escalator
escalope (eh-skah-*lop*) f escalope
escargot (eh-skahr-*goa*) m snail
escarpé (eh-skahr-*pay*) adj steep
escorte (eh-*skort*) f escort
escorter (eh-skor-*tay*) v escort
escrime: *faire de l'escrime (fair der leh-*skreem*) fence
escroc (eh-*skroa*) m swindler
escroquer (eh-skro-*kay*) v swindle
escroquerie (eh-skro-*kree*) f swindle
espace (eh-*spahss*) m space; room
espacer (eh-spah-*say*) v space
Espagne (eh-*spahñ*) f Spain
espagnol (eh-spah-*ñol*) adj Spanish
espèce (eh-*spehss*) f species; breed
espérance (eh-spay-*rahngss*) f expectation
espérer (eh-spay-*ray*) v hope
espièglerie (eh-sp*ᵞ*eh-gler-*ree*) f piece of mischief; prank
espion (eh-sp*ᵞ*awng) m spy
esplanade (eh-splah-*nahd*) f esplanade
espoir (eh-*spwaar*) m hope
esprit (eh-*spree*) m spirit; soul, mind; ghost
esquisse (eh-*skeess*) f sketch
esquisser (eh-skee-*say*) v sketch
essai (ay-*say*) m trial, essay; **à l'essai** on approval
essayer (ay-say-ᵞ*ay*) v try; attempt, test; try on
essence (ay-*sahngss*) f essence; petrol, fuel; gasoline Am, gas Am
essentiel (ay-sahng-s*ᵞ*ehl) adj capital, essential

essentiellement (ay-sahng-s*ᵞ*ehl-*mahng*) adv essentially
essieu (ay-s*ᵞ*ur) m axle
essor (ay-*sawr*) m rise
essuie-glace (ay-swee-*glahss*) m windscreen wiper, windshield wiper Am
essuyer (ay-swee-ᵞ*ay*) v wipe; dry
est (ehst) m east
estampe (eh-*stahngp*) f print; engraving
estimation (eh-stee-mah-s*ᵞ*awng) f estimate
estime (eh-*steem*) f esteem; respect
estimer (eh-stee-*may*) v consider, esteem, reckon; value, estimate
estomac (eh-sto-*mah*) m stomach
estropié (eh-stro-p*ᵞ*ay) adj crippled
estuaire (eh-*stwair*) m estuary
et (ay) conj and
étable (ay-*tahbl*) f stable
établir (ay-tah-*bleer*) v establish; found; **s'établir** settle down
étage (ay-*taazh*) m floor, stor(e)y; apartment Am
étagère (ay-tah-*zhair*) f shelf
étain (ay-*tang*) m pewter, tin
étal (ay-*tahl*) m stall
étalage (ay-tah-*laazh*) m shop-window
étaler (ay-tah-*lay*) v display
étang (ay-*tahng*) m pond
étape (ay-*tahp*) f stage
Etat (ay-*tah*) m state; **Etats-Unis** United States; the States
état (ay-*tah*) m state; condition; ~ **d'urgence** emergency
et cætera (eht-tay-tay-*rah*) etcetera
été (ay-*tay*) m summer; **en plein** ~ in midsummer
*éteindre** (ay-*tangdr*) v *put out; switch off; extinguish
étendre (ay-*tahngdr*) v expand, *spread, enlarge; extend

étendu (ay-tah$\overline{ng}$-*dew*) *adj* broad, extensive; comprehensive

éternel (ay-tehr-*nehl*) *adj* eternal

éternité (ay-tehr-nee-*tay*) *f* eternity

éternuer (ay-tehr-*nway*) *v* sneeze

Ethiopie (ay-t^{y}o-*pee*) *f* Ethiopia

éthiopien (ay-t^{y}o-p^{y}a$\overline{ng}$) *adj* Ethiopian

étincelle (ay-ta$\overline{ng}$-*sehl*) *f* spark

étiqueter (ay-teek-*tay*) *v* label

étiquette (ay-tee-*keht*) *f* tag, label

étoffes (ay-*tof*) *fpl* drapery

étoile (ay-*twahl*) *f* star

étole (ay-*tol*) *f* stole

étonnant (ay-to-*nah$\overline{ng}$*) *adj* astonishing

étonnement (ay-ton-*mah$\overline{ng}$*) *m* astonishment, wonder, amazement

étonner (ay-to-*nay*) *v* amaze; astonish

étouffant (ay-too-*fah$\overline{ng}$*) *adj* stifling

étouffer (ay-too-*fay*) *v* choke

étourdi (ay-toor-*dee*) *adj* dizzy, giddy

étourneau (ay-toor-*noa*) *m* starling

étrange (ay-*trah$\overline{ng}$zh*) *adj* strange; quaint, curious, queer

étranger (ay-trah$\overline{ng}$-*zhay*) *m*, **-ère** *f* foreigner, alien, stranger; *adj* foreign, alien; **à l'étranger** abroad

étrangler (ay-trah$\overline{ng}$-*glay*) *v* choke, strangle

être (aitr) *m* being; creature; **~ humain** human being

*être (aitr) *v* *be

*étreindre (ay-*tra$\overline{ng}$dr*) *v* hug, embrace

étreinte (ay-*tra$\overline{ng}$t*) *f* grip; hug

étroit (ay-*trwah*) *adj* narrow, tight

étude (ay-*tewd*) *f* study

étudiant (ay-tew-d^y*ah$\overline{ng}$*) *m* student

étudiante (ay-tew-d^y*ah$\overline{ng}$t*) *f* student

étudier (ay-tew-d^y*ay*) *v* study

étui (ay-*twee*) *m* case; **~ à cigarettes** cigarette case

Europe (ur-*rop*) *f* Europe

Européen (ur-ro-pay-*a$\overline{ng}$*) *m*, **-ne** *f* European

européen (ur-ro-pay-*a$\overline{ng}$*) *adj* European

eux (ur) *pron* them; **eux-mêmes** *pron* themselves

évacuer (ay-vah-*kway*) *v* evacuate, clear

évaluer (ay-vah-*lway*) *v* evaluate; appreciate, estimate

évangile (ay-vah$\overline{ng}$-*zheel*) *m* gospel

évanouir (ay-vah-*nweer*) : **s'~** faint

évaporer (ay-vah-po-*ray*) *v* evaporate

évasion (ay-vah-z^y*aw$\overline{ng}$*) *f* escape

éveillé (ay-vay-^{y}*ay*) *adj* clever

éveiller (ay-vay-^{y}*ay*): **s'~** wake up

événement (ay-vehn-*mah$\overline{ng}$*) *m* event; occurrence

éventail (ay-vah$\overline{ng}$-*tigh*) *m* fan

éventuel (ay-vah$\overline{ng}$-*twehl*) *adj* possible, eventual

évêque (ay-*vehk*) *m* bishop

évidemment (ay-vee-dah-*mah$\overline{ng}$*) *adv* of course

évident (ay-vee-*dah$\overline{ng}$*) *adj* obvious, evident; self-evident

évier (ay-v^y*ay*) *m* sink

éviter (ay-vee-*tay*) *v* avoid

évolution (ay-vo-lew-s^y*aw$\overline{ng}$*) *f* evolution

évoquer (ay-vo-*kay*) *v* call to mind; evoke

exact (ehg-*zahkt*) *adj* just, precise, exact

exactement (ehg-zahk-ter-*mah$\overline{ng}$*) *adv* exactly

exactitude (ehg-zahk-tee-*tewd*) *f* correctness

exagérer (ehg-zah-zhay-*ray*) *v* exaggerate

examen (ehg-zah-*ma$\overline{ng}$*) *m* examination; checkup

examiner (ehg-zah-mee-*nay*) *v* examine

excéder (ehk-say-*day*) *v* exceed

excellent (ehk-seh-*lah$\overline{ng}$*) *adj* excellent

exceller (ehk-say-*lay*) v excel

excentrique (ehk-sahng-*treek*) adj eccentric

excepté (ehk-sehp-*tay*) prep except

exception (ehk-sehp-*s^{y}awng*) f exception

exceptionnel (ehk-sehp-s^{y}o-*nehl*) adj exceptional

excès (ehk-*say*) m excess; **~ de vitesse** speeding

excessif (ehk-say-*seef*) adj excessive

excitation (ehk-see-tah-*s^{y}awng*) f excitement

exciter (ehk-see-*tay*) v excite

exclamation (ehk-sklah-mah-*s^{y}awng*) f exclamation

exclamer (ehk-sklah-*may*) v exclaim

***exclure** (ehk-*sklewr*) v exclude

exclusif (ehk-sklew-*zeef*) adj exclusive

exclusivement (ehk-sklew-zeev-*mahng*) adv solely, exclusively

excursion (ehk-skewr-*s^{y}awng*) f trip, excursion; day trip; tour

excuse (ehk-*skewz*) f excuse, apology

excuser (ehk-skew-*zay*) v excuse; **excusez-moi!** sorry!; **s'excuser** apologize

exécuter (ehg-zay-kew-*tay*) v execute

exécutif (ehg-zay-kew-*teef*) m executive; adj executive

exécution (ehg-zay-kew-*s^{y}awng*) f execution

exemplaire (ehg-zahng-*plair*) m copy

exemple (ehg-*zahngpl*) m instance, example; **par ~** for instance, for example

exempt (ehg-*zahng*) adj exempt; **~ de droits** duty-free; **~ d'impôts** tax-free

exempter (ehg-zahng-*tay*) v exempt

exemption (ehg-zahng-*ps^{y}awng*) f exemption

exercer (ehg-zehr-*say*) v exercise; **s'exercer** practise

exercice (ehg-zehr-*seess*) m exercise

exhiber (ehg-zee-*bay*) v exhibit

exhibition (ehg-zee-bee-*s^{y}awng*) f exhibition

exhorter (ehg-zor-*tay*) v urge

exigeant (ehg-zee-*zhahng*) adj particular

exigence (ehg-zee-*zhahngss*) f requirement

exiger (ehg-zee-*zhay*) v demand, require

exile (ehg-*zeel*) m exile

exilé (ehg-zee-*lay*) m exile

existence (ehg-zee-*stahngss*) f existence

exister (ehg-zee-*stay*) v exist

exotique (ehg-zo-*teek*) adj exotic

expédier (ehk-spay-d^{y}ay) v dispatch, despatch, *send off, *send; ship

expéditeur (ehk-spay-dee-*türr*) m sender; shipper; forwarding agent

expédition (ehk-spay-dee-*s^{y}awng*) f expedition; consignment

expeditrice (ehk-spay-dee-*trees*) f sender

expérience (ehk-spay-r^{y}ahngss) f experience; experiment; *faire l'expérience de experience

expérimenter (ehk-spay-ree-mahng-*tay*) v test; experiment with; **expérimenté** experienced

expert (ehk-*spair*) adj skilled; m expert

expirer (ehk-spee-*ray*) v breathe out, expire

explicable (ehk-splee-*kahbl*) adj explicable, explainable

explication (ehk-splee-kah-*s^{y}awng*) f explanation

explicite (ehk-splee-*seet*) adj explicit

expliquer (ehk-splee-*kay*) v explain

exploitation (ehk-splwah-tah-*s^{y}awng*) f exploitation; concern; **~ minière** mining development

exploiter (ehk-splwah-*tay*) v exploit

explorer (ehk-splo-*ray*) v explore

exploser (ehk-sploa-*zay*) *v* explode

explosif (ehk-sploa-*zeef*) *m* explosive; *adj* explosive

explosion (ehk-sploa-*z²awng*) *f* explosion, blast

exportation (ehk-spor-tah-*s²awng*) *f* exports *pl*, exportation, export

exporter (ehk-spor-*tay*) *v* export

exposer (ehk-spoa-*zay*) *v* exhibit, *show

exposition (ehk-spoa-zee-*s²awng*) *f* display, exposition, exhibition, show; exposure; ~ **d'art** art exhibition

exprès[1] (ehk-*spray*) *adv* on purpose

exprès[2] (ehk-*sprehss*) *adj* express; special delivery

expression (ehk-spreh-*s²awng*) *f* expression

exprimer (ehk-spree-*may*) *v* express

expulser (ehk-spewl-*say*) *v* expel

exquis (ehk-*skee*) *adj* delicious; exquisite; select

extase (ehk-*staaz*) *m* ecstasy

exténuer (ehk-stay-*nway*) *v* exhaust

extérieur (ehk-stay-r²*urr*) *m* exterior, outside; *adj* external, exterior; **vers l'extérieur** outwards

externe (ehk-*stehrn*) *adj* outward

extincteur (ehk-stangk-*turr*) *m* fire extinguisher

extorquer (ehk-stor-*kay*) *v* extort

extorsion (ehk-stor-*s²awng*) *f* extortion

extrader (ehk-strah-*day*) *v* extradite

***extraire** (ehk-*strair*) *v* extract

extrait (ehk-*stray*) *m* excerpt

extraordinaire (ehk-strah-or-dee-*nair*) *adj* extraordinary, exceptional

extravagant (ehk-strah-vah-*gahng*) *adj* extravagant

extrême (ehk-*strehm*) *adj* extreme, utmost; *m* extreme

exubérant (ehg-zew-bay-*rahng*) *adj* exuberant

F

fable (fahbl) *f* fable

fabricant (fah-bree-*kahng*) *m* manufacturer

fabriquer (fah-bree-*kay*) *v* manufacture

façade (fah-*sahd*) *f* façade

face (fahss) *f* front; **en ~ de** facing, opposite

fâcher (fah-*shay*) *v* annoy; **fâché** cross

facile (fah-*seel*) *adj* easy

façon (fah-*sawng*) *f* way; **de la même ~** alike; **de toute ~** anyway; at any rate

façonner (fah-so-*nay*) *v* model

facteur (fahk-*turr*) *m* factor; postman

facture (fahk-*tewr*) *f* invoice, bill

facturer (fahk-tew-*ray*) *v* bill

facultatif (fah-kewl-tah-*teef*) *adj* optional

faculté (fah-kewl-*tay*) *f* faculty

faible (fehbl) *adj* feeble, weak; small, slight; faint

faiblesse (feh-*blehss*) *f* weakness

faïence (fah-²*ahngss*) *f* crockery

faillite: en ~ (ahng fah-²*eet*) bankrupt

faim (fang) *f* hunger

***faire** (fair) *v* *do; *make; cause to, *have

faisable (fer-*zahbl*) *adj* feasible

faisan (fer-*zahng*) *m* pheasant

fait (fay) *m* fact; **de ~** in fact; **en ~** as a matter of fact, in effect

falaise (fah-*laiz*) *f* cliff

*falloir (fah-*lwaar*) *v* need, *must

falsification (fahl-see-fee-kah-*s^yawng*) *f* fake

falsifier (fahl-see-f'*ay*) *v* forge

fameux (fah-*mur*) *adj* famous

familial (fah-mee-l'*ahl*) *adj* of the family

familiariser (fah-mee-l'ah-ree-*zay*) *v* familiarize, accustom

familier (fah-mee-l'*ay*) *adj* familiar

famille (fah-*meey*) *f* family

fan (fahn) *m/f* fan

fanatique (fah-nah-*teek*) *adj* fanatical

faner (fah-*nay*) *v*: **se ~** fade

fanfare (fahng-*faar*) *f* brass band

fantaisie (fahng-tay-*zee*) *f* fantasy

fantastique (fahng-tah-*steek*) *adj* fantastic

fantôme (fahng-*tōam*) *m* phantom, ghost; spook

faon (fahng) *m* fawn

farce (fahrs) *f* filling, stuffing

farci (fahr-*see*) *adj* stuffed

fardeau (fahr-*doa*) *m* burden, load

farine (fah-*reen*) *f* flour

farouche (fah-*roosh*) *adj* shy

fasciner (fah-see-*nay*) *v* fascinate

fascisme (fah-*sheesm*) *m* fascism

fasciste (fah-*sheest*) *m* fascist; *adj* fascist

fastidieux (fah-stee-d'*ur*) *adj* tedious, tiresome, boring

fatal (fah-*tahl*) *adj* (pl ~s) fatal, mortal

fatigant (fah-tee-*gahng*) *adj* tiring

fatigue (fah-*teeg*) *f* fatigue

fatiguer (fah-tee-*gay*) *v* tire; **fatigué** weary

faubourg (foa-*bōor*) *m* outskirts *pl*, suburb

fauché (foa-*shay*) *adj* broke

faucon (foa-*kawng*) *m* hawk

faute (*fōat*) *f* mistake, error; fault; **donner la ~ à** blame; **sans ~** without fail

fauteuil (foa-*tur^{ee}*) *m* armchair, easy chair; **~ d'orchestre** orchestra seat *Am*; **~ roulant** wheelchair

faux (foa) *adj* (f fausse) false; untrue

faveur (fah-*vūrr*) *f* favo(u)r; **en ~ de** on behalf of

favorable (fah-vo-*rahbl*) *adj* favo(u)rable

favori (fah-vo-*ree*) *m*, **-rite** *f* favo(u)rite; *adj* favo(u)rite; **favoris** whiskers *pl*, sideburns *pl*

favoriser (fah-vo-ree-*zay*) *v* favo(u)r

favorite (fah-vo-*reet*) *f* favo(u)rite

fax (fahks) *m* fax; **envoyer un ~** send a fax

fédéral (fay-day-*rahl*) *adj* federal

fédération (fay-day-rah-*s^yawng*) *f* federation

*feindre (fangdr) *v* pretend

félicitations (fay-lee-see-tah-*s^yawng*) *fpl* congratulations

féliciter (fay-lee-see-*tay*) *v* congratulate, compliment

femelle (fer-*mehl*) *f* female

féminin (fay-mee-*nang*) *adj* feminine, female

femme (fahm) *f* woman, wife

fendre (fahngdr) *v* *split; crack

fenêtre (fer-*naitr*) *f* window

fenouil (fer-*noo^{ee}*) *m* fennel

fente (fahngt) *f* slot, cleft

fer (fair) *m* iron; **en ~** iron; **~ à cheval** horseshoe; **~ à repasser** iron

ferme (fehrm) *f* farmhouse, farm; *adj* firm, steady; steadfast

fermenter (fehr-mahng-*tay*) *v* ferment

fermer (fehr-*may*) *v* close, *shut; fasten; turn off; **fermé** closed shut; **~ à clé** lock

fermeture (fehrm-*tewr*) *f* fastener; **~ éclair** zip, zipper *Am*

fermier (fehr-m'*ay*) *m* farmer

fermière (fehr-m'*air*) *f* farmer's wife

féroce (fay-*ross*) *adj* fierce, wild

ferraille (feh-*righ*) f scrap-iron

ferry-boat (feh-ree-*boat*) m ferryboat; train ferry

fertile (fehr-*teel*) adj fertile

fesse (fehss) f buttock

fessée (fay-*say*) f spanking

festival (feh-stee-*vahl*) m (pl ~s) festival

fête (feht) f feast

Fête-Dieu (feht-d^y*ur*) m Corpus Christi

feu (fur) m fire; ~ **arrière** taillight, rear light; ~ **de circulation** traffic light; ~ **de position** parking light

feuille (fur^{ee}) f leaf; sheet

feuilleton (fur^{ee}-*tawng*) m serial

feutre (fŭrtr) m felt

février (fay-vree-*ay*) February

fiançailles (f^{y}ahng-*sigh*) fpl engagement

fiancé (f^{y}ahng-*say*) m fiancé; adj engaged

fiancée (f^{y}ahng-*say*) f fiancée, bride

fibre (feebr) f fibre

ficelle (fee-*sehl*) f twine, string

fiche (feesh) f plug

fiction (feek-s^y*awng*) f fiction

fidèle (fee-*dehl*) adj faithful, true

fier (f^{y}air) adj proud

fièvre (f^{y}aivr) f fever

fiévreux (f^{y}ay-*vrur*) adj feverish

figue (feeg) f fig

figure (fee-*gewr*) f figure; shape, form; face; appearance; court-card

se figurer (fee-gew-*ray*) imagine

fil (feel) m thread; line, yarn; ~ **de fer** wire; ~ **électrique** electric wire

file (feel) f line

filer (fee-*lay*) v *spin

filet (fee-*lay*) m net; ~ **à bagage** luggage rack; ~ **de pêche** fishing net

fille (feey) f girl; daughter; **vieille ~** spinster

film (feelm) m film, movie; ~ **en**

couleurs colo(u)r film

filmer (feel-*may*) v film

fils (feess) m son

filtre (feeltr) m filter; ~ **à air** air-filter; ~ **à huile** oil filter

filtrer (feel-*tray*) v filter

fin (fang) f finish, ending, end; issue; adj fine, thin

final (fee-*nahl*) adj (pl ~s) final

financer (fee-nahng-*say*) v finance

finances (fee-*nahngss*) fpl finances pl

financier (fee-nahng-s^y*ay*) adj financial

finir (fee-*neer*) v finish, end; **fini** finished, over

Finlandais (fang-lahng-*day*) m Finn

finlandais (fang-lahng-*day*) adj Finnish

Finlande (fang-*lahngd*) f Finland

fissure (fee-*sewr*) f crack, fissure

fixateur (feek-sah-*tŭrr*) m setting lotion

fixe (feeks) adj fixed; permanent

fixer (feek-*say*) v attach; gaze, stare; ~ **le prix** price

flacon (flah-*kawng*) m flask

flamant (flah-*mahng*) m flamingo

flamme (flahm) f flame

flanelle (flah-*nehl*) f flannel

flâner (flah-*nay*) v stroll

flaque (flahk) f puddle

flash (flahsh) m flash-light

flasque (flahsk) adj limp

fléau (flay-*oa*) m plague

flèche (flehsh) f arrow

flétan (flay-*tahng*) m halibut

fleur (flŭrr) f flower

fleuriste (flur-*reest*) m/f flower shop, florist

fleuve (flŭrv) m river

flexible (flehk-*seebl*) adj flexible, elastic

flic (fleek) m cop, policeman

flotte (flot) f fleet

flotter (flo-*tay*) *v* float

flotteur (flo-*turr*) *m* float

fluide (flew-*eed*) *adj* fluid

flûte (flewt) *f* flute

foi (fwah) *f* faith

foie (fwah) *m* liver

foin (fwang) *m* hay

foire (fwaar) *f* fair

fois (fwah) *f* time; *prep* times; **à la ~** at the same time; **deux ~** twice; **une ~** once; some time; **une ~ de plus** once more

folie (fo-*lee*) *f* lunacy

folklore (fol-*klawr*) *m* folklore

foncé (fawng-*say*) *adj* dark

foncer (fawng-*say*) *v* *speed

fonction (fawngk-s^y*awng*) *f* function; office

fonctionnaire (fawngk-s^yo-*nair*) *m* civil servant

fonctionnement (fawngk-s^yon-*mahng*) *m* working, operation

fonctionner (fawngk-s^yo-*nay*) *v* work, operate

fond (fawng) *m* ground, bottom; essence; background; **à ~** thoroughly; **au ~** fundamentally; **~ de teint** foundation cream

fondamental (fawng-dah-mahng-*tahl*) *adj* fundamental, basic, essential

fondation (fawng-dah-s^y*awng*) *f* foundation

fondement (fawngd-*mahng*) *m* base

fonder (fawng-*day*) *v* found; **bien fondé** well-founded

fondre (fawngdr) *v* melt; thaw

fonds (fawng) *mpl* fund

fontaine (fawng-*tehn*) *f* fountain

fonte (fawngt) *f* cast iron

football (foot-*bol*) *m* soccer

force (fors) *f* force, power, strength; **~ armée** military force; **~ motrice** driving force

forcément (for-say-*mahng*) *adv* by force

forcer (for-*say*) *v* force; strain

forer (fo-*ray*) *v* drill, bore

forestier (fo-reh-st^y*ay*) *m* forester

forêt (fo-*ray*) *f* forest

foreuse (fo-*rurz*) *f* drill

forgeron (for-zher-*rawng*) *m* smith, blacksmith

formalité (for-mah-lee-*tay*) *f* formality

format (for-*mah*) *m* size

formation (for-mah-s^y*awng*) *f* formation, forming; training

forme (form) *f* shape, form; figure

formel (for-*mehl*) *adj* explicit

former (for-*may*) *v* shape, form; train, educate

formidable (for-mee-*dahbl*) *adj* fine, swell; terrific

formulaire (for-mew-*lair*) *m* form; **~ d'inscription** registration form

formule (for-*mewl*) *f* formula

fort (fawr) *adj* powerful, strong; loud

fortement (for-ter-*mahng*) *adv* tight

forteresse (for-ter-*rehss*) *f* fortress

fortuit (for-*twee*) *adj* casual, incidental

fortune (for-*tewn*) *f* fortune

fosse (foass) *f* pit

fossé (foa-*say*) *m* ditch

fou[1] (foo) *adj* (fol; *f* folle) crazy, mad; insane; lunatic

fou[2] (foo) *m* fool

foudre (foodr) *f* lightning

fouet (fway) *m* whip

fouetter (fway-*tay*) *v* whip

fouille (foo^ee) *f* search

fouiller (foo-^y*ay*) *v* search; *dig

foulard (foo-*laar*) *m* scarf

foule (fool) *f* crowd

fouler (foo-*lay*) *v* press; **se ~ la cheville** sprain one's ankle

foulure (foo-*lewr*) *f* sprain

four (foor) *m* oven; **~ à micro-ondes** microwave oven

fourbe (foorb) *adj* hypocritical

fourchette (foor-*sheht*) *f* fork

fourgon (foor-*gawng*) *m* luggage van; van

fourmi (foor-*mee*) *f* ant

fournaise (foor-*naiz*) *f* furnace

fourneau (foor-*noa*) *m* stove; ~ à gaz gas stove

fournir (foor-*neer*) *v* provide, furnish, supply

fourniture (foor-nee-*tewr*) *f* supply

fourreur (foo-*rurr*) *m* furrier

fourrure (foo-*rewr*) *f* fur

foyer (fwah-*y*ay) *m* foyer, lounge; home; focus

fracas (frah-*kah*) *m* noise

fraction (frahk-s*y*awng) *f* fraction

fracture (frahk-*tewr*) *f* break, fracture

fracturer (frahk-tew-*ray*) *v* fracture

fragile (frah-*zheel*) *adj* fragile

fragment (frahg-*mahng*) *m* extract, fragment

frais[1] (fray) *adj* (f fraîche) fresh; chilly, cool

frais[2] (fray) *mpl* expenses *pl*, expenditure; ~ de voyage travel(l)ing expenses

fraise (fraiz) *f* strawberry

framboise (frahng-*bwaaz*) *f* raspberry

franc (frahng) *adj* (f franche) open

français (frahng-*say*) *adj* French

France (frahngss) *f* France

franchir (frahng-*sheer*) *v* cross

frange (frahngzh) *f* fringe

frappant (frah-*pahng*) *adj* striking

frappé (frah-*pay*) *m* milkshake

frapper (frah-*pay*) *v* *beat; *hit, bump, tap, knock, *strike

fraternité (frah-tehr-nee-*tay*) *f* fraternity

fraude (froad) *f* fraud

frayeur (freh-*y*urr) *f* fright

fredonner (frer-do-*nay*) *v* hum

frein (frang) *m* brake; ~ à main handbrake; ~ à pédale foot brake

freiner (fray-*nay*) *v* slow down, curb

fréquemment (fray-kah-*mahng*) *adv* frequently

fréquence (fray-*kahngss*) *f* frequency

fréquent (fray-*kahng*) *adj* frequent

fréquenter (fray-kahng-*tay*) *v* see frequently, mix with

frère (frair) *m* brother

fret (fray) *m* freight

friction (freek-s*y*awng) *f* friction

frigidaire (free-zhee-*dair*) *m* refrigerator

frigo (free-*goa*) *m* fridge

fripon (free-*pawng*) *m* rascal

***frire** (freer) *v* fry

friser (free-*zay*) *v* curl

frisson (free-*sawng*) *m* shudder, chill, shiver

frissonnant (free-so-nahng) *adj* shivery

frissonner (free-so-*nay*) *v* tremble, shiver

frites (freet) *fpl* chips, *Am* French fries

froid (frwah) *m* cold; *adj* cold

froisser (frwah-*say*) *v* crease

fromage (fro-*maazh*) *m* cheese

front (frawng) *m* forehead

frontière (frawng-t*y*air) *f* border; frontier, boundary

frotter (fro-*tay*) *v* rub, scrub

fruit (frwee) *m* fruit

fugitif (few-zhee-*teef*) *m* runaway

***fuir** (fweer) *v* escape; leak

fuite (fweet) *f* flight; leak

fumée (few-*may*) *f* smoke

fumer (few-*may*) *v* smoke

fumeur (few-*murr*) *m*, **-euse** *f* smoker; compartiment fumeurs smoker

fumier (few-*m*y ay) *m* manure; dung; tas de ~ dunghill

funérailles (few-nay-*righ*) *fpl* funeral

fureur (few-*rurr*) *f* anger, rage

furibond (few-ree-*bawng*) *adj* furious

furieux (few-r*y*ur) *adj* furious

furoncle (few-*rawn̄gkl*) *m* boil
fusée (few-*zay*) *f* rocket
fusible (few-*zeebl*) *m* fuse
fusil (few-*zee*) *m* rifle, gun

fusion (few-z*yawn̄g*) *f* merger
futile (few-*teel*) *adj* petty, insignificant, idle
futur (few-*tēwr*) *adj* future

G

gâcher (gah-*shay*) *v* mess up
gâchette (gah-*sheht*) *f* trigger
gâchis (gah-*shee*) *m* mess
gadget (gah-*jeht*) *m* gadget
gadoue (gah-*doo*) *f* muck
gages (gaazh) *mpl* wages *pl*; **donner en gage** pawn
gagner (gah-*n̄ay*) *v* *win; *make, earn, gain
gai (gay) *adj* jolly, cheerful, gay
gain (gan̄g) *m* gain; **gains** earnings *pl*; winnings *pl*
gaine (gehn) *f* girdle
galerie (gahl-*ree*) *f* gallery; ~ **d'art** art gallery
galet (gah-*lay*) *m* pebble
galop (gah-*loa*) *m* gallop
gamin (gah-*man̄g*) *m* little boy
gamine (gah-*meen*) *f* little girl
gamme (gahm) *f* scale; range
gant (gahn̄g) *m* glove
garage (gah-*raazh*) *m* garage
garagiste (gah-rah-*zheest*) *m* garage proprietor
garantie (gah-rahn̄g-*tee*) *f* guarantee
garantir (gah-rahn̄g-*teer*) *v* guarantee
garçon (gahr-*sawn̄g*) *m* boy; lad; waiter
garde (gahrd) *m* guard; *f* custody; ~ **du corps** bodyguard; ***prendre** ~ watch out
garder (gahr-*day*) *v* *keep; *hold
garde-robe (gahr-*drob*) *f* wardrobe; closet *Am*

gardien (gahr-*dyan̄g*) *m* attendant, warden; caretaker; ~ **de but** goalkeeper
gardon (gahr-*dawn̄g*) *m* roach
gare (gaar) *f* station; depot *Am*
garer (gah-*ray*) *v* garage; **se** ~ park
se gargariser (gahr-gah-ree-*zay*) gargle
gars (gah) *m* fellow
gaspillage (gah-spee-*yaazh*) *m* waste
gaspiller (gah-spee-*yay*) *v* waste
gaspilleur (gah-spee-*yūrr*) *adj* wasteful
gastrique (gah-*streek*) *adj* gastric
gastro-entérite (gah-stroa-ahn̄g-tay-*reet*) *f* gastroenteritis
gâteau (gah-*toa*) *m* cake
gâter (gah-*tay*) *v* *spoil
gauche (gōash) *adj* left; **de** ~ left-hand
gaucher (goa-*shay*) *adj* left-handed
gaufre (gōafr) *f* waffle
gaufrette (goa-*freht*) *f* wafer
gaz (gaaz) *m* gas; ~ **d'échappement** exhaust gases
gazeux (gah-*zur*) *adj* gaseous; aerated, fizzy
gazole (gah-*zol*) *m* diesel
gazon (gah-*zawn̄g*) *m* lawn
géant (zhay-*ahn̄g*) *m* giant
gel (zhehl) *m* frost
gelée (zher-*lay*) *f* jelly
geler (zher-*lay*) *v* *freeze
gémir (zhay-*meer*) *v* groan, moan
gênant (zheh-*nahn̄g*) *adj*

inconvenient, troublesome

gencive (zhahng-*seev*) *f* gum

gendre (zhahngdr) *m* son-in-law

gêner (zhay-*nay*) *v* hinder; embarrass; bother; **se ~** *be embarrassed

général (zhay-nay-*rahl*) *m* general; *adj* universal, public, general; **en ~** as a rule, in general

généralement (zhay-nay-rahl-*mahng*) *adv* as a rule

générateur (zhay-nay-rah-*turr*) *m* generator

génération (zhay-nay-rah-*s*y*awng*) *f* generation

généreux (zhay-nay-*rur*) *adj* liberal, generous

générosité (zhay-nay-ro-zee-*tay*) *f* generosity

génie (zhay-*nee*) *m* genius

génital (zhay-nee-*tahl*) *adj* genital

genou (zher-*noo*) *m* (pl ~x) knee

genre (zhahngr) *m* kind; gender

gens (zhahng) *mpl/fpl* people *pl*

gentil (zhahng-*tee*) *adj* friendly, kind; nice; sweet

gentillesse (zhahng-tee-*y*ehss*) *f* politeness; **avoir la ~ de** be so kind as to

géographie (zhay-o-grah-*fee*) *f* geography

géologie (zhay-o-lo-*zhee*) *f* geology

géométrie (zhay-o-may-*tree*) *f* geometry

germe (zhehrm) *m* germ

geste (zhehst) *m* sign

gesticuler (zheh-stee-kew-*lay*) *v* gesticulate

gestion (zheh-st*y*awng*) *f* management, administration

gibier (zhee-b*y*ay*) *m* game

gigantesque (zhee-gahng-*tehsk*) *adj* gigantic, enormous

gifle (zheefl) *f* slap in the face; box on the ear

gilet (zhee-*lay*) *m* waistcoat; vest *Am*

gingembre (zhang-zhahngbr) *m* ginger

gîte (zheet) *m* resting-place, lodging; form; vein

glace (glahss) *f* ice; ice cream

glacial (glah-s*y*ahl*) *adj* freezing

glacier (glah-s*y*ay*) *m* glacier

glaçon (glah-*sawng*) *m* icicle; ice cube; ice floe

glande (glahngd) *f* gland

glissade (glee-*sahd*) *f* slide

glissant (glee-*sahng*) *adj* slippery

glisser (glee-*say*) *v* *slide, glide; slip

global (glo-*bahl*) *adj* global, total, comprehensive

globe (glob) *m* globe

gloire (glwaar) *f* glory

glousser (gloo-*say*) *v* chuckle; giggle

gluant (glew-*ahng*) *adj* sticky

gobelet (go-*blay*) *m* mug, tumbler

goéland (go-ay-*lahng*) *m* seagull

golf (golf) *m* golf; **terrain de ~** golf links, golf course

golfe (golf) *m* gulf

gomme (gom) *f* gum; rubber, eraser

gondole (gawng-*dol*) *f* gondola

gonflable (gawng-*flahbl*) *adj* inflatable

gonfler (gawng-*flay*) *v* inflate

gorge (gorzh) *f* throat; gorge

gorgée (gor-*zhay*) *f* sip

gosse (goss) *m* kid, boy

goudron (goo-*drawng*) *m* tar

goulot d'étranglement (goo-lo day-trahng-gler-*mahng*) bottleneck

gourdin (goor-*dang*) *m* club

gourmand (goor-*mahng*) *adj* greedy

gourmet (goor-*may*) *m* gourmet

goût (goo) *m* taste; ***avoir ~ de** taste

goûter (goo-*tay*) *v* taste

goutte (goot) *f* drop; gout

gouvernail (goo-vehr-*nigh*) *m* rudder

gouvernante (goo-vehr-*nahng*t) *f*

governess; housekeeper

gouvernement (goo-vehr-ner-*mahng*) m rule, government

gouverner (goo-vehr-*nay*) v rule, govern

gouverneur (goo-vehr-*nūrr*) m governor

grâce (graass) f grace; pardon; ~ à thanks to

gracieux (grah-s^yur) adj graceful; à titre ~ free of charge

grade (grahd) m grade; degree, rank

graduel (grah-*dwehl*) adj gradual

graduellement (grah-dwehl-*mahng*) adv gradually

grain (grang) m corn, grain

graisse (grehss) f grease, fat

graisser (gray-*say*) v grease

graisseux (greh-*sur*) adj greasy

grammaire (grah-*mair*) f grammar

grammatical (grah-mah-tee-*kahl*) adj grammatical

gramme (grahm) m gram

grand (grahng) adj great; tall, big, major

Grande-Bretagne (grahngd-brer-*tahñ*) f Great Britain

grandeur (grahng-*dūrr*) f size

grandiose (grahng-d^yōāz) adj superb, magnificent

grandir (grahng-*deer*) v *grow

grand-mère (grahng-*mair*) f grandmother

grand-papa (grahng-pah-*pah*) m granddad

grand-père (grahng-*pair*) m grandfather

grands-parents (grahng-pah-*rahng*) mpl grandparents pl

grange (grahngzh) f barn

granit (grah-*neet*) m granite

graphique (grah-*feek*) adj graphic; m diagram; chart

gras (grah) adj (f ~se) fatty, fat

gratitude (grah-tee-*tewd*) f gratitude

gratte-ciel (grah-ts^yehl) m skyscraper

gratter (grah-*tay*) v scratch

gratuit (grah-*twee*) adj gratis, free of charge, free

grave (graav) adj grave; bad, severe

graver (grah-*vay*) v engrave

graveur (grah-*vūrr*) m engraver

gravier (grah-v^yay) m gravel

gravillon (grah-vee-^yawng) m grit

gravité (grah-vee-*tay*) f gravity

gravure (grah-*vēwr*) f engraving; carving

grec (grehk) adj (f grecque) Greek

Grèce (grehss) f Greece

grêle (grehl) f hail

grenier (grer-n^yay) m attic

grenouille (grer-*noo*^{ee}) f frog

grève (graiv) f strike; *faire ~ *strike

gréviste (gray-*veest*) m/f striker

griffe (greef) f claw

grill (greel) m steakhouse

grillade (gree-^yahd) f grilled meat

grille (greey) f gate; grate

griller (gree-^yay) v roast; grill

grillon (gree-^yawng) m cricket

grimper (grang-*pay*) v climb

grincer (grang-*say*) v creak

grippe (greep) f flu, influenza

gris (gree) adj grey

grive (greev) f thrush

grogner (gro-*ñay*) v grumble, growl

grondement (grawngd-*mahng*) m roar

gronder (grawng-*day*) v rumble; scold

gros (groa) adj (f -se) big; thick, fat, corpulent, stout

groseille (groa-*zay*) f currant; ~ à maquereau gooseberry

grosse (grōāss) f gross

grossesse (groa-*sehss*) f pregnancy

grossier (groa-s^yay) adj coarse, gross, rude

grossir (gro-*seer*) v increase; *put on weight

grossiste (groa-*seest*) *m* wholesale dealer
grotesque (gro-*tehsk*) *adj* ludicrous
grotte (grot) *f* cave; grotto
groupe (groop) *m* group; party
grouper (groo-*pay*) *v* group
grue (grew) *f* crane
grumeau (grew-*moa*) *m* lump
grumeleux (grewm-*lur*) *adj* lumpy
gruyère (grew-*ᵞair*) *m* Swiss cheese
guêpe (gehp) *f* wasp
guère: ne ... ~ (ner ... gair) scarcely
guérir (gay-*reer*) *v* cure; heal, recover
guérison (gay-ree-*zawng*) *f* recovery, cure
guérisseur (gay-ree-*surr*) *m* quack
guerre (gair) *f* war; **d'avant-guerre** pre-war; **~ mondiale** world war

guetter (gay-*tay*) *v* watch for
gueule (gurl) *f* mouth; **~ de bois** hangover
guichet (gee-*shay*) *m* box office; **~ de location** box office
guide (geed) *m* guidebook; *m/f* guide
guider (gee-*day*) *v* *lead
guidon (gee-*dawng*) *m* handlebars *pl*
guillemets (geey-*may*) *mpl* quotation marks
guitare (gee-*taar*) *f* guitar
gymnase (zheem-*naaz*) *m* gymnasium
gymnaste (zheem-*nahst*) *m/f* gymnast
gymnastique (zheem-nah-*steek*) *f* gymnastics *pl*
gynécologue (zhee-nay-ko-*log*) *m/f* gyn(a)ecologist

H

habile (ah-*beel*) *adj* skil(l)ful; skilled
habileté (ah-beel-*tay*) *f* skill, art
habiller (ah-bee-*ᵞay*) *v* dress
habitable (ah-bee-*tahbl*) *adj* inhabitable, habitable
habitant (ah-bee-*tahng*) *m* inhabitant
habitation (ah-bee-tah-*sᵞawng*) *f* house
habiter (ah-bee-*tay*) *v* inhabit, live
habits (ah-*bee*) *mpl* clothes *pl*
habitude (ah-bee-*tewd*) *f* habit; custom; ***avoir l'habitude de** would; **d'habitude** usually
habitué (ah-bee-*tway*) *adj* accustomed; ***être ~ à** *be used to
habituel (ah-bee-*twehl*) *adj* common, habitual, ordinary
habituellement (ah-bee-twehl-*mahng*) *adv* usually
habituer (ah-bee-*tway*): **s'~** *get

accustomed
hache ('*ahsh*) *f* axe
hacher ('ah-*shay*) *v* chop, mince
haie ('*ay*) *f* hedge
haine ('*ehn*) *f* hatred, hate
***haïr** ('ah-*eer*) *v* hate
hâlé ('ah-*lay*) *adj* tanned
haleter ('ahl-*tay*) *v* pant
hamac ('ah-*mahk*) *m* hammock
hameau ('ah-*moa*) *m* hamlet
hameçon (ahm-*sawng*) *m* fishing hook
hanche ('*ahngsh*) *f* hip
handicapé ('ahng-dee-kah-*pay*) *adj* disabled, handicapped
hardi ('ahr-*dee*) *adj* bold
hareng ('ah-*rahng*) *m* herring
haricot ('ah-ree-*koa*) *m* bean
harmonie (ahr-mo-*nee*) *f* harmony
harmonieux (ahr-mo-*nᵞur*) *adj* tuneful
harpe ('*ahrp*) *f* harp

hasard 70

hasard ('ah-*zaar*) *m* chance, luck; hazard; **par ~** by chance

hâte ('aat) *f* hurry, speed, haste

hâter ('ah-*tay*) *v*: **se ~** hasten

hausse ('ōass) *f* rise

haut ('oa) *m* top side; *adj* high, tall; **en ~** upstairs, above, overhead; up; **vers le ~** upwards

hautain (oa-*tañg*) *adj* haughty

hauteur (oa-*tūrr*) *f* height; ***être à la ~ de** *keep up with

haut-parleur ('oa-pahr-*lūrr*) *m* loudspeaker

hebdomadaire (ehb-do-mah-*dair*) *adj* weekly

héberger (ay-behr-*zhay*) *v* accommodate, put up, take in

hébreu (ay-*brur*) *m* Hebrew

hélas ('ay-*laass*) *adv* unfortunately

hélice (ay-*leess*) *f* propeller

hémorragie (ay-mo-rah-*zhee*) *f* h(a)emorrhage

hémorroïdes (ay-mo-ro-*eed*) *fpl* piles *pl*, h(a)emorrhoids *pl*

herbe (ehrb) *f* grass; herb; **mauvaise ~** weed

héréditaire (ay-ray-dee-*tair*) *adj* hereditary

hérisson ('ay-ree-*sawñg*) *m* hedgehog

héritage (ay-ree-*taazh*) *m* inheritance

hériter (ay-ree-*tay*) *v* inherit

hermétique (ehr-may-*teek*) *adj* airtight

hernie ('ehr-*nee*) *f* hernia; **~ discale** slipped disc

héron ('ay-*rawñg*) *m* heron

héros ('ay-*roa*) *m* hero

hésiter (ay-zee-*tay*) *v* hesitate

hétérosexuel (ay-tay-ro-sehk-*swehl*) *adj* heterosexual

hêtre ('aitr) *m* beech

heure (ūrr) *f* hour; **à ... heures** at ... o'clock; **~ d'arrivée** time of arrival; **~ de départ** time of departure; **~ de pointe** rush hour; **~ d'été** summer time; **heures de bureau** office hours; **heures de consultation** consultation hours; **heures de visite** visiting hours; **heures d'ouverture** business hours; **tout à l'heure** a short while ago; shortly; **toutes les heures** hourly

heureux (ur-*rur*) *adj* fortunate, happy

heurter ('urr-*tay*) *v* knock

hibou ('ee-*boo*) *m* (pl ~x) owl

hideux ('ee-*dur*) *adj* hideous

hier (ˀair) *adv* yesterday

hiérarchie ('ˀay-rahr-*shee*) *f* hierarchy

hippodrome (ee-po-*drom*) *m* racecourse

hirondelle ('o-rawñg-*dehl*) *f* swallow

hisser ('ee-*say*) *v* hoist

histoire (ee-*stwaar*) *f* history; story; **~ d'amour** love story; **~ de l'art** art history

historien (ee-sto-rˀ*añg*) *m*, **-ne** *f* historian

historique (ee-sto-*reek*) *adj* historic; historical

hiver (ee-*vair*) *m* winter

H.L.M. (ahsh-ehl-*ehm*) *f or m* council flat

hobby ('o-*bee*) *m* hobby

hockey ('o-*kay*) *m* hockey

hollandais ('o-lahñg-*day*) *adj* Dutch

Hollande ('o-*lahñgd*) *f* Holland

homard ('o-*maar*) *m* lobster

hommage (o-*maazh*) *m* homage, tribute; **rendre ~** hono(u)r

homme (om) *m* man; **~ d'affaires** businessman; **~ d'Etat** statesman

homosexuel (o-mo-sehk-*swehl*) *adj* homosexual

Hongrie ('awñg-*gree*) *f* Hungary

hongrois ('awñg-*grwah*) *adj* Hungarian

honnête (o-*neht*) *adj* hono(u)rable, honest; fair

honnêteté (o-neht-*tay*) *f* honesty

honneur (o-*nūr*) *m* hono(u)r, glory

honorable (o-no-*rahbl*) *adj* hono(u)rable, respectable

honoraires (o-no-*rair*) *mpl* fee

honorer (o-no-*ray*) *v* hono(u)r

honte ('*awngt*) *f* shame; ***avoir ~** *be ashamed; **quelle honte!** shame!

honteux ('awng-*tur*) *adj* ashamed

hôpital (o-pee-*tahl*) *m* hospital

hoquet ('o-*kay*) *m* hiccup

horaire (o-*rair*) *m* timetable, schedule

horizon (o-ree-*zawng*) *m* horizon

horizontal (o-ree-zawng-*tahl*) *adj* horizontal

horloge (or-*lawzh*) *f* clock

horloger (or-lo-*zhay*) *m* watchmaker

horreur (o-*rūr*) *f* horror

horrible (o-*reebl*) *adj* horrible

horrifiant (o-ree-f'*ahng*) *adj* horrible

hors ('awr) *adv* out; **~ de** outside

hors d'œuvre ('or-*dūrvr*) *m* hors-d'œuvre

horticulture (or-tee-kewl-*tewr*) *f* horticulture

hospice (o-*speess*) *m* home

hospitalier (o-spee-tah-l'*ay*) *adj* hospitable

hospitalité (o-spee-tah-lee-*tay*) *f* hospitality

hostile (o-*steel*) *adj* hostile

hôte (*ōat*) *m* host; guest

hôtel (oa-*tehl*) *m* hotel; **~ de ville** town hall

hôtel-Dieu (oa-tehl-*d'ur*) *m* general hospital

hôtesse (oa-*tehss*) *f* hostess; receptionist; **~ de l'air** stewardess

houblon ('oo-*blawng*) *m* hop

housse ('ooss) *f* sleeve

hublot ('ew-*bloa*) *m* porthole

huile (weel) *f* oil; **~ capillaire** hair oil; **~ de table** salad oil; **~ d'olive** olive oil; **~ solaire** suntan oil

huiler (wee-*lay*) *v* lubricate

huileux (wee-*lur*) *adj* oily

huit ('weet) *num* eight

huitième ('wee-t'*ehm*) *num* eighth

huître (weetr) *f* oyster

humain (ew-*mang*) *adj* human

humanité (ew-mah-nee-*tay*) *f* mankind, humanity

humble (urngbl) *adj* humble

humecter (ew-mehk-*tay*) *v* moisten

humeur (ew-*mūrr*) *f* mood, spirit

humide (ew-*meed*) *adj* humid; wet, damp

humidifier (ew-mee-dee-f'*ay*) *v* damp

humidité (ew-mee-dee-*tay*) *f* humidity, moisture, damp

humour (ew-*mōor*) *m* humo(u)r

hurler ('ewr-*lay*) *v* yell, scream

hutte ('ewt) *f* hut

hydrogène (ee-dro-*zhehn*) *m* hydrogen

hygiène (ee-zh'*ehn*) *f* hygiene

hygiénique (ee-zh'ay-*neek*) *adj* hygienic

hymne (eemn) *m* hymn; **~ national** national anthem

hypermarché (ee-pehr-mahr-*shay*) *m* superstore, hypermarket

hypocrisie (ee-po-kree-*zee*) *f* hypocrisy

hypocrite (ee-po-*kreet*) *m* hypocrite; *adj* hypocritical

hypothèque (ee-po-*tehk*) *f* mortgage

hystérique (ee-stay-*reek*) *adj* hysterical

I

ici (ee-*see*) *adv* here

icône (ee-*kōan*) *f* icon

idéal[1] (ee-day-*ahl*) *adj* (pl -aux) ideal

idéal[2] (ee-day-*ahl*) *m* (pl ~s, -aux) ideal

idée (ee-*day*) *f* idea; opinion; ~ **lumineuse** brain wave

identification (ee-dahng-tee-fee-kah-*s*[y]*awng*) *f* identification

identifier (ee-dahng-tee-*f*[y]*ay*) *v* identify

identique (ee-dahng-*teek*) *adj* identical

identité (ee-dahng-tee-*tay*) *f* identity

idiot (ee-*d*[y]*oa*) *adj* idiotic; *m*, **-e** *f* fool, idiot

idole (ee-*dol*) *f* idol

idylle (ee-*deel*) *f* romance

ignorant (ee-ño-*rahng*) *adj* ignorant; uneducated

ignorer (ee-ño-*ray*) *v* ignore; overlook

il (eel) *pron* he

île (eel) *f* island

illégal (ee-lay-*gahl*) *adj* illegal

illettré (ee-leh-*tray*) *m* illiterate

illicite (ee-lee-*seet*) *adj* unlawful, unauthorized

illimité (ee-lee-mee-*tay*) *adj* unlimited

illisible (ee-lee-*zeebl*) *adj* illegible

illumination (ee-lew-mee-nah-*s*[y]*awng*) *f* illumination

illuminer (ee-lew-mee-*nay*) *v* illuminate

illusion (ee-lew-*z*[y]*awng*) *f* illusion

illustration (ee-lew-strah-*s*[y]*awng*) *f* illustration; picture

illustre (ee-*lewstr*) *adj* noted

illustré (ee-lew-*stray*) *m* comic

illustrer (ee-lew-*stray*) *v* illustrate

ils (eel) *pron* they

image (ee-*maazh*) *f* picture, image

imaginaire (ee-mah-zhee-*nair*) *adj* imaginary

imagination (ee-mah-zhee-nah-*s*[y]*awng*) *f* fancy, imagination

imaginer (ee-mah-zhee-*nay*) *v* fancy, imagine; **s'imaginer** fancy, imagine

imitation (ee-mee-tah-*s*[y]*awng*) *f* imitation

imiter (ee-mee-*tay*) *v* imitate, copy

immaculé (ee-mah-kew-*lay*) *adj* stainless, spotless

immangeable (ang-mahng-*zhahbl*) *adj* inedible

immédiat (ee-may-*d*[y]*ah*) *adj* immediate

immédiatement (ee-may-d[y]aht-*mahng*) *adv* at once, instantly, immediately

immense (ee-*mahngss*) *adj* immense; vast, huge

immérité (ee-may-ree-*tay*) *adj* unearned

immeuble (ee-*murbl*) *m* house; ~ **d'habitation** block of flats; apartment house *Am*

immigrant (ee-mee-*grahng*) *m*, **-e** *f* immigrant

immigration (ee-mee-grah-*s*[y]*awng*) *f* immigration

immigrer (ee-mee-*gray*) *v* immigrate

immobile (ee-mo-*beel*) *adj* motionless

immodeste (ee-mo-*dehst*) *adj* immodest

immuniser (ee-mew-nee-*zay*) *v* immunize

immunité (ee-mew-nee-*tay*) *f* immunity

impair (ang-*pair*) *adj* odd

imparfait (ang-pahr-*fay*) *adj* imperfect; faulty

impartial (ang-pahr-*s*[y]*ahl*) *adj* impartial

impasse (ang-*pahss*) *f* dead end,

blind alley; deadlock

impatient (ang-pah-s^yahng) *adj* impatient; eager

impeccable (ang-peh-*kahbl*) *adj* faultless

impératrice (ang-pay-rah-*treess*) *f* empress

imperfection (ang-pehr-fehk-s^yawng) *f* fault

impérial (ang-pay-r^yahl) *adj* imperial

imperméable (ang-pehr-may-*ahbl*) *m* mackintosh, raincoat; *adj* waterproof, rainproof

impersonnel (ang-pehr-so-*nehl*) *adj* impersonal

impertinence (ang-pehr-tee-*nahngss*) *f* impertinence

impertinent (ang-pehr-tee-*nahng*) *adj* impertinent

impétueux (ang-pay-*twur*) *adj* impetuous, fiery; raging

impliquer (ang-plee-*kay*) *v* involve, imply

impoli (ang-po-*lee*) *adj* impolite

impopulaire (ang-po-pew-*lair*) *adj* unpopular

importance (ang-por-*tahngss*) *f* importance; ***avoir de l'importance** matter; **sans ~** insignificant

important (ang-por-*tahng*) *adj* important; considerable, big

importateur (ang-por-tah-*turr*) *m* importer

importation (ang-por-tah-s^yawng) *f* import; **taxe d'importation** import duty

importer (ang-por-*tay*) *v* import

imposable (ang-poa-zahbl) *adj* dutiable

imposant (ang-poa-*zahng*) *adj* imposing

imposer (ang-poa-*zay*) *v* tax

impossible (ang-po-*seebl*) *adj* impossible

impôt (ang-*poa*) *m* tax; **~ sur le chiffre d'affaires** turnover tax; **~ sur le revenu** income tax

impotence (ang-po-*tahngss*) *f* impotence

impotent (ang-po-*tahng*) *adj* impotent

impraticable (ang-prah-tee-*kahbl*) *adj* impassable

impression (ang-*preh*-s^yawng) *f* impression; ***faire ~ sur** impress

impressionnant (ang-preh-s^yo-*nahng*) *adj* impressive

impressionner (ang-preh-s^yo-*nay*) *v* impress

imprévu (ang-pray-*vew*) *adj* unexpected

imprimé (ang-pree-*may*) *m* printed matter

imprimer (ang-pree-*may*) *v* print

imprimerie (ang-preem-*ree*) *f* printing office

improbable (ang-pro-*bahbl*) *adj* improbable, unlikely

impropre (ang-*propr*) *adj* improper, unfit; wrong

improviser (ang-pro-vee-*zay*) *v* improvise

imprudent (ang-prew-*dahng*) *adj* unwise

impuissant (ang-pwee-*sahng*) *adj* powerless

impulsif (ang-pewl-*seef*) *adj* impulsive

impulsion (ang-pewl-s^yawng) *f* urge, impulse

inabordable (ee-nah-bor-*dahbl*) *adj* prohibitive

inacceptable (ee-nahk-sehp-*tahbl*) *adj* unacceptable

inaccessible (ee-nahk-say-*seebl*) *adj* inaccessible

inadéquat (ee-nah-day-*kwah*) *adj* inadequate, unsuitable

inadvertance (ee-nahd-vehr-*tahngss*) *f* oversight

inattendu (ee-nah-tahn̄g-*dew*) *adj*
unexpected

inattentif (ee-nah-tahn̄g-*teef*) *adj*
careless

incapable (an̄g-kah-*pahbl*) *adj*
incapable, unable

incassable (an̄g-kah-*sahbl*) *adj*
unbreakable

incendie (an̄g-sahn̄g-*dee*) *m* fire;
alarme d'incendie fire alarm

incertain (an̄g-sehr-*tan̄g*) *adj* doubtful,
uncertain

incident (an̄g-see-*dahn̄g*) *m* incident

incinérer (an̄g-see-nay-*ray*) *v* cremate

incision (an̄g-see-z^y*awn̄g*) *f* cut

inciter (an̄g-see-*tay*) *v* incite

inclinaison (an̄g-klee-neh-*zawn̄g*) *f*
gradient

inclination (an̄g-klee-nah-s^y*awn̄g*) *f*
tendency; ~ **de la tête** nod

incliné (an̄g-klee-*nay*) *adj* slanting

incliner (an̄g-klee-*nay*): **s'~** slant

*inclure (an̄g-*klēwr*) *v* include,
enclose; comprise, count

incompétent (an̄g-kawn̄g-pay-*tahn̄g*)
adj incompetent, unqualified

incomplet (an̄g-kawn̄g-*play*) *adj* (f
-plète) incomplete

inconcevable (an̄g-kawn̄g-*svahbl*) *adj*
inconceivable

inconditionnel (an̄g-kawn̄g-dee-s^{y}o-
nehl) *adj* unconditional

inconfortable (an̄g-kawn̄g-for-*tahbl*)
adj uncomfortable

inconnu (an̄g-ko-*new*) *adj* unknown;
m stranger

inconscient (an̄g-kawn̄g-s^y*ahn̄g*) *adj*
unconscious; unaware

inconsidéré (an̄g-kawn̄g-see-day-*ray*)
adj rash

inconvénient (an̄g-kawn̄g-vay-
n^y*ahn̄g*) *m* inconvenience

incorrect (an̄g-ko-*rehkt*) *adj* incorrect,
inaccurate, wrong

incroyable (an̄g-krwah-^{y}*ahbl*) *adj*
incredible

inculte (an̄g-*kewlt*) *adj* uncultivated

incurable (an̄g-kew-*rahbl*) *adj*
incurable

Inde (an̄gd) *f* India

indécent (an̄g-day-*sahn̄g*) *adj* indecent

indéfini (an̄g-day-fee-*nee*) *adj*
indefinite

indemne (an̄g-*dehmn*) *adj* unhurt

indemnité (an̄g-dehm-nee-*tay*) *f*
compensation, indemnity

indépendance (an̄g-day-pahn̄g-
dahn̄gss) *f* independence

indépendant (an̄g-day-pahn̄g-*dahn̄g*)
adj independent; self-employed

indésirable (an̄g-day-zee-*rahbl*) *adj*
undesirable

index (an̄g-*dehks*) *m* index finger;
index

indicatif (an̄g-dee-kah-*teef*) *m* area
code

indication (an̄g-dee-kah-s^y*awn̄g*) *f*
indication

Indien (an̄g-d^y*an̄g*) *m* Indian

indien (an̄g-d^y*an̄g*) *adj* Indian

indifférent (an̄g-dee-fay-*rahn̄g*) *adj*
indifferent

indigène (an̄g-dee-*zhehn*) *m/f* native;
adj native

indigent (an̄g-dee-*zhahn̄g*) *adj* poor

indigestion (an̄g-dee-zheh-st^y*awn̄g*) *f*
indigestion

indignation (an̄g-dee-ñah-s^y*awn̄g*) *f*
indignation

indiquer (an̄g-dee-*kay*) *v* point out,
indicate; declare

indirect (an̄g-dee-*rehkt*) *adj* indirect

indispensable (an̄g-dee-spahn̄g-
sahbl) *adj* essential

indisposé (an̄g-dee-spoa-*zay*) *adj*
unwell

indistinct (an̄g-dee-*stan̄g*) *adj*
indistinct, vague

individu (ang-dee-vee-*dew*) *m*
  individual

individuel (ang-dee-vee-*dwehl*) *adj*
  individual

Indonésie (ang-do-nay-*zee*) *f*
  Indonesia

Indonésien (ang-do-nay-*z*ʸ*ang*) *m*
  Indonesian

indonésien (ang-do-nay-*z*ʸ*ang*) *adj*
  Indonesian

industrie (ang-dew-*stree*) *f* industry

industriel (ang-dew-stree-*ehl*) *adj*
  industrial

inefficace (ee-nay-fee-*kahss*) *adj*
  inefficient

inégal (ec-nay-*gahl*) *adj* uneven,
  unequal

inéquitable (ee-nay-kee-*tahbl*) *adj*
  unfair

inestimable (ee-neh-stee-*mahbl*) *adj*
  priceless

inévitable (ee-nay-vee-*tahbl*) *adj*
  inevitable, unavoidable

inexact (ee-nehg-*zahkt*) *adj*
  inaccurate, inexact

inexpérimenté (ee-nehk-spay-ree-
  mahng-*tay*) *adj* inexperienced

inexplicable (ee-nehk-splee-*kahbl*)
  adj inexplicable

infâme (ang-*faam*) *adj* foul

infanterie (ang-fahng-*tree*) *f* infantry

infecter (ang-fehk-*tay*) *v* infect;
  s'infecter *become septic

infectieux (ang-fehk-s*ʸur*) *adj*
  infectious

infection (ang-fehk-s*ʸawng*) *f* infection

inférieur (ang-fay-r*ʸurr*) *adj* inferior,
  bottom

infidèle (ang-fee-*dehl*) *adj* unfaithful

infini (ang-fee-*nee*) *adj* infinite, endless

infinitif (ang-fee-nee-*teef*) *m* infinitive

infirme (ang-*feerm*) *m* invalid; *adj*
  invalid

infirmière (ang-feer-*m*ʸ*air*) *f* nurse

inflammable (ang-flah-*mahbl*) *adj*
  inflammable

inflammation (ang-flah-mah-s*ʸawng*) *f*
  inflammation

inflation (ang-flah-s*ʸawng*) *f* inflation

influence (ang-flew-*ahngss*) *f*
  influence

influencer (ang-flew-ahng-*say*) *v*
  influence

influent (ang-flew-*ahng*) *adj*
  influential

information (ang-for-mah-s*ʸawng*) *f*
  information; enquiry

informer (ang-for-*may*) *v* inform;
  s'informer inquire, enquire, query

infortune (ang-for-*tewn*) *f* misfortune

infortuné (ang-for-tew-*nay*) *adj*
  unlucky

infraction (ang-frahk-s*ʸawng*) *f*
  offence, offense *Am*

infrarouge (ang-frah-*roozh*) *adj*
  infrared

infructueux (ang-frewk-*twur*) *adj*
  unsuccessful

infusion (ang-few-z*ʸawng*) *f* infusion;
  herb tea

ingénieur (ang-zhay-n*ʸurr*) *m*
  engineer

ingénu (ang-zhay-*new*) *adj* simple

ingérence (ang-zhay-*rahngss*) *f*
  interference

ingrat (ang-*grah*) *adj* ungrateful

ingrédient (ang-gray-d*ʸahng*) *m*
  ingredient

inhabitable (ee-nah-bee-*tahbl*) *adj*
  uninhabitable

inhabité (ee-nah-bee-*tay*) *adj*
  uninhabited

inhabitué (ee-nah-bee-*tway*) *adj*
  unaccustomed

inhabituel (ee-nah-bee-*twehl*) *adj*
  unusual, uncommon

inhaler (ee-nah-*lay*) *v* inhale

ininterrompu (ee-nang-teh-rawng-

pew) *adj* continuous

initial (ee-nee-*s*ʸ*ahl*) *adj* initial

initiale (ee-nee-*s*ʸ*ahl*) *f* initial

initiative (ee-nee-*s*ʸah-*teev*) *f* initiative

injecter (ang-zhehk-*tay*) *v* inject

injection (ang-zhehk-*s*ʸ*awng*) *f* injection

injurier (ang-zhew-*r*ʸ*ay*) *v* abuse, insult

injuste (ang-*zhewst*) *adj* unjust, unfair

injustice (ang-zhew-*steess*) *f* injustice

inné (ee-*nay*) *adj* natural

innocence (ee-no-*sahngss*) *f* innocence

innocent (ee-no-*sahng*) *adj* innocent

inoculer (ee-no-kew-*lay*) *v* inoculate

inoffensif (ee-no-fahng-*seef*) *adj* harmless

inondation (ee-nawng-dah-*s*ʸ*awng*) *f* flood

inopportun (ee-no-por-*turng*) *adj* inconvenient, misplaced

inquiet (ang-*k*ʸ*ay*) *adj* (f -ète) anxious; restless

inquiétant (ang-k*ʸ*ay-*tahng*) *adj* scary

inquiéter (ang-k*ʸ*ay-*tay*): **s'~** worry

inquiétude (ang-k*ʸ*ay-*tewd*) *f* worry; unrest

insatisfaisant (ang-sah-teess-fer-*zahng*) *adj* unsatisfactory

insatisfait (ang-sah-tee-*sfay*) *adj* dissatisfied

inscription (ang-skree-*ps*ʸ*awng*) *f* inscription; registration; entry

*inscrire (ang-*skreer*) *v* enter, book; list; **s'*inscrire** check in, register

insecte (ang-*sehkt*) *m* insect; bug *Am*

insecticide (ang-sehk-tee-*seed*) *m* insecticide

insensé (ang-sahng-*say*) *adj* crazy, senseless, mad

insensible (ang-sahng-*seebl*) *adj* insensitive; imperceptible

insérer (ang-say-*ray*) *v* insert

insignifiant (ang-see-ñee-*f*ʸ*ahng*) *adj* petty, insignificant, unimportant

insipide (ang-see-*peed*) *adj* tasteless

insister (ang-see-*stay*) *v* insist

insolation (ang-so-lah-*s*ʸ*awng*) *f* sunstroke

insolence (ang-so-*lahngss*) *f* insolence

insolent (ang-so-*lahng*) *adj* insolent, impudent, impertinent

insolite (ang-so-*leet*) *adj* unusual

insomnie (ang-som-*nee*) *f* insomnia

insonorisé (ang-so-noa-ree-*zay*) *adj* soundproof

insouciant (ang-soo-*s*ʸ*ahng*) *adj* carefree

inspecter (ang-spehk-*tay*) *v* inspect

inspecteur (ang-spehk-*turr*) *m* (*f* -trice) inspector

inspection (ang-spehk-*s*ʸ*awng*) *f* inspection

inspectrice (ang-spehk-*trees*) *f* inspector

inspirer (ang-spee-*ray*) *v* inspire

instable (ang-*stahbl*) *adj* unsteady, unstable

installation (ang-stah-lah-*s*ʸ*awng*) *f* installation

installer (ang-stah-*lay*) *v* instal(l;) furnish

instant (ang-*stahng*) *m* instant, moment; second

instantané (ang-stahng-tah-*nay*) *m* snapshot; *adj* prompt

instantanément (ang-stahng-tah-nay-*mahng*) *adv* instantly

instinct (ang-*stang*) *m* instinct

instituer (ang-stee-*tway*) *v* institute

institut (ang-stee-*tew*) *m* institute; **~ de beauté** beauty parlo(u)r

instituteur (ang-stee-tew-*turr*) *m* master, teacher, schoolteacher, schoolmaster

institution (ang-stee-tew-*s*ʸ*awng*) *f* institution; institute

instructeur (ang-strewk-*turr*) *m*

instructor

instructif (aṅg-strewk-*teef*) adj instructive

instruction (aṅg-strewk-*s^yawṅg*) f instruction, direction

*****instruire** (aṅg-*strweer*) v instruct

instrument (aṅg-strew-*mahṅg*) m instrument; tool, implement; **~ de musique** musical instrument

insuffisant (aṅg-sew-fee-*zahṅg*) adj insufficient

insulte (aṅg-*sewlt*) f insult

insulter (aṅg-sewl-*tay*) v insult; scold

insupportable (aṅg-sew-por-*tahbl*) adj unbearable

insurrection (aṅg-sew-rehk-*s^yawṅg*) f revolt, uprising

intact (aṅg-*tahkt*) adj whole, intact, unbroken

intellect (aṅg-teh-*lehkt*) m intellect

intellectuel (aṅg-teh-lehk-*twehl*) adj intellectual

intelligence (aṅg-teh-lee-*zhahṅgss*) f intelligence, intellect, brain

intelligent (aṅg-teh-lee-*zhahṅg*) adj intelligent, bright, clever

intense (aṅg-*tahṅgss*) adj intense; heavy

intention (aṅg-tahṅg-*s^yawṅg*) f intention, purpose; *****avoir l'intention de** intend

intentionnel (aṅg-tahṅg-*s^yo-nehl*) adj intentional, on purpose

interdiction (aṅg-tehr-deek-*s^yawṅg*) f prohibition

*****interdire** (aṅg-tehr-*deer*) v *forbid, prohibit

interdit (aṅg-tehr-*dee*) adj prohibited; **~ aux piétons** no pedestrians

intéressant (aṅg-tay-reh-*sahṅg*) adj interesting

intéresser (aṅg-tay-ray-*say*) v interest

intérêt (aṅg-tay-*ray*) m interest

intérieur (aṅg-tay-r^y*ūrr*) m interior, inside; adj internal, inside, inner; indoor; domestic; **à l'intérieur** inside; indoors, within; **à l'intérieur de** inside; **vers l'intérieur** inwards

intérim (aṅg-tay-*reem*) m interim

interloqué (aṅg-tehr-lo-*kay*) adj speechless

interlude (aṅg-tehr-*lewd*) m interlude

intermédiaire (aṅg-tehr-may-*d^yair*) m/f intermediary; *****servir d'intermédiaire** mediate

internat (aṅg-tehr-*nah*) m boarding school

international (aṅg-tehr-nah-s^yo-*nahl*) adj international

interne (aṅg-*tehrn*) adj internal, resident

Internet (aṅg-tehr-*neht*) m internet

interprète (aṅg-tehr-*preht*) m/f interpreter

interpréter (aṅg-tehr-pray-*tay*) v interpret

interrogatif (aṅg-teh-ro-gah-*teef*) adj interrogative

interrogatoire (aṅg-teh-ro-gah-*twaar*) m interrogation, examination

interroger (aṅg-teh-ro-*zhay*) v interrogate

*****interrompre** (aṅg-teh-*rawṅgpr*) v interrupt; **s'*interrompre** *break off

interruption (aṅg-teh-rew-*ps^yawṅg*) f interruption

intersection (aṅg-tehr-sehk-*s^yawṅg*) f intersection

intervalle (aṅg-tehr-*vahl*) m interval; space

*****intervenir** (aṅg-tehr-ver-*neer*) v intervene, interfere

intervertir (aṅg-tehr-vehr-*teer*) v invert

interview (aṅg-tehr-*v^yoo*) f interview

intestin (aṅg-teh-*staṅg*) m intestine, gut; **intestins** bowels pl

intime (aṅg-*teem*) adj intimate, cosy, cozy Am

intimité (ang-tee-mee-*tay*) *f* privacy

intolérable (ang-to-lay-*rahbl*) *adj* intolerable

intoxication alimentaire (ang-tok-see-kah-s^{y}awng ah-lee-mahng-*tair*) food poisoning

intrigue (ang-*treeg*) *f* intrigue; plot

introduction (ang-tro-dewk-s^{y}awng) *f* introduction

*introduire (ang-tro-*dweer*) *v* introduce

intrus (ang-*trew*) *m* trespasser

inutile (ee-new-*teel*) *adj* useless

inutilement (ee-new-teel-*mahng*) *adv* in vain

invalide (ang-vah-*leed*) *adj* disabled, handicapped

invasion (ang-vah-z^{y}awng) *f* invasion

inventaire (ang-vahng-*tair*) *m* inventory

inventer (ang-vahng-*tay*) *v* invent

inventeur (ang-vahng-*tūrr*) *m* inventor

inventif (ang-vahng-*teef*) *adj* inventive

invention (ang-vahng-s^{y}awng) *f* invention

inverse (ang-*vehrs*) *adj* reverse

investigation (ang-veh-stee-gah-s^{y}awng) *f* investigation, enquiry

investir (ang-veh-*steer*) *v* invest

investissement (ang-veh-stee-*smahng*) *m* investment

investisseur (ang-veh-stee-*sūrr*) *m* investor

invisible (ang-vee-*zeebl*) *adj* invisible

invitation (ang-vee-tah-s^{y}awng) *f* invitation

invité (ang-vee-*tay*) *m* guest

inviter (ang-vee-*tay*) *v* invite

involontaire (ang-vo-lawng-*tair*) *adj* unintentional

iode (^{y}od) *m* iodine

Irak (ee-*rahk*) *m* Iraq

Irakien (ee-rah-k^{y}ang) *m* Iraqi

irakien (ee-rah-k^{y}ang) *adj* Iraqi

Iran (ee-*rahng*) *m* Iran

iranien (ee-rah-n^{y}ang) *adj* Iranian

irascible (ee-rah-*seebl*) *adj* quick-tempered

irlandais (eer-lahng-*day*) *adj* Irish

Irlande (eer-*lahngd*) *f* Ireland

ironie (ee-ro-*nee*) *f* irony

ironique (ee-ro-*neek*) *adj* ironical

irréel (ee-ray-*ehl*) *adj* unreal

irrégulier (ee-ray-gew-l^{y}ay) *adj* irregular, uneven

irréparable (ee-ray-pah-*rahbl*) *adj* irreparable

irrétrécissable (ee-ray-tray-see-*sahbl*) *adj* shrinkproof

irrévocable (ee-ray-vo-*kahbl*) *adj* irrevocable

irritable (ee-ree-*tahbl*) *adj* irritable

irrité (ee-ree-*tay*) *adj* angry, annoyed

irriter (ee-ree-*tay*) *v* irritate

islandais (ee-slahng-*day*) *adj* Icelandic

Islande (ee-*slahngd*) *f* Iceland

isolateur (ee-zo-lah-*tūrr*) *m* insulator

isolation (ee-zo-lah-s^{y}awng) *f* isolation, insulation

isolement (ee-zol-*mahng*) *m* isolation

isoler (ee-zo-*lay*) *v* isolate, insulate

Israël (ee-srah-*ehl*) *m* Israel

israélien (ee-srah-ay-l^{y}ang) *adj* Israeli

issue (ee-*sew*) *f* issue

Italie (ee-tah-*lee*) *f* Italy

italien (ee-tah-l^{y}ang) *adj* Italian

itinéraire (ee-tee-nay-*rair*) *m* itinerary

ivoire (ee-*vwaar*) *m* ivory

ivre (eevr) *adj* drunk; intoxicated

J

jadis (zhah-*deess*) *adv* formerly

jalousie (zhah-loo-*zee*) *f* jealousy

jaloux (zhah-*loo*) *adj* jealous, envious

jamais (zhah-*may*) *adv* ever; **ne ... ~** never

jambe (zhahnḡb) *f* leg

jambon (zhahnḡ-*bawnḡ*) *m* ham

jante (zhahnḡt) *f* rim

janvier (zhahnḡ-*v*ʸ*ay*) January

Japon (zhah-*pawnḡ*) *m* Japan

Japonais (zhah-po-*nay*) *m* Japanese

japonais (zhah-po-*nay*) *adj* Japanese

jaquette (zhah-*keht*) *f* jacket

jardin (zhahr-*danḡ*) *m* garden; **~ potager** kitchen garden; **~ public** public garden; **~ zoologique** zoological gardens

jardinier (zhahr-dee-*n*ʸ*ay*) *m* gardener

jarre (zhaar) *f* jar

jauge (zhōazh) *f* gauge

jaune (zhōan) *adj* yellow; **~ d'œuf** yolk, egg yolk

jaunisse (zhoa-*neess*) *f* jaundice

je (zher) *pron* I

jersey (zhehr-*zay*) *m* jersey

jet (zhay) *m* cast; jet, squirt, spout

jetée (zher-*tay*) *f* jetty, pier

jeter (zher-*tay*) *v* *cast, *throw; **à ~** disposable

jeton (zher-*tawnḡ*) *m* token, chip

jeu (zhur) *m* play, game; set; **carte de ~** playing card; **~ concours** quiz; **~ de dames** draughts; checkers *plAm*; **~ de quilles** ninepins, skittles; **terrain de jeux** playground

jeudi (zhur-*dee*) *m* Thursday

jeune (zhurn) *adj* young

jeunesse (zhur-*nehss*) *f* youth

joaillerie (zhwigh-*ree*) *f* jewellery, jewelry *Am*

joaillier (zhwigh-*yay*) *m*, **-ière** *f* jewel(l)er

jockey (zho-*kay*) *m* jockey

joie (zhwah) *f* joy, gladness

*joindre (zhwanḡdr) *v* join, connect; attach, enclose

jointure (zhwanḡ-*tewr*) *f* knuckle

joli (zho-*lee*) *adj* fine, nice, pretty, good-looking

jonc (zhawnḡ) *m* rush

jonction (zhawnḡk-*s*ʸ*awnḡ*) *f* junction

jonquille (zhawnḡ-*keey*) *f* daffodil

Jordanie (zhor-dah-*nee*) *f* Jordan

jordanien (zhor-dah-*n*ʸ*anḡ*) *adj* Jordanian

joue (zhoo) *f* cheek

jouer (zhoo-*ay*) *v* play; act

jouet (zhoo-*ay*) *m* toy

joueur (zhoo-*ūrr*) *m*, **-euse** *f* player

joug (zhoo) *m* yoke

jouir de (zhoo-*eer*) enjoy

jour (zhōor) *m* day; **de ~** by day; **~ de fête** holiday; **~ de la semaine** weekday; **~ ouvrable** working day; **l'autre ~** recently; **par ~** per day; **un ~ ou l'autre** some day

journal (zhoor-*nahl*) *m* newspaper, paper; diary; **~ du matin** morning paper

journalier (zhoor-nah-*l*ʸ*ay*) *adj* daily

journalisme (zhoor-nah-*leesm*) *m* journalism

journaliste (zhoor-nah-*leest*) *m/f* journalist

journée (zhoor-*nay*) *f* day

joyau (zhwah-ʸ*oa*) *m* gem

joyeux (zhwah-ʸ*ur*) *adj* joyful, cheerful, merry, glad

juge (zhēwzh) *m* judge

jugement (zhewzh-*mahnḡ*) *m* judgment; sentence

juger (zhew-*zhay*) *v* judge

juif (zhweef) *adj* Jewish; *m* Jew

juillet (zhwee-ʸ*ay*) July

juin (zhwa̅ng) June

juive (zheef) *adj* Jewish; *f* Jew

jumeaux (zhew-*moa*) *mpl* twins *pl*

jumelage (zhew-mer-*laazh*) *m* twinning

jumelles (zhew-*mehl*) *fpl* field glasses, binoculars *pl*

jument (zhew-*mah̅ng*) *f* mare

jungle (zhaw̅nggl) *f* jungle

jupe (zhewp) *f* skirt

jupon (zhew-*paw̅ng*) *m* underskirt

jurer (zhew-*ray*) *v* vow; *swear; curse

juridique (zhew-ree-*deek*) *adj* legal

juriste (zhew-*reest*) *m* lawyer

juron (zhew-*raw̅ng*) *m* curse

jury (zhew-*ree*) *m* jury

jus (zhew) *m* juice; gravy; **~ de fruits** fruit juice

jusque (zhewsk) *prep* to; **jusqu'à** *prep* till; until; **jusqu'à ce que** till

juste (zhewst) *adj* just, righteous, right, fair; appropriate, proper, correct, exact; tight; *adv* just

justement (zhew-ster-*mah̅ng*) *adv* rightly

justice (zhew-*steess*) *f* justice

justifier (zhew-stee-*fʸay*) *v* justify

juteux (zhew-*tur*) *adj* juicy

juvénile (zhew-vay-*neel*) *adj* juvenile

K

kaki (kah-*kee*) *m* khaki

kangourou (kah̅ng-goo-*roo*) *m* kangaroo

Kenya (kay-*nʸah*) *m* Kenya

kilo (kee-*loa*) *m* kilogram

kilométrage (kee-lo-may-*traazh*) *m* distance in kilometres (kilometers *Am*)

kilomètre (kee-lo-*mehtr*) *m* kilometre, kilometer *Am*

kiosque (kʸosk) *m* kiosk; **~ à journaux** newsstand

klaxon (klahk-*saw̅ng*) *m* hooter; horn

klaxonner (klahk-so-*nay*) *v* hoot; toot *Am*, honk *Am*

L

la (lah) *art* the; *pron* her

là (lah) *adv* there

là-bas (lah-*bah*) *adv* over there

labeur (lah-*bŭrr*) *m* labo(u)r

laboratoire (lah-bo-rah-*twaar*) *m* laboratory; **~ de langues** language laboratory

labourer (lah-boo-*ray*) *v* plough

labyrinthe (lah-bee-*ra̅ngt*) *m* maze, labyrinth

lac (lahk) *m* lake

lacet (lah-*say*) *m* shoelace, lace

lâche (laash) *m* coward; *adj* cowardly; loose

lâcher (lah-*shay*) *v* *let go

lagune (lah-*gewn*) *f* lagoon

laid (lay) *adj* ugly

laine (lehn) *f* wool; **en ~** wool(l)en; **~ à**

repriser darning wool

laisse (lehss) *f* leash, lead

laisser (lay-*say*) *v* *let, *leave; *leave behind

lait (lay) *m* milk

laiterie (leh-*tree*) *f* dairy

laiteux (lay-*tur*) *adj* milky

laitier (lay-t^y*ay*) *m* milkman

laiton (lay-*tawng*) *m* brass

laitue (lay-*tew*) *f* lettuce

lame (lahm) *f* blade; ~ **de rasoir** razor blade

lamentable (lah-mahng-*tahbl*) *adj* lamentable

lampadaire (lahng-pah-*dair*) *m* lamppost

lampe (lahngp) *f* lamp; ~ **de poche** torch; ~ **de travail** reading lamp; **lampe-tempête** *f* hurricane lamp

lance (lahngss) *f* spear

lancement (lahng-*smahng*) *m* throw; launching

lancer (lahng-*say*) *v* *cast, toss, *throw; launch

lande (lahngd) *f* heath, moor

langage (lahng-*gaazh*) *m* language

langue (lahngg) *f* tongue; language; ~ **maternelle** native language, mother tongue

lanterne (lahng-*tehrn*) *f* lantern

lapin (lah-*pang*) *m* rabbit

laque (lahk) *f* varnish; ~ **capillaire** hair spray

lard (laar) *m* bacon

lardon (lahr-*dawng*) *m* piece of larding bacon; kid, baby

large (lahrzh) *adj* wide, broad; generous, liberal

largeur (lahr-*zhurr*) *f* width, breadth

larme (lahrm) *f* tear

laryngite (lah-rang-*zheet*) *f* laryngitis

las (lah) *adj* (f ~se) weary; ~ **de** tired of

latitude (lah-tee-*tewd*) *f* latitude

lavable (lah-*vahbl*) *adj* washable

lavabo (lah-vah-*boa*) *m* washbasin

lavage (lah-*vaazh*) *m* washing

laver (lah-*vay*) *v* wash

laverie automatique (lah-vree oa-toa-mah-*teek*) launderette

lave-vaisselle (lahv-veh-*sehl*) *m* dish washer

laxatif (lahk-sah-*teef*) *m* laxative

le[1] (ler) *art* (f la, pl les) the

le[2] (ler) *pron* (f la) him; it

leader (lee-*dair*) *m* leader

lécher (lay-*shay*) *v* lick

lèche-vitrines (lehsh-vee-*treen*) *m*windowshopping

leçon (ler-*sawng*) *f* lesson

lecteur (lehk-*turr*) *m*, **-trice** *f* reader

lecture (lehk-*tewr*) *f* reading

légal (lay-*gahl*) *adj* legal, lawful

léger (lay-*zhay*) *adj* (f légère) slight, light; weak, gentle

légitime (lay-zhee-*teem*) *adj* legitimate, legal; just

légume (lay-*gewm*) *m* vegetable

lendemain (lahngd-*mang*) *m* next day

lent (lahng) *adj* slow; sluggish

lentille (lahng-*teey*) *f* lens

lèpre (lehpr) *f* leprosy

lequel (ler-*kehl*) *pron* (f laquelle; pl lesquels, lesquelles) which

les (lay) *art* the; *pron* them

lésion (lay-z^y*awng*) *f* injury

lessive (lay-*seev*) *f* washing, laundry

lettre (lehtr) *f* letter; **boîte aux lettres** letterbox, mailbox *Am*; ~ **de crédit** letter of credit; ~ **de recommandation** letter of recommendation; ~ **recommandée** registered letter

leur (lurr) *adj* their; *pron* them

levée (ler-*vay*) *f* collection

lever (ler-*vay*) *v* lift; ~ **du jour** daybreak; **se** ~ *rise, *get up

levier (ler-v^y*ay*) *m* lever; ~ **de vitesse** gear lever

lèvre (laivr) f lip

lévrier (lay-vr^yay) m greyhound

levure (ler-vẽwr) f yeast

liaison (l^yay-zawng) f connection; affair

Liban (lee-bahng) m Lebanon

libanais (lee-bah-nay) adj Lebanese

libéral (lee-bay-rahl) adj liberal

libération (lee-bay-rah-s^yawng) f liberation

libérer (lee-bay-ray) v release; liberate

Libéria (lee-bay-r^yah) m Liberia

libérien (lee-bay-r^yang) adj Liberian

liberté (lee-behr-tay) f freedom, liberty

libraire (lee-brair) m/f bookseller

librairie (lee-bray-ree) f bookstore

libre (leebr) adj free

libre-service (leebr-sehr-veess) m self-service

licence (lee-sahngss) f permission, licence, license Am

licencier (lee-sahng-s^yay) v fire

lien (l^yang) m band; link

lier (lee-ay) v *bind

lierre (l^yair) m ivy

lieu (l^yur) m spot; **au ~ de** instead of; *avoir ~ *take place; **~ de naissance** place of birth; **~ de rencontre** meeting place

lièvre (l^yaivr) m hare

ligne (leeñ) f line; **~ aérienne** airline; **~ d'arrivée** finish; **~ de pêche** fishing line; **~ intérieure** extension; **~ principale** main line

ligue (leeg) f union, league

lime (leem) f file; **~ à ongles** nail file

limette (lee-meht) f lime

limite (lee-meet) f limit, boundary, bound; **~ de vitesse** speed limit

limiter (lee-mee-tay) v limit

limonade (lee-mo-nahd) f lemonade

linge (langzh) m linen

lingerie (lang-zhree) f lingerie

lion (l^yawng) m lion

liqueur (lee-kūrr) f liqueur

liquide (lee-keed) m fluid; adj liquid

***lire** (leer) v *read

lis (leess) m lily

lisible (lee-zeebl) adj legible

lisse (leess) adj smooth

liste (leest) f list; **~ d'attente** waiting list

lit (lee) m bed; **~ de camp** camp bed; cot Am; **lits jumeaux** twin beds

literie (lee-tree) f bedding

litige (lee-teezh) m dispute

litre (leetr) m liter Am, litre

littéraire (lee-tay-rair) adj literary

littérature (lee-tay-rah-tẽwr) f literature

littoral (lee-to-rahl) m sea-coast

livraison (lee-vreh-zawng) f delivery

livre¹ (leevr) m book; **~ de cuisine** cookery book; cookbook Am; **~ de poche** paperback

livre² (leevr) f pound

livrer (lee-vray) v deliver

local (lo-kahl) adj local

localiser (lo-kah-lee-zay) v locate

localité (lo-kah-lee-tay) f locality

locataire (lo-kah-tair) m tenant

location (lo-kah-s^yawng) f lease; **donner en ~** lease; **~ de voitures** car hire; car rental Am

locomotive (lo-ko-mo-teev) f locomotive, engine

locution (lo-kew-s^yawng) f phrase

loge (lozh) f dressing room

logement (lozh-mahng) m lodgings pl, accommodation

loger (lo-zhay) v accommodate; lodge

logeur (lo-zhūrr) m landlord

logeuse (lo-zhũrz) f landlady

logique (lo-zheek) f logic; adj logical

loi (lwah) f law

loin (lwang) adv away, far; **plus ~** further

lointain (lwang-*tang*) *adj* far-off, remote

loisir (lwah-*zeer*) *m* leisure

long (lawng) *adj* (f longue) long; **en ~** lengthways; **le ~ de** past, along

longitude (lawng-zhee-*tewd*) *f* longitude

longtemps (lawng-*tahng*) *adv* long

longueur (lawng-*gurr*) *f* length; **~ d'onde** wavelength

lopin (lo-*pang*) *m* plot

lors de (lor der) at the time of

lorsque (lorsk) *conj* when

lot (loa) *m* batch

loterie (lo-*tree*) *f* lottery

lotion (lo-s*ʸawng*) *f* lotion

louange (loo-ahngzh) *f* glory

louche (loosh) *adj* cross-eyed

louer (loo-*ay*) *v* hire, rent, lease; *let; praise; **à ~** for hire

loup (loo) *m* wolf

lourd (loor) *adj* heavy

loyal (lwah-*ʸahl*) *adj* true, loyal

loyer (lwah-*ʸay*) *m* rent

lubie (lew-*bee*) *f* whim

lubrifiant (lew-bree-f*ʸahng*) *m* lubrication oil

lubrification (lew-bree-fee-kah-s*ʸawng*) *f* lubrication

lubrifier (lew-bree-f*ʸay*) *v* lubricate

lueur (lwurr) *f* gleam

luge (lewzh) *f* sleigh, sled(ge)

lugubre (lew-*gewbr*) *adj* creepy

lui (lwee) *pron* him; her; **lui-même** *pron* himself

luisant (lwee-*zahng*) *adj* glossy

lumbago (lawng-bah-*goa*) *m* lumbago

lumière (lew-m*ʸair*) *f* light; **~ du jour** daylight; **~ du soleil** sunlight; **~ latérale** sidelight

lumineux (lew-mee-*nur*) *adj* luminous

lundi (lurng-*dee*) *m* Monday

lune (lewn) *f* moon; **clair de ~** moonlight; **~ de miel** honeymoon

lunettes (lew-*neht*) *fpl* spectacles, glasses; **~ de plongée** goggles *pl*; **~ de soleil** sunglasses *pl*

lustre (lewstr) *m* gloss

lustrer (lew-*stray*) *v* lustre; *shine

lutte (lewt) *f* fight, combat, battle, struggle

lutter (lew-*tay*) *v* struggle; combat

luxe (lewks) *m* luxury

luxueux (lewk-*swur*) *adj* luxurious

lycée (lee-*say*) *m* (state) secondary school

M

mâcher (mah-*shay*) *v* chew

machine (mah-*sheen*) *f* engine, machine; **~ à coudre** sewing machine; **~ à écrire** typewriter; **~ à laver** washing machine

machinerie (mah-sheen-*ree*) *f* machinery

mâchoire (mah-*shwaar*) *f* jaw

maçon (mah-*sawng*) *m* bricklayer

madame (mah-*dahm*) madam

mademoiselle (mahd-mwah-*zehl*) miss

magasin (mah-gah-*zang*) *m* store, warehouse, store house; **grand ~** department store; **~ de chaussures** shoe shop; **~ de jouets** toyshop; **~ de spiritueux** off-licence, liquor store *Am*

magazine (mah-gah-*zeen*) *m* magazine

magie (mah-*zhee*) f magic
magique (mah-*zheek*) adj magic
magistrat (mah-zhee-*strah*) m magistrate
magnétique (mah-ñay-*teek*) adj magnetic
magnéto (mah-ñay-*toa*) f magneto
magnétophone (mah-ñay-to-*fon*) m tape recorder
magnétoscope (mah-ñay-to-*skop*) m video recorder
magnifique (mah-ñee-*feek*) adj splendid, gorgeous, magnificent
mai (may) May
maigre (maigr) adj thin, lean
maigrir (meh-*greer*) v slim
maille (migh) f mesh
maillet (mah-*ʸay*) m mallet
maillot de bain (mah-*ʸ*oa der *bang*) bathing suit, swimsuit
main (*mang*) f hand; **fait à la ∼** hand-made
main-d'œuvre (mang-*dūrvr*) f manpower
maintenant (mangt-*nahng*) adv now; **jusqu'à ∼** so far
*maintenir (mangt-*neer*) v maintain
maire (mair) m mayor
mairie (may-*ree*) f town hall
mais (may) conj but
maïs (mah-*eess*) m maize, corn Am; **∼ en épi** corn on the cob
maison (may-*zawng*) f house; home; **à la ∼** at home; **fait à la ∼** home-made; **maison-bateau** houseboat; **∼ de campagne** country house; **∼ de repos** rest home
maître (maitr) m master; **∼ d'école** teacher, schoolmaster; **∼ d'hôtel** head waiter
maîtresse (meh-*trehss*) f mistress; **∼ de maison** mistress
maîtriser (meh-tree-*zay*) v master
majeur (mah-*zhūrr*) adj major;

superior, main; of age
majorité (mah-zho-ree-*tay*) f bulk, majority
majuscule (mah-zhew-*skewl*) f capital letter
mal (mahl) m (pl maux) evil, harm; mischief; ***faire du ∼** harm; ***faire ∼** ache; ***hurt; ∼ à l'aise** uneasy; **∼ au cœur** sickness; **∼ au dos** backache; **∼ au ventre** stomachache; **∼ aux dents** toothache; **∼ de gorge** sore throat; **∼ de l'air** airsickness; **∼ de mer** seasickness; **∼ d'estomac** stomach ache; **∼ de tête** headache; **∼ d'oreille** earache; **∼ du pays** homesickness
malade (mah-*lahd*) adj sick, ill
maladie (mah-lah-*dee*) f sickness, illness, disease; **∼ vénérienne** venereal disease
maladroit (mah-lah-*drwah*) adj clumsy, awkward
Malais (mah-*lay*) m Malay
malaisien (mah-lay-*zʸang*) adj Malaysian
malaria (mah-lah-*rʸah*) f malaria
malchance (mahl-*shahngss*) f bad luck
mâle (maal) adj male
malentendu (mah-lahng-tahng-*dew*) m misunderstanding
malgré (mahl-*gray*) prep in spite of, despite
malheur (mah-*lūrr*) m misfortune
malheureusement (mah-lur-rurz-*mahng*) adv unfortunately
malheureux (mah-lur-*rur*) adj unhappy, unfortunate; miserable, sad
malhonnête (mah-lo-*neht*) adj dishonest, crooked
malice (mah-*leess*) f mischief
malicieux (mah-lee-*sʸur*) adj mischievous
malin (mah-*lang*) adj (f maligne) malignant; sly; bright
malle (mahl) f trunk

mallette (mah-*leht*) f suitcase; ~ **de voyage** grip Am

malodorant (mah-lo-do-*rahng*) adj smelly

malpropre (mahl-*propr*) adj foul, unclean

malsain (mahl-*sang*) adj unsound, unhealthy

malveillant (mahl-veh-*yahng*) adj spiteful; malicious

maman (mah-*mahng*) f mum

mammifère (mah-mee-*fair*) m mammal

manche (mahngsh) m handle; f sleeve; **La Manche** English Channel

manchette (mahng-*sheht*) f cuff; headline

mandarine (mahng-dah-*reen*) f tangerine, mandarin

mandat (mahng-*dah*) m mandate

manège (mah-*naizh*) m riding school

mangeoire (mahng-*zhwaar*) f manger

manger (mahng-*zhay*) v *eat; m food

maniable (mah-*nyahbl*) adj manageable

manier (mah-*nyay*) v handle

manière (mah-*nyair*) f way, manner; **de la même** ~ likewise; **de** ~ **que** so that

manifestation (mah-nee-feh-stah-*syawng*) f demonstration

manifestement (mah-nee-feh-ster-*mahng*) adv apparently

manifester (mah-nee-feh-*stay*) v express; demonstrate

manipuler (mah-nee-pew-*lay*) v handle

mannequin (mahn-*kang*) m model, mannequin

manoir (mah-*nwaar*) m mansion, manor house

manquant (mahng-*kahng*) adj missing

manque (mahngk) m want, shortage, lack

manquer (mahng-*kay*) v fail, lack; miss

manteau (mahng-*toa*) m coat, cloak; ~ **de fourrure** fur coat

manucure (mah-new-*kewr*) f manicure

manuel (mah-*nwehl*) m textbook, handbook; adj manual; ~ **de conversation** phrase book

manuscrit (mah-new-*skree*) m manuscript

maquereau (mah-*kroa*) m mackerel

maquillage (mah-kee-*yaazh*) m make-up

marais (mah-*ray*) m marsh, swamp, bog

marbre (mahrbr) m marble

marchand (mahr-*shahng*) m, -e f merchant; tradesman, dealer; ~ **de journaux** newsagent; ~ **de légumes** greengrocer; vegetable merchant; ~ **de volaille** poulterer

marchander (mahr-shahng-*day*) v bargain

marchandise (mahr-shahng-*deez*) f merchandise; wares pl, goods pl

marche (mahrsh) f march; step; *faire ~ arrière** reverse

marché (mahr-*shay*) m market; **bon** ~ cheap; inexpensive; ~ **des valeurs** stock market; ~ **noir** black market; **place du** ~ marketplace

marcher (mahr-*shay*) v walk, step, *go; march; *faire ~ fool

mardi (mahr-*dee*) m Tuesday

marée (mah-*ray*) f tide; ~ **basse** low tide; ~ **haute** flood; high tide

margarine (mahr-gah-*reen*) f margarine

marge (mahrzh) f margin

mari (mah-*ree*) m husband

mariage (mah-*ryaazh*) m matrimony, marriage; wedding

marié (mah-*ryay*) m bridegroom

marier: se ~ (mah-*ryay*) marry

marin (mah-*rang*) *m* sailor; seaman

marinade (mah-ree-*nahd*) *f* marinade *f*

marine (mah-*reen*) *f* navy; seascape

maritime (mah-ree-*teem*) *adj* maritime

marmelade (mahr-mer-*lahd*) *f* marmalade

marmite (mahr-*meet*) *f* pot

Maroc (mah-*rok*) *m* Morocco

marocain (mah-ro-*kang*) *adj* Moroccan

maroquinerie (mah-ro-keen-*ree*) *f* leather goods *pl*

marque (mahrk) *f* mark; sign, brand; ~ **de fabrique** trademark

marquer (mahr-*kay*) *v* mark

marquise (mahr-*keez*) *f* awning

marrant (mah-*rahng*) *adj* funny; odd

marron (mah-*rawng*) *m* chestnut

mars (mahrs) March

marteau (mahr-*toa*) *m* hammer

marteler (mahr-ter-*lay*) *v* thump

martyr (mahr-*teer*) *m*, **-e** *f* martyr

masculin (mah-skew-*lang*) *adj* masculine

masque (mahsk) *m* mask; ~ **de beauté** face pack

massage (mah-*saazh*) *m* massage; ~ **facial** face massage

masse (mahss) *f* mass; bulk; crowd

masser (mah-*say*) *v* massage

masseur (mah-*surr*) *m* masseur

massif (mah-*seef*) *adj* massive, solid

massue (mah-*sew*) *f* club

mat (maht) *adj* mat, dull, dim

mât (mah) *m* mast

match (mahch) *m* match; ~ **de boxe** boxing match; ~ **de football** football match

matelas (mah-*tlah*) *m* mattress

matériau (mah-tay-*r*ʸ*oa*) *m* material

matériel (mah-tay-*r*ʸ*ehl*) *m* material; *adj* material; substantial

maternel (mah-tehr-*nehl*) *adj* motherly

mathématique (mah-tay-mah-*teek*) *adj* mathematical

mathématiques (mah-tay-mah-*teek*) *fpl* mathematics

matière (mah-*t*ʸ*air*) *f* matter; ~ **première** raw material

matin (mah-*tang*) *m* morning; **ce** ~ this morning

matinée (mah-tee-*nay*) *f* morning

maturité (mah-tew-ree-*tay*) *f* maturity

***maudire** (moa-*deer*) *v* curse

mausolée (moa-zo-*lay*) *m* mausoleum

mauvais (moa-*vay*) *adj* bad; wicked, ill, evil; **le plus** ~ worst

mauve (mōav) *adj* mauve

maximum (mahk-see-*mom*) *m* maximum; **au** ~ at most

mayonnaise (mah-ʸo-*naiz*) *f* mayonnaise

mazout (mah-*zoot*) *m* fuel oil

me (mer) *pron* me; myself

mécanicien (may-kah-nee-s*ʸang*) *m* mechanic

mécanique (may-kah-*neek*) *adj* mechanical

mécanisme (may-kah-*neesm*) *m* mechanism, machinery

méchant (may-*shahng*) *adj* evil; naughty, nasty, ill

mèche (mehsh) *f* fuse

mécontent (may-kawng-*tahng*) *adj* discontented

médaille (may-*digh*) *f* medal

médecin (may-*dsang*) *m* physician, doctor; ~ **généraliste** general practitioner

médecine (may-*dseen*) *f* medicine

médiateur (may-d*ʸ*ah-*tūrr*) *m*, **-trice** *f* mediator

médical (may-dee-*kahl*) *adj* medical

médicament (may-dee-kah-*mahng*) *m* medicine, drug

médiéval (may-d*ʸ*ay-*vahl*) *adj*

mediaeval

méditer (may-dee-*tay*) *v* meditate

Méditerranée (may-dee-tay-rah-*nay*) *f* Mediterranean

méduse (may-*dēwz*) *f* jellyfish

méfiance (may-f'*ahngss*) *f* suspicion

méfiant (may-f'*ahng*) *adj* suspicious

méfier (may-f'*ay*) *v*: **se ~ de** mistrust

meilleur (meh-*yūrr*) *adj* better; **le ~** best

mélancolie (may-lahng-ko-*lee*) *f* melancholy

mélancolique (may-lahng-ko-*leek*) *adj* melancholy

mélange (may-*lahngzh*) *m* mixture

mélanger (may-lahng-*zhay*) *v* mix

mêler (may-*lay*) *v* mix; **se ~ de** interfere with

mélo (may-*loa*) *m* tear-jerker

mélodie (may-lo-*dee*) *f* melody

mélodrame (may-lo-*drahm*) *m* melodrama

melon (mer-*lawng*) *m* melon

membre (*mahngbr*) *m* member, associate; limb

mémé (may-*may*) *f* granny

même (mehm) *adj* same; *adv* even; **de ~** also

mémoire (may-*mwaar*) *f* memory

mémorable (may-mo-*rahbl*) *adj* memorable

mémorandum (may-mo-rahng-*dom*) *m* memo

mémorial (may-mo-r'*ahl*) *m* memorial

menaçant (mer-nah-*sahng*) *adj* threatening

menace (mer-*nahss*) *f* threat

menacer (mer-nah-*say*) *v* threaten

ménage (may-*naazh*) *m* housekeeping, household

ménagère (may-nah-*zhair*) *f* housewife

mendiant (mahng-d'*ahng*) *m*, **-e** *f* beggar

mendier (mahng-d'*ay*) *v* beg

mener (mer-*nay*) *v* *take, *lead

menottes (mer-*not*) *fpl* handcuffs *pl*

mensonge (mahng-*sawngzh*) *m* lie

menstruation (mahng-strew-ah-s'*awng*) *f* menstruation

mensuel (mahng-*swehl*) *adj* monthly

mental (mahng-*tahl*) *adj* mental; **aliéné ~** lunatic

menthe (mahngt) *f* peppermint, mint

mention (mahng-s'*awng*) *f* mention

mentionner (mahng-s'o-*nay*) *v* mention

***mentir** (mahng-*teer*) *v* lie

menton (mahng-*tawng*) *m* chin

menu[1] (mer-*new*) *m* menu; **~ fixe** set menu

menu[2] (mer-*new*) *adj* minor

menuisier (mer-nwee-z'*ay*) *m* carpenter

mépris (may-*pree*) *m* contempt, scorn

méprise (may-*preez*) *f* mistake

mépriser (may-pree-*zay*) *v* despise, scorn

mer (mair) *f* sea

merci (mehr-*see*) thank you

mercredi (mehr-krer-*dee*) *m* Wednesday

mercure (mehr-*kēwr*) *m* mercury

merde (mehrd) *f* shit

mère (mair) *f* mother

méridional (may-ree-d'o-*nahl*) *adj* southern, southerly

mérite (may-*reet*) *m* merit

mériter (may-ree-*tay*) *v* merit, deserve

merlan (mehr-*lahng*) *m* whiting

merle (mehrl) *m* blackbird

merveille (mehr-*vay*) *f* marvel

merveilleux (mehr-veh-'*ur*) *adj* marvel(l)ous; fine, wonderful

mesquin (meh-*skang*) *adj* mean, stingy

message (meh-*saazh*) *m* message

messager (meh-sah-*zhay*) *m*
messenger

messe (mehss) *f* mass

mesure (mer-*zewr*) *f* measure; size; **en ~ able**; **fait sur ~** tailor-made

mesurer (mer-zew-*ray*) *v* measure

métal (may-*tahl*) *m* metal

métallique (may-tah-*leek*) *adj* metal

météo (may-tay-*oa*) *f* weather report; *m* meteorologist

méthode (may-*tod*) *f* method

méthodique (may-to-*deek*) *adj* methodical

méticuleux (may-tee-kew-*lur*) *adj* meticulous

métier (may-*tʸay*) *m* trade, profession

mètre (mehtr) *m* meter *Am*, metre

métrique (may-*treek*) *adj* metric

métro (may-*troa*) *m* underground; subway *Am*

***mettre** (mehtr) *v* *put; *put on

meuble (murbl) *m* piece of furniture; **meubles** furniture

meubler (mur-*blay*) *v* furnish

meunier (mur-*nʸay*) *m* miller

meurtrier (murr-tree-*ay*) *m*, **-ière** *f* murderer

mexicain (mehk-see-*kaṉg*) *adj* Mexican

Mexique (mehk-*seek*) *m* Mexico

mi-bas (mee-*bah*) *m* knee-length sock

miche (meesh) *f* loaf

microbe (mee-*krob*) *m* germ

microphone (mee-kro-*fon*) *m* microphone

microsillon (mee-kro-see-*ʸawṉg*) *m* long-playing record

midi (mee-*dee*) *m* midday, noon

miel (mʸehl) *m* honey

mien: le ~ (ler mʸaṉg) mine

miette (mʸeht) *f* crumb

mieux (mʸur) *adv* better

mignon (mee-*ñawṉg*) *adj* dainty, nice, sweet; **péché ~** little weakness

migraine (mee-*grehn*) *f* migraine

milieu (mee-*lʸur*) *m* middle, midst; milieu; **au ~ de** among, amid; **du ~** middle

militaire (mee-lee-*tair*) *adj* military

mille (meel) *num* thousand; *m* mile

million (mee-*lʸawṉg*) *m* million

millionnaire (mee-lʸo-*nair*) *m/f* millionaire

mince (maṉgss) *adj* slim, thin

mine¹ (meen) *f* pit, mine; **~ d'or** goldmine

mine² (meen) *f* look

minerai (meen-*ray*) *m* ore

minéral (mee-nay-*rahl*) *m* mineral

minet (mee-*nay*) *m* pussy-cat

mineur (mee-*nūrr*) *m* miner; minor; *adj* minor; under age

miniature (mee-nʸah-*fewr*) *f* miniature

mini-jupe (mee-nee-*zhewp*) *f* miniskirt

minimum (mee-nee-*mom*) *m* minimum

ministère (mee-nee-*stair*) *m* ministry

ministre (mee-*neestr*) *m* minister; **premier ~** Prime Minister

minorité (mee-no-ree-*tay*) *f* minority

minuit (mee-*nwee*) midnight

minuscule (mee-new-*skewl*) *adj* tiny, minute

minute (mee-*newt*) *f* minute

minutieux (mee-new-*sʸur*) *adj* thorough

miracle (mee-*raakl*) *m* miracle, wonder

miraculeux (mee-rah-kew-*lur*) *adj* miraculous

miroir (mee-*rwaar*) *m* looking-glass, mirror

misérable (mee-zay-*rahbl*) *adj* miserable

misère (mee-*zair*) *f* misery

miséricorde (mee-zay-ree-*kord*) *f* mercy

miséricordieux (mee-zay-ree-kor-d^{y}ur) *adj* merciful

mite (meet) *f* moth

mi-temps (mee-tah$\overline{ng}$) *f* half time

mixeur (meek-s$\overline{u}$rr) *m* mixer

mobile (mo-*beel*) *adj* mobile; movable

mode[1] (mod) *f* fashion; **à la ~** fashionable

mode[2] (mod) *m* fashion, manner; **~ d'emploi** directions for use

modèle (mo-*dehl*) *m* model

modeler (mo-*dlay*) *v* model

modéré (mo-day-*ray*) *adj* moderate

moderne (mo-*dehrn*) *adj* modern

modeste (mo-*dehst*) *adj* modest

modestie (mo-deh-*stee*) *f* modesty

modification (mo-dee-fee-kah-s^{y}aw$\overline{ng}$) *f* change, alteration

modifier (mo-dee-*f^{y}ay*) *v* change, modify, alter

moelle (mwahl) *f* marrow

moelleux (mwah-*lur*) *adj* mellow

mœurs (murrs) *fpl* morals

mohair (mo-*air*) *m* mohair

moi (mwah) *pron* me; **moi-même** *pron* myself

moindre (mwa$\overline{ng}$dr) *adj* least; inferior

moine (mwahn) *m* monk

moineau (mwah-*noa*) *m* sparrow

moins (mwa$\overline{ng}$) *adv* less; *prep* minus; **à ~ que** unless; **au ~** at least

mois (mwah) *m* month

moisi (mwah-*zee*) *adj* mouldy

moisissure (mwah-zee-s$\overline{e}$wr) *f* mildew

moisson (mwah-saw$\overline{ng}$) *f* harvest

moite (mwaht) *adj* moist; damp

moitié (mwah-*t^{y}ay*) *f* half; **à ~** half

molaire (mo-*lair*) *f* molar

mollet (mo-*lay*) *m* calf

moment (mo-*mah$\overline{ng}$*) *m* moment; while

momentané (mo-mahng-tah-*nay*) *adj* momentary

mon (maw$\overline{ng}$) *adj* (f ma, pl mes) my

monarchie (mo-nahr-*shee*) *f* monarchy

monarque (mo-*nahrk*) *m* monarch, ruler

monastère (mo-nah-*stair*) *m* monastery

monde (maw$\overline{ng}$d) *m* world; **tout le ~** everyone

mondial (maw$\overline{ng}$-d^y*ahl*) *adj* worldwide; global

monétaire (mo-nay-*tair*) *adj* monetary

monnaie (mo-*nay*) *f* currency; **~ étrangère** foreign currency; **petite ~** petty cash, change; **pièce de ~** coin

monopole (mo-no-*pol*) *m* monopoly

monotone (mo-no-*ton*) *adj* monotonous

monsieur (mer-s^{y}ur) *m* (pl messieurs) gentleman; mister; sir

mont (maw$\overline{ng}$) *m* mount

montagne (maw$\overline{ng}$-*tahñ*) *f* mountain

montagneux (maw$\overline{ng}$-tah-*ñur*) *adj* mountainous

montant (maw$\overline{ng}$-*tah$\overline{ng}$*) *m* amount

montée (maw$\overline{ng}$-*tay*) *f* rise; ascent

monter (maw$\overline{ng}$-*tay*) *v* *rise; ascend; *get on; assemble; mount; **se ~ à** amount to

monteur (maw$\overline{ng}$-*t$\overline{u}$rr*) *m* mechanic

monticule (maw$\overline{ng}$-tee-*kewl*) *m* hillock

montre (maw$\overline{ng}$tr) *f* watch; **~ à affichage numérique** digital watch

montrer (maw$\overline{ng}$-*tray*) *v* *show; display; **~ du doigt** point

monture (maw$\overline{ng}$-*tewr*) *f* frame

monument (mo-new-*mah$\overline{ng}$*) *m* monument

moquer (mo-*kay*): **se ~ de** mock

moquerie (mo-*kree*) *f* mockery

moral (mo-*rahl*) *adj* moral; *m* spirits

morale (mo-*rahl*) *f* moral

moralité (mo-rah-lee-*tay*) *f* morality

morceau (mor-*soa*) *m* piece, part; morsel, fragment, scrap, bit, lump; ~ **de sucre** lump of sugar

mordre (mordr) *v* *bite

morphine (mor-*feen*) *f* morphine, morphia

morsure (mor-*sewr*) *f* bite

mort (mawr) *f* death; *adj* dead

mortel (mor-*tehl*) *adj* fatal; mortal

morue (mo-*rew*) *f* cod

mosaïque (mo-zah-*eek*) *f* mosaic

mosquée (mo-*skay*) *f* mosque

mot (moa) *m* word; ~ **de passe** password

motel (mo-*tehl*) *m* motel

moteur (mo-*tūrr*) *m* motor, engine

motif (mo-*teef*) *m* cause, motive; pattern

moto (mo-*toa*) *f* motor bike

motocyclette (mo-to-see-*kleht*) *f* motorcycle

mou (moo) *adj* (f molle) soft

moucher (moo-*shay*) wipe (*s.o.'s*) nose; snuff; snub

mouche (moosh) *f* fly

mouchoir (moo-*shwaar*) *m* handkerchief; ~ **de papier** tissue

*moudre (moodr) *v* *grind

mouette (mweht) *f* gull; seagull

moufles (moofl) *fpl* mittens *pl*

mouiller (moo-*ʸay*) *v* wet; **mouillé** wet, moist

moule (mool) *f* mussel

moulin (moo-*laṅg*) *m* mill; ~ **à paroles** chatterbox; ~ **à vent** windmill

*mourir (moo-*reer*) *v* die

mousse (mooss) *f* foam; moss

mousser (moo-*say*) *v* foam

mousseux (moo-*sur*) *adj* sparkling

moustache (moo-*stahsh*) *f* moustache

moustiquaire (moo-stee-*kair*) *f* mosquito net

moustique (moo-*steek*) *m* mosquito

moutarde (moo-*tahrd*) *f* mustard

mouton (moo-*tawṅg*) *m* sheep; mutton

mouvement (moov-*mahṅg*) *m* motion, movement

*mouvoir (moo-*vwaar*): **se ~** move

moyen (mwah-*ʸaṅg*) *m* means; *adj* medium, average

moyen-âge (mwah-*ʸeh-naazh*) *m* Middle Ages

moyenne (mwah-*ʸehn*) *f* mean, average; **en ~** on the average

muet (mway) *adj* dumb, mute

mugir (mew-*zheer*) *v* roar

muguet (mew-*gay*) *m* lily of the valley; thrush

mule (mewl) *f* mule

mulet (mew-*lay*) *m* mule

multiplication (mewl-tee-plee-kah-*sʸawṅg*) *f* multiplication

multiplier (mewl-tee-plee-*ay*) *v* multiply

municipal (mew-nee-see-*pahl*) *adj* municipal

municipalité (mew-nee-see-pah-lee-*tay*) *f* municipality

munir (mew-*neer*): ~ **de** provide with

mur (mēwr) *m* wall

mûr (mēwr) *adj* mature, ripe

mûre (mēwr) *f* blackberry

muscade (mew-*skahd*) *f* nutmeg

muscle (mewskl) *m* muscle

musclé (mew-*sklay*) *adj* muscular

museau (mew-*zoa*) *m* snout

musée (mew-*zay*) *m* museum

musical (mew-zee-*kahl*) *adj* musical

musicien (mew-zee-*sʸaṅg*) *m*, **-ne** *f* musician

musique (mew-*zeek*) *f* music; ~ **pop** pop music

musulman (mew-zewl-*mahṅg*) *adj* Moslem; *m*, **-e** *f* Moslem, Muslim

mutinerie (mew-teen-*ree*) *f* mutiny

mutuel (mew-*twehl*) *adj* mutual

myope (mʸop) *adj* short-sighted

mystère (mee-*stair*) *m* mystery
mystérieux (mee-stay-*r^{y}ur*) *adj*

mysterious
mythe (meet) *m* myth

N

nacre (nahkr) *f* mother of pearl
nager (nah-*zhay*) *v* *swim
nageur (nah-*zhūrr*) *m* swimmer
naïf (nah-*eef*) *adj* naïve
nain (na$\overline{ng}$) *m* dwarf
naissance (nay-*sah$\overline{ngss}$*) *f* birth
***naître** (naitr) *v* *be born
nappe (nahp) *f* tablecloth
narcose (nahr-*k$\overline{oaz}$*) *f* narcosis
narcotique (nahr-ko-*teek*) *m* narcotic
narine (nah-*reen*) *f* nostril
natation (nah-tah-*s^{y}aw$\overline{ng}$*) *f* swimming
nation (nah-*s^{y}aw$\overline{ng}$*) *f* nation
national (nah-s^{y}o-*nahl*) *adj* national
nationaliser (nah-s^{y}o-nah-lee-*zay*) *v* nationalize
nationalité (nah-s^{y}o-nah-lee-*tay*) *f* nationality
nature (nah-*tēwr*) *f* nature; essence
naturel (nah-tew-*rehl*) *adj* natural
naturellement (nah-tew-rehl-*mah$\overline{ng}$*) *adv* naturally
naufrage (noa-*fraazh*) *m* shipwreck
nausée (noa-*zay*) *f* nausea
naval (nah-*vahl*) *adj* (pl ~s) naval
navette (nah-*veht*) *f* shuttle (service); ~ **spatiale** space shuttle; **faire la ~** commute
navigable (nah-vee-*gahbl*) *adj* navigable
navigation (nah-vee-gah-*s^{y}aw$\overline{ng}$*) *f* navigation
naviguer (nah-vee-*gay*) *v* navigate; sail
navire (nah-*veer*) *m* ship; ~ **de guerre** man-of-war
né (nay) *adj* born

néanmoins (nay-ah$\overline{ng}$-*mwa$\overline{ng}$*) *adv* nevertheless
nébuleux (nay-bew-*lur*) *adj* hazy
nécessaire (nay-say-*sair*) *adj* necessary; ~ **de toilette** toilet case
nécessité (nay-say-see-*tay*) *f* need, necessity
nécessiter (nay-say-see-*tay*) *v* require
néerlandais (nay-ehr-lah$\overline{ng}$-*day*) *adj* Dutch
néfaste (nay-*fahst*) *adj* fatal
négatif (nay-gah-*teef*) *m* negative; *adj* negative
négligé (nay-glee-*zhay*) *m* negligee
négligence (nay-glee-*zhah$\overline{ng}$ss*) *f* neglect
négligent (nay-glee-*zhah$\overline{ng}$*) *adj* careless, neglectful
négliger (nay-glee-*zhay*) *v* neglect
négociant (nay-go-*s^{y}ah$\overline{ng}$*) *m* dealer; ~ **en vins** wine merchant
négociation (nay-go-s^{y}ah-s^{y}aw$\overline{ng}$*) *f* negotiation
négocier (nay-go-*s^{y}ay*) *v* negotiate
neige (naizh) *f* snow
neiger (nay-*zhay*) *v* snow
neigeux (neh-*zhur*) *adj* snowy
néon (nay-*aw$\overline{ng}$*) *m* neon
nerf (nair) *m* nerve
nerveux (nehr-*vur*) *adj* nervous
n'est-ce pas? (nehss-*pah*) *adv* isn't it
net (neht) *adj* distinct; net
nettoyage (neh-twah-*^{y}aazh*) *m* cleaning
nettoyer (neh-twah-*^{y}ay*) *v* clean; ~ **à sec** dry-clean

neuf¹ (nurf) *adj* (f neuve) new
neuf² (nurf) *num* nine
neutre (nūrtr) *adj* neuter; neutral
neuvième (nur-*v*ʸ*ehm*) *num* ninth
neveu (ner-*vur*) *m* nephew
névralgie (nay-vrahl-*zhee*) *f* neuralgia
névrose (nay-*vrōaz*) *f* neurosis
nez (nay) *m* nose; **saignement de ~** nosebleed
ni … ni (nee) neither … nor
nickel (nee-*kehl*) *m* nickel
nicotine (nee-ko-*teen*) *f* nicotine
nid (nee) *m* nest
nièce (nʸehss) *f* niece
nier (nee-ay) *v* deny
Nigeria (nee-zhay-rʸah) *m* Nigeria
nigérien (nee-zhay-rʸaṅg) *adj* Nigerian
niveau (nee-voa) *m* level; **~ de vie** standard of living; **passage à ~** level crossing
niveler (nee-vlay) *v* level
noble (nobl) *adj* noble
noblesse (no-*blehss*) *f* nobility
nocturne (nok-*tewrn*) *adj* nightly
Noël (no-*ehl*) Christmas, Xmas
nœud (nur) *m* knot; **~ papillon** bow tie
Noir (nwaar) *m* black
noir (nwaar) *adj* black
noisette (nwah-*zeht*) *f* hazelnut
noix (nwah) *f* nut; walnut; **~ de coco** coconut
nom (nawṅg) *m* name; noun; denomination; **au ~ de** in the name of, on behalf of; **~ de famille** family name, surname; **~ de jeune fille** maiden name
nombre (nawṅgbr) *m* number; quantity; numeral
nombreux (nawṅg-*brur*) *adj* numerous
nombril (nawṅg-*bree*) *m* navel
nomination (no-mee-nah-sʸawṅg) *f* nomination, appointment

nommer (no-*may*) *v* name; nominate, appoint
non (nawṅg) no
non-fumeur (nawṅg-few-mūrr)* *m* nonsmoker
nord (nawr) *m* north
nord-est (no-*rehst*) *m* north-east
nord-ouest (no-*rwehst*) *m* north-west
normal (nor-*mahl*) *adj* normal, regular
norme (norm) *f* standard
Norvège (nor-*vaizh*) *f* Norway
norvégien (nor-vay-zhʸaṅg) *adj* Norwegian
notaire (no-*tair*) *m* notary
notamment (no-tah-*mahṅg*) *adv* namely
note (not) *f* note; mark; bill; check *Am*
noter (no-*tay*) *v* note, *write down; notice
notifier (no-tee-fʸay) *v* notify
notion (noa-sʸawṅg) *f* notion; idea
notoire (no-*twaar*) *adj* notorious
notre (notr) *adj* our
nouer (noo-ay) *v* tie, knot
nougat (noo-gah) *m* nougat
nourrir (noo-*reer*) *v* *feed;
nourrissant nourishing
nourrisson (noo-ree-*sawṅg*) *m* infant
nourriture (noo-ree-*tewr*) *f* food
nous (noo) *pron* we; ourselves, us; **nous-mêmes** *pron* ourselves
nouveau (noo-voa) *adj* (nouvel; f nouvelle) new; **de ~** again; **Nouvel An** New Year
nouvelle (noo-*vehl*) *f* notice; **nouvelles** news
Nouvelle-Zélande (noo-vehl-zay-lahṅgd) *f* New Zealand
novembre (no-*vahṅgbr*) November
noyau (nwah-ʸoa) *m* stone; nucleus
noyer (nwah-ʸay) *v* drown; **se ~** *be drowned
nu (new) *adj* naked, nude; bare; *m* nude

nuage (nwaazh) *m* cloud; **nuages** clouds

nuageux (nwah-*zhur*) *adj* cloudy, overcast

nuance (nwahn͞gss) *f* nuance; shade

nucléaire (new-klay-*air*) *adj* atomic, nuclear

***nuire** (nweer) *v* harm

nuisible (nwee-*zeebl*) *adj* harmful

nuit (nwee) *f* night; **boîte de ~** cabaret; **cette ~** tonight; **de ~** by night, overnight; **tarif de ~** night rate

nul (newl) *adj* (f nulle) invalid, void

numéro (new-may-*roa*) *m* number; act; **~ d'immatriculation** registration number; license number *Am*

nuque (newk) *f* nape of the neck

nutritif (new-tree-*teef*) *adj* nutritious

nylon (nee-*law͞ng*) *m* nylon

O

oasis (oa-ah-*zeess*) *f* oasis

obéir (o-bay-*eer*) *v* obey

obéissance (o-bay-ee-*sahn͞gss*) *f* obedience

obéissant (o-bay-ee-*sahng*) *adj* obedient

obèse (o-*baiz*) *adj* stout, corpulent

obésité (o-bay-zee-*tay*) *f* fatness

objecter (ob-zhehk-*tay*) *v* object

objectif (ob-zhehk-*teef*) *m* target, objective, object, goal; *adj* objective

objection (ob-zhehk-*s^yaw͞ng*) *f* objection; ***faire ~ à** object to

objet (ob-*zhay*) *m* object; **objets de valeur** valuables *pl*; **objets trouvés** lost and found

obligation (o-blee-gah-*s^yaw͞ng*) *f* bond

obligatoire (o-blee-gah-*twaar*) *adj* compulsory, obligatory

obligeant (o-blee-*zhahn͞g*) *adj* obliging

obliger (o-blee-*zhay*) *v* oblige; force

oblique (o-*bleek*) *adj* slanting

oblong (o-*blaw͞ng*) *adj* (f oblongue) oblong

obscène (o-*psehn*) *adj* obscene

obscur (op-*skewr*) *adj* obscure; dim, dark

obscurité (op-skew-ree-*tay*) *f* dark

observation (o-psehr-vah-*s^yaw͞ng*) *f* observation

observatoire (o-psehr-vah-*twaar*) *m* observatory

observer (o-psehr-*vay*) *v* watch, observe; notice, note

obsession (o-pseh-*s^yaw͞ng*) *f* obsession

obstacle (op-*stahkl*) *m* obstacle

obstiné (op-stee-*nay*) *adj* stubborn, obstinate; dogged

obstruer (op-strew-*ay*) *v* block

***obtenir** (op-ter-*neer*) *v* *get; obtain

occasion (o-kah-*z^yaw͞ng*) *f* chance, opportunity; occasion; **d'occasion** second-hand

occident (ok-see-*dahng*) *m* west

occidental (ok-see-dahng-*tahl*) *adj* western, westerly

occupant (o-kew-*pahn͞g*) *m* occupant

occupation (o-kew-pah-*s^yaw͞ng*) *f* occupation; business

occuper (o-kew-*pay*) *v* occupy; *take up; **occupé** busy, engaged, occupied; **s'occuper de** attend to, look after; *take care of, see to, *deal with

océan (o-say-*ahng*) *m* ocean; **Océan**

Atlantique Atlantic; **Océan Pacifique** Pacific Ocean

octobre (ok-*tobr*) October

oculiste (o-kew-*leest*) *m/f* oculist

odeur (o-*dūrr*) *f* smell, odo(u)r

œil (ur^ee) *m* (pl yeux) eye; **coup d'œil** look; glance; glimpse

œuf (urf) *m* egg; **œufs de poisson** roe

œuvre (ūrvr) *m* work; **~ d'art** work of art

offense (o-*fahngss*) *f* offence, offense *Am*

offenser (o-fahng-*say*) *v* injure, *hurt, wound, offend; **s'offenser de** resent

offensif (o-fahng-*seef*) *adj* offensive

offensive (o-fahng-*seev*) *f* offensive

office (o-*fees*)* *m* office; agency; service

officiel (o-fee-s^y*ehl*) *adj* official

officier (o-fee-s^y*ay*) *m* officer

officieux (o-fee-s^y*ur*) *adj* unofficial

offre (ofr) *f* offer; supply

***offrir** (o-*freer*) *v* offer

oie (wah) *f* goose

oignon (o-*ñawng*) *m* onion; bulb

oiseau (wah-*zoa*) *m* bird; **~ de mer** seabird

oisif (wah-*zeef*) *adj* idle

olive (o-*leev*) *f* olive

ombragé (awng-brah-*zhay*) *adj* shady

ombre (awngbr) *f* shadow, shade; **~ à paupières** eye shadow

omelette (om-*leht*) *f* omelette

***omettre** (o-*mehtr*) *v* *leave out, omit; fail

omnibus (om-nee-*bewss*) *m* slow train

omnipotent (om-nee-po-*tahng*) *adj* omnipotent

on (awng) *pron* one

oncle (awngkl) *m* uncle

ondulation (awng-dew-lah-s^y*awng*) *f* wave

ondulé (awng-dew-*lay*) *adj* wavy, undulating

ongle (awnggl) *m* nail

onguent (awng-*gahng*) *m* ointment, salve

onze (awngz) *num* eleven

onzième (awng-z^y*ehm*) *num* eleventh

opéra (o-pay-*rah*) *m* opera; opera house

opération (o-pay-rah-s^y*awng*) *f* operation, surgery

opérer (o-pay-*ray*) *v* operate

opérette (o-pay-*reht*) *f* operetta

opiniâtre (o-pee-n^y*aatr*) *adj* obstinate

opinion (o-pee-n^y*awng*) *f* view, opinion

opposé (o-poa-*zay*) *adj* contrary, opposite

opposer (o-poa-*zay*): **s'~** oppose

opposition (o-poa-zee-s^y*awng*) *f* opposition

oppresser (o-pray-*say*) *v* oppress

opprimer (o-pree-*may*) *v* oppress

opticien (op-tee-s^y*ang*) *m*, **-ne** *f* optician

optimisme (op-tee-*meesm*) *m* optimism

optimiste (op-tee-*meest*) *m/f* optimist; *adj* optimistic

or (awr) *m* gold; **en ~** golden; **~ en feuille** gold leaf

orage (o-*raazh*) *m* thunderstorm

orageux (o-rah-*zhur*) *adj* thundery, stormy

oral (o-*rahl*) *adj* oral

orange (o-*rahngzh*) *f* orange; *adj* orange

orchestre (or-*kehstr*) *m* orchestra; band; **fauteuil d'orchestre** seat in the stalls

ordinaire (or-dee-*nair*) *adj* plain, simple, usual, regular, customary; common

ordinateur (or-dee-nah-*tūrr*) *n* computer; **~ portable** lap-top computer

ordonnance (or-do-*nahng̅ss*)* f
arrangement, layout, organisation;
prescription

ordonner (or-do-*nay*) v arrange; order;
ordonné adj tidy

ordre (ordr) m order; method;
command; ~ **du jour** agenda

ordures (or-*dēwr*) fpl garbage

oreille (o-*ray*) f ear

oreiller (o-ray-*ᵞay*) m pillow; **taie
d'oreiller** pillowcase

oreillons (o-reh-*ᵞawng̅*) mpl mumps

orfèvre (or-*faivr*) m goldsmith;
silversmith

organe (or-*gahn*) m organ

organique (or-gah-*neek*) adj organic

organisation (or-gah-nee-zah-*sᵞawng̅*)
f organization

organiser (or-gah-nee-*zay*) v organize

orgue (org) m (pl f) organ; ~ **de
Barbarie** street-organ

orgueil (or-*gurᵉᵉ*) m pride

orgueilleux (or-gur-*ᵞur*) adj proud

Orient (o-rᵞ*ahng̅*) m Orient

oriental (o-rᵞ*ahng̅-tahl*) adj oriental;
eastern, easterly

orienter (o-rᵞ*ahng̅-tay*): **s'~** orientate

originairement (o-ree-zhee-nehr-
mahng̅) adv originally

original (o-ree-zhee-*nahl*) adj original

origine (o-ree-*zheen*) f origin

ornement (or-ner-*mahng̅*) m
ornament

ornemental (or-ner-mahng̅-*tahl*) adj
ornamental

orphelin (or-fer-*lang̅*) m, **-e** f orphan

orteil (or-*tay*) m toe

orthodoxe (or-to-*doks*) adj orthodox

orthographe (or-to-*grahf*) f spelling

os (oss) m (pl ~) bone

oser (oa-*zay*) v dare

otage (o-*taazh*) m hostage

ôter (oa-*tay*) v *take out; wipe

ou (oo) conj or; ~ ... **ou** either ... or

où (oo) adv where; pron where;
n'importe ~ anywhere

ouate (waht) f cotton wool

oublier (oo-blee-*ay*) v *forget

oublieux (oo-blee-*ur*) adj forgetful

ouest (wehst) m west

oui (wee) yes

ouïe (oo-*ee*) f hearing

ouragan (oo-rah-*gahng̅*) m hurricane

ourlet (oor-*lay*) m hem

ours (oors) m bear

oursin (oor-*sang̅*) m sea urchin

outil (oo-*tee*) m tool, utensil,
implement

outrage (oo-*traazh*) m outrage;
offence, offense Am

outrager (oo-trah-*zhay*) v offend

outre (ootr) prep beyond, besides;
d'outre-mer overseas; **en ~**
furthermore, besides

ouvert (oo-*vair*) adj open

ouverture (oo-vehr-*tēwr*) f opening;
overture

ouvrage (oo-*vraazh*) m work

ouvre-boîte (oo-vrer-*bwaht*) m tin
opener, can opener Am

ouvre-bouteille (oo-vrer-boo-*tay*) m
bottle opener

ouvreur (oo-*vrurr*) m usher

ouvreuse (oo-*vrūrz*) f usherette

ouvrier (oo-vree-*ay*) m, **-ière** f worker

*ouvrir (oo-*vreer*) v open; unlock; turn
on

ovale (o-*vahl*) adj oval

oxygène (ok-see-*zhehn*) m oxygen

P

pacifisme (pah-see-*feesm*) *m* pacifism

pacifiste (pah-see-*feest*) *adj* pacifist; *m/f* pacifist

pagaie (pah-*gay*) *f* paddle

pagaille (pah-*gigh*) *f* muddle

page (paazh) *f* page; *m* pageboy

paie (pay) *f* salary

paiement (pay-*mahng*) *m* payment; ~ **échelonné** payment by insta(l)lments

païen (pah-*y*ang) *m* pagan, heathen; *adj* pagan, heathen

paille (pigh) *f* straw

pain (pang) *m* bread; ~ **complet** wholemeal bread; **petit** ~ roll

pair (pair) *adj* even

paire (pair) *f* pair

paisible (pay-*zeebl*) *adj* peaceful, quiet

paix (pay) *f* peace

Pakistan (pah-kee-*stahng*) *m* Pakistan

pakistanais (pah-kee-stah-*nay*) *adj* Pakistani

palais (pah-*lay*) *m* palace; palate

pâle (paal) *adj* pale

palmier (pahl-*m*²*ay*) *m* palm (tree)

palper (pahl-*pay*) *v* *feel

palpitation (pahl-pee-tah-*s*²*awng*) *f* palpitation

pamplemousse (pahng-pler-*mooss*) *m* grapefruit

panier (pah-*n*²*ay*) *m* basket

panique (pah-*neek*) *f* panic; scare

panne (pahn) *f* breakdown; **tomber en** ~ *break down

panneau (pah-*noa*) *m* panel

pansement (pahng-*smahng*) *m* bandage

panser (pahng-*say*) *v* dress

pantalon (pahng-tah-*lawng*) *m* trousers *pl*, slacks *pl*; pants *plAm*; **ensemble-pantalon** pant suit; ~ **de**

ski ski pants

pantoufle (pahng-*toofl*) *f* slipper

paon (pahng) *m* peacock

papa (pah-*pah*) *m* daddy

pape (pahp) *m* pope

papeterie (pah-peh-*tree*) *f* stationer's; stationery

papier (pah-*p*²*ay*) *m* paper; **en** ~ paper; ~ **de brouillon** rough paper; ~ **à lettres** notepaper, writing paper; ~ **à machine** typing paper; ~ **buvard** blotting paper; ~ **carbone** carbon paper; ~ **d'emballage** wrapping paper; ~ **d'étain** tinfoil; ~ **de verre** sandpaper; ~ **hygiénique** toilet paper; ~ **peint** wallpaper

papillon (pah-pee-*y*awng) *m* butterfly

paquebot (pahk-*boa*) *m* liner

Pâques (paak) Easter

paquet (pah-*kay*) *m* parcel, packet; bundle

par (pahr) *prep* by; for

parade (pah-*rahd*) *f* parade

paragraphe (pah-rah-*grahf*) *m* paragraph

***paraître** (pah-*raitr*) *v* seem, appear

parallèle (pah-rah-*lehl*) *m* parallel; *adj* parallel

paralyser (pah-rah-lee-*zay*) *v* paralyze; **paralysé** paralyzed

parapluie (pah-rah-*plwee*) *m* umbrella

parasol (pah-rah-*sol*) *m* sunshade

parc (pahrk) *m* park; ~ **de stationnement** car park; ~ **national** national park

parce que (pahr-sker) as, because

parcmètre (pahrk-mehtr) *m* parking meter

***parcourir** (pahr-koo-*reer*) *v* *go through; cover

parcours (pahr-*koor*) *m* distance; route; course

par-dessus (pahr-der-*sew*) *prep* over

pardessus (pahr-der-*sew*) *m* coat, overcoat

pardon (pahr-*dawng*) *m* pardon; **pardon!** sorry!

pardonner (pahr-do-*nay*) *v* *forgive

pare-brise (pahr-*breez*) *m* windscreen, windshield *Am*

pare-choc (pahr-*shok*) *m* bumper

pareil (pah-*ray*) *adj* alike, like; **sans ~** unsurpassed

parent (pah-*rahng*) *m* relative, relation; **parents** parents *pl*; **parents nourriciers** foster parents *pl*

paresseux (pah-reh-*sur*) *adj* lazy

parfait (pahr-*fay*) *adj* perfect; faultless

parfois (pahr-*fwah*) *adv* sometimes

parfum (pahr-*furng*) *m* scent; perfume

parfumerie (pahr-fewm-*ree*) *f* perfumery

pari (pah-*ree*) *m* bet

parier (pah-r^y*ay*) *v* *bet

parking (pahr-*keeng*) *m* parking lot *Am*

parlement (pahr-ler-*mahng*) *m* parliament

parlementaire (pahr-ler-mahng-*tair*) *adj* parliamentary

parler (pahr-*lay*) *v* talk, *speak

parmi (pahr-*mee*) *prep* among, amid

paroisse (pah-*rwahss*) *f* parish

parole (pah-*rol*) *f* speech

parrain (pah-*rang*) *m* godfather

part (paar) *f* part, share; **à ~** separately, apart; aside; **nulle ~** nowhere; **quelque ~** somewhere

partager (pahr-tah-*zhay*) *v* share

partenaire (pahr-ter-*nair*) *m*/*f* associate, partner

parti (pahr-*tee*) *m* party; side

partial (pahr-s^y*ahl*) *adj* partial

participant (pahr-tee-see-*pahng*) *m*, -**e** *f* participant

participer (pahr-tee-see-*pay*) *v* participate

particularité (pahr-tee-kew-lah-ree-*tay*) *f* particularity, characteristic

particulier (pahr-tee-kew-l^y*ay*) *adj* particular, special; individual, private; peculiar; *m* private individual; **en ~** in particular

particulièrement (pahr-tee-kew-l^yehr-*mahng*) *adv* specially

partie (pahr-*tee*) *f* part; **en ~** partly

partiel (pahr-s^y*ehl*) *adj* partial

partiellement (pahr-s^yehl-*mahng*) *adv* partly

***partir** (pahr-*teer*) *v* *leave; *go away; *set out, depart, pull out; **à partir de** as from, from; **parti** gone

partisan (pahr-tee-*zahng*) *m* advocate

partout (pahr-*too*) *adv* throughout, everywhere; **~ où** wherever

***parvenir à** (pahr-ver-*neer*) achieve

pas (pah) *m* step; pace, move; **faux ~** slip; **ne ... ~** not

passablement (pah-sah-bler-*mahng*) *adv* pretty, rather, fairly

passage (pah-*saazh*) *m* passage; crossing; aisle; **~ à niveau** crossing; **~ clouté** pedestrian crossing; **~ pour piétons** crosswalk *Am*

passager (pah-sah-*zhay*) *m*, -**ère** *f* passenger

passant (pah-*sahng*) *m* passer-by

passé (pah-*say*) *m* past; *adj* past; *prep* over

passeport (pah-*spawr*) *m* passport

passer (pah-*say*) *v* pass; *give; **en passant** casually; **~ à côté** pass by; **~ en contrebande** smuggle; **se ~** occur; **se ~ de** spare

passerelle (pah-*srehl*) *f* gangway

passe-temps (pah-*stahng*) *m* hobby

passif (pah-*seef*) *adj* passive

passion (pah-s^y*awng*) *f* passion

passionnant (pah-s^yo-*nahng*) *adj* exciting

passionné (pah-s^yo-*nay*) *adj* passionate; keen

passoire (pah-*swaar*) *f* sieve; strainer

pastèque (pah-*stehk*) *f* watermelon

pasteur (pah-*stūrr*) *m* clergyman; parson, minister, rector

pastille (pah-*steey*) *f* pastille, lozenge

patauger (pah-toa-*zhay*) *v* wade

pâte (paat) *f* paste; dough, batter; pie; ~ **dentifrice** toothpaste

patère (pah-*tair*) *f* peg

paternel (pah-tehr-*nehl*) *adj* fatherly

patience (pah-s^y*ahngss*) *f* patience

patient (pah-s^y*ahng*) *adj* patient; *m*, **-e** *f* patient

patin (pah-*tang*) *m* skate

patinage (pah-tee-*naazh*) *m* skating; ~ **à roulettes** roller-skating

patiner (pah-tee-*nay*) *v* skate

patinette (pah-tee-*neht*) *f* scooter

patinoire (pah-tee-*nwaar*) *f* skating rink

pâtisserie (pah-tee-*sree*) *f* cake, pastry; pastry shop

patrie (pah-*tree*) *f* native country

patriote (pah-tree-*ot*) *m* patriot

patron (pah-*trawng*) *m* master, boss

patronne (pah-*tron*) *f* mistress

patrouille (pah-*troo*^{ee}) *f* patrol

patrouiller (pah-troo-^y*ay*) *v* patrol

patte (paht) *f* paw

pâture (pah-*tewr*) *f* pasture

paume (pōam) *f* palm

paupière (poa-*p*^y*air*) *f* eyelid

pause (pōaz) *f* pause; break

pauvre (pōavr) *adj* poor

pauvreté (poa-vrer-*tay*) *f* poverty

paver (pah-*vay*) *v* pave

pavillon (pah-vee-^y*awng*) *m* pavilion; ~ **de chasse** lodge

pavot (pah-*voa*) *m* poppy

payable (pay-^y*ahbl*) *adj* due

paye (pay) *f* pay

payer (pay-^y*ay*) *v* *pay; ~ **comptant**

*pay cash

pays (pay-*ee*) *m* country, land; ~ **boisé** woodland; ~ **natal** native country

paysage (pay-ee-*zaazh*) *m* landscape, scenery

paysan (pay-ee-*zahng*) *m* peasant

Pays-Bas (pay-ee-*bah*) *mpl* the Netherlands

péage (pay-*aazh*) *m* toll

peau (poa) *f* skin; hide; ~ **de porc** pigskin

péché (pay-*shay*) *m* sin

pêche[1] (pehsh) *f* peach

pêche[2] (pehsh) *f* fishing industry; **attirail de** ~ fishing tackle, fishing gear

pêcher (pay-*shay*) *v* fish; ~ **à la ligne** angle

pêcheur (peh-*shūrr*) *m* fisherman

pédale (pay-*dahl*) *f* pedal

pédiatre (pay-*dyaatr*) *m* p(a)ediatrist

peigne (pehñ) *m* comb

peigner (pay-*ñay*) *v* comb

peignoir (peh-*ñwaar*) *m* bathrobe

***peindre** (pangdr) *v* paint

peine (pehn) *f* trouble, pains, difficulty; penalty; **à** ~ hardly; just, barely, scarcely; ***avoir de la** ~ grieve; ~ **de mort** death penalty

peiner (pay-*nay*) *v* labo(u)r

peintre (pangtr) *m* painter

peinture (pang-*tewr*) *f* paint; picture, painting; ~ **à l'huile** oil painting

peler (per-*lay*) *v* peel

pèlerin (pehl-*rang*) *m* pilgrim

pèlerinage (pehl-ree-*naazh*) *m* pilgrimage

pélican (pay-lee-*kahng*) *m* pelican

pelle (pehl) *f* spade, shovel

pellicule (peh-lee-*kewl*) *f* film; **pellicules** dandruff

pelouse (per-*lōōz*) *f* lawn

pelure (per-*lēwr*) *f* peel

penchant (pahng-*shahng*) *m*

inclination

pencher (pahng-*shay*) v: **se ~** *bend down

pendant (pahng-*dahng*) prep for; during; **~ que** while

pendentif (pahng-dahng-*teef*) m pendant

pendre (pahngdr) v *hang

pénétrer (pay-nay-*tray*) v penetrate

pénible (pay-*neebl*) adj laborious; painful

pénicilline (pay-nee-see-*leen*) f penicillin

péninsule (pay-nang-*sewl*) f peninsula

pensée (pahng-*say*) f thought; idea

penser (pahng-*say*) v *think; **~ à** *think of

pensif (pahng-*seef*) adj thoughtful

pension (pahng-s^y*awng*) f guesthouse, pension, boardinghouse; board; **~ complète** room and board, full board, bed and board, board and lodging

pensionnaire (pahng-s^yo-*nair*) m/f boarder

pente (pahngt) f incline; ramp; **en ~** sloping, slanting

Pentecôte (pahngt-*koat*) f Whitsun, Pentecost Am

pénurie (pay-new-*ree*) f scarcity

pépé (pay-*pay*) m grandad

pépin (pay-*pang*) m pip

pépinière (pay-pee-n^y*air*) f nursery

perceptible (pehr-sehp-*teebl*) adj noticeable, perceptible

perception (pehr-seh-ps^y*awng*) f perception

percer (pehr-*say*) v pierce

***percevoir** (pehr-ser-*vwaar*) v perceive; sense

perche (pehrsh) f perch, bass

percolateur (pehr-ko-lah-*tūrr*) m percolator

perdre (pehrdr) v *lose

perdrix (pehr-*dree*) f partridge

père (pair) m father

perfection (pehr-fehk-s^y*awng*) f perfection

performance (pehr-for-*mahngss*) f achievement; performance

péril (pay-*reel*) m peril

périlleux (pay-ree-^y*ur*) adj perilous

périmé (pay-ree-*may*) adj expired

période (pay-r^y*od*) f period; term

périodique (pay-r^yo-*deek*) adj periodical; m journal, periodical

périr (pay-*reer*) v perish

périssable (pay-ree-*sahbl*) adj perishable

perle (pehrl) f pearl; bead

permanent (pehr-mah-*nahng*) adj permanent

permanente (pehr-mah-*nahngt*) f permanent wave

***permettre** (pehr-*mehtr*) v permit, allow; enable; **se ~** afford

permis (pehr-*mee*) m permit; permission, licence; **~ de conduire** driver's license Am, driving licence; **~ de pêche** fishing licence; **~ de séjour** residence permit; **~ de travail** work permit; labor permit Am

permission (pehr-mee-s^y*awng*) f authorization, permission; leave

perpendiculaire (pehr-pahng-dee-kew-*lair*) adj perpendicular

perroquet (peh-ro-*kay*) m parrot

perruche (peh-*rewsh*) f parakeet

perruque (peh-*rewk*) f wig

persan (pehr-*sahng*) adj Persian

Perse (pehrs) f Persia

persévérer (pehr-say-vay-*ray*) v *keep up

persienne (pehr-s^y*ehn*) f blind; shutter

persil (pehr-*see*) m parsley

persister (pehr-see-*stay*) v insist

personnalité (pehr-so-nah-lee-*tay*) f personality

personne (pehr-*son*) *f* person; **ne ... personne** nobody, no one; **par ~** per person

personnel (pehr-so-*nehl*) *m* personnel, staff; *adj* personal, private

perspective (pehr-spehk-*teev*) *f* perspective, prospect

persuader (pehr-swah-*day*) *v* persuade

perte (pehrt) *f* loss

pertinent (pehr-tee-*nahng*) *adj* proper

peser (per-*zay*) *v* weigh

pessimisme (peh-see-*meesm*) *m* pessimism

pessimiste (peh-see-*meest*) *m/f* pessimist; *adj* pessimistic

pétale (pay-*tahl*) *m* petal

pétanque (pay-*tahngk*) *f* petanque

pétillement (pay-teey-*mahng*) *m* fizz

petit (per-*tee*) *adj* small, little; petty, short, minor

petite-fille (per-teet-*feey*) *f* granddaughter

petit-fils (per-tee-*feess*) *m* grandson

pétition (pay-tee-*s*ʸ*awng*) *f* petition

petits pois (per-tee-*pwah*)* *pl* peas

pétrole (pay-*trol*) *m* petroleum, oil; kerosene, paraffin; **gisement de ~** oil well

peu (pur) *adj* little; *m* bit; **à ~ près** approximately, about; almost; **~ de** few; **quelque ~** somewhat; **sous ~** soon, shortly; **un ~** some

peuple (purpl) *m* people; nation

peur (pūrr) *f* fear, fright; ***avoir ~** *be afraid

peut-être (pur-*taitr*) *adv* maybe, perhaps

phare (faar) *m* lighthouse; headlight, headlamp; **~ anti-brouillard** foglamp

pharmacie (fahr-mah-*see*) *f* pharmacy, chemist's; drugstore *Am*

pharmacien (fahr-mah-*s*ʸ*ang*) *m*, **-ne** *f* chemist, pharmacist *Am*

pharmacologie (fahr-mah-ko-lo-*zhee*) *f* pharmacology

phase (faaz) *f* phase, stage

philippin (fee-lee-*pang*) *adj* Philippine

Philippines (fee-lee-*peen*) *fpl* Philippines *pl*

philosophe (fee-lo-*zof*) *m* philosopher

philosophie (fee-lo-zo-*fee*) *f* philosophy

phonétique (fo-nay-*teek*) *adj* phonetic

phoque (fok) *m* seal

photo (fo-*toa*) *f* photo; **~ d'identité** passport photograph

photocopie (fo-to-ko-*pee*) *f* photocopy

photographe (fo-to-*grahf*) *m/f* photographer

photographie (fo-to-grah-*fee*) *f* photography; photograph

photographier (fo-to-grah-*f*ʸ*ay*) *v* photograph

phrase (fraaz) *f* sentence

physicien (fee-zee-*s*ʸ*ang*) *m*, **-ne** *f* physicist

physique (fee-*zeek*) *f* physics; *adj* physical

pianiste (pʸah-*neest*) *m/f* pianist

piano (pʸah-*noa*) *m* piano; **~ à queue** grand piano

pickpocket (peek-po-*keht*)* *m* pickpocket

pie (pee) *f* magpie

pièce (pʸehss) *f* piece; room, chamber; **~ de monnaie** coin; **~ de rechange** spare part; **~ détachée** spare part; **~ de théâtre** play

pied (pʸay) *m* foot; leg; **à ~** walking, on foot

piège (pʸaizh) *m* trap

pierre (pʸair) *f* stone; **en ~** stone; **~ à briquet** flint; **~ ponce** pumice stone; **~ précieuse** gem; stone; **~ tombale** tombstone, gravestone

piétiner (pʸay-tee-*nay*) *v* stamp

piéton (p^yay-*tawng*) m pedestrian
piètre (p^yehtr) adj poor
pieuvre (p^yūrvr) f octopus
pieux (p^yur) adj pious
pigeon (pee-*zhawng*) m pigeon
pignon (pee-ñawng) m gable
pile (peel) f stack; battery
pilier (pee-l^yay) m pillar
pilote (pee-*lot*) m pilot
pilule (pee-*lewl*) f pill
piment (pee-*mahng*)* m red pepper; spice
pin (pang) m pine
pince (pangss) f pliers pl, tongs pl; tweezers pl; ~ **à cheveux** hairgrip; bobby pin Am
pinceau (pang-*soa*) m brush; paintbrush
pincer (pang-*say*) v pinch
pincettes (pang-*seht*) fpl tweezers pl
pingouin (pang-*gwang*) m penguin
ping-pong (peeng-*pong*) m table tennis
pion (p^yawng) m pawn
pionnier (p^yo-n^yay) m pioneer
pipe (peep) f pipe
piquant (pee-*kahng*) adj savo(u)ry
pique-nique (peek-*neek*) m picnic
pique-niquer (peek-nee-*kay*) v picnic
piquer (pee-*kay*) v *sting, prick
piqûre (pee-*kēwr*) f shot; sting, bite
pirate (pee-*raht*) m pirate
pire (peer) adj worse; **le** ~ worst
pis (pee) adv worse; **tant pis!** never mind!
piscine (pee-*seen*) f swimming pool
pissenlit (pee-sahng-*lee*) m dandelion
pistache (pee-*stahsh*)* f pistachio nut
piste (peest) f trail; track; ring; ~ **de courses** racetrack; ~ **de décollage** runway
pistolet (pee-sto-*lay*) m pistol
piston (pee-*stawng*) m piston; **segment de** ~ piston ring

pitié (pee-t^yay) f pity; ***avoir** ~ **de** pity
pittoresque (pee-to-*rehsk*) adj picturesque, scenic
pizza (pee-*tsah*)* f pizza
placard (plah-*kaar*) m closet, cupboard
place (plahss) f place; seat; room; square; ~ **forte** stronghold
placement (plah-*smahng*) m investment
placer (plah-*say*) v place; *put, *lay; invest
plafond (plah-*fawng*) m ceiling
plage (plaazh) f beach; ~ **pour nudistes** nudist beach
plaider (play-*day*) v plead
plaidoyer (pleh-dwah-^yay) m plea
plaie (play) f wound
*plaindre (plangdr) v: **se** ~ complain
plaine (plehn) f plain, lowlands pl
plainte (plangt) f complaint
*plaire (plair) v please; **s'il vous plaît** please
plaisant (pleh-*zahng*) adj pleasant; nice, enjoyable, amusing
plaisanter (pleh-zahng-*tay*) v joke
plaisanterie (play-zahng-*tree*) f joke
plaisir (play-*zeer*) m pleasure; joy, delight, fun, enjoyment; **avec** ~ gladly; ***prendre** ~ enjoy
plan (plahng) m plan, project; map; scheme; adj flat, level, even; **premier** ~ foreground
planche (plahngsh) f plank, board
plancher (plahng-*shay*) m floor
planétarium (plah-nay-tah-r^yom) m planetarium
planète (plah-*neht*) f planet
planeur (plah-*nūr*) m glider
planifier (plah-nee-f^yay) v plan
plantation (plahng-tah-s^yawng) f plantation
plante (plahngt) f plant
planter (plahng-*tay*) v plant

plaque (plahk) *f* plate; sheet; ~ **d'immatriculation** registration plate; license plate *Am*

plastique (plah-*steek*) *adj* plastic; *m* plastic

plat (plah) *m* dish; course; *adj* flat, plane, smooth, level

plateau (plah-*toa*) *m* plateau; tray

plate-bande (plaht-*bahnḡd*) *f* flowerbed

platine (plah-*teen*) *m* platinum

plâtre (plaatr) *m* plaster

plein (planḡ) *adj* full; ***faire le ~** fill up; **pleine saison** high season

pleurer (plur-*ray*) *v* *weep, cry

***pleuvoir** (plur-*vwaar*) *v* rain

pli (plee) *m* fold; crease; ~ **permanent** permanent press

plie (plee) *f* plaice

plier (plee-*ay*) *v* fold

plomb (plawnḡ) *m* lead; **sans ~** unleaded

plombage (plawnḡ-*baazh*) *m* filling

plombier (plawnḡ-*b*ʸ*ay*) *m* plumber

plonger (plawnḡ-*zhay*) *v* dive

pluie (plwee) *f* rain

plume (plewm) *f* feather; pen

plupart (plew-*paar*): **(la) ~** most

pluriel (plew-*r*ʸ*ehl*) *m* plural

plus (plewss) *adj* more; *prep* plus; **de ~** moreover; **le ~** most; **ne … ~** no longer; **~ … plus** the … the

plusieurs (plew-*z*ʸ*ūr*) *adj* several

plutôt (plew-*toa*) *adv* fairly, pretty, rather, quite; sooner

pluvieux (plew-*v*ʸ*ur*) *adj* rainy

pneu (pnur) *m* (pl ~s) tire *Am*, tyre; ~ **crevé** flat tyre (tire *Am*); ~ **de rechange** spare tyre (tire *Am*)

pneumatique (pnur-mah-*teek*) *adj* pneumatic

pneumonie (pnur-mo-*nee*) *f* pneumonia

poche (posh) *f* pocket; **lampe de ~** flashlight

pochette (po-*sheht*) *f* pouch

poêle (pwahl) *f* saucepan; *m* stove; ~ **à frire** frying pan

poème (po-*ehm*) *m* poem; ~ **épique** epic

poésie (po-ay-*zee*) *f* poetry

poète (po-*eht*) *m* poet

poids (pwah) *m* weight

poignée (pwah-*ñay*) *f* handle; handful; ~ **de main** handshake

poignet (pwah-*ñay*) *m* wrist

poil (pwahl) *m* hair

poing (pwanḡ) *m* fist

point (pwanḡ) *m* point; item; period, full stop; stitch; ~ **de congélation** freezing point; ~ **de départ** starting point; ~ **de repère** landmark; ~ **de vue** view, outlook; ~ **d'interrogation** question mark; **point-virgule** *m* semicolon

pointe (pwanḡt) *f* point; **heure de ~** peak hour

pointer (pwanḡ-*tay*) *v* tick off

pointu (pwanḡ-*tew*) *adj* pointed

pointure (pwanḡ-*tēwr*)* *f* size

poire (pwaar) *f* pear

poireau (pwah-*roa*) *m* leek

pois (pwah) *m* pea

poison (pwah-*zawnḡ*) *m* poison

poisson (pwah-*sawnḡ*) *m* fish

poissonnerie (pwah-son-*ree*) *f* fish shop

poitrine (pwah-*treen*) *f* chest; bosom

poivre (pwaavr) *m* pepper

pôle nord (poal nawr) North Pole

pôle sud (poal sewd) South Pole

poli (po-*lee*) *adj* polite; civil

police (po-*leess*) *f* police *pl*; policy; **commissariat de ~** police station; ~ **d'assurance** insurance policy

policier (po-lee-*s*ʸ*ay*) *m* policeman

poliomyélite (po-l*ʸ*o-m*ʸ*ay-*leet*)* *f* polio

polir (po-*leer*) *v* polish

polisson (po-lee-*sawng*) *adj* naughty

politicien (po-lee-tee-*s*ʸ*ang*) *m*, **-ne** *f* politician

politique (po-lee-*teek*) *f* politics; policy; *adj* political

pollution (po-lew-*s*ʸ*awng*) *f* pollution

Pologne (po-*loñ*) *f* Poland

Polonais (po-lo-*nay*) *m* Pole

polonais (po-lo-*nay*) *adj* Polish

pomme (pom) *f* apple; ~ **de terre** potato; **pommes frites** chips, French fries *Am*

pompe (*pawng*p) *f* pump; ~ **à eau** water pump; ~ **à essence** petrol pump, gas pump *Am*

pomper (*pawng*-pay) *v* pump

pompier (*pawng*-*p*ʸ*ay*) *m* fireman; **pompiers** fire brigade, fire department *Am*

ponctuel (*pawng*k-*twehl*) *adj* punctual

pondéré (*pawng*-day-ray) *adj* level-minded

pondre (*pawng*dr) *v* *lay

poney (po-*nay*) *m* pony

pont (*pawng*) *m* bridge; deck; **pontlevis** *m* drawbridge; ~ **principal** main deck; ~ **suspendu** suspension bridge

populaire (po-pew-*lair*) *adj* popular

population (po-pew-lah-*s*ʸ*awng*) *f* population

populeux (po-pew-*lur*) *adj* populous

porc (pawr) *m* pork

porcelaine (por-ser-*lehn*) *f* porcelain, china

porc-épic (por-kay-*peek*) *m* porcupine

port[1] (pawr) *m* port, harbo(u)r; ~ **de mer** seaport

port[2] (pawr) *m* postage; ~ **payé** postage paid, post-paid

portatif (por-tah-*teef*) *adj* portable

porte (port) *f* door; gate; ~ **coulissante** sliding door; ~ **tournante** revolving door

porte-bagages (port-bah-*gaazh*) *m* luggage rack

porte-bonheur (port-bo-*nurr*) *m* lucky charm

portée (por-*tay*) *f* reach; litter

portefeuille (por-ter-*fur*ᵉᵉ) *m* wallet, billfold *Am*

porte-manteau (port-mahng-*toa*) *m* hat rack

porte-monnaie (port-mo-*nay*) *m* purse

porter (por-*tay*) *v* carry; *bear; *wear; ~ **sur** concern; **se ~ bien** *be in good health

porteur (por-*turr*) *m* bearer; porter

portier (por-*t*ʸ*ay*) *m* porter, doorman, doorkeeper

portière (por-*t*ʸ*air*)* *f* door

portion (por-*s*ʸ*awng*) *f* helping, portion

portrait (por-*tray*) *m* portrait

Portugais (por-tew-*gay*) *m* Portuguese

portugais (por-tew-*gay*) *adj* Portuguese

Portugal (por-tew-*gahl*) *m* Portugal

poser (poa-*zay*) *v* place; *put, *lay, *set

positif (poa-zee-*teef*) *m* positive; *adj* positive

position (poa-zee-*s*ʸ*awng*) *f* position

posséder (po-say-*day*) *v* possess, own

possession (po-seh-*s*ʸ*awng*) *f* possession

possibilité (po-see-bee-lee-*tay*) *f* possibility

possible (po-*seebl*) *adj* possible

poste[1] (post) *f* post; ***mettre à la ~** mail; ~ **aérienne** airmail; ~ **restante** poste restante

poste[2] (post) *m* station; post; ~ **de secours** first aid post; ~ **d'essence** petrol station, gas station *Am*

poster (po-*stay*) *v* post

postérieur (po-stay-*r*ʸ*urr*) *m* bottom;

adj subsequent

postiche (po-*steesh*) *m* hair piece

pot (poa) *m* pot

potable (po-*tahbl*) *adj* for drinking

potage (po-*taazh*) *m* soup

poteau (po-*toa*) *m* post, pole; ~ **indicateur** milepost, signpost

potelé (po-*tlay*) *adj* plump

poterie (po-*tree*) *f* pottery, crockery

pou (poo) *m* (pl ~x) louse

poubelle (poo-*behl*) *f* rubbish bin

pouce (pooss) *m* thumb

poudre (poodr) *f* powder; ~ **à canon** gunpowder; ~ **dentifrice** toothpowder; ~ **de riz** face powder; ~ **pour les pieds** foot powder; **savon en ~** soap powder

poudrier (poo-dree-*ay*) *m* powder compact

poule (pool) *f* hen

poulet (poo-*lay*) *m* chicken

pouls (poo) *m* pulse

poumon (poo-*mawng*) *m* lung

poupée (poo-*pay*) *f* doll

pour (poor) *prep* for, to; ~ **que** so that

pourboire (poor-*bwaar*) *m* tip, gratuity

pourcentage (poor-sahng-*taazh*) *m* percentage

pourchasser (poor-shah-*say*) *v* chase

pourpre (poorpr) *adj* purple

pourquoi (poor-*kwah*) *adv* why; what for

pourrir (poo-*reer*) *v* rot; **pourri** rotten

***poursuivre** (poor-*sweevr*) *v* carry on, continue, pursue

pourtant (poor-*tahng*) *adv* however, yet; though

pourvu que (poor-vew ker) provided that

poussée (poo-*say*) *f* push

pousser (poo-*say*) *v* push

poussette (poo-*seht*) *f* baby carriage *Am*

poussière (poo-s^y*air*) *f* dust

poussiéreux (poo-s^{y}ay-*rur*) *adj* dusty

poutre (pootr) *f* beam

pouvoir (poo-*vwaar*) *m* power; authority; ~ **exécutif** executive

***pouvoir** (poo-*vwaar*) *v* *can, *be able to; *might, *may

praline (prah-*leen*) *f* chocolate

pratique (prah-*teek*) *f* practice; *adj* practical, convenient

pratiquer (prah-tee-*kay*) *v* practise

pré (pray) *m* meadow

préalable (pray-ah-*lahbl*) *adj* previous

précaire (pray-*kair*) *adj* precarious, critical

précaution (pray-koa-s^y*awng*) *f* precaution

précédemment (pray-say-dah-*mahng*) *adv* before

précédent (pray-say-*dahng*) *adj* preceding, previous, last; former

précéder (pray-say-*day*) *v* precede

prêcher (pray-*shay*) *v* preach

précieux (pray-s^y*ur*) *adj* valuable; precious

précipice (pray-see-*peess*) *m* precipice

précipitation (pray-see-pee-tah-s^y*awng*) *f* precipitation

précipité (pray-see-pee-*tay*) *adj* hasty

se précipiter (pray-see-pee-*tay*) dash

précis (pray-*see*) *adj* precise; accurate

préciser (pray-see-*zay*) *v* specify

précision (pray-see-z^y*awng*) *f* precision; **précisions** points *pl*

***prédire** (pray-*deer*) *v* predict

préférable (pray-fay-*rahbl*) *adj* preferable

préférence (pray-fay-*rahngss*) *f* preference

préférer (pray-fay-*ray*) *v* prefer; **préféré** favo(u)rite

préjudiciable (pray-zhew-dee-s^y*ahbl*) *adj* harmful

préjugé (pray-zhew-*zhay*) *m* prejudice

prélever (prayl-*vay*) v impose; deduct; *withdraw

préliminaire (pray-lee-mee-*nair*) adj preliminary

prématuré (pray-mah-tew-*ray*) adj premature

premier (prer-*m*ᵞ*ay*) num first; adj foremost, primary; ~ **ministre** premier

*****prendre** (prahnḡdr) v *take; collect; v *catch; capture; ~ **garde** look out, beware; ~ **soin de** look after

prénom (pray-*nawnḡ*) m first name, Christian name

préparation (pray-pah-rah-*s*ᵞ*awnḡ*) f preparation

préparer (pray-pah-*ray*) v prepare; arrange; cook

préposition (pray-poa-zee-*s*ᵞ*awnḡ*) f preposition

près (pray) adv near; **à peu ~** about; **~ de** by, near

prescription (preh-skree-*ps*ᵞ*awnḡ*) f prescription

*****prescrire** (preh-*skreer*) v prescribe

présence (pray-*zahnḡss*) f presence

présent (pray-*zahnḡ*) m present; adj present; **jusqu'à ~** so far

présentation (pray-zahnḡ-tah-*s*ᵞ*awnḡ*) f introduction

présenter (pray-zahnḡ-*tay*) v present; introduce; **se ~** appear; report

préservatif (pray-sehr-vah-*teef*) m condom

président (pray-zee-*dahnḡ*) m, **-e** f president, chairman

présomptueux (pray-zawnḡp-*twur*) adj presumptuous

presque (prehsk) adv nearly, almost

presqu'île (preh-*skeel*) f peninsula

pressant (preh-*sahnḡ*) adj pressing

presse (prehss) f press

presser (pray-*say*) v press; **se ~** hurry, rush

pression (preh-*s*ᵞ*awnḡ*) f pressure; **~ atmosphérique** atmospheric pressure; **~ des pneus** tyre (tire Am) pressure; **~ d'huile** oil pressure

prestidigitateur (preh-stee-dee-zhee-tah-*turr*) m magician

prestige (preh-*steezh*) m prestige

présumer (pray-zew-*may*) v assume

prêt (pray) m loan; adj ready; prepared

prétendre (pray-*tahnḡdr*) v claim, pretend

prétentieux (pray-tahnḡ-*s*ᵞ*ur*) adj conceited

prétention (pray-tahnḡ-*s*ᵞ*awnḡ*) f claim

prêter (pray-*tay*) v *lend; **~ attention à** attend to, mind

prétexte (pray-*tehkst*) m pretence, pretext

prêtre (praitr) m priest

preuve (prūrv) f proof, evidence

prévenant (preh-*vnahnḡ*) adj considerate, thoughtful

*****prévenir** (preh-*vneer*) v warn; prevent, anticipate

préventif (preh-vahnḡ-*teef*) adj preventive

prévenu (preh-*vnew*) m, **-e** f accused

prévision (pray-vee-*z*ᵞ*awnḡ*) f forecast, outlook

*****prévoir** (pray-*vwaar*) v forecast; anticipate

prier (pree-*ay*) v pray; ask

prière (pree-*air*) f prayer

primaire (pree-*mair*) adj primary

prime (preem) f premium

primordial (pree-mor-*d*ᵞ*ahl*) adj primary

prince (pranḡss) m prince

princesse (pranḡ-*sehss*) f princess

principal (pranḡ-see-*pahl*) adj principal; cardinal, chief, leading, main

principalement (pranḡ-see-pahl-

mahng) *adv* especially, mainly

principe (prang-*seep*) *m* principle

printemps (prang-*tahng*) *m* spring; springtime

priorité (pree-o-ree-*tay*) *f* priority; ~ **de passage** right of way

prise (preez) *f* grip, clutch, grasp; capture; ~ **de vue** shot

prison (pree-*zawng*) *f* prison; jail

prisonnier (pree-zo-*n*ʸ*ay*) *m*, **-ière** *f* prisoner; ***faire** ~ capture; ~ **de guerre** prisoner of war

privation (pree-vah-*s*ʸ*awng*) *f* deprivation, deprival

privé (pree-*vay*) *adj* private

priver de (pree-*vay*) deprive of

privilège (pree-vee-*laizh*) *m* privilege

prix (pree) *m* price; charge, cost; award, prize; ~ **courant** *m* price list; ~ **d'achat** purchase price; ~ **de consolation** consolation prize; ~ **d'entrée** entrance fee; ~ **du voyage** fare

probable (pro-*bahbl*) *adj* probable; presumable, likely

probablement (pro-bah-bler-*mahng*) *adv* probably

problème (pro-*blehm*) *m* problem; question

procédé (pro-say-*day*) *m* process

procéder (pro-say-*day*) *v* proceed

procédure (pro-say-*dewr*) *f* procedure

procès (pro-*say*) *m* process; trial, lawsuit

procession (pro-seh-*s*ʸ*awng*) *f* procession

processus (pro-say-*sewss*) *m* process

prochain (pro-*shang*) *adj* following, next

prochainement (pro-shehn-*mahng*) *adv* soon, shortly

proche (prosh) *adj* close, near; nearby; oncoming

proclamer (pro-klah-*may*) *v* proclaim

procurer (pro-kew-*ray*) *v* furnish; **se** ~ obtain

prodigue (pro-*deeg*) *adj* extravagant; generous

producteur (pro-dewk-*tūrr*) *m*, **-trice** *f* producer

production (pro-dewk-*s*ʸ*awng*) *f* production; output; ~ **en série** mass production

***produire** (pro-*dweer*) *v* produce; generate; **se** ~ occur, happen

produit (pro-*dwee*) *m* product; produce

prof (prof) *m or f* teacher

profane (pro-*fahn*) *m* layman

professer (pro-fay-*say*) *v* confess

professeur (pro-feh-*sūrr*) *m* teacher; professor

profession (pro-feh-*s*ʸ*awng*) *f* profession

professionnel (pro-feh-*s*ʸo-*nehl*) *adj* professional

profit (pro-*fee*) *m* profit, benefit

profitable (pro-fee-*tahbl*) *adj* profitable

profiter (pro-fee-*tay*) *v* profit, benefit

profond (pro-*fawng*) *adj* deep; low; profound

profondeur (pro-fawng-*dūrr*) *f* depth

programme (pro-*grahm*) *m* programme

progrès (pro-*gray*) *m* progress

progresser (pro-gray-*say*) *v* *get on

progressif (pro-gray-*seef*) *adj* progressive

projecteur (pro-zhehk-*tūrr*) *m* spotlight; searchlight

projet (pro-*zhay*) *m* project; scheme

prolongation (pro-lawng-gah-*s*ʸ*awng*) *f* extension

prolonger (pro-lawng-*zhay*) *v* prolong, extend

promenade (prom-*nahd*) *f* walk, stroll; promenade; ~ **en voiture** drive

promener (prom-*nay*) v: **se ~** go for a walk

promeneur (prom-*nūrr*) m walker

promesse (pro-*mehss*) f promise

*promettre (pro-*mehtr*) v promise

promontoire (pro-mawng-*twaar*) m headland

promotion (pro-mo-s^y*awng*) f promotion

*promouvoir (pro-moo-*vwaar*) v promote

prompt (prawng) adj prompt; fast

prononcer (pro-nawng-*say*) v pronounce

prononciation (pro-nawng-s^yah-s^y*awng*) f pronunciation

proportion (pro-por-s^y*awng*) f proportion

proportionnel (pro-por-s^yo-*nehl*) adj proportional

propos (pro-*poa*) m intention; **à ~** by the way; **à ~ de** regarding

proposer (pro-poa-*zay*) v propose

proposition (pro-poa-zee-s^y*awng*) f proposition, proposal

propre (propr) adj clean; own

propriétaire (pro-pree-*ay*-tair) m/f owner, proprietor; landlord

propriété (pro-pree-ay-*tay*) f property; estate

propulser (pro-pewl-*say*) v propel

prospectus (pro-spehk-*tewss*) m prospectus

prospère (pro-*spair*) adj prosperous

prospérité (pro-spay-ree-*tay*) f prosperity

prostituée (pro-stee-*tway*) f prostitute

protection (pro-tehk-s^y*awng*) f protection

protéger (pro-tay-*zhay*) v protect

protestant (pro-teh-*stahng*) adj Protestant

protestation (pro-teh-stah-s^y*awng*) f protest

protester (pro-teh-*stay*) v protest

prouver (proo-*vay*) v prove

provenance (pro-*vnahngss*) f origin

*provenir de (pro-*vneer*) *come from

proverbe (pro-*vehrb*) m proverb

province (pro-*vangss*) f province

provincial (pro-vang-s^y*ahl*) adj provincial

proviseur (pro-vee-*zūrr*) m principal

provision (pro-vee-z^y*awng*) f store; provisions pl

provisoire (pro-vee-*zwaar*) adj temporary, provisional

provoquer (pro-vo-*kay*) v cause

prudence (prew-*dahngss*) f caution

prudent (prew-*dahng*) adj careful; cautious, wary

prune (prewn) f plum

pruneau (prew-*noa*) m prune

prurit (prew-*reet*) m pruritus

psychiatre (psee-k^y*aatr*) m psychiatrist

psychique (psee-*sheek*) adj psychic

psychologie (psee-ko-lo-*zhee*) f psychology

psychologique (psee-ko-lo-*zheek*) adj psychological

psychologue (psee-ko-*log*) m/f psychologist

public (pew-*bleek*) m audience, public; adj public

publication (pew-blee-kah-s^y*awng*) f publication

publicité (pew-blee-see-*tay*) f advertising, publicity; advertisement

publier (pew-blee-*ay*) v publish

puer (pway) v *stink

puis (pwee) adv then

puisque (pweesk) conj as

puissance (pwee-*sahngss*) f might, force; power, energy

puissant (pwee-*sahng*) adj powerful, mighty; strong

puits (pwee) m well; **~ de pétrole** oil well

pull(-over) (pew-lo-*vair*) *m* pullover

pulvérisateur (pewl-vay-ree-zah-*tūrr*) *m* atomizer

pulvériser (pewl-vay-ree-*zay*) *v* *grind

punaise (pew-*naiz*) *f* bug; drawing pin; thumbtack *Am*

punir (pew-*neer*) *v* punish

punition (pew-nee-*s^yawng*) *f* punishment

pupitre (pew-*peetr*) *m* desk; pulpit

pur (pewr) *adj* pure; clean; sheer, neat

pus (pew) *m* pus

pustule (pew-*stewl*) *f* pimple

putain (pew-*tang*) *f* whore

puzzle (purzl) *m* jigsaw puzzle

pyjama (pee-zhah-*mah*) *m* pyjamas *pl*

Q

quai (kay) *m* wharf, dock, quay; platform

qualification (kah-lee-fee-kah-*s^yawng*) *f* qualification

qualifié (kah-lee-*f^yay*) *adj* qualified; **être ~* qualify; *non ~* unskilled

qualité (kah-lee-*tay*) *f* quality; *de première ~* first-class; first-rate

quand (kahng) *adv* when; *conj* when; *n'importe ~* whenever

quant à (kahng-*tah*) as regards

quantité (kahng-tee-*tay*) *f* quantity, amount; lot

quarantaine (kah-rahng-*tehn*) *f* quarantine

quarante (kah-*rahngt*) *num* forty

quart (kaar) *m* quarter; *~ d'heure* quarter of an hour

quartier (kahr-*t^yay*) *m* district, quarter; *bas ~* slum; *~ général* headquarters *pl*

quatorze (kah-*torz*) *num* fourteen

quatorzième (kah-tor-*z^yehm*) *num* fourteenth

quatre (kahtr) *num* four

quatre-vingt-dix (kah-trer-vang-*deess*) *num* ninety

quatre-vingts (kah-trer-*vang*) *num* eighty

quatrième (kah-*tr^yehm*) *num* fourth

que (ker) *conj* that; as, than; *adv* how; *ce ~* what

quel (kehl) *pron* which; *n'importe ~* any; whichever

quelquefois (kehl-ker-*fwah*) *adv* sometimes

quelques (kehlk) *adj* some, some

quelqu'un (kehl-*kurng*) *pron* someone, somebody

querelle (ker-*rehl*) *f* dispute, row, quarrel

question (keh-*st^yawng*) *f* question; inquiry, query; matter, issue, problem

quêter (kay-*tay*) *v* collect

queue (kur) *f* tail; queue; **faire la ~* queue; stand in line *Am*

qui (kee) *pron* who; which, that; *à ~* whom; *n'importe ~* anybody

quiche (keesh) *f* quiche

quille (keey) *f* keel

quincaillerie (kang-kigh-*ree*) *f* hardware; hardware store

quinze (kangz) *num* fifteen; *~ jours* fortnight

quinzième (kang-*z^yehm*) *num* fifteenth

quitter (kee-*tay*) *v* *leave

quoi (kwah) *pron* what; *n'importe ~* anything

quoique (kwahk) *conj* though,

although; **quoiqu'il en soit** at any rate

quote-part (kot-*paar*) *f* quota

R

rabais (rah-*bay*) *m* discount, reduction, rebate

raccourcir (rah-koor-*seer*) *v* shorten

racial (rah-s*ˢahl*) *adj* racial

racine (rah-*seen*) *f* root

racler (rah-*klay*) *v* scrape

raconter (rah-kaw*ng*-*tay*) *v* *tell

radeau (rah-*doa*) *m* raft

radiateur (rah-d*ʸ*ah-*tūrr*) *m* radiator

radical (rah-dee-*kahl*) *adj* radical

radio (rah-d*ʸoa*) *f* wireless, radio

radiographie (rah-d*ʸ*oa-grah-*fee*) *f* X-ray

radiographier (rah-d*ʸ*oa-grah-*fʸay*) *v* X-ray

radis (rah-*dee*) *m* radish

radotage (rah-do-*taazh*) *m* rubbish

rafale (rah-*fahl*) *f* gust

raffinerie (rah-feen-*ree*) *f* refinery; **~ de pétrole** oil refinery

rafraîchir (rah-fray-*sheer*) *v* refresh

rafraîchissement (rah-freh-shee-*smahng*) *m* refreshment

rage (raazh) *f* rabies; rage; craze

rager (rah-*zhay*) *v* rage

raide (rehd) *adj* stiff

raie (ray) *f* stripe; parting

raifort (ray-*fawr*) *m* horseradish

rail (righ) *m* rail

raisin (ray-*zang*) *m* grapes *pl*; **~ sec** currant, raisin

raison (ray-*zawng*) *f* reason; cause; wits *pl*, sense; ***avoir ~** * be right; **en ~ de** for, owing to, because of

raisonnable (ray-zo-*nahbl*) *adj*

reasonable; sensible

raisonner (ray-zo-*nay*) *v* reason

ralentir (rah-lah*ng*-*teer*) *v* slow down

rallonge (rah-*lawngzh*) *f* extension cord

ramasser (rah-mah-*say*) *v* pick up

rame (rahm) *f* oar

ramener (rahm-*nay*) *v* *bring back

ramer (rah-*may*) *v* row

rampe (rah*ng*p) *f* railing

ramper (rah*ng*-*pay*) *v* *creep, crawl

rance (rah*ng*ss) *adj* rancid

rançon (rah*ng*-*sawng*) *f* ransom

randonnée (rah*ng*-do-*nay*) *f* tour, excursion; (long) trip; outing; hike

rang (rah*ng*) *m* row, rank

rangée (rah*ng*-*zhay*) *f* line

ranger (rah*ng*-*zhay*) *v* sort; tidy up, *put away

râpe (raap) *f* grater

râper (rah-*pay*) *v* grate

rapide (rah-*peed*) *adj* quick; fast, swift, rapid; *m* rapids *pl*

rapidement (rah-peed-*mahng*) *adv* soon

rapidité (rah-pee-dee-*tay*) *f* speed

rappeler (rah-*play*) *v* remind; recall; **se ~** remember, recall

rapport (rah-*pawr*) *m* report; connection, relation; **rapports** intercourse

rapporter (rah-por-*tay*) *v* *bring back; report

rapprocher (rah-pro-*shay*) *v* *bring closer

rare (raar) *adj* rare; uncommon, scarce

rarement (rahr-*mahng*) *adv* seldom, rarely

raser (rah-*zay*): **se ~** shave

raseur (rah-*zūr*) *m* bore

rasoir (rah-*zwaar*) *m* razor; **~ électrique** electric razor; shaver

rassemblement (rah-sahng-bler-*mahng*) *m* rally

rassembler (rah-sahng-*blay*) *v* assemble; collect

rassis (rah-*see*) *adj* stale

rassurer (rah-sew-*ray*) *v* reassure

rat (rah) *m* rat

râteau (rah-*toa*) *m* rake

ration (rah-sᵉ*awng*) *f* ration

rauque (rōak) *adj* hoarse

ravissant (rah-vee-*sahng*) *adj* lovely, delightful, enchanting

rayé (ray-ᵉ*ay*) *adj* striped

rayon (ray-ᵉ*awng*) *m* beam, ray; radius; spoke

rayure (ray-ᵉ*ēwr*) *f* scratch

réaction (ray-ahk-sᵉ*awng*) *f* reaction

réalisable (ray-ah-lee-*zahbl*) *adj* feasible; realizable

réalisation (ray-ah-lee-zah-sᵉ*awng*) *f* realization; direction

réaliser (ray-ah-lee-*zay*) *v* realize; carry out, implement

réaliste (ray-ah-*leest*) *adj* matter-of-fact

réalité (ray-ah-lee-*tay*) *f* reality; **en ~** actually; really

rébellion (ray-beh-lᵉ*awng*) *f* revolt, rebellion

rebord (rer-*bawr*) *m* edge, rim; **~ de fenêtre** windowsill

rebut (rer-*bew*) *m* junk, refuse

récemment (ray-sah-*mahng*) *adv* lately, recently

récent (ray-*sahng*) *adj* recent

réception (ray-seh-psᵉ*awng*) *f* receipt; reception; reception office

recette (rer-*seht*) *f* recipe; **recettes** revenue

*recevoir (rer-*svwaar*) *v* receive; entertain

recharge (rer-*shahrzh*) *f* refill

réchaud (ray-*shoa*)* *m* (portable) stove

réchauffer (ray-shoa-*fay*) *v* warm up

recherche (rer-*shehrsh*) *f* research

rechercher (rer-shehr-*shay*) *v* search for

récif (ray-*seef*) *m* reef

récipient (ray-see-pᵉ*ahng*) *m* container, vessel

réciproque (ray-see-*prok*) *adj* mutual

récit (ray-*see*) *m* tale; account

récital (ray-see-*tahl*) *m* (pl ~s) recital

réclamation (ray-klah-mah-sᵉ*awng*) *f* claim

réclame (ray-*klahm*) *f* publicity

réclamer (ray-klah-*may*) *v* claim

récolte (ray-*kolt*) *f* crop

recommandation (rer-ko-mahng-dah-sᵉ*awng*) *f* recommendation

recommander (rer-ko-mahng-*day*) *v* recommend; register

recommencer (rer-ko-mahng-*say*) *v* recommence

récompense (ray-kawng-*pahngss*) *f* reward, prize

récompenser (ray-kawng-pahng-*say*) *v* reward

réconciliation (ray-kawng-see-lᵉah-sᵉ*awng*) *f* reconciliation

réconfort (ray-kawng-*fawr*) *m* comfort

reconnaissance (rer-ko-nay-sahngss) *f* recognition

reconnaissant (rer-ko-nay-sahng) *adj* thankful, grateful

*reconnaître (rer-ko-*naitr*) *v* recognize; acknowledge; admit

record (rer-*kawr*) *m* record

*recouvrir (rer-koo-*vreer*) *v* cover; re-cover

récréation (ray-kray-ah-*s^yawng*) *f* recreation

rectangle (rehk-*tahnggl*) *m* rectangle; oblong

rectangulaire (rehk-tahng-gew-*lair*) *adj* rectangular

rectification (rehk-tee-fee-kah-*s^yawng*) *f* correction

reçu (rer-*sew*) *m* receipt; voucher

***recueillir** (rer-kur-^yeer*) *v* gather

reculer (rer-kew-*lay*) *v* step back; back up

récupérer (ray-kew-pay-*ray*) *v* recover

rédacteur (ray-dahk-*turr*) *m* editor

rédiger (ray-dee-*zhay*) *v* *draw up

redouter (rer-doo-*tay*) *v* fear

réduction (ray-dewk-*s^yawng*) *f* discount, reduction

***réduire** (ray-*dweer*) *v* reduce; decrease, *cut

réduit (ray-*dwee*) *m* shed

rééducation (ray-ay-dew-kah-*s^yawng*) *f* rehabilitation

réel (ray-*ehl*) *adj* real; true, factual, actual, substantial

réellement (ray-ehl-*mahng*) *adv* really

référence (ray-fay-*rahngss*) *f* reference

réfléchir (ray-flay-*sheer*) *v* *think; ~ à *think over

réflecteur (ray-flehk-*turr*) *m* reflector

reflet (rer-*flay*) *m* reflection

refléter (rer-flay-*tay*) *v* reflect

réforme (ray-*form*) *f* reformation

réfrigérateur (ray-free-zhay-rah-*turr*) *m* fridge, refrigerator

refroidir (rer-frwah-*deer*) *v* cool off

refuge (rer-*fewzh*) *m* refuge

réfugié (ray-few-zh^y*ay*) *m*, **-e** *f* refugee

refus (rer-*few*) *m* refusal

refuser (rer-few-*zay*) *v* refuse; deny, reject

regard (rer-*gaar*) *m* look

regarder (rer-gahr-*day*) *v* look; watch, look at; concern

régime (ray-*zheem*) *m* régime; rule, government; diet

région (ray-zh^y*awng*) *f* region; area, zone

régional (ray-zh^yo-*nahl*) *adj* regional

règle (raigl) *f* rule; ruler; **en ~** in order

règlement (reh-gler-*mahng*) *m* regulation; arrangement; settlement

régler (ray-*glay*) *v* regulate; settle

réglisse (ray-*gleess*) *f* liquorice

règne (rehñ) *m* reign; dominion, rule

régner (ray-*ñay*) *v* reign; rule

regret (rer-*gray*) *m* regret

regretter (rer-gray-*tay*) *v* regret

régulier (ray-gew-l^y*ay*) *adj* regular

rein (rang) *m* kidney

reine (rehn) *f* queen

rejeter (rerzh-*tay*) *v* reject; turn down

***rejoindre** (rer-zhwangdr) *v* rejoin

relater (rer-lah-*tay*) *v* relate; report

relatif (rer-lah-*teef*) *adj* relative; comparative; **~ à** with reference to, concerning

relation (rer-lah-*s^yawng*) *f* connection; relation

relayer (rer-lay-^y*ay*) *v* relieve

relèvement (rer-lehv-*mahng*) *m* increase

relever (rerl-*vay*) *v* raise

relief (rer-l^y*ehf*) *m* relief

relier (rer-l^y*ay*) *v* link; *bind

religieuse (rer-lee-zh^y*ürz*) *f* nun

religieux (rer-lee-zh^y*ur*) *adj* religious

religion (rer-lee-zh^y*awng*) *f* religion

relique (rer-*leek*) *f* relic

reliure (rer-l^y*ewr*) *f* binding

remarquable (rer-mahr-*kahbl*) *adj* remarkable; noticeable, striking

remarque (rer-*mahrk*) *f* remark

remarquer (rer-mahr-*kay*) *v* notice; remark

remboursement (rahng-boor-ser-*mahng*) *m* repayment, refund

rembourser (rahng-boor-*say*) *v*

*repay, reimburse, refund

remède (rer-*mehd*) *m* remedy

remerciement (rer-mehr-see-*mahng*) *m* thanks *pl*

remercier (rer-mehr-*s*ʸ*ay*) *v* thank

*remettre (rer-*mehtr*) *v* deliver; commit; hand over; remit; **se ~** recover

remise (rer-*meez*) *f* delivery

remonter (rer-mawng-*tay*) *v* *wind up

remorque (rer-*mork*) *f* trailer

remorquer (rer-mor-*kay*) *v* tow, tug

remorqueur (rer-mor-*kūrr*) *m* tug

rémoulade (ray-moo-*lahd*) *f* remoulade-sauce

remplacer (rahng-plah-*say*) *v* replace

remplir (rahng-*pleer*) *v* fill; fill in; fill out *Am*

remue-ménage (rer-mew-may-*naazh*) *m* bustle

remuer (rer-*mway*) *v* stir

rémunération (ray-mew-nay-rah-*s*ʸ*awng*) *f* remuneration

rémunérer (ray-mew-nay-*ray*) *v* remunerate

renard (rer-*naar*) *m* fox

rencontre (rahng-*kawngtr*) *f* meeting, encounter; **aller à la ~** *go and *meet

rencontrer (rahng-kawng-*tray*) *v* *meet; *come across, run into, encounter

rendement (rahng-der-*mahng*) *m* profit

rendez-vous (rahng-day-*voo*) *m* appointment, date

rendre (*rahngdr*) *v* refund; *make; **~ compte de** account for; **~ visite à** call on; **se ~** surrender; *go; **se ~ compte** realize

renommée (rer-no-*may*) *f* fame

renoncer (rer-nawng-*say*) *v* *give up

renouveler (rer-noo-*vlay*) *v* renew

renseignement (rahng-sehñ-*mahng*) *m* information; **bureau des**

renseignements inquiry office

renseigner (rahng-say-*ñay*) *v*: **se ~** inquire

rentable (rahng-*tahbl*) *adj* paying

rentrée (rahng-*tray*) *f* return; homecoming; re-entry

rentrer (rahng-*tray*) *v* *go home; reassemble

renverser (rahng-vehr-*say*) *v* knock down

*renvoyer (rahng-vwah-ʸ*ay*) *v* *send back; dismiss; **~ à** refer to; postpone

répandre (ray-*pahngdr*) *v* *shed; *spill

réparation (ray-pah-rah-*s*ʸ*awng*) *f* reparation, repair

réparer (ray-pah-*ray*) *v* repair; mend, fix

répartir (ray-pahr-*teer*) *v* divide

repas (rer-*pah*) *m* meal

repassage *m* ironing

repasser (rer-pah-*say*) *v* press, iron

repentir (rer-pahng-*teer*) *m* repentance

répertoire (ray-pehr-*twaar*) *m* repertory

répéter (ray-pay-*tay*) *v* repeat; rehearse

répétition (ray-pay-tee-*s*ʸ*awng*) *f* repetition; rehearsal

répit (ray-*pee*) *m* respite

répondre (ray-*pawngdr*) *v* reply, answer

réponse (ray-*pawngss*) *f* reply, answer; **en ~** in reply; **sans ~** unanswered

reporter (rer-por-*tay*) *m* reporter

repos (rer-*poa*) *m* rest

reposant (rer-poa-*zahng*) *adj* restful

reposer (rer-poa-*zay*) *v*: **se ~** rest

repousser (rer-poo-*say*) *v* turn down; repel; **repoussant** repulsive

*reprendre (rer-*prahngdr*) *v* resume; *take over

représentant (rer-pray-zahng-*tahng*) *m*, **-e** *f* agent

représentatif (rer-pray-zahn̄g-tah-*teef*) *adj* representative

représentation (rer-pray-zahn̄g-tah-s*y*aw*n̄g*) *f* show; representation

représenter (rer-pray-zahn̄g-*tay*) *v* represent

réprimander (ray-pree-mahn̄g-*day*) *v* reprimand

réprimer (ray-pree-*may*) *v* suppress

reprise (rer-*preez*) *f* revival; round

repriser (rer-pree-*zay*) *v* darn

reproche (rer-*prosh*) *m* reproach

reprocher (rer-pro-*shay*) *v* reproach

reproduction (rer-pro-dewk-s*y*aw*n̄g*) *f* reproduction

*reproduire (rer-pro-*dweer*) *v* reproduce

reptile (rehp-*teel*) *m* reptile

républicain (ray-pew-blee-*kan̄g*) *adj* republican

république (ray-pew-*bleek*) *f* republic

répugnance (ray-pew-ñah*n̄g*ss) *f* dislike

répugnant (ray-pew-*ñah̄ng*) *adj* repellent; filthy, disgusting, revolting

réputation (ray-pew-tah-s*y*aw*n̄g*) *f* fame, reputation

*requérir (rer-kay-*reer*) *v* request

requête (rer-*keht*) *f* request

requin (rer-*kan̄g*) *m* shark

requis (rer-*kee*) *adj* requisite

R.E.R. (ehr-er-*ehr*) *m* high-speed train service between Paris and the suburbs

réseau (ray-*zoa*) *m* network; ~ **routier** road system

réservation (ray-zehr-vah-s*y*aw*n̄g*) *f* reservation; booking

réserve (ray-*zehrv*) *f* reserve; qualification; **de** ~ spare; ~ **zoologique** game reserve

réserver (ray-zehr-*vay*) *v* reserve; book

réservoir (ray-zehr-*vwaar*) *m* reservoir; tank; ~ **d'essence** petrol tank, gas tank *Am*

résidence (ray-zee-*dah̄ngss*) *f* residence

résident (ray-zee-*dah̄ng*) *m* resident

résider (ray-zee-*day*) *v* reside

résille (ray-*zeey*) *f* hair net

résine (ray-*zeen*) *f* resin

résistance (ray-zee-*stah̄ngss*) *f* resistance

résister (ray-zee-*stay*) *v* resist

résolu (ray-zo-*lew*) *adj* determined, resolute

*résoudre (ray-*zoodr*) *v* solve

respect (reh-*spay*) *m* respect; esteem, regard

respectable (reh-spehk-*tahbl*) *adj* respectable

respecter (reh-spehk-*tay*) *v* respect

respectif (reh-spehk-*teef*) *adj* respective

respectueux (reh-spehk-*twur*) *adj* respectful

respiration (reh-spee-rah-s*y*aw*n̄g*) *f* breathing, respiration

respirer (reh-spee-*ray*) *v* breathe

resplendir (reh-splah̄ng-*deer*) *v* *shine

responsabilité (reh-spaw̄ng-sah-bee-lee-*tay*) *f* responsibility; liability

responsable (reh-spaw̄ng-*sahbl*) *adj* responsible; in charge; liable

ressemblance (rer-sah̄ng-*blah̄ngss*) *f* resemblance

ressembler à (rer-sah̄ng-*blay*) resemble

resserrer (rer-say-*ray*) *v* tighten; **se** ~ tighten

ressort (rer-*sawr*) *m* spring

ressource (rer-*soors*) *f* option; **ressources** resources *pl*; means *pl*

restant (reh-*stah̄ng*) *adj* remaining; *m* remnant, remainder

restaurant (reh-stoa-*rah̄ng*) *m* restaurant; ~ **libre service** self-service restaurant

reste (rehst) *m* rest; remnant, remainder

rester (reh-*stay*) *v* stay; remain

restituer (reh-stee-*tway*) *v* reimburse

restriction (reh-streek-*s*ʸ*awn̄g*) *f* restriction; qualification

résultat (ray-zewl-*tah*) *m* result; issue, effect, outcome

résulter (ray-zewl-*tay*) *v*: ~ **de** result from

résumé (ray-zew-*may*) *m* résumé, summary; survey

retard (rer-*taar*) *m* delay; **en** ~ overdue, late

retarder (rer-tahr-*day*) *v* delay

*retenir (rert-*neer*) *v* reserve, book; remember; restrain

rétine (ray-*teen*) *f* retina

retirer (rer-tee-*ray*) *v* *withdraw

retour (rer-*tōōr*) *m* return; **voyage de** ~ return journey

retourner (rer-toor-*nay*) *v* *get back; return, turn back, *go back; turn over, turn, turn round; **se** ~ turn round

retracer (rer-trah-*say*) *v* trace

retraite (rer-*treht*) *f* retirement; pension

retraité (rer-tray-*tay*) *adj* retired

rétrécir (ray-tray-*seer*) *v* *shrink

rétroviseur (ray-tro-vee-*zūr*) *m* driving mirror, rear-view mirror

réunion (ray-ew-*n*ʸ*awn̄g*) *f* meeting, assembly

réunir (ray-ew-*neer*) *v* join; reunite; **se** ~ gather

réussir (ray-ew-*seer*) *v* manage, succeed; pass; *make; **réussi** successful

rêve (raiv) *m* dream

réveil (ray-*vay*) *m* alarm clock

réveiller (ray-vay-ʸ*ay*) *v* *awake; *wake; **réveillé** awake; **se** ~ wake up

révélation (ray-vay-lah-*s*ʸ*awn̄g*) *f* revelation

révéler (ray-vay-*lay*) *v* reveal; *give away; **se** ~ prove

revendication (rer-vahn̄g-dee-kah-*s*ʸ*awn̄g*) *f* claim

revendiquer (rer-vahn̄g-dee-*kay*) *v* claim

*revenir (rer-*vneer*) *v* return

revenu (rer-*vnew*) *m* earnings *pl*, income, revenue

rêver (ray-*vay*) *v* *dream

revers (rer-*vair*) *m* reverse; lapel

revirement (rer-veer-*mahn̄g*) *m* reverse, turn

reviser (rer-vee-*zay*) *v* revise; overhaul

révision (ray-vee-*z*ʸ*awn̄g*) *f* revision

*revoir (rer-*vwaar*) *v* *see again; review; **au revoir!** goodbye!

révoltant (ray-vol-*tahn̄g*) *adj* revolting

révolte (ray-*volt*) *f* revolt, rebellion

révolter (ray-vol-*tay*) *v*: **se** ~ revolt

révolution (ray-vo-lew-*s*ʸ*awn̄g*) *f* revolution

revolver (ray-vol-*vair*) *m* gun, revolver

révoquer (ray-vo-*kay*) *v* recall

revue (rer-*vew*) *f* revue; review, magazine; ~ **mensuelle** monthly magazine

rez-de-chaussée (reh-dshoa-*say*) *m* ground floor

rhinocéros (ree-no-say-*ross*) *m* rhinoceros

rhubarbe (rew-*bahrb*) *f* rhubarb

rhum (rom) *m* rum

rhumatisme (rew-mah-*teesm*) *m* rheumatism

rhume (rewm) *m* cold; ~ **des foins** hay fever

riche (reesh) *adj* rich; wealthy

richesse (ree-*shehss*) *f* wealth; riches *pl*

ride (reed) *f* wrinkle

rideau (ree-*doa*) *m* curtain

ridicule (ree-dee-*kewl*) *adj* ridiculous; ludicrous

ridiculiser (ree-dee-kew-lee-*zay*) *v* ridicule

rien (r^{y}a$\overline{\text{ng}}$) *pron* nothing; nil; **ne ... ~** nothing; **~ que** only

rigoler (ree-go-*lay*) *v* laugh; have fun; be joking

rime (reem) *f* rhyme

rinçage (ra$\overline{\text{ng}}$-*saazh*) *m* rinse

rincer (ra$\overline{\text{ng}}$-*say*) *v* rinse

rire (reer) *m* laughter, laugh

*rire (reer) *v* laugh

risque (reesk) *m* risk; chance

risquer (ree-*skay*) *v* venture, risk; **risqué** risky

rivage (ree-*vaazh*) *m* shore

rival (ree-*vahl*) *m* rival

rivaliser (ree-vah-lee-*zay*) *v* rival

rivalité (ree-vah-lee-*tay*) *f* rivalry

rive (reev) *f* bank, shore

rivière (ree-*v^{y}air*) *f* river

riz (ree) *m* rice

robe (rob) *f* dress; robe, frock, gown; **~ de chambre** dressing gown

robinet (ro-bee-*nay*) *m* tap; faucet *Am*

robuste (ro-*bewst*) *adj* solid, robust

rocade (ro-*kahd*) *f* bypass

rocher (ro-*shay*) *m* rock, boulder

rocheux (ro-*shur*) *adj* rocky

roi (rwah) *m* king

rôle (r$\overline{\text{oa}}$l) *m* role

roman (ro-*ma$\overline{\text{ng}}$*) *m* novel; **~ policier** detective story

romantique (ro-ma$\overline{\text{ng}}$-*teek*) *adj* romantic

rompre (raw$\overline{\text{ng}}$pr) *v* *break

rond (raw$\overline{\text{ng}}$) *adj* round

rond-point (raw$\overline{\text{ng}}$-*pwa$\overline{\text{ng}}$*) *m* roundabout

ronfler (raw$\overline{\text{ng}}$-*flay*) *v* snore

rosaire (roa-*zair*) *m* rosary

rose (r$\overline{\text{oa}}$z) *f* rose; *adj* pink, rose

roseau (roa-*zoa*) *m* reed

rosée (roa-*zay*) *f* dew

rossignol (ro-see-*ñol*) *m* nightingale

rotation (ro-tah-*s^{y}aw$\overline{\text{ng}}$*) *f* revolution

rôti (roa-*tee*) *m* roast (meat)

rotin (ro-*ta$\overline{\text{ng}}$*) *m* rattan

rôtir (roa-*teer*) *v* roast

rôtisserie (ro-tee-*sree*) *f* grillroom

rotule (ro-*tewl*) *f* kneecap

roue (roo) *f* wheel; **~ de secours** spare wheel

rouge (r$\overline{\text{oo}}$zh) *adj* red; *m* rouge; **~ à lèvres** lipstick

rouge-gorge (roozh-*gorzh*) *m* robin

rougeole (roo-*zhol*) *f* measles

rougir (roo-*zheer*) *v* blush

rouille (roo^{ee}) *f* rust

rouillé (roo-^{y}*ay*) *adj* rusty

rouleau (roo-*loa*) *m* roll

rouler (roo-*lay*) *v* roll; *go

roulette (roo-*leht*) *f* roulette

roulotte (roo-*lot*) *f* caravan

roumain (roo-*ma$\overline{\text{ng}}$*) *adj* Rumanian

Roumanie (roo-mah-*nee*) *f* Rumania

route (root) *f* drive, road; route; **en ~ pour** bound for; **~ à péage** turnpike *Am*; **~ d'évitement** by-pass; **~ principale** thoroughfare, main road

routine (roo-*teen*) *f* routine

royal (rwah-^{y}*ahl*) *adj* royal

royaume (rwah-^{y}*$\overline{\text{oa}}$m*) *m* kingdom

ruban (rew-*bah$\overline{\text{ng}}$*) *m* ribbon; **~ adhésif** adhesive tape, scotch tape

rubrique (rew-*breek*) *f* column

ruche (rewsh) *f* beehive

rude (rewd) *adj* rough

rue (rew) *f* street; road; **~ principale** main street; **~ transversale** side street

ruelle (rwehl) *f* alley, lane

rugir (rew-*zheer*) *v* roar

rugissement (rew-zhee-*smah$\overline{\text{ng}}$*) *m* roar

rugueux (rew-*gur*) *adj* rough

ruine (rween) *f* ruins; ruin

ruiner (rwee-*nay*) *v* ruin

ruisseau (rwee-*soa*) *m* brook, stream
rumeur (rew-*mūrr*) *f* rumo(u)r
rural (rew-*rahl*) *adj* rural
rusé (rew-*zay*) *adj* cunning

russe (rewss) *adj* Russian
Russie (rew-*see*) *f* Russia
rustique (rew-*steek*) *adj* rustic
rythme (reetm) *m* rhythm; pace

S

sable (sahbl) *m* sand
sableux (sah-*blur*) *adj* sandy
sabot (sah-*boa*) *m* wooden shoe; hoof
sac (sahk) *m* bag; sack; ~ **à dos** rucksack; ~ **à glace** ice bag; ~ **à main** bag, handbag; ~ **à provisions** shopping bag; ~ **de couchage** sleeping bag; ~ **en papier** paper bag
sachet (sah-*shay*) *m* small bag; ~ **de thé** teabag
sacoche (sah-*kosh*) *f* bag
sacré (sah-*kray*) *adj* holy, sacred
sacrifice (sah-kree-*feess*) *m* sacrifice
sacrifier (sah-kree-*fʸay*) *v* sacrifice
sacrilège (sah-kree-*laizh*) *m* sacrilege
sage (saazh) *adj* wise; good
sage-femme (sahzh-*fahm*) *f* midwife
sagesse (sah-*zhehss*) *f* wisdom
saigner (say-*ñay*) *v* *bleed
sain (sañg) *adj* healthy; wholesome, well
saint (sañg) *m* saint
saisir (say-*zeer*) *v* seize; *catch, grip, *take, grasp
saison (seh-*zawñg*) *f* season; **hors ~** off season; **morte-saison** *f* low season; **pleine ~** peak season
salade (sah-*lahd*) *f* salad
salaire (sah-*lair*) *m* salary, pay
salaud (sah-*loa*) *m* bastard
sale (sahl) *adj* dirty; filthy
salé (sah-*lay*) *adj* salty
saleté (sahl-*tay*) *f* dirt
salière (sah-*lʸair*) *f* salt cellar, salt

shaker *Am*
salir (sah-*leer*) *v* soil
salive (sah-*leev*) *f* spit
salle (sahl) *f* hall; ~ **à manger** dining room; ~ **d'attente** waiting room; ~ **de bains** bathroom; ~ **de bal** ballroom; ~ **de classe** classroom; ~ **de concert** concert hall; ~ **de lecture** reading room; ~ **de séjour** living room; ~ **d'exposition** showroom
salon (sah-*lawñg*) *m* sitting room; drawing room, salon; ~ **de beauté** beauty salon; ~ **de thé** tearoom
salopette (sah-lo-*peht*) *f* overalls *pl*
saluer (sah-*lway*) *v* greet; salute
salut (sah-*lew*) *m* welfare
salutation (sah-lew-tah-*sʸawñg*) *f* greeting
samedi (sahm-*dee*) *m* Saturday
S.A.M.U. (sah-*mew*) *m* mobile accident unit
sanatorium (sah-nah-to-*rʸom*) *m* sanatorium
sanctuaire (sahñgk-*twair*) *m* shrine
sandale (sahñg-*dahl*) *f* sandal
sandwich (sahñg-*dweech*) *m* sandwich
sang (sahñg) *m* blood
sanitaire (sah-nee-*tair*) *adj* sanitary
sans (sahñg) *prep* without
santé (sahñg-*tay*) *f* health
sapin (sah-*pañg*) *m* fir-tree
sardine (sahr-*deen*) *f* sardine
satellite (sah-tay-*leet*) *m* satellite
satin (sah-*tañg*) *m* satin

satisfaction (sah-teess-fahk-*s*^y*awng*) *f* satisfaction

***satisfaire** (sah-tee-*sfair*) *v* satisfy; **satisfait** satisfied; content

sauce (*soass*) *f* sauce

saucisse (soa-*seess*) *f* sausage

saucisson (soa-see-*sawng*) *m* sausage

sauf (soaf) *prep* but

saumon (soa-*mawng*) *m* salmon

sauna (soa-*nah*) *m* sauna

saut (soa) *m* jump; hop, leap; **~ à ski** ski jump

sauter (soa-*tay*) *v* jump; skip; ***faire ~** fry

sauterelle (soa-*trehl*) *f* grasshopper

sautiller (soa-tee-*y*ay) *v* hop, skip

sauvage (soa-*vaazh*) *adj* savage; wild, fierce

sauver (soa-*vay*) *v* rescue, save

sauvetage (soav-*taazh*) *m* rescue

sauveur (soa-*vurr*) *m* savio(u)r

savant (sah-*vahng*) *m* scientist

saveur (sah-*vurr*) *f* flavour

***savoir** (sah-*vwaar*) *v* *know; *be able to

savoir-vivre (sah-vwahr-*veevr*) *m* manners *pl*

savon (sah-*vawng*) *m* soap; **~ à barbe** shaving soap; **~ en poudre** soap powder

savoureux (sah-voo-*rur*) *adj* tasty, savo(u)ry

scandale (skahng-*dahl*) *m* scandal

scandinave (skahng-dee-*naav*) *adj* Scandinavian

Scandinavie (skahng-dee-nah-*vee*) *f* Scandinavia

sceau (soa) *m* seal

scène (sehn) *f* scene; stage; **metteur en ~** director; ***mettre en ~** direct

scie (see) *f* saw

science (*s*^y*ahngss*) *f* science

scientifique (*s*^yahng-tee-*feek*) *adj* scientific

scierie (see-*ree*) *f* sawmill

scintillant (sang-tee-*y*ahng) *adj* sparkling

scolaire (sko-*lair*) *adj* school-

scooter (skoo-*tair*) *m* scooter

scout (skoot) *m* scout; boy scout

sculpteur (skewl-*turr*) *m* sculptor

sculpture (skewl-*tewr*) *f* sculpture

se (ser) *pron* himself; herself; themselves

séance (say-*ahngss*) *f* session

seau (soa) *m* bucket, pail

sec (sehk) *adj* (f sèche) dry

sèche-cheveux (sehsh-sher-*vur*) *m* hairdrier, hairdryer

sécher (say-*shay*) *v* dry

sécheresse (say-*shrehss*) *f* drought

séchoir (say-*shwaar*) *m* dryer

second (ser-*gawng*) *adj* second

secondaire (ser-gawng-*dair*) *adj* secondary; subordinate

seconde (ser-*gawng*d) *f* second

secouer (ser-*kway*) *v* *shake

secours (ser-*koor*) *m* assistance; **premier ~** first aid

secousse (ser-*kooss*) *f* jolt; jerk

secret[1] (ser-*kray*) *m* secret

secret[2] (ser-*kray*) *adj* (f secrète) secret

secrétaire (ser-kray-*tair*) *m/f* clerk, secretary

section (sehk-*s*^y*awng*) *f* section; stretch

sécurité (say-kew-ree-*tay*) *f* safety, security; **glissière de ~** crash barrier

sédatif (say-dah-*teef*) *m* sedative

***séduire** (say-*dweer*) *v* seduce

séduisant (say-dwee-*zahng*) *adj* attractive, charming

sein (sang) *m* breast; bosom

seize (saiz) *num* sixteen

seizième (seh-*z*^yehm) *num* sixteenth

séjour (say-*zhoor*) *m* stay

séjourner (say-zhoor-*nay*) *v* stay

sel (sehl) *m* salt; **sels de bain** bath

salts

sélection (say-lehk-s^y*awng*) f choice, selection

sélectionner (say-lehk-s^yo-*nay*) v select

selle (sehl) f saddle

selon (ser-*lawng*) prep according to

semaine (ser-*mehn*) f week

semblable (sahng-*blahbl*) adj alike

sembler (sahng-*blay*) v seem; look, appear

semelle (ser-*mehl*) f sole

semence (ser-*mahngss*) f seed

semer (ser-*may*) v *sow

semi- (ser-*mee*) semi-

sénat (say-*nah*) m senate

sénateur (say-nah-*türr*) m senator

sénile (say-*neel*) adj senile

sens (sahngss) m sense; reason; **bon ~** sense; **en ~ inverse** the other way round; **~ unique** one-way traffic

sensation (sahng-sah-s^y*awng*) f sensation; feeling

sensationnel (sahng-sah-s^yo-*nehl*) adj sensational

sensible (sahng-*seebl*) adj sensitive; considerable

sentence (sahng-*tahngss*) f verdict

sentier (sahng-t^y*ay*) m path; trail; **~ pour piétons** footpath

sentiment (sahng-tee-*mahng*) m feeling; emotion; consciousness, sense

sentimental (sahng-tee-mahng-*tahl*) adj sentimental

***sentir** (sahng-*teer*) v *feel; *smell; **~ mauvais** *smell

séparation (say-pah-rah-s^y*awng*) f division

séparé (say-pah-*ray*) adj separate

séparément (say-pah-ray-*mahng*) adv apart

séparer (say-pah-*ray*) v separate; divide, part

sept (seht) num seven

septembre (sehp-*tahngbr*) September

septentrional (sehp-tahng-tree-o-*nahl*) adj northern, north

septicémie (sehp-tee-say-*mee*) f bloodpoisoning

septième (seh-t^y*ehm*) num seventh

septique (sehp-*teek*) adj septic

sépulture (say-pewl-*tewr*) f burial

serein (ser-*rang*) adj serene

série (say-*ree*) f sequence; series

sérieux (say-r^y*ur*) adj serious; m seriousness

seringue (ser-*rangg*) f syringe

serment (sehr-*mahng*) m vow, oath; **faux ~** perjury

sermon (sehr-*mawng*) m sermon

serpent (sehr-*pahng*) m snake

serpentant (sehr-pahng-*tahng*) adj winding

serpenter (sehr-pahng-*tay*) v *wind

serre (sair) f greenhouse

serrer (say-*ray*) v tighten; **serré** tight, narrow

serrure (say-*rewr*) f lock; **trou de la ~** keyhole

sérum (say-*rom*) m serum

serveuse (sehr-*vürz*) f waitress

serviable (sehr-v^y*ahbl*) adj helpful

service (sehr-*veess*) m service; service charge; section; **~ à thé** tea set; **~ de table** dinner service; **~ d'étage** room service; **services postaux** postal service

serviette (sehr-v^y*eht*) f towel; napkin, serviette; briefcase; **~ de bain** bath towel; **~ de papier** paper napkin; **~ hygiénique** sanitary towel, sanitary napkin *Am*

***servir** (sehr-*veer*) v serve; attend on, wait on; *be of use; **se ~ de** apply

serviteur (sehr-vee-*türr*) m servant

seuil (sur^{ee}) m threshold

seul (surl) adv alone; adj single, only

seulement (surl-*mahng*) *adv* only; merely

sévère (say-*vair*) *adj* strict; harsh; severe

sévir (say-*veer*) *v* rage

sexe (sehks) *m* sex

sexualité (sehk-swah-lee-*tay*) *f* sexuality

sexuel (sehk-*swehl*) *adj* sexual

shampooing (shahng-*pwang*) *m* shampoo

short (short) *m* shorts

si (see) *conj* if; whether; *adv* so; **si ... ou** whether ... or

Siamois (s^yah-*mwah*) *m* Siamese

siamois (s^yah-*mwah*) *adj* Siamese

sida (see-*dah*) *m* Aids, AIDS

siècle (s^yehkl) *m* century

siège (s^yaizh) *m* chair, seat; siege

sien: le ~ (ler s^yang) his

sieste (s^yehst) *f* siesta; nap

siffler (see-*flay*) *v* whistle

sifflet (see-*flay*) *m* whistle

signal (see-*ñahl*) *m* signal; **~ de détresse** distress signal

signalement (see-ñahl-*mahng*) *m* description

signaler (see-ñah-*lay*) *v* signal; indicate

signature (see-ñah-*tewr*) *f* signature

signe (seeñ) *m* sign; token, signal, indication; ***faire ~** *make a sign, wave

signer (see-*ñay*) *v* sign

significatif (see-ñee-fee-kah-*teef*) *adj* significant

signification (see-ñee-fee-kah-s^yawng) *f* meaning, sense

signifier (see-ñee-f^yay) *v* *mean

silence (see-*lahngss*) *m* silence; quiet

silencieux (see-lahng-s^yur) *adj* silent; *m* silencer; muffler *Am*

sillon (see-^yawng) *m* groove

similaire (see-mee-*lair*) *adj* similar

similitude (see-mee-lee-*tewd*) *f* similarity

simple (sangpl) *adj* simple; plain

simplement (sang-pler-*mahng*) *adv* simply

simuler (see-mew-*lay*) *v* simulate

simultané (see-mewl-tah-*nay*) *adj* simultaneous

sincère (sang-*sair*) *adj* honest, sincere

singe (sangzh) *m* monkey

singulier (sang-gew-l^ay) *m* singular; *adj* remarkable, singular, uncommon

sinistre (see-*neestr*) *adj* sinister, ominous; *m* catastrophe

sinon (see-*nawng*) *conj* otherwise

sirène (see-*rehn*) *f* siren

sirop (see-*roa*) *m* syrup

site (seet) *m* site

situation (see-twah-s^yawng) *f* situation; position, location

situé (see-*tway*) *adj* situated

six (seess) *num* six

sixième (see-z^yehm) *num* sixth

ski (skee) *m* ski; skiing; **~ nautique** water ski

skier (skee-*ay*) *v* ski

skieur (skee-*ürr*) *m* skier

slip (sleep) *m* briefs *pl*

smoking (smo-*keeng*) *m* dinner jacket; tuxedo *Am*

S.N.C.F. (eh-sehn-say-*ehf*) *f* French national railway company

snob (snob) *adj* snooty

sobre (sobr) *adj* sober

social (so-s^yahl) *adj* social

socialisme (so-s^yah-*leesm*) *m* socialism

socialiste (so-s^yah-*leest*) *adj* socialist; *m* socialist

société (so-s^yay-*tay*) *f* community, society; company

sœur (sürr) *f* sister

soi (swah) *pron* oneself; **soi-même** *pron* oneself

soi-disant (swah-dee-*zahng*) *adj* socalled

soie (swah) *f* silk

soif (swahf) *f* thirst

soigné (swah-*ñay*) *adj* neat; thorough

soigner (swah-*ñay*) *v* treat; nurse

soigneux (swah-*ñur*) *adj* careful

soin (swang) *m* care; ***prendre ~ de** *take care of; **soins de beauté** beauty treatment

soir (swaar) *m* night, evening; **ce ~** tonight

soirée (swah-*ray*) *f* evening

soit ... soit (swah) either ... or

soixante (swah-*sahngt*) *num* sixty

soixante-dix (swah-sahngt-*deess*) *num* seventy

sol (sol) *m* floor; soil, earth, ground

soldat (sol-*dah*) *m* soldier

solde (sold) *m* balance; **soldes** sales, clearance sale

sole (sol) *f* sole

soleil (so-*lay*) *m* sun; sunshine; **coucher du ~** sunset; **coup de ~** sunburn; **lever du ~** sunrise

solennel (so-lah-*nehl*) *adj* solemn

solide (so-*leed*) *adj* solid; firm, sound; *m* solid

solitaire (so-lee-*tair*) *adj* lonely

solitude (so-lee-*tewd*) *f* loneliness

soluble (so-*lewbl*) *adj* soluble

solution (so-lew-s^y*awng*) *f* solution

sombre (*sawngbr*) *adj* somber *Am*, sombre, obscure; gloomy

sommaire (so-*mair*) *m* summary

somme (som) *f* sum; amount; *m* nap; **~ globale** lump sum

sommeil (so-*may*) *m* sleep

sommelier (so-mer-l^y*ay*) *m* winewaiter

sommet (so-*may*) *m* summit; top, peak, height; **~ de colline** hilltop

somnifère (som-nee-*fair*) *m* sleeping pill

somnolent (som-no-*lahng*) *adj* sleepy

son[1] (sawng) *adj* (f sa, pl ses) his; her

son[2] (sawng) *m* sound

songer (sawng-*zhay*) *v* *dream; **~ à** *think of

sonner (so-*nay*) *v* sound; *ring

sonnette (so-*neht*) *f* bell; doorbell

sorcière (sor-s^y*air*) *f* witch

sort (sawr) *m* fortune, lot, destiny

sorte (sort) *f* sort; **toutes sortes de** all sorts of

sortie (sor-*tee*) *f* way out, exit; **~ de secours** emergency exit

*sortir (sor-*teer*) *v* *go out

sot (soa) *adj* (f sotte) foolish, silly

sottise (so-*teez*) *f* nonsense, rubbish

souche (soosh) *f* stub

souci (soo-*see*) *m* concern, worry; care

soucier (soo-s^y*ay*) *v*: **se ~ de** care about

soucieux (soo-s^y*ur*) *adj* concerned, worried

soucoupe (soo-*koop*) *f* saucer

soudain (soo-*dang*) *adj* sudden; *adv* suddenly

souder (soo-*day*) *v* weld

souffle (soofl) *m* breath

souffler (soo-*flay*) *v* *blow

souffrance (soo-*frahngss*) *f* suffering

*souffrir (soo-*freer*) *v* suffer

souhait (sweh) *m* wish

souhaiter (sway-*tay*) *v* wish

souillé (soo-^{y}*ay*) *adj* soiled, dirty

soulagement (soo-lahzh-*mahng*) *m* relief

soulager (soo-lah-*zhay*) *v* relieve

soulever (sool-*vay*) *v* lift; *bring up

soulier (soo-l^y*ay*) *m* shoe

souligner (soo-lee-*ñay*) *v* underline; stress, emphasize

*soumettre (soo-*mehtr*) *v* subject; **se ~** submit

soupape (soo-*pahp*) *f* valve

soupçon (soop-*sawng*) *m* suspicion

soupçonner (soop-so-*nay*) *v* suspect

soupçonneux (soop-so-*nur*) *adj* suspicious

soupe (soop) *f* soup

souper (soo-*pay*) *m* supper

souple (soopl) *adj* supple; flexible

source (soors) *f* well; fountain, source, spring

sourcil (soor-*see*) *m* eyebrow

sourd (sōōr) *adj* deaf

sourire (soo-*reer*) *m* smile; ~ **forcé** forced smile

*****sourire** (soo-*reer*) *v* smile

souris (soo-*ree*) *f* mouse

sous (soo) *prep* under

sous-estimer (soo-zeh-stee-*may*) *v* underestimate

sous-locataire (soo-lo-kah-*tair*) *m* lodger

sous-marin (soo-mah-*rang*) *adj* underwater

soussigné (soo-see-*ñay*) *m* undersigned

sous-sol (soo-*sol*) *m* basement

sous-titre (soo-*teetr*) *m* subtitle

*****soustraire** (soo-*strair*) *v* subtract

sous-vêtements (soo-veht-*mahng*) *mpl* underwear

*****soutenir** (soot-*neer*) *v* support; *hold up

souterrain (soo-teh-*rang*) *adj* underground

soutien (soo-t*y*ang) *m* support; relief

soutien-gorge (soo-t*y*ang-*gorzh*) *m* bra

souvenir (soo-*vneer*) *m* memory, remembrance; souvenir; **se *souvenir** recollect

souvent (soo-*vahng*) *adv* often; **le plus ~** mostly

souverain (soo-*vrang*) *m* sovereign

spacieux (spah-s*y*ur) *adj* spacious, roomy, large

sparadrap (spah-rah-*drah*) *m* adhesive plaster

spécial (spay-s*y*ahl) *adj* special; peculiar, particular

spécialement (spay-s*y*ahl-*mahng*) *adv* especially

spécialiser (spay-s*y*ah-lee-*zay*) *v*: **se ~** specialize

spécialiste (spay-s*y*ah-*leest*) *m/f* specialist, expert

spécialité (spay-s*y*ah-lee-*tay*) *f* speciality

spécifique (spay-see-*feek*) *adj* specific

spectacle (spehk-*tahkl*) *m* spectacle; show; sight; ~ **de variétés** floor show, variety show

spectaculaire (spehk-tah-kew-*lair*) *adj* sensational

spectateur (spehk-tah-*tūrr*) *m*, **-trice** *f* spectator

spectre (spehktr) *m* spook

spéculer (spay-kew-*lay*) *v* speculate

sphère (sfair) *f* sphere

spirituel (spee-ree-*twehl*) *adj* spiritual; witty

spiritueux (spee-ree-*twur*) *mpl* liquor, spirits

splendeur (splahng-*dūrr*) *f* splendo(u)r

splendide (splahng-*deed*) *adj* splendid; wonderful, glorious, enchanting, magnificent

sport (spawr) *m* sport; **sports d'hiver** winter sports

sportif (spor-*teef*) *m* sportsman

square (skwaar) *m* square

stable (stahbl) *adj* permanent, stable; solid, fixed

stade (stahd) *m* stadium

stand (stahng) *m* stand; ~ **de livres** bookstand

standard (stahng-*daar*) *adj* standard

starter (stahr-*tair*) *m* choke

station (stah-s*y*awng) *f* station; ~ **balnéaire** seaside resort; ~ **de taxis** taxi rank; taxi stand *Am*; ~ **thermale**

spa

stationnaire (stah-s^yo-*nair*) *adj* stationary

stationnement (stah-s^yon-*mahng*) *m* parking; ~ **interdit** no parking

station-service (stah-s^yon-sehr-*veess*) *f* filling station, service station; gas station *Am*

statistique (stah-tee-*steek*) *f* statistics *pl*

statue (stah-*tew*) *f* statue

stature (stah-*tewr*) *f* figure

steak (stehk) *m* steak

stéréo (*stay*-ray-oa) *f* stereo

stérile (stay-*reel*) *adj* sterile

stériliser (stay-ree-lee-*zay*) *v* sterilize

stimulant (stee-mew-*lahng*) *m* impulse; stimulant

stimuler (stee-mew-*lay*) *v* stimulate

stock (stok) *m* stock; supply; ***avoir en ~** stock

stop! (stop) stop!

store (stawr) *m* blind

strophe (strof) *f* stanza

structure (strewk-*tewr*) *f* structure; fabric

studio (stew-*d^yoa*) *m* studio; flatlet, one-room apartment

stupide (stew-*peed*) *adj* foolish, stupid

style (steel) *m* style

stylo (stee-*loa*) *m* fountain pen; ~ **à bille** ballpoint pen

subir (sew-*beer*) *v* suffer

sublime (sew-*bleem*) *adj* grand

subordonné (sew-bor-do-*nay*) *adj* subordinate

subsistance (sewb-zee-*stahngss*) *f* livelihood

substance (sewb-*stahngss*) *f* substance

substantiel (sewb-stahng-s^y*ehl*) *adj* substantial

substantif (sewb-stahng-*teef*) *m* noun

substituer (sewb-stee-*tway*) *v* substitute

substitut (sewb-stee-*tew*) *m* substitute; deputy

subtil (sewb-*teel*) *adj* subtle

suburbain (sew-bewr-*bang*) *adj* suburban

subvention (sewb-vahng-s^y*awng*) *f* subsidy; grant

succéder (sewk-say-*day*) *v* succeed

succès (sewk-*say*) *m* success; hit

succession (sewk-seh-s^y*awng*) *f* sequence

succomber (sew-kawng-*bay*) *v* succumb

succulent (sew-kew-*lahng*) *adj* tasty

succursale (sew-kewr-*sahl*) *f* branch

sucer (sew-*say*) *v* suck

sucre (sewkr) *m* sugar

sucrer (sew-*kray*) *v* sweeten; **sucré** sweet

sud (sewd) *m* south

sud-américain (sew-dah-may-ree-*kang*) *adj* Latin-American

sud-est (sew-*dehst*) *m* southeast

sud-ouest (sew-*dwehst*) *m* southwest

Suède (swehd) *f* Sweden

suédois (sway-*dwah*) *adj* Swedish

suer (sway) *v* perspire, sweat

sueur (swurr) *f* perspiration, sweat

***suffire** (sew-*feer*) *v* *do, suffice

suffisant (sew-fee-*zahng*) *adj* enough, sufficient

suffrage (sew-*fraazh*) *m* vote

suggérer (sewg-zhay-*ray*) *v* suggest

suggestion (sewg-zheh-st^y*awng*) *f* suggestion

suicide (swee-*seed*) *m* suicide

Suisse (sweess) *f* Switzerland; *m/f* Swiss

suisse (sweess) *adj* Swiss

suite (sweet) *f* sequel; series; **et ainsi de ~** and so on; **par la ~** afterwards; **tout de ~** at once, instantly

suivant (swee-*vahng*) *adj* following, next

*suivre (sweevr) *v* follow; ***faire ~** forward

sujet (sew-*zhay*) *m* subject; issue, topic, theme; **~ à** liable to, subject to

superbe (sew-*pehrb*) *adj* superb

superficiel (sew-pehr-fee-s*^{y}ehl*) *adj* superficial

superflu (sew-pehr-*flew*) *adj* superfluous; unnecessary, redundant

supérieur (sew-pay-r*^{y}ūrr*) *adj* superior; top, upper; excellent

supermarché (sew-pehr-mahr-*shay*) *m* supermarket

superstition (sew-pehr-stee-s*^{y}awng*) *f* superstition

superviser (sew-pehr-vee-*zay*) *v* supervise

supervision (sew-pehr-vee-z*^{y}awng*) *f* supervision

supplément (sew-play-*mahng*) *m* supplement; surcharge

supplémentaire (sew-play-mahng-*tair*) *adj* additional; extra

supplier (sew-plee-*ay*) *v* beg

supporter[1] (sew-por-*tay*) *v* *bear; support

supporter[2] (sew-por-*tair*) *m* supporter

supposer (sew-poa-*zay*) *v* suppose; guess, assume, reckon

suppositoire (sew-poa-zee-*twaar*) *m* suppository

supprimer (sew-pree-*may*) *v* *do away with

suprême (sew-*prehm*) *adj* supreme

sur (sewr) *prep* upon; on; in; about

sûr (sēwr) *adj* sure; safe, secure; **bien ~** naturally

surcharge (sewr-*shahrzh*) *f* overweight

sûrement (sewr-*mahng*) *adv* surely

surface (sewr-*fahss*) *f* surface, surface area

surgelé (sewr-zher-*lay*) *adj* deep- *or* quick-frozen

surgir (sewr-*zheer*) *v* *arise

surmené (sewr-mer-*nay*) *adj* overworked

surmener (sewr-mer-*nay*) *v*: **se ~** overwork

surnom (sewr-*nawng*) *m* nickname

surpasser (sewr-pah-*say*) *v* *outdo, exceed

surplus (sewr-*plew*) *m* surplus

*surprendre (sewr-*prahngdr*) *v* surprise; amaze; *catch

surprise (sewr-*preez*) *f* surprise

surprise-partie (sewr-preez-pahr-*tee*) *f* party

surtout (sewr-*too*) *adv* most of all

surveillance (sewr-veh-*^{y}ahngss*) *f* supervision

surveillant (sewr-veh-*^{y}ahng*) *m* warden, supervisor

surveiller (sewr-vay-*^{y}ay*) *v* watch; guard, patrol

*survenir (sewr-ver-*neer*) *v* occur

survie (sewr-*vee*) *f* survival

*survivre (sewr-*veevr*) *v* survive

suspect (sew-*spehkt*) *adj* suspicious; *m* suspect

suspecter (sew-spehk-*tay*) *v* suspect

suspendre (sew-*spahngdr*) *v* *hang; discontinue, suspend

suspension (sew-spahng-s*^{y}awng*) *f* suspension

suture (sew-*tēwr*) *f* stitch

svelte (svehlt) *adj* slender

syllabe (see-*lahb*) *f* syllable

symbole (sang-*bol*) *m* symbol

sympathie (sang-pah-*tee*) *f* sympathy

sympathique (sang-pah-*teek*) *adj* nice; pleasant

symphonie (sang-fo-*nee*) *f* symphony

symptôme (sangp-*tōam*) *m* symptom

synagogue (see-nah-*gog*) *f* synagogue

syndicat (sang-dee-*kah*) *m* trade union; **~ d'initiative** tourist office

synonyme (see-no-*neem*) *m* synonym

synthétique (sañg-tay-*teek*) *adj* synthetic

Syrie (see-*ree*) *f* Syria

syrien (see-*r^y añg*) *adj* Syrian

systématique (see-stay-mah-*teek*) *adj* systematic

système (see-*stehm*) *m* system; ~ **décimal** decimal system; ~ **de lubrification** lubrication system

T

tabac (tah-*bah*) *m* tobacco; **bureau de** ~ tobacconist's; **débitant de** ~ tobacconist; ~ **à rouler** cigarette tobacco; **tabac pour pipe** pipe tobacco

table (tahbl) *f* table; ~ **des matières** table of contents

tableau (tah-*bloa*) *m* chart; board; ~ **de bord** dashboard; ~ **de conversions** conversion chart; ~ **de distribution** switchboard; ~ **noir** blackboard

tablette (tah-*bleht*) *f* tablet

tablier (tah-blee-*ay*) *m* apron

tabou (tah-*boo*) *m* taboo

tache (tahsh) *f* speck, stain, spot, blot

tâche (taash) *f* duty, task

tacher (tah-*shay*) *v* stain

tâcher (tah-*shay*) *v* try

tacheté (tahsh-*tay*) *adj* spotted

tactique (tahk-*teek*) *f* tactics *pl*

taille (tigh) *f* waist; size

taille-crayon (tigh-kreh-*^y awñg*) *m* pencil sharpener

tailler (tah-*^y ay*) *v* trim, chip; carve

tailleur (tah-*^y ūrr*) *m* tailor

***taire** (tair): **se** ~ *keep quiet, *be silent

talc (tahlk) *m* talc powder

talent (tah-*lahñg*) *m* talent; faculty, gift

talon (tah-*lawñg*) *m* heel; counterfoil

tambour (tahñg-*bōōr*) *m* drum; ~ **de frein** brake drum

tamiser (tah-mee-*zay*) *v* sift, sieve

tampon (tahñg-*pawñg*) *m* tampon

tamponner (tahñg-po-*nay*) *v* bump

tandis que (tahñg-dee ker) while; whilst

tangible (tahñg-*zheebl*) *adj* tangible

tanière (tah-*n^y air*) *f* den

tante (tahñgt) *f* aunt

tapageur (tah-pah-*zhūrr*) *adj* rowdy

taper (tah-*pay*) *v* slap; ~ **à la machine** type

tapis (tah-*pee*) *m* carpet; rug, mat

taquiner (tah-kee-*nay*) *v* kid, tease

tard (taar) *adj* late

tarif (tah-*reef*) *m* rate

tarte (tahrt) *f* tart; flan

tartine (tahr-*teen*) *f* sandwich

tas (tah) *m* pile, lot; heap

tasse (tahss) *f* cup; ~ **à thé** teacup

taureau (toa-*roa*) *m* bull

taux (toa) *m* tariff; ~ **d'escompte** bankrate

taverne (tah-*vehrn*) *f* tavern

taxe (tahks) *f* tax

taxi (tahk-*see*) *m* taxi; cab; **chauffeur de** ~ taxi driver

taximètre (tahk-see-*mehtr*) *m* taximeter

tchèque (chehk) *adj* Czech

te (ter) *pron* you; yourself

technicien (tehk-nee-*s^y añg*) *m* technician

technique (tehk-*neek*) *f* technique; *adj*

technical

technologie (tehk-no-lo-*zhee*) f technology

*teindre (ta͞ngdr) v dye

teint (ta͞ng) m complexion

teinture (ta͞ng-*tewr*) f dye

teinturerie (ta͞ng-tewr-*ree*) f dry cleaner's

tel (tehl) adj such; ~ **que** such as

télé (tay-*lay*) f television

télécarte (tay-lay-*kahrt*) f phonecard

télégramme (tay-lay-*grahm*) m cable, telegram

télé-objectif (tay-lay-ob-zhehk-*teef*) m telephoto lens

téléphone (tay-lay-*fon*) m telephone; phone; **coup de** ~ telephone call

téléphoner (tay-lay-fo-*nay*) v phone; call, ring up; call up *Am*

téléski (tay-lay-*skee*) m ski lift

téléviseur (tay-lay-vee-*zūrr*) m television set

télévision (tay-lay-vee-*z*ʸ*aw͞ng*) f television; television set; ~ **par câble** cable television; ~ **par satellite** satellite television

télex (tay-*lehks*) m telex

tellement (tehl-*mah͞ng*) adv such; so

téméraire (tay-may-*rair*) adj daring

témoignage (tay-mwah-*n*ʸ*aazh*) m testimony

témoigner (tay-mwah-*ñay*) v testify

témoin (tay-*mwa͞ng*) m witness; ~ **oculaire** eye-witness

tempe (tah͞ngp) f temple

température (tah͞ng-pay-rah-*tewr*) f temperature; ~ **ambiante** room temperature

tempête (tah͞ng-*peht*) f storm; tempest, gale; ~ **de neige** snowstorm, blizzard

temple (tah͞ngpl) m temple

temporaire (tah͞ng-po-*rair*) adj temporary

temps (tah͞ng) m time; weather; **à** ~ in

time; **ces derniers** ~ lately; **de temps en** ~ now and then, occasionally; ~ **libre** spare time

tenailles (ter-*nigh*) fpl pincers pl

tendance (tah͞ng-*dah͞ngss*) f tendency; ***avoir** ~ *be inclined to, tend

tendon (tah͞ng-*daw͞ng*) m sinew, tendon

tendre¹ (tah͞ngdr) adj delicate, tender

tendre² (tah͞ngdr) v stretch; ~ **à** tend to; **tendu** tense

tendresse (tah͞ng-*drehss*) f tenderness

ténèbres (tay-*nehbr*) fpl dark; gloom

*tenir (ter-*neer*) v *hold; *keep; **se** ~ **debout** *stand; ~ **à** care for

tennis (tay-*neess*) m tennis; ~ **de table** table tennis

tension (tah͞ng-*s*ʸ*aw͞ng*) f tension; stress, strain; pressure; ~ **artérielle** blood pressure

tentation (tah͞ng-tah-*s*ʸ*aw͞ng*) f temptation

tentative (tah͞ng-tah-*teev*) f try, attempt

tente (tah͞ngt) f tent

tenter (tah͞ng-*tay*) v try; attempt; tempt

tenue (ter-*new*) f conduct; dress; ~ **de soirée** evening dress

térébenthine (tay-ray-bah͞ng-*teen*) f turpentine

terme (tehrm) m term

terminer (tehr-mee-*nay*) v finish; **se** ~ expire

terminus (tehr-mee-*newss*) m terminal

terne (tehrn) adj dull, colo(u)rless

terrain (teh-*ra͞ng*) m terrain; grounds; ~ **d'aviation** airfield; ~ **de camping** camping site; ~ **de golf** golf course; ~ **de jeux** recreation ground

terrasse (teh-*rahss*) f terrace

terre (tair) f earth; soil, ground; **à** ~ ashore; **hautes terres** uplands pl; **par** ~ down; ~ **cuite** terracotta; ~ **ferme**

mainland

terreur (teh-*rūrr*) *f* terror

terrible (tay-*reebl*) *adj* terrible; awful, dreadful, frightful

terrifiant (teh-ree-f'*ahng*) *adj* terrifying; horrible, creepy

terrifier (teh-ree-f'*ay*) *v* terrify

territoire (teh-ree-*twaar*) *m* territory

terroir (teh-*rwaar*) *m* soil

terrorisme (teh-ro-*reesm*) *m* terrorism

terroriste (teh-ro-*reest*) *m* terrorist

test (tehst) *m* test

testament (teh-stah-*mahng*) *m* will

tête (teht) *f* head

têtu (tay-*tew*) *adj* head-strong, stubborn

texte (tehkst) *m* text

textile (tehk-*steel*) *m* textile

T.G.V. (tay-zhay-*vay*) *m* high-speed train

thaïlandais (tah-ee-lah̄ng-*day*) *adj* Thai

Thaïlande (tah-ee-*lahngd*) *f* Thailand

thé (tay) *m* tea

théâtre (tay-*aatr*) *m* theater *Am*, theatre; drama; **~ de marionnettes** puppet-show; **~ de variétés** variety theatre (theater *Am*)

théière (tay-'*air*) *f* teapot

thème (tehm) *m* theme

théologie (tay-o-lo-*zhee*) *f* theology

théorie (tay-o-*ree*) *f* theory

théorique (tay-o-*reek*) *adj* theoretical

thérapie (tay-rah-*pee*) *f* therapy

thermomètre (tehr-mo-*mehtr*) *m* thermometer

thermoplongeur (tehr-moa-plawng-*zhūrr*) *m* immersion heater

thermos (tehr-*moss*) *m* thermos flask, vacuum flask

thermostat (tehr-mo-*stah*) *m* thermostat

thèse (taiz) *f* thesis

thon (tawng) *m* tuna

thym (tang) *m* thyme

ticket (tee-*kay*) *m* ticket

tiède (t'ehd) *adj* lukewarm, tepid

tien: le ~ (ler t'ang) yours

tiers (t'air) *adj* (f tierce) third

tige (teezh) *f* stem; rod

tigre (teegr) *m* tiger

tilleul (tee-'*url*) *m* limetree, lime

timbre (tangbr) *m* stamp; tone

timbre-poste (tang-brer-*post*) *m* postage stamp

timide (tee-*meed*) *adj* timid, shy

timidité (tee-mee-dee-*tay*) *f* timidity, shyness

tirage (tee-*raazh*) *m* draw; issue

tisane (tee-*zahn*) *f* infusion; tea

tire-bouchon (teer-boo-*shawng*) *m* corkscrew

tirer (tee-*ray*) *v* *draw, pull; fire, *shoot

tiroir (tee-*rwaar*) *m* drawer

tisser (tee-*say*) *v* *weave

tissu (tee-*sew*) *m* tissue; fabric, cloth, material

tissu-éponge (tee-sew-ay-*pawngz*) *m* towel(l)ing

titre (teetr) *m* title; heading

toast (toast) *m* toast

toboggan (to-bo-*gahng*) *m* slide

toi (twah) *pron* you

toile (twahl) *f* linen; **grosse ~** canvas

toilettes (twah-*leht*) *fpl* toilet, bathroom; washroom *Am*; **~ pour dames** ladies' room; powder room; **~ pour hommes** men's room

toi-même (twah-*mehm*) *pron* yourself

toit (twah) *m* roof; **~ de chaume** *m* thatched roof

tolérable (to-lay-*rahbl*) *adj* tolerable

tolérer (to-lay-*ray*) *v* *bear

tomate (to-*maht*) *f* tomato

tombe (tawngb) *f* tomb, grave

tomber (tawng-*bay*) *v* *fall

tome (tom) *m* volume

ton[1] (taw*ng*) *adj* (f ta, pl tes) your

ton[2] (taw*ng*) *m* note, tone

tonique (to-*neek*) *m* tonic; ~ **capillaire** hair tonic

tonne (ton) *f* ton

tonneau (to-*noa*) *m* barrel; cask

tonnerre (to-*nair*) *m* thunder

torche (torsh) *f* torch

torchon (tor-*shawng*) *m* tea towel, kitchen towel *Am*

tordre (tordr) *v* twist; wrench

tordu (tor-*dew*) *adj* crooked

torsion (tor-*s*ʸ*awng*) *f* twist

tort (tawr) *m* wrong; harm; **avoir ~ *be wrong; *faire du ~ harm

tortue (tor-*tew*) *f* turtle

torture (tor-*tewr*) *f* torture

torturer (tor-tew-*ray*) *v* torture

tôt (toa) *adv* early

total (to-*tahl*) *adj* total; utter, overall; *m* total

totalement (to-tahl-*mahng*) *adv* completely

totalitaire (to-tah-lee-*tair*) *adj* totalitarian

touchant (too-*shahng*) *adj* touching

toucher (too-*shay*) *v* touch; affect; *hit; cash; *m* touch

toujours (too-*zhoor*) *adv* always; ever; ~ **et encore** again and again

tour (toor) *m* turn; move; *f* tower

tourisme (too-*reesm*) *m* tourism

touriste (too-*reest*) *m/f* tourist

tourment (toor-*mahng*) *m* torment

tourmenter (toor-mahng-*tay*) *v* torment

tournant (toor-*nahng*) *m* turn, curve; turning point

tourne-disque (toor-ner-*deesk*) *m* record player

tourner (toor-*nay*) *v* turn; *spin

tournevis (toor-ner-*veess*) *m* screwdriver

tournoi (toor-*nwah*) *m* tournament

tousser (too-*say*) *v* cough

tout (too) *adj* all; every; entire; *pron* everything; **du ~** at all; **en ~** altogether; ~ **à fait** quite; ~ **à l'heure** presently; ~ **au plus** at most; ~ **ce que** whatever; ~ **de suite** immediately, straight away; ~ **droit** straight on; ~ **le monde** everybody

toutefois (toot-*fwah*) *adv* still

toux (too) *f* cough

toxique (tok-*seek*) *adj* toxic

tracas (trah-*kah*) *m* bother

tracasser (trah-kah-*say*) *v* bother

trace (trahss) *f* trace

tracer (trah-*say*) *v* trace

tracteur (trahk-*turr*) *m* tractor

tradition (trah-dee-*s*ʸ*awng*) *f* tradition

traditionnel (trah-dee-s*ʸ*o-*nehl*) *adj* traditional

traducteur (trah-dewk-*turr*) *m*, **-trice** *f* translator

traduction (trah-dewk-*s*ʸ*awng*) *f* translation

*traduire (trah-*dweer*) *v* translate

trafic (trah-*feek*) *m* traffic

tragédie (trah-zhay-*dee*) *f* tragedy; drama

tragique (trah-*zheek*) *adj* tragic

trahir (trah-*eer*) *v* betray

trahison (trah-ee-*zawng*) *f* treason

train (tra*ng*) *m* train; ~ **de marchandises** goods train; freight train *Am*; ~ **de nuit** night train; ~ **de voyageurs** passenger train; ~ **direct** through train; ~ **express** fast train; ~ **local** local train

traîneau (treh-*noa*) *m* sled(ge); sleigh

traîner (tray-*nay*) *v* drag, haul

trait (tray) *m* line; trait; ~ **de caractère** characteristic; ~ **d'union** hyphen; ~ **du visage** feature

traite (treht) *f* draft

traité (tray-*tay*) *m* treaty

traitement (treht-*mahng*) *m* treatment

traiter (tray-*tay*) v treat; handle

traître (traitr) m traitor

trajet (trah-*zhay*) m way

tram (trahm) m tram; streetcar *Am*

tranche (trahngsh) f slice

trancher (trahng-*shay*) v *cut off; settle

tranquille (trahng-*keel*) adj calm; tranquil, quiet, still

tranquillité (trahng-kee-lee-*tay*) f quietness

transaction (trahng-zahk-s*y*aw*ng*) f transaction, deal

transatlantique (trahng-zaht-lahng-*teek*) adj transatlantic

transférer (trahng-sfay-*ray*) v transfer

transformateur (trahng-sfor-mah-*tūrr*) m transformer

transformer (trahng-sfor-*may*) v transform

transition (trahng-zee-s*y*aw*ng*) f transition

transparent (trahng-spah-*rahng*) adj transparent

transpiration (trahng-spee-rah-s*y*aw*ng*) f perspiration

transpirer (trahng-spee-*ray*) v perspire

transport (trahng-*spawr*) m transportation, transport

transporter (trahng-spor-*tay*) v transport

travail (trah-*vigh*) m (pl travaux) work, labo(u)r, job; ~ **artisanal** handwork; ~ **manuel** handicraft; **travaux ménagers** housekeeping, housework

travailler (trah-vah-*y*ay) v work

travailleur (trah-vah-*y*ūrr) m, **-euse** f worker

travers: à ~ (ah trah-*vair*) through; across

traversée (trah-vehr-*say*) f passage, crossing

traverser (trah-vehr-*say*) v cross; pass through

trébucher (tray-bew-*shay*) v stumble

trèfle (trehfl) m clover; shamrock

treize (traiz) num thirteen

treizième (treh-z*y*ehm) num thirteenth

trembler (trahng-*blay*) v tremble; shiver

tremper (trahng-*pay*) v soak

trente (trahngt) num thirty

trentième (trahng-t*y*ehm) num thirtieth

trépasser (tray-pah-*say*) v pass away

très (tray) adv very

trésor (tray-*zawr*) m treasure; darling; **Trésor** treasury

triangle (tree-*ahnggl*) m triangle

triangulaire (tree-ahng-gew-*lair*) adj triangular

tribord (tree-*bawr*) m starboard

tribu (tree-*bew*) f tribe

tribunal (tree-bew-*nahl*) m court, law court

tribune (tree-*bewn*) f stand

tricher (tree-*shay*) v cheat

tricot (tree-*koa*) m knitted wear; jersey; ~ **de corps** undershirt

tricoter (tree-ko-*tay*) v *knit

trier (tree-*ay*) v sort

trimestre (tree-*mehstr*) m quarter

trimestriel (tree-meh-stree-*ehl*) adj quarterly

triomphant (tree-awng-*fahng*) adj triumphant

triomphe (tree-*awngf*) m triumph

triompher (tree-awng-*fay*) v triumph

triste (treest) adj sad

tristesse (tree-*stehss*) f sorrow, sadness

trivial (tree-v*y*ahl) adj coarse, crude

trognon (tro-ñawng) m core

trois (trwah) num three; ~ **quarts** three-quarter

troisième (trwah-z*y*ehm) num third

tromper (trawng-*pay*) v deceive; **se ~** *be mistaken; err

tromperie (trawng-*pree*) *f* deceit

trompette (trawng-*peht*) *f* trumpet

tronc (trawng) *m* trunk

trône (troan) *m* throne

trop (troa) *adv* too

tropical (tro-pee-*kahl*) *adj* tropical

tropiques (tro-*peek*) *mpl* tropics *pl*

troquer (tro-*kay*) *v* swap

trottoir (tro-*twaar*) *m* pavement, sidewalk *Am*

trou (troo) *m* hole

trouble (troobl) *adj* turbid; dubious; *m* perturbation

troubler (troo-*blay*) *v* disturb

troupeau (troo-*poa*) *m* herd; flock

troupes (troop) *fpl* troops *pl*

trousseau (troo-*soa*) *m* kit

trousse de secours (trooss der ser-*koor*) first aid kit

trouver (troo-*vay*) *v* *find; *come across; consider

truc (trewk) *m* trick

truite (trweet) *f* trout

tu (tew) *pron* you

tube (tewb) *m* tube; ~ **de plongée** snorkel

tuberculose (tew-behr-kew-*loaz*) *f* tuberculosis

tuer (tway) *v* kill

tuile (tweel) *f* tile

tulipe (tew-*leep*) *f* tulip

tumeur (tew-*murr*) *f* tumo(u)r; growth

tunique (tew-*neek*) *f* tunic

Tunisie (tew-nee-*zee*) *f* Tunisia

tunisien (tew-nee-z^y*ang*) *adj* Tunisian

tunnel (tew-*nehl*) *m* tunnel

turbine (tewr-*been*) *f* turbine

turc (tewrk) *adj* Turkish; **Turc** *m* Turk

Turquie (tewr-*kee*) *f* Turkey

tuteur (tew-*turr*) *m* guardian, tutor

tuyau (twee-^y*oa*) *m* tube, pipe; ~ **d'échappement** exhaust

tympan (tang-*pahng*) *m* eardrum

type (teep) *m* type; guy, chap

typhoïde (tee-fo-*eed*) *f* typhoid

typique (tee-*peek*) *adj* typical

U

ulcère (ewl-*sair*) *m* ulcer; ~ **à l'estomac** gastric ulcer

ultime (ewl-*teem*) *adj* ultimate

ultra-violet (ewl-trah-v^yo-*lay*) *adj* ultraviolet

un (urng) *art* (f une) a *art*; *num* one; **l'un l'autre** each other; **l'un ou l'autre** either; **ni l'un ni l'autre** neither

unanime (ew-nah-*neem*) *adj* unanimous

uni (ew-*nee*) *adj* joint; smooth

uniforme (ew-nee-*form*) *m* uniform; *adj* uniform

unilatéral (ew-nee-lah-tay-*rahl*) *adj* one-sided

union (ew-n^y*awng*) *f* union

unique (ew-*neek*) *adj* unique; sole

uniquement (ew-neek-*mahng*) *adv* exclusively

unir (ew-*neer*) *v* unite

unité (ew-nee-*tay*) *f* unity; unit; ~ **monétaire** monetary unit

univers (ew-nee-*vair*) *m* universe

universel (ew-nee-vehr-*sehl*) *adj* universal; all-round

université (ew-nee-vehr-see-*tay*) *f* university

urbain (ewr-*bang*) *adj* urban

urgence (ewr-*zhahngss*) *f* urgency; emergency

urgent (ewr-*zhahng*) *adj* pressing, urgent

urine (ew-*reen*) *f* urine

Uruguay (ew-rew-*gay*) *m* Uruguay

uruguayen (ew-rew-gay-*yang*) *adj* Uruguayan

usage (ew-*zaazh*) *m* usage

usager (ew-zah-*zhay*) *m* user

user (ew-*zay*) *v* use up; wear out; **usé** worn; threadbare, worn-out

usine (ew-*zeen*) *f* factory; mill, plant, works *pl*; ~ **à gaz** gasworks

ustensile (ew-stahng-*seel*) *m* utensil

usuel (ew-*zwehl*) *adj* customary

utile (ew-*teel*) *adj* useful

utilisable (ew-tee-lee-*zahbl*) *adj* usable

utilisateur (ew-tee-lee-zah-*turr*) *m* consumer

utilisation (ew-tee-lee-zah-*s'awng*) *f* utilization

utiliser (ew-tee-lee-*zay*) *v* utilize, employ

utilité (ew-tee-lee-*tay*) *f* utility, use

V

vacance (vah-*kahngss*) *f* vacancy; **vacances** holiday

vacant (vah-*kahng*) *adj* vacant, unoccupied

vacarme (vah-*kahrm*) *m* noise, racket

vaccination (vahk-see-nah-*s'awng*) *f* vaccination

vacciner (vahk-see-*nay*) *v* vaccinate

vache (vahsh) *f* cow

vaciller (vah-see-*yay*) *v* falter

vagabond (vah-gah-*bawng*) *m* tramp

vagabonder (vah-gah-bawng-*day*) *v* tramp, roam

vague (vahg) *f* wave; *adj* vague; faint, obscure

vaillance (vah-*yahngss*) *f* courage

vain (vang) *adj* vain; **en** ~ in vain

***vaincre** (vangkr) *v* *overcome; conquer, defeat

vainqueur (vang-*kurr*) *m* winner

vaisseau (vay-*soa*) *m* vessel; ~ **sanguin** blood vessel

vaisselle (veh-*sehl*) *f* crockery; dishes *pl*; ***faire la** ~ wash up

valable (vah-*lahbl*) *adj* valid

valeur (vah-*lurr*) *f* value, worth; **sans** ~ worthless

valise (vah-*leez*) *f* case, bag, suitcase

vallée (vah-*lay*) *f* valley

***valoir** (vah-*lwaar*) *v* *be worth; ~ **la peine** *be worth-while

valse (vahls) *f* waltz

vanille (vah-*neey*) *f* vanilla

vaniteux (vah-nee-*tur*) *adj* vain

vanneau (vah-*noa*) *m* peewit

vanter (vahng-*tay*): **se** ~ boast

vapeur (vah-*purr*) *f* steam; vapo(u)r

vaporisateur (vah-po-ree-zah-*turr*) *m* atomizer

variable (vah-r'ahbl) *adj* variable

variation (vah-r'ah-s'awng) *f* variation

varice (vah-*reess*) *f* varicose vein

varicelle (vah-ree-*sehl*) *f* chickenpox

varier (vah-r'ay) *v* vary

variété (vah-r'ay-tay) *f* variety

variole (vah-r'ol) *f* smallpox

vase (vaaz) *m* vase; *f* mud *m*

vaseline (vah-zleen) *f* vaseline

vaste (vahst) *adj* large; wide, broad, vast; extensive

vautour (voa-toor) *m* vulture

veau (voa) *m* calf; veal; calf skin

végétarien (vay-zhay-tah-*r^{y}ang*) *m* vegetarian

végétation (vay-zhay-tah-*s^{y}awng*) *f* vegetation

véhicule (vay-ee-*kewl*) *m* vehicle

veille (*vay^y*) *f* day before

veiller (*vay-^{y}ay*) *v* stay awake; ~ **sur** watch over

veine (vain) *f* vein

vélo (vay-*loa*) *m* bicycle, cycle

vélomoteur (vay-loa-mo-*tūrr*) *m* motorbike *Am*, moped

velours (ver-*loor*) *m* velvet; ~ **côtelé** corduroy; ~ **de coton** cotton velvet

vendable (vahng-*dahbl*) *adj* saleable

vendange (vahng-*dahngzh*) *f* vintage

vendeur (vahng-*dūrr*) *m*, **-euse** *f* vendor; seller; sales clerk *Am*, shop assistant

vendre (*vahngdr*) *v* *sell; **à** ~ for sale

vendredi (vahng-drer-*dee*) *m* Friday

vénéneux (vay-nay-*nur*) *adj* poisonous

vénérable (vay-nay-*rahbl*) *adj* venerable

Venezuela (vay-nay-zway-*lah*) *m* Venezuela

vénézuélien (vay-nay-zway-*l^{y}ang*) *adj* Venezuelan

vengeance (vahng-*zhahngss*) *f* revenge

venger (vahng-*zhay*) *v* avenge

***venir** (ver-*neer*) *v* *come; ***faire** ~ *send for

vent (vahng) *m* wind; **coup de** ~ blow

vente (*vahngt*) *f* sale; ~ **aux enchères** auction; ~ **en gros** wholesale

venteux (vahng-*tur*) *adj* windy, gusty

ventilateur (vahng-tee-lah-*tūrr*) *m* fan, ventilator

ventilation (vahng-tee-lah-*s^{y}awng*) *f* ventilation

ventiler (vahng-tee-*lay*) *v* ventilate

ventre (*vahngtr*) *m* belly

venue (ver-*new*) *f* arrival

ver (vair) *m* worm

véranda (vay-rahng-*dah*) *f* veranda

verbal (vehr-*bahl*) *adj* verbal

verbe (vehrb) *m* verb

verdict (vehr-*deekt*) *m* verdict

verger (vehr-*zhay*) *m* orchard

véridique (vay-ree-*deek*) *adj* truthful

vérifier (vay-ree-*f^{y}ay*) *v* verify; check

véritable (vay-ree-*tahbl*) *adj* real

vérité (vay-ree-*tay*) *f* truth

vernir (vehr-*neer*) *v* varnish; glaze

vernis (vehr-*nee*) *m* varnish; lacquer; ~ **à ongle** nail polish

verre (vair) *m* glass; ~ **de couleur** stained glass; ~ **grossissant** magnifying glass; **verres de contact** contact lenses

verrou (veh-*roo*) *m* bolt

vers (vair) *m* verse; *prep* towards; at; ~ **le bas** downwards; ~ **le haut** up

versant (vehr-*sahng*) *m* slope

versement (vehr-ser-*mahng*) *m* deposit, remittance

verser (vehr-*say*) *v* pour; *shed

version (vehr-*s^{y}awng*) *f* version

vert (vair) *adj* green

vertical (vehr-tee-*kahl*) *adj* vertical

vertige (vehr-*teezh*) *m* dizziness, giddiness

vertu (vehr-*tew*) *f* virtue

vessie (vay-*see*) *f* bladder

veste (vehst) *f* jacket; ~ **de sport** blazer

vestiaire (vehss-t^{y}air*) *m* cloakroom; checkroom *Am*

vestibule (veh-stee-*bewl*) *m* hall, lobby

veston (veh-*stawng*) *m* jacket; ~ **sport** sports jacket

vêtements (veht-*mahng*) *mpl* clothes *pl*; ~ **de sport** sportswear

vétérinaire (vay-tay-ree-*nair*) *m/f* veterinary surgeon

***vêtir** (vay-*teer*) *v* dress

veuf (vurf) *m* widower

veuve (vūrv) f widow

via (vee-*ah*) prep via

viaduc (v^{y}ah-*dewk*) m viaduct

viande (v^{y}ah$\overline{ng}$d) f meat

vibration (vee-brah-s^{y}aw$\overline{ng}$) f vibration

vibrer (vee-*bray*) v vibrate; tremble

vicaire (vee-*kair*) m vicar

vice-président (vee-spray-zee-*dah$\overline{ng}$*) m vice president

vicieux (vee-s^{y}ur) adj vicious

victime (veek-*teem*) f victim; casualty

victoire (veek-*twaar*) f victory •

vide (veed) adj empty; m vacuum

vider (vee-*day*) v empty

vie (vee) f life; lifetime; **en ~** alive; **~ privée** privacy

vieillard (v^{y}eh-^{y}aar) m old man

vieillesse (v^{y}eh-^{y}ehss) f age, old age

vieilli (v^{y}ay-^{y}ee) adj ancient

vieillot (v^{y}eh-^{y}oa) adj quaint

vierge (v^{y}ehrzh) f virgin

vieux (v^{y}ur) adj (vieil; f vieille) old; aged, ancient

vif (veef) adj vivid; intense, brisk, lively

vigilant (vee-zhee-*lah$\overline{ng}$*) adj vigilant

vigne (veeñ) f vine

vignoble (vee-*ñobl*) m vineyard

vigoureux (vee-goo-*rur*) adj vigorous

vigueur (vee-*gūrr*) f strength

vilain (vee-*la$\overline{ng}$*) adj bad

villa (vee-*lah*) f villa; cottage

village (vee-*laazh*) m village

ville (veel) f town

vin (va$\overline{ng}$) m wine

vinaigre (vee-*naigr*) m vinegar

vingt (va$\overline{ng}$) num twenty

vingtième (va$\overline{ng}$-t^{y}ehm) num twentieth

violation (v^{y}o-lah-s^{y}aw$\overline{ng}$) f violation

violence (v^{y}o-*lah$\overline{ng}$ss*) f violence

violent (v^{y}o-*lah$\overline{ng}$*) adj violent; fierce, severe

violer (v^{y}o-*lay*) v assault, rape

violet (v^{y}o-*lay*) adj violet

violette (v^{y}o-*leht*) f violet

violon (v^{y}o-*law$\overline{ng}$*) m violin

virage (vee-*raazh*) m turning, bend

virer (vee-*ray*) v turn

virgule (veer-*gewl*) f comma

vis (veess) f screw

visa (vee-*zah*) m visa

visage (vee-*zaazh*) m face

viser (vee-*zay*) v aim at

viseur (vee-*zūrr*) m viewfinder

visibilité (vee-zee-bee-lee-*tay*) f visibility

visible (vee-*zeebl*) adj visible

vision (vee-z^{y}aw$\overline{ng}$) f vision

visite (vee-*zeet*) f visit; call; **rendre ~ à** call on

visiter (vee-zee-*tay*) v visit

visiteur (vee-zee-*tūrr*) m visitor

vital (vee-*tahl*) adj vital

vitamine (vee-tah-*meen*) f vitamin

vite (veet) adv quickly

vitesse (vee-*tehss*) f speed; gear; **en ~** in a hurry; **indicateur de ~** speedometer; **limitation de ~** speed limit; **~ de croisière** cruising speed

vitre (veetr) f window-pane

vitrine (vee-*treen*) f showcase, shopwindow

vivant (vee-*vah$\overline{ng}$*) adj alive; live

*vivre (veevr) v live; experience

vocabulaire (vo-kah-bew-*lair*) m vocabulary

vocal (vo-*kahl*) adj vocal

vœu (vur) m desire; vow

voici (vwah-*see*) adv here is

voie (vwah) f way; track; lane; **~ d'eau** waterway; **~ ferrée** railway line; railroad line Am

voilà (vwah-*lah*) adv there is; here you are

voile (vwahl) f sail; m veil

*voir (vwaar) v *see

voisin (vwah-*zang*) *m* neighbo(u)r

voisinage (vwah-zee-*naazh*) *m* vicinity, neighbo(u)rhood

voisine (vwah-*zeen*) *f* neighbo(u)r

voiture (vwah-*tewr*) *f* car; carriage; ~ d'enfant pram; ~ de sport sports car; ~ Pullman Pullman

voix (vwah) *f* voice; à haute ~ aloud

vol (vol) *m* flight; robbery, theft; ~ charter charter flight; ~ de nuit night flight; ~ de retour return flight

volaille (vo-*ligh*) *f* poultry, fowl

volant (vo-*lahng*) *m* steering wheel

volcan (vol-*kahng*) *m* volcano

voler (vo-*lay*) *v* *fly; *steal; rob

volet (vo-*lay*) *m* shutter

voleur (vo-*lurr*) *m* thief; robber

volontaire (vo-lawng-*tair*) *adj* voluntary; *m* volunteer

volonté (vo-lawng-*tay*) *f* will; willpower

volontiers (vo-lawng-t*'*ay) *adv* willingly, gladly

volt (volt) *m* volt

voltage (vol-*taazh*) *m* voltage

volume (vo-*lewm*) *m* volume

volumineux (voa-lew-mee-*nur*) *adj* bulky, big

vomir (vo-*meer*) *v* vomit

vote (vot) *m* vote; droit de ~ franchise

voter (vo-*tay*) *v* vote

votre (votr) *adj* (pl vos) your

***vouloir** (voo-*lwaar*) *v* want; *will; en ~ à resent; ~ dire *mean

vous (voo) *pron* you; yourselves; vous-même *pron* yourself; vousmêmes *pron* yourselves

voûte (voot) *f* vault, arch

voyage (vwah-*'aazh*) *m* journey; trip; voyage; ~ d'affaires business trip; ~ de retour return journey

voyager (vwah-*'*ah-*zhay*) *v* travel; ~ en auto motor

voyageur (vwah-*'*ah-*zhurr*) *m*, -euse *f* travel(l)er

voyelle (vwah-*'ehl*) *f* vowel

vrai (vray) *adj* true; very

vraiment (vray-*mahng*) *adv* really

vraisemblable (vray-sahng-*blahbl*) *adj* probable

vu (vew) *prep* considering

vue (vew) *f* sight; view; point de ~ point of view

vulgaire (vewl-*gair*) *adj* vulgar

vulnérable (vewl-nay-*rahbl*) *adj* vulnerable

W

wagon (vah-*gawng*) *m* carriage; wag(g)on, coach; passenger car *Am*;

wagon-lit sleeping car; **wagon-restaurant** dining car

Y

y (ee) *pron* there; to it

yacht (ʸot) *m* yacht

Z

zèbre (zaibr) *m* zebra
zélé (zay-*lay*) *adj* zealous
zèle (zehl) *m* zeal
zéro (zay-*roa*) *m* zero; nought
zinc (zan̄gg) *m* zinc
zodiaque (zo-dᵉ*ahk*) *m* zodiac

zone (zōān) *f* zone; area; ~ **de
stationnement** parking zone; ~
industrielle industrial area
zoo (zoa) *m* zoo
zoom (zoom) *m* zoom lens

Menu Reader
Food

à la, à l', au, aux in the manner of, as in, with

abats, abattis giblets, innards

abricot apricot

agneau lamb

aiglefin haddock

ail garlic

ailloli garlic mayonnaise

airelle a kind of cranberry

alouette sans tête slice of veal rolled and generally stuffed with minced meat, garlic and parsley

(à l')alsacienne usually garnished with sauerkraut, ham and sausages

amande almond

amuse-gueule appetizer

ananas pineapple

anchois anchovy

(à l')ancienne old style; usually with wine-flavoured cream sauce of mushrooms, onions or shallots

(à l')andalouse usually with green peppers, aubergines and tomatoes

andouille a kind of tripe sausage

andouillette smaller kind of tripe sausage

(à l')anglaise 1) usually boiled or steamed vegetables, especially potatoes 2) breaded and fried vegetables, meat, fish or fowl

anguille eel

~ au vert eel braised in a white sauce served with minced parsley and other greens

anis aniseed

artichaut (globe) artichoke

asperge asparagus

assiette plate

~ anglaise cold meat (US cold cuts)

~ de charcuterie assorted pork and other meat products

assorti assorted

aubergine aubergine (US eggplant)

ballottine (de volaille) boned fowl which is stuffed, rolled, cooked and served in gelatine

banane banana

bar bass

barbue brill

basilic basil

béarnaise sauce of egg-yolk, butter, vinegar, shallots, tarragon and white wine

bécasse woodcock

béchamel white sauce

beignet fritter generally filled with fruit, vegetables or meat

(à la) Bercy butter sauce of white wine and shallots

betterave beetroot

beurre butter

~ blanc white butter sauce of shallots, vinegar and white wine

~ maître d'hôtel butter with chopped parsley and lemon juice

~ noir browned butter sauce of vinegar and parsley

bifteck beef steak

(à la) bigarade brown sauce generally with oranges, sugar and vinegar

biscotte rusk (US zwieback)

biscuit biscuit (US cookie)

bisque cream soup of lobster or crayfish (US chowder)

blanc de volaille boned breast of fowl

blanchaille whitebait

blanquette de veau veal stew in white sauce

(au) bleu 1) of fish (usually trout), boiled very fresh 2) of cheese, blue-

veined 3) of meat, very underdone
(US rare)

bœuf beef

~ bourguignon chunks of beef
stewed in red wine with onions,
bacon and mushrooms

~ en daube larded chunks of beef
marinated in red wine with
vegetables and stewed

~ miro(n)ton cold boiled beef or beef
stew with onion sauce

~ mode larded chunks of beef braised
in red wine with carrots and onions

bolet boletus mushroom

bombe glacée moulded ice-cream
dessert

(à la) bordelaise red wine sauce with
shallots, beef marrow and boletus
mushrooms

bouchée à la reine vol-au-vent; puff-
pastry shell filled with meat,
sweetbreads or seafood and
sometimes mushrooms

boudin black pudding (US blood
sausage)

bouillabaisse assorted fish and
shellfish stewed in white wine, garlic,
saffron and olive oil

bouilli 1) boiled 2) boiled beef

bouillon bouillon, broth, stock

(à la) bourguignonne button
mushrooms, pearl onions or shallots
braised in rich red wine

braisé braised

brandade (de morue) prepared cod
with cream, oil and garlic

brie white, mellow cheese

brioche small roll or cake

(à la) broche (on a) spit

brochet pike

(en) brochette (cooked on a) skewer

cabillaud fresh cod

café glacé coffee-flavoured ice-cream
dessert

caille quail

camembert soft cheese with a thin
white rind and a yellow interior

canard (caneton) duck (duckling)

~ à l'orange roast duck braised with
oranges and orange liqueur

cannelle cinnamon

cantal smooth, firm cheese not unlike
Cheddar

câpre caper

carbonnade charcoal-grilled meat

~ flamande beef slices, onions and
herbs braised in beer

cardon cardoon (vegetable)

carotte carrot

carottes Vichy steamed carrots

carpe carp

carré loin, rack

~ de l'Est usually square-shaped soft,
mild, fermented cheese

carrelet plaice

carte des vins wine list

cassis blackcurrant

cassoulet toulousain butter-bean
stew of goose or with mutton, pork
and sometimes sausage

céleri celery (usually celery root)

~ en branche branch celery

~-rave celeriac, celery root

cèpe boletus mushroom

cerfeuil chervil

cerise cherry

cervelle brains

champignon mushroom

~ de Paris button mushroom

chanterelle chanterelle mushroom

charbonnade charcoal-grilled meat

charcuterie various kinds of cold pork
products

charlotte fruit dessert (usually apples)
made in a deep, round mould

chasse venison

chasseur hunter's style; sauce of
mushrooms, tomatoes, wine and

garlic herbs

chateaubriand thick slice of beef taken from the fillet

chaud warm

chaudrée fish and seafood stew, often with garlic, herbs, onions and white wine

chausson aux pommes apple dumpling (US turnover)

chevreuil deer

chicorée endive (US chicory)

chou cabbage

~ **de Bruxelles** brussels sprouts

~ **à la crème** cream puff

~**-fleur** cauliflower

~ **rouge** red cabbage

choucroute sauerkraut

~ **garnie** usually with ham, bacon and sausage

ciboulette chive

citron lemon

civet de lapin (lièvre) jugged rabbit (hare)

clafoutis fruit baked in pancake batter, brandy often added

clémentine pipless (US seedless) tangerine

cochon de lait suck(l)ing pig

(en) cocotte casserole

cœur heart

~ **d'artichaut** artichoke heart

(à la) Colbert dipped in egg batter and breadcrumbs, fried

colin hake

concombre cucumber

confit d'oie pieces of goose preserved in its own fat

confiture jam

consommation general word for drinks

consommé clear soup served hot or cold

~ **Célestine** with chicken and noodles

~ **aux cheveux d'ange** with thin noodles

~ **Colbert** with poached eggs, spring vegetables

~ **julienne** with shredded vegetables

~ **madrilène** cold and flavoured with tomatoes

~ **princesse** with diced chicken and asparagus tips

~ **aux vermicelles** with thin noodles

contre-filet sirloin

coq au vin chicken stewed in red wine with mushrooms, bacon, onions and herbs

coquelet cockerel

coquillage shellfish

coquille Saint-Jacques scallop gratinéed in its shell

corbeille de fruits basket of assorted fruit

cornichon small gherkin (US pickle)

côte chop or rib

~ **de bœuf** rib of beef

~ **de veau** veal chop

côtelette cutlet, chop

~ **d'agneau** lamb chop

~ **de porc** pork chop

coupe a metal or glass dish usually for individual desserts

~ **glacée** ice-cream dessert

courgette a long vegetable with a dark green skin (US zucchini)

couvert cover charge

~**, vin et service compris** price includes wine, service and cover charges

crabe crab

crème 1) a dessert with cream or a creamy dessert

~ **anglaise** custard

~ **caramel** caramel custard

~ **Chantilly** whipped cream

~ **glacée** ice-cream

crème 2) a creamy soup

crêpe large, paper-thin pancake

~**Suzette** pancake with orange sauce, flamed with brandy and often orange liqueur

cresson (water)cress

crevette shrimp

croissant crescent-shaped flaky roll (usually served for breakfast)

croque-monsieur grilled or baked ham-and-cheese sandwich

croustade pie, pastry shell filled with fish, seafood, meat or vegetables

(en) croûte (in a) pastry crust

croûton small piece of bread, toasted or fried

cru raw

crudités raw vegetables usually served sliced, grated or diced as an hors d'oeuvre

crustacé shellfish

cuisse leg or thigh

cuisses de grenouilles frogs' legs

cuit cooked

  bien ~ well-done

cumin caraway, cumin

darne thick fillet of fish, usually of salmon

datte date

daurade gilt-head

déjeuner lunch

délice often used to describe a dessert speciality of the chef

demi half

  ~**-sel** soft cream cheese, slightly salty

demoiselle de Cherbourg small rock lobster

(à la) dieppoise garnish of mussels and shrimp served in white-wine sauce

dinde, dindon turkey

dindonneau young turkey

dîner dinner

diplomate moulded custard dessert with crystallized fruit and lined with sponge fingers steeped in liqueur

dodine de canard boned duck, rolled, stuffed, sometimes served cold in gelatine

(à la) du Barry garnish of cauliflower and cheese sauce, gratinéed

(aux) duxelles with minced mushrooms sautéed with butter, white wine and herbs

échalote shallot

écrevisse (freshwater) crayfish

  ~ **à la nage** simmered in white wine, aromatic vegetables and herbs

églefin haddock

émincé slices of cooked meat in gravy or thick cream sauce

endive chicory (US endive)

  ~ **à la bruxelloise** steamed chicory rolled in a slice of ham

entrecôte rib-eye steak

entrée dish served between the hors d'oeuvre or soup and the main course; the first course in a smaller dinner (US starter)

entremets small dish served before cheese; today it often means dessert

épaule shoulder

éperlan smelt

épice spice

épicé hot, peppered

épinard spinach

escalope de veau veal scallop, thin slice of veal

escalope viennoise wiener schnitzel; breaded veal cutlet

escargot snail

estouffade braised or steamed in tightly sealed vessel with minimum of cooking liquid

estragon tarragon

étuvé steamed, stewed with minimum of cooking liquid

faisan pheasant

farci stuffed

fenouil fennel

féra dace (fish)

fève broad bean
filet meat or fish fillet
  ~ de bœuf fillet of beef (US tenderloin)
  ~ mignon small round veal or pork fillet
  ~ de sole fillet of sole
(à la) financière rich sauce of pike dumplings, truffles, mushrooms, Madeira wine, sometimes with olives and crayfish
(aux) fines herbes with herbs
(à la) flamande Flemish style; usually a garnish of braised potatoes, carrots, cabbage, turnips, bacon and sausage (sometimes simmered in beer)
flambé dish flamed usually with brandy
flétan halibut
foie liver
  ~ gras goose or duck liver
fond d'artichaut artichocke heart (US bottom)
fondue (au fromage) melted-cheese mixture in a pot into which pieces of bread are dipped
fondue bourguignonne bite-size pieces of meat dipped into boiling oil at the table and eaten with a variety of sauces
fondue chinoise paper-thin slices of beef dipped into boiling bouillon and eaten with a variety of sauces
(à la) forestière forester's style; generally sautéed in butter with morel mushrooms, potatoes and bacon
(au) four baked
frais, fraîche fresh
fraise strawberry
  ~ des bois wild strawberry
framboise raspberry
frappé chilled, iced
friand patty with meat filling

fricandeau braised, larded veal
fricassée browned pieces of meat braised with seasonings and vegetables and served in a thick sauce
frit fried
frites chips (US french fries)
friture (de poisson) fried fish
fromage cheese
  ~ frais fresh curd cheese
  ~ de tête brawn (US headcheese)
fruit confit candied fruit
fruits de mer mussels, oysters, clams
fumé smoked
galette flat, plain cake
garbure thick cabbage soup made of salted pork, spices and *confit d'oie*
garni garnished
(avec) garniture (with) vegetables
gâteau cake, flan, tart
gaufre waffle
gaufrette small, crisp, sweet wafer
(en) gelée jellied
gélinotte hazel-hen, hazel-grouse (US prairie chicken)
gibelotte de lapin rabbit stew in wine sauce
gibier game
  ~ de saison game in season
gigot d'agneau leg of lamb
girolle chanterelle mushroom
glace ice-cream
  ~ (à la) napolitaine ice-cream layers of different flavours
glacé iced, glazed
goujon gudgeon
gras-double tripe simmered in wine and onions
(au) gratin browned with breadcrumbs or cheese
gratin dauphinois sliced potatoes gratinéed in the oven with eggs, cream and cheese
gratin de fruits de mer shellfish in

heavy cream sauce and gratinéed

grillade grilled meat

grillé grilled

grive thrush

groseille à maquereau gooseberry

groseille rouge redcurrant

gruyère a hard cheese rich in flavour

haché minced, hashed

hachis mince, hash

hareng herring

haricot bean

~ **de mouton** stew of mutton with beans and potatoes

~ **vert** French bean (US green bean)

Henri IV artichoke hearts garnished with béarnaise sauce

hollandaise sauce of egg-yolks, butter and lemon juice or vinegar

homard lobster

~ **à l'américaine** (or **à l'armoricaine**) lobster flamed in brandy, simmered in white wine with garlic, tomatoes and herbs

~ **cardinal** flamed in brandy, diced, served in its shell with truffles and chopped mushrooms and gratinéed

~ **Newburg** cut into sections, cooked in brandy and fish stock

~ **Thermidor** simmered in white wine, sautéed in butter with mushrooms, herbs, spices, mustard, flamed in brandy and gratinéed with cheese**huile** oil

huître oyster

~ **belon** flat, pinkish oyster

~ **de claire** similar to bluepoint oyster

~ **portugaise** small, fat oyster

jambon ham

~ **de Bayonne** raw, with a slightly salty flavour

~ **cru** raw, cured

~ **à l'os** baked ham

jardinière cooked assorted vegetables

jarret shank, shin

julienne vegetables cut into fine strips

jus gravy, juice

lamproie lamprey

langouste spiny lobster

langoustine Norway lobster, prawn, crawfish

langue tongue

lapin rabbit

lard bacon

légume vegetable

lentille lentil

levraut young hare, leveret

lièvre hare

limande dab

livarot small, round cheese from Normandy

longe de veau loin of veal

(à la) lorraine usually braised in red wine with red cabbage

loup (de mer) (sea) bass

(à la) lyonnaise generally sautéed with onions

macédoine mixed, diced vegetables or fruit

(au) madère with Madeira wine

maigre lean

maïs maize (US corn)

maître d'hôtel sautéed in butter with chopped parsley and lemon juice

maquereau mackerel

marcassin young boar

marchand de vin red wine sauce seasoned with shallots

mariné marinated

marinière sailor's style; garnish of mussels with other seafood simmered in white wine and spices

marjolaine marjoram

maroilles strong, semi-hard cheese from Picardy

marron chestnut

matelote freshwater-fish stew (especially of eel) with wine, onions, mushrooms

médaillon small, round cut of meat

menthe mint

menu in France, generally means *menu à prix fixe*, set meal at a fixed price

merguez very spicy sausage

merlan whiting

merluche dried hake

meunière floured and sautéed in butter with lemon juice and chopped parsley

miel honey

mijoté simmered

millefeuille flaky pastry with cream filling (US napoleon)

(à la) Mirabeau with anchovies, olives, tarragon

mirabelle small yellow plum

(à la) mode in the style (of); often means made according to a local recipe

moelle marrow (bone)

morille morel mushroom

Mornay *béchamel* sauce with cheese

moule mussel

moules marinière mussels simmered in white wine with shallots, thyme and parsley

mousse 1) any frothy cream dish 2) chopped or pounded meat or fish with eggs and cream

mousseline 1) frothy mixture containing cream, usually whipped 2) variation of hollandaise sauce with whipped cream

moutarde mustard

mouton mutton

munster soft cheese with a pungent flavour

mûre mulberry or blackberry

myrtille bilberry (US blueberry)

nature/au naturel plain, without dressing, sauce or stuffing

navarin mutton stew with turnips

navet turnip

(à la/en) neige snow-like; i.e. with beaten egg-whites

(à la) niçoise Riviera style; usually with garlic, anchovies, olives, onions, tomatoes

(à la) nivernaise a garnish of carrots, onions, potatoes

noisette 1) hazelnut 2) boneless round piece of meat usually taken from loin or rib

noix walnut

~ **de coco** coconut

~ **(de) muscade** nutmeg

~ **de veau** pope's eye of veal

(à la) normande usually cooked with gudgeon, shrimps, mushrooms, cream and sometimes truffles

nouilles noodles

œuf egg

~ **brouillé** scrambled

~ **à la coque** soft-boiled

~ **dur** hard-boiled

~ **farci** stuffed

~ **en gelée** lightly poached and served in gelatine

~ **au jambon** ham and eggs

~ **au/sur le plat** fried

~ **poché** poached

~ **Rossini** with truffles and Madeira wine

oie goose

oignon onion

omble-chevalier freshwater fish of the char family

omelette omelet

~ **norvégienne** ice-cream dessert covered with beaten egg-whites, quickly browned in oven and served flaming (US baked Alaska)

ortolan small game bird like a finch

os bone

~ **à moelle** marrow bone

oseille sorrel

oursin sea urchin
pain bread
palourde clam
pamplemousse grapefruit
panaché mixed; two or more kinds of something
pané breaded, rolled in breadcrumbs
(en) papillote encased in greased paper and baked
parfait ice-cream dessert
Parmentier containing potatoes
pastèque watermelon
pâté 1) a moulded pastry case which holds meat or fish 2) a thickish paste often of liver (contained in an earthenware dish)
  ~ ardennais a purée of pork and seasonings encased in a loaf of bread, served in slices
  ~ de campagne strongly flavoured with a variety of meat
  ~ en croûte in a pastry crust
  ~ de foie gras goose (or duck) liver paste
pâtes noodles, macaroni, spaghetti
paupiette (de veau) veal bird, thin slice of veal rolled around stuffing
(à la) paysanne country style; usually containing various vegetables
pêche peach
perche perch
perdreau young partridge
perdrix partridge
(à la) périgourdine preparation with truffles
persil parsley
petit small
  ~ déjeuner breakfast
  ~ four small, fancy cake (US fancy cookie)
  ~ pain roll
  ~ pois green pea
  ~ salé (au chou) salt pork (with cabbage)

~suisse a mild-flavoured, double-cream cheese
pied de porc pig's trotter (US pig's foot)
pigeonneau squab
piment pimento
pintade guinea hen
piperade omelet with green peppers, garlic, tomatoes, ham
piquant sharp-tasting, spicy (e.g. of a sauce)
pissaladière onion and anchovy tart with black olives
plat plate
  ~ du jour speciality of the day
  ~ principal main dish
plateau de fromages cheese board
plie plaice
poché poached
(à la) poêle fried
(à) point medium
pointe d'asperge asparagus tip
poire pear
  ~ à la Condé served hot on a bed of vanilla-flavoured rice
  ~ Belle Hélène with vanilla ice-cream and chocolate sauce
poireau leek
pois pea
  ~ chiche chick pea
poisson fish
  ~ d'eau douce freshwater fish
  ~ de mer saltwater fish
poitrine breast
  ~ de bœuf brisket
(au) poivre (with) pepper
poivron sweet pepper
pomme apple
pommes (de terre) potatoes
  ~ allumettes matchstick potatoes
  ~ chips crisps (US potato chips)
  ~ dauphine potatoes mashed in butter and egg-yolks, mixed in seasoned flour and deep-fried

~ **duchesse** potatoes mashed with butter and egg-yolks

~ **en robe des champs** potatoes in their jackets

~ **frites** chips (US french fries)

~ **mousseline** mashed potatoes

~ **nature** boiled, steamed potatoes

~ **nouvelles** new potatoes

~ **vapeur** steamed, boiled potatoes

pont-l'évêque soft cheese, firmer and yellower than camembert

porc pork

port-salut soft cheese, yellow in colour, mild in taste

potage soup

~ **bonne femme** potato, leek, mushroom, onion, rice and sometimes bacon

~ **cancalais** fish consommé (often with oysters or other seafood)

~ **Condé** mashed red beans

~ **Crécy** carrots

~ **cultivateur** mixed vegetables and bacon or pork

~ **du Barry** cream of cauliflower

~ **julienne** vegetables

~ **Longchamp** peas, sorrel and chervil

~ **Saint-Germain** split-pea, leek and onion

~ **soissonnais** haricot bean

pot-au-feu 1) stockpot of beef, potatoes and aromatic vegetables 2) stew

potée boiled pork or beef with vegetables, especially cabbage

potiron pumpkin

poularde fat pullet

~ **de Bresse** grain-fed; reputedly the finest available

~ **demi-deuil** with truffles inserted under the skin and simmered in broth

poule hen

~ **au pot** stewed with vegetables

~ **au riz** stewed in bouillon and served with rice

poulet chicken

~ **Marengo** sautéed in olive oil, cooked with white wine, tomatoes, garlic, shallots and mushrooms

pourboire tip (but *service* is the percentage added to the bill)

praire clam

pré-salé lamb pastured in the salt meadows on the Atlantic seashore

(à la) printanière with spring vegetables

prix price

~ **fixe** at a fixed price

profiterole au chocolat puff pastry filled with whipped cream or custard and covered with hot chocolate

(à la) provençale often with garlic, onions, herbs, olives, oil and tomatoes

prune plum

pruneau (blue) plum

~ **sec** prune

pudding plum pudding

puits d'amour pastry shell filled with liqueur-flavoured custard

purée pulped and strained fruit or vegetables

~ **de pommes de terre** mashed potatoes

quenelle light dumpling made of fish, fowl or meat

queue tail

quiche flan, open tart with meat or vegetable filling, eggs and cream

~ **lorraine** tart with cheese, bacon, eggs and cream

râble de lièvre saddle of hare

raclette hot, melted cheese scraped from a block of cheese; accompanied with boiled potatoes and gherkins

radis radish

(en) ragoût stew(ed)

raie skate, ray

raisin grape

~ sec raisin, sultana

ramequin small cheese tart

rascasse a Mediterranean fish, an essential ingredient of *bouillabaisse*

ratatouille Mediterranean stew of tomatoes, peppers, onions, garlic and aubergines, served hot or cold

ravigote vinegar sauce with chopped hard-boiled eggs, capers and herbs

reblochon soft, mild cheese, pale cream colour (Savoy)

(à la) reine with mince meat or fowl

reine-claude greengage

repas meal

rhubarbe rhubarb

(à la) Richelieu garnish of tomatoes, peas, bacon and potatoes

rillettes usually minced pork (sometimes goose or duck) baked in its own fat

ris de veau calf sweetbread

rissole fritter, pasty

riz rice

~ pilaf rice boiled in a bouillon, sometimes with onions

rognon kidney

romarin rosemary

roquefort blue-veined cheese made from ewe's milk; strong, salty with piquant flavour

rosbif roast beef

rôti roast(ed)

rouelle de veau shank of veal (usually a round cut)

roulade 1) a rolled slice of meat or fish with stuffing 2) dessert with cream or jam stuffing (Swiss roll)

sabayon creamy dessert of egg-yolks, sugar and white wine flavoured with a citrus fruit, served warm

safran saffron

saignant underdone (US rare)

saint-pierre John Dory (fish)

salade salad

~ chiffonnade shredded lettuce and sorrel in melted butter, served with a dressing

~ de fruits fruit salad (US fruit cocktail)

~ niçoise lettuce, tomatoes, green beans, hard-boiled eggs, tunny, olives, green pepper, potatoes and anchovies

~ russe cooked vegetables in mayonnaise

~ verte green

salé salted

salmis game or fowl partially roasted, then simmered in wine and vegetable *purée*

salpicon garnish or stuffing of one or various elements held together by sauce

salsifis salsify

sandre pikeperch

sanglier wild boar

sarcelle teal, small freshwater duck

sauce sauce

~ béarnaise vinegar, egg-yolks, butter, shallots and tarragon

~ béchamel white sauce

~ au beurre blanc butter, shallots, vinegar or lemon juice

~ au beurre noir browned butter

~ bordelaise brown sauce with boletus mushrooms, red wine, shallots and beef marrow

~ bourguignonne red wine sauce with herbs, onions and spices (sometimes tarragon)

~ café de Paris cream, mustard and herbs

~ chasseur brown sauce with wine, mushrooms, onions, shallots and herbs

~ **diable** hot, spicy sauce with white wine, herbs, vinegar and cayenne pepper

~ **financière** cream, Madeira wine, herbs, spices, mushrooms, truffles and olives

~ **hollandaise** butter, egg-yolks and vinegar or lemon juice

~ **lyonnaise** onions, white wine and butter

~ **madère** brown sauce with Madeira wine base

~ **Mornay** *béchamel* sauce with cheese

~ **ravigote** vinegar sauce with chopped hardboiled eggs, capers and herbs; served cold

~ **rémoulade** mayonnaise enriched with mustard and herbs

~ **suprême** chicken-stock base, thick and bland, served with fowl

~ **tartare** mayonnaise base with gherkins, chives, capers and olives

~ **vinaigrette** oil, vinegar and herbs (sometimes mustard)

saucisse sausage

~ **de Francfort** frankfurter

saucisson a large sausage

saumon salmon

sauté lightly browned in hot butter, oil or fat, sautéed

savarin sponge cake steeped in rum and usually topped with cream

sel salt

selle saddle

selon grosseur (or **grandeur**) price according to size, e.g. of a lobster, often abbreviated **s.g. service (non) compris** service (not) included

sorbet water ice (US sherbet)

soufflé à la reine soufflé with finely chopped poultry or meat

soufflé Rothschild vanilla-flavoured soufflé with candied fruit

soupe soup

~ **au pistou** vegetables, noodles, garlic, basil and cheese

~ **à l'oignon** onion

~ **à l'oignon gratinée** onion soup topped with toast and grated cheese; gratinéed

spécialité (du chef) (chef's) speciality

steak steak

~ **haché** hamburger

~ **au poivre** broiled with crushed peppercorns (often flamed in brandy)

~ **tartare** minced beef, eaten raw, with sauce of egg-yolks, mustard, capers, onions, oil and parsley

sucre sugar

suprême de volaille boned chicken breast with creamy sauce

sur commande to your special order

(en) sus in addition, additional charge

tarte open(-faced) flan, tart

~ **Tatin** upside-down tart of caramelized apples

tartelette small tart

tendrons de veau breast of veal

(en) terrine a preparation of meat, fish, fowl or game baked in an earthenware dish called a *terrine*, served cold

tête head

thon tunny (US tuna)

(en) timbale meat, fish, seafood, fruit or vegetables cooked in a pastry case or mould

tomate tomato

tomme a mild soft cheese

topinambour Jerusalem artichoke

tortue turtle

tournedos round cut of prime beef

~ **Rossini** garnished with foie gras and truffles, served with Madeira wine sauce

tout compris all-inclusive (price of a

meal)
tranche slice
　~ napolitaine cassata; slice of layered
　ice-cream and crystallized fruit
tripes tripe
　~ à la mode de Caen baked with
　calf's trotters (US calf's feet),
　vegetables, apple brandy or cider
truffe truffle
truite trout
vacherin a mellow cheese
　~ glacé an ice-cream dessert with
　meringue
vanille vanilla
(à la) vapeur steamed
varié assorted
veau veal
velouté a creamy soup (of vegetables
　or poultry), thickened with butter

and flour
vert-pré a garnish of cress
viande meat
　~ séchée dried beef served as hors
　d'oeuvre in paper-thin slices
viandes froides various cold slices of
　meat and ham (US cold cuts)
vinaigre vinegar
vinaigrette salad sauce of vinegar, oil,
　herbs and mustard
volaille fowl
vol-au-vent puff-pastry shell filled
　with meat, sweetbreads or fish and
　sometimes mushrooms
waterzoï de poulet chicken poached in
　white wine and shredded vegetables,
　cream and egg-yolks
yaourt yoghurt

Drinks

Alsace (93 communes situated on the
River Rhine) produces virtually only
dry white wine, notably
*Gewurztraminer, Riesling, Sylvaner,
Traminer*; the terms *grand vin* and
grand cru are sometimes employed to
indicate a wine of exceptional quality
Amer Picon an aperitif with wine and
brandy base and quinine flavouring
Anjou a region of the Loire district
producing fine rosé and white wine
apéritif often bittersweet, some
aperitifs have a wine and brandy base
with herbs and bitters (like *Amer
Picon, Byrrh, Dubonnet*), others,
called *pastis*, have an aniseed base
(like *Pernod* or *Ricard*); an aperitif
may also be simply vermouth (like
Noilly Prat) or a liqueur drink like

blanc-cassis
**appellation d'origine contrôlée
(A.O.C.)** officially recognized wines
of which there are over 250 in France;
standards of quality are rigidly
checked by government inspectors
armagnac a wine-distilled brandy
from the Armagnac region, west of
Toulouse
Beaujolais Burgundy's most southerly
and extensive vineyards which
produce mainly red wine, e.g.,
*Brouilly, Chénas, Chiroubles, Côte de
Brouilly, Fleurie, Juliénas, Morgon,
Moulin-à-Vent*
Belgique Belgium; though the
Romans introduced wine-making to
Belgium, the kingdom today only
incidentally produces wine, primarily

white, sometimes rosé and sparkling wine

bénédictine forest-green liqueur; brandy base, herbs and orange peel, reputedly secret formula

Berry a region of the Loire district producing red, white and rosé wine; e.g., *Châteaumeillant, Menetou-Salon, Quincy, Reuilly, Sancerre, Sauvignon*

bière beer
~ **blonde** light
~ **(en) bouteille** bottled
~ **brune** dark
~ **pression** draught (US draft)
~ **des Trappistes** malt beer brewed by Trappist monks

blanc-cassis white wine mixed with blackcurrant liqueur

Blayais a region of Bordeaux producing mainly red and white wine

boisson drink

Bordeaux divided into several regions: Blayais, Bourgeais, Entre-Deux-Mers, Fronsac, Graves, Médoc, Pomerol, St-Emilion, Sauternais; among the officially recognized wines are 34 reds, 23 whites and two rosés divided into three categories: general (e.g., *Bordeaux* or *Bordeaux supérieur*), regional (e.g., *Entre-Deux-Mers, Graves, Médoc*) and communal (e.g., *Margaux, Pauillac, Sauternes*); Bordeaux red wine is known as claret in America and Britain

Bourgeais a region of Bordeaux producing red and white table wine

Bourgogne Burgundy, divided into five regions: Beaujolais, Chablis, Côte Chalonnaise, Côte d'Or (which comprises the Côte de Beaune and the Côte de Nuits) and Mâconnais; Burgundy counts the largest number of officially recognized wines of France's wine-growing districts; there are four categories of wine: generic or regional (e.g., *Bourgogne* red, white or rosé), subregional (e.g., *Beaujolais, Beaujolais supérieur, Beaujolais-Villages, Côte de Beaune-Villages, Mâcon, Mâcon supérieur, Mâcon-Villages*), communal (e.g., *Beaune, Chablis, Fleurie, Meursault, Nuits-St-Georges, Volnay*) and vineyard (*climat*) (e.g., *Chambertin, Clos de Vougeot, Musigny*)

brut extra dry, refers to *Champagne*

Byrrh an aperitif with wine base and quinine, fortified with brandy

cacao cocoa

café coffee
~ **complet** with bread, roll, butter and jam; the Continental breakfast
~ **crème** with cream
~ **espresso** espresso
~ **filtre** percolated or dripped through a filter
~ **frappé** iced
~ **au lait** white (with milk)
~ **liégeois** cold with ice-cream, topped with whipped cream
~ **nature, noir** simple, black
~ **sans caféine** caffeine-free

calvados an apple brandy from Normandy

cassis blackcurrant liqueur

Chablis a region of Burgundy noted for its white wine

chambrer to bring wine gently to room (*chambre*) temperature

Champagne district divided into three large regions: Côte des Blancs, Montagne de Reims and Vallée de la Marne with some 200 kilometres (120 miles) of underground caves where the wine ferments; there are ordinary red, white and rosé wines but the production is overwhelmingly centered upon the sparkling white and rosé (usually referred to in English as pink Champagne) for which the region is universally known; vineyards are of little importance in classifying wines from Champagne since, according to tradition, certain varieties of Champagne are produced by blending wine from different vineyards in proportions which are carefully-guarded secrets; sparkling Champagne is sold according to the amount of sugar added: *brut* (extra dry) contains up to 1.5 per cent sugar additive, *extra-sec* (very dry), 1.5–2.5 per cent, *sec* (dry), 2.5–5 per cent, *demi-sec* (slightly sweet), 5–8 per cent and *doux* (sweet), 8–15 per cent

Chartreuse a yellow or green liqueur of herbs and spices produced by monks of Grande Chartreuse in the French Alps

château castle; term employed traditionally in the district of Bordeaux to indicate a wine of exceptional quality; synonyms: *clos, domaine*

chocolat chocolate

cidre cider

citron pressé freshly squeezed lemon juice

citronnade lemon squash (US lemon drink)

claret see *Bordeaux*

clos vineyard; generally indicates a wine of exceptional quality

cognac cognac; the famed winedistilled brandy from the Charente and Charente-Maritime regions

Cointreau orange liqueur

Corse Corsica; this Mediterranean island, a French department, produces fine wine, particularly from the hilly areas and Cape Corsica; red, white and rosé wine is characterized by a rich, full-bodied taste; the best wine, grown near Bastia, is the rosé *Patrimonio*

Côte de Beaune the southern half of Burgundy's celebrated Côte d'Or producing chiefly red wine; e.g., the prestigious *Aloxe-Corton* as well as *Beaune, Blagny, Chassagne-Montrachet, Meursault, Pernand-Vergelesses, Puligny-Montrachet, Santenay, Savigny-lès-Beaune, Volnay*

Côte de Nuits a region of Burgundy especially noted for its red wine, e.g., *Chambolle-Musigny, Fixin, Gevrey-Chambertin, Morey-St-Denis, Nuits-St-Georges, Vosne-Romanée*

Côte d'Or a famed region of Burgundy composed of the Côte de Beaune and de Nuits which is noted for its red and white wine

Côtes du Rhône extend from Vienne to Avignon along the banks of the River Rhone between the Burgundy and Provence wine districts; over a hundred communes offer a wide diversity in white, red and rosé wine of varying character; divided into a northern and southern region with notable wine: *Château-Grillet, Châteauneuf-du-Pape, Condrieu, Cornas, Côte-Rôtie, Crozes-Hermitage, Hermitage, Lirac, St-Joseph, St-Péray, Tavel*

crème 1) cream 2) sweetened liqueur like *crème de menthe, crème de cacao*

cru growth 1) refers to a particular vineyard and its wine 2) a system of grading wine; *premier cru, grand cru, cru classé*

curaçao originally from the name of the island of the Dutch Antilles, now applied to liqueur made from orange peel

cuvée a blend of wine from various vineyards, especially, according to tradition, in the making of Champagne

domaine estate; used on a wine label it indicates a wine of exceptional quality

eau water

~ **gazeuse** fizzy (US carbonated)

~ **minérale** mineral

Entre-Deux-Mers a vast Bordeaux region called "between two seas"—actually it's between two rivers—which produces white and red wine

extra-sec very dry (of Champagne)

framboise raspberry liqueur or brandy

frappé 1) iced 2) milk shake

Fronsac a Bordeaux region producing chiefly red wine

Gueuzelambic a strong Flemish bitter beer brewed from wheat and barley

grand cru, grand vin indicates a wine of exceptional quality

Grand Marnier an orange liqueur

Graves a Bordeaux region especially noted for its white wine but also its red

Jura a six-kilometre- (four-mile-) wide strip which runs 80 kilometres (50 miles) parallel to the western Swiss border and Burgundy; offers white, red, rosé, golden and sparkling wine; there are four formally recognized wines: *Arbois*, *Château-Chalon*, *Côtes du Jura* and *l'Etoile*

kirsch spirit distilled from cherries

Kriekenlambic a strong Brussels bitter beer flavoured with morello cherries

lait milk

~ **écrémé** skimmed

Languedoc district, formerly a French province, to the south-west of the Rhone delta; its ordinary table wine is often referred to as *vin du Midi* but other officially recognized wines, mostly white, are produced, including *Blanquette de Limoux* (sparkling), *Clairette du Languedoc*, *Fitou* and the *Muscats* from Frontignan, Lunel, Mireval and St-Jean-de-Minervois

limonade 1) lemonade 2) soft drink

Loire a district of 200, 000 hectares (80,000 acres) sprawled over the vicinity of France's longest river, the Loire; produces much fine red, white and rosé wine in four regions: Anjou (e.g., *Coteaux-de-l'Aubance*, *Coteaux-du-Layon*, *Coteaux-de-la-Loire*, *Saumur*), Berry and Nivernais (*Menetou-Salon*, *Pouilly-sur-Loire*, *Quincy*, *Reuilly*, *Sancerre*), Nantais (*Muscadet*) and Touraine (*Bourgueil*, *Chinon*, *Montlouis*, *Vouvray*)

Lorraine a flourishing and renowned wine district up to the 18th century, today it is of minor importance; good red, white and rosé wine continue to be produced (e.g., *Vins de la Moselle*, *Côtes-de-Toul*)

Mâcon a region of Burgundy producing basically red wine

marc spirit distilled from grape residue

Médoc a Bordeaux region producing highly reputed red wine including *Listrac*, *Margaux*, *Moulis*, *Pauillac*, *St-Estèphe*, *St-Julien*

mirabelle a brandy made from small yellow plums, particularly produced in the Alsace-Lorraine area

Muscadet a white wine from the Nantes area (Loire)

muscat 1) a type of grape 2) name

given to dessert wine; especially renowned is the muscat from Frontignan (Languedoc)

Nantais a region of the Loire chiefly renowned for its *Muscadet* white wine but offers other wine, e.g., *Coteaux d'Ancenis, Gros-Plant*

Neuchâtel a Swiss region producing primarily white wine (e.g., *Auvernier, Cormondrèche, Cortaillod, Hauterive*)

Noilly Prat a French vermouth

orange pressée freshly squeezed orange juice

pastis aniseed-flavoured aperitif

Pernod an aniseed-flavoured aperitif

pétillant slightly sparkling

Pomerol a Bordeaux region producing red wine (e.g., *Château Pétrus, Lalande-de-Pomerol, Néac*)

Provence France's most ancient wine-producing district; it traces its history back over two-and-a-half milleniums when Greek colonists planted the first vineyards on the Mediterranean coast of Gaul; red, white and rosé wine is produced, e.g., *Bandol, Bellet, Cassis, Coteaux-d'Aix-en-Provence, Coteaux-des-Baux, Coteaux-de-Pierrevert, Côtes-de-Provence, Palette*

quetsche spirit distilled from plums

rancio dessert wine, especially from Roussillon, which is aged in oak casks under the Midi sun

Ricard an aniseed-flavoured aperitif

Roussillon district which was a French province with Perpignan as its capital; its wine is similar in character to that of the Languedoc to the immediate north; good red, white and rosé table wine, e.g., *Corbières du Roussillon* and *Roussillon Dels Aspres*; this region produces three quarters of France's naturally sweet

wine, usually referred to as *rancio*, which is aged in oak casks under the Midi sun; notable examples among them are *Banyuls, Côtes-d'Agly, Côtes-du-Haut-Roussillon; Grand-Roussillon, Muscat de Rivesaltes, Rivesaltes*

St-Emilion a Bordeaux region producing red wine including *Lussac, Montagne, Parsac, Puisseguin, St-Georges*

St-Raphaël a quinine-flavoured aperitif

Sauternais a Bordeaux region noted for its white wine (*Sauternes*), notably the prestigious *Château d'Yquem*

Savoie Savoy; the Alpine district producing primarily dry, light and often slightly acid white wine (e.g., *Crépy, Seyssel*) but also good red, rosé and sparkling wine which is chiefly produced around Chambéry

Sud-Ouest a district in southwestern France producing quite varying types of wine, mostly white but some red and even rosé; the district includes the former province of Aquitaine, Béarn, Basque Country and Languedoc; wines of particular note are *Bergerac, Côtes-de-Duras, Gaillac, Jurançon, Madiran, Monbazillac, Montravel*

Suisse Switzerland; two-thirds of the nation's wine production consists of white wine; some 230 different vineyards are scattered over a dozen of Switzerland's 23 cantons though only four have a special significance: Neuchâtel, Tessin, Valais and Vaud

Suze an aperitif based on gentian

thé tea

Touraine for 14 centuries a celebrated wine district of the Loire producing red, white and rosé wine (e.g.,

Bourgueil, Chinon, Montlouis, St-Nicolas-de-Bourgueil, Vouvray)

Triple Sec an orange liqueur

Valais sometimes referred to as the California of Switzerland, this Swiss region produces nearly a quarter of the nation's wine; the region in the Rhone Valley is noted for providing Switzerland's best red wine (e.g., *Dôle*) and much of its finest white wine (e.g., *Arvine, Ermitage, Fendant, Johannisberg, Malvoisie*)

Vaud a Swiss region producing primarily white wine (e.g., *Aigle, Dézaley, Mont-sur-Rolle, Lavaux, Yvorne*)

V.D.Q.S. (vin délimité de qualité supérieure) regional wine of exceptional quality, produced according to carefully defined specifications and checked by government inspectors

Vieille Cure a wine-distilled liqueur

vin wine

~ **blanc** white

~ **chambré** wine at room temperature

~ **doux** sweet, dessert

~ **gris** pinkish

~ **mousseux** sparkling

~ **ordinaire** table

~ **du pays** local

~ **rosé** rosé (pink in reference to Champagne)

~ **rouge** red

~ **sec** dry

V.S.O.P. (very special old pale) in reference to cognac, indicates that it has been aged at least 5 years

(vin de) xérès sherry

Mini French Grammar

Articles

All nouns in French are either masculine or feminine.

1. Definite article (the):

masc. **le train**	the train	*fem.* **la voiture**	the car

Le and **la** are contracted to **l'** when followed by a vowel or a silent **h***.

l'avion	the plane	**l'hôtel**	the hotel

Plural (masc. and fem.):

les **trains**	*les* **voitures**	*les* **avions**

2. Indefinite article (a/an):

masc. *un* **timbre**	a stamp	fem. *une* **lettre**	a letter

Plural (masc. and fem.):

des **timbres**	stamps	*des* **lettres**	letters

3. Some/any (partitive)

Expressed by **de, du, de la, de l', des** as follows:

masc. **du** (= **de** + **le**)	**de l'** when followed by a vowel
fem. **de la**	or a silent **h***

Plural (masc. and fem.): **des** (= **de** + **les**)

du **sel**	some salt	*de la* **moutarde**	some mustard
de l' **ail**	some garlic	*des* **oranges**	some oranges

In negatives sentences, **de** is generally used.

Il n'y a pas *de* **taxis.**	There aren't any taxis.
Je n'ai pas *d'* **argent.**	I haven't any money.

Note the contraction **d'** before a vowel.

---

* In French the letter *h* at the beginning of a word is not pronounced. However, in several words the *h* is what is called "aspirate", i.e., no liaison is made with the word preceding it. E.g., *le héros*. See also Guide to Pronunciation, p. 10.

Nouns

1. As already noted, nouns are either masculine or feminine. There are no short cuts for determining gender (though, note that most nouns ending in **-e, -té, -tion** are feminine). So always learn a noun together with its accompanying article.

2. The plural of the majority of nouns is formed by adding **s** to the singular. (The final **s** is not pronounced.)

3. To show possession, use the preposition **de** (of).

la fin *de* **la semaine**	the end of the week
le début *du* **mois**	the beginning of the month
le patron *de* **l'hôtel**	the owner of the hotel
les valises *des* **voyageurs**	the travellers' luggage

Adjectives

1. Adjectives agree with the noun in gender and number. Most of them form the feminine by adding **e** to the masculine (unless the word already ends in **e**). For the plural, add **s**.

a. **un grand magasin**	a big shop	**des grands magasins**
b. **une auto anglaise**	an English car	**des autos anglaises**

2. As can be seen from the above, adjectives can come (a) before the noun or (b) after the noun. Since it is basically a question of sound and idiom, rules are difficult to formulate briefly; but adjectives more often follow nouns.

3. **Demonstrative adjectives:**

this/that	**ce** (*masc.*)	these/those	**ces** (*masc. and fem.*)
	cet (*masc. before a vowel or silent* **h**)		
	cette (*fem.*)		

4. **Possessive adjectives:** These agree in number and gender with *the noun they modify*, i.e., with the thing possessed and not the possessor.

	masc.	fem.	plur.
my	**mon**	**ma**	**mes**
your	**ton**	**ta**	**tes**
his/her/its	**son**	**sa**	**ses**
our	**notre**	**notre**	**nos**
your	**votre**	**votre**	**vos**
their	**leur**	**leur**	**leurs**

Thus, depending on the context:

son **fils**	can mean *his* son or *her* son
sa **chambre**	can mean *his* room or *her* room
ses **vêtements**	can mean *his* clothes or *her* clothes

Personal pronouns

	Subject	Direct object	Indirect object	After a preposition
I	**je**	**me**	**me**	**moi**
you	**tu**	**te**	**te**	**toi**
he/it (masc.)	**il**	**le**	**lui**	**lui**
she/it (fem.)	**elle**	**la**	**lui**	**elle**
we	**nous**	**nous**	**nous**	**nous**
you	**vous**	**vous**	**vous**	**vous**
they (masc.)	**ils**	**les**	**leur**	**eux**
they (fem.)	**elles**	**les**	**leur**	**elles**

Note: There are two forms for "you" in French: **tu** is used when talking to relatives, close friends and children (and between young people); **vous** is used in all other cases, and is also the plural form of **tu.**

Adverbs

Adverbs are generally formed by adding **-ment** to the feminine form of the adjective.

masc.:	fem.:	adverb:
lent (slow)	**lente**	lentement
sérieux (serious)	**sérieuse**	sérieusement

Verbs

Three regular conjugations appear below, grouped by families according to their infinitive endings, *-er*, *-ir* and *-re*. Verbs with the ending *-er* are considered as the true regular conjugation in French. Verbs which do not follow the conjugations below are considered irregular (see irregular verb list). Note that there are some verbs which follow the regular conjugation of the category they belong to, but present some minor changes in the spelling of the stem. Example: *acheter, j'achète; broyer, je broie.*

		1st conj.	2nd conj.	3rd conj.
Infinitive		**chant er** (*sing*)	**fin ir** (*finish*)	**vend re**[1] (*sell*)
Present	je	chant e	fin is	vend s
	tu	chant es	fin is	vend s
	il	chant e	fin it	vend
	nous	chant ons	fin issons	vend ons
	vous	chant ez	fin issez	vend ez
	ils	chant ent	fin issent	vend ent
Imperfect *past*	je	chant ais	fin issais	vend ais
	tu	chant ais	fin issais	vend ais
	il	chant ait	fin issait	vend ait
	nous	chant ions	fin issions	vend ions
	vous	chant iez	fin issiez	vend iez
	ils	chant aient	fin issaient	vend aient
Future	je	chant erai	fin irai	vend rai
	tu	chant eras	fin iras	vend ras
	il	chant era	fin ira	vend ra
	nous	chant erons	fin irons	vend rons
	vous	chant erez	fin irez	vend rez
	ils	chant eront	fin iront	vend ront
Conditional	je	chant erais	fin irais	vend rais
	tu	chant erais	fin irais	vend rais
	il	chant erait	fin irait	vend rait
	nous	chant erions	fin irions	vend rions
	vous	chant eriez	fin iriez	vend riez
	ils	chant eraient	fin iraient	vend raient

[1]conjugated in the same way: all verbs ending in *-andre*, *-endre*, *-ondre*, *-erdre*, *-ordre* (except *prendre* and its compounds).

Pres. subj.[2]	je	chant **e**	fin **isse**	vend **e**
	tu	chant **es**	fin **isses**	vend **es**
	il	chant **e**	fin **isse**	vend **e**
	nous	chant **ions**	fin **issions**	vend **ions**
	vous	chant **iez**	fin **issiez**	vend **iez**
	ils	chant **ent**	fin **issent**	vend **ent**
Past part.		chant **é(e)**	fin **i(e)**	vend **u(e)**

[2]French verbs are always preceded by *que* when conjugated in all tenses of subjonctive. Examples: *que je chante, que nous finissions, qu'ils aient.*

Auxiliary verbs

	avoir (*to have*)		**être** (*to be*)	
Present	*Imperfect*	*Present*	*Imperfect*	
j', je	ai	avais	suis	étais
tu	as	avais	es	étais
il	a	avait	est	était
nous	avons	avions	sommes	étions
vous	avez	aviez	êtes	étiez
ils	ont	avaient	sont	étaient
	Future	*Conditional*	*Future*	*Conditional*
j', je	aurai	aurais	serai	serais
tu	auras	aurais	seras	serais
il	aura	aurait	sera	serait
nous	aurons	aurions	serons	serions
vous	aurez	auriez	serez	seriez
ils	auront	auraient	seront	seraient
	Pres. subj.[1]	*Pres. perf*	*Pres. subj.*[1]	*Pres. perf.*
j', je	aie	ai eu	sois	ai été
tu	aies	as eu	sois	as été
il	ait	a eu	soit	a été
nous	ayons	avons eu	soyons	avons été
vous	ayez	avez eu	soyez	avez été
ils	aient	ont eu	soient	ont été

[1]French verbs are always preceded by *que* when conjugated in all tenses of subjonctive. Examples: *que je chante, que nous finissions, qu'ils aient.*

Irregular verbs

Below is a list of the verbs and tenses commonly used in spoken French. In the listing a) stands for the present tense, b) for the imperfect, c) for the future, d) for the conditional, e) for the present subjunctive and f) for the past participle. In the present tense we have given the whole conjugation, for the other tenses the first person singular, as the conjugations for tenses other than present are similar to those used in the regular verbs. Unless otherwise indicated, verbs with prefixes (ab-, ac-, com-, con-, contre-, de-, dé-, dis-, é-, en-, entr(e)-, ex-, in-, o-, par-, pré-, pour-, re-, ré-, sous-, etc.) are conjugated like the stem verb.

absoudre
absolve
a) absous, absous, absout, absolvons, absolvez, absolvent;
b) absolvais; c) absoudrai; d) absoudrais; e) absolve;
f) absous, absoute

accroître
increase
a) accrois, accrois, accroît, accroissons, accroissez,
accroissent; b) accroissais; c) accroîtrai; d) accroîtrais;
e) accroisse; f) accru(e)

acquérir
acquire
a) acquiers, acquiers, acquiert, acquérons, acquérez, acquiè-
rent; b) acquérais; c) acquerrai; d) acquerrais; e) acquière;
f) acquis(e)

aller
go
a) vais, vas, va, allons, allez, vont; b) allais; c) irai; d) irais;
e) aille; f) allé(e)

apercevoir
perceive
→ recevoir

apparaître
appear
→ connaître

assaillir
assail
a) assaille, assailles, assaille, assaillons, assaillez, assaillent;
b) assaillais; c) assaillirai; d) assaillirais; e) assaille; f) assailli(e)

asseoir
set
a) assieds, assieds, assied, asseyons, asseyez, asseyent;
b) asseyais; c) assiérai; d) assiérais; e) asseye; f) assis(e)

astreindre
compel
→ peindre

battre
beat
a) bats, bats, bat, battons, battez, battent; b) battais; c) battrai;
d) battrais; e) batte; f) battu(e)

boire
drink
a) bois, bois, boit, buvons, buvez, boivent; b) buvais;
c) boirai; d) boirais; e) boive; f) bu(e)

bouillir
boil
a) bous, bous, bout, bouillons, bouillez, bouillent; b) bouillais;
c) bouillirai; d) bouillirais; e) bouille; f) bouilli(e)

ceindre
gird
→ peindre

circoncire
circumcise
→ suffire

circonscrire
limit
→ écrire

clore	a) je clos, tu clos, il clôt, ils closent; b) –; c) clorai; d) clorais;
close	e) close; f) clos(e)
concevoir	→ recevoir
conceive	
conclure	a) conclus, conclus, conclut, concluons, concluez, concluent;
conclude	b) concluais; c) conclurai; d) conclurais; e) conclue; f) conclu(e)
conduire	→ cuire
drive	
connaître	a) connais, connais, connaît, connaissons, connaissez,
know	connaissent; b) connaissais; c) connaîtrai; d) connaîtrais;
	e) connaisse; f) connu(e)
conquérir	→ acquérir
conquer	
construire	→ cuire
build	
contraindre	→ craindre
constrain	
contredire	→ médire
contradict	
coudre	a) couds, couds, coud, cousons, cousez, cousent; b) cousais;
sew	c) coudrai; d) coudrais; e) couse; f) cousu(e)
courir	a) cours, cours, court, courons, courez, courent; b) courais;
run	c) courrai; d) courrais; e) coure; f) couru(e)
couvrir	a) couvre, couvres, couvre, couvrons, couvrez, couvrent;
cover	b) couvrais; c) couvrirai; d) couvrirais; e) couvre; f) couvert(e)
craindre	a) crains, crains, craint, craignons, craignez, craignent;
fear	b) craignais; c) craindrai; d) craindrais; e) craigne; f) craint(e)
croire	a) crois, crois, croit, croyons, croyez, croient; b) croyais;
believe	c) croirai; d) croirais; e) croie; f) cru(e)
croître	a) croîs, croîs, croît, croissons, croissez, croissent; b) croissais;
grow	c) croîtrai; d) croîtrais; e) croisse; f) crû, crue
cueillir	a) cueille, cueilles, cueille, cueillons, cueillez, cueillent;
pick	b) cueillais; c) cueillerai; d) cueillerais; e) cueille; f) cueilli(e)
cuire	a) cuis, cuis, cuit, cuisons, cuisez, cuisent; b) cuisais;
cook	c) cuirai; d) cuirais; e) cuise; f) cuit(e)
décevoir	→ recevoir
deceive	
décrire	→ écrire
describe	
déduire	→ cuire
deduct	
détruire	→ cuire
destroy	

devoir	a) dois, dois, doit, devons, devez, doivent; b) devais;
have to	c) devrai; d) devrais; e) doive; f) dû, due
dire	a) dis, dis, dit, disons, dites, disent; b) disais; c) dirai;
say	d) dirais; e) dise; f) dit(e)
dissoudre	→ absoudre
dissolve	
dormir	a) dors, dors, dort, dormons, dormez, dorment; b) dormais;
sleep	c) dormirai; d) dormirais; e) dorme; f) dormi
échoir	a) il échoit; b) –; c) il échoira; d) il échoirait;
fall to	e) qu'il échoie; f) échu(e)
écrire	a) écris, écris, écrit, écrivons, écrivez, écrivent; b) écrivais;
write	c) écrirai; d) écrirais; e) écrive; f) écrit(e)
élire	→ lire
elect	
émettre	→ mettre
emit	
émouvoir	→ mouvoir; f) ému(e)
affect	
empreindre	→ peindre
imprint	
enduire	→ cuire
coat	
enfreindre	→ craindre
infringe	
envoyer	a) envoie, envoies, envoie, envoyons, envoyez, envoient;
send	b) envoyais; c) enverrai; d) enverrais; e) envoie; f) envoyé(e)
éteindre	→ peindre
switch off	
étreindre	→ peindre
embrace	
exclure	→ conclure
exclude	
faillir	a) –; b) –; c) faillirai; d) faillirais; e) faille; f) failli
fail	
faire	a) fais, fais, fait, faisons, faites, font; b) faisais; c) ferai;
do, make	d) ferais; e) fasse; f) fait(e)
falloir	a) il faut; b) il fallait; c) il faudra; d) il faudrait; e) qu'il faille;
have to	f) il a fallu
feindre	→ peindre
feign	
frire	→ confire
fry	
fuir	a) fuis, fuis, fuit, fuyons, fuyez, fuient; b) fuyais; c) fuirai;
escape	d) fuirais; e) fuie; f) fui

geindre	→ craindre
whine	
haïr	a) hais, hais, hait, haïssons, haïssez, haïssent; b) haïssais;
hate	c) haïrai; d) haïrais; e) haïsse; f) haï(e)
inclure	→ conclure
include	
induire	→ cuire
induce	
inscrire	→ écrire
register	
instruire	→ cuire
instruct	
interdire	→ médire
forbid	
introduire	→ cuire
introduce	
joindre	a) joins, joins, joint, joignons, joignez, joignent;
join	b) joignais; c) joindrai; d) joindrais; e) joigne; f) joint(e)
lire	a) lis, lis, lit, lisons, lisez, lisent; b) lisais; c) lirai;
read	d) lirais; e) lise; f) lu(e)
luire	a) luis, luis, luit, luisons, luisez, luisent; b) luisais;
shine	c) luirai; d) luirais; e) luise; f) lui
maudire	a) maudis, maudis, maudit, maudissons, maudissez, maudis-
curse	sent; b) maudissais; c) maudirai; d) maudirais; e) maudisse;
	f) maudit(e)
médire	a) médis, médis, médit, médisons, médisez, médisent;
speak ill of	b) médisais; c) médirai; d) médirais; e) médise; f) médit(e)
mentir	a) mens, mens, ment, mentons, mentez, mentent; b) mentais;
lie	c) mentirai; d) mentirais; e) mente; f) menti
mettre	a) mets, mets, met, mettons, mettez, mettent; b) mettais;
put	c) mettrai; d) mettrais; e) mette; f) mis(e)
moudre	a) mouds, mouds, moud, moulons, moulez, moulent;
grind	b) moulais; c) moudrai; d) moudrais; e) moule; f) moulu(e)
mourir	a) meurs, meurs, meurt, mourons, mourez, meurent; b)
die	mourais; c) mourrai; d) mourrais; e) meure; f) mort(e)
mouvoir	a) meus, meus, meut, mouvons, mouvez, meuvent; b) mouvais;
set in motion	c) mouvrai; d) mouvrais; e) meuve; f) mû, mue
naître	a) nais, nais, naît, naissons, naissez, naissent; b) naissais;
be born	c) naîtrai; d) naîtrais; e) naisse; f) né(e)
nuire	→ cuire; f) nui
harm	
offrir	→ couvrir
offer	

ouvrir → couvrir
open

paître a) pais, pais, paît, paissons, paissez, paissent; b) paissais;
graze c) paîtrai; d) paîtrais; e) paisse; f) –

paraître → connaître
appear

partir → mentir; f) parti(e)
leave

peindre a) peins, peins, peint, peignons, peignez, peignent;
paint b) peignais; c) peindrai; d) peindrais; e) peigne; f) peint(e)

percevoir → recevoir
perceive

plaindre → craindre
pity

plaire a) plais, plais, plaît, plaisons, plaisez, plaisent; b) plaisais;
please c) plairai; d) plairais; e) plaise; f) plu

pleuvoir a) il pleut; b) il pleuvait; c) il pleuvra; d) il pleuvrait;
rain e) qu'il pleuve; f) il a plu

pourvoir a) pourvois, pourvois, pourvoit, pourvoyons, pourvoyez,
provide pourvoient; b) pourvoyais; c) pourvoirai; d) pourvoirais;
  e) pourvoie; f) pourvu(e)

pouvoir a) peux (puis), peux, peut, pouvons, pouvez, peuvent;
be able to b) pouvais, c) pourrai; d) pourrais; e) puisse; f) pu

prédire a) prédis, prédis, prédit, prédisons, prédisez, prédisent;
foretell b) prédisais; c) prédirai; d) prédirais; e) prédise; f) prédit(e)

prendre a) prends, prends, prend, prenons, prenez, prennent;
take b) prenais; c) prendrai; d) prendrais; e) prenne; f) pris(e)

prescrire → écrire
prescribe

prévoir a) prévois, prévois, prévoit, prévoyons, prévoyez, prévoient;
foresee b) prévoyais; c) prévoirai; d) prévoirais; e) prévoie; f) prévu(e)

produire → cuire
produce

proscrire → écrire
outlaw

recevoir a) reçois, reçois, reçoit, recevons, recevez, reçoivent;
receive b) recevais; c) recevrai; d) recevrais; e) reçoive; f) reçu(e)

requérir → acquérir
require

restreindre → peindre
restrict

rire a) ris, ris, rit, rions, riez, rient; b) riais; c) rirai;
laugh d) rirais; e) rie; f) ri

savoir	a) sais, sais, sait, savons, savez, savent; b) savais; c) saurai; d)
know	saurais; e) sache; f) su(e)
séduire	→ cuire
seduce	
sentir	→ mentir; f) senti(e)
feel	
servir	a) sers, sers, sert, servons, servez, servent; b) servais;
serve	c) servirai; d) servirais; e) serve; f) servi(e)
sortir	→ mentir; f) sorti(e)
go out	
souffrir	→ couvrir
suffer	
souscrire	→ écrire
subscribe	
suffire	a) suffis, suffis, suffit, suffisons, suffisez, suffisent; b) suffisais;
be enough	c) suffirai; d) suffirais; e) suffise; e) suffi
suivre	a) suis, suis, suit, suivons, suivez, suivent; b) suivais;
follow	c) suivrai; d) suivrais; e) suive; f) suivi(e)
taire	a) tais, tais, tait, taisons, taisez, taisent; b) taisais;
be silent	c) tairai; d) tairais; e) taise; f) tu(e)
teindre	→ peindre
dye	
tenir	a) tiens, tiens, tient, tenons, tenez, tiennent; b) tenais;
hold	c) tiendrai; d) tiendrais; e) tienne; f) tenu(e)
traduire	→ cuire
translate	
traire	a) trais, trais, trait, trayons, trayez, traient; b) trayais;
milk (cow)	c) trairai; d) trairais; e) traie; f) trait(e)
transcrire	→ écrire
transcribe	
tressaillir	→ assaillir
startle	
vaincre	a) vaincs, vaincs, vainc, vainquons, vainquez, vainquent;
defeat	b) vainquais; c) vaincrai; d) vaincrais; e) vainque; f) vaincu(e)
valoir	a) vaux, vaux, vaut, valons, valez, valent; b) valais; c) vaudrai;
be worth	d) vaudrais; e) vaille; f) valu(e)
venir	→ tenir
come	
vêtir	a) vêts, vêts, vêt, vêtons, vêtez, vêtent; b) vêtais; c) vêtirai;
dress	d) vêtirais; e) vête; f) vêtu(e)
vivre	a) vis, vis, vit, vivons, vivez, vivent; b) vivais; c) vivrai;
live	d) vivrais; e) vive; f) vécu(e)

voir a) vois, vois, voit, voyons, voyez, voient; b) voyais; c) verrai;
see d) verrais; e) voie; f) vu(e)

vouloir a) veux, veux, veut, voulons, voulez, veulent; b) voulais;
want c) voudrai; d) voudrais; e) veuille; f) voulu(e)

French Abbreviations

ACF	*Automobile-Club de France*	Automobile Association of France
ACS	*Automobile-Club de Suisse*	Swiss Automobile Association
AELE	*Association européenne de libre-échange*	EFTA, European Free Trade Association
apr. J.-C.	*après Jésus-Christ*	A.D.
av. J.-C.	*avant Jésus-Christ*	B.C.
bd	*boulevard*	boulevard
c.-à-d.	*c'est-à-dire*	i.e.
c/c	*compte courant*	current account
CCP	*compte de chèques postaux*	postal account
CFF	*Chemins de fer fédéraux*	Swiss Federal Railways
ch	*chevaux-vapeur*	horsepower
Cie, Co.	*compagnie*	company
CRS	*Compagnies républicaines de sécurité*	French order and riot police
ct	*courant*	of the month
CV	*chevaux-vapeur*	horsepower
EU	*Etats-Unis*	United States
exp.	*expéditeur*	sender
Fs/Fr.s.	*franc suisse*	Swiss franc
h.	*heure*	hour, o'clock
hab.	*habitants*	inhabitants, population
M.	*Monsieur*	Mr.
Me	*Maître*	title for barrister or lawyer
Mgr	*Monseigneur*	ecclesiastic title for the rank of bishop
Mlle	*Mademoiselle*	Miss
MM.	*Messieurs*	gentlemen, Messrs.
Mme	*Madame*	Mrs.
n°	*numéro*	number
ONU	*Organisation des Nations Unies*	UN
OTAN	*Organisation du Traité de l'Atlantique Nord*	NATO, North Atlantic Treaty Organization
PCV	*paiement contre vérification*	reverse-charge call (collect call)
PDG	*président-directeur général*	chairman of the board
p.ex.	*par exemple*	e.g.
PJ	*police judiciaire*	criminal investigation department
p.p.	*port payé*	postage paid

P & T	*Postes et Télécommunications*	post and telecommunications (France)
PTT	*Postes, Télégraphes, Téléphones*	Post, Telegraph, Telephone (Belgium and Switzerland)
RATP	*Régie autonome des transports parisiens*	Parisian transport authority
RF	*République française*	the French Republic
RN	*route nationale*	national highway
RP	*Révérend Père*	Reverend Father
RSVP	*répondez, s'il vous plaît*	RSVP, please reply
s/	*sur*	on, at
SA	*société anonyme*	Ltd., Inc.
S.A.R.L.	*société à responsabilité limitée*	limited liability company
SE	*Son Eminence; Son Excellence*	His Eminence; His/Her Excellency
SI	*Syndicat d'Initiative*	tourist office
SIDA	*syndrome immuno-déficitaire acquis*	AIDS
SM	*Sa Majesté*	His/Her Majesty
SNCB	*Société nationale des chemins de fer belges*	Belgian National Railways
SNCF	*Société nationale des chemins de fer français*	French National Railways
St, Ste	*saint, sainte*	saint
succ.	*successeur; succursale*	successor; branch office
s. v. p.	*s'il vous plaît*	please
TCB	*Touring-Club royal de Belgique*	Royal Touring Club of Belgium
TCF	*Touring-Club de France*	Touring Club of France
TCS	*Touring-Club Suisse*	Swiss Touring Club
TGV	*train à grande vitesse*	high-speed train
t. s. v. p.	*tournez, s'il vous plaît*	please turn over
TVA	*taxe à la valeur ajoutée*	VAT, value added tax
UE	*Union européenne*	European Union
Vve	*veuve*	widow

Numerals

Cardinal numbers

0	zéro
1	un
2	deux
3	trois
4	quatre
5	cinq
6	six
7	sept
8	huit
9	neuf
10	dix
11	onze
12	douze
13	treize
14	quatorze
15	quinze
16	seize
17	dix-sept
18	dix-huit
19	dix-neuf
20	vingt
21	vingt et un
22	vingt-deux
30	trente
40	quarante
50	cinquante
60	soixante
70	soixante-dix
71	soixante et onze
72	soixante-douze
80	quatre-vingts
81	quatre-vingt-un
90	quatre-vingt-dix
100	cent
101	cent un
230	deux cent trente
1 000	mille
1 107	onze cent sept
2 000	deux mille
1 000 000	un million

Ordinal numbers

1er	premier
2^e	deuxième (second)
3^e	troisième
4^e	quatrième
5^e	cinquième
6^e	sixième
7^e	septième
8^e	huitième
9^e	neuvième
10^e	dixième
11^e	onzième
12^e	douzième
13^e	treizième
14^e	quatorzième
15^e	quinzième
16^e	seizième
17^e	dix-septième
18^e	dix-huitième
19^e	dix-neuvième
20^e	vingtième
21^e	vingt et unième
22^e	vingt-deuxième
23^e	vingt-troisième
30^e	trentième
40^e	quarantième
50^e	cinquantième
60^e	soixantième
70^e	soixante-dixième
71^e	soixante et onzième
72^e	soixante-douzième
80^e	quatre-vingtième
81^e	quatre-vingt-unième
90^e	quatre-vingt-dixième
100^e	centième
101^e	cent unième
200^e	deux centième
330^e	trois cent trentième
$1 000^e$	millième
$1 107^e$	onze cent septième
$2 000^e$	deux millième

Time

Although official time in France is based on the 24-hour clock, the 12-hour system is used in conversation.

If you have to indicate that it is a.m. or p.m., add *du matin*, *de l'après-midi* or *du soir*.

Thus:

huit heures du matin	8 a.m.
deux heures de l'après-midi	2 p.m.
huit heures du soir	8 p.m.

Days of the Week

dimanche	Sunday	*jeudi*	Thursday
lundi	Monday	*vendredi*	Friday
mardi	Tuesday	*samedi*	Saturday
mercredi	Wednesday		

Some Basic Phrases

Please.	S'il vous plaît.
Thank you very much.	Merci beaucoup.
Don't mention it.	Il n'y a pas de quoi.
Good morning.	Bonjour (*matin*).
Good afternoon.	Bonjour (*après-midi*).
Good evening.	Bonsoir.
Good night.	Bonne nuit.
Good-bye.	Au revoir.
See you later.	A bientôt.
Where is/Where are...?	Où se trouve/Où se trouvent...?
What do you call this?	Comment appelez-vous ceci?
What does that mean?	Que veut dire cela?
Do you speak English?	Parlez-vous anglais?
Do you speak German?	Parlez-vous allemand?
Do you speak French?	Parlez-vous français?
Do you speak Spanish?	Parlez-vous espagnol?
Do you speak Italian?	Parlez-vous italien?
Could you speak more slowly, please?	Pourriez-vous parler plus lentement, s'il vous plaît?
I don't understand.	Je ne comprends pas.
Can I have...?	Puis-je avoir...?
Can you show me...?	Pouvez-vous m'indiquer...?
Can you tell me...?	Pouvez-vous me dire...?
Can you help me, please?	Pouvez-vous m'aider, s'il vous plaît?
I'd like...	Je voudrais...
We'd like...	Nous voudrions...
Please give me...	S'il vous plaît, donnez-moi...
Please bring me...	S'il vous plaît, apportez-moi...
I'm hungry.	J'ai faim.
I'm thirsty.	J'ai soif.
I'm lost.	Je me suis perdu.
Hurry up!	Dépêchez-vous!
There is/There are...	Il y a...
There isn't/There aren't...	Il n'y a pas...

Arrival

Your passport, please.	Votre passeport, s'il vous plaît.
Have you anything to declare?	Avez-vous quelque chose à déclarer?
No, nothing at all.	Non, rien du tout.

Can you help me with my luggage, please?	Pouvez-vous prendre mes bagages, s'il vous plaît?
Where's the bus to the centre of town, please?	Où est le bus pour le centre de la ville, s'il vous plaît?
This way, please.	Par ici, s'il vous plaît.
Where can I get a taxi?	Où puis-je trouver un taxi?
What's the fare to…?	Quel est le tarif pour…?
Take me to this address, please.	Conduisez-moi à cette adresse, s'il vous plaît.
I'm in a hurry.	Je suis pressé.

Hotel / Hôtel

My name is…	Je m'appelle…
Have you a reservation?	Avez-vous réservé?
I'd like a room with a bath.	J'aimerais une chambre avec bains.
What's the price per night?	Quel est le prix pour une nuit?
May I see the room?	Puis-je voir la chambre?
What's my room number, please?	Quel est le numéro de ma chambre, s'il vous plaît?
There's no hot water.	Il n'y a pas d'eau chaude.
May I see the manager, please?	Puis-je voir le directeur, s'il vous plaît?
Did anyone telephone me?	Y a-t-il eu des appels pour moi?
Is there any mail for me?	Y a-t-il du courrier pour moi?
May I have my bill (check), please?	Puis-je avoir ma note, s'il vous plaît?

Eating out / Restaurant

Do you have a fixed-price menu?	Avez-vous un menu?
May I see the menu?	Puis-je voir la carte?
May we have an ashtray, please?	Pouvons-nous avoir un cendrier, s'il vous plaît?
Where's the toilet, please?	Où sont les toilettes, s'il vous plaît?
I'd like an hors d'uvre (starter).	Je voudrais un hors-d'uvre.
Have you any soup?	Avez-vous du potage?
I'd like some fish.	J'aimerais du poisson.
What kind of fish do you have?	Qu'avez-vous comme poisson?
I'd like a steak.	Je voudrais un steak.
What vegetables have you got?	Quels légumes servez-vous?
Nothing more, thanks.	Je suis servi, merci.
What would you like to drink?	Qu'aimeriez-vous boire?
I'll have a beer, please.	J'aimerais une bière, s'il vous plaît.
I'd like a bottle of wine.	Je voudrais une bouteille de vin.
May I have the bill (check), please?	Puis-je avoir l'addition, s'il vous plaît?
Is service included?	Le service est-il compris?
Thank you, that was a very good meal.	Merci, c'était très bon.

Travelling

Voyages

Where's the railway station, please?	Où se trouve la gare, s'il vous plaît?
Where's the ticket office, please?	Où est le guichet, s'il vous plaît?
I'd like a ticket to...	J'aimerais un billet pour...
First or second class?	Première ou deuxième classe?
First class, please.	Première classe, s'il vous plaît.
Single or return (one way or roundtrip)?	Aller simple ou aller et retour?
Do I have to change trains?	Est-ce que je dois changer de train?
What platform does the train for ... leave from?	De quel quai part le train pour...?
Where's the nearest underground (subway) station?	Où est la station de métro la plus proche?
Where's the bus station, please?	Où est la gare routière, s'il vous plaît?
When's the first bus to...?	A quelle heure part le premier autobus pour...?
Please let me off at the next stop.	S'il vous plaît, déposez-moi au prochain arrêt.

Relaxing

Distractions

What's on at the cinema (movies)?	Que joue-t-on au cinéma?
What time does the film begin?	A quelle heure commence le film?
Are there any tickets for tonight?	Reste-t-il encore des places pour ce soir?
Where can we go dancing?	Où pouvons-nous aller danser?

Meeting people

Rencontres

How do you do.	Bonjour, Madame/Mademoiselle/Monsieur.
How are you?	Comment allez-vous?
Very well, thank you. And you?	Très bien, merci. Et vous?
May I introduce...?	Puis-je vous présenter...?
My name is...	Je m'appelle...
I'm very pleased to meet you.	Enchanté de faire votre connaissance.
How long have you been here?	Depuis combien de temps êtes-vous ici?
It was nice meeting you.	Enchanté d'avoir fait votre connaissance.
Do you mind if I smoke?	Est-ce que ça vous dérange que je fume?
Do you have a light, please?	Avez-vous du feu, s'il vous plaît?
May I get you a drink?	Puis-je vous offrir un verre?
May I invite you for dinner tonight?	Puis-je vous inviter à dîner ce soir?
Where shall we meet?	Où nous retrouverons-nous?

Shops, stores and services

Where's the nearest bank, please?

Where can I cash some travellers' cheques?

Can you give me some small change, please?

Where's the nearest chemist's (pharmacy)?

How do I get there?

Is it within walking distance?

Can you help me, please?

How much is this? And that?

It's not quite what I want.

I like it.

Can you recommend something for sunburn?

I'd like a haircut, please.

I'd like a manicure, please.

Magasins et services

Où se trouve la banque la plus proche, s'il vous plaît?

Où puis-je changer des chèques de voyage?

Pouvez-vous me donner de la monnaie, s'il vous plaît?

Où est la pharmacie la plus proche?

Comment puis-je m'y rendre?

Peut-on y aller à pied?

Pouvez-vous m'aider, s'il vous plaît?

Combien coûte ceci? Et cela?

Ce n'est pas exactement ce que je désire.

Cela me plaît.

Pouvez-vous me conseiller quelque chose contre les coups de soleil?

Je voudrais me faire couper les cheveux, s'il vous plaît.

Je voudrais une manucure, s'il vous plaît.

Street directions

Can you show me on the map where I am?

You are on the wrong road.

Go/Walk straight ahead.

It's on the left/on the right.

Directions

Pouvez-vous me montrer sur la carte où je me trouve?

Vous n'êtes pas sur la bonne route.

Continuez tout droit.

C'est à gauche/à droite.

Emergencies

Call a doctor quickly.

Call an ambulance.

Please call the police.

Urgences

Appelez vite un médecin.

Appelez une ambulance.

Appelez la police, s'il vous plaît.

Anglais-Français

English-French

Introduction

Ce dictionnaire a été conçu dans un but pratique. Vous n'y trouverez donc pas d'information linguistique inutile. Les adresses sont classées par ordre alphabétique, sans tenir compte du fait qu'un mot peut être simple ou composé, avec ou sans trait d'union.

Lorsqu'une adresse est suivie d'adresses secondaires (p. ex. expressions usuelles ou locutions), ces dernières sont également rangées par ordre alphabétique sous le mot vedette.

Chaque mot souche est suivi d'une transcription phonétique (voir le Guide de prononciation) et, s'il y a lieu, de l'indication de la catégorie grammaticale (substantif, verbe, adjectif, etc.). Lorsqu'un mot souche peut appartenir à plusieurs catégories grammaticales, les traductions qui s'y réfèrent sont groupées derrière chacune d'elles.

Les pluriels irréguliers des substantifs sont toujours donnés, de même que certains pluriels pouvant prêter à hésitation.

Pour éviter toute répétition, nous avons utilisé un tilde (~) en lieu et place de l'adresse principale.

Dans le pluriel des mots composés, le tiret (-) remplace la partie du mot qui demeure inchangée.

Un astérisque (*) signale les verbes irréguliers. Pour plus de détails, consulter la liste de ces verbes.

Ce dictionnaire tient compte de l'épellation anglaise. Les mots et les définitions des termes typiquement américains ont été indiqués comme tels (voir la liste des abréviations utilisées dans le texte).

Abréviations

adj	adjectif	*num*	numéral
adv	adverbe	*p*	imparfait
Am	américain	*pl*	pluriel
art	article	*plAm*	pluriel (américain)
conj	conjonction	*pp*	participe passé
f	féminin	*pr*	présent
fpl	féminin pluriel	*pref*	préfixe
m	masculin	*prep*	préposition
mpl	masculin pluriel	*pron*	pronom
n	nom	*v*	verbe
nAm	nom (américain)	*vAm*	verbe (américain)

Guide de prononciation

Chaque article de cette partie du dictionnaire est accompagné d'une transcription phonétique qui vous indique la prononciation des mots. Vous la lirez comme si chaque lettre ou groupe de lettres avait la même valeur qu'en français. Au-dessous figurent uniquement les lettres et les symboles ambigus ou particulièrement difficiles à comprendre. *Toutes* les consonnes, y compris celles placées à la fin d'une syllabe ou d'un mot, doivent être prononcées.

Les traits d'union séparent chaque syllabe. Celles que l'on doit accentuer sont imprimées en *italique*.

Les sons de deux langues ne coïncident jamais parfaitement; mais si vous suivez soigneusement nos indications, vous pourrez prononcer les mots étrangers de façon à vous faire comprendre. Pour faciliter votre tâche, nos transcriptions simplifient parfois légèrement le système phonétique de la langue, mais elles reflètent néanmoins les différences de son essentielles.

Consonnes

ð	le **th** anglais de **th**e; **z** dit en zézayant
gh	comme **g** dans **g**ai
h	doit être prononcé en expirant fortement; rappelle le **h** de l'interjection **h**ue!
ng/nng	comme dans campi**ng**; ou comme le dernier son de pai**n**, prononcé avec l'accent du Midi
s	toujours comme dans **s**i
θ	le **th** anglais de **th**ink; **s** dit en zézayant
y	toujours comme dans **y**eux

Au début ou à la fin d'un mot anglais, **b, d, v, z** sont moins sonores qu'en français. C'est également le cas avec **gh** et **ð.**

Voyelles et diphtongues

æ	entre **a** et **è**
i	entre **i** et **é**
ii	comme **i** dans l**i**re
o	proche du **o** de p**o**mme, mais avec la langue placée plus bas et plus retirée dans la bouche et avec les lèvres plus arrondies

1) Les voyelles longues sont indiquées par un dédoublement (p.ex. **oo**) ou par un accent circonflexe placé sur le second élément (p.ex. **eû**).

2) Nos transcriptions comprenant un **ï** doivent être lues comme des diphtongues; le **ï** ne doit pas être séparé de la voyelle qui le précède (comme dans tr**ahi**), mais doit se fondre dans celle-ci (comme dans **ail**).

3) Les lettres imprimées en petits caractères et dans une position surélevée doivent être prononcées d'une façon assez faible et rapide (p.ex. ^{ou}**ï**, **i**^{eu}).

Prononciation américaine

Notre transcription correspond à la prononciation anglaise habituelle. Si la langue américaine varie grandement d'une région à l'autre, elle présente tout de même quelques différences marquantes par rapport à l'anglais de Grande-Bretagne. Ainsi par exemple:

1) Le **r**, qu'il soit placé devant une consonne ou à la fin d'un mot, se prononce toujours (contrairement à l'habitude anglaise).

2) Le **ââ** devient **ææ** dans certains mots, tels que *ask*, *castle*, *laugh*, etc.

3) Le **o** anglais se prononce **a** ou souvent **oo**.

4) Placé devant **oû**, le son **y** est fréquemment omis (ainsi: *duty*, *tune*, *new*, etc.)

5) Enfin, l'accent tonique de certains mots peut varier considérablement.

A

a (éï, eu) *art* (an) un *art*

abbey (*æ*-bi) *n* abbaye *f*

abbreviation (eu-brii-vi-*éï*-cheunn) *n* abréviation *f*

ability (eu-*bi*-leu-ti) *n* capacité *f*

able (*éï*-beul) *adj* en mesure; capable; ***be ~ to** *être capable de; *savoir, *pouvoir

aboard (eu-*bood*) *adv* à bord

abolish (eu-*bo*-lich) *v* abolir

abortion (eu-*boo*-cheunn) *n* avortement *m*

about (eu-*baout*) *prep* de; concernant, sur; autour de; *adv* à peu près; autour

above (eu-*bav*) *prep* au-dessus de; *adv* en haut

abroad (eu-*brood*) *adv* à l'étranger

abscess (*æb*-sèss) *n* abcès *m*

absence (*æb*-seunns) *n* absence *f*

absent (*æb*-seunnt) *adj* absent

absolutely (*æb*-seu-loût-li) *adv* absolument

abstain from (eub-*stéïn*) s'*abstenir de

abstract (*æb*-strækt) *adj* abstrait

absurd (eub-*seûd*) *adj* absurde

abundance (eu-*bann*-deunns) *n* abondance *f*

abundant (eu-*bann*-deunnt) *adj* abondant

abuse (eu-*byoûss*) *n* abus *m*

abyss (eu-*biss*) *n* abîme *m*

academy (eu-*kæ*-deu-mi) *n* académie *f*

accelerate (euk-*sè*-leu-réït) *v* accélérer

accelerator (euk-*sè*-leu-réï-teu) *n* accélérateur *m*

accent (*æk*-seunnt) *n* accent *m*

accept (euk-*sèpt*) *v* accepter

access (*æk*-sèss) *n* accès *m*

accessible (euk-*sè*-seu-beul) *adj* accessible

accessories (euk-*sè*-seu-riz) *pl* accessoires *mpl*

accident (*æk*-si-deunnt) *n* accident *m*

accidental (*æk*-si-*dèn*-teul) *adj* accidentel

accommodate (eu-*ko*-meu-déït) *v* loger

accommodation (eu-ko-meu-*déï*-cheunn) *n* accommodation *f*, logement *m*

accompany (eu-*kamm*-peu-ni) *v* accompagner

accomplish (eu-*kamm*-plich) *v* achever; accomplir

accordance: in ~ with (inn eu-*koo*-deunns ^{ou}ið) conformément à

according to (eu-*koo*-dinng toû) d'après, selon; conformément à

account (eu-*kaount*) *n* compte *m*; récit *m*; **~ for** rendre compte de; **on ~ of** à cause de

accountable (eu-*kaoun*-teu-beul) *adj* responsable

accurate (*æ*-kyou-reut) *adj* précis

accuse (eu-*kyoûz*) *v* accuser

accused (eu-*kyoûzd*) *n* prévenu *m*, -e *f*

accustom (eu-*ka*-steumm) *v* familiariser; **accustomed** accoutumé, habitué

ache (éïk) *v* *faire mal; *n* douleur *f*

achieve (eu-*tchiiv*) *v* *parvenir à; accomplir

achievement (eu-*tchiiv*-meunnt) *n* performance *f*

acid (*æ*-sid) *n* acide *m*

acknowledge (euk-*no*-lidj) *v* *reconnaître; *admettre; confirmer

acne (*æk*-ni) *n* acné *f*

acquaintance (eu-*kouéïn*-teunns) *n* connaissance *f*

acquire (eu-*kouaïeu*) *v* *acquérir

acquisition (æ-k^{ou}i-*zi*-cheunn) *n* acquisition *f*

acquittal (eu-*koui*-teul) *n* acquittement *m*

across (eu-*kross*) *prep* à travers; de l'autre côté de; *adv* de l'autre côté

act (ækt) *n* acte *m*; numéro *m*; *v* agir; se *conduire; jouer

action (*æk*-cheunn) *n* action *f*

active (*æk*-tiv) *adj* actif; animé

activity (æk-*ti*-veu-ti) *n* activité *f*

actor (*æk*-teu) *n* acteur *m*

actress (*æk*-triss) *n* actrice *f*

actual (*æk*-tchou-eul) *adj* véritable, réel

actually (*æk*-tchou-eu-li) *adv* en réalité

acute (eu-*kyoût*) *adj* aigu

adapt (eu-*dæpt*) *v* adapter

add (æd) *v* additionner; ajouter

addition (eu-*di*-cheunn) *n* addition *f*

additional (eu-*di*-cheu-neul) *adj* supplémentaire; accessoire

address (eu-*drèss*) *n* adresse *f*; *v* adresser; s'adresser à

addressee (æ-drè-*sii*) *n* destinataire *m*

adequate (*æ*-di-k^{ou}eut) *adj* adéquat; approprié

adjective (*æ*-djik-tiv) *n* adjectif *m*

adjourn (eu-*djeûnn*) *v* ajourner

adjust (eu-*djast*) *v* ajuster; rectifier; régler

administer (eud-*mi*-ni-steu) *v* administrer

administration (eud-mi-ni-*strëï*-cheunn) *n* administration *f*; gestion *f*

administrative (eud-*mi*-ni-streu-tiv) *adj* administratif; **~ law** droit administratif

admiration (æd-meu-*rëï*-cheunn) *n* admiration *f*

admire (eud-*maïeu*) *v* admirer

admission (eud-*mi*-cheunn) *n* admission *f*

admit (eud-*mit*) *v* *admettre; *reconnaître

admittance (eud-*mi*-teunns) *n* accès *m*; **no ~** entrée interdite

adopt (eu-*dopt*) *v* adopter

adoption (eu-*dop*-cheunn) *n* adoption *f*

adorable (eu-*doo*-reu-beul) *adj* adorable

adult (*æ*-dalt) *n* adulte *m*; *adj* adulte

advance (eud-*vââns*) *n* avancement *m*; avance *f*; *v* avancer; **in ~** à l'avance, d'avance

advanced (eud-*vâânst*) *adj* avancé

advantage (eud-*vâân*-tidj) *n* avantage *m*

advantageous (æd-veunn-*tëï*-djeuss) *adj* avantageux

adventure (eud-*vèn*-tcheu) *n* aventure *f*

advertise (*æd*-veu-taïz) *v* faire de la réclame (pour), annoncer, faire connaître; insérer une annonce

advertisement (eud-*veû*-tiss-meunnt) *n* annonce *f*; publicité *f*

advertising (*æd*-veu-taï-zinng) *n* publicité *f*

advice (eud-*vaïss*) *n* avis *m*, conseil *m*

advise (eud-*vaïz*) *v* donner des conseils, conseiller

advocate (*æd*-veu-keut) *n* partisan *m*

aerial (*èeu*-ri-eul) *n* antenne *f*

aeroplane (*èeu*-reu-pléïn) *n* avion *m*

affair (eu-*fèeu*) *n* affaire *f*; liaison *f*, affaire de cœur

affect (eu-*fèkt*) *v* affecter; toucher

affected (eu-*fèk*-tid) *adj* affecté

affection (eu-*fèk*-cheunn) *n* affection *f*

affectionate (eu-*fèk*-cheu-nit) *adj* affectueux

affiliated (eu-*fi*-li-éï-tid) *adj* affilié

affirm (eu-*feûm*) *v* affirmer, soutenir

affirmative (eu-*feû*-meu-tiv) *adj* affirmatif

afford (eu-*food*) *v* se *permettre

afraid (eu-*frèïd*) *adj* apeuré, effrayé; *be ~ *avoir peur

Africa (*æ*-fri-keu) Afrique *f*

African (*æ*-fri-keunn) *adj* africain; *n* Africain *m*

after (*ââf*-teu) *prep* après; derrière; *conj* après que

afternoon (ââf-teu-*noûn*) *n* après-midi *m/f*

afterwards (*ââf*-teu-^{ou}eudz) *adv* après; par la suite, ensuite

again (eu-*ghèn*) *adv* encore; de nouveau; ~ **and again** toujours et encore

against (eu-*ghènst*) *prep* contre

age (éïdj) *n* âge *m*; vieillesse *f*; **of ~** majeur; **under ~** mineur

aged (*éï*-djid) *adj* âgé; vieux

agency (*éï*-djeunn-si) *n* agence *f*; bureau *m*

agenda (éï-*djèn*-deu) *n* ordre du jour

agent (*éï*-djeunnt) *n* agent *m*, représentant *m*

aggressive (eu-*ghrè*-siv) *adj* agressif

ago (eu-*ghôou*) *adv* il y a

agree (eu-*ghrii*) *v* *être d'accord; *consentir; concorder

agreeable (eu-*ghrii*-eu-beul) *adj* agréable

agreement (eu-*ghrii*-meunnt) *n* contrat *m*; accord *m*; entente *f*

agriculture (*æ*-ghri-kal-tcheu) *n* agriculture *f*

ahead (eu-*hèd*) *adv* en avant; ~ **of** devant; *go ~ continuer; **straight ~** tout droit

aid (éïd) *n* aide *f*; *v* assister, aider

aim (éïm) *n* but *m*; ~ **at** viser; aspirer à

air (è^{eu}) *n* air *m*; *v* aérer; ~ **conditioning** climatisation *f*

air-conditioned *adj* climatisé

aircraft (*èeu*-krââft) *n* (pl ~) avion *m*; appareil *m*

airfield (*èeu*-fiild) *n* terrain d'aviation

air-filter (*èeu*-fil-teu) *n* filtre à air

airline (*èeu*-laïn) *n* ligne aérienne

airmail (*èeu*-méïl) *n* poste aérienne

airplane (*èeu*-pléïn) *n*Am avion *m*

airport (*èeu*-poot) *n* aéroport *m*

airsickness (*èeu*-sik-neuss) *n* mal de l'air

airtight (*èeu*-taït) *adj* hermétique

airy (*èeu*-ri) *adj* aéré

aisle (aïl) *n* bas-côté *m*; passage *m*

alarm (eu-*lââm*) *n* alerte *f*; *v* alarmer; ~ **clock** réveil *m*

album (*æl*-beumm) *n* album *m*

alcohol (*æl*-keu-hol) *n* alcool *m*

alcoholic (æl-keu-*ho*-lik) *adj* alcoolique

ale (éïl) *n* bière *f*

Algeria (æl-*djïeu*-ri-eu) Algérie *f*

Algerian (æl-*djïeu*-ri-eunn) *adj* algérien; *n* Algérien *m*

alien (*éï*-li-eunn) *n* étranger *m*, -ère *f*; *adj* étranger

alike (eu-*laïk*) *adj* pareil, semblable; *adv* de la même façon

alive (eu-*laïv*) *adj* en vie, vivant

all (ool) *adj* tout; ~ **in** tout compris; ~ **right!** bien!; **at ~** du tout

allergy (*æ*-leu-dji) *n* allergie *f*

alley (*æ*-li) *n* ruelle *f*

alliance (eu-*laï*-eunns) *n* alliance *f*

Allies (*æ*-laïz) *pl* Alliés

allot (eu-*lot*) *v* assigner

allow (eu-*laou*) *v* autoriser, *permettre; ~ **to** autoriser à; *be allowed *être autorisé

allowance (eu-*laou*-eunns) *n* allocation *f*

all-round (ool-*raound*) *adj* universel

almond (*ââ*-meunnd) *n* amande *f*

almost (*ool*-mô^{ou}st) *adv* presque; à peu près

alone (eu-*lôoun*) *adv* seul

along (eu-*lonng*) *prep* le long de

aloud (eu-*laoud*) *adv* à haute voix

alphabet (*æl*-feu-bèt) *n* alphabet *m*

already (ool-*rè*-di) *adv* déjà

also (*ool*-sô^{ou}) *adv* aussi; de même, également

altar (*ool*-teu) *n* autel *m*

alter (*ool*-teu) *v* changer, modifier

alteration (ool-teu-*réï*-cheunn) *n* changement *m*, modification *f*

alternate (ool-*teû*-neut) *adj* alternatif

alternative (ool-*teû*-neu-tiv) *n* alternative *f*

although (ool-*ðôou*) *conj* quoique, bien que

altitude (*æl*-ti-tyoûd) *n* altitude *f*

alto (*æl*-tô^{ou}) *n* (pl ∼s) contralto *m*

altogether (ool-teu-*ghè*-ðeu) *adv* entièrement; en tout

always (*ool*-^{ou}éïz) *adv* toujours

am (æm) *v* (pr be)

amaze (eu-*méïz*) *v* étonner, *surprendre

amazement (eu-*méïz*-meunnt) *n* étonnement *m*

amazing (eu-*méï*-zinng) *adj* stupéfiant, étonnant

ambassador (æm-*bæ*-seu-deu) *n* ambassadeur *m*

amber (*æm*-beu) *n* ambre *m*

ambiguous (æm-*bi*-ghyou-euss) *adj* ambigu; équivoque

ambition (æm-*bi*-cheunn) *n* ambition *f*

ambitious (æm-*bi*-cheuss) *adj* ambitieux

ambulance (*æm*-byou-leunns) *n* ambulance *f*

America (eu-*mè*-ri-keu) Amérique *f*

American (eu-*mè*-ri-keunn) *adj* américain; *n* Américain *m*

amid (eu-*mid*) *prep* entre; parmi, au milieu de

ammonia (eu-*môou*-ni-eu) *n* ammoniaque *f*

amnesty (*æm*-ni-sti) *n* amnistie *f*

among (eu-*manng*) *prep* parmi; au milieu de, entre; ∼ **other things** entre autres

amount (eu-*maount*) *n* quantité *f*; montant *m*, somme *f*; ∼ **to** se monter à

amuse (eu-*myoûz*) *v* divertir, amuser

amusement (eu-*myoûz*-meunnt) *n* amusement *m*, divertissement *m*

amusing (eu-*myoû*-zinng) *adj* plaisant

anaemia (eu-*nii*-mi-eu) *n* anémie *f*

anaesthesia (æ-niss-*θii*-zi-eu) *n* anesthésie *f*

anaesthetic (æ-niss-*θè*-tik) *n* anesthésique *m*

analyse (*æ*-neu-laïz) *v* analyser

analysis (eu-*næ*-leu-siss) *n* (pl -ses) analyse *f*

analyst (*æ*-neu-list) *n* analyste *m/f*; psychanalyste *m/f*

anarchy (*æ*-neu-ki) *n* anarchie *f*

anatomy (eu-*næ*-teu-mi) *n* anatomie *f*

ancestor (*æn*-sè-steu) *n* ancêtre *m/f*

anchor (*æng*-keu) *n* ancre *f*

anchovy (*æn*-tcheu-vi) *n* anchois *m*

ancient (*éïn*-cheunnt) *adj* vieux, ancien; antique

and (ænd, eunnd) *conj* et

angel (*éïn*-djeul) *n* ange *m*

anger (*æng*-gheu) *n* colère *f*; fureur *f*

angle (*æng*-gheul) *v* pêcher à la ligne; *n* angle *m*

angry (*æng*-ghri) *adj* en colère

animal (*æ*-ni-meul) *n* animal *m*

ankle (*æng*-keul) *n* cheville *f*

annex¹ (æ-nèks) *n* annexe *f*

annex² (eu-*nèks*) *v* annexer

anniversary (æ-ni-*veû*-seu-ri) *n* anniversaire *m*

announce (eu-*naouns*) *v* annoncer

announcement (eu-*naouns*-meunnt)

n annonce *f*

annoy (eu-*noï*) *v* agacer, fâcher;
ennuyer

annoyance (eu-*noï*-eunns) *n* ennui *m*

annoying (eu-*noï*-inng) *adj* ennuyeux

annual (*æ*-nyou-eul) *adj* annuel; *n*
annuaire *m*

annum: per ~ (peur *æ*-neumm) par an

anonymous (eu-*no*-ni-meuss) *adj*
anonyme

another (eu-*na*-ðeu) *adj* encore un; un
autre

answer (*âân*-seu) *v* répondre à; *n*
réponse *f*

ant (ænt) *n* fourmi *f*

antibiotic (æn-ti-baï-*o*-tik) *n*
antibiotique *m*

anticipate (æn-*ti*-si-péït) *v* *prévoir,
anticiper; *prévenir

antifreeze (*æn*-ti-friiz) *n* antigel *m*

antipathy (æn-*ti*-peu-θi) *n* antipathie *f*

antique (æn-*tiik*) *adj* antique; *n*
antiquité *f*; **~ dealer** antiquaire *m/f*

antiquity (æn-*ti*-k^{ou}eu-ti) *n* Antiquité;
antiquities *pl* antiquités

anxiety (æng-*zaï*-eu-ti) *n* anxiété *f*

anxious (*ængk*-cheuss) *adj* désireux;
inquiet

any (è-ni) *adj* n'importe quel

anybody (è-ni-bo-di) *pron* n'importe
qui

anyhow (è-ni-haou) *adv* n'importe
comment

anyone (è-ni-^{ou}ann) *pron* chacun

anything (è-ni-θinng) *pron* n'importe
quoi

anyway (è-ni-^{ou}éï) *adv* de toute façon

anywhere (è-ni-^{ou}è^{eu}) *adv* n'importe
où

apart (eu-*pâât*) *adv* à part,
séparément; **~ from** abstraction faite
de

apartment (eu-*pâât*-meunnt) *nAm*
appartement *m*; étage *m*; **~ house**

Am immeuble d'habitation

aperitif (eu-*pè*-reu-tiv) *n* apéritif *m*

apologize (eu-*po*-leu-djaïz) *v*
s'excuser

apology (eu-*po*-leu-dji) *n* excuse *f*

apparatus (æ-peu-*réï*-teuss) *n*
dispositif *m*, appareil *m*

apparent (eu-*pæ*-reunnt) *adj* apparent

apparently (eu-*pæ*-reunnt-li) *adv*
apparemment; manifestement

appeal (eu-*pül*) *n* appel *m*

appear (eu-*pieu*) *v* sembler, *paraître;
*apparaître; se présenter

appearance (eu-*pieu*-reunns) *n*
apparence *f*; aspect *m*; entrée *f*

appendicitis (eu-pèn-di-*saï*-tiss) *n*
appendicite *f*

appendix (eu-*pèn*-diks) *n* (pl -dices,
-dixes) appendice *m*

appetite (*æ*-peu-taït) *n* appétit *m*

appetizer (*æ*-peu-taï-zeu) *n*
amusegueule *m*

appetizing (*æ*-peu-taï-zinng) *adj*
appétissant

applaud (eu-*plood*) *v* applaudir

applause (eu-*plooz*) *n*
applaudissements *mpl*

apple (*æ*-peul) *n* pomme *f*

appliance (eu-*plaï*-eunns) *n* appareil
m

application (æ-pli-*kéï*-cheunn) *n*
application *f*; demande *f*; candidature
f

apply (eu-*plaï*) *v* appliquer; se *servir
de; solliciter un emploi; s'appliquer à

appoint (eu-*poïnt*) *v* désigner,
nommer

appointment (eu-*poïnt*-meunnt) *n*
rendez-vous *m*; nomination *f*

appreciate (eu-*prii*-chi-éït) *v* évaluer;
apprécier

appreciation (eu-prii-chi-*éï*-cheunn) *n*
appréciation *f*

apprentice (eu-*prèn*-tiss) *n* apprenti

m, **-e** *f*

approach (eu-*prôoutch*) *v* approcher; *n* approche *f*; accès *m*

appropriate (eu-*prôou*-pri-eut) *adj* juste, approprié, adéquat

approval (eu-*proû*-veul) *n* approbation *f*; consentement *m*, accord *m*; **on ~** à l'essai

approve (eu-*proûv*) *v* approuver; **~ of** *être d'accord avec

approximate (eu-*prok*-si-meut) *adj* approximatif

approximately (eu-*prok*-si-meut-li) *adv* à peu près, approximativement

apricot (*éï*-pri-kot) *n* abricot *m*

April (*éï*-preul) avril

apron (*éï*-preunn) *n* tablier *m*

Arab (*æ*-reub) *adj* arabe; *n* Arabe *m/f*

arbitrary (*ââ*-bi-treu-ri) *adj* arbitraire

arcade (ââ-*kéïd*) *n* arcade *f*

arch (ââtch) *n* arche *f*; voûte *f*

arch(a)eologist (ââ-ki-*o*-leu-djist) *n* archéologue *m/f*

arch(a)eology (ââ-ki-*o*-leu-dji) *n* archéologie *f*

archbishop (ââtch-*bi*-cheup) *n* archevêque *m*

arched (ââtcht) *adj* arqué

architect (*ââ*-ki-tèkt) *n* architecte *m/f*

architecture (*ââ*-ki-tèk-tcheu) *n* architecture *f*

archives (*ââ*-kaïvz) *pl* archives *fpl*

are (ââ) *v* (pr be)

area (*èeu*-ri-eu) *n* région *f*; zone *f*; **~ code** indicatif *m*

Argentina (ââ-djeunn-*tii*-neu) Argentine *f*

Argentinian (ââ-djeunn-*ti*-ni-eunn) *adj* argentin; *n* Argentin *m*

argue (*ââ*-ghyoû) *v* argumenter, discuter; disputer

argument (*ââ*-ghyou-meunnt) *n* argument *m*; discussion *f*; dispute *f*

***arise** (eu-*raïz*) *v* surgir

arm (ââm) *n* bras *m*; arme *f*; *v* armer

armchair (*ââm*-tchè*eu*) *n* fauteuil *m*

armed (ââmd) *adj* armé; **~ forces** forces armées

armour (*ââ*-meu) *n* armure *f*

army (*ââ*-mi) *n* armée *f*

aroma (eu-*rôou*-meu) *n* arôme *m*

around (eu-*raound*) *prep* autour de; *adv* autour

arrange (eu-*réïndj*) *v* classer, arranger; préparer

arrangement (eu-*réïndj*-meunnt) *n* règlement *m*

arrest (eu-*rèst*) *v* arrêter; *n* arrestation *f*

arrival (eu-*raï*-veul) *n* arrivée *f*; venue *f*

arrive (eu-*raïv*) *v* arriver

arrow (*æ*-rô*ou*) *n* flèche *f*

art (âât) *n* art *m*; habileté *f*; **~ collection** collection d'art; **~ exhibition** exposition d'art; **~ gallery** galerie d'art; **~ history** histoire de l'art; **arts and crafts** arts et métiers; **~ school** académie des beaux-arts

artery (*ââ*-teu-ri) *n* artère *f*

artichoke (*ââ*-ti-tchô*ou*k) *n* artichaut *m*

article (*ââ*-ti-keul) *n* article *m*

artificial (ââ-ti-*fi*-cheul) *adj* artificiel

artist (*ââ*-tist) *n* artiste *m/f*

artistic (ââ-*ti*-stik) *adj* artistique

as (æz) *conj* comme; aussi; que; puisque, parce que; **~ from** à partir de; **~ if** comme si

asbestos (æz-*bè*-stoss) *n* amiante *m*

ascend (eu-*sènd*) *v* monter; *faire l'ascension de

ascent (eu-*sènt*) *n* montée *f*

ascertain (æ-seu-*téïn*) *v* établir; vérifier

ash (æch) *n* cendre *f*

ashamed (eu-*chéïmd*) *adj* honteux; ***be ~** *avoir honte

ashore (eu-*choo*) *adv* à terre

ashtray (*æch*-tréï) *n* cendrier *m*

Asia (*éï*-cheu) Asie *f*

Asian (*éï*-cheunn) *adj* asiatique; *n* Asiatique *m/f*

aside (eu-*saïd*) *adv* de côté, à part

ask (âask) *v* demander; prier

asleep (eu-*sliip*) *adj* endormi

asparagus (eu-*spæ*-reu-gheuss) *n* asperge *f*

aspect (*æ*-spèkt) *n* aspect *m*

asphalt (*æss*-fælt) *n* asphalte *m*

aspire (eu-*spaïeu*) *v* aspirer

aspirin (*æ*-speu-rinn) *n* aspirine *f*

assassination (eu-sæ-si-si-*néï*-cheunn) *n* assassinat *m*

assault (eu-*soolt*) *v* attaquer; violer

assemble (eu-*sèm*-beul) *v* rassembler; monter, assembler

assembly (eu-*sèm*-bli) *n* réunion *f*, assemblée *f*

assignment (eu-*saïn*-meunnt) *n* tâche assignée

assign to (eu-*saïn*) assigner à; attribuer à

assist (eu-*sist*) *v* assister

assistance (eu-si-*steunns*) *n* secours *m*; aide *f*, assistance *f*

assistant (eu-si-*steunnt*) *n* assistant *m*, -e *f*

associate (eu-*sôou*-chi-eut) *n* partenaire *m/f*, associé *m*, -e *f*; allié *m*; membre *m*; *v* associer; ~ **with** fréquenter

association (eu-sô^{ou}-si-*éï*-cheunn) *n* association *f*

assort (eu-*soot*) *v* classer

assortment (eu-*soot*-meunnt) *n* assortiment *m*

assume (eu-*syoûm*) *v* supposer, présumer

assure (eu-*choueu*) *v* assurer

asthma (*æss*-meu) *n* asthme *m*

astonish (eu-*sto*-nich) *v* étonner

astonishing (eu-*sto*-ni-chinng) *adj* étonnant

astonishment (eu-*sto*-nich-meunnt) *n* étonnement *m*

astronaut (*æss*-treu-noot) *n* astronaute *m/f*

astronomy (eu-*stro*-neu-mi) *n* astronomie *f*

asylum (eu-*saï*-leumm) *n* asile *m*

at (æt) *prep* à, chez; vers

ate (èt) *v* (p eat)

athlete (*æθ*-liit) *n* athlète *m*

athletics (æθ-lè-tiks) *pl* athlétisme *m*

Atlantic (eut-*læn*-tik) Océan Atlantique

atmosphere (*æt*-meuss-fi^{eu}) *n* atmosphère *f*; ambiance *f*

atomic (eu-*to*-mik) *adj* atomique; nucléaire

attach (eu-*tætch*) *v* attacher; fixer; *joindre

attack (eu-*tæk*) *v* attaquer; *n* attaque *f*

attain (eu-*téïn*) *v* *atteindre

attainable (eu-*téï*-neu-beul) *adj* accessible

attempt (eu-*tèmpt*) *v* tenter; essayer; *n* tentative *f*

attend (eu-*tènd*) *v* assister à; ~ **on** *servir; ~ **to** s'occuper de; *faire attention à, prêter attention à

attendance (eu-*tèn*-deunns) *n* assistance *f*

attendant (eu-*tèn*-deunnt) *n* gardien *m*, gardienne *f*

attention (eu-*tèn*-cheunn) *n* attention *f*; *pay* ~ *faire attention

attentive (eu-*tèn*-tiv) *adj* attentif

attest (eu-*tèst*) *v* attester; ~ **to** témoigner de

attic (*æ*-tik) *n* grenier *m*

attitude (*æ*-ti-tyoûd) *n* attitude *f*

attorney (eu-*teû*-ni) *n* avocat *m*, -e *f*

attract (eu-*trækt*) *v* attirer

attraction (eu-*træk*-cheunn) *n*

attraction *f*; attrait *m*
attractive (eu-*træk*-tiv) *adj* séduisant
auction (*ook*-cheunn) *n* vente aux enchères
audible (*oo*-di-beul) *adj* audible
audience (*oo*-di-eunns) *n* public *m*
auditor (*oo*-di-teu) *n* auditeur *m*, -trice *f*
August (*oo*-gheust) août
aunt (âânt) *n* tante *f*
Australia (o-*stréï*-li-eu) Australie *f*
Australian (o-*stréï*-li-eunn) *adj* australien; *n* Australien *m*
Austria (*o*-stri-eu) Autriche *f*
Austrian (*o*-stri-eunn) *adj* autrichien; *n* Autrichien *m*
authentic (oo-*θèn*-tik) *adj* authentique
author (*oo*-θeu) *n* auteur *m*
authoritarian (oo-θo-ri-*tèeu*-ri-eunn) *adj* autoritaire
authority (oo-*θo*-reu-ti) *n* autorité *f*; pouvoir *m*
authorization (oo-θeu-raï-*zéï*-cheunn) *n* autorisation *f*; permission *f*
authorize (*oo*-θeu-raïz) *v* autoriser
automatic (oo-teu-*mæ*-tik) *adj* automatique
automation (oo-teu-*méï*-cheunn) *n* automatisation *f*

automobile (*oo*-teu-meu-biil) *n* auto *f*; ~ **club** club automobile
autonomous (oo-*to*-neu-meuss) *adj* autonome
autumn (*oo*-teumm) *n* automne *m*
available (eu-*véï*-leu-beul) *adj* disponible
avalanche (*æ*-veu-lâânch) *n* avalanche *f*
avenue (*æ*-veu-nyoû) *n* avenue *f*
average (*æ*-veu-ridj) *adj* moyen; *n* moyenne *f*; **on the ~** en moyenne
averse (eu-*veûss*) *adj* ennemi, peu disposé
aversion (eu-*veû*-cheunn) *n* aversion *f*
avert (eu-*veût*) *v* détourner
avoid (eu-*voïd*) *v* éviter
await (eu-ouéït) *v* attendre
awake (eu-ouéïk) *adj* réveillé
***awake** (eu-ouéïk) *v* réveiller
award (eu-ouood) *n* prix *m*; *v* décerner
aware (eu-ouèeu) *adj* conscient
away (eu-ouéï) *adv* loin; ***go ~** s'en *aller
awful (*oo*-feul) *adj* terrible
awkward (*oo*-k^ou^eud) *adj* embarrassant; maladroit
awning (*oo*-ninng) *n* marquise *f*
axe (æks) *n* hache *f*
axle (*æk*-seul) *n* essieu *m*

B

baby (*béï*-bi) *n* bébé *m*; ~ **carriage** *Am* poussette *f*
babysitter (*béï*-bi-si-teu) *n* baby-sitter *m*
bachelor (*bæ*-tcheu-leu) *n* célibataire *m*
back (bæk) *n* dos *m*; *adv* en arrière; ***go ~** retourner

backache (*bæ*-kéïk) *n* mal au dos
backbone (*bæk*-bô^ou^n) *n* épine dorsale
background (*bæk*-ghraound) *n* fond *m*
backwards (*bæk*-^ou^eudz) *adv* en arrière
bacon (*béï*-keunn) *n* lard *m*

bacterium (bæk-*tii*-ri-eumm) *n* (pl -ria) bactérie *f*

bad (bæd) *adj* mauvais; grave; vilain

bag (bægh) *n* sac *m*; sac à main; valise *f*

baggage (*bæ*-ghidj) *n* bagage *m*; ~ **check** *Am* consigne *f*; **hand** ~ *Am* bagage à main

bail (béïl) *n* caution *f*

bait (béït) *n* amorce *f*

bake (béïk) *v* *cuire au four

baker (*béï*-keu) *n* boulanger *m*

bakery (*béï*-keu-ri) *n* boulangerie *f*

balance (*bæ*-leunns) *n* équilibre *m*; bilan *m*; solde *m*

balcony (*bæl*-keu-ni) *n* balcon *m*

bald (boold) *adj* chauve

ball (bool) *n* ballon *m*, balle *f*; bal *m*

ballet (*bæ*-léï) *n* ballet *m*

balloon (beu-*loûn*) *n* ballon *m*

ballpoint pen (*bool*-poïnt-pèn) *n* stylo à bille

ballroom (*bool*-roûm) *n* salle de bal

bamboo (bæm-*boû*) *n* (pl ~s) bambou *m*

banana (beu-*nââ*-neu) *n* banane *f*

band (bænd) *n* orchestre *m*; lien *m*

bandage (*bæn*-didj) *n* pansement *m*

bandit (*bæn*-dit) *n* bandit *m*

bangle (*bæng*-gheul) *n* bracelet *m*

bank (bængk) *n* rive *f*; banque *f*; *v* déposer en banque; ~ **account** compte en banque

banknote (*bængk*-nô^{ou}t) *n* billet de banque

bank rate (*bængk*-réït) *n* taux d'escompte

bankrupt (*bængk*-rapt) *adj* en faillite

banner (*bæ*-neu) *n* bannière *f*

banquet (*bæng*-k^{ou}it) *n* banquet *m*

baptism (*bæp*-ti-zeumm) *n* baptême *m*

baptize (bæp-*taïz*) *v* baptiser

bar (bââ) *n* bar *m*; barre *f*; barreau *m*

barbecue (*bââ*-bi-kyoû) *n* barbecue *m*; *v* griller au charbon de bois; rôtir tout entier

barber (*bââ*-beu) *n* coiffeur *m*

bare (bè^{eu}) *adj* nu

barely (*bèu*-li) *adv* à peine

bargain (*bââ*-ghinn) *n* bonne affaire; *v* marchander

baritone (*bæ*-ri-tô^{ou}n) *n* bariton *m*

bark (bââk) *n* écorce *f*; *v* aboyer

barley (*bââ*-li) *n* orge *f*

barman (*bââ*-meunn) *n* (pl -men) barman *m*

barn (bâân) *n* grange *f*

barometer (beu-*ro*-mi-teu) *n* baromètre *m*

baroque (beu-*rok*) *adj* baroque

barracks (*bæ*-reuks) *pl* caserne *f*

barrel (*bæ*-reul) *n* tonneau *m*, baril *m*

barrier (*bæ*-ri-eu) *n* barrière *f*

barrister (*bæ*-ri-steu) *n* avocat *m*

bartender (*bææ*-tèn-deu) *n* barman *m*

base (béïss) *n* base *f*; fondement *m*; *v* baser

baseball (*béïss*-bool) *n* base-ball *m*

basement (*béïss*-meunnt) *n* sous-sol *m*

basic (*béï*-sik) *adj* fondamental

basilica (beu-*zi*-li-keu) *n* basilique *f*

basin (*béï*-seunn) *n* bol *m*, bassin *m*

basis (*béï*-siss) *n* (pl bases) base *f*

basket (*bââ*-skit) *n* panier *m*

bass¹ (béïss) *n* basse *f*

bass² (bæss) *n* (pl ~) perche *f*

bastard (*bââ*-steud) *n* bâtard *m*; salaud *m*

batch (bætch) *n* lot *m*

bath (bââθ) *n* bain *m*; ~ **salts** sels de bain; ~ **towel** serviette de bain

bathe (béïð) *v* se baigner

bathing cap (*béï*-ðinng-kæp) *n* bonnet de bain

bathing suit (*béï*-ðinng-soût) *n* maillot de bain

bathing trunks (*béï*-ðinng-tranngks)

n caleçon de bain

bathrobe (*bââθ*-rô^oub) *n* peignoir *m*

bathroom (*bââθ*-roûm) *n* salle de bains

batter (*bæ*-teu) *n* pâte *f*

battery (*bæ*-teu-ri) *n* pile *f*; accumulateur *m*

battle (*bæ*-teul) *n* bataille *f*; lutte, combat *m*; *v* *combattre

bay (béï) *n* baie *f*; *v* aboyer

***be** (bii) *v* *être

beach (biitch) *n* plage *f*; **nudist ~** plage pour nudistes

bead (biid) *n* perle *f*; **beads** *pl* collier *m*; chapelet *m*

beak (biik) *n* bec *m*

beam (biim) *n* rayon *m*; poutre *f*

bean (biin) *n* haricot *m*

bear (bè^eu) *n* ours *m*

***bear** (bè^eu) *v* porter; tolérer; supporter

beard (bi^eud) *n* barbe *f*

bearer (*bèeu*-reu) *n* porteur *m*

beast (biist) *n* bête *f*; **~ of prey** bête de proie

***beat** (biit) *v* frapper; *battre

beautiful (*byoû*-ti-feul) *adj* beau

beauty (*byoû*-ti) *n* beauté *f*; **~ parlo(u)r** institut de beauté; **~ salon** salon de beauté; **~ treatment** soins de beauté

beaver (*bii*-veu) *n* castor *m*

because (bi-*koz*) *conj* parce que; **~ of** en raison de, à cause de

***become** (bi-*kamm*) *v* *devenir

bed (bèd) *n* lit *m*; **~ and board** pension complète; **~ and breakfast** chambre et petit déjeuner

bedding (*bè*-dinng) *n* literie *f*

bedroom (*bèd*-roûm) *n* chambre à coucher

bee (bii) *n* abeille *f*

beech (bii-tch) *n* hêtre *m*

beef (biif) *n* bœuf *m*

beehive (*bii*-haïv) *n* ruche *f*

been (biin) *v* (pp be)

beer (bi^eu) *n* bière *f*

beet (biit) *n* betterave *f*

beetroot (*biit*-roût) *n* betterave *f*

before (bi-*foo*) *prep* avant; devant; *conj* avant que; *adv* d'avance; précédemment, avant

beg (bègh) *v* mendier; supplier; demander

beggar (*bè*-gheu) *n* mendiant *m*, -e *f*

***begin** (bi-*ghinn*) *v* commencer; débuter

beginner (bi-*ghi*-neu) *n* débutant *m*, -e *f*

beginning (bi-*ghi*-ninng) *n* commencement *m*; début *m*

behalf: on ~ of (onn bi-*hââf* ov) au nom de; en faveur de

behave (bi-*héïv*) *v* se comporter

behavio(u)r (bi-*héï*-vyeu) *n* comportement *m*

behind (bi-*haïnd*) *prep* derrière; *adv* en arrière

beige (béïj) *adj* beige

being (*bii*-inng) *n* être *m*

Belgian (*bèl*-djeunn) *adj* belge; *n* Belge *m*

Belgium (*bèl*-djeumm) Belgique *f*

belief (bi-*liif*) *n* croyance *f*

believe (bi-*liiv*) *v* *croire

bell (bèl) *n* cloche *f*; sonnette *f*

bellboy (*bèl*-boï) *n* chasseur *m*

belly (*bè*-li) *n* ventre *m*

belong (bi-*lonng*) *v* *appartenir

belongings (bi-*lonng*-inngz) *pl* affaires *fpl*

beloved (bi-*lavd*) *adj* aimé

below (bi-*lôou*) *prep* au-dessous de; en bas de; *adv* en dessous

belt (bèlt) *n* ceinture *f*

bench (bèntch) *n* banc *m*

bend (bènd) *n* virage *m*, courbe *f*

***bend** (bènd) *v* courber; **~ down** se

pencher

beneath (bi-*niiθ*) *prep* en dessous de; *adv* au-dessous

benefit (*bè*-ni-fit) *n* profit *m*, bénéfice *m*; avantage *m*; *v* profiter

bent (bènt) *adj* (pp bend) tordu

beret (*bè*-réï) *n* béret *m*

berry (*bè*-ri) *n* baie *f*

beside (bi-*saïd*) *prep* à côté de

besides (bi-*saïdz*) *adv* en outre; d'ailleurs; *prep* outre

best (bèst) *adj* le meilleur

bet (bèt) *n* pari *m*

*bet** (bèt) *v* parier

betray (bi-*tréï*) *v* trahir

better (*bè*-teu) *adj* meilleur

between (bi-*touiin*) *prep* entre

beverage (*bè*-veu-ridj) *n* boisson *f*

beware (bi-*ouèu*) *v* *prendre garde, *faire attention

bewitch (bi-*ouitch*) *v* ensorceler, enchanter

beyond (bi-*yonnd*) *prep* au delà de; outre; *adv* au delà

bible (*baï*-beul) *n* Bible *f*

bicycle (*baï*-si-keul) *n* bicyclette *f*; vélo *m*

bid (bid) *v* commander; dire; faire une offre de; **a ~ to** un effort pour

big (bigh) *adj* grand; volumineux; gros; important

bike (baïk) *n* vélo *m*

bile (baïl) *n* bile *f*

bilingual (baï-*linng*-gh^{ou}eul) *adj* bilingue

bill (bil) *n* facture *f*; addition *f*, note *f*; *v* facturer

billiards (*bil*-yeudz) *pl* billard *m*

billion (*bil*-yeunn) *n* billion *m*, Am milliard *m*

*bind** (baïnd) *v* lier

binding (*baïn*-dinng) *n* reliure *f*

binoculars (bi-*no*-kyeu-leuz) *pl* jumelles *fpl*

biology (baï-*o*-leu-dji) *n* biologie *f*

birch (beûtch) *n* bouleau *m*

bird (beûd) *n* oiseau *m*

Biro (*baï*-rô^{ou}) *n* crayon à bille *m*

birth (beûθ) *n* naissance *f*

birthday (*beûθ*-déï) *n* anniversaire *m*

biscuit (*biss*-kit) *n* biscuit *m*

bishop (*bi*-cheup) *n* évêque *m*

bit (bit) *n* morceau *m*; peu *m*

bitch (bitch) *n* chienne *f*

bite (baït) *n* bouchée *f*; morsure *f*; piqûre *f*

*bite** (baït) *v* mordre

bitter (*bi*-teu) *adj* amer

black (blæk) *adj* noir; **~ market** marché noir

blackberry (*blæk*-beu-ri) *n* mûre *f*

blackbird (*blæk*-beûd) *n* merle *m*

blackboard (*blæk*-bood) *n* tableau noir

blackcurrant (blæk-*ka*-reunnt) *n* cassis *m*

blackmail (*blæk*-méïl) *n* chantage *m*; *v* *faire chanter

blacksmith (*blæk*-smiθ) *n* forgeron *m*

bladder (*blæ*-deu) *n* vessie *f*

blade (bléïd) *n* lame *f*; **~ of grass** brin d'herbe

blame (bléïm) *n* blâme *m*; *v* donner la faute à, blâmer

blank (blængk) *adj* blanc

blanket (*blæng*-kit) *n* couverture *f*

blast (blââst) *n* explosion *f*

blazer (*bléï*-zeu) *n* veste de sport, blazer *m*

bleach (bliitch) *v* décolorer

bleak (bliik) *adj* morne; désolé

*bleed** (bliid) *v* saigner

bless (blèss) *v* bénir

blessing (*blè*-sinng) *n* bénédiction *f*

blind (blaïnd) *n* store *m*, persienne *f*; *adj* aveugle; *v* aveugler

blinker (*blinng*-keu) *n* clignotant *m*

blister (*bli*-steu) *n* ampoule *f*, cloque *f*

blizzard (*bli*-zeud) n tempête de neige

block (blok) v obstruer, bloquer; n bloc m; ~ **of flats** immeuble d'habitation

blond(e) (blonnd) n blonde f

blood (blad) n sang m; ~ **poisoning** septicémie f; ~ **pressure** tension artérielle; ~ **vessel** vaisseau sanguin**bloody** (*bla*-di) adj ensanglanté; sanguinaire; sacré; vachement

blossom (*blo*-seum) n fleur f; v fleurir

blot (blot) n tache f; **blotting paper** papier buvard

blouse (blaouz) n chemisier m

blow (blô^{ou}) n claque f, coup m; coup de vent

***blow** (blô^{ou}) v souffler

blowout (*blôou*-aout) n éclatement m

blue (bloû) adj bleu; déprimé

blunt (blannt) adj émoussé

blush (blach) v rougir

board (bood) n planche f; tableau m; pension f; conseil m; ~ **and lodging** pension complète

boarder (*boo*-deu) n pensionnaire m/f

boardinghouse (*boo*-dinng-haouss) n pension f

boarding school (*boo*-dinng-skoûl) n internat m

boast (bô^{ou}st) v se vanter

boat (bô^{ou}t) n navire m, bateau m

body (*bo*-di) n corps m

bodyguard (*bo*-di-ghââd) n garde du corps

bog (bogh) n marais m

boil (boïl) v *bouillir; n furoncle m

bold (bô^{ou}ld) adj audacieux; effronté, hardi

Bolivia (beu-*li*-vi-eu) Bolivie f

Bolivian (beu-*li*-vi-eunn) adj bolivien; n Bolivien m

bolt (bô^{ou}lt) n verrou m; boulon m

bomb (bomm) n bombe f; v bombarder

bond (bonnd) n obligation f

bone (bô^{ou}n) n os m; arête f; v désosser

bonnet (*bo*-nit) n capot m

book (bouk) n livre m; v *retenir, réserver; *inscrire, enregistrer

booking (*bou*-kinng) n réservation f

bookseller (*bouk*-sè-leu) n libraire m/f

bookstand (*bouk*-stænd) n stand de livres

bookstore (*bouk*-stoo) n librairie f

boot (boût) n botte f; coffre m

booth (boûð) n échoppe f; cabine f

border (*boo*-deu) n frontière f; bord m

bore¹ (boo) v ennuyer; forer; n raseur m

bore² (boo) v (p bear)

boring (*boo*-rinng) adj ennuyeux

born (boon) adj né

borrow (*bo*-rô^{ou}) v emprunter

bosom (*bou*-zeumm) n poitrine f, sein m

boss (boss) n chef m, patron m

botany (*bo*-teu-ni) n botanique f

both (bô^{ou}θ) adj les deux; **both ... and** aussi bien que

bother (*bo*-ðeu) v gêner, tracasser; n tracas m

bottle (*bo*-teul) n bouteille f; ~ **opener** ouvre-bouteilles m; **hotwater ~** bouillotte f

bottleneck (*bo*-teul-nèk) n goulot d'étranglement

bottom (*bo*-teumm) n fond m; postérieur m, derrière m; adj inférieur

bought (boot) v (p, pp buy)

boulder (*bô^{ou}l*-deu) n rocher m

bound (baound) n limite f; *be ~ to *devoir; ~ for en route pour

boundary (*baoun*-deu-ri) n limite f;

frontière f

bouquet (bou-*kéï*) n bouquet m

bourgeois (*boueu*-j^{ou}ââ) adj bourgeois

boutique (bou-*tiik*) n boutique f

bow¹ (baou) v courber

bow² (bô^{ou}) n arc m; ~ **tie** nœud papillon

bowels (baou^{eu}lz) pl intestins

bowl (bô^{ou}l) n bol m

bowling (*bôou*-linng) n bowling m; ~ **alley** bowling m

box¹ (boks) v boxer; **boxing match** match de boxe

box² (boks) n boîte f

box office (*boks*-o-fiss) n guichet de location, guichet m

boy (boï) n garçon m; gamin m, gosse m; serviteur m; ~ **scout** scout m

bra (brââ) n soutien-gorge m

bracelet (*bréïss*-lit) n bracelet m

braces (*bréï*-siz) pl bretelles fpl

brain (bréïn) n cerveau m; intelligence f; ~ **wave** idée lumineuse

brake (bréïk) n frein m; ~ **drum** tambour de frein

branch (brâântch) n branche f; succursale f

brand (brænd) n marque f

brand-new (brænd-*nyoû*) adj flambant neuf

brass (brââss) n laiton m; cuivre m, cuivre jaune; ~ **band** n fanfare f

brave (bréïv) adj courageux, brave

Brazil (breu-*zil*) Brésil m

Brazilian (breu-*zil*-yeunn) adj brésilien; n Brésilien m

breach (briitch) n brèche f

bread (bréd) n pain m; **wholemeal** ~ pain complet

breadth (brèdθ) n largeur f

break (bréïk) n fracture f; pause f

***break** (bréïk) v rompre, casser; ~ **down** tomber en panne; analyser

breakdown (*bréïk*-daoun) n panne f

breakfast (*brèk*-feust) n petit déjeuner

breast (brèst) n sein m

breaststroke (*brèst*-strô^{ou}k) n brasse f

breath (brèθ) n souffle m

breathe (briið) v respirer

breathing (*brii*-ðinng) n respiration f

breed (briid) n race f; espèce f

***breed** (briid) v élever

breeze (briiz) n brise f

brew (broû) v brasser

brewery (*broû*-eu-ri) n brasserie f

bribe (braïb) v *corrompre

bribery (*braï*-beu-ri) n corruption f

brick (brik) n brique f

bricklayer (*brik*-léï^{eu}) n maçon m

bride (braïd) n fiancée f

bridegroom (*braïd*-ghroûm) n marié m

bridge (bridj) n pont m; bridge m

brief (briif) adj bref

briefcase (*briif*-kéïss) n serviette f

briefs (briifs) pl slip m, caleçon m

bright (braït) adj brillant; malin, intelligent

brighten (*braï*-teunn) v faire briller; éclairer; égayer; v s'éclaircir; s'allumer; s'animer

brilliant (*bril*-yeunnt) adj brillant

brim (brimm) n bord m

***bring** (brinng) v apporter; amener; ~ **back** rapporter, ramener; ~ **up** élever; soulever

brisk (brisk) adj vif

Britain (*bri*-teunn) Angleterre f

British (*bri*-tich) adj britannique

Briton (*bri*-teunn) n Britannique m; Anglais m

broad (brood) adj large; vaste, étendu

broadcast (*brood*-kââst) n émission f

***broadcast** (*brood*-kââst) v *émettre

brochure (*brôou*-chou^{eu}) n brochure f

broke¹ (brô^{ou}k) v (p break)

broke² (brô^{ou}k) adj fauché

broken (brôou-keunn) adj (pp break) cassé, brisé; en dérangement

broker (brôou-keu) n courtier m

bronchitis (bronng-kaï-tiss) n bronchite f

bronze (bronnz) n bronze m; adj en bronze

brooch (brôoutch) n broche f

brook (brouk) n ruisseau m

broom (broûm) n balai m

brothel (bro-œul) n bordel m

brother (bra-ðeu) n frère m

brother-in-law (bra-ðeu-rinn-loo) n (pl brothers-) beau-frère m

brought (broot) v (p, pp bring)

brown (braoun) adj brun

bruise (broûz) n bleu m, contusion f; v contusionner

brunette (broû-nèt) n brunette f

brush (brach) n brosse f; pinceau m; v lustrer, brosser

brutal (broû-teul) adj brutal

bubble (ba-beul) n bulle f

buck (bak) m mâle; Am colloquial dollar m; chevalet; v ruer; ~ off jeter, désarçonner; colloquial ~ up se remuer; prendre courage; résister à, opposer; remonter le moral à

bucket (ba-kit) n seau m

buckle (ba-keul) n boucle f

bud (bad) n bourgeon m

buddy (ba-di) n Am colloquial ami m; copain m

budget (ba-djit) n budget m

buffet (bou-féï) n buffet m

bug (bagh) n punaise f; coléoptère m; nAm insecte m

***build** (bild) v bâtir

building (bil-dinng) n construction f

bulb (balb) n bulbe m; oignon m; **light ~** ampoule f

Bulgaria (bal-ghèeu-ri-eu) Bulgarie f

Bulgarian (bal-ghèeu-ri-eunn) adj bulgare; n Bulgare m

bulk (balk) n masse f; majorité f

bulky (bal-ki) adj volumineux

bull (boul) n taureau m

bullet (bou-lit) n balle f

bulletin (bou-li-tinn) n bulletin m, communiqué m; informations pl; Am **bulletin board** tableau m d'affichage

bullfight (boul-faït) n corrida f

bullring (boul-rinng) n arène f

bump (bammp) v cogner; tamponner; frapper; n coup m

bumper (bamm-peu) n pare-choc m

bumpy (bamm-pi) adj cahoteux

bun (bann) n brioche f

bunch (banntch) n bouquet m; bande f

bundle (bann-deul) n paquet m; v empaqueter, lier ensemble

bunk (banngk) n couchette f

buoy (boï) n bouée f

burden (beû-deunn) n fardeau m

bureau (byoueu-rôou) n (pl ~x, ~s) bureau m; nAm commode f

bureaucracy (byoueu-ro-kreu-si) n bureaucratie f

burglar (beû-ghleu) n cambrioleur m, -euse f

burgle (beû-gheul) v cambrioler

burial (bè-ri-eul) n sépulture f, enterrement m

burn (beûnn) n brûlure f

***burn** (beûnn) v brûler

***burst** (beûst) v éclater

bury (bè-ri) v enterrer

bus (bass) n autobus m

bush (bouch) n buisson m

business (biz-neuss) n affaires fpl, commerce m; entreprise f, affaire f; occupation f; ~ **hours** heures d'ouverture, heures de bureau; ~ **trip** voyage d'affaires; **on ~** pour affaires

businessman (biz-neuss-meunn) n (pl -men) homme d'affaires

businesswoman (*biz*-neuss-^{ou}ou-meunn) *n* (pl -women) femme d'affaires

bust (bast) *n* buste *m*

bustle (*ba*-seul) *n* remue-ménage *m*

busy (*bi*-zi) *adj* occupé; animé, affairé

but (bat) *conj* mais; cependant; *prep* sauf

butcher (*bou*-tcheu) *n* boucher *m*

butter (*ba*-teu) *n* beurre *m*

butterfly (*ba*-teu-flaï) *n* papillon *m*; ~ **stroke** brasse papillon

buttock (*ba*-teuk) *n* fesse *f*

button (*ba*-teunn) *n* bouton *m*; *v* boutonner

buttonhole (*ba*-teunn-hô^{ou}l) *n* boutonnière *f*

***buy** (baï) *v* acheter; *acquérir

buyer (*baï*-eu) *n* acheteur *m*, -euse *f*

buzz (baz) *n* bourdonnement *m*; *Am* ~ **saw** scie *f* circulaire; *colloquial* **give someone a** ~ donner un coup de fil à quelqu'un; bourdonner

by (baï) *prep* par; en; près de

bye-bye (*baï-baï*) *colloquial* au revoir!; adieu!

by-pass (*baï*-pââss) *n* route d'évitement; *v* contourner

C

cab (kæb) *n* taxi *m*

cabaret (*kæ*-beu-réï) *n* cabaret *m*; boîte de nuit

cabbage (*kæ*-bidj) *n* chou *m*

cab driver (*kæb*-draï-veu) *n* chauffeur de taxi

cabin (*kæ*-binn) *n* cabine *f*; cabane *f*

cabinet (*kæ*-bi-neut) *n* cabinet *m*

cable (*kéï*-beul) *n* câble *m*; télégramme *m*

café (*kæ*-féï) *n* café *m*

cafeteria (kæ-feu-*tieu*-ri-eu) *n* cafétéria *f*

caffeine (*kæ*-fiin) *n* caféine *f*

cage (kéïdj) *n* cage *f*

cake (kéïk) *n* gâteau *m*; pâtisserie *f*

calamity (keu-*læ*-meu-ti) *n* calamité *f*, catastrophe *f*

calcium (*kæl*-si-eumm) *n* calcium *m*

calculate (*kæl*-kyou-léït) *v* calculer

calculation (kæl-kyou-*léï*-cheunn) *n* calcul *m*

calculator (*kæl*-kyou-léï-teu) *n* calculatrice *f*

calendar (*kæ*-leunn-deu) *n* calendrier *m*

calf (kââf) *n* (pl calves) veau *m*; mollet *m*; ~ **skin** veau *m*

call (kool) *v* appeler; téléphoner; *n* appel *m*; visite *f*; coup de téléphone; ***be called** s'appeler; ~ **names** injurier; ~ **on** rendre visite à; ~ **up** *Am* téléphoner

calm (kââm) *adj* tranquille, calme; ~ **down** calmer

calorie (*kæ*-leu-ri) *n* calorie *f*

came (kéïm) *v* (p come)

camel (*kæ*-meul) *n* chameau *m*

camera (*kæ*-meu-reu) *n* appareil photographique; caméra *f*; ~ **shop** magasin de photographe

camp (kæmp) *n* camp *m*; *v* camper; ~ **bed** lit de camp

campaign (kæm-*péïn*) *n* campagne *f*

camper (*kæm*-peu) *n* campeur *m*

camping (*kæm*-pinng) *n* camping *m*; ~ **site** terrain de camping

can (kæn) *n* boîte *f*; ~ **opener**

ouvreboîte *m*; **canned food**
conserves *fpl*

*can (kæn) *v* *pouvoir

Canada (*kæ*-neu-deu) Canada *m*

Canadian (keu-*néï*-di-eunn) *adj*
canadien; *n* Canadien *m*

canal (keu-*næl*) *n* canal *m*

canary (keu-*nèeu*-ri) *n* canari *m*

cancel (*kæn*-seul) *v* annuler

cancellation (kæn-seu-*léï*-cheunn) *n*
annulation *f*

cancer (*kæn*-seu) *n* cancer *m*

candidate (*kæn*-di-deut) *n* candidat *m*

candle (*kæn*-deul) *n* bougie *f*

candy (*kæn*-di) *nAm* bonbon *m*;
confiserie *f*; **~ store** *Am* confiserie *f*

cane (kéïn) *n* canne *f*

canister (*kæ*-ni-steu) *n* boîte
métallique

canoe (keu-*noû*) *n* canot *m*

canteen (kæn-*tiin*) *n* cantine *f*

canvas (*kæn*-veuss) *n* grosse toile

cap (kæp) *n* casquette *f*

capable (*kéï*-peu-beul) *adj* capable

capacity (keu-*pæ*-seu-ti) *n* capacité *f*;
compétence *f*

cape (kéïp) *n* cape *f*; cap *m*

capital (*kæ*-pi-teul) *n* capitale *f*;
capital *m*; *adj* capital, essentiel; **~
letter** majuscule *f*

capitalism (*kæ*-pi-teu-li-zeumm) *n*
capitalisme *m*

capitulation (keu-pi-tyou-*léï*-cheunn)
n capitulation *f*

capsule (*kæp*-syoûl) *n* capsule *f*

captain (*kæp*-tinn) *n* capitaine *m*;
commandant *m*

capture (*kæp*-tcheu) *v* *faire
prisonnier, capturer; *prendre; *n*
capture *f*; prise *f*

car (kââ) *n* voiture *f*; **~ hire** location de
voitures; **~ park** parc de
stationnement; **~ rental** *Am* location
de voitures

caramel (*kæ*-reu-meul) *n* caramel *m*

caravan (*kæ*-reu-væn) *n* caravane *f*;
roulotte *f*

carburettor (kââ-byou-*rè*-teu) *n*
carburateur *m*

card (kââd) *n* carte *f*; carte postale

cardboard (*kââd*-bood) *n* carton *m*;
adj en carton

cardigan (*kââ*-di-gheunn) *n* cardigan
m

cardinal (*kââ*-di-neul) *n* cardinal *m*;
adj cardinal, principal

care (kè^{eu}) *n* soin *m*; souci *m*; **~ about**
se soucier de; **~ for** *tenir à; ***take ~ of**
*prendre soin de, s'occuper de

career (keu-*rieu*) *n* carrière *f*

carefree (*kèeu*-frii) *adj* insouciant

careful (*kèeu*-feul) *adj* prudent;
soigneux, attentif

careless (*kèeu*-leuss) *adj* inattentif,
négligent

caretaker (*kèeu*-téï-keu) *n* gardien *m*

cargo (*kââ*-ghô^{ou}) *n* (pl ~es)
chargement *m*, cargaison *f*

carnival (*kââ*-ni-veul) *n* carnaval *m*

carp (kââp) *n* (pl ~) carpe *f*

carpenter (*kââ*-pinn-teu) *n* menuisier
m

carpet (*kââ*-pit) *n* tapis *m*

carriage (*kæ*-ridj) *n* wagon *m*;
carrosse *m*, voiture *f*

carrot (*kæ*-reut) *n* carotte *f*

carry (*kæ*-ri) *v* porter; *conduire; **~ on**
continuer; *poursuivre; **~ out** réaliser

carrycot (*kæ*-ri-kot) *n* berceau de
voyage

cart (kâât) *n* charrette *f*

cartilage (*kââ*-ti-lidj) *n* cartilage *m*

carton (*kââ*-teunn) *n* carton *m*;
cartouche *f*

cartoon (kââ-*toûn*) *n* dessins animés

cartridge (*kââ*-tridj) *n* cartouche *f*

carve (kââv) *v* découper; entailler,
tailler

carving (*kââ*-vinng) *n* gravure *f*

case (kéïss) *n* cas *m*; affaire *f*; valise *f*; étui *m*; **in ~ of** au cas où; **in ~ of** en cas de

cash (kæch) *n* argent liquide, argent comptant; *v* toucher, encaisser; **~ dispenser** distributeur automatique *m*

cashier (kæ-*chieu*) *n* caissier *m*, caissière *f*

cashmere (*kæch*-mi^eu) *n* cachemire *m*

casino (keu-*sii*-nô^ou) *n* (pl ~s) casino *m*

cask (kââsk) *n* baril *m*, tonneau *m*

cassette (kæ-*sèt*) *n* cassette *f*; **~ player** lecteur *m* de cassettes; **~ recorder** magnétophone *m* à cassettes

cast (kââst) *n* jet *m*

*cast (kââst) *v* lancer, jeter; **cast iron** fonte *f*

castle (*kââ*-seul) *n* château *m*

casual (*kæ*-jou-eul) *adj* sans façons; fait en passant, fortuit

casualty (*kæ*-jou-eul-ti) *n* victime *f*

cat (kæt) *n* chat *m*

catacomb (*kæ*-teu-kô^ou m) *n* catacombe *f*

catalogue (*kæ*-teu-logh) *n* catalogue *m*

catarrh (keu-*tââ*) *n* catarrhe *m*

catastrophe (keu-*tæ*-streu-fi) *n* sinistre *m*

*catch (kætch) *v* attraper; saisir; *surprendre; *prendre

category (*kæ*-ti-gheu-ri) *n* catégorie *f*

cathedral (keu-θ*ii*-dreul) *n* cathédrale *f*

catholic (*kæ*-θeu-lik) *adj* catholique

cattle (*kæ*-teul) *pl* bétail *m*

caught (koot) *v* (p, pp catch)

cauliflower (*ko*-li-flaou^eu) *n* choufleur

cause (kooz) *v* causer; provoquer; *n* cause *f*; raison *f*, motif *m*; **~ to** *faire

causeway (kooz-^ou éï) *n* chaussée *f*

caution (*koo*-cheunn) *n* prudence *f*; *v* avertir

cautious (*koo*-cheuss) *adj* prudent

cave (kéïv) *n* grotte *f*

cavern (*kæ*-veunn) *n* caverne *f*

caviar (*kæ*-vi-ââ) *n* caviar *m*

cavity (*kæ*-veu-ti) *n* cavité *f*

cd (sii-*dii*) *n* cd *m*; **~ player** lecteur de cd

cease (siiss) *v* cesser

cease-fire (*siiss*-faï^eu) *n* cessez-le-feu *m*

ceiling (*sii*-linng) *n* plafond *m*

celebrate (*sè*-li-bréït) *v* célébrer

celebration (sè-li-*bréï*-cheunn) *n* célébration *f*

celebrity (si-*lè*-breu-ti) *n* célébrité *f*

celery (*sè*-leu-ri) *n* céleri *m*

cell (sèl) *n* cellule *f*

cellar (*sè*-leu) *n* cave *f*

cell phone (sèl-fô^ou n) *n* (téléphone) portable

cement (si-*mènt*) *n* ciment *m*

cemetery (*sè*-mi-tri) *n* cimetière *m*

censorship (*sèn*-seu-chip) *n* censure *f*

center (*sèn*-teu) *n* centre *m*

centigrade (*sèn*-ti-ghréïd) *adj* centigrade

centimetre, *Am* **centimeter** (*sèn*-ti-mii-teu) *n* centimètre *m*

central (*sèn*-treul) *adj* central; **~ heating** chauffage central; **~ station** gare centrale

centralize (*sèn*-treu-laïz) *v* centraliser

centre (*sèn*-teu) *n* centre *m*

century (*sèn*-tcheu-ri) *n* siècle *m*

ceramics (si-*ræ*-miks) *pl* céramique *f*

ceremony (*sè*-reu-meu-ni) *n* cérémonie *f*

certain (*seû*-teunn) *adj* certain

certificate (seu-*ti*-fi-keut) *n* certificat *m*; attestation *f*, document *m*, diplôme *m*

chain (tchéïn) *n* chaîne *f*

chair (tchè^{eu}) *n* chaise *f*; siège *m*

chairman (*tchèu*-meunn) *n* (pl -men) président *m*

chalet (*chœ*-léï) *n* chalet *m*

chalk (tchook) *n* craie *f*

challenge (*tchœ*-leunndj) *v* défier; *n* défi *m*

chamber (*tchéïm*-beu) *n* pièce *f*

champagne (chœm-*péïn*) *n* champagne *m*

champion (*tchœm*-pyeunn) *n* champion *m*, -ne *f*; défenseur *m*

chance (tchââns) *n* hasard *m*; chance *f*, occasion *f*; risque *m*; **by ~** par hasard

change (tchéïndj) *v* modifier, changer; se changer; *n* modification *f*, changement *m*; petite monnaie, change *m*

channel (*tchœ*-neul) *n* canal *m*; **English Channel** La Manche

chaos (*kéï*-oss) *n* chaos *m*

chaotic (kéï-*o*-tik) *adj* chaotique

chap (tchœp) *n* type *m*

chapel (*tchœ*-peul) *n* église *f*, chapelle *f*

chaplain (*tchœ*-plinn) *n* chapelain *m*

character (*kœ*-reuk-teu) *n* caractère *m*

characteristic (kœ-reuk-teu-*ri*-stik) *adj* caractéristique; *n* caractéristique *f*; trait de caractère

characterize (*kœ*-reuk-teu-raïz) *v* caractériser

charcoal (*tchââ*-kô^{ou}l) *n* charbon de bois

charge (tchââdj) *v* demander; charger; accuser; *n* prix *m*; charge *f*, chargement *m*; accusation *f*; **~ card** *Am* carte de crédit; **free of ~** à titre gracieux; **in ~ of** chargé de; ***take ~ of** se charger de

charity (*tchœ*-reu-ti) *n* charité *f*

charm (tchââm) *n* attraits, charme *m*; amulette *f*

charming (*tchââ*-minng) *adj* séduisant

chart (tchâât) *n* tableau *m*; graphique *m*; carte marine; **conversion ~** tableau de conversions

chase (tchéïss) *v* pourchasser; poursuivre, chasser; *n* chasse *f*

chasm (*kœ*-zeumm) *n* gouffre *m*, abîme *m*

chassis (*chœ*-si) *n* (pl ~) châssis *m*

chaste (tchéïst) *adj* chaste

chat (tchœt) *v* bavarder, causer; *n* causette *f*, bavardage *m*

chatterbox (*tchœ*-teu-boks) *n* moulin à paroles

cheap (tchiip) *adj* bon marché; avantageux

cheat (tchiit) *v* tricher; duper

check (tchèk) *v* contrôler, vérifier; *n* damier *m*; *nAm* note *f*; chèque *m*; **check!** échec!; **~ in** s'*inscrire; **~ out** *partir

checkbook (*tchèk*-bouk) *nAm* carnet de chèques

checkerboard (*tchè*-keu-bood) *nAm* échiquier *m*

checkers (*tchè*-keuz) *plAm* jeu de dames

checkroom (*tchèk*-roûm) *nAm* vestiaire *m*

checkup (*tchè*-kap) *n* examen *m*

cheek (tchiik) *n* joue *f*

cheeky (*tchii*-ki) *adj colloquial* insolent, effronté

cheer (tchi^{eu}) *v* acclamer; **~ up** égayer

cheerful (*tchieu*-feul) *adj* joyeux, gai

cheese (tchiiz) *n* fromage *m*

chef (chèf) *n* chef cuisinier

chemical (*kè*-mi-keul) *adj* chimique

chemist (*kè*-mist) *n* pharmacien *m*, pharmacienne *f*; **chemist's** pharmacie *f*

chemistry (*kè*-mi-stri) *n* chimie *f*

cheque (tchèk) n chèque m
chequebook (tchèk-bouk) n carnet de chèques
chequered (tchè-keud) adj à carreaux, à damiers
cherry (tchè-ri) n cerise f
chess (tchèss) n échecs
chest (tchèst) n poitrine f; coffre m; ~ **of drawers** commode f
chestnut (tchèss-nat) n marron m
chew (tchoû) v mâcher
chewing gum (tchoû-inng-ghamm) n chewing gum m
chicken (tchi-kinn) n poulet m
chickenpox (tchi-kinn-poks) n varicelle f
chief (tchiif) n chef m; adj principal
chieftain (tchiif-teunn) n chef m
child (tchaïld) n (pl children) enfant m
childbirth (tchaïld-beûθ) n accouchement m
childhood (tchaïld-houd) n enfance f
Chile (tchi-li) Chili m
Chilean (tchi-li-eunn) adj chilien; n Chilien m
chill (tchil) n frisson m
chilly (tchi-li) adj frais
chimes (tchaïmz) pl carillon m
chimney (tchimm-ni) n cheminée f
chin (tchinn) n menton m
China (tchaï-neu) Chine f
china (tchaï-neu) n porcelaine f
Chinese (tchaï-niiz) adj chinois; n Chinois m
chip (tchip) n éclat m; jeton m; v tailler, ébrécher; **chips** pommes frites
chives (tchaïvz) pl ciboulette f
chlorine (kloo-riin) n chlore m
chock-full (tchok-foul) adj plein à craquer, bourré
chocolate (tcho-kleut) n chocolat m; praline f
choice (tchoïss) n choix m; sélection f

choir (kᵒᵘaïᵉᵘ) n chœur m
choke (tchôᵘk) v étrangler, étouffer; n starter m
***choose** (tchoûz) v choisir
chop (tchop) n côte f, côtelette f; v hacher
christen (kri-seunn) v baptiser
christening (kri-seu-ninng) n baptême m
Christian (kriss-tcheunn) adj chrétien; ~ **name** prénom m
Christmas (kriss-meuss) Noël
chronic (kro-nik) adj chronique
chronological (kro-neu-lo-dji-keul) adj chronologique
chuckle (tcha-keul) v glousser
chunk (tchanngk) n gros morceau
church (tcheûtch) n église f
churchyard (tcheûtch-yââd) n cimetière m
cigar (si-ghââ) n cigare m; ~ **shop** bureau de tabac
cigarette (si-gheu-rèt) n cigarette f; ~ **case** étui à cigarettes; ~ **lighter** briquet m
cinema (si-neu-meu) n cinéma m
cinnamon (si-neu-meunn) n cannelle f
circle (seû-keul) n cercle m; balcon m; v encercler, entourer
circulation (seû-kyou-léï-cheunn) n circulation f
circumstance (seû-keumm-stæns) n circonstance f
circus (seû-keuss) n cirque m
citizen (si-ti-zeunn) n citoyen m, -ne f
citizenship (si-ti-zeunn-chip) n citoyenneté f
city (si-ti) n cité f
civic (si-vik) adj civique
civil (si-veul) adj civil; poli; ~ **law** droit civil; ~ **servant** fonctionnaire m
civilian (si-vil-yeunn) adj civil; n civil m

civilization (si-veu-laï-*zéï*-cheunn) *n* civilisation *f*

civilized (*si*-veu-laïzd) *adj* civilisé

claim (kléïm) *v* revendiquer, réclamer; prétendre; *n* revendication *f*, prétention *f*

clamp (klæmp) *n* mordache *f*; crampon *m*

clap (klæp) *v* applaudir

clarify (*klæ*-ri-faï) *v* éclaircir, clarifier

class (klââss) *n* classe *f*

classical (*klæ*-si-keul) *adj* classique

classify (*klæ*-si-faï) *v* classer

classmate (*klââss*-méït) *n* camarade de classe

classroom (*klââss*-roûm) *n* salle de classe

claw (kloo) *n* griffe *f*

clay (kléï) *n* argile *f*

clean (kliin) *adj* pur, propre; *v* nettoyer

cleaning (*klii*-ninng) *n* nettoyage *m*; ~ **fluid** détachant *m*

clear (kli\u1d49u) *adj* clair; *v* nettoyer

clearing (*klieu*-rinng) *n* clairière *f*

cleft (klèft) *n* fente *f*

clergyman (*kleû*-dji-meunn) *n* (*pl* -men) pasteur *m*; ecclésiastique *m*

clerk (klââk) *n* employé(e) de bureau; greffier *m*; secrétaire *m/f*

clever (*klè*-veu) *adj* intelligent, astucieux, éveillé

click (klik) *n* cliquetis *m*, bruit *m* sec; cliquet *m*; déclic *m*; *v* cliqueter; faire un déclic; *colloquial* become clear; ~ **with** plaire à

client (*klaï*-eunnt) *n* client *m*, -e *f*

cliff (klif) *n* falaise *f*

climate (*klaï*-mit) *n* climat *m*

climb (klaïm) *v* grimper; *n* ascension *f*

cling (klinng) *v* s'accrocher, se cramponner; adhérer (**to** à)

clinic (*kli*-nik) *n* clinique *f*

cloak (klô\u1d52uk) *n* manteau *m*

cloakroom (*klô\u1d52uk*-roûm) *n* vestiaire *m*

clock (klok) *n* horloge *f*; **at ... o'clock** à ... heures

cloister (*kloï*-steu) *n* cloître *m*

close¹ (klô\u1d52uz) *v* fermer; **closed** *adj* fermé, clos

close² (klô\u1d52uss) *adj* proche

closet (*klo*-zit) *n* placard *m*; *nAm* garde-robe *f*

cloth (kloθ) *n* tissu *m*; chiffon *m*

clothes (klô\u1d52uðz) *pl* habits *mpl*, vêtements *mpl*

clothing (*klôou*-ðinng) *n* habillement *m*

cloud (klaoud) *n* nuage *m*

cloudy (*klaou*-di) *adj* nuageux

clover (*klôou*-veu) *n* trèfle *m*

clown (klaoun) *n* clown *m*

club (klab) *n* club *m*; cercle *m*, association *f*; gourdin *m*, massue *f*

clumsy (*klamm*-zi) *adj* maladroit

clutch (klatch) *n* embrayage *m*; prise *f*

coach (kô\u1d52utch) *n* car *m*; wagon *m*; carrosse *m*; entraîneur *m*

coal (kô\u1d52ul) *n* charbon *m*

coarse (kooss) *adj* grossier

coast (kô\u1d52ust) *n* côte *f*

coat (kô\u1d52ut) *n* pardessus *m*, manteau *m*; ~ **hanger** cintre *m*

cocaine (kô\u1d52u-*kéïn*) *n* cocaïne *f*

cock (kok) *n* coq *m*

cocktail (*kok*-téïl) *n* cocktail *m*

coconut (*kôou*-keu-nat) *n* noix de coco

cod (kod) *n* (*pl* ~) morue *f*

code (kô\u1d52ud) *n* code *m*

coffee (*ko*-fi) *n* café *m*

coherence (kô\u1d52u-*hieu*-reunns) *n* cohérence *f*

coin (koïn) *n* pièce de monnaie *f*

coincide (kô\u1d52u-inn-*saïd*) *v* coïncider

cold (kô\u1d52uld) *adj* froid; *n* froid *m*; rhume *m*; **catch a** ~ s'enrhumer

collaborate (keu-*læ*-beu-réït) *v*

collaborer

collapse (keu-*læps*) v s'effondrer, s'écrouler

collar (*ko*-leu) n collier m; col m; ~ **stud** bouton de col

collarbone (*ko*-leu-bô^{ou}n) n clavicule f

colleague (*ko*-liigh) n collègue m

collect (keu-*lèkt*) v rassembler; *prendre; *aller chercher; quêter

collection (keu-*lèk*-cheunn) n collection f; levée f

collective (keu-*lèk*-tiv) adj collectif

collector (keu-*lèk*-teu) n collectionneur

college (*ko*-lidj) n collège m

collide (keu-*laïd*) v entrer en collision

collision (keu-*li*-jeunn) n collision f; abordage m

colloquial (ko-*lô^{ou}*-k^{ou}i-eul) adj familier

Colombia (keu-*lomm*-bi-eu) Colombie f

Colombian (keu-*lomm*-bi-eunn) adj colombien; n Colombien m

colonel (keû-neul) n colonel m

colony (*ko*-leu-ni) n colonie f

colo(u)r (*ka*-leu) n couleur f; v colorer; ~ **film** film en couleurs

colo(u)r-blind (*ka*-leu-blaïnd) adj daltonien

colo(u)red (*ka*-leud) adj de couleur

colo(u)rful (*ka*-leu-feul) adj coloré

column (*ko*-leumm) n colonne f; rubrique f

coma (*kôou*-meu) n coma m

comb (kô^{ou}m) v peigner; n peigne m

combat (*komm*-bæt) n lutte f, combat m; v *combattre, lutter

combination (komm-bi-*néï*-cheunn) n combinaison f

combine (keumm-*baïn*) v combiner

*come (kamm) v *venir; ~ **across** rencontrer; trouver

comedian (keu-*mii*-di-eunn) n comédien m, -ne f; comique m

comedy (*ko*-meu-di) n comédie f; **musical** ~ comédie musicale

comfort (*kamm*-feut) n bien-être m, commodité f, confort m; réconfort m; v consoler

comfortable (*kamm*-feu-teu-beul) adj confortable

comic (*ko*-mik) adj comique

comics (*ko*-miks) pl bandes dessinées

coming (*ka*-minng) n arrivée f

comma (*ko*-meu) n virgule f

command (keu-*mâând*) v commander; n ordre m

commander (keu-*mâân*-deu) n commandant m

commemoration (keu-mè-meu-*réï*-cheunn) n commémoration f

commence (keu-*mèns*) v commencer

comment (*ko*-mènt) n commentaire m; v commenter

commerce (*ko*-meûss) n commerce m

commercial (keu-*meû*-cheul) adj commercial; n annonce publicitaire; ~ **law** droit commercial

commission (keu-*mi*-cheunn) n commission f

commit (keu-*mit*) v *remettre, confier; *commettre

committee (keu-*mi*-ti) n commission f, comité m

common (*ko*-meunn) adj commun; habituel; ordinaire

communicate (keu-*myoû*-ni-kéït) v communiquer

communication (keu-myoû-ni-*kéï*-cheunn) n communication f

communism (*ko*-myou-ni-zeumm) n communisme m

community (keu-*myoû*-neu-ti) n société f, communauté f

commuter (keu-*myoû*-teu) n navetteur m

compact (*komm*-pækt) *adj* compact

compact disc (*komm*-pækt disk) *n* compact disc *m*; ~ **player** lecteur de compact disc *m*

companion (keumm-*pæ*-nyeunn) *n* compagnon *m*, compagne *f*

company (*kamm*-peu-ni) *n* compagnie *f*; entreprise *f*, société *f*

comparative (keumm-*pæ*-reu-tiv) *adj* relatif

compare (keumm-*pèeu*) *v* comparer

comparison (keumm-*pæ*-ri-seunn) *n* comparaison *f*

compartment (keumm-*pâât*-meunnt) *n* compartiment *m*

compass (*kamm*-peuss) *n* boussole *f*

compel (keumm-*pèl*) *v* *contraindre

compensate (*komm*-peunn-séït) *v* compenser

compensation (komm-peunn-*séï*-cheunn) *n* compensation *f*; indemnité *f*

compete (keumm-*piit*) *v* *concourir

competition (komm-peu-*ti*-cheunn) *n* compétition *f*

competitor (keumm-*pè*-ti-teur) *n* concurrent *m*

compile (keumm-*païl*) *v* compiler

complain (keumm-*plèïn*) *v* se *plaindre

complaint (keumm-*plèïnt*) *n* plainte *f*; **complaints book** cahier de doléances

complete (keumm-*pliit*) *adj* entier, complet; *v* achever

completely (keumm-*pliit*-li) *adv* entièrement, totalement, complètement

complex (*komm*-plèks) *n* complexe *m*; *adj* complexe

complexion (keumm-*plèk*-cheunn) *n* teint *m*

complicated (*komm*-pli-kéï-tid) *adj* compliqué

compliment (*komm*-pli-meunnt) *n* compliment *m*; *v* complimenter, féliciter

compose (keumm-*pôouz*) *v* composer

composer (keumm-*pôou*-zeu) *n* compositeur *m*, -trice *f*

comprehensive (komm-pri-*hèn*-siv) *adj* étendu

comprise (keumm-*praïz*) *v* *comprendre, *inclure

compromise (*komm*-preu-maïz) *n* compromis *m*

compulsory (keumm-*pal*-seu-ri) *adj* obligatoire

computer (komm-*pyou*-teu) *n* ordinateur *m*; **lap-top** ~ ordinateur portable

comrade (*komm*-réïd) *n* camarade *m*

conceal (keunn-*siil*) *v* dissimuler

conceited (keunn-*sii*-tid) *adj* prétentieux

conceive (keunn-*siiv*) *v* *concevoir

concentrate (*konn*-seunn-tréït) *v* concentrer

concentration (konn-seunn-*tréï*-cheunn) *n* concentration *f*

conception (keunn-*sèp*-cheunn) *n* conception *f*

concern (keunn-*seûnn*) *v* regarder, concerner; *n* souci *m*; affaire *f*

concerned (keunn-*seûnnd*) *adj* soucieux; concerné

concerning (keunn-*seû*-ninng) *prep* relatif à, concernant

concert (*konn*-seut) *n* concert *m*; ~ **hall** salle de concert

concession (keunn-*sè*-cheunn) *n* concession *f*

concierge (kon-si-*èeuj*) *n* concierge *m*

concise (keunn-*saïss*) *adj* concis

conclusion (keunng-*kloû*-jeunn) *n* conclusion *f*

concrete (*konng*-kriit) *adj* concret; *n*

béton *m*

concussion (keunng-*ka*-cheunn) *n* commotion cérébrale

condition (keunn-*di*-cheunn) *n* condition *f*; état *m/f*; circonstance *f*

condom (*konn*-dom) *n* préservatif *m*

conduct¹ (*konn*-dakt) *n* conduite *f*

conduct² (keunn-*dakt*) *v* *conduire; diriger

conductor (keunn-*dak*-teu) *n* conducteur *m*, -trice *f*; chef d'orchestre

confectioner (keunn-*fèk*-cheu-neu) *n* confiseur *m*, -seuse *f*

conference (*konn*-feu-reunns) *n* conférence *f*

confess (keunn-*fèss*) *v* *reconnaître; confesser; professer

confession (keunn-*fè*-cheunn) *n* confession *f*

confidence (*konn*-fi-deunns) *n* confiance *f*

confident (*konn*-fi-deunnt) *adj* confiant

confidential (konn-fi-*dèn*-cheul) *adj* confidentiel

confirm (keunn-*feûmm*) *v* confirmer

confirmation (konn-feu-*méï*-cheunn) *n* confirmation *f*

confiscate (*konn*-fi-skéït) *v* confisquer

conflict (*konn*-flikt) *n* conflit *m*

confuse (keunn-*fyoûz*) *v* confondre; **confused** *adj* confus

confusion (keunn-*fyoû*-jeunn) *n* confusion *f*

congratulate (keunng-*ghræ*-tchou-léït) *v* congratuler, féliciter

congratulations (keunng-ghræ-tchou-*léï*-cheunnz) *n* félicitations *fpl*

congregation (konng-ghri-*ghéï*-cheunn) *n* congrégation *f*

congress (*konng*-ghrèss) *n* congrès *m*

connect (keu-*nèkt*) *v* *joindre;

*mettre en communication; brancher

connection (keu-*nèk*-cheunn) *n* relation *f*; rapport *m*; communication *f*, correspondance *f*

connoisseur (ko-neu-*seû*) *n* connaisseur *m*

connotation (ko-neu-*téï*-cheunn) *n* connotation *f*

conquer (*konng*-keu) *v* *conquérir; *vaincre

conqueror (*konng*-keu-reu) *n* conquérant *m*

conquest (*konng*-k^{ou}èst) *n* conquête *f*

conscience (*konn*-cheunns) *n* conscience *f*

conscious (*konn*-cheuss) *adj* conscient

consciousness (*konn*-cheuss-neuss) *n* conscience *f*

conscript (*konn*-skript) *n* conscrit *m*

consent (keunn-*sènt*) *v* *consentir; approuver; *n* assentiment *m*, consentement *m*

consequence (*konn*-si-k^{ou}eunns) *n* effet *m*, conséquence *f*

consequently (*konn*-si-k^{ou}eunnt-li) *adv* par conséquent

conservative (keunn-*seû*-veu-tiv) *adj* conservateur

consider (keunn-*si*-deu) *v* considérer; envisager; trouver, estimer

considerable (keunn-*si*-deu-reu-beul) *adj* considérable; important, sensible

considerate (keunn-*si*-deu-reut) *adj* prévenant

consideration (keunn-si-deu-*réï*-cheunn) *n* considération *f*; égards *mpl*, attention *f*

considering (keunn-*si*-deu-rinng) *prep* vu

consignment (keunn-*saïn*-meunnt) *n* expédition *f*

consist (keunn-*sist*) *v* ~ **in** consister

en; consister à; **~ of** se composer de

conspire (keunn-*spaïeu*) *v* conspirer

constant (*konn*-steunnt) *adj* constant

constipation (konn-sti-*péï*-cheunn) *n* constipation *f*

constituency (keunn-*sti*-tchou-eunn-si) *n* circonscription électorale

constitution (konn-sti-*tyoû*-cheunn) *n* constitution *f*

construct (keunn-*strakt*) *v* *construire; bâtir, édifier

construction (keunn-*strak*-cheunn) *n* construction *f*; édification *f*; édifice *m*

consulate (*konn*-syou-leut) *n* consulat *m*

consult (keunn-*salt*) *v* consulter

consultation (konn-seul-*téï*-cheunn) *n* consultation *f*; **~ hours** *n* heures de consultation

consume (keunn-*syoûm*) *v* consommer; consumer

consumer (keunn-*syoû*-meu) *n* utilisateur *m*, consommateur *m*, -trice *f*

contact (*konn*-tækt) *n* contact *m*; *v* contacter; **~ lenses** verres de contact

contagious (keunn-*téï*-djeuss) *adj* contagieux

contain (keunn-*téïn*) *v* *contenir; *comprendre

container (keunn-*téï*-neu) *n* récipient *m*; conteneur *m*

contemporary (keunn-*tèm*-peu-reu-ri) *adj* contemporain; de l'époque; *n* contemporain *m*

contempt (keunn-*tèmpt*) *n* dédain *m*, mépris *m*

content (keunn-*tènt*) *adj* satisfait

contents (*konn*-tènts) *pl* contenu *m*

contest (*konn*-tèst) *n* combat *m*; concours *m*

continent (*konn*-ti-neunnt) *n* continent *m*

continental (konn-ti-*nèn*-teul) *adj* continental

continual (keunn-*ti*-nyou-eul) *adj* continuel

continue (keunn-*ti*-nyoû) *v* continuer; *poursuivre, durer

continuous (keunn-*ti*-nyou-euss) *adj* continuel, continu, ininterrompu

contour (*konn*-tou^eu) *n* contour *m*

contraceptive (konn-treu-*sèp*-tiv) *n* contraceptif *m*

contract[1] (*konn*-trækt) *n* contrat *m*

contract[2] (keunn-*trækt*) *v* attraper

contractor (keunn-*træk*-teu) *n* entrepreneur *m*

contradict (konn-treu-*dikt*) *v* *contredire

contradictory (konn-treu-*dik*-teu-ri) *adj* contradictoire

contrary (*konn*-treu-ri) *n* contraire *m*; *adj* opposé; **on the ~** au contraire

contrast (*konn*-trââst) *n* contraste *m*; différence *f*

contribution (konn-tri-*byoû*-cheunn) *n* contribution *f*

control (keunn-*trôoul*) *n* contrôle *m*; *v* contrôler

controversial (konn-treu-*veû*-cheul) *adj* discuté, controversé

convenience (keunn-*vii*-nyeunns) *n* commodité *f*

convenient (keunn-*vii*-nyeunnt) *adj* pratique; approprié, qui convient, commode

convent (*konn*-veunnt) *n* couvent *m*

conversation (konn-veu-*séï*-cheunn) *n* entretien *m*, conversation *f*

convert (keunn-*veût*) *v* convertir

convict[1] (keunn-*vikt*) *v* déclarer coupable

convict[2] (*konn*-vikt) *n* condamné *m*

conviction (keunn-*vik*-cheunn) *n* conviction *f*; condamnation *f*

convince (keunn-*vinns*) *v*

*convaincre

convulsion (keunn-*val*-cheunn) n
convulsion f

cook (kouk) n cuisinier m; v *cuire;
préparer

cookbook (kouk-bouk) nAm livre de
cuisine

cooker (*kou*-keu) n cuisinière f; **gas ~**
cuisinière à gaz

cookery book (*kou*-keu-ri-bouk) n
livre de cuisine

cookie (*kou*-ki) nAm biscuit m

cool (koûl) adj frais

cooperation (kô^{ou}-o-peu-*réï*-cheunn)
n coopération f; collaboration f

cooperative (kô^{ou}-o-peu-reu-tiv) adj
coopératif; coopérant; n coopérative
f

coordinate (kô^{ou}-*oo*-di-néït) v
coordonner

coordination (kô^{ou}-oo-di-*néï*-
cheunn) n coordination f

cope (kô^{ou}p) v se débrouiller, s'en
tirer, *colloquial* se défendre; **~ with**
tenir tête à, faire face à; s'occuper de;
venir à bout de

copper (*ko*-peu) n cuivre m

copy (*ko*-pi) n copie f; exemplaire m; v
copier; imiter; **carbon ~** copie f

coral (*ko*-reul) n corail m

cord (kood) n corde f; cordon m

cordial (*koo*-di-eul) adj cordial

corduroy (*koo*-deu-roï) n velours
côtelé

core (koo) n cœur m; trognon m

cork (kook) n bouchon m

corkscrew (*kook*-skroû) n tire-
bouchon m

corn (koon) n grain m; céréale f; blé m;
durillon m, cor au pied; **~ on the cob**
maïs en épi

corner (*koo*-neu) n coin m

cornfield (*koon*-fiild) n champ de blé

corpse (koops) n cadavre m

corpulent (*koo*-pyou-leunnt) adj
corpulent; gros, obèse

correct (keu-*rèkt*) adj juste, correct; v
corriger

correction (keu-*rèk*-cheunn) n
correction f; rectification f

correctness (keu-*rèkt*-neuss) n
exactitude f

correspond (ko-ri-*sponnd*) v
correspondre; *être conforme

correspondence (ko-ri-*sponn*-
deunns) n correspondance f

correspondent (ko-ri-*sponn*-deunnt)
n correspondant m, -e f

corridor (*ko*-ri-doo) n corridor m

corrupt (keu-*rapt*) adj corrompu; v
*corrompre

corruption (keu-*rap*-cheunn) n
corruption f

corset (*koo*-sit) n corset m

cosmetics (koz-*mè*-tiks) pl
cosmétiques mpl, produits de beauté

cost (kost) n coût m; prix m

*cost (kost) v coûter

cosy (*kô^{ou}*-zi) adj intime, confortable

cot (kot) nAm lit de camp

cottage (*ko*-tidj) n villa f

cotton (*ko*-teunn) n coton m; en
coton; **~ wool** ouate f

couch (kaoutch) n canapé m

cough (kof) n toux f; v tousser

could (koud) v (p can)

council (*kaoun*-seul) n conseil m

councillor (*kaoun*-seu-leu) n
conseiller m

counsel (*kaoun*-seul) n conseil m

counsellor (*kaoun*-seu-leu) n
conseiller m

count (kaount) v compter; *inclure; n
comte m

counter (*kaoun*-teu) n comptoir m;
barre f

counterfeit (*kaoun*-teu-fiit) v
*contrefaire

counterfoil (*kaoun*-teu-foïl) n talon m

countess (*kaoun*-tiss) n comtesse f

country (*kann*-tri) n pays m; campagne f; région f; ~ **house** maison de campagne

countryman (*kann*-tri-meunn) n (pl -men) **fellow** ~ compatriote m

countryside (*kann*-tri-saïd) n campagne f

county (*kaoun*-ti) n comté m

couple (*ka*-peul) n couple m

coupon (*koû*-ponn) n coupon m

courage (*ka*-ridj) n vaillance f, courage m

courageous (keu-*réï*-djeuss) adj brave, courageux

course (kooss) n cap m; plat m; cours m; **crash** ~ cours accéléré; **of** ~ évidemment

court (koot) n tribunal m; cour f

courteous (*keû*-ti-euss) adj courtois

cousin (*ka*-zeunn) n cousine f, cousin m

cover (*ka*-veu) v *couvrir; n abri m; couvercle m; couverture f

cow (kaou) n vache f

coward (*kaou*-eud) n lâche m

cowardly (*kaou*-eud-li) adj lâche

crab (kræb) n crabe m

crack (kræk) n craquement m; fissure f; v craquer; fendre

cracker (*kræ*-keu) nAm biscuit m

cradle (*kréï*-deul) n berceau m

cramp (kræmp) n crampe f

crane (kréïn) n grue f

crash (kræch) n collision f; v entrer en collision; s'écraser; ~ **barrier** glissière de sécurité

crate (kréït) n caisse f

crater (*kréï*-teu) n cratère m

crawl (krool) v ramper; n crawl m

craze (kréïz) n rage f

crazy (*kréï*-zi) adj fou; insensé

creak (kriik) v grincer

cream (kriim) n crème f; crème fraîche; adj crème

creamy (*krii*-mi) adj crémeux

crease (kriiss) v froisser; n pli m; faux pli

create (kri-*éït*) v créer

creative (kri-*éï*-tiv) adj créateur, créatif

creature (*krii*-tcheu) n créature f; être m

credible (*krè*-di-beul) adj croyable

credit (*krè*-dit) n crédit m; v créditer; ~ **card** carte de crédit

creditor (*krè*-di-teu) n créditeur m

credulous (*krè*-dyou-leuss) adj crédule

creek (kriik) n baie f, crique f

*creep (kriip) v ramper

creepy (*krii*-pi) adj lugubre, terrifiant

cremate (kri-*méït*) v incinérer

crew (kroû) n équipage m

cricket (*kri*-kit) n cricket m; grillon m

crime (kraïm) n crime m

criminal (*kri*-mi-neul) n délinquant m, criminel m; adj criminel; ~ **law** droit pénal

criminality (kri-mi-*næ*-leu-ti) n criminalité f

crimson (*krimm*-zeunn) adj cramoisi

crippled (*kri*-peuld) adj estropié

crisis (*kraï*-siss) n (pl crises) crise f

crisp (krisp) adj croustillant

critic (*kri*-tik) n critique m/f

critical (*kri*-ti-keul) adj critique; précaire, délicat

criticism (*kri*-ti-si-zeumm) n critique f

criticize (*kri*-ti-saïz) v critiquer

crochet (*krôou*-chéï) v *faire du crochet

crockery (*kro*-keu-ri) n poterie f, faïence f

crocodile (*kro*-keu-daïl) n crocodile m

crooked (*krou*-kid) adj tordu;

malhonnête

crop (krop) n récolte f

cross (kross) v traverser; adj en
colère, fâché; n croix f

cross-eyed (kross-aïd) adj louche

crossing (kro-sinng) n traversée f;
croisement m; passage m; passage à
niveau

crossroads (kross-rô^{ou}dz) n
carrefour m

crosswalk (kross-^{ou}ook) nAm
passage pour piétons

crow (krô^{ou}) n corneille f

crowd (kraoud) n masse f, foule f

crowded (kraou-did) adj animé;
bondé

crown (kraoun) n couronne f; v
couronner

crucifix (kroû-si-fiks) n crucifix m

crucifixion (kroû-si-fik-cheunn) n
crucifixion f

crucify (kroû-si-faï) v crucifier

cruel (krou^{eu}l) adj cruel

cruise (kroûz) n croisière f

crumb (kramm) n miette f

crust (krast) n croûte f

crutch (kratch) n béquille f

cry (kraï) v pleurer; crier; appeler; n
cri m; appel m

crystal (kri-steul) n cristal m; adj en
cristal

Cuba (kyoû-beu) Cuba m

Cuban (kyoû-beunn) adj cubain; n
Cubain m

cube (kyoûb) n cube m

cuckoo (kou-koû) n coucou m

cucumber (kyoû-keumm-beu) n
concombre m

cuddle (ka-deul) v câliner

cuff (kaf) n manchette f; ~ **links**
boutons de manchettes

cuff-links (kaf-linngks) pl boutons de
manchettes

cultivate (kal-ti-véït) v cultiver

culture (kal-tcheu) n culture f

cultured (kal-tcheud) adj cultivé

cunning (ka-ninng) adj rusé

cup (kap) n tasse f; coupe f

cupboard (ka-beud) n placard m

curb (keûb) n bord du trottoir; v
freiner

cure (kyou^{eu}) v guérir; n cure f,
guérison f

curiosity (kyou^{eu}-ri-o-seu-ti) n
curiosité f

curious (kyoueu-ri-euss) adj curieux;
étrange

curl (keûl) v boucler; friser; n boucle f

curler (keû-leu) n bigoudi m

curly (keû-li) adj bouclé

currant (ka-reunnt) n raisin sec;
groseille f

currency (ka-reunn-si) n monnaie f;
foreign ~ monnaie étrangère

current (ka-reunnt) n courant m; adj
courant; **alternating** ~ courant
alternatif; **direct** ~ courant continu

curry (ka-ri) n curry m

curse (keûss) v jurer; *maudire; n
juron m

curtain (keû-teunn) n rideau m

curve (keûv) n courbe f; tournant m

curved (keûvd) adj courbe, courbé

cushion (kou-cheunn) n coussin m

custody (ka-steu-di) n garde f à vue;
garde f

custom (ka-steumm) n coutume f,
habitude f

customary (ka-steu-meu-ri) adj
usuel, coutumier, ordinaire

customer (ka-steu-meu) n client m

Customs (ka-steummz) pl douane f; ~
duty droit de douane; ~ **officer**
douanier m

cut (kat) n incision f; coupure f

***cut** (kat) v couper; *réduire; ~ **off**
couper; ~ **out** découper

cutlery (kat-leu-ri) n couvert m

cutlet (*kat*-leut) *n* côtelette *f*
cycle (*saï*-keul) *n* vélo *m*; bicyclette *f*; cycle *m*
cyclist (*saï*-klist) *n* cycliste *m*
cylinder (*si*-linn-deu) *n* cylindre *m*; ~ **head** tête de cylindre

cystitis (si-*staï*-tiss) *n* cystite *f*
Czech (tchèk) *adj* tchèque; *n* Tchèque *m*
Czech Republic (tchèk ri-*pa*-blik) République Tchèque

D

dad (dæd) *n* papa *m*
daddy (*dæ*-di) *n* papa *m*
daffodil (*dæ*-feu-dil) *n* jonquille *f*
daily (*déï*-li) *adj* journalier, quotidien; *n* quotidien *m*
dairy (*dèeu*-ri) *n* laiterie *f*
dam (dæm) *n* barrage *m*; digue *f*
damage (*dæ*-midj) *n* dommage *m*; *v* endommager
damn (dæm) *v* condamner; maudire
damned (dæmd) *adj* sacré, fichu
damp (dæmp) *adj* humide; moite; *n* humidité *f*; *v* humidifier
dance (dââns) *v* danser; *n* danse *f*
dandelion (*dæn*-di-laï-eunn) *n* pissenlit *m*
dandruff (*dæn*-dreuf) *n* pellicules
Dane (déïn) *n* Danois *m*
danger (*déïn*-djeu) *n* danger *m*
dangerous (*déïn*-djeu-reuss) *adj* dangereux
Danish (*déï*-nich) *adj* danois
dare (dè^eu) *v* oser
daring (*dèeu*-rinng) *adj* téméraire
dark (dââk) *adj* obscur; *n* obscurité *f*, ténèbres *fpl*
darling (*dââ*-linng) *n* trésor *m*, chéri *m*
darn (dâân) *v* repriser
dash (dæch) *v* se précipiter
dashboard (*dæch*-bood) *n* tableau de bord
data (*déï*-teu) *pl* données *fpl*

date[1] (déït) *n* date *f*; rendez-vous *m*; *v* dater; **out of** ~ démodé
date[2] (déït) *n* datte *f*
daughter (*doo*-teu) *n* fille *f*; ~**-in-law** belle-fille *f*
dawn (doon) *n* aube *f*; aurore *f*
day (déï) *n* jour *m*; **by** ~ de jour; ~ **trip** excursion *f*; **per** ~ par jour; **the** ~ **before yesterday** avant-hier
daybreak (*déï*-bréïk) *n* lever du jour
daylight (*déï*-laït) *n* lumière du jour
dead (dèd) *adj* mort; décédé
deaf (dèf) *adj* sourd
deal (diil) *n* transaction *f*, affaire *f*
***deal** (diil) *v* distribuer; ~ **with** *v* s'occuper de; *faire des affaires avec
dealer (*dii*-leu) *n* négociant *m*; marchand *m*, -e *f*
dear (di^eu) *adj* cher
death (dèθ) *n* mort *f*; ~ **penalty** peine de mort
debate (di-*béït*) *n* débat *m*
debit (*dè*-bit) *n* débit *m*
debt (dèt) *n* dette *f*
decaffeinated (dii-*kæ*-fi-néï-tid) *adj* décaféiné
deceit (di-*siit*) *n* tromperie *f*
deceive (di-*siiv*) *v* tromper
December (di-*sèm*-beu) décembre
decency (*dii*-seunn-si) *n* décence *f*
decent (*dii*-seunnt) *adj* décent
decide (di-*saïd*) *v* décider

decision (di-*si*-jeunn) *n* décision *f*

deck (dèk) *n* pont *m*; ~ **cabin** cabine de pont; ~ **chair** chaise longue

declaration (dè-kleu-*réï*-cheunn) *n* déclaration *f*

declare (di-*klèeu*) *v* déclarer; indiquer

decorate (dè-keu-réït) *v* décorer; orner; peindre (et tapisser)

decoration (dè-keu-*réï*-cheunn) *n* décoration *f*

decrease (dii-*kriiss*) *v* *réduire; diminuer; *n* diminution *f*

dedicate (dè-di-kéït) *v* dédier

deduce (di-*dyoûss*) *v* *déduire

deduct (di-*dakt*) *v* *déduire

deed (diid) *n* action *f*, acte *m*

deep (diip) *adj* profond

deep-freeze (diip-*friiz*) *n* congélateur *m*

deer (di^{eu}) *n* (pl ~) daim *m*

defeat (di-*fiit*) *v* *vaincre; *n* défaite *f*

defective (di-*fèk*-tiv) *adj* défectueux

defence (di-*fèns*) *n* défense *f*

defend (di-*fènd*) *v* défendre

defense *Am* (di-*fèns*) *n* défense *f*

deficiency (di-*fi*-cheunn-si) *n* déficience *f*

deficit (dè-fi-sit) *n* déficit *m*

define (di-*faïn*) *v* définir, déterminer

definite (dè-fi-nit) *adj* déterminé

definition (dè-fi-*ni*-cheunn) *n* définition *f*

deformed (di-*foomd*) *adj* contrefait, difforme

degree (di-*ghrii*) *n* degré *m*; grade *m*

delay (di-*léï*) *v* retarder; différer; *n* retard *m*; ajournement *m*

delegate (dè-li-gheut) *n* délégué *m*

delegation (dè-li-*ghéï*-cheunn) *n* délégation *f*

deliberate[1] (di-*li*-beu-réït) *v* discuter, délibérer

deliberate[2] (di-*li*-beu-reut) *adj* délibéré

deliberation (di-li-beu-*réï*-cheunn) *n* discussion *f*, délibération *f*

delicacy (dè-li-keu-si) *n* délicatesse *f*

delicate (dè-li-keut) *adj* délicat; tendre

delicatessen (dè-li-keu-*tè*-seunn) *n* épicerie fine

delicious (di-*li*-cheuss) *adj* exquis, délicieux

delight (di-*laït*) *n* délice *m*, plaisir *m*; *v* enchanter

delightful (di-*laït*-feul) *adj* délicieux, ravissant

deliver (di-*li*-veu) *v* *remettre, livrer; délivrer

delivery (di-*li*-veu-ri) *n* remise *f*; livraison *f*; accouchement *m*; délivrance *f*; ~ **van** camion de livraison

demand (di-*mâând*) *v* exiger, réclamer; *n* demande *f*

democracy (di-*mo*-kreu-si) *n* démocratie *f*

democratic (dè-meu-*krœ*-tik) *adj* démocratique

demolish (di-*mo*-lich) *v* démolir

demolition (dè-meu-*li*-cheunn) *n* démolition *f*

demonstrate (dè-meunn-stréït) *v* démontrer; manifester

demonstration (dè-meunn-*stréï*-cheunn) *n* démonstration *f*; manifestation *f*

den (dèn) *n* tanière *f*

Denmark (*dèn*-mââk) Danemark *m*

denomination (di-no-mi-*néï*-cheunn) *n* dénomination *f*

dense (dèns) *adj* dense

dent (dènt) *n* bosse *f*

dentist (*dèn*-tist) *n* dentiste *m*

denture (*dèn*-tcheu) *n* dentier *m*

deny (di-*naï*) *v* nier; dénier, refuser

deodorant (dii-*ôou*-deu-reunnt) *n* désodorisant *m*

depart (di-*pâât*) *v* s'en *aller, *partir; ~

this world trépasser

department (di-*pâât*-meunnt) n
division f, département m; **~ store**
grand magasin

departure (di-*pââ*-tcheu) n départ m

depend (di-*pènd*): **~ on** dépendre de

dependent (di-*pèn*-deunnt) adj
dépendant

deposit (di-*po*-zit) n versement m;
consigne f; dépôt m; v déposer

depository (di-*po*-zi-teu-ri) n
entrepôt m

depot (dè-*pô*ou) n dépôt m; nAm gare
f

depress (di-*prèss*) v déprimer

depression (di-*prè*-cheunn) n
dépression f

deprive of (di-*praïv*) priver de

depth (dèpθ) n profondeur f

deputy (*dè*-pyou-ti) n député m/f;
substitut m

descend (di-*sènd*) v descendre

descendant (di-*sèn*-deunnt) n
descendant m, -e f

descent (di-*sènt*) n descente f

describe (di-*skraïb*) v *décrire

description (di-*skrip*-cheunn) n
description f; signalement m

desert¹ (*dè*-zeut) n désert m; adj
désert

desert² (di-*zeût*) v déserter;
abandonner

deserve (di-*zeûv*) v mériter

design (di-*zaïn*) v créer; n dessein m

designate (*dè*-zigh-néït) v désigner

desirable (di-*zaïeu*-reu-beul) adj
désirable

desire (di-*zaïeu*) n vœu m; envie f,
désir m; v *avoir envie de, désirer

desk (dèsk) n bureau m; pupitre m;
banc d'école

despair (di-*spèeu*) n désespoir m; v
désespérer

despatch (di-*spætch*) v expédier

desperate (*dè*-speu-reut) adj
désespéré

despise (di-*spaïz*) v mépriser

despite (di-*spaït*) prep malgré

dessert (di-*zeût*) n dessert m

destination (dè-sti-*néï*-cheunn) n
destination f

destine (*dè*-stinn) v destiner

destiny (*dè*-sti-ni) n destin m, sort m

destroy (di-*stroï*) v dévaster, *détruire

destruction (di-*strak*-cheunn) n
destruction f; anéantissement m

detach (di-*tætch*) v détacher

detail (*dii*-téïl) n détail m

detailed (*dii*-téïld) adj détaillé

detect (di-*tèkt*) v détecter

detective (di-*tèk*-tiv) n détective m; **~
story** roman policier

detergent (di-*teû*-djeunnt) n
détergent m

determine (di-*teû*-minn) v définir,
déterminer

determined (di-*teû*-minnd) adj résolu

detest (di-*tèst*) v détester

detour (*dii*-tou^eu) n détour m;
déviation f

devaluation (dii-væl-you-*éï*-cheunn) n
dévaluation f

devalue (dii-*væl*-yoû) v dévaluer

develop (di-*vè*-leup) v développer

development (di-*vè*-leup-meunnt) n
développement m

deviate (*dii*-vi-éït) v dévier

devil (*dè*-veul) n diable m

devise (di-*vaïz*) v *concevoir

devote (di-*vôout*) v consacrer

dew (dyoû) n rosée f

diabetes (daï-eu-*bii*-tiiz) n diabète m

diabetic (daï-eu-*bè*-tik) n diabétique
m/f

diagnose (daï-eugh-*nôouz*) v
diagnostiquer

diagnosis (daï-eugh-*nôou*-siss) n (pl
-ses) diagnostic m

diagonal (daï-*æ*-gheu-neul) *n*
diagonale *f*; *adj* diagonale

diagram (*daï*-eu-ghræm) *n*
diagramme *m*; graphique *m*

dial (daï^{eu}l) *n* cadran *m*; *v* composer,
faire

dial(l)ing tone (*daï*-eu-linng-tô^{ou}n) *n*
tonalité *f*

dialect (*daï*-eu-lèkt) *n* dialecte *m*

diamond (*daï*-eu-meunnd) *n* diamant
m

diaper (*daï*-eu-peu) *nAm* couche *f*

diarrh(o)ea (daï-eu-*ri*-eu) *n* diarrhée *f*

diary (*daï*-eu-ri) *n* agenda *m*; journal
m

dictate (dik-*têït*) *v* dicter

dictation (dik-*têï*-cheunn) *n* dictée *f*

dictionary (*dik*-cheu-neu-ri) *n*
dictionnaire *m*

did (did) *v* (p do)

die (daï) *v* *mourir

diesel (*dii*-zeul) *n* diesel *m*

diet (*daï*-eut) *n* régime *m*

differ (*di*-feu) *v* différer

difference (*di*-feu-reunns) *n*
différence *f*; distinction *f*

different (*di*-feu-reunnt) *adj* différent;
autre

difficult (*di*-fi-keult) *adj* difficile

difficulty (*di*-fi-keul-ti) *n* difficulté *f*;
peine *f*

*dig (digh) *v* creuser; fouiller

digest (di-*djèst*) *v* digérer

digestible (di-*djè*-steu-beul) *adj*
digestible

digestion (di-*djèss*-tcheunn) *n*
digestion *f*

digit (*di*-djit) *n* chiffre *m*

dignified (*digh*-ni-faïd) *adj* digne

dignity (*digh*-ni-ti) *n* dignité *f*

dike (daïk) *n* digue *f*

dilapidated (di-*læ*-pi-déï-tid) *adj*
délabré

diligence (*di*-li-djeunns) *n* assiduité *f*,
application *f*

diligent (*di*-li-djeunnt) *adj* laborieux,
assidu

dilute (daï-*lyoût*) *v* allonger, diluer

dim (dimm) *adj* terne, mat; obscur

dine (daïn) *v* dîner

dinghy (*dinng*-ghi) *n* canot *m*

dining car (*daï*-ninng-kââ) *n* wagon-
restaurant

dining room (*daï*-ninng-roûm) *n* salle
à manger

dinner (*di*-neu) *n* dîner *m*; ~ **jacket**
smoking *m*; ~ **service** service de
table

diphtheria (dif-*θ*eu-ri-eu) *n* diphtérie
f

diploma (di-*plôou*-meu) *n* diplôme *m*

diplomat (*di*-pleu-mæt) *n* diplomate
m

direct (di-*rèkt*) *adj* direct; *v* diriger;
administrer; *mettre en scène

direction (di-*rèk*-cheunn) *n* direction
f; instruction *f*; réalisation *f*;
directions for use mode d'emploi

directive (di-*rèk*-tiv) *n* directive *f*

director (di-*rèk*-teu) *n* directeur *m*,
-trice *f*; metteur en scène

directory (di-*rèk*-teu-ri) *n* répertoire
m d'adresses; annuaire *m* (des
téléphones); ~ **assistance**, ~
enquiry renseigements *pl*

dirt (deût) *n* saleté *f*

dirty (*deû*-ti) *adj* sale, souillé

disabled (di-*séï*-beuld) *adj* handicapé,
invalide

disadvantage (di-seud-*vâân*-tidj) *n*
désavantage *m*

disagree (di-seu-*ghrii*) *v* *être en
désaccord

disagreeable (di-seu-*ghrii*-eu-beul)
adj désagréable

disappear (di-seu-*pieu*) *v* *disparaître

disappoint (di-seu-*poïnt*) *v* *décevoir

disappointment (di-seu-*poïnt*-

meunnt) *n* déception *f*

disapprove (di-seu-*proûv*) *v* désapprouver

disaster (di-*zââ*-steu) *n* désastre *m*; catastrophe *f*, calamité *f*

disastrous (di-*zââ*-streuss) *adj* désastreux

disc (disk) *n* disque *m*; **slipped ~** hernie discale

discard (di-*skââd*) *v* se débarrasser de

discharge (diss-*tchââdj*) *v* décharger; **~ of** dispenser de

discipline (*di*-si-plinn) *n* discipline *f*

discolo(u)r (di-*ska*-leu) *v* décolorer

disconnect (di-skeu-*nèkt*) *v* *disjoindre; débrancher

discontented (di-skeunn-*tèn*-tid) *adj* mécontent

discontinue (di-skeunn-*ti*-nyoû) *v* suspendre, cesser

discount (*di*-skaount) *n* réduction *f*, rabais *m*

discourage (di-*ska*-ridj *v* décourager (**from** de)

discover (di-*ska*-veu) *v* *découvrir

discovery (di-*ska*-veu-ri) *n* découverte *f*

discuss (di-*skass*) *v* discuter; *débattre

discussion (di-*ska*-cheunn) *n* discussion *f*; conversation *f*, délibération *f*, débat *m*

disease (di-*ziiz*) *n* maladie *f*

disembark (di-simm-*bââk*) *v* débarquer

disgrace (diss-*ghréïss*) *n* déshonneur *m*

disguise (diss-*ghaïz*) *v* se déguiser; *n* déguisement *m*

disgust (diss-*ghast*) *n* dégoût *m*; répugnance *f*; *v* dégoûter

disgusting (diss-*gha*-stinng) *adj* répugnant, dégoûtant

dish (dich) *n* assiette *f*; plat *m*

dishonest (di-*so*-nist) *adj* malhonnête

dishwasher (*dich*-^ou^o-cheu) *n* laveur *m* de vaisselle; lave-vaisselle *m*

disinfect (di-sinn-*fèkt*) *v* désinfecter

disinfectant (di-sinn-*fèk*-teunnt) *n* désinfectant *m*

dislike (di-*slaïk*) *v* détester, ne pas aimer; *n* répugnance *f*, aversion *f*, antipathie *f*

dislocated (*di*-sleu-kéï-tid) *adj* disloqué

dismiss (diss-*miss*) *v* *renvoyer

disorder (di-*soo*-deu) *n* désordre *m*; confusion *f*

dispatch (di-*spætch*) *v* *envoyer, expédier

display (di-*splèï*) *v* étaler; montrer; *n* exposition *f*

displease (di-*spliiz*) *v* *déplaire

disposable (di-*spôou*-zeu-beul) *adj* à jeter

disposal (di-*spôou*-zeul) *n* disposition *f*

dispose of (di-*spôouz*) disposer de

dispute (di-*spyoût*) *n* discussion *f*; querelle *f*, litige *m*; *v* se disputer, contester

dissatisfied (di-*sæ*-tiss-faïd) *adj* insatisfait

dissolve (di-*zolv*) *v* *dissoudre, diluer

dissuade from (di-*souéïd*) dissuader

distance (*di*-steunns) *n* distance *f*; **~ in kilometres,** *Am* **kilometers** kilométrage *m*

distant (*di*-steunnt) *adj* éloigné

distinct (di-*stinngkt*) *adj* net; distinct

distinction (di-*stinngk*-cheunn) *n* distinction *f*

distinguish (di-*stinng*-gh^ou^ich) *v* distinguer, discerner

distinguished (di-*stinng*-gh^ou^icht) *adj* distingué

distress (di-*strèss*) *n* détresse *f*; **~ signal** signal de détresse

distribute (di-*stri*-byoût) *v* distribuer

distributor (di-*stri*-byou-teu) *n* concessionnaire *m*; distributeur *m*

district (*di*-strikt) *n* district *m*; région *f*; quartier *m*

disturb (di-*steûb*) *v* déranger

disturbance (di-*steû*-beunns) *n* dérangement *m*; agitation *f*

ditch (ditch) *n* fossé *m*

dive (daïv) *v* plonger

diversion (daï-*veû*-cheunn) *n* déviation *f*; diversion *f*

divide (di-*vaïd*) *v* diviser; répartir; séparer

divine (di-*vaïn*) *adj* divin

division (di-*vi*-jeunn) *n* division *f*; séparation *f*; département *m*

divorce (di-*vooss*) *n* divorce *m*; *v* divorcer

dizziness (di-*zi*-neuss) *n* vertige *m*

dizzy (*di*-zi) *adj* étourdi

***do** (doû) *v* *faire; *suffire

dock (dok) *n* dock *m*; quai *m*; *v* accoster

docker (*do*-keu) *n* docker *m*

doctor (*dok*-teu) *n* médecin *m*, docteur *m*

document (*do*-kyou-meunnt) *n* document *m*

dog (dogh) *n* chien *m*

dogged (*do*-ghid) *adj* obstiné

doll (dol) *n* poupée *f*

dollar (*do*-leu) *n* dollar *m*

dome (dô^{ou}m) *n* dôme *m*

domestic (deu-*mè*-stik) *adj* domestique; intérieur; *n* domestique *m*

domicile (*do*-mi-saïl) *n* domicile *m*

domination (do-mi-*néï*-cheunn) *n* domination *f*

dominion (deu-*mi*-nyeunn) *n* règne *m*

donate (dô^{ou}-*néït*) *v* donner

donation (dô^{ou}-*néï*-cheunn) *n* don *m*, donation *f*

done (dann) *v* (pp do)

donkey (*donng*-ki) *n* âne *m*

donor (*dôou*-neu) *n* donateur *m*

door (doo) *n* porte *f*; **revolving ~** porte tournante; **sliding ~** porte coulissante

doorbell (*doo*-bèl) *n* sonnette *f*

doorkeeper (*doo*-kii-peu) *n* portier *m*

doorman (*doo*-meunn) *n* (pl -men) portier *m*

dormitory (*doo*-mi-tri) *n* dortoir *m*

dose (dô^{ou}ss) *n* dose *f*

dot (dot) *n* point *m*

double (*da*-beul) *adj* double

doubt (daout) *v* douter de, douter; *n* doute *m*; **without ~** sans aucun doute

doubtful (*daout*-feul) *adj* douteux; incertain

dough (dô^{ou}) *n* pâte *f*

down[1] (daoun) *adv* en bas; vers le bas, par terre; *adj* déprimé; *prep* le long de, en bas de; **~ payment** acompte *m*

down[2] (daoun) *n* duvet *m*

downpour (*daoun*-poo) *n* averse *f*

downstairs (daoun-*stèeuz*) *adv* en bas

downstream (daoun-*striim*) *adv* en aval

downwards (daoun-^{ou}eudz) *adv* vers le bas

dozen (*da*-zeunn) *n* (pl ~, ~s) douzaine *f*

draft[1] (drââft) *n* traite *f*

draft[2] (drââft) *n* courant *m* d'air

drag (drægh) *v* traîner

dragon (*dræ*-gheunn) *n* dragon *m*

drain (dréïn) *v* assécher; drainer; *n* égout *m*

drama (*drââ*-meu) *n* drame *m*; tragédie *f*; théâtre *m*

dramatic (dreu-*mæ*-tik) *adj* dramatique

dramatist (*dræ*-meu-tist) *n* dramaturge *m*

drank (drængk) *v* (p drink)

drapery (*dréï*-peu-ri) *n* étoffes *fpl*

draught (drââft) *n* courant d'air;
draughts jeu de dames

draw (droo) *n* tirage *m*

*draw (droo) *v* dessiner; tirer; **~ up**
rédiger

drawbridge (droo-bridj) *n* pont-levis
m

drawer (*droo*-eu) *n* tiroir *m*; **drawers**
caleçon *m*

drawing (*droo*-inng) *n* dessin *m*; **~ pin**
punaise *f*; **~ room** (*droo*-inng-roûm)
n salon *m*

dread (drèd) *v* *craindre; *n* crainte *f*

dreadful (*drèd*-feul) *adj* terrible,
affreux

dream (driim) *n* rêve *m*

*dream (driim) *v* rêver, songer

dress (drèss) *v* habiller; se *vêtir,
s'habiller, *vêtir; panser; *n* robe *f*

dressing gown (*drè*-sinng-ghaoun) *n*
robe de chambre

dressing room (*drè*-sinng-roûm) *n*
loge *f*

dressing table (*drè*-sinng-téï-beul) *n*
coiffeuse *f*

dressmaker (*drèss*-méï-keu) *n*
couturière *f*

drill (dril) *v* forer; entraîner; *n* foreuse *f*

drink (drinngk) *n* apéritif *m*, boisson *f*

*drink (drinngk) *v* *boire

drinking water (*drinng*-kinng-^{ou}oo-
teu) *n* eau potable

drip-dry (drip-*draï*) *adj* qui ne
nécessite aucun repassage

drive (draïv) *n* route *f*; promenade en
voiture

*drive (draïv) *v* *conduire

driver (*draï*-veu) *n* conducteur *m*

drizzle (*dri*-zeul) *n* crachin *m*

drop (drop) *v* laisser tomber; *n* goutte
f

drought (draout) *n* sécheresse *f*

drown (draoun) *v* noyer; ***be drowned**
se noyer

drug (dragh) *n* drogue *f*; médicament
m

drugstore (*dragh*-stoo) *nAm*
drugstore *m*

drum (dramm) *n* tambour *m*

drunk (dranngk) *adj* (pp drink) ivre

dry (draï) *adj* sec; *v* sécher; essuyer

dry-clean (draï-*kliin*) *v* nettoyer à sec

dry cleaner's (draï-*klii*-neuz) *n*
teinturerie *f*

dryer (*draï*-eu) *n* séchoir *m*

duchess (da-tchiss) *n* duchesse *f*

duck (dak) *n* canard *m*

due (dyou) *adj* attendu; payable; dû

dues (dyoûz) *pl* droits

dug (dagh) *v* (p, pp dig)

duke (dyoûk) *n* duc *m*

dull (dal) *adj* ennuyeux; terne, mat;
émoussé

dumb (damm) *adj* muet; bête

dune (dyoûn) *n* dune *f*

dung (danng) *n* fumier *m*

dunghill (*danng*-hil) *n* tas de fumier

duration (dyou-*réï*-cheunn) *n* durée *f*

during (*dyoueu*-rinng) *prep* durant,
pendant

dusk (dask) *n* crépuscule *m*

dust (dast) *n* poussière *f*

dustbin (*dast*-binn) *n* boîte à ordures

dusty (*da*-sti) *adj* poussiéreux

Dutch (datch) *adj* néerlandais,
hollandais

duty (*dyoû*-ti) *n* devoir *m*; tâche *f*;
droit d'importation; **Customs ~** droit
de douane

duty-free (dyoû-ti-*frii*) *adj* exempt de
droits

dwarf (d^{ou}oof) *n* nain *m*

dye (daï) *v* *teindre; *n* teinture *f*

dynamo (*daï*-neu-mô^{ou}) *n* (pl ~s)
dynamo *f*

E

each (iitch) *adj* chaque; ~ **other** l'un
l'autre

eager (*ii*-gheu) *adj* désireux, impatient

eagle (*ii*-gheul) *n* aigle *m*

ear (i^{eu}) *n* oreille *f*

earache (*ieu*-réík) *n* mal d'oreille

eardrum (*ieu*-dramm) *n* tympan *m*

earl (eûl) *n* comte *m*

early (eû-li) *adj* tôt

earn (eûnn) *v* gagner

earnest (eû-nist) *n* sérieux *m*

earnings (eû-ninngz) *pl* revenu *m*,
gains

earring (*ieu*-rinng) *n* boucle d'oreille

earth (eûθ) *n* terre *f*; sol *m*

earthquake (eû$θ$-k^{ou}éík) *n*
tremblement de terre

ease (iiz) *n* aisance *f*; aise *f*

east (iist) *n* est *m*

Easter (*ii*-steu) Pâques

easterly (*ii*-steu-li) *adj* oriental

eastern (*ii*-steunn) *adj* oriental

easy (*ii*-zi) *adj* facile; commode; ~
chair fauteuil *m*

easy-going (*ii*-zi-ghô^{ou}-inng) *adj*
décontracté

***eat** (iit) *v* manger; dîner

eavesdrop (*iivz*-drop) *v* écouter aux
portes

ebony (*è*-beu-ni) *n* ébène *f*

eccentric (ik-*sèn*-trik) *adj* excentrique

echo (*è*-kô^{ou}) *n* (pl ~es) écho *m*

eclipse (i-*klips*) *n* éclipse *f*

economic (ii-keu-*no*-mik) *adj*
économique

economical (ii-keu-*no*-mi-keul) *adj*
parcimonieux, économe

economist (i-*ko*-neu-mist) *n*
économiste *m*

economize (i-*ko*-neu-maïz) *v*
économiser

economy (i-*ko*-neu-mi) *n* économie *f*

ecstasy (*èk*-steu-zi) *n* extase *m*

Ecuador (*è*-k^{ou}eu-doo) Equateur *m*

Ecuadorian (è-k^{ou}eu-*doo*-ri-eunn) *n*
Ecuadorien *m*

eczema (*èk*-si-meu) *n* eczéma *m*

edge (èdj) *n* rebord *m*, bord *m*

edible (*è*-di-beul) *adj* comestible

edit (*è*-dit) *v* éditer; diriger

edition (i-*di*-cheunn) *n* édition *f*;
morning ~ édition du matin

editor (*è*-di-teu) *n* rédacteur *m*

educate (*è*-djou-kéít) *v* former,
éduquer

education (è-djou-*kéí*-cheunn) *n*
éducation *f*

eel (iil) *n* anguille *f*

effect (i-*fèkt*) *n* résultat *m*, effet *m*; *v*
effectuer; **in** ~ en fait

effective (i-*fèk*-tiv) *adj* efficace,
effectif

efficient (i-*fi*-cheunnt) *adj* efficace

effort (*è*-feut) *n* effort *m*

egg (ègh) *n* œuf *m*; ~ **yolk** jaune d'œuf

eggcup (*ègh*-kap) *n* coquetier *m*

eggplant (*ègh*-plâânt) *n* aubergine *f*

ego(t)istic (è-ghô^{ou}-*i*-stik) *adj* égoïste

Egypt (*ii*-djipt) Egypte *f*

Egyptian (i-*djip*-cheunn) *adj* égyptien;
n Egyptien *m*

eiderdown (*aï*-deu-daoun) *n* édredon
m

eight (éít) *num* huit

eighteen (éí-*tiin*) *num* dix-huit

eighteenth (éí-*tiin*θ) *num* dix-
huitième

eighth (éítθ) *num* huitième

eighty (*éí*-ti) *num* quatre-vingts

either (*aï*-ðeu) *pron* l'un ou l'autre;
either ... or ou ... ou, soit ... soit

elaborate (i-*læ*-beu-réít) *v* élaborer

elastic (i-*læ*-stik) *adj* élastique;
flexible; élastique *m*

elasticity (è-læ-*sti*-seu-ti) *n* élasticité *f*

elbow (*èl*-bô^{ou}) *n* coude *m*

elder (*èl*-deu) *adj* plus âgé

elderly (*èl*-deu-li) *adj* âgé

eldest (*èl*-dist) *adj* le plus âgé

elect (i-*lèkt*) *v* *élire

election (i-*lèk*-cheunn) *n* élection *f*

electric (i-*lèk*-trik) *adj* électrique; ~ **razor** rasoir électrique; ~ **wire** fil électrique

electrician (i-lèk-*tri*-cheunn) *n* électricien *m*

electricity (i-lèk-*tri*-seu-ti) *n* électricité *f*

electronic (i-lèk-*tro*-nik) *adj* électronique

elegance (è-li-gheunns) *n* élégance *f*

elegant (è-li-gheunnt) *adj* élégant

element (è-li-meunnt) *n* élément *m*

elephant (è-li-feunnt) *n* éléphant *m*

elevator (è-li-véï-teu) *nAm* ascenseur *m*

eleven (i-*lè*-veunn) *num* onze

eleventh (i-*lè*-veunnθ) *num* onzième

eliminate (i-*li*-mi-néït) *v* éliminer

else (èls) *adv* autrement

elsewhere (èl-*soueu*) *adv* ailleurs

elucidate (i-*loû*-si-déït) *v* élucider

e-mail (i-méïl) *n* e-mail *m*; message électronique

emancipation (i-mæn-si-*péï*-cheunn) *n* émancipation *f*

embankment (imm-*bængk*-meunnt) *n* berge *f*

embargo (èm-*bââ*-ghô^{ou}) *n* (pl ~es) embargo *m*

embark (imm-*bââk*) *v* embarquer

embarkation (èm-bââ-*kéï*-cheunn) *n* embarquement *m*

embarrass (imm-*bæ*-reuss) *v* embarrasser; gêner;

embarrassed (imm-*bæ*-reust) *adj* confus

embarrassment (imm-*bæ*-reuss-meunnt) *n* embarras *m*; gêne *f*

embassy (*èm*-beu-si) *n* ambassade *f*

emblem (*èm*-bleumm) *n* emblème *m*

embrace (imm-*bréïss*) *v* *étreindre; *n* enlacement *m*

embroider (imm-*broï*-deu) *v* broder

embroidery (imm-*broï*-deu-ri) *n* broderie *f*

emerald (è-meu-reuld) *n* émeraude *f*

emergency (i-*meû*-djeunn-si) *n* cas d'urgence, urgence *f*; état d'urgence; ~ **exit** sortie de secours

emigrant (è-mi-ghreunnt) *n* émigrant *m*

emigrate (è-mi-ghréït) *v* émigrer

emigration (è-mi-*ghréï*-cheunn) *n* émigration *f*

emotion (i-*môou*-cheunn) *n* émoi *m*, émotion *f*

emotional (i-*môou*-cheu-neul) *adj* émotionnel; émotif ; qui fait appel aux émotions, touchant, émouvant

emperor (*èm*-peu-reu) *n* empereur *m*

emphasize (*èm*-feu-saïz) *v* souligner

empire (*èm*-paï^{eu}) *n* empire *m*

employ (imm-*ploï*) *v* employer; utiliser

employee (èm-ploï-*ii*) *n* employé *m*, -e *f*

employer (imm-*ploï*-eu) *n* employeur *m*, -se *f*

employment (imm-*ploï*-meunnt) *n* emploi *m*; ~ **exchange** bureau de l'emploi

empress (*èm*-priss) *n* impératrice *f*

empty (*èmp*-ti) *adj* vide; *v* vider

enable (i-*néï*-beul) *v* *permettre

enamel (i-*næ*-meul) *n* émail *m*

enamelled (i-*næ*-meuld) *adj* émaillé

enchanting (inn-*tchâân*-tinng) *adj* splendide, ravissant

encircle (inn-*seû*-keul) *v* encercler, entourer

enclose (inng-*klôouz*) *v* *inclure,

*joindre

enclosure (inng-*klôou*-jeu) *n* pièce jointe

encounter (inng-*kaoun*-teu) *v* rencontrer; *n* rencontre *f*

encourage (inng-*ka*-ridj) *v* encourager

encyclop(a)edia (èn-saï-kleu-*pii*-di-eu) *n* encyclopédie *f*

end (ènd) *n* fin *f*, bout *m*; conclusion *f*; *v* finir

ending (*èn*-dinng) *n* fin *f*

endless (*ènd*-leuss) *adj* infini

endorse (inn-*dooss*) *v* endosser

endure (inn-*dyoueu*) *v* endurer

enemy (*è*-neu-mi) *n* ennemi *m*, -e *f*

energetic (è-neu-*djè*-tik) *adj* énergique

energy (*è*-neu-dji) *n* énergie *f*; puissance *f*

engage (inng-*ghéïdj*) *v* engager; s'engager; **engaged** fiancé; occupé

engagement (inng-*ghéïdj*-meunnt) *n* fiançailles *fpl*; engagement *m*; **~ ring** bague de fiançailles

engine (*èn*-djinn) *n* machine *f*, moteur *m*; locomotive *f*

engineer (èn-dji-*nieu*) *n* ingénieur *m*

England (*inng*-ghleunnd) Angleterre *f*

English (*inng*-ghlich) *adj* anglais

Englishman (*inng*-ghlich-meunn) *n* (pl -men) Anglais *m*

Englishwoman (*inng*-ghlich-ᵒᵘou-meunn) *n* (pl -women) Anglaise *f*

engrave (inng-*ghréïv*) *v* graver

engraver (inng-*ghréï*-veu) *n* graveur *m*

engraving (inng-*ghréï*-vinng) *n* estampe *f*; gravure *f*

enigma (i-*nigh*-meu) *n* énigme *f*

enjoy (inn-*djoï*) *v* jouir de, *prendre plaisir

enjoyable (inn-*djoï*-eu-beul) *adj* agréable, plaisant; bon

enjoyment (inn-*djoï*-meunnt) *n* plaisir *m*

enlarge (inn-*lââdj*) *v* agrandir; étendre

enlargement (inn-*lââdj*-meunnt) *n* agrandissement *m*

enormous (i-*noo*-meuss) *adj* gigantesque, énorme

enough (i-*naf*) *adv* assez; *adj* suffisant

enquire (inng-*kouaïeu*) *v* s'informer; enquêter

enquiry (inng-*kouaïeu*-ri) *n* information *f*; investigation *f*; enquête *f*

enter (*èn*-teu) *v* entrer; *inscrire

enterprise (*èn*-teu-praïz) *n* entreprise *f*

entertain (èn-teu-*téïn*) *v* divertir, amuser; *recevoir

entertainer (èn-teu-*téï*-neu) *n* animateur *m*

entertaining (èn-teu-*téï*-ninng) *adj* amusant, divertissant

entertainment (èn-teu-*téïn*-meunnt) *n* amusement *m*, divertissement *m*

enthusiasm (inn-θ*yoû*-zi-æ-zeumm) *n* enthousiasme *m*

enthusiastic (inn-θ*yoû*-zi-æ-stik) *adj* enthousiaste

entire (inn-*taïeu*) *adj* tout, entier

entirely (inn-*taïeu*-li) *adv* entièrement

entrance (*èn*-treunns) *n* entrée *f*; accès *m*; **~ fee** prix d'entrée

entry (*èn*-tri) *n* entrée *f*; admission *f*; inscription *f*; **no ~** défense d'entrer

envelop (inn- *vè*-leup) *v* envelopper

envelope (*èn*-veu-lôᵒᵘp) *n* enveloppe *f*

envious (*èn*-vi-euss) *adj* envieux, jaloux

environment (inn-*vaïeu*-reunn-meunnt) *n* environnement *m*; environs *mpl*

envoy (*èn*-voï) *n* envoyé *m*

envy (*èn*-vi) *n* envie *f*; *v* envier

epic (*è*-pik) *n* poème épique; *adj* épique

epidemic (è-pi-*dè*-mik) *n* épidémie *f*

epilepsy (*è*-pi-lèp-si) *n* épilepsie *f*

episode (*è*-pi-sô^{ou}d) *n* épisode *m*

equal (*ii*-k^{ou}eul) *adj* égal; *v* égaler

equality (i-*kouo*-leu-ti) *n* égalité *f*

equalize (*ii*-k^{ou}eu-laïz) *v* égaliser

equally (*ii*-k^{ou}eu-li) *adv* également

equator (i-*kouéi*-teu) *n* équateur *m*

equip (i-*kouip*) *v* équiper

equipment (i-*kouip*-meunnt) *n* équipement *m*

equivalent (i-*koui*-veu-leunnt) *adj* équivalent

eraser (i-*réï*-zeu) *n* gomme *f*

erect (i-*rèkt*) *v* ériger; *adj* debout, droit

err (eû) *v* se tromper, errer

errand (*è*-reunnd) *n* commission *f*

error (*è*-reu) *n* faute *f*, erreur *f*

escalator (*è*-skeu-léï-teu) *n* escalier roulant

escape (i-*skéïp*) *v* échapper; *fuir; *n* évasion *f*

escort[1] (*è*-skoot) *n* escorte *f*

escort[2] (i-*skoot*) *v* escorter

especially (i-*spè*-cheu-li) *adv* principalement, spécialement

esplanade (è-spleu-*néïd*) *n* esplanade *f*

essay (*è*-séï) *n* essai *m*; dissertation *f*, composition *f*

essence (*è*-seunns) *n* essence *f*; fond *m*, nature *f*

essential (i-*sèn*-cheul) *adj* indispensable; fondamental, essentiel

essentially (i-*sèn*-cheu-li) *adv* essentiellement

establish (i-*stæ*-blich) *v* établir

estate (i-*stéït*) *n* propriété *f*

esteem (i-*stiim*) *n* respect *m*, estime *f*;

v estimer

estimate[1] (*è*-sti-méït) *v* évaluer, estimer

estimate[2] (*è*-sti-meut) *n* estimation *f*

estuary (*èss*-tchou-eu-ri) *n* estuaire *m*

etcetera (èt-sè-*teu*-reu) et cætera

etching (*è*-tchinng) *n* eau-forte *f*

eternal (i-*teû*-neul) *adj* éternel

eternity (i-*teû*-neu-ti) *n* éternité *f*

Ethiopia (i-θi-*ôou*-pi-eu) Ethiopie *f*

Ethiopian (i-θi-*ôou*-pi-eunn) *adj* éthiopien; *n* Ethiopien *m*

Euro (*youeu*-reu) *n* euro *m*

Europe (*youeu*-reup) Europe *f*

European (you^{eu}-reu-*pii*-eunn) *adj* européen; *n* Européen *m*

evacuate (i-*væ*-kyou-éït) *v* évacuer

evade (i-*véïd*) *v* éviter, échapper à; éluder

evaluate (i-*væl*-you-éït) *v* évaluer

evaporate (i-*væ*-peu-réït) *v* évaporer

even (*ii*-veunn) *adj* plan, égal; constant; pair; *adv* même

evening (*iiv*-ninng) *n* soir *m*; ~ **dress** tenue de soirée

event (i-*vènt*) *n* événement *m*; cas *m*

eventual (i-*vèn*-tchou-eul) *adj* éventuel

ever (*è*-veu) *adv* jamais; toujours

every (*èv*-ri) *adj* tout, chaque

everybody (*èv*-ri-bo-di) *pron* tout le monde

everyday (*èv*-ri-déï) *adj* quotidien

everyone (*èv*-ri-^{ou}ann) *pron* chacun, tout le monde

everything (*èv*-ri-θinng) *pron* tout

everywhere (*èv*-ri-^{ou}è^{eu}) *adv* partout

evidence (*è*-vi-deunns) *n* preuve *f*

evident (*è*-vi-deunnt) *adj* évident

evil (*ii*-veul) *n* mal *m*; *adj* méchant, mauvais

evolution (ii-veu-*loû*-cheunn) *n* évolution *f*

exact (igh-*zækt*) *adj* juste, exact

exactly (igh-*zækt*-li) *adv* exactement

exaggerate (igh-*zæ*-djeu-réït) *v* exagérer

exam (igh-*zæm*) *n colloquial* examen *m*

examination (igh-zæ-mi-*néï*-cheunn) *n* examen *m*; interrogatoire *m*

examine (igh-*zæ*-minn) *v* examiner

example (igh-*zââm*-peul) *n* exemple *m*; **for ~** par exemple

exceed (ik-*siid*) *v* excéder; surpasser

excel (ik-*sèl*) *v* exceller

excellent (*èk*-seu-leunnt) *adj* excellent

except (ik-*sèpt*) *prep* excepté

exception (ik-*sèp*-cheunn) *n* exception *f*

exceptional (ik-*sèp*-cheu-neul) *adj* extraordinaire, exceptionnel

excerpt (*èk*-seûpt) *n* extrait *m*

excess (ik-*sèss*) *n* excès *m*

excessive (ik-*sè*-siv) *adj* excessif

exchange (iks-*tchéïndj*) *v* échanger, changer; *n* bourse *f*; **~ office** bureau de change; **~ rate** taux de change

excite (ik-*saït*) *v* exciter

excitement (ik-*saït*-meunnt) *n* agitation *f*, excitation *f*

exciting (ik-*saï*-tinng) *adj* passionnant

exclaim (ik-*skléïm*) *v* exclamer

exclamation (èk-skleu-*méï*-cheunn) *n* exclamation *f*

exclude (ik-*skloûd*) *v* *exclure

exclusive (ik-*skloû*-siv) *adj* exclusif

exclusively (ik-*skloû*-siv-li) *adv* exclusivement, uniquement

excursion (ik-*skeû*-cheunn) *n* excursion *f*

excuse[1] (ik-*skyoûss*) *n* excuse *f*

excuse[2] (ik-*skyoûz*) *v* excuser

execute (*èk*-si-kyoût) *v* exécuter

execution (èk-si-*kyoû*-cheunn) *n* exécution *f*

executive (igh-*zè*-kyou-tiv) *adj* exécutif; *n* pouvoir exécutif; exécutif *m*

exempt (igh-*jèmpt*) *v* dispenser, exempter; *adj* exempt

exemption (igh-*zèmp*-cheunn) *n* exemption *f*

exercise (*èk*-seu-saïz) *n* exercice *m*; *v* exercer

exhale (èks-*héïl*) *v* expirer

exhaust (igh-*zoost*) *n* tuyau d'échappement, échappement *m*; *v* exténuer; **~ gases** gaz d'échappement

exhibit (igh-*zi*-bit) *v* exposer; exhiber

exhibition (èk-si-*bi*-cheunn) *n* exhibition *f*, exposition *f*

exile (*èk*-saïl) *n* exile *m*; exilé *m*

exist (igh-*zist*) *v* exister

existence (igh-*zi*-steunns) *n* existence *f*

exit (*èk*-sit) *n* sortie *f*

exotic (igh-*zo*-tik) *adj* exotique

expand (ik-*spænd*) *v* étendre; déployer

expansion (ik-*spæn*-cheunn) *n* expansion *f*; dilatation *f*; développement *m*

expect (ik-*spèkt*) *v* attendre

expectation (èk-spèk-*téï*-cheunn) *n* espérance *f*

expedition (èk-speu-*di*-cheunn) *n* expédition *f*

expel (ik-*spèl*) *v* expulser

expenditure (ik-*spèn*-di-tcheu) *n* dépense *f*

expense (ik-*spèns*) *n* dépense *f*; **expenses** *pl* frais *mpl*

expensive (ik-*spèn*-siv) *adj* cher; coûteux

experience (ik-*spieu*-ri-eunns) *n* expérience *f*; *v* éprouver, *vivre, *faire l'expérience de; **experienced** expérimenté

experiment (ik-*spè*-ri-meunnt) *n* épreuve *f*, expérience *f*; *v* expérimenter

expert (*èk*-speût) *n* spécialiste *m*, expert *m*; *adj* compétent

expire (ik-*spaïeu*) *v* *venir à échéance, se terminer, expirer; **expired** périmé

expiry (ik-*spaïeu*-ri) *n* expiration *f*

explain (ik-*spléïn*) *v* expliquer

explanation (èk-spleu-*néï*-cheunn) *n* éclaircissement *m*, explication *f*

explicit (ik-*spli*-sit) *adj* formel, explicite

explode (ik-*splôoud*) *v* exploser

exploit (ik-*sploït*) *v* exploiter

explore (ik-*sploo*) *v* explorer

explosion (ik-*splôo*-jeunn) *n* explosion *f*

explosive (ik-*splôou*-siv) *adj* explosif; *n* explosif *m*

export¹ (ik-*spoot*) *v* exporter

export² (*èk*-spoot) *n* exportation *f*

exportation (èk-spoo-*téï*-cheunn) *n* exportation *f*

exports (*èk*-spoots) *n pl* exportation *f*

expose (ik-*spôouz*) *v* exposer; démasquer; dévoiler

exposition (èk-speu-*zi*-cheunn) *n* exposition *f*

exposure (ik-*spôou*-jeu) *n* exposition *f*

express (ik-*sprèss*) *v* exprimer; manifester; *adj* exprès; explicite; ~ **train** rapide *m*

expression (ik-*sprè*-cheunn) *n* expression *f*

exquisite (ik-*skoui*-zit) *adj* exquis

extend (ik-*stènd*) *v* étendre; agrandir

extension (ik-*stèn*-cheunn) *n* prolongation *f*; agrandissement *m*; ligne intérieure; ~ **cord** rallonge *f*

extensive (ik-*stèn*-siv) *adj* considérable; vaste, étendu

extent (ik-*stènt*) *n* dimension *f*

exterior (èk-*stieu*-ri-eu) *adj* extérieur; *n* extérieur *m*

external (èk-*steû*-neul) *adj* extérieur

extinguish (ik-*stinng*-gh^(ou)ich) *v* *éteindre

extort (ik-*stoot*) *v* extorquer

extortion (ik-*stoo*-cheunn) *n* extorsion *f*

extra (*èk*-streu) *adj* supplémentaire

extract¹ (ik-*strækt*) *v* arracher, *extraire

extract² (*èk*-strækt) *n* fragment *m*

extradite (*èk*-streu-daït) *v* extrader

extraordinary (ik-*stroo*-deunn-ri) *adj* extraordinaire

extravagant (ik-*stræ*-veu-gheunnt) *adj* exagéré, extravagant

extreme (ik-*striim*) *adj* extrême; *n* extrême *m*

exuberant (igh-*zyoû*-beu-reunnt) *adj* exubérant

eye (aï) *n* œil *m*; ~ **shadow** ombre à paupières

eyebrow (*aï*-braou) *n* sourcil *m*; ~ **pencil** crayon pour les yeux

eyelash (*aï*-læch) *n* cil *m*

eyelid (*aï*-lid) *n* paupière *f*

eyewitness (*aï*-^(ou)it-neuss) *n* témoin oculaire

F

fable (*féï*-beul) *n* fable *f*

fabric (*fæ*-brik) *n* tissu *m*; structure *f*

façade (feu-*sââd*) *n* façade *f*

face (féïss) *n* visage *m*; *v* affronter; ~ **cream** crème de beauté; ~ **massage** massage facial; ~ **pack** masque de

beauté; **~ powder** poudre de riz;
facing en face de

fact (fækt) *n* fait *m*; **in ~** de fait

factor (*fæk*-teu) *n* facteur *m*

factory (*fæk*-teu-ri) *n* usine *f*

factual (*fæk*-tchou-eul) *adj* réel

faculty (*fæ*-keul-ti) *n* faculté *f*; don *m*,
talent *m*, aptitude *f*

fade (féïd) *v* se faner, *déteindre

fail (féïl) *v* échouer; manquer;
*omettre; **without ~** sans faute

failure (*féïl*-yeu) *n* échec *m*

faint (féïnt) *v* s'évanouir; *adj* faible,
vague, défaillant

fair (fèᵉu) *n* foire *f*; *adj* honnête, juste;
blond; beau

fairly (*fèᵉu*-li) *adv* assez, plutôt

fairy (*fèᵉu*-ri) *n* fée *f*

fairytale (*fèᵉu*-ri-téïl) *n* conte de fées

faith (féïθ) *n* foi *f*; confiance *f*

faithful (*féïθ*-foul) *adj* fidèle

fake (féïk) *n* falsification *f*

fall (fool) *n* chute *f*; *nAm* automne *m*

***fall** (fool) *v* tomber

false (fools) *adj* faux; **~ teeth** dentier
m

falter (*fool*-teu) *v* vaciller; balbutier

fame (féïm) *n* renommée *f*, célébrité *f*;
réputation *f*

familiar (feu-*mil*-yeu) *adj* familier

family (*fæ*-meu-li) *n* famille *f*; **~ name**
nom de famille

famous (*féï*-meuss) *adj* fameux

fan (fæn) *n* ventilateur *m*; éventail *m*;
fan *m/f*; **~ belt** courroie de ventilateur

fanatical (feu-*næ*-ti-keul) *adj*
fanatique

fancy (*fæn*-si) *v* aimer, *avoir envie de;
s'imaginer, imaginer; *n* caprice *m*;
imagination *f*

fantastic (fæn-*tæ*-stik) *adj* fantastique

fantasy (*fæn*-teu-zi) *n* fantaisie *f*

far (fââ) *adj* loin; *adv* beaucoup; **by ~**
de beaucoup; **so ~** jusqu'à
maintenant

far-away (*fââ*-reu-ᵒᵘéï) *adj* éloigné

fare (fèᵉu) *n* prix du voyage; chère *f*,
nourriture *f*

farm (fââm) *n* ferme *f*

farmer (*fââ*-meu) *n* fermier *m*;
farmer's wife fermière *f*

farmhouse (*fââm*-haouss) *n* ferme *f*

far-off (*fââ*-rof) *adj* lointain

fascinate (*fæ*-si-néït) *v* fasciner

fascism (*fæ*-chi-zeumm) *n* fascisme *m*

fascist (*fæ*-chist) *adj* fasciste

fashion (*fæ*-cheunn) *n* mode *f*; mode
m

fashionable (*fæ*-cheu-neu-beul) *adj* à
la mode

fast (fââst) *adj* prompt, rapide; ferme

fasten (*fââ*-seunn) *v* attacher; fermer

fastener (*fââ*-seu-neu) *n* fermeture *f*

fat (fæt) *adj* gras, gros; *n* graisse *f*

fatal (*féï*-teul) *adj* néfaste, mortel,
fatal

fate (féït) *n* destin *m*

father (*fââ*-ðeu) *n* père *m*

father-in-law (*fââ*-ðeu-rinn-loo) *n* (pl
fathers-) beau-père *m*

fatness (*fæt*-neuss) *n* obésité *f*

fatty (*fæ*-ti) *adj* gras

faucet (*foo*-sit) *nAm* robinet *m*

fault (foolt) *n* faute *f*; imperfection *f*,
défaut *m*

faultless (*foolt*-leuss) *adj* impeccable;
parfait

faulty (*fool*-ti) *adj* imparfait,
défectueux

favo(u)r (*féï*-veu) *n* faveur *f*; *v*
favoriser

favo(u)rable (*féï*-veu-reu-beul) *adj*
favorable

favo(u)rite (*féï*-veu-rit) *n* favori *m*, -te
f; *adj* préféré

fax (faks) *n* fax *m*; **send a ~** envoyer un
fax

fear (fiᵉu) *n* crainte *f*, peur *f*; *v*

*craindre

feasible (*fii-zeu-beul*) *adj* faisable

feast (fiist) *n* fête *f*

feat (fiit) *n* exploit *m*, prouesse *f*

feather (*fè-ðeu*) *n* plume *f*

feature (*fii-tcheu*) *n* caractéristique *f*; trait du visage

February (*fè-brou-eu-ri*) février

federal (*fè-deu-reul*) *adj* fédéral

federation (*fè-deu-réï-cheunn*) *n* fédération *f*

fee (fii) *n* honoraires *mpl*

feeble (*fii-beul*) *adj* faible

***feed** (fiid) *v* nourrir; **fed up with** dégoûté

***feel** (fiil) *v* *sentir; palper; ~ **like** *avoir envie de

feeling (*fii-linng*) *n* sensation *f*

feet (fiit) *n* (pl foot)

fell (fèl) *v* (p fall)

fellow (*fè-lô*ou) *n* gars *m*

felt[1] (fèlt) *n* feutre *m*

felt[2] (fèlt) *v* (p, pp feel)

female (*fii-méïl*) *adj* féminin

feminine (*fè-mi-ninn*) *adj* féminin

fence (fèns) *n* clôture *f*; barrière *f*; *v* *faire de l'escrime

ferment (*feû-mènt*) *v* fermenter

ferry-boat (*fè-ri-bô*ou*t*) *n* ferry-boat *m*

fertile (*feû-taïl*) *adj* fertile

festival (*fè-sti-veul*) *n* festival *m*

festive (*fè-stiv*) *adj* de fête

fetch (fètch) *v* apporter; *aller chercher

fever (*fii-veu*) *n* fièvre *f*

feverish (*fii-veu-rich*) *adj* fiévreux

few (fyoû) *adj* peu de

fiancé (fi-*an-séï*) *n* fiancé *m*

fiancée (fi-*an-séï*) *n* fiancée *f*

fibre (*faï-beu*) *n* fibre *f*

fiction (*fik-cheunn*) *n* fiction *f*

field (fiild) *n* champ *m*; domaine *m*; ~ **glasses** jumelles *fpl*

fierce (fi*eu*ss) *adj* féroce; sauvage,

violent

fifteen (fif-*tiin*) *num* quinze

fifteenth (fif-*tiinθ*) *num* quinzième

fifth (fifθ) *num* cinquième

fifty (*fif-*ti) *num* cinquante

fig (figh) *n* figue *f*

fight (faït) *n* lutte *f*, combat *m*

***fight** (faït) *v* se *battre, *combattre

figure (*fi-gheu*) *n* stature *f*, forme *f*; chiffre *m*

file (faïl) *n* lime *f*; dossier *m*

fill (fil) *v* remplir; ~ **in** remplir; **filling station** station-service *f*; ~ **out** *Am* remplir; ~ **up** *faire le plein

filling (*fi-linng*) *n* plombage *m*; farce *f*

film (film) *n* film *m*; pellicule *f*; *v* filmer

filter (*fil-teu*) *n* filtre *m*

filthy (*fil-θi*) *adj* répugnant, sale

final (*faï-neul*) *adj* final

finally (*faï-neu-li*) *adv* enfin; définitivement

finance (faï-*næns*) *v* financer

finances (faï-*næn*-siz) *pl* finances *fpl*

financial (faï-*næn*-cheul) *adj* financier

***find** (faïnd) *v* trouver

fine (faïn) *n* amende *f*, *adj* fin; joli; formidable, merveilleux; ~ **arts** beaux-arts *mpl*

finger (*finng-gheu*) *n* doigt *m*; **little** ~ auriculaire *m*

fingerprint (*finng-gheu-prinnt*) *n* empreinte digitale

finish (*fi-nich*) *v* achever, finir; terminer; *n* fin *f*; ligne d'arrivée

Finland (*finn-leunnd*) Finlande *f*

Finn (finn) *n* Finlandais *m*

Finnish (*fi-nich*) *adj* finlandais

fire (faï*eu*) *n* feu *m*; incendie *m*; *v* tirer; licencier; ~ **alarm** alarme d'incendie; ~ **brigade**, *Am* **fire department** pompiers; ~ **escape** escalier de secours; ~ **extinguisher** extincteur *m*

fireplace (*faïeu-pléïss*) *n* cheminée *f*

fireproof (*faïeu-proûf*) *adj* ignifuge;

qui va au four

firm (feûmm) *adj* ferme; solide; *n* firme *f*

first (feûst) *num* premier; **at ~** d'abord; au début; **~ name** prénom *m*

first aid (feûst-*éïd*) *n* premier secours; **~ kit** trousse de secours; **~ post** poste de secours

first-class (feûst-*klââss*) *adj* de première qualité

first-rate (feûst-*réït*) *adj* de premier ordre, de première qualité

fir tree (feû-trii) *n* sapin *m*

fish[1] (fich) *n* (pl ~, ~es) poisson *m*; **~ shop** poissonnerie *f*

fish[2] (fich) *v* pêcher; **fishing gear** attirail de pêche; **fishing hook** hameçon *m*; **fishing industry** pêche *f*; **fishing licence (license** *Am*) permis de pêche; **fishing line** ligne de pêche; **fishing net** filet de pêche; **fishing rod** canne à pêche; **fishing tackle** attirail de pêche

fishbone (*fich*-bôᵒᵘn) *n* arête *f*

fisherman (*fi*-cheu-meunn) *n* (pl -men) pêcheur *m*

fist (fist) *n* poing *m*

fit (fit) *adj* convenable; *n* attaque *f*; *v* *convenir; **fitting room** cabine d'essayage

five (faïv) *num* cinq

fix (fiks) *v* réparer

fixed (fikst) *adj* fixe

fizz (fiz) *n* pétillement *m*

flag (flægh) *n* drapeau *m*

flame (fléïm) *n* flamme *f*

flamingo (fleu-*minng*-ghôᵒᵘ) *n* (pl ~s, ~es) flamant *m*

flannel (*flæ*-neul) *n* flanelle *f*

flash (flæch) *n* éclair *m*; **~ bulb** ampoule de flash

flashlight (*flæch*-laït) *n* lampe de poche

flask (flââsk) *n* flacon *m*; **thermos ~**

thermos *m*

flat (flæt) *adj* plan, plat; *n* appartement *m*; **~ tire** *Am*, **~ tyre** pneu crevé

flavour (*fléï*-veu) *n* saveur *f*; *v* assaisonner

flee (flii) *v* s'enfuir; fuir

fleet (fliit) *n* flotte *f*

flesh (flèch) *n* chair *f*

flew (floû) *v* (p fly)

flex (flèks) *n* fil souple

flexible (*flèk*-si-beul) *adj* flexible; souple

flight (flaït) *n* vol *m*; **charter ~** vol charter

flint (flinnt) *n* pierre à briquet

float (flôᵒᵘt) *v* flotter; *n* flotteur *m*

flock (flok) *n* troupeau *m*

flood (flad) *n* inondation *f*; marée haute

floor (floo) *n* sol *m*; étage *m*; **~ show** spectacle de variétés

florist (*flo*-rist) *n* fleuriste *m/f*

flour (flaouᵉᵘ) *n* farine *f*

flow (flôᵒᵘ) *v* s'écouler, couler

flower (flaouᵉᵘ) *n* fleur *f*; **~ shop** fleuriste *m*

flowerbed (*flaoueu*-bèd) *n* plate-bande *f*

flown (flôᵒᵘn) *v* (pp fly)

flu (floû) *n* grippe *f*

fluently (*floû*-eunnt-li) *adv* couramment

fluid (*floû*-id) *adj* fluide; *n* liquide *m*

flute (floût) *n* flûte *f*

fly (flaï) *n* mouche *f*; braguette *f*

***fly** (flaï) *v* voler

foam (fôᵒᵘm) *n* mousse *f*, *v* mousser; **~ rubber** caoutchouc mousse

focus (*fôou*-keuss) *n* foyer *m*

fog (fogh) *n* brouillard *m*

foggy (*fo*-ghi) *adj* brumeux

foglamp (*fogh*-læmp) *n* phare antibrouillard

fold (fôᵒᵘld) *v* plier; *n* pli *m*

folk (fô^{ou}k) *n* gens *mpl*; **~ dance** danse folklorique; **~ song** chanson populaire

folklore (*fô*ouk-loo) *n* folklore *m*

follow (fo-lô^{ou}) *v* *suivre; **following** *adj* prochain, suivant

fond: *be ~ of (bii fonnd ov) aimer

food (foûd) *n* nourriture *f*; manger *m*; **~ poisoning** intoxication alimentaire

foodstuffs (foûd-stafs) *pl* aliments *mpl*

fool (foûl) *n* idiot *m*/fou *m*; *v* *faire marcher

foolish (foû-lich) *adj* sot, stupide; absurde

foot (fout) *n* (pl feet) pied *m*; **~ brake** frein à pédale; **~ powder** poudre pour les pieds; **on ~** à pied

football (*fout*-bool) *n* ballon *m*; **~ match** match de football

footpath (*fout*-pââθ) *n* sentier pour piétons

footwear (*fout*-ou è^{eu}) *n* chaussures

for (foo, feu) *prep* pour; pendant; à cause de, en raison de, par; *conj* car

*forbid (feu-*bid*) *v* *interdire

force (fooss) *v* obliger, forcer; *n* puissance *f*, force *f*; **by ~** forcément; **driving ~** force motrice

forecast (*foo*-kââst) *n* prévision *f*; *v* *prévoir

foreground (*foo*-ghraound) *n* premier plan

forehead (fo-rèd) *n* front *m*

foreign (fo-rinn) *adj* étranger

foreigner (fo-ri-neu) *n* étranger *m*

foreman (*foo*-meunn) *n* (pl -men) contremaître *m*

foremost (*foo*-mô^{ou}st) *adj* premier

forest (fo-rist) *n* bois *m*/forêt *f*

forester (fo-ri-steu) *n* forestier *m*

forge (foodj) *v* falsifier

*forget (feu-*ghèt*) *v* oublier

forgetful (feu-*ghèt*-feul) *adj* oublieux

*forgive (feu-*ghiv*) *v* pardonner

fork (fook) *n* fourchette *f*; bifurcation *f*; *v* bifurquer

form (foom) *n* forme *f*; formulaire *m*; classe *f*; *v* former

formal (*foo*-meul) *adj* cérémonieux

formality (foo-*mæ*-leu-ti) *n* formalité *f*

former (*foo*-meu) *adj* ancien; précédent; **formerly** antérieurement, auparavant

formula (*foo*-myou-leu) *n* (pl ~e, ~s) formule *f*

fortnight (*foot*-naït) *n* quinze jours

fortress (*foo*-triss) *n* forteresse *f*

fortunate (*foo*-tcheu-neut) *adj* heureux

fortunately (*foo*-tcheu-neut-li) *adv* par bonheur, heureusement

fortune (*foo*-tchoûn) *n* fortune *f*; sort *m*, chance *f*

forty (*foo*-ti) *num* quarante

forward (*foo*-ou eud) *adv* en avant; *v* *faire suivre

foster parents (fo-steu-pè^{eu}-reunnts) *pl* parents nourriciers

fought (foot) *v* (p, pp fight)

foul (faoul) *adj* malpropre; infâme

found[1] (faound) *v* (p, pp find)

found[2] (faound) *v* fonder, établir

foundation (faoun-*dé*ï-cheunn) *n* fondation *f*; **~ cream** fond de teint

fountain (*faoun*-tinn) *n* fontaine *f*; source *f*; **~ pen** stylo *m*

four (foo) *num* quatre

fourteen (foo-*tiin*) *num* quatorze

fourteenth (foo-*tiin*θ) *num* quatorzième

fourth (fooθ) *num* quatrième

fowl (faoul) *n* (pl ~s, ~) volaille *f*

fox (foks) *n* renard *m*

fraction (*fræk*-cheunn) *n* fraction *f*

fracture (*fræk*-tcheu) *v* fracturer; *n* fracture *f*

fragile (*fræ*-djaïl) *adj* fragile

fragment (*frægh*-meunnt) n fragment m; morceau m

frame (fréïm) n cadre m; monture f

France (frââns) France f

franchise (*fræn*-tchaïz) n droit de vote

fraternity (freu-*teû*-neu-ti) n fraternité f

fraud (frood) n fraude f

fray (fréï) v s'effilocher

free (frii) adj libre; gratuit; ~ of charge gratuit; ~ ticket billet gratuit

freedom (*frii*-deumm) n liberté f

*freeze (friiz) v geler

freezer (*frii*-zeu) n congélateur m

freezing (*frii*-zinng) adj glacial; ~ point point de congélation

freight (fréït) n fret m, chargement m; ~ train train de marchandises

French (frèntch) adj français

French fries (frèntch-fraïz) nAm pommes de terre frites fpl

frequency (*frii*-k^ou eunn-si) n fréquence f

frequent (*frii*-k^ou eunnt) adj courant, fréquent

fresh (frèch) adj frais; ~ water eau douce

friction (*frik*-cheunn) n friction f

Friday (*fraï*-di) vendredi m

fridge (fridj) n réfrigérateur m, frigo m

friend (frènd) n ami m, -e f

friendly (*frènd*-li) adj gentil; amical

friendship (*frènd*-chip) n amitié f

fright (fraït) n peur f, frayeur f

frighten (*fraï*-teunn) v effrayer

frightened (*fraï*-teunnd) adj effrayé; *be ~ *être effrayé

frightful (*fraït*-feul) adj terrible, affreux

fringe (frinndj) n frange f

frock (frok) n robe f

frog (frogh) n grenouille f

from (fromm) prep de; à partir de

front (frannt) n face f; in ~ of devant

frontier (*frann*-ti^eu) n frontière f

frost (frost) n gel m

froth (froθ) n écume f

frozen (*frôou*-zeunn) adj congelé; ~ food aliments surgelés

fruit (froût) n fruits; fruit m

fry (fraï) v *faire sauter; *frire

frying pan (*fraï*-inng-pæn) n poêle à frire

fuel (*fyoû*-eul) n combustible m; essence f; ~ pump Am distributeur d'essence

full (foul) adj plein; ~ board pension complète; ~ stop point m; ~ up complet

fun (fann) n divertissement m, plaisir m

function (*fanngk*-cheunn) n fonction f

fund (fannd) n fonds mpl

fundamental (fann-deu-*mèn*-teul) adj fondamental

funeral (*fyoû*-neu-reul) n funérailles fpl

funnel (*fa*-neul) n entonnoir m

funny (*fa*-ni) adj drôle, amusant; bizarre

fur (feû) n fourrure f; ~ coat manteau de fourrure

furious (*fyoueu*-ri-euss) adj furibond, furieux

furnace (*feû*-niss) n fournaise f

furnish (*feû*-nich) v fournir, procurer; installer, meubler; ~ with approvisionner en

furniture (*feû*-ni-tcheu) n meubles

furrier (*fa*-ri-eu) n fourreur m

further (*feû*-ðeu) adj plus loin; complémentaire

furthermore (*feû*-ðeu-moo) adv en outre

furthest (*feû*-ðist) adj le plus éloigné

fuse (fyoûz) n fusible m; mèche f

fuss (fass) *n* agitation *f*; embarras *m*, chichi *m*

future (fyoû-tcheu) *n* avenir *m*; *adj* futur

G

gable (ghéï-beul) *n* pignon *m*

gadget (ghæ-djit) *n* gadget *m*

gain (ghéïn) *v* gagner; *n* gain *m*

gale (ghéïl) *n* tempête *f*

gall (ghool) *n* bile *f*; **~ bladder** vésicule biliaire

gallery (ghæ-leu-ri) *n* galerie *f*

gallon (ghæ-leun) *n* gallon *m*

gallop (ghæ-leup) *n* galop *m*

gallstone (ghool-stô^ou n) *n* calcul biliaire

game (ghéïm) *n* jeu *m*; gibier *m*; **~ reserve** réserve zoologique

gang (ghæng) *n* bande *f*; équipe *f*

gangway (ghæng-^ou éï) *n* passerelle *f*

gap (ghæp) *n* brèche *f*

garage (ghæ-râåj) *n* garage *m*; *v* garer

garbage (ghââ-bidj) *n* détritus *m*, ordures *fpl*

garden (ghââ-deunn) *n* jardin *m*; **public ~** jardin public; **zoological gardens** jardin zoologique

gardener (ghââ-deu-neu) *n* jardinier *m*, -ière *f*

gargle (ghââ-gheul) *v* se gargariser

garlic (ghââ-lik) *n* ail *m*

gas (ghæss) *n* gaz *m*; *nAm* essence *f*; **~ cooker** cuisinière à gaz; **~ pump** *Am* pompe à essence; **~ station** *Am* station-service *f*; **~ stove** fourneau à gaz; **~ tank** réservoir d'essence

gasoline (ghæ-seu-liin) *nAm* essence *f*

gastric (ghæ-strik) *adj* gastrique; **~ ulcer** ulcère à l'estomac

gasworks (ghæss-^ou eûks) *n* usine à gaz

gate (ghéït) *n* porte *f*; grille *f*

gather (ghæ-ðeu) *v* collectionner; se réunir

gauge (ghéïdj) *n* jauge *f*

gave (ghéïv) *v* (p give)

gay (ghéï) *adj* gai; éclatant

gaze (ghéïz) *v* fixer

gear (ghi^eu) *n* vitesse *f*; équipement *m*; **change ~** changer de vitesse; **~ lever** levier de vitesse

gearbox (ghieu-boks) *n* boîte de vitesse

geese (ghiiz) *n* (pl goose)

gem (djèm) *n* joyau *m*, pierre précieuse; bijou *m*

gender (djèn-deu) *n* genre *m*

general (djè-neu-reul) *adj* général; *n* général *m*; **~ practitioner** médecin généraliste; **in ~** en général

generate (djè-neu-réït) *v* *produire

generation (djè-neu-*réï*-cheunn) *n* génération *f*

generator (djè-neu-réï-teur) *n* générateur *m*

generosity (djè-neu-*ro*-seu-ti) *n* générosité *f*

generous (djè-neu-reuss) *adj* large, généreux

genital (djè-ni-teul) *adj* génital

genius (djii-ni-euss) *n* génie *m*

gentle (djèn-teul) *adj* doux; léger; délicat

gentleman (djèn-teul-meunn) *n* (pl -men) monsieur *m*

genuine (djè-nyou-inn) *adj* authentique

geography (dji-*o*-ghreu-fi) *n* géographie *f*

geology (dji-*o*-leu-dji) *n* géologie *f*

geometry (dji-*o*-meu-tri) *n* géométrie *f*

germ (djeûmm) *n* microbe *m*; germe *m*

German (*djeû*-meunn) *adj* allemand; *n* Allemand *m*

Germany (*djeû*-meu-ni) Allemagne *f*

gesticulate (dji-*sti*-kyou-léït) *v* gesticuler

*****get** (ghèt) *v* *obtenir; *aller prendre; *devenir; ~ **back** retourner; ~ **off** descendre; ~ **on** monter; progresser; ~ **up** se lever

ghost (ghô^{ou}st) *n* fantôme *m*; esprit *m*

giant (*djaï*-eunnt) *n* géant *m*

giddiness (*ghi*-di-neuss) *n* vertige *m*

giddy (*ghi*-di) *adj* étourdi

gift (ghift) *n* don *m*, cadeau *m*; talent *m*

gifted (*ghif*-tid) *adj* doué

gigantic (djaï-*ghæn*-tik) *adj* gigantesque

giggle (*ghi*-gheul) *v* glousser

gill (ghil) *n* branchie *f*

gilt (ghilt) *adj* doré

ginger (*djinn*-djeu) *n* gingembre *m*

girdle (*gheû*-deul) *n* gaine *f*

girl (gheûl) *n* fille *f*; ~ **guide** scout *m*

girlfriend (*gheûl*-frènd) *n* amie *f*; petite amie *f*

*****give** (ghiv) *v* donner; passer; ~ **away** révéler; ~ **in** céder; ~ **up** renoncer

glacier (*ghlæ*-si-eu) *n* glacier *m*

glad (ghlæd) *adj* joyeux, content; **gladly** avec plaisir, volontiers

gladness (*ghlæd*-neuss) *n* joie *f*

glamorous (*ghlæ*-meu-reuss) *adj* enchanteur, charmant

glamour (*ghlæ*-meu) *n* charme *m*

glance (ghlââns) *n* coup d'œil; *v* jeter un coup d'œil

gland (ghlænd) *n* glande *f*

glare (ghlè^{eu}) *n* éclat *m*; éblouissement *m*

glaring (*ghlèeu*-rinng) *adj* éblouissant

glass (ghlââss) *n* verre *m*; de verre; **glasses** lunettes *fpl*; **magnifying** ~ verre grossissant

glaze (ghléïz) *v* vernir

glide (ghlaïd) *v* glisser

glider (*ghlaï*-deu) *n* planeur *m*

glimpse (ghlimmps) *n* aperçu *m*; coup d'œil; *v* *entrevoir

global (*ghlôou*-beul) *adj* mondial

globe (ghlô^{ou}b) *n* globe *m*

gloom (ghloûm) *n* ténèbres *fpl*

gloomy (*ghloû*-mi) *adj* sombre

glorious (*ghloo*-ri-euss) *adj* splendide

glory (*ghloo*-ri) *n* gloire *f*; honneur *m*, louange *f*

gloss (ghloss) *n* lustre *m*

glossy (*ghlo*-si) *adj* luisant

glove (ghlav) *n* gant *m*

glow (ghlô^{ou}) *v* briller; *n* éclat *m*

glue (ghloû) *n* colle *f*

*****go** (ghô^{ou}) *v* se rendre, *aller; marcher; *devenir; ~ **ahead** continuer; ~ **away** *partir; ~ **back** retourner; ~ **home** rentrer; ~ **in** entrer; ~ **on** continuer; ~ **out** *sortir; ~ **through** endurer

goal (ghô^{ou}l) *n* objectif *m*, but *m*

goalkeeper (*ghôoul*-kii-peu) *n* gardien de but

goat (ghô^{ou}t) *n* bouc *m*, chèvre *f*

god (ghod) *n* dieu *m*

godfather (*ghod*-fââ-ðeu) *n* parrain *m*

goggles (*gho*-gheulz) *pl* lunettes de plongée

gold (ghô^{ou}ld) *n* or *m*; ~ **leaf** or en feuille

golden (*ghôoul*-deunn) *adj* en or

goldmine (*ghôould*-maïn) *n* mine d'or

goldsmith (*ghôould*-smiθ) *n* orfèvre

m

golf (gholf) *n* golf *m*; ~ **course** terrain de golf; ~ **links** terrain de golf

golfclub (*golf*-klab) *n* club de golf

gondola (*ghonn*-deu-leu) *n* gondole *f*

gone (ghonn) *adv* (pp go) parti

good (ghoud) *adj* bon; sage, brave

goodbye! (ghoud-*baï*) au revoir!

good-humoured (ghoud-*hyoû*-meud) *adj* de bonne humeur

good-looking (ghoud-*lou*-kinng) *adj* joli

good-natured (ghoud-*néï*-tcheud) *adj* de bon caractère

goods (ghoudz) *pl* marchandise *f*, biens *mpl*; ~ **train** train de marchandises

good-tempered (ghoud-*tèm*-peud) *adj* de bonne humeur

goodwill (ghoud-*ouil*) *n* bienveillance *f*

goose (ghoûss) *n* (pl geese) oie *f*; ~ **bumps**, ~ **flesh**, ~ **pimples** chair de poule

gooseberry (*ghouz*-beu-ri) *n* groseille à maquereau

gorge (ghoodj) *n* gorge *f*

gorgeous (*ghoo*-djeuss) *adj* magnifique

gospel (*gho*-speul) *n* évangile *m*

gossip (*gho*-sip) *n* commérage *m*; *v* *faire des commérages

got (ghot) *v* (p, pp get)

gout (ghaout) *n* goutte *f*

govern (*gha*-veunn) *v* gouverner

governess (*gha*-veu-niss) *n* gouvernante *f*

government (*gha*-veunn-meunnt) *n* régime *m*, gouvernement *m*

governor (*gha*-veu-neu) *n* gouverneur *m*

gown (ghaoun) *n* robe *f*

grace (ghréïss) *n* grâce *f*; clémence *f*

graceful (*ghréïss*-feul) *adj* charmant, gracieux

grade (ghréïd) *n* grade *m*; *v* classer

gradient (*ghréï*-di-eunnt) *n* inclinaison *f*

gradual (*ghræ*-djou-eul) *adj* graduel

graduate (*ghræ*-djou-éït) *v* *obtenir un diplôme

grain (ghréïn) *n* grain *m*, blé *m*, céréale *f*

gram (ghræm) *n* gramme *m*

grammar (*ghræ*-meu) *n* grammaire *f*

grammatical (ghreu-*mæ*-ti-keul) *adj* grammatical

grand (ghrænd) *adj* sublime

grandchild (*ghræn*-tchaïld) *n* petit-fils *m*,-fille *f*

granddad (*ghræn*-dæd) *n* grand-papa *m*

granddaughter (*ghræn*-doo-teu) *n* petite-fille *f*

grandfather (*ghræn*-fââ-ðeu) *n* grandpère *m*

grandmother (*ghræn*-ma-ðeu) *n* grand-mère *f*

grandparents (*ghræn*-pè^{eu}-reunnts) *pl* grands-parents *mpl*

grandson (*ghræn*-sann) *n* petit-fils *m*

granite (*ghræ*-nit) *n* granit *m*

grant (ghrâânt) *v* accorder; concéder; *n* subvention *f*, bourse *f*

grapefruit (*ghréïp*-froût) *n* pamplemousse *m*

grapes (ghréïps) *pl* raisin *m*

graph (ghræf) *n* diagramme *m*

graphic (*ghræ*-fik) *adj* graphique

grasp (ghrââsp) *v* saisir; *n* prise *f*

grass (ghrââss) *n* herbe *f*

grasshopper (*ghrââss*-ho-peu) *n* sauterelle *f*

grate (ghréït) *n* grille *f*; *v* râper

grateful (*ghréït*-feul) *adj* reconnaissant

grater (*ghréï*-teu) *n* râpe *f*

gratis (*ghræ*-tiss) *adj* gratuit

gratitude (*ghræ*-ti-tyoûd) n gratitude f
gratuity (greu-*tyoû*-eu-ti) n pourboire m
grave (ghréïv) n tombe f; adj grave
gravel (*ghræ*-veul) n gravier m
gravestone (*ghréïv*-stô^ou^n) n pierre tombale
graveyard (*ghréïv*-yââd) n cimetière m
gravity (*ghræ*-veu-ti) n gravité f
gravy (*ghréï*-vi) n jus m
graze (ghréïz) v *paître; n égratignure f
grease (ghriiss) n graisse f; v graisser
greasy (*ghrii*-si) adj graisseux
great (ghréït) adj grand; **Great Britain** Grande-Bretagne f
Greece (ghriiss) Grèce f
greed (ghriid) n cupidité f
greedy (*ghrii*-di) adj cupide; gourmand
Greek (ghriik) adj grec; n Grec m
green (ghriin) adj vert; ~ **card** carte verte
greengrocer (*ghriin*-ghrô^ou^-seu) n marchand de légumes
greenhouse (*ghriin*-haouss) n serre f
greens (ghriinz) pl légumes mpl
greet (ghriit) v saluer
greeting (*ghrii*-tinng) n salutation f
grey (ghréï) adj gris
greyhound (*ghréï*-haound) n lévrier m
grief (ghriif) n chagrin m; affliction f, douleur f
grieve (ghriiv) v *avoir de la peine
grill (ghril) n grill m; v griller
grillroom (*ghril*-roûm) n rôtisserie f
grim (ghrimm) adj sinistre; sévère; farouche
grin (ghrinn) n large sourire
*****grind** (ghraïnd) v *moudre; pulvériser
grip (ghrip) v saisir; n prise f, étreinte

f; nAm mallette de voyage
grit (ghrit) n gravillon m
groan (ghrô^ou^n) v gémir
grocer (*ghrôou*-seu) n épicier m; **grocer's, grocery** épicerie f
groceries (*ghrôou*-seu-riz) pl articles d'épicerie
groin (ghroïn) n aine f
groom (ghroûm) n palefrenier m; marié m; v panser; soigner; former, façonner
groove (ghroûv) n sillon m
gross[1] (ghrô^ou^ss) n (pl ~) grosse f
gross[2] (ghrô^ou^ss) adj grossier; brut
grotto (*ghro*-tô^ou^) n (pl ~es, ~s) grotte f
ground[1] (ghraound) n fond m, sol m; ~ **floor** rez-de-chaussée m; **grounds** terrain m
ground[2] (ghraound) v (p, pp grind)
group (ghroûp) n groupe m
grouse (ghraouss) n (pl ~) grouse f
grove (ghrô^ou^v) n bosquet m
*****grow** (ghrô^ou^) v grandir; cultiver
growl (ghraoul) v grogner
grown-up (*ghrôoun*-ap) adj adulte; n adulte m/f
growth (ghrô^ou^θ) n croissance f; tumeur f
grudge (ghradj) v envier
grumble (*ghramm*-beul) v grogner
guarantee (ghæ-reunn-*tii*) n garantie f; caution f, v garantir
guard (ghââd) n garde m; v surveiller
guardian (*ghââ*-di-eunn) n tuteur m
guess (ghèss) v deviner; *croire, supposer; n conjecture f
guest (ghèst) n hôte m, invité m; ~ **room** chambre d'ami
guesthouse (*ghèst*-haouss) n pension f
guide (ghaïd) n guide m; v *conduire; ~ **dog** chien d'aveugle
guidebook (*ghaïd*-bouk) n guide m

guilt (ghilt) *n* culpabilité *f*

guilty (*ghil*-ti) *adj* coupable

guinea pig (*ghi*-ni-pigh) *n* cochon d'Inde

guitar (ghi-*tââ*) *n* guitare *f*

gulf (ghalf) *n* golfe *m*

gull (ghal) *n* mouette *f*

gum (ghamm) *n* gencive *f*; gomme *f*; colle *f*

gun (ghann) *n* fusil *m*; revolver *m*; canon *m*

gunpowder (*ghann*-paou-deu) *n* poudre à canon

gust (ghast) *n* rafale *f*

gusty (*gha*-sti) *adj* venteux

gut (ghat) *n* intestin *m*; **guts** cran *m*

gutter (*gha*-teu) *n* caniveau *m*

guy (ghaï) *n* type *m*

gym (djimm) *n colloquial* gymnase *f*; gym(nastique) *f*; de gymnastique; ~ **shoes** tennis *pl*, baskets *pl*

gymnasium (djimm-*néï*-zi-eumm) *n* (pl ~s, -sia) gymnase *m*

gymnast (*djimm*-næst) *n* gymnaste *m*

gymnastics (djimm-*næ*-stiks) *pl* gymnastique *f*

gyn(a)ecologist (ghaï-neu-*ko*-leu-djist) *n* gynécologue *m*/*f*

H

habit (*hæ*-bit) *n* habitude *f*

habitable (*hæ*-bi-teu-beul) *adj* habitable

habitual (heu-*bi*-tchou-eul) *adj* habituel

had (hæd) *v* (p, pp have)

haddock (*hæ*-deuk) *n* (pl ~) aiglefin *m*

h(a)emorrhage (*hè*-meu-ridj) *n* hémorragie *f*

h(a)emorrhoids (*hè*-meu-roïdz) *pl* hémorroïdes *fpl*

hail (héïl) *n* grêle *f*

hair (he^eu) *n* cheveu *m*; ~ **cream** crème capillaire; ~ **gel** gel pour les cheveux *m*; ~ **net** résille *f*; ~ **oil** huile capillaire; ~ **piece** postiche *m*; ~ **rollers** bigoudis *mpl*

hairbrush (*hè*eu-brach) *n* brosse à cheveux

haircut (*hè*eu-kat) *n* coupe de cheveux

hairdo (*hè*eu-doû) *n* coiffure *f*

hairdresser (*hè*eu-drè-seu) *n* coiffeur *m*, -se *f*

hairdrier, hairdryer (*hè*eu-draï-eu) *n* sèche-cheveux *m*

hairgrip (*hè*eu-ghrip) *n* pince à cheveux

hairpin (*hè*eu-pinn) *n* épingle à cheveux

hair spray (*hè*eu-spréï) *n* laque capillaire

hairy (*hè*eu-ri) *adj* chevelu

half[1] (hââf) *adj* demi; *adv* à moitié

half[2] (hââf) *n* (pl halves) moitié *f*

half time (hââf-*taïm*) *n* mi-temps *f*

halfway (hââf-*ouéï*) *adv* à mi-chemin

halibut (*hæ*-li-beut) *n* (pl ~) flétan *m*

hall (hool) *n* vestibule *m*; salle *f*

halt (hoolt) *v* s'arrêter

halve (hââv) *v* diviser en deux

ham (hæm) *n* jambon *m*

hamlet (*hæm*-leut) *n* hameau *m*

hammer (*hæ*-meu) *n* marteau *m*

hammock (*hæ*-meuk) *n* hamac *m*

hamper (*hæm*-peu) *n* panier d'osier

hand (hænd) *n* main *f*; ~ **cream** crème pour les mains; ~ **over** *remettre

handbag (*hænd*-bægh) *n* sac à main

handbook (*hænd*-bouk) *n* manuel *m*

handbrake (*hænd*-bréïk) *n* frein à main

handcuffs (*hænd*-kafs) *pl* menottes *fpl*

handful (*hænd*-foul) *n* poignée *f*

handicap (*hæn*-di-kæp) *n* handicap *m*; *v* handicaper

handicapped (*hæn*-di-kæpt) *adj* handicapé

handicraft (*hæn*-di-krâât) *n* travail manuel; artisanat *m*

handkerchief (*hæng*-keu-tchif) *n* mouchoir *m*

handle (*hæn*-deul) *n* manche *m*, poignée *f*; *v* manipuler; traiter

hand-made (hænd-*méïd*) *adj* fait à la main

handshake (*hænd*-chéïk) *n* poignée de main

handsome (*hæn*-seumm) *adj* beau

handwork (*hænd*-^{ou}eûk) *n* travail artisanal

handwriting (*hænd*-raï-tinng) *n* écriture *f*

handy (*hæn*-di) *adj* commode

***hang** (hæng) *v* suspendre; pendre

hanger (*hæng*-eu) *n* cintre *m*

hangover (*hæng*-ô^{ou}-veu) *n* gueule de bois

happen (*hæ*-peunn) *v* se *produire, arriver

happening (*hæ*-peu-ninng) *n* événement *m*

happiness (*hæ*-pi-neuss) *n* bonheur *m*

happy (*hæ*-pi) *adj* content, heureux

harbo(u)r (*hââ*-beu) *n* port *m*

hard (hââd) *adj* dur; difficile; **hardly** à peine

hardware (*hââd*-^{ou}è^{eu}) *n* quincaillerie *f*; **~ store** quincaillerie *f*

hare (hè^{eu}) *n* lièvre *m*

harm (hââm) *n* mal *m*; tort *m*; *v* *faire du mal

harmful (*hââm*-feul) *adj* préjudiciable, nuisible

harmless (*hââm*-leuss) *adj* inoffensif

harmony (*hââ*-meu-ni) *n* harmonie *f*

harp (hââp) *n* harpe *f*

harpsichord (*hââp*-si-kood) *n* clavecin *m*

harsh (hââch) *adj* âpre; sévère; cruel

harvest (*hââ*-vist) *n* moisson *f*

has (hæz) *v* (pr have)

haste (héïst) *n* hâte *f*

hasten (*héï*-seunn) *v* se hâter

hasty (*héï*-sti) *adj* précipité

hat (hæt) *n* chapeau *m*; **~ rack** porte-manteau *m*

hate (héït) *v* détester; *haïr; *n* haine *f*

hatred (*héï*-trid) *n* haine *f*

haughty (*hoo*-ti) *adj* hautain

haul (hool) *v* traîner

***have** (hæv) *v* *avoir; *faire; **~ to** *devoir

hawk (hook) *n* faucon *m*

hay (héï) *n* foin *m*; **~ fever** rhume des foins

hazard (*hæ*-zeud) *n* hasard *m*

haze (héïz) *n* brume *f*

hazelnut (*héï*-zeul-nat) *n* noisette *f*

hazy (*héï*-zi) *adj* brumeux; nébuleux

he (hii) *pron* il

head (hèd) *n* tête *f*; *v* diriger; **~ of state** chef d'Etat; **~ teacher** directeur d'école; **~ waiter** maître d'hôtel

headache (*hè*-déïk) *n* mal de tête

heading (*hè*-dinng) *n* titre *m*

headlamp (*hèd*-læmp) *n* phare *m*

headland (*hèd*-leunnd) *n* promontoire *m*

headlight (*hèd*-laït) *n* phare *m*

headline (*hèd*-laïn) *n* manchette *f*

headmaster (hèd-*mââ*-steu) *n* directeur d'école

headquarters (hèd-*kouoo*-teuz) *pl* quartier général

head-strong (*hèd*-stronng) *adj* têtu

heal (hiil) *v* guérir

health (hèlθ) *n* santé *f*; ~ **centre** dispensaire *m*; ~ **certificate** certificat médical

healthy (*hèl*-θi) *adj* sain

heap (hiip) *n* amoncellement *m*, tas *m*

*****hear** (hi^{eu}) *v* entendre

hearing (*hieu*-rinng) *n* ouïe *f*

heart (hâât) *n* cœur *m*; **by ~** par cœur; ~ **attack** crise cardiaque

heartburn (*hâât*-beûnn) *n* brûlures d'estomac

hearth (hââθ) *n* cheminée *f*

heartless (*hâât*-leuss) *adj* insensible

hearty (*hââ*-ti) *adj* cordial

heat (hiit) *n* chaleur *f*; *v* chauffer; **heating pad** coussin chauffant

heater (*hii*-teu) *n* appareil de chauffage; **immersion ~** thermoplongeur *m*

heath (hiiθ) *n* lande *f*

heathen (*hii*-ðeunn) *n* païen *m*

heather (*hè*-ðeu) *n* bruyère *f*

heating (*hii*-tinng) *n* chauffage *m*

heaven (*hè*-veunn) *n* ciel *m*

heavy (*hè*-vi) *adj* lourd

Hebrew (*hii*-broû) *n* hébreu *m*

hedge (hèdj) *n* haie *f*

hedgehog (*hèdj*-hogh) *n* hérisson *m*

heel (hiil) *n* talon *m*

height (haït) *n* hauteur *f*; sommet *m*, apogée *m*

heir (hè^{eu}) *n* héritier *m* (**to** de); ~ **apparent** héritier *m* présomptif

heir-at-law (*hèeu*-reut-loo) *n* héritier *m* légitime

heiress (*hèeu*-resse) *n* héritière *f*

helicopter (*hè*-li-kop-teu) *n* hélicoptère *m*

hell (hèl) *n* enfer *m*

hello! (hè-*lôou*) bonjour!

helm (hèlm) *n* barre *f*

helmet (*hèl*-mit) *n* casque *m*

help (hèlp) *v* aider; *n* aide *f*

helper (*hèl*-peu) *n* aide *m/f*

helpful (*hèlp*-feul) *adj* serviable

helping (*hèl*-pinng) *n* portion *f*

hem (hèm) *n* ourlet *m*

hemp (hèmp) *n* chanvre *m*

hen (hèn) *n* poule *f*

her (heû) *pron* la *art/pron*, lui; *adj* son

herb (heûb) *n* herbe *f*

herd (heûd) *n* troupeau *m*

here (hi^{eu}) *adv* ici; ~ **you are** voilà

hereditary (hi-*rè*-di-teu-ri) *adj* héréditaire

hernia (*heû*-ni-eu) *n* hernie *f*

hero (*hieu*-rô^{ou}) *n* (pl ~es) héros *m*

heron (*hè*-reunn) *n* héron *m*

herring (*hè*-rinng) *n* (pl ~, ~s) hareng *m*

herself (heû-*sèlf*) *pron* se; elle-même

hesitate (*hè*-zi-téît) *v* hésiter

heterosexual (hè-teu-reu-*sèk*-chou-eul) *adj* hétérosexuel

hiccup (*hi*-kap) *n* hoquet *m*

hide (haïd) *n* peau *f*

*****hide** (haïd) *v* cacher; dissimuler

hideous (*hi*-di-euss) *adj* hideux

hierarchy (*haïeu*-rââ-ki) *n* hiérarchie *f*

high (haï) *adj* haut

highway (*haï*-^{ou}éï) *n* route nationale; *nAm* autoroute *f*

hijack (*haï*-djæk) *v* détourner

hike (haïk) *v* faire des randonnées

hill (hil) *n* colline *f*

hillock (*hi*-leuk) *n* monticule *m*

hillside (*hil*-saïd) *n* coteau *m*

hilltop (*hil*-top) *n* sommet de colline

hilly (*hi*-li) *adj* accidenté

him (himm) *pron* le, lui

himself (himm-*sèlf*) *pron* se; lui-même

hinder (*hinn*-deu) *v* gêner

hinge (hinndj) *n* charnière *f*

hint (hinnt) *n* allusion *f*; signe *m*; *v* suggérer; faire allusion (**at** à)

hip (hip) *n* hanche *f*

hire (haï^eu) *v* louer; **for ~** à louer

hire purchase (haï^eu-*peû*-tcheuss) *n* achat à tempérament

his (hiz) *adj* son

historian (hi-*stoo*-ri-eunn) *n* historien *m*, -ne *f*

historic (hi-*sto*-rik) *adj* historique

historical (hi-*sto*-ri-keul) *adj* historique

history (*hi*-steu-ri) *n* histoire *f*

hit (hit) *n* succès *m*

***hit** (hit) *v* frapper; toucher

hitchhike (*hitch*-haïk) *v* *faire de l'auto-stop

hitchhiker (*hitch*-haï-keu) *n* auto-stoppeur *m*, -se *f*

hoarse (hooss) *adj* rauque, enroué

hobby (*ho*-bi) *n* hobby *m*, passetemps *m*

hockey (*ho*-ki) *n* hockey *m*

hoist (hoïst) *v* hisser

hold (hô^ould) *n* cale *f*

***hold** (hô^ould) *v* *tenir; garder; **~ on** s'accrocher; **~ up** *soutenir

hold-up (*hôoul*-dap) *n* attaque *f*

hole (hô^ul) *n* trou *m*

holiday (*ho*-leu-di) *n* vacances; jour de fête; **~ camp** camp de vacances; **on ~** en vacances

Holland (*ho*-leunnd) Hollande *f*

hollow (*ho*-lô^ou) *adj* creux

holy (*hô*ou-li) *adj* sacré

homage (*ho*-midj) *n* hommage *m*

home (hô^um) *n* maison *f*; foyer *m*, demeure *f*; *adv* chez soi; **at ~** à la maison

home-made (hô^um-*méïd*) *adj* fait à la maison

homesickness (*hôoum*-sik-neuss) *n* mal du pays

homosexual (hô^ou-meu-*sèk*-chou-

eul) *adj* homosexuel

honest (*o*-nist) *adj* honnête; sincère

honesty (*o*-ni-sti) *n* honnêteté *f*

honey (*ha*-ni) *n* miel *m*

honeymoon (*ha*-ni-moûn) *n* lune de miel

honk (hanngk) *vAm* klaxonner

hono(u)r (*o*-neu) *n* honneur *m*; *v* honorer, rendre hommage

hono(u)rable (*o*-neu-reu-beul) *adj* honorable; honnête

hood (houd) *n* capuchon *m*; *nAm* capot *m*

hoof (hoûf) *n* sabot *m*

hook (houk) *n* crochet *m*

hoot (hoût) *v* klaxonner

hooter (*hoû*-teu) *n* klaxon *m*

hoover (*hoû*-veu) *v* passer l'aspirateur

hop¹ (hop) *v* sautiller; *n* saut *m*

hop² (hop) *n* houblon *m*

hope (hô^up) *n* espoir *m*; *v* espérer

hopeful (*hôoup*-feul) *adj* plein d'espoir

hopeless (*hôoup*-leuss) *adj* désespéré

horizon (heu-*raï*-zeunn) *n* horizon *m*

horizontal (ho-ri-*zonn*-teul) *adj* horizontal

horn (hoon) *n* corne *f*; cor *m*; klaxon *m*

horrible (*ho*-ri-beul) *adj* horrible; terrifiant, atroce, horrifiant

horror (*ho*-reu) *n* épouvante *f*, horreur *f*

horse (hooss) *n* cheval *m*

horseman (*hooss*-meunn) *n* (pl -men) cavalier *m*

horsepower (*hooss*-paou^eu) *n* chevalvapeur *m*

horserace (*hooss*-réïss) *n* course de chevaux

horseradish (*hooss*-ræ-dich) *n* raifort *m*

horseshoe (*hooss*-choû) *n* fer à cheval

horticulture (*hoo*-ti-kal-tcheu) *n*

horticulture *f*

hospitable (*ho*-spi-teu-beul) *adj* hospitalier

hospital (*ho*-spi-teul) *n* hôpital *m*

hospitality (ho-spi-*tæ*-leu-ti) *n* hospitalité *f*

host (hô^{ou}st) *n* hôte *m*

hostage (*ho*-stidj) *n* otage *m*

hostel (*ho*-steul) *n* auberge *f*

hostess (*hôou*-stiss) *n* hôtesse *f*

hostile (*ho*-staïl) *adj* hostile

hot (hot) *adj* chaud

hotel (hô^{ou}-*tèl*) *n* hôtel *m*

hot-tempered (hot-*tèm*-peud) *adj* coléreux

hour (aou^{eu}) *n* heure *f*

hourly (*aoueu*-li) *adj* toutes les heures

house (haouss) *n* maison *f*; habitation *f*; immeuble *m*; ~ **agent** agent immobilier; ~ **block** *Am* pâté de maisons; **public** ~ café *m*

houseboat (*haouss*-bô^{ou}t) *n* maisonbateau

household (*haouss*-hô^{ou}ld) *n* ménage *m*

housekeeper (*haouss*-kii-peu) *n* gouvernante *f*

housekeeping (*haouss*-kii-pinng) *n* travaux ménagers, ménage *m*

housemaid (*haouss*-méïd) *n* bonne *f*

housewife (*haouss*-^{ou}aïf) *n* ménagère *f*

housework (*haouss*-^{ou}eûk) *n* travaux ménagers

how (haou) *adv* comment; que; ~ **many** combien; ~ **much** combien

however (haou-è-veu) *conj* pourtant, cependant

hug (hagh) *v* *étreindre; *n* étreinte *f*

huge (hyoûdj) *adj* immense, énorme

hum (hamm) *v* fredonner

human (*hyoû*-meunn) *adj* humain; ~ **being** être humain

humanity (hyou-*mæ*-neu-ti) *n* humanité *f*

humble (*hamm*-beul) *adj* humble

humid (*hyoû*-mid) *adj* humide

humidity (hyou-*mi*-deu-ti) *n* humidité *f*

humorous (*hyoû*-meu-reuss) *adj* comique, drôle

humour (*hyoû*-meu) *n* humour *m*

hundred (*hann*-dreud) *n* cent

Hungarian (hanng-*ghèeu*-ri-eunn) *adj* hongrois; *n* Hongrois *m*

Hungary (*hanng*-gheu-ri) Hongrie *f*

hunger (*hanng*-gheu) *n* faim *f*

hungry (*hanng*-ghri) *adj* affamé

hunt (hannt) *v* chasser; *n* chasse *f*; ~ **for** chercher

hunter (*hann*-teu) *n* chasseur *m*

hurricane (*ha*-ri-keunn) *n* ouragan *m*; ~ **lamp** lampe-tempête *f*

hurry (*ha*-ri) *v* se dépêcher, se presser; *n* hâte *f*; **in a** ~ en vitesse

*hurt (heût) *v* *faire mal, blesser; offenser

hurtful (*heût*-feul) *adj* nuisible

husband (*haz*-beunnd) *n* époux *m*, mari *m*

hut (hat) *n* hutte *f*

hydrogen (*haï*-dreu-djeunn) *n* hydrogène *m*

hygiene (*haï*-djiin) *n* hygiène *f*

hygienic (haï-*djii*-nik) *adj* hygiénique

hymn (himm) *n* hymne *m*

hyphen (*haï*-feunn) *n* trait d'union

hypocrisy (hi-*po*-kreu-si) *n* hypocrisie *f*

hypocrite (*hi*-peu-krit) *n* hypocrite *m*

hypocritical (hi-peu-*kri*-ti-keul) *adj* hypocrite, fourbe

hysterical (hi-*stè*-ri-keul) *adj* hystérique

I

I (aï) *pron* je

ice (aïss) *n* glace *f*; **~ bag** sac à glace; **~ cream** crème glacée, glace *f*

Iceland (aïss-leunnd) Islande *f*

Icelander (aïss-leunn-deu) *n* Islandais *m*

Icelandic (aïss-læn-dik) *adj* islandais

icon (aï-konn) *n* icône *f*

idea (aï-*dieu*) *n* idée *f*; pensée *f*; notion *f*, concept *m*

ideal (aï-*dieul*) *adj* idéal; *n* idéal *m*

identical (aï-*dèn*-ti-keul) *adj* identique

identification (aï-dèn-ti-fi-*kéï*-cheunn) *n* identification *f*

identify (aï-*dèn*-ti-faï) *v* identifier

identity (aï-*dèn*-teu-ti) *n* identité *f*; **~ card** carte d'identité

idiot (*i*-di-eut) *n* idiot *m*

idiotic (i-di-*o*-tik) *adj* idiot

idle (*aï*-deul) *adj* oisif; futile

idol (*aï*-deul) *n* idole *f*

if (if) *conj* si

ignition (igh-*ni*-cheunn) *n* allumage *m*; **~ coil** bobine d'allumage

ignorant (*igh*-neu-reunnt) *adj* ignorant

ignore (igh-*noo*) *v* ignorer

ill (il) *adj* malade; mauvais; méchant

illegal (i-*lii*-gheul) *adj* illégal

illegible (i-*lè*-djeu-beul) *adj* illisible

illiterate (i-*li*-teu-reut) *n* illettré *m*

illness (*il*-neuss) *n* maladie *f*

illuminate (i-*loû*-mi-néït) *v* illuminer

illumination (i-loû-mi-*néï*-cheunn) *n* illumination *f*

illusion (i-*loû*-jeunn) *n* illusion *f*

illustrate (*i*-leu-stréït) *v* illustrer

illustration (i-leu-*stréï*-cheunn) *n* illustration *f*

image (*i*-midj) *n* image *f*

imaginary (i-*mæ*-dji-neu-ri) *adj* imaginaire

imagination (i-mæ-dji-*néï*-cheunn) *n* imagination *f*

imagine (i-*mæ*-djinn) *v* imaginer; s'imaginer; se figurer

imitate (*i*-mi-téït) *v* imiter

imitation (i-mi-*téï*-cheunn) *n* imitation *f*

immediate (i-*mii*-dyeut) *adj* immédiat

immediately (i-*mii*-dyeut-li) *adv* surle-champ, tout de suite, immédiatement

immense (i-*mèns*) *adj* immense, énorme

immigrant (*i*-mi-ghreunnt) *n* immigrant *m*

immigrate (*i*-mi-ghréït) *v* immigrer

immigration (i-mi-*ghréï*-cheunn) *n* immigration *f*

immodest (i-*mo*-dist) *adj* immodeste

immunity (i-*myoû*-neu-ti) *n* immunité *f*

immunize (*i*-myou-naïz) *v* immuniser

impartial (imm-*pââ*-cheul) *adj* impartial

impassable (imm-*pââ*-seu-beul) *adj* impraticable

impatient (imm-*péï*-cheunnt) *adj* impatient

impede (imm-*piid*) *v* entraver

impediment (imm-*pè*-di-meunnt) *n* entrave *f*

imperfect (imm-*peû*-fikt) *adj* imparfait

imperial (imm-*pi*eu-ri-eul) *adj* impérial

impersonal (imm-*peû*-seu-neul) *adj* impersonnel

impertinence (imm-*peû*-ti-neunns) *n* impertinence *f*

impertinent (imm-*peû*-ti-neunnt) *adj* insolent, effronté, impertinent

implement[1] (*imm*-pli-meunnt) *n*

instrument *m*, outil *m*
implement² (*imm*-pli-mènt) *v* réaliser
imply (imm-*plaï*) *v* impliquer;
comporter
impolite (imm-peu-*laït*) *adj* impoli
import¹ (imm-*poot*) *v* importer
import² (*imm*-poot) *n* importation *f*; ~
duty taxe d'importation
importance (imm-*poo*-teunns) *n*
importance *f*
important (imm-*poo*-teunnt) *adj*
important
importer (imm-*poo*-teu) *n*
importateur *m*
imposing (imm-*pôou*-zinng) *adj*
imposant
impossible (imm-*po*-seu-beul) *adj*
impossible
impotence (*imm*-peu-teunns) *n*
impotence *f*
impotent (*imm*-peu-teunnt) *adj*
impotent
impress (imm-*près*) *v* *faire
impression sur, impressionner
impression (imm-*prè*-cheunn) *n*
impression *f*
impressive (imm-*prè*-siv) *adj*
impressionnant
imprison (imm-*pri*-zeunn) *v*
emprisonner
imprisonment (imm-*pri*-zeunn-
meunnt) *n* emprisonnement *m*
improbable (imm-*pro*-beu-beul) *adj*
improbable
improper (imm-*pro*-peu) *adj*
impropre
improve (imm-*proûv*) *v* améliorer
improvement (imm-*proûv*-meunnt) *n*
amélioration *f*
improvise (*imm*-preu-vaïz) *v*
improviser
impudent (imm-pyou-deunnt) *adj*
insolent
impulse (*imm*-pals) *n* impulsion *f*;

stimulant *m*
impulsive (imm-*pal*-siv) *adj* impulsif
in (inn) *prep* en; dans, sur; *adv* dedans
inaccessible (i-næk-*sè*-seu-beul) *adj*
inaccessible
inaccurate (i-*næ*-kyou-reut) *adj*
incorrect
inadequate (i-*næ*-di-kᵒᵘeut) *adj*
inadéquat
incapable (inng-*kéï*-peu-beul) *adj*
incapable
incense (*inn*-sèns) *n* encens *m*
inch (inntch) *n* pouce *m*; pas *m*; **by
inches** peu à peu, petit à petit;
within an ~ of àdeux doigts de; **inch
one's way** avancer petit à petit
incident (*inn*-si-deunnt) *n* incident *m*
incidental (inn-si-*dèn*-teul) *adj* fortuit
incite (inn-*saït*) *v* inciter
inclination (inng-kli-*néï*-cheunn) *n*
penchant *m*
incline (inng-*klaïn*) *n* pente *f*
inclined (inng-*klaïnd*) *adj* disposé,
enclin; *be ~ to *v* *avoir tendance
include (inng-*kloûd*) *v* *comprendre,
*inclure
inclusive (inng-*kloû*-siv) *adj* compris
income (*inng*-keumm) *n* revenu *m*; ~
tax impôt sur le revenu
incompetent (inng-*komm*-peu-
teunnt) *adj* incompétent
incomplete (inn-keumm-*pliit*) *adj*
incomplet
inconceivable (inng-keunn-*sii*-veu-
beul) *adj* inconcevable
inconspicuous (inng-keunn-*spi*-
kyou-euss) *adj* qui passe inaperçu;
discret
inconvenience (inng-keunn-*vii*-
nyeunns) *n* désagrément *m*,
inconvénient *m*
inconvenient (inng-keunn-*vii*-
nyeunnt) *adj* inopportun; gênant
incorrect (inng-keu-*rèkt*) *adj* incorrect

increase¹ (inng-*kriiss*) v augmenter;
s'accumuler, *croître

increase² (*inng*-kriiss) n
augmentation f; relèvement m

incredible (inng-*krè*-deu-beul) adj
incroyable

incurable (inng-*kyoueu*-reu-beul) adj
incurable

indecent (inn-*dii*-seunnt) adj indécent

indeed (inn-*diid*) adv en effet

indefinite (inn-*dè*-fi-nit) adj indéfini

indemnity (inn-*dèm*-neu-ti) n
dédommagement m, indemnité f

independence (inn-di-*pèn*-deunns) n
indépendance f

independent (inn-di-*pèn*-deunnt) adj
indépendant; autonome

index (*inn*-dèks) n index m; ~ **finger**
index m

India (*inn*-di-eu) Inde f

Indian (*inn*-di-eunn) adj indien; n
Indien m

indicate (*inn*-di-kéït) v signaler,
indiquer

indication (inn-di-*kéï*-cheunn) n signe
m, indication f

indicator (*inn*-di-kéï-teu) n clignotant
m

indifferent (inn-*di*-feu-reunnt) adj
indifférent

indigestion (inn-di-*djèss*-tcheunn) n
indigestion f

indignation (inn-digh-*néï*-cheunn) n
indignation f

indirect (inn-di-*rèkt*) adj indirect

individual (inn-di-*vi*-djou-eul) adj
particulier, individuel; n individu m

Indonesia (inn-deu-*nii*-zi-eu)
Indonésie f

Indonesian (inn-deu-*nii*-zi-eunn) adj
indonésien; n Indonésien m

indoor (*inn*-doo) adj intérieur

indoors (inn-*dooz*) adv à l'intérieur

indulge (inn-*daldj*) v céder

industrial (inn-*da*-stri-eul) adj
industriel; ~ **area** zone industrielle

industrious (inn-*da*-stri-euss) adj
industrieux

industry (*inn*-deu-stri) n industrie f

inedible (i-*nè*-di-beul) adj
immangeable

inefficient (i-ni-*fi*-cheunnt) adj
inefficace

inevitable (i-*nè*-vi-teu-beul) adj
inévitable

inexpensive (i-nik-*spèn*-siv) adj bon
marché

inexperienced (i-nik-*spieu*-ri-eunnst)
adj inexpérimenté

infant (*inn*-feunnt) n nourrisson m

infantry (*inn*-feunn-tri) n infanterie f

infect (inn-*fèkt*) v infecter

infection (inn-*fèk*-cheunn) n infection
f

infectious (inn-*fèk*-cheuss) adj
infectieux

infer (inn-*feû*) v *déduire

inferior (inn-*fieu*-ri-eu) adj moindre,
inférieur

infinite (*inn*-fi-neut) adj infini

infinitive (inn-*fi*-ni-tiv) n infinitif m

inflammable (inn-*flæ*-meu-beul) adj
inflammable

inflammation (inn-fleu-*méï*-cheunn)
n inflammation f

inflatable (inn-*fléï*-teu-beul) adj
gonflable

inflate (inn-*fléït*) v gonfler

inflation (inn-*fléï*-cheunn) n inflation f

inflict (inn-*flikt*) v infliger (**on** à)

influence (*inn*-flou-eunns) n
influence f; v influencer

influential (inn-flou-*èn*-cheul) adj
influent

influenza (inn-flou-*èn*-zeu) n grippe f

inform (inn-*foom*) v informer; *mettre
au courant, communiquer

informal (inn-*foo*-meul) adj sans

cérémonie

information (inn-feu-*méï*-cheunn) *n* information *f*; renseignement *m*, communication *f*; ~ **office** bureau des renseignements

infra-red (inn-freu-*rèd*) *adj* infrarouge

infrequent (inn-*frii*-k^(ou)eunnt) *adj* peu fréquent

ingredient (inng-*ghrii*-di-eunnt) *n* ingrédient *m*

inhabit (inn-*hæ*-bit) *v* habiter

inhabitable (inn-*hæ*-bi-teu-beul) *adj* habitable

inhabitant (inn-*hæ*-bi-teunnt) *n* habitant *m*

inhale (inn-*héïl*) *v* inhaler

inherit (inn-*hè*-rit) *v* hériter

inheritance (inn-*hè*-ri-teunns) *n* héritage *m*

inhibit (inn-*hi*-bit) *v* empêcher; inhiber

initial (i-*ni*-cheul) *adj* initial; *n* initiale *f*; *v* parapher

initiate (i-*ni*-chi-éït) *v* lancer, entreprendre; inaugurer; ~ **into** initier à

initiative (i-*ni*-cheu-tiv) *n* initiative *f*

inject (inn-*djèkt*) *v* injecter

injection (inn-*djèk*-cheunn) *n* injection *f*

injure (*inn*-djeu) *v* blesser; offenser

injury (*inn*-djeu-ri) *n* blessure *f*; lésion *f*

injustice (inn-*dja*-stiss) *n* injustice *f*

ink (inngk) *n* encre *f*

inlet (*inn*-lèt) *n* crique *f*

inn (inn) *n* auberge *f*

inner (*i*-neu) *adj* intérieur; ~ **tube** chambre à air

innocence (*i*-neu-seunns) *n* innocence *f*

innocent (*i*-neu-seunnt) *adj* innocent

inoculate (i-*no*-kyou-léït) *v* inoculer

inquire (inng-*kouaïeu*) *v* se

renseigner, s'informer

inquiry (inng-*kouaïeu*-ri) *n* question *f*, enquête *f*; ~ **office** bureau de renseignements

inquisitive (inng-*koui*-zeu-tiv) *adj* curieux

insane (inn-*séïn*) *adj* fou

inscription (inn-*skrip*-cheunn) *n* inscription *f*

insect (*inn*-sèkt) *n* insecte *m*; ~ **repellent** insectifuge *m*

insecticide (inn-*sèk*-ti-saïd) *n* insecticide *m*

insensitive (inn-*sèn*-seu-tiv) *adj* insensible

insert (inn-*seût*) *v* insérer

inside (inn-*saïd*) *n* intérieur *m*; *adj* intérieur; *adv* à l'intérieur; dedans; *prep* dans, à l'intérieur de; ~ **out** à l'envers; **insides** ventre *m*

insight (*inn*-saït) *n* compréhension *f*

insignificant (inn-sigh-*ni*-fi-keunnt) *adj* insignifiant; sans importance; futile

insist (inn-*sist*) *v* insister; persister

insolence (*inn*-seu-leunns) *n* insolence *f*

insolent (*inn*-seu-leunnt) *adj* insolent

insomnia (inn-*somm*-ni-eu) *n* insomnie *f*

inspect (inn-*spèkt*) *v* inspecter

inspection (inn-*spèk*-cheunn) *n* inspection *f*; contrôle *m*

inspector (inn-*spèk*-teu) *n* inspecteur *m*, -trice *f*

inspire (inn-*spaïeu*) *v* inspirer

insta(l)l (inn-*stool*) *v* installer

installation (inn-steu-*léï*-cheunn) *n* installation *f*

instal(l)ment (inn-*stool*-meunnt) *n* versement partiel; **payment by instalments** paiement échelonné

instance (*inn*-steunns) *n* exemple *m*; cas *m*; **for** ~ par exemple

instant (*inn*-steunnt) *n* instant *m*

instantly (*inn*-steunnt-li) *adv* instantanément, tout de suite, immédiatement

instead of (inn-*stèd* ov) au lieu de

instinct (*inn*-stinngkt) *n* instinct *m*

institute (*inn*-sti-tyoût) *n* institut *m*; institution *f*; *v* instituer

institution (inn-sti-*tyoû*-cheunn) *n* institution *f*

instruct (inn-*strakt*) *v* *instruire

instruction (inn-*strak*-cheunn) *n* instruction *f*

instructive (inn-*strak*-tiv) *adj* instructif

instructor (inn-*strak*-teu) *n* instructeur *m*

instrument (*inn*-strou-meunnt) *n* instrument *m*; **musical ~** instrument de musique

insufficient (*inn*-seu-*fi*-cheunnt) *adj* insuffisant

insulate (*inn*-syou-léït) *v* isoler

insulation (inn-syou-*léï*-cheunn) *n* isolation *f*

insulator (*inn*-syou-léï-teu) *n* isolateur *m*

insult[1] (inn-*salt*) *v* insulter

insult[2] (*inn*-salt) *n* insulte *f*

insurance (inn-*choueu*-reunns) *n* assurance *f*; **~ policy** police d'assurance

insure (inn-*choueu*) *v* assurer

intact (inn-*tækt*) *adj* intact

integrate (*inn*-ti-ghréït) *v* (s')intégrer

intellect (*inn*-teu-lèkt) *n* intellect *m*, intelligence *f*

intellectual (inn-teu-*lèk*-tchou-eul) *adj* intellectuel

intelligence (inn-*tè*-li-djeunns) *n* intelligence *f*

intelligent (inn-*tè*-li-djeunnt) *adj* intelligent

intend (inn-*tènd*) *v* *avoir l'intention de

intense (inn-*tèns*) *adj* intense; vif

intensify (inn-*tèn*-si-faï) *v* (s')intensifier

intention (inn-*tèn*-cheunn) *n* intention *f*

intentional (inn-*tèn*-cheu-neul) *adj* intentionnel

intercourse (*inn*-teu-kooss) *n* rapports *mpl*

interest (*inn*-treust) *n* intérêt *m*; *v* intéresser

interesting (*inn*-treu-stinng) *adj* intéressant

interfere (inn-teu-*fieu*) *v* *intervenir; **~ with** se mêler de

interference (inn-teu-*fieu*-reunns) *n* ingérence *f*

interim (*inn*-teu-rimm) *n* intérim *m*

interior (inn-*tieu*-ri-eu) *n* intérieur *m*

interlude (*inn*-teu-loûd) *n* interlude *m*

intermediary (inn-teu-*mii*-dyeu-ri) *n* intermédiaire *m/f*

intermission (inn-teu-*mi*-cheunn) *n* entracte *m*

internal (inn-*teû*-neul) *adj* intérieur, interne

international (inn-teu-*næ*-cheu-neul) *adj* international

interpret (inn-*teû*-prit) *v* interpréter

interpreter (inn-*teû*-pri-teu) *n* interprète *m/f*

interrogate (inn-*tè*-reu-ghéït) *v* interroger

interrogation (inn-tè-reu-*ghéï*-cheunn) *n* interrogatoire *m*

interrogative (inn-teu-*ro*-gheu-tiv) *adj* interrogatif

interrupt (inn-teu-*rapt*) *v* *interrompre

interruption (inn-teu-*rap*-cheunn) *n* interruption *f*

intersection (inn-teu-*sèk*-cheunn) *n* intersection *f*

interval (*inn*-teu-veul) *n* entracte *m*; intervalle *m*

intervene (inn-teu-*viin*) *v* *intervenir

interview (*inn*-teu-vyoû) *n* entrevue *f*, interview *f*

intestine (inn-*tè*-stinn) *n* intestin *m*

intimate (*inn*-ti-meut) *adj* intime

into (*inn*-tou) *prep* dans

intolerable (inn-*to*-leu-reu-beul) *adj* intolérable

intoxicated (inn-tok-si-kéï-tid) *adj* ivre

intrigue (inn-*triigh*) *n* intrigue *f*

introduce (inn-treu-*dyoûss*) *v* présenter; *introduire

introduction (inn-treu-*dak*-cheunn) *n* présentation *f*; introduction *f*

invade (inn-*véïd*) *v* envahir

invalid¹ (*inn*-veu-liid) *n* infirme *m*; *adj* infirme

invalid² (inn-*væ*-lid) *adj* nul

invasion (inn-*véï*-jeunn) *n* invasion *f*

invent (inn-*vènt*) *v* inventer

invention (inn-*vèn*-cheunn) *n* invention *f*

inventive (inn-*vèn*-tiv) *adj* inventif

inventor (inn-*vèn*-teu) *n* inventeur *m*

inventory (*inn*-veunn-tri) *n* inventaire *m*

invert (inn-*veût*) *v* intervertir

invest (inn-*vèst*) *v* investir; placer

investigate (inn-vè-sti-*ghéït*) *v* enquêter

investigation (inn-vè-sti-*ghéï*-cheunn) *n* investigation *f*

investment (inn-*vèst*-meunnt) *n* investissement *m*; placement *m*

investor (inn-*vè*-steu) *n* investisseur *m*

invisible (inn-*vi*-zeu-beul) *adj* invisible

invitation (inn-vi-*téï*-cheunn) *n* invitation *f*

invite (inn-*vaït*) *v* inviter

invoice (*inn*-voïss) *n* facture *f*

involve (inn-*volv*) *v* impliquer

inwards (*inn*-ᵒᵘeudz) *adv* vers l'intérieur

iodine (*aï*-eu-diin) *n* iode *m*

Iran (i-*râân*) Iran *m*

Iranian (i-*réï*-ni-eunn) *adj* iranien; *n* Iranien *m*

Iraq (i-*rââ*) Irak *m*

Iraqi (i-*rââ*-ki) *adj* irakien; *n* Irakien *m*

Ireland (*aïeu*-leunnd) Irlande *f*

Irish (*aïeu*-rich) *adj* irlandais

iron (*aï*-eunn) *n* fer *m*; fer à repasser; en fer; *v* repasser

ironical (aï-*ro*-ni-keul) *adj* ironique

irony (*aïeu*-reu-ni) *n* ironie *f*

irregular (i-*rè*-ghyou-leu) *adj* irrégulier

irreparable (i-*rè*-peu-reu-beul) *adj* irréparable

irrevocable (i-*rè*-veu-keu-beul) *adj* irrévocable

irritable (*i*-ri-teu-beul) *adj* irritable

irritate (*i*-ri-téït) *v* agacer, irriter

is (iz) *v* (pr be)

island (*aï*-leunnd) *n* île *f*

isolate (*aï*-seu-léït) *v* isoler

isolation (aï-seu-*léï*-cheunn) *n* isolement *m*; isolation *f*

Israel (*iz*-réïl) Israël *m*

Israeli (iz-*réï*-li) *adj* israélien; *n* Israélien *m*

issue (*i*-choû) *v* distribuer; *n* émission *f*, tirage *m*, édition *f*; question *f*, sujet *m*; issue *f*, résultat *m*, conclusion *f*, fin *f*

it (it) *pron* le

Italian (i-*tæl*-yeunn) *adj* italien; *n* Italien *m*

Italy (*i*-teu-li) Italie *f*

itch (itch) *n* démangeaison *f*; *v* démanger

item (*aï*-teumm) *n* article *m*; point *m*

its (its) *adj* son, sa; ses

itself (it-*sèlf*) lui-même, elle-même;

se, soi; **by ~** à part; tout seul; **in ~** en lui-même ; en soi, de soi; **of ~** tout seul; de lui-même, d'elle-même
itinerary (aï-*ti*-neu-reu-ri) *n* itinéraire *m*

ivory (aï-veu-ri) *n* ivoire *m*
ivy (*aï*-vi) *n* lierre *m*

J

jack (djæk) *n* cric *m*
jacket (*djæ*-kit) *n* veste *f*, veston *m*; jaquette *f*
jade (djéïd) *n* jade *m*
jail (djéïl) *n* prison *f*
jam (djæm) *n* confiture *f*; embouteillage *m*
janitor (*djæ*-ni-teu) *n* concierge *m*
January (*djæ*-nyou-eu-ri) janvier
Japan (djeu-*pæn*) Japon *m*
Japanese (djæ-peu-*niiz*) *adj* japonais; *n* Japonais *m*
jar (djââ) *n* jarre *f*
jaundice (*djoon*-diss) *n* jaunisse *f*
jaw (djoo) *n* mâchoire *f*
jealous (*djè*-leuss) *adj* jaloux
jealousy (*djè*-leu-si) *n* jalousie *f*
jeans (djiinz) *pl* blue-jean *m*
jelly (*djè*-li) *n* gelée *f*
jellyfish (*djè*-li-fich) *n* méduse *f*
jersey (*djeû*-zi) *n* jersey *m*; chandail *m*
jet (djèt) *n* jet *m*; avion à réaction
jetty (*djè*-ti) *n* jetée *f*
Jew (djoû) *n* juif *m*, juive *f*
jewel (*djoû*-eul) *n* bijou *m*
jewel(l)er (*djoû*-eu-leu) *n* bijoutier *m*
jewellery, Am jewelry (*djoû*-eul-ri) *n* bijoux; joaillerie *f*
Jewish (*djoû*-ich) *adj* juif
job (djob) *n* boulot *m*; emploi *m*, travail *m*
jobless (*djob*-lèss) *adj* sans travail
jockey (*djo*-ki) *n* jockey *m*
join (djoïn) *v* *joindre; s'affilier à;

adhérer à; assembler, réunir
joint (djoïnt) *n* articulation *f adj* uni, conjoint
jointly (*djoïnt*-li) *adv* conjointement
joke (djô^{ou}k) *n* blague *f*, plaisanterie *f*
jolly (*djo*-li) *adj* gai
Jordan (*djoo*-deunn) Jordanie *f*
Jordanian (djoo-*déï*-ni-eunn) *adj* jordanien; *n* Jordanien *m*
journal (*djeû*-neul) *n* périodique *m*
journalism (*djeû*-neu-li-zeumm) *n* journalisme *m*
journalist (*djeû*-neu-list) *n* journaliste *m/f*
journey (*djeû*-ni) *n* voyage *m*
joy (djoï) *n* plaisir *m*, joie *f*
joyful (*djoï*-feul) *adj* joyeux
jubilee (*djoû*-bi-lii) *n* anniversaire *m*
judge (djadj) *n* juge *m*; *v* juger; apprécier
judgment (*djadj*-meunnt) *n* jugement *m*
jug (djagh) *n* cruche *f*
Jugoslav (yoû-gheu-*slââv*) *adj* yougoslave; *n* Yougoslave *m*
Jugoslavia (yoû-gheu-*slââ*-vi-eu) Yougoslavie *f*
juice (djoûss) *n* jus *m*
juicy (*djoû*-si) *adj* juteux
July (djou-*laï*) juillet
jump (djammp) *v* sauter; *n* bond *m*, saut *m*
jumper (*djamm*-peu) *n* chandail *m*, pull *m*; *Am* robe à bretelles

junction (*djann**gk**-cheunn*) *n* carrefour *m*; jonction *f*

June (*djoûn*) juin

jungle (*djann**g**-gheul*) *n* jungle *f*

junior (*djoû-nyeu*) *adj* cadet

junk (*djanngk*) *n* rebut *m*

jury (*djoueu-ri*) *n* jury *m*

just (*djast*) *adj* légitime, juste; exact; *adv* à peine; juste

justice (*dja-stiss*) *n* droit *m*; justice *f*

justify (*dja-sti-faï*) *v* justifier

juvenile (*djoû-veu-naïl*) *adj* juvénile

K

kangaroo (*kæng-gheu-roû*) *n* kangourou *m*

keel (*kiil*) *n* quille *f*

keen (*kiin*) *adj* passionné; aigu

*keep (*kiip*) *v* *tenir; garder; continuer; **~ away from** se *tenir éloigné de; **~ off** ne pas toucher; **~ on** continuer; **~ quiet** se *taire; **~ up** persévérer; **~ up with** *être à la hauteur de

kennel (*kè-neul*) *n* chenil *m*

Kenya (*kè-nyeu*) Kenya *m*

kerosene (*kè-reu-siin*) *n* pétrole *m*

kettle (*kè-teul*) *n* bouilloire *f*

key (*kii*) *n* clé *f*

keyboard (*kii-bood*) *n* clavier *m*

keyhole (*kii-hô*ᵘ*l*) *n* trou de la serrure

khaki (*kââ-ki*) *n* kaki *m*

kick (*kik*) *v* donner des coups de pied; *n* coup de pied

kickoff (*ki-kof*) *n* coup d'envoi

kid (*kid*) *n* enfant *m*, gosse *m*; chevreau *m*; *v* taquiner

kidney (*kid-ni*) *n* rein *m*

kill (*kil*) *v* tuer

kilogram (*ki-leu-ghræm*) *n* kilo *m*

kilometer *Am*, **kilometre** (*ki-leu-mii-teu*) *n* kilomètre *m*

kind (*kaïnd*) *adj* gentil, aimable; bon; *n* genre *m*

kindergarten (*kinn-deu-ghââ-teunn*) *n* école maternelle

king (*kinng*) *n* roi *m*

kingdom (*kinng-deumm*) *n* royaume *m*

kiosk (*kii-osk*) *n* kiosque *m*

kiss (*kiss*) *n* baiser *m*; *v* embrasser

kit (*kit*) *n* trousseau *m*

kitchen (*ki-tchinn*) *n* cuisine *f*; **~ garden** jardin potager, **~ towel** torchon *m*

knapsack (*næp-sæk*) *n* havresac *m*

knave (*néïv*) *n* valet *m*

knee (*nii*) *n* genou *m*

kneecap (*nii-kæp*) *n* rotule *f*

*kneel (*niil*) *v* s'agenouiller

knew (*nyoû*) *v* (p know)

knife (*naïf*) *n* (pl knives) couteau *m*

knight (*naït*) *n* chevalier *m*

*knit (*nit*) *v* tricoter

knob (*nob*) *n* bouton *m*

knock (*nok*) *v* frapper; *n* coup *m*; **~ against** cogner contre; **~ down** renverser

knot (*not*) *n* nœud *m*; *v* nouer

*know (*nô*ᵘ) *v* *savoir, *connaître

knowledge (*no-lidj*) *n* connaissance *f*

knuckle (*na-keul*) *n* jointure *f*

L

label (*léï*-beul) *n* étiquette *f*; *v* étiqueter

laboratory (leu-*bo*-reu-teu-ri) *n* laboratoire *m*

labo(u)r (*léï*-beu) *n* travail *m*, labeur *m*; douleurs; *v* bûcher, peiner; **labor permit** *Am* permis de travail

labo(u)rer (*léï*-beu-reu) *n* travailleur *m*, travailleuse *f*

labo(u)r-saving (*léï*-beu-séï-vinng) *adj* qui économise du travail

labyrinth (*læ*-beu-rinnθ) *n* labyrinthe *m*

lace (léïss) *n* dentelle *f*; lacet *m*

lack (læk) *n* manque *m*; *v* manquer

lacquer (*læ*-keu) *n* vernis *m*

lad (læd) *n* garçon *m*

ladder (*læ*-deu) *n* échelle *f*

lady (*léï*-di) *n* dame *f*; **ladies' room** toilettes pour dames

lagoon (leu-*ghoûn*) *n* lagune *f*

lake (léïk) *n* lac *m*

lamb (læm) *n* agneau *m*

lame (léïm) *adj* paralysé, boiteux

lamentable (*læ*-meunn-teu-beul) *adj* lamentable

lamp (læmp) *n* lampe *f*

lamppost (*læmp*-pôᵘst) *n* lampadaire *m*

lampshade (*læmp*-chéïd) *n* abat-jour *m*

land (lænd) *n* pays *m*, terre *f*; *v* atterrir; débarquer

landlady (*lænd*-léï-di) *n* logeuse *f*

landlord (*lænd*-lood) *n* propriétaire *m*; logeur *m*

landmark (*lænd*-mââk) *n* point de repère

landscape (*lænd*-skéïp) *n* paysage *m*

lane (léïn) *n* ruelle *f*, chemin *m*; voie *f*

language (*læng*-ghᵒᵘidj) *n* langue *f*; ~ **laboratory** laboratoire de langues

lantern (*læn*-teunn) *n* lanterne *f*

lap (læp) *n* pan *m*; tour *m* (de piste); *v* laper; envelopper (**in** de); clapoter; ~ **of hono(u)r** tour *m* d'honneur; **in** (*or* **on**) **someone's** ~ sur les genoux de quelqu'un

lapel (leu-*pèl*) *n* revers *m*

large (lââdj) *adj* vaste; spacieux

largely (*lââdj*-li) *adv* en grande partie

lark (lââk) *n* alouette *f*

laryngitis (læ-rinn-*djaï*-tiss) *n* laryngite *f*

last (lââst) *adj* dernier; précédent; *v* durer; **at** ~ enfin; en fin de compte

lasting (*lââ*-stinng) *adj* durable

latchkey (*lætch*-kii) *n* clé de la maison

late (léït) *adj* tard; en retard

lately (*léït*-li) *adv* ces derniers temps, dernièrement, récemment

lather (*lââ*-ðeu) *n* écume *f*

Latin America (*læ*-tinn eu-*mè*-ri-keu) Amérique latine

Latin-American (læ-tinn-eu-*mè*-ri-keunn) *adj* sud-américain

latitude (*læ*-ti-tyoûd) *n* latitude *f*

laugh (lââf) *v* *rire; *n* rire *m*

laughter (*lââf*-teu) *n* rire *m*

launch (loontch) *v* lancer; *n* bateau à moteur

launching (*loon*-tchinng) *n* lancement *m*

launderette (loon-deu-*rèt*) *n* laverie automatique

laundry (*loon*-dri) *n* blanchisserie *f*; lessive *f*

lavatory (*læ*-veu-teu-ri) *n* cabinet *m*

lavish (*læ*-vich) *adj* prodigue

law (loo) *n* loi *f*; droit *m*; ~ **court** tribunal *m*

lawful (*loo*-feul) *adj* légal

lawn (loon) *n* gazon *m*, pelouse *f*

lawsuit (*loo*-soût) *n* procès *m*

lawyer (*loo*-yeu) *n* avocat *m*; juriste *m*

laxative (*læk*-seu-tiv) *n* laxatif *m*

*lay (léï) *v* placer, poser; ~ **bricks** maçonner

layer (léï^eu) *n* couche *f*

layman (*léï*-meunn) *n* profane *m*

lazy (*léï*-zi) *adj* paresseux

lead[1] (liid) *n* avance *f*; conduite *f*; laisse *f*

lead[2] (lèd) *n* plomb *m*

*lead (liid) *v* diriger

leader (*lii*-deu) *n* leader *m*, dirigeant *m*

leadership (*lii*-deu-chip) *n* direction *f*

leading (*lii*-dinng) *adj* dominant, principal

leaf (liif) *n* (pl leaves) feuille *f*

league (liigh) *n* ligue *f*

leak (liik) *v* *fuir; *n* fuite *f*

leaky (*lii*-ki) *adj* ayant une fuite

lean (liin) *adj* maigre

*lean (liin) *v* s'appuyer

leap (liip) *n* saut *m*

*leap (liip) *v* bondir

leap year (liip-yi^eu) *n* année bissextile

*learn (leûnn) *v* *apprendre

learner (*leû*-neu) *n* débutant *m*

lease (liiss) *n* location *f*; bail *m*; *v* donner en location, louer

leash (liich) *n* laisse *f*

least (liist) *adj* moindre; **at** ~ au moins

leather (*lè*-ðeu) *n* cuir *m*; en cuir

leave (liiv) *n* permission *f*

*leave (liiv) *v* *partir, quitter; laisser; ~ **out** *omettre

Lebanese (lè-beu-*niiz*) *adj* libanais; *n* Libanais *m*

Lebanon (*lè*-beu-neunn) Liban *m*

lecture (*lèk*-tcheu) *n* cours *m*, conférence *f*

left[1] (lèft) *adj* gauche

left[2] (lèft) *v* (p, pp leave)

left-hand (*lèft*-hænd) *adj* à gauche, de gauche

left-handed (lèft-*hæn*-did) *adj* gaucher

leg (lègh) *n* pied *m*, jambe *f*

legacy (*lè*-gheu-si) *n* legs *m*

legal (*lii*-gheul) *adj* légitime, légal; juridique

legible (*lè*-dji-beul) *adj* lisible

legitimate (li-*dji*-ti-meut) *adj* légitime

leisure (*lè*-jeu) *n* loisir *m*; aise *f*

lemon (*lè*-meunn) *n* citron *m*

lemonade (lè-meu-*néïd*) *n* limonade *f*

*lend (lènd) *v* prêter

length (lèngθ) *n* longueur *f*

lengthen (*lèng*-θeunn) *v* allonger

lengthways (*lèng*θ^ou éïz) *adv* en long

lens (lènz) *n* lentille *f*; **telephoto** ~ télé-objectif *m*; **zoom** ~ zoom *m*

leprosy (*lè*-preu-si) *n* lèpre *f*

less (lèss) *adv* moins

lessen (*lè*-seunn) *v* diminuer

lesson (*lè*-seunn) *n* leçon *f*

*let (lèt) *v* laisser; louer; ~ **down** *décevoir

letter (*lè*-teu) *n* lettre *f*, ~ **of credit** lettre de crédit; ~ **of recommendation** lettre de recommandation; ~ **opener** coupe-papier *m*

letterbox (*lè*-teu-boks) *n* boîte aux lettres

lettuce (*lè*-tiss) *n* laitue *f*

level (*lè*-veul) *adj* égal; plat, plan; *n* niveau *m*; *v* égaliser, niveler; ~ **crossing** passage à niveau

lever (*lii*-veu) *n* levier *m*

liability (laï-eu-*bi*-leu-ti) *n* responsabilité *f*

liable (*laï*-eu-beul) *adj* responsable; ~ **to** sujet à

liar (*laï*-eu) *n* menteur *m*, menteuse *f*

liberal (*li*-beu-reul) *adj* libéral; généreux, large

liberation (li-beu-*réï*-cheunn) *n* libération *f*

Liberia (laï-*bieu*-ri-eu) Libéria *m*

Liberian (laï-*bieu*-ri-eunn) *adj* libérien; *n* Libérien *m*

liberty (*li*-beu-ti) *n* liberté *f*

library (*laï*-breu-ri) *n* bibliothèque *f*

licence (*laï*-seunns) *n* licence *f*; permis *m*; **driving** ~ permis de conduire

license (*laï*-seunns) *v* autoriser; *nAm* licence *f*; permis *m*; **driver's** ~ permis de conduire; ~ **number** numéro d'immatriculation; ~ **plate** plaque d'immatriculation

lick (lik) *v* lécher

lid (lid) *n* couvercle *m*

lie (laï) *v* *mentir; *n* mensonge *m*

*lie (laï) *v* *être couché; ~ **down** se coucher

life (laïf) *n* (pl lives) vie *f*; ~ **insurance** assurance-vie *f*

lifebelt (*laïf*-bèlt) *n* bouée de sauvetage

lifetime (*laïf*-taïm) *n* vie *f*

lift (lift) *v* soulever, lever; *n* ascenseur *m*

light (laït) *n* lumière *f*; *adj* léger; clair; ~ **bulb** ampoule *f*

*light (laït) *v* allumer

lighter (*laï*-teu) *n* briquet *m*

lighthouse (*laït*-haouss) *n* phare *m*

lighting (*laï*-tinng) *n* éclairage *m*

lightning (*laït*-ninng) *n* éclair *m*

like (laïk) *v* aimer; bien aimer; *adj* pareil; *conj* comme

likely (*laï*-kli) *adj* probable

like-minded (laïk-*maïn*-did) *adj* de même opinion

likewise (*laïk*-ᵒᵘaïz) *adv* de la même manière, également

lily (*li*-li) *n* lis *m*

limb (limm) *n* membre *m*

lime (laïm) *n* chaux *f*; tilleul *m*; limette *f*

limetree (*laïm*-trii) *n* tilleul *m*

limit (*li*-mit) *n* limite *f*; *v* limiter

limp (limmp) *v* boiter; *adj* flasque

line (laïn) *n* ligne *f*; trait *m*; fil *m*; rangée *f*; **stand in** ~ *Am* *faire la queue

linen (*li*-ninn) *n* toile *f*; linge *m*

liner (*laï*-neu) *n* paquebot *m*

lining (*laï*-ninng) *n* doublure *f*

link (linngk) *v* relier; *n* lien *m*; maillon *m*

lion (*laï*-eunn) *n* lion *m*

lip (lip) *n* lèvre *f*

lipstick (*lip*-stik) *n* rouge à lèvres

liqueur (li-*kyoueu*) *n* liqueur *f*

liquid (*li*-kᵒᵘid) *adj* liquide; *n* liquide *m*

liquor (*li*-keu) *n* spiritueux *mpl*; ~ **store** magasin de vins et spiritueux

liquorice (*li*-keu-riss) *n* réglisse *f*

list (list) *n* liste *f*; *v* *inscrire

listen (*li*-seunn) *v* écouter

listener (*liss*-neu) *n* auditeur *m*

liter (*lii*-teu) *nAm* litre *m*

literary (*li*-treu-ri) *adj* littéraire

literature (*li*-treu-tcheu) *n* littérature *f*

litre (*li*-teu) *n* litre *m*

litter (*li*-teu) *n* détritus *m*; immondices *fpl*; portée *f*

little (*li*-teul) *adj* petit; peu

live¹ (liv) *v* *vivre; habiter

live² (laïv) *adj* vivant

livelihood (*laïv*-li-houd) *n* subsistance *f*

lively (*laïv*-li) *adj* vif

liver (*li*-veu) *n* foie *m*

living (*li*-vinng) *adj* vivant, en vie; *n* vie *f*, gagne-pain *m*; **make** (or **earn**) **a** ~ gagner sa vie (**by** en); ~ **room** living *m*, (salle *f* de) séjour *m*; ~ **space** espace *m* vital; ~ **standard** niveau *m* de vie

lizard (*li*-zeud) *n* lézard *m*

load (lôᵒud) *n* chargement *m*; fardeau *m*; *v* charger

loaf (lôᵒuf) *n* (pl loaves) miche *f*

loan (lô^{ou}n) *n* prêt *m*

lobby (*lo*-bi) *n* vestibule *m*

lobster (*lob*-steu) *n* homard *m*

local (*lô*ou-keul) *adj* local; ~ **call** communication locale; ~ **train** train local

locality (lô^{ou}-*kæ*-leu-ti) *n* localité *f*

locate (lô^{ou}-*kéït*) *v* localiser

location (lô^{ou}-*kéï*-cheunn) *n* situation *f*

lock (lok) *v* fermer à clé; *n* serrure *f*; écluse *f*; ~ **up** enfermer

locker (*lo*-keu) *n* casier *m*

locomotive (lô^{ou}-keu-*môou*-tiv) *n* locomotive *f*

lodge (lodj) *v* loger; *n* pavillon de chasse

lodger (*lo*-djeu) *n* sous-locataire *m*

lodgings (*lo*-djinngz) *pl* logement *m*

log (logh) *n* bûche *f*

logic (*lo*-djik) *n* logique *f*

logical (*lo*-dji-keul) *adj* logique

lonely (*lô*oun-li) *adj* solitaire

long (lonng) *adj* long; ~ **for** désirer; **no longer** ne … plus

longing (*lonng*-inng) *n* envie *f*

longitude (*lonn*-dji-tyoûd) *n* longitude *f*

look (louk) *v* regarder; sembler, *avoir l'air; *n* coup d'œil, regard *m*; apparence *f*, aspect *m*; ~ **after** s'occuper de, *prendre soin de; ~ **at** regarder; ~ **for** chercher; ~ **out** *prendre garde, *faire attention; ~ **up** chercher

looking-glass (*lou*-kinng-ghlââss) *n* miroir *m*

loop (loûp) *n* boucle *f*

loose (loûss) *adj* lâche

loosen (*loû*-seunn) *v* desserrer

lord (lood) *n* lord *m*

lorry (*lo*-ri) *n* camion *m*

***lose** (loûz) *v* perdre

loser (*loû*-zeu) *n* perdant *m*, perdante *f*

loss (loss) *n* perte *f*

lost (lost) *adj* égaré; disparu; ~ **and found** objets trouvés; ~ **property office** bureau des objets trouvés

lot (lot) *n* sort *m*; tas *m*, quantité *f*

lotion (*lô*ou-cheunn) *n* lotion *f*; **aftershave** ~ after-shave *m*

lottery (*lo*-teu-ri) *n* loterie *f*

loud (laoud) *adj* fort

loudspeaker (laoud-*spii*-keu) *n* haut-parleur *m*

lounge (laoundj) *n* foyer *m*

louse (laouss) *n* (pl lice) pou *m*

love (lav) *v* aimer; *n* amour *m*; **in** ~ amoureux; ~ **story** histoire d'amour

lovely (*lav*-li) *adj* délicieux, ravissant, beau

lover (*la*-veu) *n* amant *m*

low (lô^{ou}) *adj* bas; profond; déprimé; ~ **tide** marée basse

lower (*lô*ou-eu) *v* baisser; amener; *adj* inférieur, bas

lowlands (*lô*ou-leunndz) *pl* plaine *f*

loyal (*loï*-eul) *adj* loyal

lubricate (*loû*-bri-kéït) *v* huiler, lubrifier

lubrication (loû-bri-*kéï*-cheunn) *n* lubrification *f*; ~ **oil** lubrifiant *m*; ~ **system** système de lubrification

luck (lak) *n* chance *f*; hasard *m*; **bad** ~ malchance *f*

lucky (*la*-ki) *adj* chanceux; ~ **charm** porte-bonheur *m*

ludicrous (*loû*-di-kreuss) *adj* ridicule, grotesque

luggage (*la*-ghidj) *n* bagage *m*; **hand** ~ bagage à main; **left** ~ **office** consigne *f*; ~ **rack** porte-bagages *m*/ filet à bagage; ~ **van** fourgon *m*

lukewarm (*loûk*-ou oom) *adj* tiède

lumbago (lamm-*béï*-ghô^{ou}) *n* lumbago *m*

luminous (*loû*-mi-neuss) *adj*

lumineux

lump (lammp) *n* morceau *m*, grumeau *m*; bosse *f*; ~ **of sugar** morceau de sucre; ~ **sum** somme globale

lumpy (*lamm*-pi) *adj* grumeleux

lunacy (*loû*-neu-si) *n* folie *f*

lunatic (*loû*-neu-tik) *adj* fou; *n* aliéné mental

lunch (lanntch) *n* lunch *m*, déjeuner *m*

luncheon (*lann*-tcheunn) *n* déjeuner *m*

lung (lanng) *n* poumon *m*

luxurious (lagh-*joueu*-ri-euss) *adj* luxueux

luxury (*lak*-cheu-ri) *n* luxe *m*

M

machine (meu-*chiin*) *n* appareil *m*, machine *f*

machinery (meu-*chii*-neu-ri) *n* machinerie *f*; mécanisme *m*

mackerel (*mæ*-kreul) *n* (pl ~) maquereau *m*

mackintosh (*mæ*-kinn-toch) *n* imperméable *m*

mad (mæd) *adj* dément, insensé, fou; enragé

madam (*mæ*-deumm) *n* madame

madness (*mæd*-neuss) *n* démence *f*

magazine (mæ-gheu-*ziin*) *n* revue *f*

magic (*mæ*-djik) *n* magie *f*; *adj* magique

magician (meu-*dji*-cheunn) *n* prestidigitateur *m*

magistrate (*mæ*-dji-stréït) *n* magistrat *m*

magnetic (mægh-*nè*-tik) *adj* magnétique

magneto (mægh-*nii*-tô^(ou)) *n* (pl ~s) magnéto *f*

magnificent (mægh-*ni*-fi-seunnt) *adj* magnifique; grandiose, splendide

magnify (*mægh*-ni-faï) *v* grossir; **magnifying glass** *n* loupe *f*

magpie (*mægh*-paï) *n* pie *f*

maid (méïd) *n* bonne *f*

maiden name (*méï*-deunn néïm) nom de jeune fille

mail (méïl) *n* courrier *m*; *v* *mettre à la poste; ~ **order** *Am* mandat-poste *m*

mailbox (*méïl*-boks) *nAm* boîte aux lettres

main (méïn) *adj* principal; majeur; ~ **deck** pont principal; ~ **line** ligne principale; ~ **road** route principale; ~ **street** rue principale

mainland (*méïn*-leunnd) *n* terre ferme

mainly (*méïn*-li) *adv* principalement

mains (méïnz) *pl* secteur *m*

maintain (méïn-*téïn*) *v* *maintenir

maintenance (*méïn*-teu-neunns) *n* entretien *m*

maize (méïz) *n* maïs *m*

major (*méï*-djeu) *adj* grand; majeur

majority (meu-*djo*-reu-ti) *n* majorité *f*

*make (méïk) *v* *faire, rendre; gagner; réussir; ~ **do with** se débrouiller avec; ~ **good** compenser; ~ **up** dresser

make-up (*méï*-kap) *n* maquillage *m*

malaria (meu-*lèeu*-ri-eu) *n* malaria *f*

Malay (meu-*léï*) *n* Malais *m*

Malaysia (meu-*léï*-zi-eu) Malaysia *m*

Malaysian (meu-*léï*-zi-eunn) *adj* malaisien

male (méïl) *adj* mâle

malicious (meu-*li*-cheuss) *adj* malveillant

malignant (meu-*ligh*-neunnt) *adj* malin

mallet (*mæ*-lit) *n* maillet *m*

malnutrition (mæl-nyou-*tri*-cheunn) *n* dénutrition *f*

mammal (*mæ*-meul) *n* mammifère *m*

man (mæn) *n* (pl men) homme *m*; **men's room** toilettes pour hommes

manage (*mæ*-nidj) *v* diriger; réussir

manageable (*mæ*-ni-djeu-beul) *adj* maniable

management (*mæ*-nidj-meunnt) *n* direction *f*; gestion *f*

manager (*mæ*-ni-djeu) *n* chef *m*, directeur *m*, -trice *f*

mandarin (*mæn*-deu-rinn) *n* mandarine *f*

mandate (*mæn*-déït) *n* mandat *m*

manger (*méïn*-djeu) *n* mangeoire *f*

manicure (*mæ*-ni-kyou^eu) *n* manicure *f*; *v* soigner les ongles

manipulate (meu-*ni*-pyou-léït) *v* manipuler ; manœuvrer

mankind (mæn-*kaïnd*) *n* humanité *f*

mannequin (*mæ*-neu-kinn) *n* mannequin *m*

manner (*mæ*-neu) *n* mode *m*, manière *f*; **manners** *pl* savoir-vivre *m*

manor house (*mæ*-neu-haouss) *n* manoir *m*

mansion (*mæn*-cheunn) *n* manoir *m*

manual (*mæ*-nyou-eul) *adj* manuel

manufacture (mæ-nyou-*fæk*-tcheu) *v* fabriquer

manufacturer (mæ-nyou-*fæk*-tcheu-reu) *n* fabricant *m*

manure (meu-*nyoueu*) *n* fumier *m*

manuscript (*mæ*-nyou-skript) *n* manuscrit *m*

many (*mè*-ni) *adj* beaucoup de

map (mæp) *n* carte *f*; plan *m*

maple (*méï*-peul) *n* érable *m*

marble (*mââ*-beul) *n* marbre *m*; bille *f*

March (mââtch) mars

march (mââtch) *v* marcher; *n* marche *f*

mare (mè^eu) *n* jument *f*

margarine (mââ-djeu-*riin*) *n* margarine *f*

margin (*mââ*-djinn) *n* marge *f*

maritime (*mæ*-ri-taïm) *adj* maritime

mark (mââk) *v* marquer; caractériser; *n* marque *f*; note *f*; cible *f*

market (*mââ*-kit) *n* marché *m*

marketplace (*mââ*-kit-pléïss) *n* place du marché

marmalade (*mââ*-meu-léïd) *n* marmelade *f*

marriage (*mæ*-ridj) *n* mariage *m*

married (*mæ*-rid) *adj* marié ; conjugal; **~ couple** ménage *m*

marrow (*mæ*-rô^ou) *n* moelle *f*

marry (*mæ*-ri) *v* épouser, se marier

marsh (mââch) *n* marais *m*

martyr (*mââ*-teu) *n* martyr *m*

marvel (*mââ*-veul) *n* merveille *f*; *v* s'émerveiller

marvel(l)ous (*mââ*-veu-leuss) *adj* merveilleux

mascara (mæ-*skââ*-reu) *n* cosmétique pour les cils

masculine (*mæ*-skyou-linn) *adj* masculin

mash (mæch) *v* écraser

mask (mââsk) *n* masque *m*

mass¹ (mæss) *n* messe *f*

mass² (mæss) *n* masse *f*; **~ production** production en série

massage (*mæ*-sââj) *n* massage *m*; *v* masser

masseur (mæ-*seû*) *n* masseur *m*

massive (*mæ*-siv) *adj* massif

mast (mââst) *n* mât *m*

master (*mââ*-steu) *n* maître *m*; patron *m*; professeur *m*, instituteur *m*; *v* maîtriser

masterpiece (*mââ*-steu-piiss) *n* chef-d'œuvre *m*

mat (mæt) *n* tapis *m*; *adj* mat

match (mætch) n allumette f; match m; v s'accorder avec

matchbox (mætch-boks) n boîte d'allumettes

material (meu-tieu-ri-eul) n matériel m; tissu m; adj matériel

mathematical (mæ-Œu-mæ-ti-keul) adj mathématique

mathematics (mæ-Œu-mæ-tiks) n mathématiques fpl

matrimony (mæ-tri-meu-ni) n mariage m

matter (mæ-teu) n matière f; affaire f, question f; v *avoir de l'importance; **as a ~ of fact** effectivement, en fait

matter-of-fact (mæ-teu-reuv-fækt) adj réaliste

mattress (mæ-treuss) n matelas m

mature (meu-tyoueu) adj mûr

maturity (meu-tyoueu-reu-ti) n maturité f

mausoleum (moo-seu-lii-eumm) n mausolée m

mauve (môᵒᵘv) adj mauve

May (méï) mai

***may** (méï) v *pouvoir

maybe (méï-bii) adv peut-être

mayor (mèᵉᵘ) n maire m

maze (méïz) n labyrinthe m

me (mii) pron moi; me

meadow (mè-dôᵒᵘ) n pré m

meal (miil) n repas m

mean (miin) adj mesquin; n moyenne f

***mean** (miin) v signifier; *vouloir dire

meaning (mii-ninng) n signification f

meaningless (mii-ninng-leuss) adj dénué de sens

means (miinz) n moyen m; **by no ~** aucunement, en aucun cas

in the meantime (inn ðeu miin-taïm) en attendant, entre-temps

meanwhile (miin-ᵒᵘaïl) adv entretemps

measles (mii-zeulz) n rougeole f

measure (mè-jeu) v mesurer; n mesure f

meat (miit) n viande f

mechanic (mi-kæ-nik) n monteur m, mécanicien m

mechanical (mi-kæ-ni-keul) adj mécanique

mechanism (mè-keu-ni-zeumm) n mécanisme m

medal (mè-deul) n médaille f

media (mii-di-eu)n pl medias mpl

mediaeval (mè-di-ii-veul) adj médiéval

mediate (mii-di-éït) v *servir d'intermédiaire

mediator (mii-di-éï-teu) n médiateur m

medical (mè-di-keul) adj médical

medicine (mèd-sinn) n médicament m; médecine f

medieval (mè-di-ii-veul) adj médiéval

meditate (mè-di-téït) v méditer

Mediterranean (mè-di-teu-réï-ni-eunn) Méditerranée f

medium (mii-di-eumm) adj moyen

***meet** (miit) v rencontrer

meeting (mii-tinng) n assemblée f, réunion f; rencontre f; **~ place** lieu de rencontre

melancholy (mè-leunng-keu-li) n mélancolie f

mellow (mè-lôᵒᵘ) adj moelleux

melodrama (mè-leu-drââ-meu) n mélodrame m

melody (mè-leu-di) n mélodie f

melon (mè-leunn) n melon m

melt (mèlt) v fondre

member (mèm-beu) n membre m; **Member of Parliament** député m

membership (mèm-beu-chip) n affiliation f

memo (mè-môᵒᵘ) n (pl ~s) mémorandum m

memorable (mè-meu-reu-beul) adj

mémorable

memorial (meu-*moo*-ri-eul) *n*
mémorial *m*

memorize (*mè*-meu-raïz) *v*
*apprendre par cœur

memory (*mè*-meu-ri) *n* mémoire *f*;
souvenir *m*

mend (mènd) *v* réparer

menstruation (mèn-strou-*éï*-cheunn)
n menstruation *f*

mental (*mèn*-teul) *adj* mental

mention (*mèn*-cheunn) *v* mentionner;
n mention *f*

menu (*mè*-nyou) *n* carte *f*, menu *m*

merchandise (*meû*-tcheunn-daïz) *n*
marchandise *f*

merchant (*meû*-tcheunnt) *n*
commerçant *m*, marchand *m*

merciful (*meû*-si-feul) *adj*
miséricordieux

mercury (*meû*-kyou-ri) *n* mercure *m*

mercy (*meû*-si) *n* miséricorde *f*,
clémence *f*

mere (mi^eu^) *adj* pur

merely (*mieu*-li) *adv* seulement

merge (meûdj) *v* fusionner;
amalgamer (**with, into** avec); se
fondre (**with, into** dans);
s'amalgamer

merger (*meû*-djeu) *n* fusion *f*

merit (*mè*-rit) *v* mériter; *n* mérite *m*

merry (*mè*-ri) *adj* joyeux

merry-go-round (*mè*-ri-ghô^ou^-
raound) *n* chevaux de bois

mesh (mèch) *n* maille *f*

mess (mèss) *n* désordre *m*, gâchis *m*; ~
up gâcher

message (*mè*-sidj) *n* commission *f*,
message *m*

messenger (*mè*-sinn-djeu) *n*
messager *m*

metal (*mè*-teul) *n* métal *m*; métallique

meter (*mii*-teu) *n* compteur *m*

method (*mè*-θeud) *n* méthode *f*; ordre

m

methodical (meu-θ*o*-di-keul) *adj*
méthodique

metre (*mii*-teu) *n* mètre *m*

metric (*mè*-trik) *adj* métrique

Mexican (*mèk*-si-keunn) *adj* mexicain;
n Mexicain *m*

Mexico (*mèk*-si-kô^ou^) Mexique *m*

microphone (*maï*-kreu-fô^ou^n) *n*
microphone *m*

microwave oven (*maï*-kreu-^ou^éiv a-
veunn) *n* four à micro-ondes *m*

midday (*mid*-déï) *n* midi *m*

middle (*mi*-deul) *n* milieu *m*; *adj* du
milieu; **Middle Ages** moyen-âge *m*; ~
class classe moyenne; **middle-class**
adj bourgeois

midnight (*mid*-naït) *n* minuit *m*

midsummer (*mid*-sa-meu) *n* milieu *m*
de l'été; **in ~** en plein été

midwife (*mid*-^ou^aïf) *n* (pl -wives)
sagefemme *f*

might (maït) *n* puissance *f*

*might (maït) *v* *pouvoir

mighty (*maï*-ti) *adj* puissant

mild (maïld) *adj* doux

mildew (*mil*-dyou) *n* moisissure *f*

mile (maïl) *n* mille *m*

mileage (*maï*-lidj) *n* nombre de milles

milepost (*maïl*-pô^ou^st) *n* poteau
indicateur

milestone (*maïl*-stô^ou^n) *n* borne
routière

milieu (*mii*-lyeû) *n* milieu *m*

military (*mi*-li-teu-ri) *adj* militaire; ~
force force armée

milk (milk) *n* lait *m*

milkman (*milk*-meunn) *n* (pl -men)
laitier *m*

milkshake (*milk*-chéïk) *n* frappé *m*

milky (*mil*-ki) *adj* laiteux

mill (mil) *n* moulin *m*; usine *f*

miller (*mi*-leu) *n* meunier *m*

million (*mil*-yeunn) *n* million *m*

millionaire (mil-yeu-*nèeu*) *n* millionnaire *m/f*

mince (minns) *v* hacher

mind (maïnd) *n* esprit *m*; *v* prêter attention à

mine (maïn) *n* mine *f*

miner (*maï*-neu) *n* mineur *m*

mineral (*mi*-neu-reul) *n* minéral *m*; ~ **water** eau minérale

mingle (*minng*-gheul) *v* (se) mêler (**with** à); (se) mélanger (**with** avec)

miniature (*minn*-yeu-tcheu) *n* miniature *f*

minimum (*mi*-ni-meumm) *n* minimum *m*

mining (*maï*-ninng) *n* exploitation minière

minister (*mi*-ni-steu) *n* ministre *m*; pasteur *m*; **Prime Minister** premier ministre

ministry (*mi*-ni-stri) *n* ministère *m*

minor (*maï*-neu) *adj* petit, menu, mineur; *n* mineur *m*

minority (maï-*no*-reu-ti) *n* minorité *f*

mint (minnt) *n* menthe *f*

minus (*maï*-neuss) *prep* moins

minute[1] (*mi*-nit) *n* minute *f*; **minutes** compte rendu

minute[2] (maï-*nyoût*) *adj* minuscule

miracle (*mi*-reu-keul) *n* miracle *m*

miraculous (mi-*ræ*-kyou-leuss) *adj* miraculeux

mirror (*mi*-reu) *n* miroir *m*

misbehave (miss-bi-*héïv*) *v* se *conduire mal

miscarriage (miss-*kæ*-ridj) *n* fausse couche

miscellaneous (mi-seu-*léï*-ni-euss) *adj* divers

mischief (*miss*-tchif) *n* espièglerie *f*; mal *m*, dommage *m*, malice *f*

mischievous (*miss*-tchi-veuss) *adj* malicieux

miserable (*mi*-zeu-reu-beul) *adj* misérable, malheureux

misery (*mi*-zeu-ri) *n* détresse *f*, misère *f*

misfortune (miss-*foo*-tchèn) *n* infortune *f*, malheur *m*

mishap (*miss*-hæp) *n* mésaventure *f*; accident *m*

***mislay** (miss-*léï*) *v* égarer

misplaced (miss-*pléïst*) *adj* inopportun; mal placé

mispronounce (miss-preu-*naouns*) *v* mal prononcer

miss[1] (miss) mademoiselle, demoiselle *f*

miss[2] (miss) *v* manquer

missing (*mi*-sinng) *adj* manquant; ~ **person** disparu *m*

mist (mist) *n* brume *f*, brouillard *m*

mistake (mi-*stéïk*) *n* méprise *f*, faute *f*, erreur *f*

***mistake** (mi-*stéïk*) *v* confondre

mistaken (mi-*stéï*-keunn) *adj* erroné; ***be** ~ se tromper

mister (*mi*--steu) monsieur *m*

mistress (*mi*-streuss) *n* maîtresse de maison; patronne *f*; maîtresse *f*

mistrust (miss-*trast*) *v* se méfier de

misty (*mi*-sti) *adj* brumeux

***misunderstand** (mi-sann-deu-*stænd*) *v* mal *comprendre

misunderstanding (mi-sann-deu-*stæn*-dinng) *n* malentendu *m*

misuse (miss-*yoûss*) *n* abus *m*

mittens (*mi*-teunnz) *pl* moufles *fpl*

mix (miks) *v* mélanger, mêler; ~ **with** fréquenter

mixed (mikst) *adj* mêlé, mélangé

mixer (*mik*-seu) *n* mixeur *m*

mixture (*miks*-tcheu) *n* mélange *m*

moan (mô^{ou}n) *v* gémir

moat (mô^{ou}t) *n* douve *f*

mobile (*môou*-baïl) *adj* mobile; ~ **phone** (téléphone) portable; téléphone mobile

mock (mok) *v* se moquer de

mockery (*mo-keu-ri*) *n* moquerie *f*

model (*mo-deul*) *n* modèle *m*; mannequin *m*; *v* façonner, modeler

moderate (*mo-deu-reut*) *adj* modéré

modern (*mo-deunn*) *adj* moderne

modest (*mo-dist*) *adj* modeste

modesty (*mo-di-sti*) *n* modestie *f*

modify (*mo-di-faï*) *v* modifier

mohair (*môou-hè^{eu}*) *n* mohair *m*

moist (moïst) *adj* mouillé, moite

moisten (*moï-seunn*) *v* humecter

moisture (*moïss-tcheu*) *n* humidité *f*; **moisturizing cream** crème hydratante

molar (*môou-leu*) *n* molaire *f*

moment (*môou-meunnt*) *n* instant *m*, moment *m*

momentary (*môou-meunn-teu-ri*) *adj* momentané

monarch (*mo-neuk*) *n* monarque *m*

monarchy (*mo-neu-ki*) *n* monarchie *f*

monastery (*mo-neu-stri*) *n* monastère *m*

Monday (*mann-di*) lundi *m*

monetary (*ma-ni-teu-ri*) *adj* monétaire; **~ unit** unité monétaire

money (*ma-ni*) *n* argent *m*; **~ exchange** bureau de change; **~ order** mandat-poste *m*

monk (manngk) *n* moine *m*

monkey (*manng-ki*) *n* singe *m*

monologue (*mo-no-logh*) *n* monologue *m*

monopoly (*meu-no-peu-li*) *n* monopole *m*

monotonous (*meu-no-teu-neuss*) *adj* monotone

month (mannθ) *n* mois *m*

monthly (*mannθ-li*) *adj* mensuel; **~ magazine** revue mensuelle

monument (*mo-nyou-meunnt*) *n* monument *m*

mood (moûd) *n* humeur *f*

moon (moûn) *n* lune *f*

moonlight (*moûn-laït*) *n* clair de lune

moor (*mou^{eu}*) *n* bruyère *f*, lande *f*

moose (moûss) *n* (pl ~, ~s) élan *m*

moped (*môou-pèd*) *n* vélomoteur *m*

moral (*mo-reul*) *n* morale *f*; *adj* moral; **morals** mœurs *fpl*

morality (*meu-ræ-leu-ti*) *n* moralité *f*

more (moo) *adj* plus; **once ~** une fois de plus

moreover (*moo-rôou-veu*) *adv* d'ailleurs, de plus

morning (*moo-ninng*) *n* matin *m*; **~ paper** journal du matin

Moroccan (*meu-ro-keunn*) *adj* marocain; *n* Marocain *m*

Morocco (*meu-ro-kô^{ou}*) Maroc *m*

morphia (*moo-fi-eu*) *n* morphine *f*

morphine (*moo-fiin*) *n* morphine *f*

morsel (*moo-seul*) *n* morceau *m*

mortal (*moo-teul*) *adj* fatal, mortel

mortgage (*moo-ghidj*) *n* hypothèque *f*

mosaic (*meu-zé^ï-ik*) *n* mosaïque *f*

mosque (mosk) *n* mosquée *f*

mosquito (*meu-skii-tô^{ou}*) *n* (pl ~es) moustique *m*; **~ net** moustiquaire *f*

moss (moss) *n* mousse *f*

most (mô^{ou}st) *adj* le plus; **at ~** au maximum, tout au plus; **~ of all** surtout

mostly (*môoust-li*) *adv* le plus souvent

motel (*mô^{ou}-tèl*) *n* motel *m*

moth (moθ) *n* mite *f*

mother (*ma-ðeu*) *n* mère *f*; **~ tongue** langue maternelle; **~ of pearl** nacre *f*

mother-in-law (*ma-ðeu-rinn-loo*) *n* (pl mothers-) belle-mère *f*

motion (*môou-cheunn*) *n* mouvement *m*

motivate (*môou-ti-véït*) *v* motiver

motive (*môou-tiv*) *n* motif *m*

motor (*môou-teu*) *n* moteur *m*; *v* voyager en auto; **~ body** *Am* carrosserie *f*; **starter ~** démarreur *m*

motorbike (*môou*-teu-baïk) *nAm* vélomoteur *m*

motorboat (*môou*-teu-bô^out) *n* canot automobile

motorcar (*môou*-teu-kââ) *n* automobile *f*

motorcycle (*môou*-teu-saï-keul) *n* motocyclette *f*

motorist (*môou*-teu-rist) *n* automobiliste *m*

motorway (*môou*-teu-^ouéï) *n* autoroute *f*

motto (*mo*-tô^ou) *n* (pl ~es, ~s) devise *f*

mouldy (*môoul*-di) *adj* moisi

mound (maound) *n* butte *f*

mount (maount) *v* monter; *n* mont *m*

mountain (*maoun*-tinn) *n* montagne *f*; ~ **pass** col *m*; ~ **range** chaîne de montagnes

mountaineering (maoun-ti-*nieu*-rinng) *n* alpinisme *m*

mountainous (*maoun*-ti-neuss) *adj* montagneux

mourning (*moo*-ninng) *n* deuil *m*

mouse (mauss) *n* (pl mice) souris *f*

moustache (meu-*stââch*) *n* moustache *f*

mouth (maouθ) *n* bouche *f*; gueule *f*; embouchure *f*

mouthwash (*maouθ*-^ouoch) *n* eau dentifrice

movable (*moû*-veu-beul) *adj* mobile

move (moûv) *v* bouger; déplacer; se *mouvoir; déménager; *émouvoir; *n* tour *m*, pas *m*; déménagement *m*

movement (*moûv*-meunnt) *n* mouvement *m*

movie (*moû*-vi) *n* film *m*; **movies** *Am* cinéma *m*; ~ **theatre,** cinéma *m*

much (match) *adj* beaucoup de; *adv* beaucoup; **as ~** autant

muck (mak) *n* gadoue *f*

mud (mad) *n* boue *f*

muddle (*ma*-deul) *n* fouillis *m*,

pagaille *f*, confusion *f*; *v* embrouiller

muddy (*ma*-di) *adj* boueux

muffler (*maf*-leu) *nAm* silencieux *m*

mug (magh) *n* gobelet *m*, chope *f*

mule (myoûl) *n* mulet *m*, mule *f*

multiplication (mal-ti-pli-*kéï*-cheunn) *n* multiplication *f*

multiply (*mal*-ti-plaï) *v* multiplier

mumps (mammps) *n* oreillons *mpl*

municipal (myoû-*ni*-si-peul) *adj* municipal

municipality (myoû-ni-si-*pæ*-leu-ti) *n* municipalité *f*

murder (*meû*-deu) *n* assassinat *m*; *v* assassiner

murderer (*meû*-deu-reu) *n* meurtrier *m*, -ière *f*

muscle (*ma*-seul) *n* muscle *m*

muscular (*ma*-skyou-leu) *adj* musclé

museum (myoû-*zii*-eumm) *n* musée *m*

mushroom (*mach*-roûm) *n* champignon *m*

music (*myoû*-zik) *n* musique *f*; ~ **academy** conservatoire *m*; ~ **hall** music-hall *m*

musical (*myoû*-zi-keul) *adj* musical; *n* comédie musicale

musician (myoû-*zi*-cheunn) *n* musicien *m*, -ienne *f*

mussel (*ma*-seul) *n* moule *f*

***must** (mast) *v* *falloir

mustard (*ma*-steud) *n* moutarde *f*

mute (myoût) *adj* muet

mutiny (*myoû*-ti-ni) *n* mutinerie *f*

mutton (*ma*-teunn) *n* mouton *m*

mutual (*myoû*-tchou-eul) *adj* mutuel, réciproque

my (maï) *adj* mon

myself (maï-*sèlf*) *pron* me; moi-même

mysterious (mi-*stieu*-ri-euss) *adj* mystérieux

mystery (*mi*-steu-ri) *n* énigme *f*, mystère *m*

myth (miθ) *n* mythe *m*

N

nail (néïl) *n* ongle *m*; clou *m*; **~ file** lime à ongles; **~ polish** vernis à ongle; **~ scissors** ciseaux à ongles

nailbrush (néïl-brach) *n* brosse à ongles

naïve (nââ-*iiv*) *adj* naïf

naked (néï-kid) *adj* nu; dénudé

name (néïm) *n* nom *m*; *v* nommer; **in the ~ of** au nom de

namely (néïm-li) *adv* notamment

nap (næp) *n* somme *m*

napkin (næp-kinn) *n* serviette *f*

nappy (næ-pi) *n* couche *f*

narcosis (nââ-*kôou*-siss) *n* (pl -ses) narcose *f*

narcotic (nââ-*ko*-tik) *n* narcotique *m*

narrow (næ-rô^{ou}) *adj* serré, étroit

narrow-minded (næ-rô^{ou}-*maïn*-did) *adj* borné

nasty (nââ-sti) *adj* antipathique, désagréable; méchant

nation (néï-cheunn) *n* nation *f*; peuple *m*

national (næ-cheu-neul) *adj* national; de l'Etat; **~ anthem** hymne national; **~ dress** costume national; **~ park** parc national

nationality (næ-cheu-næ-leu-ti) *n* nationalité *f*

nationalize (næ-cheu-neu-laïz) *v* nationaliser

native (néï-tiv) *n* indigène *m/f*; *adj* indigène; **~ country** patrie *f*, pays natal; **~ language** langue maternelle

natural (næ-tcheu-reul) *adj* naturel; inné

naturally (næ-tcheu-reu-li) *adv* bien sûr, naturellement

nature (néï-tcheu) *n* nature *f*

naughty (noo-ti) *adj* polisson, méchant

nausea (noo-si-eu) *n* nausée *f*

naval (néï-veul) *adj* naval

navel (néï-veul) *n* nombril *m*

navigable (næ-vi-gheu-beul) *adj* navigable

navigate (næ-vi-ghéït) *v* naviguer

navigation (næ-vi-*ghéï*-cheunn) *n* navigation *f*

navy (néï-vi) *n* marine *f*

near (ni^{eu}) *prep* près de; *adj* proche, près

nearby (nieu-baï) *adj* proche

nearly (nieu-li) *adv* presque

neat (niit) *adj* soigné; pur

necessary (nè-seu-seu-ri) *adj* nécessaire

necessity (neu-*sè*-seu-ti) *n* nécessité *f*

neck (nèk) *n* cou *m*; **nape of the ~** nuque *f*

necklace (*nèk*-leuss) *n* collier *m*

necktie (*nèk*-taï) *n* cravate *f*

need (niid) *v* *falloir, *avoir besoin de; *n* besoin *m*; nécessité *f*; **~ to** *devoir

needle (nii-deul) *n* aiguille *f*

needlework (nii-deul-^{ou}eûk) *n* travail à l'aiguille

negative (nè-gheu-tiv) *adj* négatif; *n* négatif *m*

neglect (ni-*ghlèkt*) *v* négliger; *n* négligence *f*

neglectful (ni-*ghlèkt*-feul) *adj* négligent

negligee (nè-ghli-jéï) *n* négligé *m*

negotiate (ni-*ghôou*-chi-éït) *v* négocier

negotiation (ni-ghô^{ou}-chi-éï-cheunn) *n* négociation *f*

neighbour (néï-beu) *n* voisin *m*, -e *f*

neighbo(u)rhood (néï-beu-houd) *n* voisinage *m*

neighbo(u)ring (néï-beu-rinng) *adj* contigu, avoisinant

neither (naï-ðeu) *pron* ni l'un ni

l'autre; **neither … nor** ni … ni

neon (*nii*-onn) *n* néon *m*

nephew (*nè*-fyoû) *n* neveu *m*

nerve (neûv) *n* nerf *m*; audace *f*

nervous (*neû*-veuss) *adj* nerveux

nest (nèst) *n* nid *m*

net (nèt) *n* filet *m*; *adj* net

Netherlands (*nè*-ðeu-leunndz): **the ~**
Pays-Bas *mpl*

network (*nèt*-ᵒᵘeûk) *n* réseau *m*

neuralgia (nyou*eu*-*ræl*-djeu) *n*
névralgie *f*

neurosis (nyou*eu*-*rôou*-siss) *n* névrose
f

neuter (*nyoû*-teu) *adj* neutre

neutral (*nyoû*-treul) *adj* neutre

never (*nè*-veu) *adv* ne … jamais

nevertheless (nè-veu-ðeu-*lèss*) *adv*
néanmoins

new (nyoû) *adj* nouveau

news (nyoûz) *n* nouvelles, nouvelle *f*;
actualités

newsagent (*nyoû*-zéï-djeunnt) *n*
marchand de journaux

newspaper (*nyoûz*-péï-peu) *n* journal
m

newsreel (*nyoûz*-riil) *n* actualités

newsstand (*nyoûz*-stænd) *n* kiosque à
journaux

New Year (nyoû yi*eu*) Nouvel An; **New
Year's Eve** la Saint-Sylvestre

New Zealand (nyoû *zii*-leunnd)
Nouvelle-Zélande *f*

next (nèkst) *adj* prochain, suivant; **~ to**
à côté de

next-door (nèkst-*doo*) *adv* à côté

nice (naïss) *adj* gentil, joli, plaisant;
bon; sympathique

nickel (*ni*-keul) *n* nickel *m*

nickname (*nik*-néïm) *n* surnom *m*

nicotine (*ni*-keu-tiin) *n* nicotine *f*

niece (niiss) *n* nièce *f*

Nigeria (naï-*djieu*-ri-eu) Nigeria *m*

Nigerian (naï-*djïeu*-ri-eunn) *adj*

nigérien; *n* Nigérien *m*

night (naït) *n* nuit *f*; soir *m*; **by ~** de
nuit; **~ cream** crème de nuit; **~ flight**
vol de nuit; **~ rate** tarif de nuit; **~ train**
train de nuit

nightclub (*naït*-klab) *n* boîte de nuit

nightdress (*naït*-drèss) *n* chemise de
nuit

nightingale (*naï*-tinng-ghéïl) *n*
rossignol *m*

nightly (*naït*-li) *adj* nocturne

nightmare (*naït*-mè*eu*) *n* cauchemar
m

nil (nil) rien

nine (naïn) *num* neuf

nineteen (naïn-*tiin*) *num* dix-neuf

nineteenth (naïn-*tiinθ*) *num* dix-
neuvième

ninety (*naïn*-ti) *num* quatre-vingt-dix

ninth (naïnθ) *num* neuvième

no (nô*ou*) non; *adj* aucun; **~ one** ne …
personne

nobility (nô*ou*-*bi*-leu-ti) *n* noblesse *f*

noble (*nôou*-beul) *adj* noble

nobody (*nôou*-bo-di) *pron* ne …
personne

nod (nod) *n* inclination de la tête; *v*
opiner de la tête

noise (noïz) *n* bruit *m*; fracas *m*,
vacarme *m*

noisy (*noï*-zi) *adj* bruyant; sonore

nominate (*no*-mi-néït) *v* nommer

nomination (no-mi-*néï*-cheunn) *n*
nomination *f*

none (nann) *pron* aucun

nonsense (*nonn*-seunns) *n* sottise *f*

non-smoker (*nonn*-smô*ou*-keu) *n*
non-fumeur *m*

noon (noûn) *n* midi *m*

nor (noo): **neither ~** ni; ne … pas non
plus; **nor do I** (ni) moi non plus

normal (*noo*-meul) *adj* normal

north (nooθ) *n* nord *m*; *adj*
septentrional; **North Pole** pôle nord

north-east (nooθ-*iist*) n nord-est m

northerly (*noo*-ðeu-li) adj du nord

northern (*noo*-ðeunn) adj septentrional

north-west (nooθ-*ouèst*) n nord-ouest m

Norway (*noo*-^{ou}éï) Norvège f

Norwegian (noo-*ouii*-djeunn) adj norvégien; n Norvégien m

nose (nô^{ou}z) n nez m

nosebleed (*nôouz*-bliid) n saignement de nez

nostril (*no*-stril) n narine f

nosy (*nôou*-zi) adj colloquial curieux; indiscret

not (not) adv ne … pas

notary (*nôou*-teu-ri) n notaire m

note (nô^{ou}t) n note f; ton m; v noter; observer, constater

notebook (*nôout*-bouk) n carnet m

noted (*nôou*-tid) adj illustre

notepaper (*nôout*-péï-peu) n papier à lettres

nothing (*na*-θinng) n rien, ne … rien

notice (*nôou*-tiss) v observer, noter, remarquer; n avis m, nouvelle f; attention f

noticeable (*nôou*-ti-seu-beul) adj perceptible; remarquable

notify (*nôou*-ti-faï) v notifier; avertir

notion (*nôou*-cheunn) n notion f

notorious (nô^{ou}-*too*-ri-euss) adj notoire

nougat (*noû*-ghââ) n nougat m

nought (noot) n zéro m

noun (naoun) n nom m, substantif m

nourishing (*na*-ri-chinng) adj nourrissant

novel (*no*-veul) n roman m

November (nô^{ou}-*vèm*-beu) novembre

now (naou) adv maintenant; à l'heure actuelle; ~ **and then** de temps en temps

nowadays (*naou*-eu-déïz) adv actuellement

nowhere (*nôou*-^{ou}è^{eu}) adv nulle part

nozzle (*no*-zeul) n bec m

nuance (nyoû-*anss*) n nuance f

nuclear (*nyoû*-kli-eu) adj nucléaire; ~ **energy** énergie nucléaire

nucleus (*nyoû*-kli-euss) n noyau m

nude (nyoûd) adj nu; n nu m

nuisance (*nyoû*-seunns) n ennui m

numb (namm) adj engourdi

number (*namm*-beu) n numéro m; chiffre m, nombre m

numeral (*nyoû*-meu-reul) n nombre m

numerous (*nyoû*-meu-reuss) adj nombreux

nun (nann) n religieuse f

nunnery (*na*-neu-ri) n couvent m

nurse (neûss) n infirmière f; bonne d'enfants; v soigner; allaiter

nursery (*neû*-seu-ri) n chambre d'enfants; crèche f; pépinière f

nut (nat) n noix f; écrou m

nutcrackers (*nat*-kræ-keuz) pl cassenoix m

nutmeg (*nat*-mègh) n muscade f

nutritious (nyoû-*tri*-cheuss) adj nutritif

nutshell (*nat*-chèl) n coquille de noix

nylon (*naï*-lonn) n nylon m

O

oak (ô^{ou}k) *n* chêne *m*

oar (oo) *n* rame *f*

oasis (ô^{ou}-*éï*-siss) *n* (pl oases) oasis *f*

oath (ô^{ou}θ) *n* serment *m*

oats (ô^{ou}ts) *pl* avoine *f*

obedience (eu-*bii*-di-eunns) *n* obéissance *f*

obedient (eu-*bii*-di-eunnt) *adj* obéissant

obey (eu-*béï*) *v* obéir

object¹ (*ob*-djikt) *n* objet *m*; objectif *m*

object² (eub-*djèkt*) *v* objecter; **~ to** *faire objection à

objection (eub-*djèk*-cheunn) *n* objection *f*

objective (eub-*djèk*-tiv) *adj* objectif; *n* objectif *m*

obligatory (eu-*bli*-gheu-teu-ri) *adj* obligatoire

oblige (eu-*blaïdj*) *v* obliger; ***be obliged to** *être obligé de; *devoir

obliging (eu-*blaï*-djinng) *adj* obligeant

oblong (*ob*-lonng) *adj* oblong; *n* rectangle *m*

obscene (eub-*siin*) *adj* obscène

obscure (eub-*skyoueu*) *adj* vague, sombre, obscur

observation (ob-zeu-*véï*-cheunn) *n* observation *f*

observatory (eub-*zeû*-veu-tri) *n* observatoire *m*

observe (eub-*zeûv*) *v* observer

obsession (eub-*sè*-cheunn) *n* obsession *f*

obstacle (*ob*-steu-keul) *n* obstacle *m*

obstinate (*ob*-sti-neut) *adj* obstiné; opiniâtre

obtain (eub-*téïn*) *v* se procurer, *obtenir

obtainable (eub-*téï*-neu-beul) *adj* disponible

obvious (*ob*-vi-euss) *adj* évident

occasion (eu-*kéï*-jeunn) *n* occasion *f*

occasionally (eu-*kéï*-jeu-neu-li) *adv* de temps en temps

occupant (*o*-kyou-peunnt) *n* occupant *m*

occupation (o-kyou-*péï*-cheunn) *n* occupation *f*

occupy (*o*-kyou-paï) *v* occuper

occur (eu-*keû*) *v* se passer, se *produire, *survenir

occurrence (eu-*ka*-reunns) *n* événement *m*

ocean (ô*ou*-cheunn) *n* océan *m*

October (ok-*tôou*-beu) octobre

octopus (*ok*-teu-peuss) *n* pieuvre *f*

oculist (*o*-kyou-list) *n* oculiste *m/f*

odd (od) *adj* bizarre; impair

odo(u)r (ô*ou*-deu) *n* odeur *f*

of (ov, euv) *prep* de

off (of) *prep* de

offence (eu-*fèns*) *n* infraction *f*; offense *f*, outrage *m*

offend (eu-*fènd*) *v* blesser, offenser; outrager

offense (eu-*fèns*) *nAm* infraction *f*; offense *f*, outrage *m*

offensive (eu-*fèn*-siv) *adj* offensif; grossier; *n* offensive *f*

offer (*o*-feu) *v* *offrir; *n* offre *f*

office (*o*-fiss) *n* bureau *m*; fonction *f*; **~ hours** heures de bureau

officer (*o*-fi-seu) *n* officier *m*

official (eu-*fi*-cheul) *adj* officiel

off-licence (*of*-laï-seunns) *n* magasin de spiritueux

often (*o*-feunn) *adv* souvent

oil (oïl) *n* huile *f*; pétrole *m*; **fuel ~** mazout *m*; **~ filter** filtre à huile; **~ painting** peinture à l'huile; **~ pressure** pression d'huile; **~ refinery** raffinerie de pétrole; **~ well** gisement de pétrole, puits de pétrole

oily (*oï*-li) *adj* huileux

ointment (*oïnt*-meunnt) *n* onguent *m*

okay! (ô^{ou}-*kéï*) d'accord!

old (ô^{ou}ld) *adj* vieux; ~ **age** vieillesse *f*

old-fashioned (ô^{ou}ld-*fæ*-cheunnd) *adj* démodé

olive (*o*-liv) *n* olive *f*; ~ **oil** huile d'olive

omelette (*omm*-leut) *n* omelette *f*

ominous (*o*-mi-neuss) *adj* sinistre

omit (eu-*mit*) *v* *omettre

omnipotent (omm-*ni*-peu-teunnt) *adj* omnipotent

on (onn) *prep* sur; à

once (^{ou}anns) *adv* une fois; **at ~** immédiatement, tout de suite; **for ~** pour un coup; ~ **more** une fois de plus

oncoming (*onn*-ka-minng) *adj* venant en sens inverse; proche

one (^{ou}ann) *num* un; *pron* on

oneself (^{ou}ann-*sèlf*) *pron* soi-même

onion (*a*-nyeunn) *n* oignon *m*

only (*ô^{ou}n*-li) *adj* seul; *adv* rien que, seulement; *conj* cependant

onwards (*onn*-^{ou}eudz) *adv* en avant

open (*ô^{ou}*-peunn) *v* *ouvrir; *adj* ouvert; franc

opener (*ô^{ou}*-peu-neu) *n* ouvreur *m*

opening (*ô^{ou}*-peu-ninng) *n* ouverture *f*

opera (*o*-peu-reu) *n* opéra *m*; ~ **house** opéra *m*

operate (*o*-peu-réït) *v* opérer, fonctionner

operation (o-peu-*réï*-cheunn) *n* fonctionnement *m*; opération *f*

operator (*o*-peu-réï-teu) *n* standardiste *m/f*

operetta (o-peu-*rè*-teu) *n* opérette *f*

opinion (eu-*pi*-nyeunn) *n* idée *f*, opinion *f*

opponent (eu-*pôou*-neunnt) *n* adversaire *m/f*

opportunity (o-peu-*tyoû*-neu-ti) *n* occasion *f*

oppose (eu-*pôouz*) *v* s'opposer

opposite (*o*-peu-zit) *prep* en face de; *adj* opposé, contraire

opposition (o-peu-*zi*-cheunn) *n* opposition *f*

oppress (eu-*prèss*) *v* oppresser, opprimer

optician (op-*ti*-cheunn) *n* opticien *m*, -ienne *f*

optimism (*op*-ti-mi-zeumm) *n* optimisme *m*

optimist (*op*-ti-mist) *n* optimiste *m/f*

optimistic (op-ti-*mi*-stik) *adj* optimiste

optional (*op*-cheu-neul) *adj* facultatif

or (oo) *conj* ou

oral (*o*o**-reul) *adj* oral

orange (*o*-rinndj) *n* orange *f*; *adj* orange

orbit (*oo*-bit) *n* orbite *f*; *v* tourner autour de

orchard (*oo*-tcheud) *n* verger *m*

orchestra (*oo*-ki-streu) *n* orchestre *m*; ~ **seat** *Am* fauteuil d'orchestre

order (*oo*-deu) *v* commander; *n* ordre *m*; commandement *m*; commande *f*; ~ **form** bon de commande; **in ~ to** afin de; **in ~** en règle; **made to ~** fait sur commande; **out of ~** en dérangement; **postal ~** mandat-poste *m*

ordinary (*oo*-deunn-ri) *adj* commun, habituel

ore (oo) *n* minerai *m*

organ (*oo*-gheunn) *n* organe *m*; orgue *m*

organic (oo-*ghæ*-nik) *adj* organique

organization (oo-gheu-naï-*zéï*-cheunn) *n* organisation *f*

organize (*oo*-gheu-naïz) *v* organiser

Orient (*oo*-ri-eunnt) *n* Orient *m*

oriental (oo-ri-*èn*-teul) *adj* oriental

orientate (*oo*-ri-eunn-téït) *v* s'orienter

origin (*o*-ri-djinn) *n* origine *f*; descendance *f*, provenance *f*

original (eu-*ri*-dji-neul) *adj* authentique, original

originally (eu-*ri*-dji-neu-li) *adv* originairement

orlon (*oo*-lonn) *n* orlon *m*

ornament (*oo*-neu-meunnt) *n* ornement *m*

ornamental (oo-neu-*mèn*-teul) *adj* ornemental

orphan (*oo*-feunn) *n* orphelin *m*

orthodox (*oo*-œu-doks) *adj* orthodoxe

ostrich (*o*-stritch) *n* autruche *f*

other (*a*-ðeu) *adj* autre

otherwise (*a*-ðeu-ᵒᵘaïz) *conj* sinon; *adv* autrement

*ought to (oot) **devoir

ounce (aouns) *n* once *f*

our (aouᵉᵘ) *adj* notre

ours (aouᵉᵘz) le (la) nôtre, les nôtres; à nous; **a ... of ~** un(e) de nos ...

ourselves (aouᵉᵘ-*sèlv*z) *pron* nous; nous-mêmes

out (aout) *adv* dehors, hors; **~ of** en dehors de, de

outbreak (aout-bréïk) *n* déchaînement *m*

outburst (*aout*-beûst) *n* explosion *f*, éruption *f*

outcome (aout-kamm) *n* résultat *m*

*outdo (aout-*doû*) *v* surpasser

outdoors (aout-*dooz*) *adv* dehors

outer (*aou*-teu) *adj* extérieur

outfit (*aout*-fit) *n* équipement *m*

outline (*aout*-laïn) *n* contour *m*; *v* esquisser

outlook (*aout*-louk) *n* prévision *f*; point de vue

output (*aout*-pout) *n* production *f*

outrage (*aout*-réïdj) *n* outrage *m*

outside (aout-*saïd*) *adv* dehors; *prep* hors de; *n* extérieur *m*

outsize (aout-saïz) *n* hors série

outskirts (*aout*-skeûts) *pl* faubourg *m*

outstanding (aout-*stæn*-dinng) *adj* éminent

outward (*aout*-ᵒᵘeud) *adj* externe

outwards (*aout*-ᵒᵘeudz) *adv* vers l'extérieur

oval (*ôou*-veul) *adj* ovale

oven (*a*-veunn) *n* four *m*

over (*ôou*-veu) *prep* au-dessus de, pardessus; passé; *adv* au-dessus; *adj* fini; **~ there** là-bas

overall (*ôou*-veu-rool) *adj* total

overalls (*ôou*-veu-roolz) *pl* salopette *f*

overcast (*ôou*-veu-kâast) *adj* nuageux

overcoat (*ôou*-veu-kôᵒᵘt) *n* pardessus *m*

*overcome (ô^{ou}-veu-*kamm*) *v* *vaincre

overdo (ô^{ou}-veu-*doû*) *v* exagérer; prendre trop de; excéder; trop cuire

overdraw (ô^{ou}-veu-*droo*) *v* exagérer; mettre à découvert

overdue (ô^{ou}-veu-*dyoû*) *adj* en retard; arriéré

overgrown (ô^{ou}-veu-*ghrôoun*) *adj* couvert de verdure

overhaul (ô^{ou}-veu-*hool*) *v* reviser

overhead (ô^{ou}-veu-*hèd*) *adv* en haut

overlook (ô^{ou}-veu-*louk*) *v* ignorer

overnight (ô^{ou}-veu-*naït*) *adv* de nuit

overseas (ô^{ou}-veu-*siiz*) *adj* d'outremer

oversight (*ôou*-veu-saït) *n* inadvertance *f*

*oversleep (ô^{ou}-veu-*sliip*) *v* *dormir trop longtemps

overstrung (ô^{ou}-veu-*stranng*) *adj* à cordes croisées

*overtake (ô^{ou}-veu-*téïk*) *v* dépasser; **no overtaking** défense de doubler

over-tired (ô^{ou}-veu-*taïeud*) *adj* épuisé

overture (*ôou*-veu-tcheu) *n* ouverture *f*

overweight (*ôou*-veu-*ou*éït) *n* surcharge *f*

overwhelm (ô*ou*-veu-*ouèlm*) *v* accabler; écraser

overwork (ô*ou*-veu-*oueûk*) *v* se surmener

owe (ô*ou*) *v* *devoir; **owing to** en raison de

owl (aoul) *n* hibou *m*

own (ô*ou*n) *v* posséder; *adj* propre

owner (*ôou*-neu) *n* propriétaire *m/f*

ox (oks) *n* (pl oxen) bœuf *m*

oxygen (*ok*-si-djeunn) *n* oxygène *m*

oyster (*oï*-steu) *n* huître *f*

ozone (*ôou*-zô*ou*n) *n* ozone *m*

P

pace (péïss) *n* allure *f*; pas *m*; rythme *m*

Pacific Ocean (peu-*si*-fik ô*ou*-cheunn) Océan Pacifique

pacifism (*pæ*-si-fi-zeumm) *n* pacifisme *m*

pacifist (*pæ*-si-fist) *n* pacifiste *m*

pack (pæk) *v* emballer; **~ up** emballer

package (*pæ*-kidj) *n* colis *m*

packet (*pæ*-kit) *n* paquet *m*

packing (*pæ*-kinng) *n* emballage *m*

pact (pækt) *n* pacte *m*, contrat *m*

pad (pæd) *n* coussinet *m*; bloc-notes *m*

paddle (*pæ*-deul) *n* pagaie *f*

padlock (*pæd*-lok) *n* cadenas *m*

pagan (*péï*-gheunn) *adj* païen; *n* païen *m*

page (péïdj) *n* page *f*

pageboy (*péïdj*-boï) *n* page *m*

pail (péïl) *n* seau *m*

pain (péïn) *n* douleur *f*; **pains** peine *f*

painful (*péïn*-feul) *adj* douloureux

painkiller (*péïn*-ki-leu) *n* analgésique *m*

painless (*péïn*-leuss) *adj* sans douleur

paint (péïnt) *n* peinture *f*; *v* *peindre

paintbox (*péïnt*-boks) *n* boîte de couleurs

paintbrush (*péïnt*-brach) *n* pinceau *m*

painter (*péïn*-teu) *n* peintre *m*

painting (*péïn*-tinng) *n* peinture *f*

pair (pè*eu*) *n* paire *f*

Pakistan (pââ-ki-*stâân*) Pakistan *m*

Pakistani (pââ-ki-*stââ*-ni) *adj* pakistanais; *n* Pakistanais *m*

pal (pæl) *n colloquial* copain *m*, copine *f*

palace (*pæ*-leuss) *n* palais *m*

pale (péïl) *adj* pâle

palm (pââm) *n* palme *f*; paume *f*; **~ (tree)** palmier *m*

palpitation (pæl-pi-*téï*-cheunn) *n* palpitation *f*

pan (pæn) *n* casserole *f*

pancake (*pæn*-kéïk) *n* crêpe *f*

pane (péïn) *n* carreau *m*

panel (*pæ*-neul) *n* panneau *m*

panic (*pæ*-nik) *n* panique *f*

pant (pænt) *v* haleter

panties (*pæn*-tiz) *pl* culotte *f*

pants (pænts) *pl* caleçon *m*; *plAm* pantalon *m*

pant suit (*pænt*-soût) *n* ensemble-pantalon

panty hose (*pæn*-ti-hô*ou*z) *n* collants *mpl*

paper (*péï*-peu) *n* papier *m*; journal *m*; en papier; **carbon ~** papier carbone; **~ bag** sac en papier; **~ knife** coupe-papier *m*; **~ napkin** serviette de papier; **typing** ~ papier à machine; **wrapping** ~ papier d'emballage

paperback (*péï*-peu-bæk) *n* livre de poche

parade (peu-*réïd*) *n* parade *f*

paradise (*pæ*-reu-daïs) *n* paradis *m*

paraffin (*pæ*-reu-finn) *n* pétrole *m*

paragraph (*pæ*-reu-ghrââf) *n* paragraphe *m*

parakeet (*pæ*-reu-kiit) *n* perruche *f*

parallel (*pæ*-reu-lèl) *adj* parallèle; *n* parallèle *m*

paralyse, *Am* **paralyze** (*pæ*-reu-laïz) *v* paralyser

parcel (*pââ*-seul) *n* colis *m*, paquet *m*

pardon (*pââ*-deunn) *n* pardon *m*; grâce *f*

parent (*pèeu*-reunnt) *n* père *m*, mère *f*; **parents** *pl* parents *pl*

parents-in-law (*pèeu*-reunnts-inn-loo) *pl* beaux-parents *mpl*

parish (*pæ*-rich) *n* paroisse *f*

park (pââk) *n* parc *m*; *v* se garer

parking (*pââ*-kinng) *n* stationnement *m*; **no** ~ stationnement interdit; ~ **fee** droit de stationnement; ~ **light** feu de position; ~ **lot** *Am* parking *m*; ~ **meter** parcomètre *m*; ~ **zone** zone de stationnement

parliament (*pââ*-leu-meunnt) *n* parlement *m*

parliamentary (pââ-leu-*mèn*-teu-ri) *adj* parlementaire

parrot (*pæ*-reut) *n* perroquet *m*

parsley (*pââ*-sli) *n* persil *m*

parson (*pââ*-seunn) *n* pasteur *m*

parsonage (*pââ*-seu-nidj) *n* presbytère *m*

part (pâât) *n* part *f*, partie *f*, morceau *m*; *v* séparer; **spare** ~ pièce de rechange

partial (*pââ*-cheul) *adj* partiel; partial

participant (pââ-*ti*-si-peunnt) *n* participant *m*, -e *f*

participate (pââ-*ti*-si-péït) *v* participer

particular (peu-*ti*-kyou-leu) *adj* spécial, particulier; exigeant; **in** ~ en particulier

parting (*pââ*-tinng) *n* adieu *m*; raie *f*

partition (pââ-*ti*-cheunn) *n* cloison *f*

partly (*pâât*-li) *adv* en partie, partiellement

partner (*pâât*-neu) *n* partenaire *m/f*; associé *m*

partridge (*pââ*-tridj) *n* perdrix *f*

party (*pââ*-ti) *n* parti *m*; surprise-partie *f*; groupe *m*

pass (pââss) *v* passer, dépasser; réussir; *vAm* doubler; **no passing** *Am* défense de doubler; ~ **by** passer à côté; ~ **through** traverser

passage (*pæ*-sidj) *n* passage *m*; traversée *f*

passenger (*pæ*-seunn-djeu) *n* passager *m*, passagère *f*; ~ **car** *Am* wagon *m*; ~ **train** train de voyageurs

passer-by (pââ-seu-*baï*) *n* passant *m*

passion (*pæ*-cheunn) *n* passion *f*; colère *f*

passionate (*pæ*-cheu-neut) *adj* passionné

passive (*pæ*-siv) *adj* passif

passport (*pââss*-poot) *n* passeport *m*; ~ **control** contrôle des passeports; ~ **photograph** photo d'identité

password (*pââss*-^{ou}eûd) *n* mot de passe

past (pâât) *n* passé *m*; *adj* passé, dernier; *prep* le long de, au delà de

paste (péïst) *n* pâte *f*; *v* coller

pastime (*pââss*-taïm) *n* passe-temps *m*; distraction *f*

pastry (*péï*-stri) *n* pâtisserie *f*; ~ **shop** pâtisserie *f*

pasture (*pââss*-tcheu) *n* pâture *f*

patch (pætch) *v* rapiécer; ~ **up** réparer

patent (*péï*-teunnt) *n* brevet *m*

path (pââθ) *n* sentier *m*

patience (*péï*-cheunns) *n* patience *f*

patient (*péï*-cheunnt) *adj* patient; *n* patient *m*, -e *f*

patriot (*péï*-tri-eut) *n* patriote *m*

patrol (peu-*trôoul*) *n* patrouille *f*; *v* patrouiller; surveiller

pattern (*pæ*-teunn) *n* motif *m*, dessin *m*

pause (pooz) *n* pause *f*; *v* *faire une pause

pave (péïv) *v* paver

pavement (*péïv*-meunnt) *n* trottoir *m*; pavage *m*

pavilion (peu-*vil*-yeunn) *n* pavillon *m*

paw (poo) *n* patte *f*

pawn (poon) *v* donner en gage, *mettre en gage; *n* pion *m*

pay (péï) *n* salaire *m*, paye *f*

***pay** (péï) *v* payer; ~ **attention to** *faire attention à; ~ **cash** payer comptant; ~ **desk** caisse *f*; **paying** rentable; ~ **off** amortir

payee (péï-*ii*) *n* bénéficiaire *m/f*

payment (*péï*-meunnt) *n* paiement *m*

PC (pii-*sii*) *n* micro *m*; P.C. *m*

pea (pii) *n* pois *m*

peace (piiss) *n* paix *f*

peaceful (*piiss*-feul) *adj* paisible

peach (piitch) *n* pêche *f*

peacock (*pii*-kok) *n* paon *m*

peak (piik) *n* sommet *m*; apogée *m*; ~ **hour** heure de pointe; ~ **season** pleine saison

peanut (*pii*-nat) *n* cacahuète *f*

pear (pè^{eu}) *n* poire *f*

pearl (peûl) *n* perle *f*

peasant (*pè*-zeunnt) *n* paysan *m*

pebble (*pè*-beul) *n* galet *m*

peculiar (pi-*kyoûl*-yeu) *adj* spécial, particulier

peculiarity (pi-kyoû-li-*æ*-reu-ti) *n* particularité *f*

pedal (*pè*-deul) *n* pédale *f*

pedestrian (pi-*dè*-stri-eunn) *n* piéton

m; **no pedestrians** interdit aux piétons; ~ **crossing** passage clouté

peel (piil) *v* peler; *n* pelure *f*

peep (piip) *v* épier

peewit (*pii*-^{ou}it) *n* vanneau *m*

peg (pègh) *n* patère *f*

pelican (*pè*-li-keunn) *n* pélican *m*

pelvis (*pèl*-viss) *n* bassin *m*

pen (pèn) *n* plume *f*

penalty (*pè*-neul-ti) *n* amende *f*; peine *f*; ~ **kick** penalty *m*

pencil (*pèn*-seul) *n* crayon *m*; ~ **sharpener** taille-crayon *m*

pendant (*pèn*-deunnt) *n* pendentif *m*

penetrate (*pè*-ni-tréït) *v* pénétrer

penguin (*pèng*-gh^{ou}inn) *n* pingouin *m*

penicillin (pè-ni-*si*-linn) *n* pénicilline *f*

peninsula (peu-*ninn*-syou-leu) *n* péninsule *f*

penknife (*pèn*-naïf) *n* (pl -knives) canif *m*

penny (*pè*-ni) *n* (pl pence, pennies) penny *m*

pension[1] (*pan*-si-on) *n* pension *f*

pension[2] (*pèn*-cheunn) *n* pension *f*

Pentecost (*pèn*-ti-kost) *n* Pentecôte *f*

people (*pii*-peul) *pl* gens *mpl/fpl*; *n* peuple *m*

pepper (*pè*-peu) *n* poivre *m*

peppermint (*pè*-peu-minnt) *n* menthe *f*

perceive (peu-*siiv*) *v* *percevoir

percent (peu-*sènt*) *n* pour cent

percentage (peu-*sèn*-tidj) *n* pourcentage *m*

perceptible (peu-*sèp*-ti-beul) *adj* perceptible

perception (peu-*sèp*-cheunn) *n* perception *f*

perch (peûtch) (pl ~) perche *f*

percolator (*peû*-keu-léï-teu) *n* percolateur *m*

perfect (*peû*-fikt) *adj* parfait

perfection (peu-*fèk*-cheunn) *n*

perfection *f*

perform (peu-*foom*) *v* accomplir

performance (peu-*foo*-meunns) *n* performance *f*

perfume (*peû*-fyoûm) *n* parfum *m*

perhaps (peu-*hæps*) *adv* peut-être

peril (*pè*-ril) *n* péril *m*

perilous (*pè*-ri-leuss) *adj* périlleux

period (*pieu*-ri-eud) *n* époque *f*, période *f*; point *m*

periodical (pi^{eu}-ri-*o*-di-keul) *n* périodique *m*; *adj* périodique

perish (*pè*-rich) *v* périr

perishable (*pè*-ri-cheu-beul) *adj* périssable

perjury (*peû*-djeu-ri) *n* faux serment

permanent (*peû*-meu-neunnt) *adj* durable, permanent; stable, fixe; ~ **press** pli permanent; ~ **wave** permanente *f*

permission (peu-*mi*-cheunn) *n* permission *f*, autorisation *f*; permis *m*, licence *f*

permit[1] (peu-*mit*) *v* *permettre

permit[2] (*peû*-mit) *n* permis *m*

peroxide (peu-*rok*-saïd) *n* eau oxygénée

perpendicular (peû-peunn-*di*-kyou-leu) *adj* perpendiculaire

Persia (*peû*-cheu) Perse *f*

Persian (*peû*-cheunn) *adj* persan; *n* Persan *m*

person (*peû*-seunn) *n* personne *f*; **per** ~ par personne

personal (*peû*-seu-neul) *adj* personnel

personality (peû-seu-*næ*-leu-ti) *n* personnalité *f*

personnel (peû-seu-*nèl*) *n* personnel *m*

perspective (peu-*spèk*-tiv) *n* perspective *f*

perspiration (peû-speu-*rêî*-cheunn) *n* transpiration *f*, sueur *f*

perspire (peu-*spaïeu*) *v* transpirer, suer

persuade (peu-*souêïd*) *v* persuader; *convaincre

persuasion (peu-*souêî*-jeunn) *n* conviction *f*

pessimism (*pè*-si-mi-zeumm) *n* pessimisme *m*

pessimist (*pè*-si-mist) *n* pessimiste *m/f*

pessimistic (pè-si-*mi*-stik) *adj* pessimiste

pet (pèt) *n* animal familier; chouchou *m*

petal (*pè*-teul) *n* pétale *m*

petition (pi-*ti*-cheunn) *n* pétition *f*

petrol (*pè*-treul) *n* essence *f*; ~ **pump** pompe à essence; ~ **station** poste d'essence; ~ **tank** réservoir d'essence

petroleum (pi-*trôou*-li-eumm) *n* pétrole *m*

petty (*pè*-ti) *adj* petit, futile, insignifiant; ~ **cash** petite monnaie

pewter (*pyoû*-teu) *n* étain *m*

phantom (*fæn*-teumm) *n* fantôme *m*

pharmacist (*fââ*-meu-sist) *n* pharmacien *m*, pharmacienne *f*

pharmacology (fââ-meu-*ko*-leu-dji) *n* pharmacologie *f*

pharmacy (*fââ*-meu-si) *n* pharmacie *f*

phase (féïz) *n* phase *f*

pheasant (*fè*-zeunnt) *n* faisan *m*

Philippine (*fi*-li-païn) *adj* philippin

Philippines (*fi*-li-piinz) *pl* Philippines *fpl*

philosopher (fi-*lo*-seu-feu) *n* philosophe *m*

philosophy (fi-*lo*-seu-fi) *n* philosophie *f*

phone (fô^{ou}n) *n* téléphone *m*; *v* téléphoner

phonetic (feu-*nè*-tik) *adj* phonétique

photo (*fôou*-tô^{ou}) *n* (pl ~s) photo *f*

photocopy (*fôou*-teu-ko-pi) *n*

photocopie *f*; *v* photocopier
photograph (*fôou*-teu-ghrââf) *n*
photographie *f*; *v* photographier
photographer (feu-*to*-ghreu-feu) *n*
photographe *m*
photography (feu-*to*-ghreu-fi) *n*
photographie *f*
phrase (fréiz) *n* locution *f*; ~ **book**
manuel de conversation
physical (*fi*-zi-keul) *adj* physique
physician (fi-*zi*-cheunn) *n* médecin *m*
physicist (*fi*-zi-sist) *n* physicien *m*
physics (*fi*-ziks) *n* physique *f*
pianist (*pii*-eu-nist) *n* pianiste *m*
piano (pi-*æ*-nô^ou) *n* piano *m*; **grand ~**
piano à queue
pick (pik) *v* *cueillir; choisir; *n* choix
m; ~ **up** ramasser; *aller chercher;
pick-up van camionnette *f*
pickles (*pi*-keulz) *pl* conserves au
vinaigre, marinades *fpl*
picnic (*pik*-nik) *n* pique-nique *m*; *v*
pique-niquer
picture (*pik*-tcheu) *n* peinture *f*;
illustration *f*; image *f*; ~ **postcard**
carte postale, carte postale illustrée;
pictures cinéma *m*
picturesque (pik-tcheu-*rèsk*) *adj*
pittoresque
pie (païe) *n* pâté *m*; tourte *f*
piece (piiss) *n* morceau *m*, pièce *f*
pier (pi^eu) *n* jetée *f*
pierce (pi^euss) *v* percer
pig (pigh) *n* cochon *m*
pigeon (*pi*-djeunn) *n* pigeon *m*
pig-headed (pigh-*hè*-did) *adj* obstiné
piglet (*pigh*-leut) *n* cochon de lait
pigskin (*pigh*-skinn) *n* peau de porc
pike (païk) (pl ~) brochet *m*
pile (païl) *n* tas *m*; *v* entasser; **piles** *pl*
hémorroïdes *fpl*
pilgrim (*pil*-ghrimm) *n* pèlerin *m*
pilgrimage (*pil*-ghri-midj) *n*
pèlerinage *n*

pill (pil) *n* pilule *f*
pillar (*pi*-leu) *n* colonne *f*, pilier *m*
pillow (*pi*-lô^ou) *n* oreiller *m*
pillowcase (*pi*-lô^ou-kéïss) *n* taie
d'oreiller
pilot (*païe*-leut) *n* pilote *m*
pimple (*pimm*-peul) *n* pustule *f*
pin (pinn) *n* épingle *f*; *v* épingler;
bobby ~ *Am* pince à cheveux
pincers (*pinn*-seuz) *pl* tenailles *fpl*
pinch (pinntch) *v* pincer
pineapple (*païe*-næ-peul) *n* ananas *m*
ping-pong (*pinng*-ponng) *n* ping-
pong *m*
pink (pinngk) *adj* rose
pint (païnt) *n* pinte *f*
pioneer (païe-eu-*nieu*) *n* pionnier *m*
pious (*païe*-euss) *adj* pieux
pip (pip) *n* pépin *m*
pipe (païp) *n* pipe *f*; tuyau *m*; ~
cleaner cure-pipe *m*; ~ **tobacco**
tabac pour pipe
pipeline (*païp*-laïn) *n* pipe-line *m*
pirate (*païe*-eu-reut) *n* pirate *m*
pistol (*pi*-steul) *n* pistolet *m*
piston (*pi*-steunn) *n* piston *m*; ~ **ring**
segment de piston
pit (pit) *n* fosse *f*; mine *f*
pitcher (*pi*-tcheu) *n* cruche *f*
pity (*pi*-ti) *n* pitié *f*; *v* *avoir pitié de;
what a pity! dommage!
placard (*plæ*-kââd) *n* affiche *f*
place (pléïss) *n* place *f*; *v* poser, placer;
~ **of birth** lieu de naissance; *take ~
*avoir lieu
plague (pléïgh) *n* fléau *m*
plaice (pléïss) (pl ~) plie *f*
plain (pléïn) *adj* clair; ordinaire,
simple; *n* plaine *f*
plan (plæn) *n* plan *m*; *v* planifier
plane (pléïn) *adj* plat; *n* avion *m*; ~
crash accident d'avion
planet (*plæ*-nit) *n* planète *f*
planetarium (plæ-ni-*tèeu*-ri-eumm) *n*

planétarium *m*

plank (plængk) *n* planche *f*

plant (plâânt) *n* plante *f*; usine *f*; *v* planter

plantation (plæn-*téï*-cheunn) *n* plantation *f*

plaster (*plââ*-steu) *n* plâtre *m*; sparadrap *m*

plastic (*plæ*-stik) *adj* plastique; *n* plastique *m*

plate (pléït) *n* assiette *f*; plaque *f*

plateau (*plæ*-tô^{ou}) *n* (pl ∼x, ∼s) plateau *m*

platform (*plæt*-foom) *n* quai *m*; ∼ **ticket** billet de quai

platinum (*plæ*-ti-neumm) *n* platine *m*

play (pléï) *v* jouer; *n* jeu *m*; pièce de théâtre; **one-act** ∼ pièce en un acte; ∼ **truant** *faire l'école buissonnière

player (pléï^{eu}) *n* joueur *m*, joueuse *f*

playground (*pléï*-ghraound) *n* terrain de jeux

playing card (*pléï*-inng-kââd) *n* carte de jeu

playwright (*pléï*-raït) *n* dramaturge *m*

plea (plii) *n* plaidoyer *m*

plead (pliid) *v* plaider

pleasant (*plè*-zeunnt) *adj* plaisant, sympathique, agréable

please (pliiz) s'il vous plaît; *v* *plaire; **pleased** content; **pleasing** agréable

pleasure (*plè*-jeu) *n* agrément *m*, divertissement *m*, plaisir *m*

plentiful (*plèn*-ti-feul) *adj* abondant

plenty (*plèn*-ti) *n* abondance *f*

pliers (plaï^{eu}z) *pl* pince *f*

plimsolls (*plimm*-seulz) *pl* chaussures de basket

plot (plot) *n* conspiration *f*, complot *m*; intrigue *f*; lopin *m*

plough (plaou) *n* charrue *f*; *v* labourer

plucky (*pla*-ki) *adj* courageux

plug (plagh) *n* fiche *f*; ∼ **in** brancher

plum (plamm) *n* prune *f*

plumber (*pla*-meu) *n* plombier *m*

plump (plammp) *adj* potelé

plural (*ploueu*-reul) *n* pluriel *m*

plus (plass) *prep* plus

pneumatic (nyoû-*mæ*-tik) *adj* pneumatique

pneumonia (nyoû-*môou*-ni-eu) *n* pneumonie *f*

poach (pô^{ou}tch) *v* braconner

pocket (*po*-kit) *n* poche *f*

pocketknife (*po*-kit-naïf) *n* (pl -knives) couteau de poche

poem (*pôou*-imm) *n* poème *m*

poet (*pôou*-it) *n* poète *m*

poetry (*pôou*-i-tri) *n* poésie *f*

point (poïnt) *n* point *m*; pointe *f*; *v* montrer du doigt; ∼ **of view** point de vue; ∼ **out** indiquer

pointed (*poïn*-tid) *adj* pointu

poison (*poï*-zeunn) *n* poison *m*; *v* empoisonner

poisonous (*poï*-zeu-neuss) *adj* vénéneux

Poland (*pôou*-leunnd) Pologne *f*

Pole (pô^{ou}l) *n* Polonais *m*

pole (pô^{ou}l) *n* poteau *m*

police (peu-*liiss*) *pl* police *f*; ∼ **station** commissariat de police

policeman (peu-*liiss*-meunn) *n* (pl -men) agent de police, policier *m*

policewoman (peu-*liiss*-^{ou}ou-meunn) *n* (pl-women) femme policier

policy (*po*-li-si) *n* politique *f*; police *f*

polio (*pôou*-li-ô^{ou}) *n* poliomyélite *f*

Polish (*pôou*-lich) *adj* polonais

polish (*po*-lich) *v* polir

polite (peu-*laït*) *adj* poli

political (peu-*li*-ti-keul) *adj* politique

politician (po-li-*ti*-cheunn) *n* politicien *m*, politicienne *f*

politics (*po*-li-tiks) *n* politique *f*

poll (pô^{ou}l) *n* vote *m* (par bulletins); scrutin *m*; *v* sonder l'opinion de; réunir; **(opinion)** ∼ sondage *m*

(d'opinion)

pollution (peu-*loû*-cheunn) *n*
pollution *f*

pond (ponnd) *n* étang *m*

pony (*pôou*-ni) *n* poney *m*

pool (poûl) *n* flaque *f* d'eau; mare *f*

poor (pou^eu^) *adj* pauvre; indigent;
piètre

pope (pô^ou^p) *n* pape *m*

pop music (pop *myoû*-zik) musique
pop

poppy (*po*-pi) *n* coquelicot *m*; pavot *m*

popular (*po*-pyou-leu) *adj* populaire

population (po-pyou-*léï*-cheunn) *n*
population *f*

populous (*po*-pyou-leuss) *adj*
populeux

porcelain (*poo*-seu-linn) *n* porcelaine
f

porcupine (*poo*-kyou-païn) *n* porc-
épic *m*

pork (pook) *n* porc *m*

port (poot) *n* port *m*; bâbord *m*

portable (*poo*-teu-beul) *adj* portatif

porter (*poo*-teu) *n* porteur *m*; portier
m

porthole (*poot*-hô^ou^l) *n* hublot *m*

portion (*poo*-cheunn) *n* portion *f*

portrait (*poo*-trit) *n* portrait *m*

Portugal (*poo*-tyou-gheul) Portugal
m

Portuguese (poo-tyou-*ghiiz*) *adj*
portugais; *n* Portugais *m*

posh (poch) *adj colloquial* chic,
chouette

position (peu-*zi*-cheunn) *n* position *f*;
situation *f*; attitude *f*

positive (*po*-zeu-tiv) *adj* positif; *n*
positif *m*

possess (peu-*zèss*) *v* posséder;
possessed *adj* possédé

possession (peu-*zè*-cheunn) *n*
possession *f*; **possessions** biens *mpl*

possibility (po-seu-*bi*-leu-ti) *n*
possibilité *f*

possible (*po*-seu-beul) *adj* possible;
éventuel

post (pô^ou^st) *n* poteau *m*; poste *m*;
poste *f*; *v* poster; ~ **box** boîte *f* postale
~**office** bureau de poste

postage (*pôou*-stidj) *n* port *m*; ~ **paid**
port payé; ~ **stamp** timbre-poste *m*

postcard (*pôoust*-kââd) *n* carte
postale

poster (*pôou*-steu) *n* affiche *f*

poste restante (pô^ou^st rè-*stant*) poste
restante

postman (*pôoust*-meunn) *n* (pl -men)
facteur *m*

post-paid (pô^ou^st-*péïd*) *adj* port payé

postpone (peu-*spôoun*) *v* ajourner,
*renvoyer à

pot (pot) *n* pot *m*

potato (peu-*téï*-tô^ou^) *n* (pl ~es)
pomme de terre

pottery (*po*-teu-ri) *n* poterie *f*

pouch (paoutch) *n* pochette *f*

poulterer (*pôoul*-teu-reu) *n* marchand
de volaille

poultry (*pôoul*-tri) *n* volaille *f*

pound (paound) *n* livre *f*

pour (poo) *v* verser

poverty (*po*-veu-ti) *n* pauvreté *f*

powder (*paou*-deu) *n* poudre *f*; ~
compact poudrier *m*; ~ **room**
toilettes pour dames; **talc** ~ talc *m*

power (paou^eu^) *n* force *f*, puissance *f*;
énergie *f*; pouvoir *m*; ~ **station**
centrale *f*

powerful (*paoueu*-feul) *adj* puissant;
fort

powerless (*paoueu*-leuss) *adj*
impuissant

practical (*præk*-ti-keul) *adj* pratique

practically (*præk*-ti-kli) *adv*
pratiquement

practice (*præk*-tiss) *n* pratique *f*

practise (*præk*-tiss) *v* pratiquer;

s'exercer
praise (préïz) *v* louer; *n* éloge *m*
pram (præm) *n* voiture d'enfant
prawn (proon) *n* crevette *f*, crevette rose
pray (préï) *v* prier
prayer (prè^{eu}) *n* prière *f*
preach (priitch) *v* prêcher
precarious (pri-*kèeu*-ri-euss) *adj* précaire
precaution (pri-*koo*-cheunn) *n* précaution *f*
precede (pri-*siid*) *v* précéder
preceding (pri-*sii*-dinng) *adj* précédent
precious (*prè*-cheuss) *adj* précieux
precipice (*prè*-si-piss) *n* précipice *m*
precipitation (pri-si-pi-*téï*-cheunn) *n* précipitation *f*
precise (pri-*saïss*) *adj* précis, exact; méticuleux
predict (pri-*dikt*) *v* *prédire
prefer (pri-*feû*) *v* aimer mieux, préférer
preferable (*prè*-feu-reu-beul) *adj* préférable
preference (*prè*-feu-reunns) *n* préférence *f*
pregnant (*prègh*-neunnt) *adj* enceinte
prejudice (*prè*-djeu-diss) *n* préjugé *m*
preliminary (pri-*li*-mi-neu-ri) *adj* préliminaire
premature (*prè*-meu-tchou^{eu}) *adj* prématuré
premier (*prèm*-i^{eu}) *n* premier ministre
premises (*prè*-mi-siz) *pl* locaux *mpl*
premium (*prii*-mi-eumm) *n* prime *f*
prepaid (prii-*pèïd*) *adj* payé d'avance
preparation (prè-peu-*réï*-cheunn) *n* préparation *f*
prepare (pri-*pèeu*) *v* préparer
prepared (pri-*pèeud*) *adj* prêt
preposition (prè-peu-*zi*-cheunn) *n* préposition *f*

prescribe (pri-*skraïb*) *v* *prescrire
prescription (pri-*skrip*-cheunn) *n* prescription *f*
presence (*prè*-zeunns) *n* présence *f*
present[1] (*prè*-zeunnt) *n* cadeau *m*; présent *m*; *adj* actuel; présent
present[2] (pri-*zènt*) *v* présenter
presently (*prè*-zeunnt-li) *adv* tout à l'heure
preservation (prè-zeu-*véï*-cheunn) *n* conservation *f*
preserve (pri-*zeûv*) *v* conserver; *mettre en conserve
president (*prè*-zi-deunnt) *n* président *m*, -e *f*
press (prèss) *n* presse *f*; *v* appuyer, presser; repasser; **~ conference** conférence de presse
pressing (*prè*-sinng) *adj* pressant, urgent
pressure (*prè*-cheu) *n* pression *f*; tension *f*; **atmospheric ~** pression atmosphérique
prestige (prè-*stiij*) *n* prestige *m*
presumable (pri-*zyoû*-meu-beul) *adj* probable
presume (pri-*zyoûm*) *v* présumer; prendre des libertés; se permettre (**to** de); **~ (up)on** abuser de
presumptuous (pri-*zammp*-cheuss) *adj* présomptueux
pretence (pri-*tèns*) *n* prétexte *m*
pretend (pri-*tènd*) *v* *feindre, prétendre
pretext (*prii*-tèkst) *n* prétexte *m*
pretty (*pri*-ti) *adj* beau, joli; *adv* assez, plutôt, passablement
prevent (pri-*vènt*) *v* empêcher; *prévenir
preventive (pri-*vèn*-tiv) *adj* préventif
preview (*prii*-vyoû) *n* avant-première *f*; aperçu *m*
previous (*prii*-vi-euss) *adj* précédent, antérieur, préalable

pre-war (prii-*ouoo*) *adj* d'avant-guerre

price (praïss) *v* fixer le prix; **~ list** prix courant *m*

priceless (*praïss*-leuss) *adj* inestimable

prick (prik) *v* piquer

pride (praïd) *n* orgueil *m*

priest (priist) *n* prêtre *m*

primary (*praï*-meu-ri) *adj* primaire; premier, primordial; élémentaire

prince (prinns) *n* prince *m*

princess (prinn-*sèss*) *n* princesse *f*

principal (*prinn*-seu-peul) *adj* principal; *n* proviseur *m*, directeur *m*

principle (*prinn*-seu-peul) *n* principe *m*

print (prinnt) *v* imprimer; *n* épreuve *f*; estampe *f*; **printed matter** imprimé *m*

printer (*prinn*-teu) *n* imprimeur *m*; imprimante *f*

prior (praï^eu) *adj* antérieur

priority (praï-*o*-reu-ti) *n* priorité *f*

prison (*pri*-zeunn) *n* prison *f*

prisoner (*pri*-zeu-neu) *n* détenu *m*, -e *f*, prisonnier *m*, prisonnière *f*; **~ of war** prisonnier de guerre

privacy (*praï*-veu-si) *n* intimité *f*, vie privée

private (*praï*-vit) *adj* particulier, privé; personnel

privilege (*pri*-vi-lidj) *n* privilège *m*

prize (praïz) *n* prix *m*; récompense *f*

probable (*pro*-beu-beul) *adj* vraisemblable, probable

probably (*pro*-beu-bli) *adv* probablement

problem (*pro*-bleumm) *n* problème *m*; question *f*

procedure (preu-*sii*-djeu) *n* procédure *f*

proceed (preu-*siid*) *v* procéder

process (*prôou*-sèss) *n* processus *m*,

procédé *m*; procès *m*

procession (preu-*sè*-cheunn) *n* procession *f*, cortège *m*

proclaim (preu-*klêïm*) *v* proclamer

produce[1] (preu-*dyoûss*) *v* *produire

produce[2] (*prod*-yoûss) *n* produit *m*

producer (preu-*dyoû*-seu) *n* producteur *m*

product (*pro*-dakt) *n* produit *m*

production (preu-*dak*-cheunn) *n* production *f*

profession (preu-*fè*-cheunn) *n* métier *m*, profession *f*

professional (preu-*fè*-cheu-neul) *adj* professionnel

professor (preu-*fè*-seu) *n* professeur *m*

profit (*pro*-fit) *n* bénéfice *m*, profit *m*; avantage *m*; *v* profiter

profitable (*pro*-fi-teu-beul) *adj* profitable

profound (preu-*faound*) *adj* profond

programme (*prôou*-ghræm) *n* programme *m*

progress[1] (*prôou*-ghrèss) *n* progrès *m*

progress[2] (preu-*ghrèss*) *v* avancer

progressive (preu-*ghrè*-siv) *adj* progressif

prohibit (preu-*hi*-bit) *v* *interdire

prohibition (prô^ou-i-*bi*-cheunn) *n* interdiction *f*

prohibitive (preu-*hi*-bi-tiv) *adj* inabordable

project (*pro*-djèkt) *n* plan *m*, projet *m*

promenade (pro-meu-*nââd*) *n* promenade *f*

promise (*pro*-miss) *n* promesse *f*; *v* *promettre

promote (preu-*môout*) *v* *promouvoir

promotion (preu-*môou*-cheunn) *n* promotion *f*

prompt (prommpt) *adj* instantané, prompt

pronounce (preu-*naouns*) *v*

prononcer

pronunciation (preu-nann-si-*éï*-cheunn) *n* prononciation *f*

proof (proûf) *n* preuve *f*

propel (preu-*pèl*) *v* propulser

propeller (preu-*pè*-leu) *n* hélice *f*

proper (*pro*-peu) *adj* juste; convenable, pertinent, adéquat, approprié

property (*pro*-peu-ti) *n* propriété *f*

proportion (preu-*poo*-cheunn) *n* proportion *f*

proportional (preu-*poo*-cheu-neul) *adj* proportionnel

proposal (preu-*pôou*-zeul) *n* proposition *f*

propose (preu-*pôouz*) *v* proposer

proposition (pro-peu-*zi*-cheunn) *n* proposition *f*

proprietor (preu-*praï*-eu-teu) *n* propriétaire *m/f*

prospect (*pro*-spèkt) *n* perspective *f*

prospectus (preu-*spèk*-teuss) *n* prospectus *m*

prosperity (pro-*spè*-reu-ti) *n* prospérité *f*

prosperous (*pro*-speu-reuss) *adj* prospère

prostitute (*pro*-sti-tyoût) *n* prostituée *f*

protect (preu-*tèkt*) *v* protéger

protection (preu-*tèk*-cheunn) *n* protection *f*

protest[1] (*prôou*-tèst) *n* protestation *f*

protest[2] (preu-*tèst*) *v* protester

Protestant (*pro*-ti-steunnt) *adj* protestant

proud (praoud) *adj* fier; orgueilleux

prove (proûv) *v* démontrer, prouver; se révéler

proverb (*pro*-veûb) *n* proverbe *m*

provide (preu-*vaïd*) *v* fournir; **provided that** pourvu que

province (*pro*-vinns) *n* province *f*

provincial (preu-*vinn*-cheul) *adj* provincial

provisional (preu-*vi*-jeu-neul) *adj* provisoire

provisions (preu-*vi*-jeunnz) *pl* provision *f*

prune (proûn) *n* pruneau *m*

psychiatrist (saï-*kaï*-eu-trist) *n* psychiatre *m*

psychic (*saï*-kik) *adj* psychique

psychological (saï-ko-*lo*-dji-keul) *adj* psychologique

psychologist (saï-*ko*-leu-djist) *n* psychologue *m*

psychology (saï-*ko*-leu-dji) *n* psychologie *f*

pub (pab) *n* bistrot *m*

public (*pa*-blik) *adj* public; général; *n* public *m*; **~ garden** jardin public; **~ house** café *m*

publication (pa-bli-*kéï*-cheunn) *n* publication *f*

publicity (pa-*bli*-seu-ti) *n* publicité *f*

publish (*pa*-blich) *v* publier

publisher (*pa*-bli-cheu) *n* éditeur *m*, éditrice *f*

puddle (*pa*-deul) *n* flaque *f*

pull (poul) *v* tirer; **~ out** *partir; **~ up** s'arrêter

Pullman (*poul*-meunn) *n* voiture Pullman

pullover (pou-lô^{ou}-veu) *n* pull-over *m*

pulpit (*poul*-pit) *n* pupitre *m*, chaire *f*

pulse (pals) *n* pouls *m*

pump (pammp) *n* pompe *f*; *v* pomper

pun (pann) *n* jeu *m* de mots

punch (panntch) *v* donner des coups de poing; *n* coup de poing

punctual (*panngk*-tchou-eul) *adj* ponctuel

puncture (*panngk*-tcheu) *n* crevaison *f*

punctured (*panngk*-tcheud) *adj* crevé

punish (*pa*-nich) *v* punir

punishment (*pa*-nich-meunnt) *n* punition *f*

pupil (*pyoû*-peul) *n* élève *m/f*

puppet-show (*pa*-pit-chô^{ou}) *n* théâtre de marionnettes

purchase (*peû*-tcheuss) *v* acheter; *n* acquisition *f*, achat *m*; ~ **price** prix d'achat

purchaser (*peû*-tcheu-seu) *n* acheteur *m*, acheteuse *f*

pure (pyou^{eu}) *adj* pur

purple (*peû*-peul) *adj* pourpre

purpose (*peû*-peuss) *n* intention *f*, but *m*; **on ~** intentionnel

purse (peûss) *n* bourse *f*, porte-monnaie *m*

pursue (peu-*syoû*) *v* *poursuivre; aspirer à

pus (pass) *n* pus *m*

push (pouch) *n* poussée *f*, coup *m*; *v* pousser

***put** (pout) *v* placer, poser, *mettre; ~ **away** ranger; ~ **off** ajourner; ~ **on** *mettre; ~ **out** *éteindre

puzzle (*pa*-zeul) *n* casse-tête *m*; énigme *f*; *v* embarrasser; **jigsaw ~** puzzle *m*

puzzling (*paz*-linng) *adj* embarrassant

pyjamas (peu-*djââ*-meuz) *pl* pyjama *m*

Q

quail (k^{ou}éïl) *n* (pl ~, ~s) caille *f*

quaint (k^{ou}éïnt) *adj* étrange; vieillot

qualification (k^{ou}o-li-fi-*kéï*-cheunn) *n* qualification *f*; réserve *f*, restriction *f*

qualified (*kouo*-li-faïd) *adj* qualifié; compétent

qualify (*kouo*-li-faï) *v* *être qualifié

quality (*kouo*-leu-ti) *n* qualité *f*; caractéristique *f*

quantity (*kouonn*-teu-ti) *n* quantité *f*; nombre *m*

quarantine (*kouo*-reunn-tiin) *n* quarantaine *f*

quarrel (*kouo*-reul) *v* se disputer; *n* querelle *f*

quarry (*kouo*-ri) *n* carrière *f*

quarter (*kouou*-teu) *n* quart *m*; trimestre *m*; quartier *m*; ~ **of an hour** quart d'heure

quarterly (*kouoo*-teu-li) *adj* trimestriel

quay (kii) *n* quai *m*

queen (k^{ou}iin) *n* reine *f*

queer (k^{ou}i^{eu}) *adj* étrange; drôle

query (*kouieu*-ri) *n* question *f*; *v* s'informer; *mettre en doute

question (*kouèss*-tcheunn) *n* question *f*; problème *m*; *v* interroger; *mettre en doute; ~ **mark** point d'interrogation

queue (kyoû) *n* queue *f*; *v* *faire la queue

quick (k^{ou}ik) *adj* rapide

quick-tempered (k^{ou}ik-*tèm*-peud) *adj* irascible

quiet (*kouaï*-eut) *adj* paisible, calme, tranquille; *n* silence *m*, tranquillité *f*

quilt (k^{ou}ilt) *n* courtepointe *f*

quit (k^{ou}it) *v* cesser

quite (k^{ou}aït) *adv* entièrement, tout à fait; assez, plutôt

quiz (k^{ou}iz) *n* (pl ~zes) jeu concours *m*

quota (*kouôou*-teu) *n* quote-part *f*

quotation (k^{ou}ô^{ou}-*téï*-cheunn) *n* citation *f*; ~ **marks** guillemets *mpl*

quote (k^{ou}ô^{ou}t) *v* citer

R

rabbit (*ræ*-bit) *n* lapin *m*

rabies (*réï*-biz) *n* rage *f*

race (réïss) *n* course *f*

racecourse (*réïss*-kooss) *n* champ de courses, hippodrome *m*

racehorse (*réïss*-hooss) *n* cheval de course

racetrack (*réïss*-træk) *n* piste de courses

racial (*réï*-cheul) *adj* racial

racket (*ræ*-kit) *n* vacarme *m*; raquette *f*

radiator (*réï*-di-éï-teu) *n* radiateur *m*

radical (*ræ*-di-keul) *adj* radical

radio (*réï*-di-ô^{ou}) *n* radio *f*

radish (*ræ*-dich) *n* radis *m*

radius (*réï*-di-euss) *n* (pl radii) rayon *m*

raft (rââft) *n* radeau *m*

rag (rægh) *n* chiffon *m*

rage (réïdj) *n* fureur *f*, rage *f*; *v* rager, sévir

raid (réïd) *n* raid *m*

rail (réïl) *n* balustrade *f*, barre *f*

railing (*réï*-linng) *n* rampe *f*

railroad (*réïl*-rô^{ou}d) *nAm* voie ferrée, chemin de fer

railway (*réïl*-^{ou}éï) *n* chemin de fer, voie ferrée

rain (réïn) *n* pluie *f*; *v* *pleuvoir

rainbow (*réïn*-bô^{ou}) *n* arc-en-ciel *m*

raincoat (*réïn*-kô^{ou}t) *n* imperméable *m*

rainproof (*réïn*-proûf) *adj* imperméable

rainy (*réï*-ni) *adj* pluvieux

raise (réïz) *v* élever; relever; cultiver; *nAm* augmentation de salaire

raisin (*réï*-zeunn) *n* raisin sec

rake (réïk) *n* râteau *m*

rally (*ræ*-li) *n* rassemblement *m*

ramp (ræmp) *n* pente *f*

rancid (*ræn*-sid) *adj* rance

rang (ræng) *v* (p ring)

range (réïndj) *n* gamme *f*

rank (rængk) *n* grade *m*; rang *m*

ransom (*ræn*-seumm) *n* rançon *f*

rape (réïp) *v* violer

rapid (*ræ*-pid) *adj* rapide

rapids (*ræ*-pidz) *pl* rapide *m*

rare (rè^{eu}) *adj* rare

rarely (*rèeu*-li) *adv* rarement

rascal (*rââ*-skeul) *n* coquin *m*, fripon *m*

rash (ræch) *n* éruption *f*; *adj* imprudent, inconsidéré

raspberry (*rââz*-beu-ri) *n* framboise *f*

rat (ræt) *n* rat *m*

rate (réït) *n* tarif *m*; vitesse *f*; **at any ~** de toute façon, quoiqu'il en soit; **~ of exchange** cours du change

rather (*rââ*-ðeu) *adv* assez, passablement, plutôt

ration (*ræ*-cheunn) *n* ration *f*

rattan (*ræ*-tæn) *n* rotin *m*

raven (*réï*-veunn) *n* corbeau *m*

raw (roo) *adj* cru; **~ material** matière première

ray (réï) *n* rayon *m*

razor (*réï*-zeu) *n* rasoir *m*; **~ blade** lame de rasoir

reach (riitch) *v* *atteindre; *n* portée *f*

react (ri-*ækt*) *v* réagir

reaction (ri-*æk*-cheunn) *n* réaction *f*

***read** (riid) *v* *lire

reader (*rii*-deu) *n* lecteur *m*, lectrice *f*; maître *m* de conférences; livre *m* de lecture

reading (*rii*-dinng) *n* lecture *f*; **~ lamp** lampe de travail; **~ room** salle de lecture

ready (rè-di) *adj* prêt

ready-made (rè-di-*méïd*) *adj* de confection

real (*ri*ᵉᵘl) *adj* réel

reality (ri-*æ*-leu-ti) *n* réalité *f*

realizable (*rieu*-laï-zeu-beul) *adj* réalisable

realize (*rieu*-laïz) *v* se rendre compte; réaliser

really (*rieu*-li) *adv* vraiment, réellement; en réalité

rear (ri*ᵉᵘ*) *n* arrière *m*; *v* élever; **~ light** feu arrière

reason (*rii*-zeunn) *n* cause *f*, raison *f*; sens *m*; *v* raisonner

reasonable (*rii*-zeu-neu-beul) *adj* raisonnable; équitable

reassure (rii-eu-*choueu*) *v* rassurer

rebate (*rii*-béït) *n* réduction *f*, rabais *m*

rebellion (ri-*bèl*-yeunn) *n* révolte *f*, rébellion *f*

recall (ri-*kool*) *v* se rappeler; rappeler; révoquer

receipt (ri-*siit*) *n* reçu *m*; réception *f*

receive (ri-*siiv*) *v* *recevoir

receiver (ri-*sii*-veu) *n* combiné *m*

recent (*rii*-seunnt) *adj* récent

recently (*rii*-seunnt-li) *adv* l'autre jour, récemment

reception (ri-*sèp*-cheunn) *n* réception *f*; accueil *m*; **~ office** réception *f*

receptionist (ri-*sèp*-cheu-nist) *n* hôtesse *f*

recipe (*rè*-si-pi) *n* recette *f*

recital (ri-*saï*-teul) *n* récital *m*

reckon (*rè*-keunn) *v* calculer; estimer; supposer

recognition (rè-keugh-*ni*-cheunn) *n* reconnaissance *f*

recognize (*rè*-keugh-naïz) *v* *reconnaître

recollect (rè-keu-*lèkt*) *v* se *souvenir

recommence (rii-keu-*mèns*) *v* recommencer

recommend (rè-keu-*mènd*) *v* recommander; conseiller

recommendation (rè-keu-mèn-*déï*-cheunn) *n* recommandation *f*

reconciliation (rè-keunn-si-li-*éï*-cheunn) *n* réconciliation *f*

record[1] (*rè*-kood) *n* disque *m*; record *m*; dossier *m*; **long-playing ~** microsillon *m*; **~ player** tourne-disque *m*

record[2] (ri-*kood*) *v* enregistrer

recorder (ri-*koo*-deu) *n* magnétophone *m*

recording (ri-*koo*-dinng) *n* enregistrement *m*

recover (ri-*ka*-veu) *v* récupérer; se *remettre, guérir

recovery (ri-*ka*-veu-ri) *n* guérison *f*

recreation (rè-kri-*éï*-cheunn) *n* récréation *f*; **~ centre** centre de loisirs; **~ ground** terrain de jeux

rectangle (*rèk*-tæng-gheul) *n* rectangle *m*

rectangular (rèk-*tæng*-ghiou-leu) *adj* rectangulaire

rector (*rèk*-teu) *n* pasteur *m*, recteur *m*

rectory (*rèk*-teu-ri) *n* presbytère *m*

red (rèd) *adj* rouge

redeem (ri-*diim*) *v* racheter, compenser

reduce (ri-*dyoûss*) *v* *réduire, diminuer

reduction (ri-*dak*-cheunn) *n* rabais *m*, réduction *f*

redundant (ri-*dann*-deunnt) *adj* superflu

reed (riid) *n* roseau *m*

reef (riif) *n* récif *m*

referee (rè-feu-*rii*) *n* arbitre *m*; *v* arbitrer; *v* être arbitre, faire fonction d'arbitre

reference (*rèf*-reunns) *n* référence *f*; rapport *m*; **with ~ to** relatif à

refer to (ri-*feû*) *renvoyer à

refill (*rii*-fil) *n* recharge *f*

refinery (ri-*faï*-neu-ri) *n* raffinerie *f*

reflect (ri-*flèkt*) *v* refléter

reflection (ri-*flèk*-cheunn) *n* reflet *m*

reflector (ri-*flèk*-teu) *n* réflecteur *m*

reformation (rè-feu-*méï*-cheunn) *n* réforme *f*

refresh (ri-*frèch*) *v* rafraîchir

refreshment (ri-*frèch*-meunnt) *n* rafraîchissement *m*

refrigerator (ri-*fri*-djeu-réï-teu) *n* frigidaire *m*, réfrigérateur *m*

refugee (rè-fyoû-*djii*) *n* réfugié *m*, réfugiée *f*

refund¹ (ri-*fannd*) *v* rendre, rembourser

refund² (*rii*-fannd) *n* remboursement *m*

refusal (ri-*fyoû*-zeul) *n* refus *m*

refuse¹ (ri-*fyoûz*) *v* refuser

refuse² (*rè*-fyoûss) *n* rebut *m*

regard (ri-*ghââd*) *v* considérer; *n* respect *m*; **as regards** quant à, concernant, en ce qui concerne

regarding (ri-*ghââ*-dinng) *prep* en ce qui concerne, concernant; à propos de

régime (réï-*jiim*) *n* régime *m*

region (*rii*-djeunn) *n* région *f*

regional (*rii*-djeu-neul) *adj* régional

register (*rè*-dji-steu) *v* s'*inscrire; recommander; **registered letter** lettre recommandée

registration (rè-dji-*strèï*-cheunn) *n* inscription *f*, ~ **form** formulaire d'inscription; ~ **number** numéro d'immatriculation; ~ **plate** plaque d'immatriculation

regret (ri-*ghrèt*) *v* regretter; *n* regret *m*

regular (*rè*-ghyou-leu) *adj* régulier; ordinaire, normal

regulate (*rè*-ghyou-léït) *v* régler

regulation (rè-ghyou-*léï*-cheunn) *n* règlement *m*

rehabilitation (rii-heu-bi-li-*téï*-cheunn) *n* rééducation *f*

rehearsal (ri-*heû*-seul) *n* répétition *f*

rehearse (ri-*heûss*) *v* répéter

reign (réïn) *n* règne *m*; *v* régner

reimburse (rii-imm-*beûss*) *v* restituer, rembourser

reject (ri-*djèkt*) *v* refuser, rejeter

relate (ri-*léït*) *v* relater

related (ri-*léï*-tid) *adj* apparenté

relation (ri-*léï*-cheunn) *n* rapport *m*, relation *f*; parent *m*

relationship (ri-*léï*-cheunn-chip) *n* rapport *m*; parenté *f*

relative (*rè*-leu-tiv) *n* parent *m*; *adj* relatif

relax (ri-*læks*) *v* se détendre

relaxation (ri-læk-*séï*-cheunn) *n* détente *f*

reliable (ri-*laï*-eu-beul) *adj* digne de confiance

relic (*rè*-lik) *n* relique *f*

relief (ri-*liif*) *n* soulagement *m*; soutien *m*; relief *m*

relieve (ri-*liiv*) *v* soulager; relayer

religion (ri-*li*-djeunn) *n* religion *f*

religious (ri-*li*-djeuss) *adj* religieux

rely on (ri-*laï*) compter sur

remain (ri-*méïn*) *v* rester

remainder (ri-*méïn*-deu) *n* restant *m*, reste *m*

remaining (ri-*méï*-ninng) *adj* restant

remark (ri-*mââk*) *n* remarque *f*; *v* remarquer

remarkable (ri-*mââ*-keu-beul) *adj* remarquable

remedy (*rè*-meu-di) *n* remède *m*

remember (ri-*mèm*-beu) *v* se rappeler; *retenir

remembrance (ri-*mèm*-breunns) *n* souvenir *m*

remind (ri-*maïnd*) *v* rappeler

remit (ri-*mit*) *v* *remettre

remittance (ri-*mi*-teunns) *n* versement *m*

remnant (*rèm*-neunnt) *n* reste *m*, restant *m*

remote (ri-*môout*) *adj* éloigné, lointain

removal (ri-*moû*-veul) *n* déplacement *m*

remove (ri-*moûv*) *v* enlever

remunerate (ri-*myoû*-neu-réït) *v* rémunérer

remuneration (ri-myoû-neu-*réï*-cheunn) *n* rémunération *f*

renew (ri-*nyoû*) *v* renouveler

rent (rènt) *v* louer; *n* loyer *m*

repair (ri-*pèeu*) *v* réparer; *n* réparation *f*

reparation (rè-peu-*réï*-cheunn) *n* réparation *f*

*repay (ri-*péï*) *v* rembourser

repayment (ri-*péï*-meunnt) *n* remboursement *m*

repeat (ri-*piit*) *v* répéter

repellent (ri-*pè*-leunnt) *adj* écœurant, répugnant

repentance (ri-*pèn*-teunns) *n* repentir *m*

repertory (*rè*-peu-teu-ri) *n* répertoire *m*

repetition (rè-peu-*ti*-cheunn) *n* répétition *f*

replace (ri-*pléïss*) *v* remplacer

reply (ri-*plaï*) *v* répondre; *n* réponse *f*; **in ~** en réponse

report (ri-*poot*) *v* relater; rapporter; se présenter; *n* compte rendu, rapport *m*

reporter (ri-*poo*-teu) *n* reporter *m*

represent (rè-pri-*zènt*) *v* représenter

representation (rè-pri-zèn-*téï*-cheunn) *n* représentation *f*

representative (rè-pri-*zèn*-teu-tiv) *adj* représentatif

reprimand (*rè*-pri-mâând) *v* réprimander

reproach (ri-*prôoutch*) *n* reproche *m*; *v* reprocher

reproduce (rii-preu-*dyoûss*) *v* *reproduire

reproduction (rii-preu-*dak*-cheunn) *n* reproduction *f*

reptile (*rèp*-taïl) *n* reptile *m*

republic (ri-*pa*-blik) *n* république *f*

republican (ri-*pa*-bli-keunn) *adj* républicain

repulsive (ri-*pal*-siv) *adj* repoussant

reputation (rè-pyou-*téï*-cheunn) *n* réputation *f*

request (ri-*kouèst*) *n* requête *f*; demande *f*; *v* *requérir

require (ri-*kouaïeu*) *v* exiger

requirement (ri-*kouaïeu*-meunnt) *n* exigence *f*

requisite (rè-k^{ou}i-zit) *adj* requis

rescue (*rè*-skyoû) *v* sauver; *n* sauvetage *m*

research (ri-*seûtch*) *n* recherche *f*

resemblance (ri-*zèm*-bleunns) *n* ressemblance *f*

resemble (ri-*zèm*-beul) *v* ressembler à

resent (ri-*zènt*) *v* s'offenser de, en *vouloir à

reservation (rè-zeu-*véï*-cheunn) *n* réservation *f*

reserve (ri-*zeûv*) *v* réserver; *retenir; *n* réserve *f*

reserved (ri-*zeûvd*) *adj* réservé

reservoir (*rè*-zeu-v^{ou}ââ) *n* réservoir *m*

reside (ri-*zaïd*) *v* résider

residence (*rè*-zi-deunns) *n* résidence *f*; **~ permit** permis de séjour

resident (*rè*-zi-deunnt) *n* résident *m*; *adj* domicilié; interne

resign (ri-*zaïn*) *v* démissionner

resignation (rè-zigh-*néï*-cheunn) *n* démission *f*

resin (*rè*-zinn) *n* résine *f*

resist (ri-*zist*) *v* résister

resistance (ri-*zi*-steunns) *n* résistance *f*

resolute (*rè*-zeu-loût) *adj* résolu, déterminé

respect (ri-*spèkt*) *n* respect *m*; estime *f*, considération *f*; *v* respecter

respectable (ri-*spèk*-teu-beul) *adj* honorable, respectable

respectful (ri-*spèkt*-feul) *adj* respectueux

respective (ri-*spèk*-tiv) *adj* respectif

respiration (rè-speu-*réï*-cheunn) *n* respiration *f*

respite (*rè*-spaït) *n* répit *m*

responsibility (ri-sponn-seu-*bi*-leu-ti) *n* responsabilité *f*

responsible (ri-*sponn*-seu-beul) *adj* responsable

rest (rèst) *n* repos *m*; reste *m*; *v* se reposer; ~ **home** maison de repos; ~ **room** toilettes

restaurant (*rè*-steu-ron) *n* restaurant *m*

restful (*rèst*-feul) *adj* reposant

restless (*rèst*-leuss) *adj* agité; inquiet

restrain (ri-*stréïn*) *v* *contenir, *retenir

restriction (ri-*strik*-cheunn) *n* restriction *f*

result (ri-*zalt*) *n* résultat *m*; effet *m*; *v* résulter

resume (ri-*zyoûm*) *v* *reprendre

résumé (*rè*-zyou-méï) *n* résumé *m*; *Am* curriculum vitae *m*; C.V. *m*

retail (*rii*-téïl) *v* détailler; ~ **trade** commerce de détail

retailer (*rii*-téï-leu) *n* détaillant *m*, -e *f*

retina (*rè*-ti-neu) *n* rétine *f*

retired (ri-*taïeud*) *adj* retraité

return (ri-*teûnn*) *v* *revenir, retourner; *n* retour *m*; ~ **flight** vol de retour; ~ **journey** voyage de retour

reunite (rii-yoû-*naït*) *v* réunir

reveal (ri-*viil*) *v* révéler

revelation (rè-veu-*léï*-cheunn) *n* révélation *f*

revenge (ri-*vèndj*) *n* vengeance *f*

revenue (*rè*-veu-nyoû) *n* recettes,

revenu *m*

reverse (ri-*veûss*) *n* contraire *m*; revers *m*; marche arrière; revirement *m*; *adj* inverse; *v* *faire marche arrière

review (ri-*vyoû*) *n* critique *f*; revue *f*

revise (ri-*vaïz*) *v* reviser

revision (ri-*vi*-jeunn) *n* révision *f*

revival (ri-*vaï*-veul) *n* reprise *f*

revolt (ri-*vôoult*) *v* se révolter; *n* rébellion *f*, révolte *f*

revolting (ri-*vôoul*-tinng) *adj* dégoûtant, révoltant, répugnant

revolution (rè-veu-*loû*-cheunn) *n* révolution *f*, rotation *f*

revolver (ri-*vol*-veu) *n* revolver *m*

revue (ri-*vyoû*) *n* revue *f*

reward (ri-*ouood*) *n* récompense *f*; *v* récompenser

rheumatism (*roû*-meu-ti-zeumm) *n* rhumatisme *m*

rhinoceros (raï-*no*-seu-reuss) *n* (pl ~, ~es) rhinocéros *m*

rhubarb (*roû*-bââb) *n* rhubarbe *f*

rhyme (raïm) *n* rime *f*

rhythm (*ri*-ðeumm) *n* rythme *m*

rib (rib) *n* côte *f*

ribbon (*ri*-beunn) *n* ruban *m*

rice (raïss) *n* riz *m*

rich (ritch) *adj* riche

riches (*ri*-tchiz) *pl* richesse *f*

rid (rid) *v* débarrasser (**of** de); **get** ~ **of** se débarrasser de

riddle (*ri*-deul) *n* énigme *f*

ride (raïd) *n* course *f*

*ride (raïd) *v* aller; monter à cheval

rider (*raï*-deu) *n* cavalier *m*

ridge (ridj) *n* arête *f*

ridicule (*ri*-di-kyoûl) *v* ridiculiser

ridiculous (ri-*di*-kyou-leuss) *adj* ridicule

riding (*raï*-dinng) *n* équitation *f*; ~ **school** manège *m*

rifle (*raï*-feul) *v* fusil *m*

right (raït) *n* droit *m*; *adj* correct, juste; droit; équitable; **all ~!** d'accord!; ***be ~ *avoir raison; ~ of way** priorité de passage

righteous (*raï*-tcheuss) *adj* juste

right-hand (*raït*-hænd) *adj* à droite, de droite

rightly (*raït*-li) *adv* justement

rim (rimm) *n* jante *f*; rebord *m*

ring (rinng) *n* bague *f*; cercle *m*; piste *f*

***ring** (rinng) *v* sonner; **~ up** téléphoner

rinse (rinns) *v* rincer; *n* rinçage *m*

riot (*raï*-eut) *n* émeute *f*

rip (rip) *v* déchirer

ripe (raïp) *adj* mûr

rise (raïz) *n* augmentation de salaire, augmentation *f*; élévation *f*; montée *f*; essor *m*

***rise** (raïz) *v* se lever; monter

rising (*raï*-zinng) *n* insurrection *f*

risk (risk) *n* risque *m*; danger *m*; *v* risquer

risky (*ri*-ski) *adj* dangereux, risqué

rival (*raï*-veul) *n* rival *m*, -e *f*; concurrent *m*, -e *f*; *v* rivaliser

rivalry (*raï*-veul-ri) *n* rivalité *f*; concurrence *f*

river (*ri*-veu) *n* fleuve *m*; **~ bank** rive *f*

riverside (*ri*-veu-saïd) *n* bord de la rivière

roach (rô^{ou}tch) *n* (pl ~) gardon *m*

road (rô^{ou}d) *n* rue *f*, route *f*; **~ fork** bifurcation *f*; **~ map** carte routière; **~ system** réseau routier; **~ up** attention travaux

roadhouse (*rôoud*-haouss) *n* auberge *f*

roadside (*rôoud*-saïd) *n* bord de la route; **~ restaurant** auberge *f*

roadway (*rôoud*-^{ou}éï) *n* Am chaussée *f*

roam (rô^{ou}m) *v* vagabonder

roar (roo) *v* mugir, rugir; *n* rugissement *m*, grondement *m*

roast (rô^{ou}st) *v* griller, rôtir

rob (rob) *v* voler

robber (*ro*-beu) *n* voleur *m*

robbery (*ro*-beu-ri) *n* vol *m*

robe (rô^{ou}b) *n* robe *f*

robin (*ro*-binn) *n* rouge-gorge *m*

robust (rô^{ou}-*bast*) *adj* robuste

rock (rok) *n* rocher *m*; *v* balancer

rocket (*ro*-kit) *n* fusée *f*

rocky (*ro*-ki) *adj* rocheux

rod (rod) *n* barre *f*, tige *f*

roe (rô^{ou}) *n* œufs de poisson, laitance *f*

role, rôle (rô^{ou}l) *n* rôle *m*

roll (rô^{ou}l) *v* rouler; *n* rouleau *m*; petit pain

roller-skating (*rôou*-leu-skéï-tinng) *n* patinage à roulettes

Roman Catholic (*rôou*-meunn kæ-Œu-lik) catholique

romance (reu-*mæns*) *n* idylle *f*

romantic (reu-*mæn*-tik) *adj* romantique

roof (roûf) *n* toit *m*; **thatched ~** toit de chaume *m*

room (roûm) *n* pièce *f*, chambre *f*; espace *m*, place *f*; **~ and board** pension complète; **~ service** service d'étage; **~ temperature** température ambiante

roomy (*roû*-mi) *adj* spacieux

root (roût) *n* racine *f*

rope (rô^{ou}p) *n* corde *f*

rosary (*rôou*-zeu-ri) *n* rosaire *m*

rose (rô^{ou}z) *n* rose *f*; *adj* rose

rotten (*ro*-teunn) *adj* pourri

rouge (roûj) *n* rouge *m*

rough (raf) *adj* rugueux

roulette (roû-*lèt*) *n* roulette *f*

round (raound) *adj* rond; *prep* autour de; *n* reprise *f*; **~ trip** *Am* aller et retour

roundabout (*raoun*-deu-baout) *n* rond-point *m*

rounded (*raoun*-did) *adj* arrondi

route (roût) *n* route *f*

routine (roû-*tiin*) *n* routine *f*

row¹ (rô^{ou}) *n* rang *m*; *v* ramer

row² (raou) *n* querelle *f*

rowdy (raou-di) *adj* tapageur

rowing boat (*rôou*-inng-bô^{ou}t) *n* bateau à rames

royal (*roï*-eul) *adj* royal

rub (rab) *v* frotter

rubber (*ra*-beu) *n* caoutchouc *m*; gomme *f*; ~ **band** élastique *m*

rubbish (*ra*-bich) *n* détritus *m*; radotage *m*, sottise *f*; ~ **bin** poubelle *f*; **talk** ~ baratiner

rucksack (*rak*-sæk) *n* sac à dos

rudder (*ra*-deu) *n* gouvernail *m*

rude (roûd) *adj* grossier

rug (ragh) *n* tapis *m*

ruin (*roû*-inn) *v* ruiner; *n* ruine *f*

rule (roûl) *n* règle *f*; régime *m*, gouvernement *m*, règne *m*; *v* régner, gouverner; **as a** ~ généralement, en général

ruler (*roû*-leu) *n* monarque *m*, dirigeant *m*; règle *f*

Rumania (roû-*mêi*-ni-eu) Roumanie *f*

Rumanian (roû-*mêi*-ni-eunn) *adj* roumain; *n* Roumain *m*

rumo(u)r (*roû*-meu) *n* rumeur *f*

*****run** (rann) *v* *courir; ~ **into** rencontrer

runaway (*ra*-neu-^{ou}éï) *n* fugitif *m*

rung (rann) *v* (pp ring)

runner (*ra*-neu) *n* coureur *m*, coureuse *f*; patin *m*; coulisseau *m*

runway (*rann*-^{ou}éï) *n* piste de décollage

rural (*roueu*-reul) *adj* rural

ruse (roûz) *n* ruse *f*

rush (rach) *v* se presser; *n* jonc *m*; ~ **hour** heure de pointe

Russia (*ra*-cheu) Russie *f*

Russian (*ra*-cheunn) *adj* russe; *n* Russe *m*

rust (rast) *n* rouille *f*

rustic (*ra*-stik) *adj* rustique

rusty (*ra*-sti) *adj* rouillé

S

sack (sæk) *n* sac *m*

sacred (*séï*-krid) *adj* sacré

sacrifice (*sæ*-kri-faïss) *n* sacrifice *m*; *v* sacrifier

sacrilege (*sæ*-kri-lidj) *n* sacrilège *m*

sad (sæd) *adj* triste; malheureux, affligé

saddle (*sæ*-deul) *n* selle *f*

sadness (*sæd*-neuss) *n* tristesse *f*

safe (séïf) *adj* sûr; *n* coffre-fort *m*

safety (*séïf*-ti) *n* sécurité *f*; ~ **belt** ceinture de sécurité; ~ **pin** épingle de sûreté

sail (séïl) *v* naviguer; *n* voile *f*

sailing boat (*séï*-linng-bô^{ou}t) *n* bateau à voiles

sailor (*séï*-leu) *n* marin *m*

saint (séïnt) *n* saint *m*

salad (*sæ*-leud) *n* salade *f*; ~ **oil** huile de table

salary (*sæ*-leu-ri) *n* paie *f*, salaire *m*

sale (séïl) *n* vente *f*; **clearance** ~ soldes; **for** ~ à vendre; **sales** soldes

saleable (*séï*-leu-beul) *adj* vendable

salesgirl (*séïlz*-gheûl) *n* vendeuse *f*

salesman (*séïlz*-meunn) *n* (pl -men) vendeur *m*

salmon (*sæ*-meunn) *n* (pl ~) saumon

m

salon (*sæ*-lon) *n* salon *m*

saloon (seu-*loûn*) *n* café *m*

salt (soolt) *n* sel *m*; ~ **cellar**, *Am* ~ **shaker** salière *f*

salty (*sool*-ti) *adj* salé

salute (seu-*loût*) *v* saluer

salve (sââv) *n* onguent *m*

same (séïm) *adj* même

sample (*sââm*-peul) *n* échantillon *m*

sanatorium (sæ-neu-*too*-ri-eumm) *n* (pl ~s, -ria) sanatorium *m*

sand (sænd) *n* sable *m*

sandal (*sæn*-deul) *n* sandale *f*

sandpaper (*sænd*-péï-peu) *n* papier de verre

sandwich (*sæn*-^{ou}idj) *n* sandwich *m*; tartine *f*

sandy (*sæn*-di) *adj* sableux

sanitary (*sæ*-ni-teu-ri) *adj* sanitaire; ~ **towel** (*Am* ~ **napkin**) serviette hygiénique

sardine (sââ-*diin*) *n* sardine *f*

satchel (*sæ*-tcheul) *n* cartable *m*

satellite (*sæ*-teu-laït) *n* satellite *m*

satin (*sæ*-tinn) *n* satin *m*

satisfaction (sæ-tiss-*fæk*-cheunn) *n* satisfaction *f*

satisfactory (sæ-tiss-*fæk*-teu-ri) *adj* satisfaisant

satisfy (*sæ*-tiss-faï) *v* *satisfaire

Saturday (*sæ*-teu-di) samedi *m*

sauce (sooss) *n* sauce *f*

saucepan (*sooss*-peunn) *n* poêle *f*

saucer (*soo*-seu) *n* soucoupe *f*

Saudi Arabia (saou-di-eu-*réï*-bi-eu) Arabie Séoudite

sauna (*soo*-neu) *n* sauna *m*

sausage (*so*-sidj) *n* saucisse *f*

savage (*sæ*-vidj) *adj* sauvage

save (séïv) *v* sauver; épargner

savings (*séï*-vinngz) *pl* économies; ~ **bank** caisse d'épargne

savio(u)r (*séï*-vyeu) *n* sauveur *m*

savo(u)ry (*séï*-veu-ri) *adj* savoureux; piquant

saw[1] (soo) *v* (p see)

saw[2] (soo) *n* scie *f*

sawmill (*soo*-mil) *n* scierie *f*

***say** (séï) *v* *dire

scaffolding (*skæ*-feul-dinng) *n* échafaudage *m*

scale (skéïl) *n* échelle *f*; gamme *f*; écaille *f*; **scales** *pl* balance *f*

scandal (*skæn*-deul) *n* scandale *m*

Scandinavia (skæn-di-*néï*-vi-eu) Scandinavie *f*

Scandinavian (skæn-di-*néï*-vi-eunn) *adj* scandinave; *n* Scandinave *m*

scapegoat (*skéïp*-ghô^{ou}t) *n* bouc émissaire

scar (skââ) *n* cicatrice *f*

scarce (ske^{eu}ss) *adj* rare

scarcely (*skèeu*-sli) *adv* à peine

scarcity (*skèeu*-seu-ti) *n* pénurie *f*

scare (skè^{eu}) *v* effrayer; *n* panique *f*

scarf (skââf) *n* (pl ~s, scarves) écharpe *f*

scarlet (*skââ*-leut) *adj* écarlate

scary (*skèeu*-ri) *adj* inquiétant

scatter (*skæ*-teu) *v* disperser

scene (siin) *n* scène *f*

scenery (*sii*-neu-ri) *n* paysage *m*

scenic (*sii*-nik) *adj* pittoresque

scent (sènt) *n* parfum *m*

schedule (*chè*-dyoûl) *n* horaire *m*

scheme (skiim) *n* plan *m*; projet *m*

scholar (*sko*-leu) *n* érudit *m*; élève *m*/

scholarship (*sko*-leu-chip) *n* bourse d'études

school (skoûl) *n* école *f*

schoolboy (*skoûl*-boï) *n* écolier *m*

schoolgirl (*skoûl*-gheûl) *n* écolière *f*

schoolmaster (*skoûl*-mââ-steu) *n* instituteur *m*, maître d'école

schoolteacher (*skoûl*-tii-tcheu) *n* instituteur *m*, institutrice *f*

science (*saï*-eunns) n science f

scientific (saï-eunn-*ti*-fik) adj scientifique

scientist (*saï*-eunn-tist) n savant m

scissors (*si*-zeuz) pl ciseaux mpl

scold (skô^{ou}ld) v gronder; insulter

scooter (*skoû*-teu) n scooter m; patinette f

score (skoo) n nombre de points; v marquer

scorn (skoon) n dédain m, mépris m; v mépriser

Scot (skot) n Ecossais m

Scotch (skotch) adj écossais; **scotch tape** ruban adhésif

Scotland (*skot*-leunnd) Ecosse f

Scottish (*sko*-tich) adj écossais

scout (skaout) n scout m

scrap (skræp) n morceau m

scrapbook (*skræp*-bouk) n album de collage

scrape (skréïp) v racler

scratch (skrætch) v érafler, gratter; n rayure f, égratignure f

scream (skriim) v hurler, crier; n cri m

screen (skriin) n écran m

screw (skroû) n vis f

screwdriver (*skroû*-draï-veu) n tournevis m

scrub (skrab) v frotter; n buisson m

sculptor (*skalp*-teu) n sculpteur m

sculpture (*skalp*-tcheu) n sculpture f

sea (sii) n mer f; ~ **urchin** oursin m; ~ **water** eau de mer

seabird (*sii*-beûd) n oiseau de mer

sea-coast (*sii*-kô^{ou}st) n littoral m

seafood (*sii*-foûd) n fruits mpl de mer

seagull (*sii*-ghal) n mouette f, goéland m

seal (siil) n sceau m; phoque m

seam (siim) n couture f

seaman (*sii*-meunn) n (pl -men) marin m

seamless (*siim*-leuss) adj sans couture

seaport (*sii*-poot) n port de mer

search (seûtch) v chercher; fouiller; n fouille f

searchlight (*seûtch*-laït) n projecteur m

seascape (*sii*-skéïp) n marine f

seashell (*sii*-chèl) n coquillage m

seashore (*sii*-choo) n bord de la mer

seasick (*sii*-sik) adj souffrant du mal de mer

seasickness (*sii*-sik-neuss) n mal de mer

seaside (*sii*-saïd) n bord de la mer; ~ **resort** station balnéaire

season (*sii*-zeunn) n saison f; **high** ~ pleine saison; **low** ~ morte-saison f; **off** ~ hors saison; ~ **ticket** carte d'abonnement

seat (siit) n siège m; place f; ~ **belt** ceinture de sécurité

second (*sè*-keunnd) num deuxième; n seconde f; instant m

secondary (*sè*-keunn-deu-ri) adj secondaire; ~ **school** école secondaire

second-hand (sè-keunnd-*hænd*) adj d'occasion

secret (*sii*-kreut) n secret m; adj secret

secretary (*sè*-kreu-tri) n secrétaire f; secrétaire m

section (*sèk*-cheunn) n section f; case f, service m

secure (si-*kyoueu*) adj sûr; v s'assurer de

security (si-*kyoueu*-reu-ti) n sécurité f; caution f

sedative (*sè*-deu-tiv) n sédatif m

seduce (si-*dyoûss*) v *séduire

***see** (sii) v *voir; *comprendre, se rendre compte; ~ **to** s'occuper de

seed (siid) n semence f

***seek** (siik) v chercher

seem (siim) v *paraître, sembler

seen (siin) *v* (pp see)

seesaw (*sii*-soo) *n* balançoire *f*

seize (siiz) *v* saisir

seldom (*sèl*-deumm) *adv* rarement

select (si-*lèkt*) *v* sélectionner, choisir; *adj* exquis, choisi

selection (si-*lèk*-cheunn) *n* choix *m*, sélection *f*

self (sèlf) (*pl* selves) **the ~** le moi

self-... (sèlf) *pref* de soi; auto-; automatique(ment)

self-centered *Am*, **self-centred** (sèlf-*sèn*-teud) *adj* égocentrique

self-employed (sèl-fimm-*ploïd*) *adj* indépendant

self-evident (sèl-*fè*-vi-deunnt) *adj* évident

self-government (sèlf-*gha*-veu-meunnt) *n* autonomie *f*

selfish (*sèl*-fich) *adj* égoïste

selfishness (*sèl*-fich-neuss) *n* égoïsme *m*

self-service (sèlf-*seû*-viss) *n* libre-service *m*

*sell (sèl) *v* vendre

semblance (*sèm*-bleunns) *n* apparence *f*

semi- (*sè*-mi) semi-

semicircle (*sè*-mi-seû-keul) *n* demicercle *m*

semicolon (*sè*-mi-*kôou*-leunn) *n* point-virgule *m*

senate (*sè*-neut) *n* sénat *m*

senator (*sè*-neu-teu) *n* sénateur *m*

*send (sènd) *v* expédier, *envoyer; **~ back** *renvoyer; **~ for** *faire venir; **~ off** expédier

sender (*sèn*-deu) *n* expéditeur *m*, expéditrice *f*

senile (*sii*-naïl) *adj* sénile

senior (*sii*-nyeu) *adj* aîné; plus âgé (**to** que); supérieur (**to** à); premier; **~ citizens** *pl* personnes *pl* âgées; **~ partner** associé *m* principal; aîné *m*,

aîne *f*; le plus ancien *m*, la plus ancienne *f*; supérieur *m*, supérieure *f*

sensation (sèn-*séï*-cheunn) *n* sensation *f*

sensational (sèn-*séï*-cheu-neul) *adj* spectaculaire, sensationnel

sense (sèns) *n* sens *m*; bon sens, raison *f*; signification *f*; *v* *percevoir; **~ of honour** sens de l'honneur

senseless (*sèns*-leuss) *adj* insensé

sensible (*sèn*-seu-beul) *adj* raisonnable

sensitive (*sèn*-si-tiv) *adj* sensible

sentence (*sèn*-teunns) *n* phrase *f*; jugement *m*; *v* condamner

sentimental (sèn-ti-*mèn*-teul) *adj* sentimental

separate¹ (*sè*-peu-réït) *v* séparer

separate² (*sè*-peu-reut) *adj* distinct, séparé

separately (*sè*-peu-reut-li) *adv* à part

September (sèp-*tèm*-beu) septembre

septic (*sèp*-tik) *adj* septique; ***become ~** s'infecter

sequel (*sii*-k^{ou}eul) *n* suite *f*

sequence (*sii*-k^{ou}eunns) *n* succession *f*; série *f*

serene (seu-*riin*) *adj* serein; clair

serial (*sieu*-ri-eul) *n* feuilleton *m*

series (*sieu*-riiz) *n* (*pl* ~) suite *f*, série *f*

serious (*sieu*-ri-euss) *adj* sérieux

seriousness (*sieu*-ri-euss-neuss) *n* sérieux *m*

sermon (*seû*-meunn) *n* sermon *m*

serum (*sieu*-reumm) *n* sérum *m*

servant (*seû*-veunnt) *n* domestique *m*

serve (seûv) *v* *servir

service (*seû*-viss) *n* service *m*; **~ charge** service *m*; **~ station** station-service *f*

serviette (seû-vi-*èt*) *n* serviette *f*

session (*sè*-cheunn) *n* séance *f*

set (sèt) *n* jeu *m*

*set (sèt) *v* poser; **~ menu** menu fixe; **~**

out *partir

setting (*sè*-tinng) *n* cadre *m*; ~ **lotion** fixateur *m*

settle (*sè*-teul) *v* régler, arranger; ~ **down** s'établir

settlement (*sè*-teul-meunnt) *n* règlement *m*, arrangement *m*, accord *m*

seven (*sè*-veunn) *num* sept

seventeen (*sè*-veunn-*tiin*) *num* dixsept

seventeenth (*sè*-veunn-*tiin*θ) *num* dix-septième

seventh (*sè*-veunnθ) *num* septième

seventy (*sè*-veunn-ti) *num* soixantedix

several (*sè*-veu-reul) *adj* divers, plusieurs

severe (si-*vieu*) *adj* violent, sévère, grave

sew (sô^{ou}) *v* *coudre

sewer (*soû*-eu) *n* égout *m*

sewing machine (*sôou*-inng-meu-chiin) *n* machine à coudre

sex (sèks) *n* sexe *m*

sexual (*sèk*-chou-eul) *adj* sexuel

sexuality (sèk-chou-*æ*-leu-ti) *n* sexualité *f*

shade (chéïd) *n* ombre *f*; nuance *f*

shadow (*chæ*-dô^{ou}) *n* ombre *f*

shady (*chéï*-di) *adj* ombragé

*shake (chéïk) *v* secouer

*shall (chæl) *v* *devoir

shallow (*chæ*-lô^{ou}) *adj* peu profond

shame (chéïm) *n* honte *f*; déshonneur *m*; **shame!** quelle honte!

shampoo (chæm-*poû*) *n* shampooing *m*

shamrock (*chæm*-rok) *n* trèfle *m*

shape (chéïp) *n* forme *f*; *v* former

share (chè^{eu}) *v* partager; *n* part *f*; action *f*

shark (chââk) *n* requin *m*

sharp (chââp) *adj* aigu

sharpen (*chââ*-peunn) *v* affiler, aiguiser

shave (chéïv) *v* se raser

shaver (*chéï*-veu) *n* rasoir électrique

shaving brush (*chéï*-vinng-brach) *n* blaireau *m*

shaving cream (*chéï*-vinng-kriim) *n* crème à raser

shaving soap (*chéï*-vinng-sô^{ou}p) *n* savon à barbe

shawl (chool) *n* châle *m*

she (chii) *pron* elle

shed (chèd) *n* réduit *m*

*shed (chèd) *v* verser; répandre

sheep (chiip) *n* (pl ~) mouton *m*

sheer (chi^{eu}) *adj* absolu, pur

sheet (chiit) *n* drap *m*; feuille *f*; plaque *f*

shelf (chèlf) *n* (pl shelves) étagère *f*

shell (chèl) *n* coquille *f*

shellfish (*chèl*-fich) *n* crustacé *m*

shelter (*chèl*-teu) *n* abri *m*; *v* abriter

shepherd (*chè*-peud) *n* berger *m*

shift (chift) *n* équipe *f*

*shine (chaïn) *v* briller; resplendir

ship (chip) *n* navire *m*; *v* expédier; **shipping line** compagnie de navigation

shipowner (*chi*-pô^{ou}-neu) *n* armateur *m*

shipyard (*chip*-yââd) *n* chantier naval

shirt (cheût) *n* chemise *f*

shiver (*chi*-veu) *v* trembler, frissonner; *n* frisson *m*

shock (chok) *n* choc *m*; *v* choquer; ~ **absorber** amortisseur *m*

shocking (*cho*-kinng) *adj* choquant

shoe (choû) *n* chaussure *f*; **gym shoes** chaussures de gymnastique; ~ **polish** cirage *m*; ~ **shop** magasin de chaussures

shoelace (*choû*-léïss) *n* lacet *m*

shoemaker (*choû*-méï-keu) *n* cordonnier *m*

shook (chouk) v (p shake)

*shoot (choût) v tirer

shop (chop) n boutique f; v *faire des achats; ~ assistant vendeur m, vendeuse f

shopping (cho-pinng) n achats pl; go ~ *faire des achats; ~ bag sac à provisions; ~ centre centre commercial

shopkeeper (chop-kii-peu) n commerçant m, commerçante f

shopwindow (chop-ouinn-dô^ou) n vitrine f

shore (choo) n rive f, rivage m

short (choot) adj court; petit; ~ circuit court-circuit m

shortage (choo-tidj) n carence f, manque m

shorten (choo-teunn) v raccourcir

shortly (choot-li) adv sous peu, prochainement, bientôt

shorts (choots) pl short m; plAm caleçon m

short-sighted (choot-saï-tid) adj myope

shot (chot) n coup de feu; piqûre f; prise de vue

*should (choud) v *devoir

shoulder (chôoul-deu) n épaule f

shout (chaout) v crier; n cri m

shovel (cha-veul) n pelle f

show (chô^ou) n représentation f, spectacle m; exposition f

*show (chô^ou) v montrer; exposer; démontrer

showcase (chôou-kéïss) n vitrine f

shower (chaou^eu) n douche f; averse f

showroom (chôou-roûm) n salle d'exposition

shriek (chriik) v pousser des cris; n cri aigu

shrimp (chrimmp) n crevette f

shrine (chraïn) n sanctuaire m

*shrink (chrinngk) v rétrécir

shrinkproof (chrinngk-proûf) adj irrétrécissable

shrub (chrab) n arbuste m

shudder (cha-deu) n frisson m

shuffle (cha-feul) v *battre

*shut (chat) v fermer; shut clos, fermé; ~ in enfermer

shutter (cha-teu) n persienne f, volet m

shy (chaï) adj farouche, timide

shyness (chaï-neuss) n timidité f

Siamese (saï-eu-miiz) adj siamois; n Siamois m

sick (sik) adj malade; ayant mal au cœur

sickness (sik-neuss) n maladie f; mal au cœur

side (saïd) n côté m; parti m; onesided adj unilatéral; ~ street rue transversale

sideburns (saïd-beûnnz) pl favoris

sidelight (saïd-laït) n lumière latérale

sidewalk (saïd-^ouook) nAm trottoir m

sideways (saïd-^ouéïz) adv de côté

siege (siidj) n siège m

sieve (siv) n passoire f; v tamiser

sift (sift) v tamiser

sight (saït) n vue f; spectacle m; curiosité f

sightseeing (saït-sii-inng) n visite f (de la ville)

sign (saïn) n marque f, signe m; geste m; v signer

signal (sigh-neul) n signal m; signe m; v signaler

signature (sigh-neu-tcheu) n signature f

significant (sigh-ni-fi-keunnt) adj significatif

signpost (saïn-pô^oust) n poteau indicateur

silence (saï-leunns) n silence m; v *faire taire

silencer (saï-leunn-seu) n silencieux

m

silent (*saï*-leunnt) *adj* silencieux; ***be ~** se *taire

silk (silk) *n* soie *f*

silly (*si*-li) *adj* bête, sot

silver (*sil*-veu) *n* argent *m*; en argent

silversmith (*sil*-veu-smiθ) *n* orfèvre *m*

silverware (*sil*-veu-ᵒᵘèᵉᵘ) *n* argenterie *f*

similar (*si*-mi-leu) *adj* analogue, similaire

similarity (si-mi-*læ*-reu-ti) *n* similitude *f*

simple (*simm*-peul) *adj* ingénu, simple; ordinaire

simply (*simm*-pli) *adv* simplement

simulate (*si*-myou-léït) *v* simuler

simultaneous (si-meul-*téï*-ni-euss) *adj* simultané

sin (sinn) *n* péché *m*

since (sinns) *prep* depuis; *adv* depuis; *conj* depuis que; comme

sincere (sinn-*sieu*) *adj* sincère; **Yours sincerely** sincères salutations; veuillez agréer, chère Madame / cher Monsieur, l'expression de mes sentiments distingués

sinew (*si*-nyoû) *n* tendon *m*

*sing (sinng) *v* chanter

singer (*sinng*-eu) *n* chanteur *m*, chanteuse *f*

single (*sinng*-gheul) *adj* seul; célibataire

singular (*sinng*-ghyou-leu) *n* singulier *m*; *adj* singulier

sinister (*si*-ni-steu) *adj* sinistre

sink (sinngk) *n* évier *m*

*sink (sinngk) *v* s'enfoncer

sip (sip) *n* gorgée *f*

sir (seû) monsieur *m*

siren (*saïeu*-reunn) *n* sirène *f*

sister (*si*-steu) *n* sœur *f*

sister-in-law (*si*-steu-rinn-loo) *n* (pl sisters-) belle-sœur *f*

*sit (sit) *v* *être assis; **~ down** s'*asseoir

site (saït) *n* site *m*

sitting room (*si*-tinng-roûm) *n* salon *m*

situated (*si*-tchou-éï-tid) *adj* situé

situation (si-tchou-*éï*-cheunn) *n* situation *f*

six (siks) *num* six

sixteen (siks-*tiin*) *num* seize

sixteenth (siks-*tiin*θ) *num* seizième

sixth (siksθ) *num* sixième

sixty (*siks*-ti) *num* soixante

size (saïz) *n* taille *f*, mesure *f*; dimension *f*, grandeur *f*; format *m*

skate (skéït) *v* patiner; *n* patin *m*

skating (*skéï*-tinng) *n* patinage *m*; **~ rink** patinoire *f*

sketch (skètch) *n* dessin *m*, esquisse *f*; *v* dessiner, esquisser

ski¹ (skii) *v* skier

ski² (skii) *n* (pl ~, ~s) ski *m*; **~ boots** chaussures de ski; **~ jump** saut à ski; **~ lift** téléski *m* **~ pants** pantalon de ski; **~ poles** *Am* bâtons de ski; **~ sticks** bâtons de ski

skid (skid) *v* déraper

skier (*skii*-eu) *n* skieur *m*, skieuse *f*

skiing (*skii*-inng) *n* ski *m*

skil(l)ful (*skil*-feul) *adj* habile, adroit

skill (skil) *n* habileté *f*

skilled (skild) *adj* habile; expert

skin (skinn) *n* peau *f*; **~ cream** crème de beauté

skip (skip) *v* sautiller; sauter

skirt (skeût) *n* jupe *f*

skull (skal) *n* crâne *m*

sky (skaï) *n* ciel *m*; air *m*

skyscraper (*skaï*-skréï-peu) *n* gratteciel *m*

slack (slæk) *adj* lâche; faible

slacks (slæks) *pl* pantalon *m*

slam (slæm) *v* claquer

slander (*slâân*-deu) *n* calomnie *f*

slang (slæng) n argot m
slant (slâânt) v s'incliner
slanting (slâân-tinng) adj oblique, en pente, incliné
slap (slæp) v *battre; n claque f
slate (sléit) n ardoise f
slave (sléiv) n esclave m
sledge (slèdj) n luge f, traîneau m
sleep (sliip) n sommeil m
*****sleep** (sliip) v *dormir
sleeping bag (slii-pinng-bægh) n sac de couchage
sleeping car (slii-pinng-kââ) n wagonlit
sleeping pill (slii-pinng-pil) n somnifère m
sleepless (sliip-leuss) adj sans sommeil
sleepy (slii-pi) adj somnolent
sleeve (sliiv) n manche f; housse f
sleigh (sléi) n luge f, traîneau m
slender (slèn-deu) adj svelte
slice (slaïss) n tranche f
slide (slaïd) n glissade f; toboggan m; diapositive f
*****slide** (slaïd) v glisser
slight (slaït) adj léger; faible
slim (slimm) adj mince; v maigrir
slip (slip) v déraper, glisser; s'échapper; n faux pas; combinaison f
slipper (sli-peu) n pantoufle f
slippery (sli-peu-ri) adj glissant
slope (slôoup) n versant m; v décliner
sloping (slôou-pinng) adj en pente
sloppy (slo-pi) adj négligé
slot (slot) n fente f; ~ **machine** appareil à jetons
slovenly (sla-veunn-li) adj mal soigné
slow (slôou) adj lent; ~ **down** ralentir; freiner
sluice (sloûss) n écluse f
slum (slamm) n bas quartier
slump (slammp) n baisse des prix
slush (slach) n boue f

sly (slaï) adj malin
smack (smæk) v donner une claque; n claque f
small (smool) adj petit; faible
smallpox (smool-poks) n variole f
smart (smâât) adj élégant; adroit, alerte
smash (smæch) v (se)briser, (se)fracasser; n fracas m; coup m (violent); collision f; ~ **hit** succès m
smell (smèl) n odeur f
*****smell** (smèl) v *sentir; *sentir mauvais
smelly (smè-li) adj malodorant
smile (smaïl) v *sourire; n sourire m
smith (smiθ) n forgeron m
smog (smoog) n smog m
smoke (smôouk) v fumer; n fumée f; **no smoking** défense de fumer
smoker (smôou-keu) n fumeur m; compartiment fumeurs
smoking compartment (smôou-kinng-keumm-pâât-meunnt) n compartiment fumeurs
smooth (smoûð) adj uni, plat, lisse; doux
smuggle (sma-gheul) v passer en contrebande
snack (snæk) n casse-croûte m; ~ **bar** snack-bar m
snail (snéil) n escargot m
snake (snéik) n serpent m
snapshot (snæp-chot) n instantané m
sneakers (snii-keuz) plAm chaussures de gymnastique
sneeze (sniiz) v éternuer
snooty (snoû-ti) adj snob
snore (snoo) v ronfler
snorkel (snoo-keul) n tube de plongée
snout (snaout) n museau m
snow (snôou) n neige f; v neiger
snowstorm (snôou-stoom) n tempête de neige
snowy (snôou-i) adj neigeux

so (sô^{ou}) *conj* donc; *adv* ainsi; tellement, si; **and ~ on** et ainsi de suite; **~ far** jusqu'à présent; **~ that** de manière que, pour que, afin que

soak (sô^{ou}k) *v* tremper

soap (sô^{ou}p) *n* savon *m*; **~ powder** savon en poudre

sober (sôou-beu) *adj* sobre; sérieux, posé

so-called (sôou-koold) *adj* soi-disant

soccer (so-keu) *n* football *m*; **~ team** équipe *f*

social (sôou-cheul) *adj* social

socialism (sôou-cheu-li-zeumm) *n* socialisme *m*

socialist (sôou-cheu-list) *adj* socialiste; *n* socialiste *m*

society (seu-saï-eu-ti) *n* société *f*; association *f*; compagnie *f*

sock (sok) *n* chaussette *f*

socket (so-kit) *n* douille *f*

soda water (sôou-deu-^{ou}oo-teu) *n* eau de Seltz

sofa (sôou-feu) *n* canapé *m*

soft (soft) *adj* mou; **~ drink** boisson non alcoolisée

soften (so-feunn) *v* adoucir

software (soft- ouèeu) *n* logiciel *m*

soil (soïl) *n* sol *m*; terroir *m*, terre *f*

soiled (soïld) *adj* souillé

solar (sôou-leu) *adj* solaire; **~ cell** cellule *f* photovoltaïque; **~ eclipse** éclipse *f* du soleil; **~ plexus** plexus *m* solaire

sold (sô^{ou}ld) *v* (p, pp sell); **~ out** épuisé

soldier (sôoul-djeu) *n* soldat *m*

sole[1] (sô^{ou}l) *adj* unique

sole[2] (sô^{ou}l) *n* semelle *f*; sole *f*

solely (sôoul-li) *adv* exclusivement

solemn (so-leumm) *adj* solennel

solicitor (seu-li-si-teu) *n* avoué *m*, avocat *m*

solid (so-lid) *adj* robuste, solide; massif; *n* solide *m*

soluble (so-lyou-beul) *adj* soluble

solution (seu-loû-cheunn) *n* solution *f*

solve (solv) *v* *résoudre

somber *Am*, **somber** (somm-beu) *adj* sombre

some (samm) *adj* quelques; *pron* certains, quelques; un peu; **~ day** un jour ou l'autre; **~ more** encore un peu; **~ time** une fois

somebody (samm-beu-di) *pron* quelqu'un

somehow (samm-haou) *adv* d'une manière ou d'une autre

someone (samm-^{ou}ann) *pron* quelqu'un

something (samm-θinng) *pron* quelque chose

sometimes (samm-taïmz) *adv* parfois

somewhat (samm-^{ou}ot) *adv* quelque peu

somewhere (samm-^{ou}è^eu) *adv* quelque part

son (sann) *n* fils *m*

song (sonng) *n* chanson *f*

son-in-law (sa-ninn-loo) *n* (pl sons-) gendre *m*

soon (soûn) *adv* rapidement, sous peu, prochainement, bientôt; **as ~ as** dès que

sooner (soû-neu) *adv* plutôt

sore (soo) *adj* douloureux; *n* plaie *f*; **~ throat** mal de gorge

sorrow (so-rô^{ou}) *n* tristesse *f*, douleur *f*, chagrin *m*

sorry (so-ri) *adj* désolé; **sorry!** excusez-moi!, pardon!

sort (soot) *v* classer, ranger; *n* catégorie *f*, sorte *f*; **all sorts of** toutes sortes de

soul (sô^{ou}l) *n* âme *f*; esprit *m*

sound (saound) *n* son *m*; *v* sonner; *adj* solide

soundproof (saound-proûf) *adj*

insonorisé

soup (soûp) n soupe f

sour (saou^eu) adj aigre

source (sooss) n source f

south (saouθ) n sud m; **South Pole** pôle sud

South Africa (saouθ æ-fri-keu) Afrique du Sud

South America (saouθ eu-mè-ri-keu) Amérique du Sud

southeast (saouθ-iist) n sud-est m

southerly (sa-ðeu-li) adj méridional

southern (sa-ðeunn) adj méridional

southwest (saouθ-ouèst) n sud-ouest m

souvenir (soû-veu-ni^eu) n souvenir m

sovereign (sov-rinn) n souverain m

*****sow** (sô^ou) v semer

spa (spââ) n station thermale

space (spéïss) n espace m; distance f, intervalle m; v espacer

spacious (spéï-cheuss) adj spacieux

spade (spéïd) n bêche f, pelle f

Spain (spéïn) Espagne f

Spanish (spæ-nich) adj espagnol

spanking (spæng-kinng) n fessée f

spanner (spæ-neu) n clé à écrous

spare (spè^eu) adj de réserve, disponible; v se passer de; ~ **part** pièce détachée; ~ **room** chambre d'ami; ~ **time** temps libre; ~ **tyre** (Am **tire**) pneu de rechange; ~ **wheel** roue de secours

spark (spââk) n étincelle f

sparking plug (spââ-kinng-plagh) n bougie d'allumage

sparkle (spââ-keul) v briller

sparkling (spââ-klinng) adj scintillant; mousseux

sparrow (spæ-rô^ou) n moineau m

*****speak** (spiik) v parler

speaker (spii-keu) n parleur m, parleuse f; haut-parleur m

spear (spi^eu) n lance f

special (spè-cheul) adj particulier, spécial; ~ **delivery** exprès

specialist (spè-cheu-list) n spécialiste m/f

speciality (spè-chi-æ-leu-ti) n spécialité f

specialize (spè-cheu-laïz) v se spécialiser

specially (spè-cheu-li) adv particulièrement

species (spii-chiiz) n (pl ~) espèce f

specific (speu-si-fik) adj spécifique

speck (spèk) n tache f

spectacle (spèk-teu-keul) n spectacle m; **spectacles** lunettes fpl

spectator (spèk-téï-teu) n spectateur m, spectatrice f

speculate (spè-kyou-léït) v spéculer

speech (spiitch) n parole f; allocution f, discours m

speechless (spiitch-leuss) adj interloqué

speed (spiid) n vitesse f; rapidité f, hâte f; **cruising** ~ vitesse de croisière; ~ **limit** limite de vitesse, limitation de vitesse

*****speed** (spiid) v foncer; rouler trop vite

speeding (spii-dinng) n excès de vitesse

speedometer (spii-do-mi-teu) n indicateur de vitesse

spell (spèl) n enchantement m

*****spell** (spèl) v épeler

spelling (spè-linng) n orthographe f

*****spend** (spènd) v dépenser; employer

sphere (sfi^eu) n sphère f

spice (spaïss) n épice f

spiced (spaïst) adj épicé

spicy (spaï-si) adj épicé

spider (spaï-deu) n araignée f; **spider's web** toile d'araignée

*****spill** (spil) v répandre

*****spin** (spinn) v filer; tourner

spinach (*spi*-nidj) *n* épinards *mpl*

spine (spaïn) *n* épine dorsale

spinster (*spinn*-steu) *n* vieille fille

spire (spaï^{eu}) *n* aiguille *f*

spirit (*spi*-rit) *n* esprit *m*; humeur *f*;
spirits boissons alcoolisées,
spiritueux *mpl*; moral *m*; ~ **stove**
réchaud à alcool

spiritual (*spi*-ri-tchou-eul) *adj*
spirituel

spit (spit) *n* crachat *m*, salive *f*; broche
f

***spit** (spit) *v* cracher

spite: in ~ of (inn spaït ov) en dépit de,
malgré

spiteful (*spaït*-feul) *adj* malveillant

splash (splæch) *v* éclabousser

splendid (*splèn*-did) *adj* magnifique,
splendide

splendo(u)r (*splèn*-deu) *n* splendeur *f*

splint (splinnt) *n* éclisse *f*

splinter (*splinn*-teu) *n* écharde *f*

***split** (split) *v* fendre

***spoil** (spoïl) *v* gâter

spoke[1] (spô^{ou}k) *v* (p speak)

spoke[2] (spô^{ou}k) *n* rayon *m*

sponge (spanndj) *n* éponge *f*

spook (spoûk) *n* spectre *m*, fantôme
m

spool (spoûl) *n* bobine *f*

spoon (spoûn) *n* cuillère *f*

spoonful (*spoûn*-foul) *n* cuillerée *f*

sport (spoot) *n* sport *m*

sports car (*spoots*-kââ) *n* voiture de
sport

sports jacket (*spoots*-djæ-kit) *n*
veston sport

sportsman (*spoots*-meunn) *n* (pl
-men) sportif *m*

sportswear (*spoots*-^{ou}è^{eu}) *n*
vêtements de sport

spot (spot) *n* tache *f*; lieu *m*, endroit *m*

spotless (*spot*-leuss) *adj* immaculé

spotlight (*spot*-laït) *n* projecteur *m*

spotted (*spo*-tid) *adj* tacheté

spout (spaout) *n* jet *m*

sprain (spréïn) *v* fouler; *n* foulure *f*

spray (spréï) *n* spray *m*, aérosol *m*; *v*
vaporiser; arroser

***spread** (sprèd) *v* étendre

spring (sprinng) *n* printemps *m*;
ressort *m*; source *f*

springtime (*sprinng*-taïm) *n*
printemps *m*

sprouts (spraouts) **Brussels ~** *pl*
choux de Bruxelles

spy (spaï) *n* espion *m*

square (sk^{ou}è^{eu}) *adj* carré; *n* carré *m*;
square *m*, place *f*

squash (sk^{ou}och) *n* sirop *m*; Am
courgette

squeeze (sk^{ou}iiz) *v* serrer; presser;
extorquer (**from** à); ~ **out** exprimer

squirrel (sk^{ou}i-reul) *n* écureuil *m*

squirt (sk^{ou}eût) *n* jet *m*

stable (*stéï*-beul) *adj* stable; *n* étable *f*

stack (stæk) *n* pile *f*

stadium (*stéï*-di-eumm) *n* stade *m*

staff (stââf) *n* personnel *m*

stage (stéïdj) *n* scène *f*; phase *f*, étape *f*

stain (stéïn) *v* tacher; *n* tache *f*;
stained glass verre de couleur; ~
remover détachant *m*

stainless (*stéïn*-leuss) *adj* immaculé; ~
steel acier inoxydable

staircase (*stèeu*-kéïss) *n* escalier *m*

stairs (stè^{eu}z) *pl* escalier *m*

stale (stéïl) *adj* rassis

stall (stool) *n* étal *m*; **seat in the stalls**
fauteuil d'orchestre

stamp (stæmp) *n* timbre *m*; *v*
affranchir; piétiner; ~ **machine**
distributeur de timbres

stand (stænd) *n* stand *m*; tribune *f*

***stand** (stænd) *v* se *tenir debout

standard (*stæn*-deud) *n* norme *f*;
standard; ~ **of living** niveau de vie

stanza (*stæn*-zeu) *n* strophe *f*

staple (*stéï*-peul) *n* agrafe *f*

star (*stââ*) *n* étoile *f*

starboard (*stââ*-beud) *n* tribord *m*

stare (*stè*^{eu}) *v* fixer

starling (*stââ*-linng) *n* étourneau *m*

start (*stâât*) *v* commencer; *n* début *m*

starting point (*stââ*-tinng-poïnt) *n* point de départ

state (*stéït*) *n* Etat *m*; état *m*; *v* déclarer; **the States** les Etats-Unis

statement (*stéït*-meunnt) *n* déclaration *f*

statesman (*stéïts*-meunn) *n* (pl -men) homme d'Etat

station (*stéï*-cheunn) *n* gare *f*; poste *m*

stationary (*stéï*-cheu-neu-ri) *adj* stationnaire

stationer's (*stéï*-cheu-neuz) *n* papeterie *f*

stationery (*stéï*-cheu-neu-ri) *n* papeterie *f*

statistics (steu-*ti*-stiks) *pl* statistique *f*

statue (*stæ*-tchoû) *n* statue *f*

stay (*stéï*) *v* rester; séjourner; *n* séjour *m*

steadfast (*stèd*-fââst) *adj* ferme

steady (*stè*-di) *adj* ferme

steak (*stéïk*) *n* bifteck *m*

*steal (stiil) *v* voler

steam (stiim) *n* vapeur *f*

steamer (*stii*-meu) *n* bateau à vapeur *m*

steel (stiil) *n* acier *m*

steep (stiip) *adj* abrupt, escarpé

steeple (*stii*-peul) *n* clocher *m*

steering column (*stieu*-rinng-koleumm) *n* colonne de direction

steering wheel (*stieu*-rinng-^{ou}iil) *n* volant *m*

stem (stèm) *n* tige *f*

step (stèp) *n* pas *m*; marche *f*; *v* marcher

stepchild (*stèp*-tchaïld) *n* (pl -children) enfant d'un autre lit

stepfather (*stèp*-fââ-ðeu) *n* beau-père *m*

stepmother (*stèp*-ma-ðeu) *n* belle-mère *f*

stereo (*stè*-ri-ô^{ou}) *n* stéréo *f*

sterile (*stè*-raïl) *adj* stérile

sterilize (*stè*-ri-laïz) *v* stériliser

stern (steûn) *adj* sévère

steward (*styoû*-eud) *n* steward *m*

stewardess (*styoû*-eu-dèss) *n* hôtesse de l'air

stick (stik) *n* bâton *m*

*stick (stik) *v* coller

sticky (*sti*-ki) *adj* gluant

stiff (stif) *adj* raide

still (stil) *adv* encore; toutefois; *adj* tranquille

stimulant (*sti*-myou-leunnt) *n* stimulant *m*

stimulate (*sti*-myou-léït) *v* stimuler

sting (stinng) *n* piqûre *f*

*sting (stinng) *v* piquer

stingy (*stinn*-dji) *adj* mesquin

*stink (stinngk) *v* puer

stir (steû) *v* bouger; remuer

stitch (stitch) *n* point *m*, point de côté; suture *f*

stock (stok) *n* stock *m*; *v* *avoir en stock; ~ **exchange** bourse des valeurs, bourse *f*; ~ **market** marché des valeurs; **stocks and shares** actions

stocking (*sto*-kinng) *n* bas *m*

stole¹ (stô^{ou}l) *v* (p steal)

stole² (stô^{ou}l) *n* étole *f*

stomach (*sta*-meuk) *n* estomac *m*; ~ **ache** mal au ventre, mal d'estomac

stone (stô^{ou}n) *n* pierre *f*; pierre précieuse; noyau *m*; en pierre; **pumice** ~ pierre ponce

stood (stoud) *v* (p, pp stand)

stop (stop) *v* arrêter; cesser; *n* arrêt *m*; **stop!** stop!

stopper (*sto*-peu) *n* bouchon *m*

storage (*stoo*-ridj) *n* emmagasinage *m*

store (stoo) *n* provision *f*; magasin *m*; *v* emmagasiner; **~ house** magasin *m*

stor(e)y (*stoo*-ri) *n* étage *m*

stork (stook) *n* cigogne *f*

storm (stoom) *n* tempête *f*

stormy (*stoo*-mi) *adj* orageux

story (*stoo*-ri) *n* histoire *f*

stout (staout) *adj* gros, obèse, corpulent

stove (stô^{ou}v) *n* fourneau *m*; cuisinière *f*

straight (stréit) *adj* droit; *adv* directement; **~ ahead** tout droit; **~ away** directement, tout de suite; **~ on** tout droit

strain (stréïn) *n* effort *m*; tension *f*; *v* forcer

strainer (*stréï*-neu) *n* passoire *f*

strange (stréïndj) *adj* étrange; bizarre

stranger (*stréïn*-djeu) *n* étranger *m*; inconnu *m*

strangle (*stræng*-gheul) *v* étrangler

strap (stræp) *n* courroie *f*

straw (stroo) *n* paille *f*

strawberry (*stroo*-beu-ri) *n* fraise *f*

stream (striim) *n* ruisseau *m*; courant *m*; *v* couler

street (striit) *n* rue *f*

streetcar (*striit*-kââ) *nAm* tram *m*

strength (strèngθ) *n* vigueur *f*, force *f*

stress (strèss) *n* tension *f*; accent *m*; *v* souligner

stretch (strètch) *v* tendre; *n* section *f*

strict (strikt) *adj* sévère

strike (straïk) *n* grève *f*

***strike** (straïk) *v* frapper; *faire grève; amener

striking (*straï*-kinng) *adj* frappant, remarquable

string (strinng) *n* ficelle *f*; corde *f*

strip (strip) *n* bande *f*

stripe (straïp) *n* raie *f*

striped (straïpt) *adj* rayé

stroke (strô^{ou}k) *n* attaque *f*

stroll (strô^{ou}l) *v* flâner; *n* promenade *f*

strong (stronng) *adj* fort; puissant

stronghold (*stronng*-hô^{ou}ld) *n* place forte

structure (*strak*-tcheu) *n* structure *f*

struggle (*stra*-gheul) *n* combat *m*, lutte *f*; *v* lutter

stub (stab) *n* souche *f*

stubborn (*sta*-beunn) *adj* têtu

student (*styoû*-deunnt) *n* étudiant *m*; étudiante *f*

study (*sta*-di) *v* étudier; *n* étude *f*; cabinet *m*

stuff (staf) *n* substance *f*; fatras *m*

stuffed (staft) *adj* farci

stuffing (*sta*-finng) *n* farce *f*

stuffy (*sta*-fi) *adj* mal aéré

stumble (*stamm*-beul) *v* trébucher

stung (stanng) *v* (p, pp sting)

stupid (*styoû*-pid) *adj* stupide

style (staïl) *n* style *m*

stylish (*staï*-lich) *adj* élégant; chic; à la mode

subject¹ (*sab*-djikt) *n* sujet *m*; **~ to** sujet à

subject² (seub-*djèkt*) *v* *soumettre

submarine (sab-meu-*riin*) *n* sous-marin *m*

submit (seub-*mit*) *v* se *soumettre

subordinate (seu-*boo*-di-neut) *adj* subordonné; secondaire

subscriber (seub-*skraï*-beu) *n* abonné *m*

subscription (seub-*skrip*-cheunn) *n* abonnement *m*

subsequent (*sab*-si-k^{ou}eunnt) *adj* postérieur

subsidy (*sab*-si-di) *n* subvention *f*

substance (*sab*-steunns) *n* substance *f*

substantial (seub-*stæn*-cheul) *adj* matériel; réel; substantiel

substitute (*sab*-sti-tyoût) *v* substituer; *n* substitut *m*

subtitle (*sab*-taï-teul) *n* sous-titre *m*

subtle (*sa*-teul) *adj* subtil

subtract (seub-*trækt*) *v* *soustraire

suburb (*sa*-beûb) *n* banlieue *f*, faubourg *m*

suburban (seu-*beû*-beunn) *adj* suburbain

subway (*sab*-⁰ᵘéï) *nAm* métro *m*

succeed (seuk-*siid*) *v* réussir; succéder

success (seuk-*sèss*) *n* succès *m*

successful (seuk-*sèss*-feul) *adj* réussi

succumb (seu-*kamm*) *v* succomber

such (satch) *adj* tel; *adv* tellement; ~ **as** tel que

suck (sak) *v* sucer

sudden (*sa*-deunn) *adj* soudain

suddenly (*sa*-deunn-li) *adv* soudain

suede (s⁰ᵘéïd) *n* daim *m*

suffer (*sa*-feu) *v* *souffrir; subir

suffering (*sa*-feu-rinng) *n* souffrance *f*

suffice (seu-*faïss*) *v* *suffire

sufficient (seu-*fi*-cheunnt) *adj* adéquat, suffisant

suffrage (*sa*-fridj) *n* droit de vote, suffrage *m*

sugar (*chou*-gheu) *n* sucre *m*

suggest (seu-*djèst*) *v* suggérer

suggestion (seu-*djèss*-tcheunn) *n* suggestion *f*

suicide (*soû*-i-saïd) *n* suicide *m*

suit (soût) *v* *convenir; adapter à; bien *aller; *n* complet *m*

suitable (*soû*-teu-beul) *adj* qui convient, approprié

suitcase (*soût*-kéïss) *n* valise *f*

suite (s⁰ᵘiit) *n* appartement *m*

sum (samm) *n* somme *f*

summary (*sa*-meu-ri) *n* sommaire *m*, résumé *m*

summer (*sa*-meu) *n* été *m*; ~ **time** heure d'été

summit (*sa*-mit) *n* sommet *m*

sun (sann) *n* soleil *m*

sunbathe (*sann*-béïð) *v* *prendre un bain de soleil

sunburn (*sann*-beûnn) *n* coup de soleil

Sunday (*sann*-di) dimanche *m*

sunglasses (*sann*-ghlââ-siz) *pl* lunettes de soleil

sunlight (*sann*-laït) *n* lumière du soleil

sunny (*sa*-ni) *adj* ensoleillé

sunrise (*sann*-raïz) *n* lever du soleil

sunset (*sann*-sèt) *n* coucher du soleil

sunshade (*sann*-chéïd) *n* parasol *m*

sunshine (*sann*-chaïn) *n* soleil *m*

sunstroke (*sann*-strô⁰ᵘk) *n* insolation *f*

suntan oil (*sann*-tæn-oïl) huile solaire

super (*soû*-peu) *adj colloquial* super

superb (sou-*peûb*) *adj* grandiose, superbe

superficial (soû-peu-*fi*-cheul) *adj* superficiel

superfluous (sou-*peû*-flou-euss) *adj* superflu

superior (sou-*pieu*-ri-eu) *adj* supérieur, majeur

supermarket (*soû*-peu-mââ-kit) *n* supermarché *m*

superstition (soû-peu-*sti*-cheunn) *n* superstition *f*

supervise (*soû*-peu-vaïz) *v* superviser

supervision (soû-peu-*vi*-jeunn) *n* supervision *f*, surveillance *f*

supervisor (*soû*-peu-vaï-zeu) *n* surveillant *m*

supper (*sa*-peu) *n* souper *m*

supple (*sa*-peul) *adj* souple

supplement (*sa*-pli-meunnt) *n* supplément *m*

supply (seu-*plaï*) *n* fourniture *f*; stock *m*; offre *f*; *v* fournir

support (seu-*poot*) *v* supporter, *soutenir; *n* soutien *m*; ~ **hose** bas élastiques

supporter (seu-*poo*-teu) *n* supporter *m*

suppose (seu-*pôouz*) *v* supposer; **supposing that** en admettant que

suppository (seu-*po*-zi-teu-ri) *n* suppositoire *m*

suppress (seu-*prèss*) *v* réprimer

surcharge (*seû*-tchââdj) *n* supplément *m*

sure (chou^eu) *adj* sûr

surely (*choueu*-li) *adv* sûrement

surface (*seû*-fiss) *n* surface *f*

surgeon (*seû*-djeunn) *n* chirurgien *m*; **veterinary ~** vétérinaire *m*

surgery (*seû*-djeu-ri) *n* opération *f*; cabinet de consultations

surname (*seû*-néïm) *n* nom de famille

surplus (*seû*-pleuss) *n* surplus *m*

surprise (seu-*praïz*) *n* surprise *f*; *v* *surprendre

surrender (seu-*rèn*-deu) *v* se rendre; *n* reddition *f*

surround (seu-*raound*) *v* entourer

surrounding (seu-*raoun*-dinng) *adj* environnant

surroundings (seu-*raoun*-dinngz) *pl* alentours *mpl*

survey (*seû*-véï) *n* résumé *m*

survival (seu-*vaï*-veul) *n* survie *f*

survive (seu-*vaïv*) *v* *survivre

suspect[1] (seu-*spèkt*) *v* soupçonner; suspecter

suspect[2] (*sa*-spèkt) *n* suspect *m*, -e *f*

suspend (seu-*spènd*) *v* suspendre

suspenders (seu-*spèn*-deuz) *plAm* bretelles *fpl*

suspension (seu-*spèn*-cheunn) *n* suspension *f*; **~bridge** pont suspendu

suspicion (seu-*spi*-cheunn) *n* soupçon *m*; soupçons *mpl*

suspicious (seu-*spi*-cheuss) *adj* suspect; soupçonneux, méfiant

sustain (seu-*stéïn*) *v* endurer

swallow (*souo*-lô^ou) *v* avaler; *n* hirondelle *f*

swam (s^ou æm) *v* (p swim)

swamp (s^ou ommp) *n* marais *m*

swan (s^ou onn) *n* cygne *m*

swap (s^ou op) *v* troquer

***swear** (s^ou è^eu) *v* jurer

sweat (s^ou èt) *n* sueur *f*; *v* suer

sweater (*souè*-teu) *n* chandail *m*

Swede (s^ou iid) *n* Suédois *m*

Sweden (*souii*-deunn) Suède *f*

Swedish (*souii*-dich) *adj* suédois

***sweep** (s^ou iip) *v* balayer

sweet (s^ou iit) *adj* sucré; gentil; *n* bonbon *m*; dessert *m*; **sweets** douceurs *fpl*, bonbons

sweeten (*souii*-teunn) *v* sucrer

sweetheart (*souiit*-hâât) *n* mon amour, chéri *m*

sweetshop (*souiit*-chop) *n* confiserie *f*

swell (s^ou èl) *adj* formidable

***swell** (s^ou èl) *v* enfler

swelling (*souè*-linng) *n* enflure *f*

swift (s^ou ift) *adj* rapide

***swim** (s^ou imm) *v* nager

swimmer (*soui*-meu) *n* nageur *m*, nageuse *f*

swimming (*soui*-minng) *n* natation *f*; **~ pool** piscine *f*

swimmingtrunks (*soui*-minng-tranngks) *n* caleçon de bain

swimsuit (*souimm*-soût) *n* maillot de bain

swindle (*souinn*-deul) *v* escroquer; escroquerie *f*

swindler (*souinn*-dleu) *n* escroc *m*

swing (s^ou inng) *n* balançoire *f*

***swing** (s^ou inng) *v* balancer

Swiss (s^ou iss) *adj* suisse; *n* Suisse *m*

switch (s^ou itch) *n* commutateur *m*; *v* changer; **~ off** *éteindre; **~ on** allumer

switchboard (*souitch*-bood) *n* tableau de distribution

Switzerland (*souit*-seu-leunnd) Suisse *f*

sword (sood) *n* épée *f*

swum (s^{ou}amm) *v* (pp swim)

syllable (*si*-leu-beul) *n* syllabe *f*

symbol (*simm*-beul) *n* symbole *m*

sympathetic (simm-peu-θè-tik) *adj* compatissant, de sympathie

sympathy (*simm*-peu-θi) *n* sympathie *f*; compassion *f*

symphony (*simm*-feu-ni) *n* symphonie *f*

symptom (*simm*-teumm) *n* symptôme *m*

synagogue (*si*-neu-ghogh) *n* synagogue *f*

synonym (*si*-neu-nimm) *n* synonyme

m

synthetic (sinn-θè-tik) *adj* synthétique

syphon (*saï*-feunn) *n* siphon *m*

Syria (*si*-ri-eu) Syrie *f*

Syrian (*si*-ri-eunn) *adj* syrien; *n* Syrien *m*

syringe (si-*rinndj*) *n* seringue *f*

syrup (*si*-reup) *n* sirop *m*

system (*si*-steumm) *n* système *m*; **decimal ~** système décimal

systematic (si-steu-*mæ*-tik) *adj* systématique

T

table (*téi*-beul) *n* table *f*; **~ of contents** table des matières; **~ tennis** ping-pong *m*

tablecloth (*téi*-beul-kloθ) *n* nappe *f*

tablespoon (*téi*-beul-spoûn) *n* cuillère *f*

tablet (*tæ*-blit) *n* tablette *f*

taboo (teu-*boû*) *n* tabou *m*

tactics (*tæk*-tiks) *pl* tactique *f*

tag (tægh) *n* étiquette *f*

tail (téil) *n* queue *f*

taillight (*téil*-laït) *n* feu arrière

tailor (*téi*-leu) *n* tailleur *m*

tailor-made (*téi*-leu-méïd) *adj* fait sur mesure

*take (téïk) *v* *prendre; saisir; *conduire; **~ away** emporter; enlever; **~ off** décoller; **~ out** ôter; **~ over** *reprendre; **~ place** *avoir lieu; **~ up** occuper

take-off (*téï*-kof) *n* décollage *m*

tale (téïl) *n* conte *m*, récit *m*

talent (*tæ*-leunnt) *n* don *m*, talent *m*

talented (*tæ*-leunn-tid) *adj* doué

talk (took) *v* parler; *n* conversation *f*

talkative (*too*-keu-tiv) *adj* bavard

tall (tool) *adj* haut; grand

tame (téïm) *adj* domestiqué, apprivoisé; *v* apprivoiser

tampon (*tæm*-peunn) *n* tampon *m*

tangerine (tæn-djeu-*riin*) *n* mandarine *f*

tangible (*tæn*-dji-beul) *adj* tangible

tank (tængk) *n* réservoir *m*

tanker (*tæng*-keu) *n* bateau-citerne *m*

tanned (tænd) *adj* hâlé

tap (tæp) *n* robinet *m*; coup *m*; *v* frapper

tape (téïp) *n* bande *f*, ruban *m*; **adhesive ~** ruban adhésif; **~ recorder** magnétophone *m*

tar (tââ) *n* goudron *m*

target (*tââ*-ghit) *n* objectif *m*, cible *f*

tariff (*tæ*-rif) *n* taux *m*

task (tââsk) *n* tâche *f*

taste (téïst) *n* goût *m*; *v* *avoir goût de; goûter

tasteless (*téïst*-leuss) *adj* insipide

tasty (*téï*-sti) *adj* succulent, savoureux

taught (toot) *v* (p, pp teach)

tavern (*tæ*-veunn) *n* taverne *f*

tax (tæks) *n* impôt *m*; *v* imposer

tax-free (*tæks*-frii) *adj* exempt d'impôts

taxi (*tæk*-si) *n* taxi *m*; ~ **driver** chauffeur de taxi; ~ **rank** station de taxis; ~ **stand** *Am* station de taxis

taximeter (*tæk*-si-mii-teu) *n* taximètre *m*

tea (tii) *n* thé *m*; ~ **set** service à thé; ~ **towel** torchon *m*

teach (tiitch) *v* *apprendre, enseigner

teacher (*tii*-tcheu) *n* professeur *m*, maître *m*; instituteur *m*, institutrice *f*, maître d'école

teachings (*tii*-tchinngz) *pl* enseignements

teacup (*tii*-kap) *n* tasse à thé

team (tiim) *n* équipe *f*

teapot (*tii*-pot) *n* théière *f*

tear[1] (ti*eu*) *n* larme *f*

tear[2] (tè*eu*) *n* déchirure *f*; *tear *v* déchirer

tear-jerker (*tieu*-djeû-keu) *n* mélo *m*

tease (tiiz) *v* taquiner

teashop (*tii*-chop) *n* pâtisserie-salon de thé

teaspoon (*tii*-spoun) *n* cuillère à thé

teaspoonful (*tii*-spoûn-foul) *n* cuillerée à thé

technical (*tèk*-ni-keul) *adj* technique

technician (tèk-*ni*-cheunn) *n* technicien *m*

technique (tèk-*niik*) *n* technique *f*

technology (tèk-*no*-leu-dji) *n* technologie *f*

teenager (*tii*-néï-djeu) *n* adolescent *m*, -e *f*

teetotaller (tii-*tôou*-teu-leu) *n* antialcoolique *m*

telegram (*tè*-li-ghræm) *n* télégramme *m*

telephone (*tè*-li-fô*ou*n) *n* téléphone *m*; ~ **book** *Am* annuaire téléphonique; ~ **booth** cabine téléphonique; ~ **call** coup de téléphone, appel téléphonique; ~ **directory** annuaire téléphonique, bottin *m*; ~ **exchange** central téléphonique

television (*tè*-li-vi-jeunn) *n* télévision *f*; ~ **set** télévision *f*; **cable** ~ télévision par câble; **satellite** ~ télévision par satellite

telex (*tè*-lèks) *n* télex *m*

tell (tèl) *v* *dire; raconter

telly (*tè*-li) *n colloquial* télé *f*

temper (*tèm*-peu) *n* colère *f*

temperature (*tèm*-preu-tcheu) *n* température *f*

tempest (*tèm*-pist) *n* tempête *f*

temple (*tèm*-peul) *n* temple *m*; tempe *f*

temporary (*tèm*-peu-reu-ri) *adj* provisoire, temporaire

tempt (tèmpt) *v* tenter

temptation (tèmp-*téï*-cheunn) *n* tentation *f*

ten (tèn) *num* dix

tenant (*tè*-neunnt) *n* locataire *m*

tend (tènd) *v* *avoir tendance; soigner; ~ **to** tendre à

tendency (*tèn*-deunn-si) *n* inclination *f*, tendance *f*

tender (*tèn*-deu) *adj* tendre, délicat

tendon (*tèn*-deunn) *n* tendon *m*

tennis (*tè*-niss) *n* tennis *m*; ~ **court** court de tennis; ~ **shoes** chaussures de tennis

tense (tèns) *adj* tendu

tension (*tèn*-cheunn) *n* tension *f*

tent (tènt) *n* tente *f*

tenth (tènθ) *num* dixième

tepid (*tè*-pid) *adj* tiède

term (teûmm) *n* terme *m*; période *f*; condition *f*

terminal (*teû*-mi-neul) *n* terminus *m*

terrace (tè-reuss) n terrasse f

terrain (tè-rě́in) n terrain m

terrible (tè-ri-beul) adj épouvantable, terrible

terrific (teu-ri-fik) adj formidable

terrify (tè-ri-faï) v terrifier

territory (tè-ri-teu-ri) n territoire m

terror (tè-reu) n terreur f

terrorism (tè-reu-ri-zeumm) n terrorisme m

terrorist (tè-reu-rist) n terroriste m/f

test (tèst) n test m, épreuve f; v essayer, éprouver

testify (tè-sti-faï) v témoigner

text (tèkst) n texte m

textbook (tèks-bouk) n manuel m

textile (tèk-staïl) n textile m

Thai (taï) adj thaïlandais; n Thaïlandais m

Thailand (taï-lænd) Thaïlande f

than (ðæn) conj que

thank (θængk) v remercier; ~ you merci

thankful (θængk-feul) adj reconnaissant

that (ðæt) adj ce; pron celui-là, cela; qui; conj que

thaw (θoo) v dégeler, fondre; n dégel m

the (ðeu, ði) art le art; **the ... the** plus ... plus

theater Am, **theatre** (θieu-teu) n théâtre m

theft (θèft) n vol m

their (ðè^{eu}) adj leur

them (ðèm) pron les; leur

theme (θiim) n thème m, sujet m

themselves (ðeumm-sèlvz) pron se; eux-mêmes

then (ðèn) adv alors; ensuite, puis

theology (θi-o-leu-dji) n théologie f

theoretical (θi^{eu}-rè-ti-keul) adj théorique

theory (θieu-ri) n théorie f

therapy (θè-reu-pi) n thérapie f

there (ðè^{eu}) adv là

therefore (ðèeu-foo) conj donc

thermometer (θeu-mo-mi-teu) n thermomètre m

thermostat (θeû-meu-stæt) n thermostat m

these (ðiiz) adj ces

thesis (θii-siss) n (pl theses) thèse f

they (ðéï) pron ils

thick (θik) adj gros; épais

thicken (θi-keunn) v épaissir

thickness (θik-neuss) n épaisseur f

thief (θiif) n (pl thieves) voleur m, voleuse f

thigh (θaï) n cuisse f

thimble (θimm-beul) n dé m

thin (θinn) adj mince; maigre

thing (θinng) n chose f

*think (θinngk) v penser; réfléchir; ~ of penser à; songer à; ~ over réfléchir à

third (θeûd) num troisième

thirst (θeûst) n soif f

thirsty (θeû-sti) adj assoiffé

thirteen (θeû-tiin) num treize

thirteenth (θeû-tiinθ) num treizième

thirtieth (θeû-ti-euθ) num trentième

thirty (θeû-ti) num trente

this (ðiss) adj ce; pron ceci

thistle (θi-seul) n chardon m

thorn (θoon) n épine f

thorough (θa-reu) adj minutieux, soigné

thoroughfare (θa-reu-fè^{eu}) n route principale, artère f

those (ðô^{ou}z) adj ces; pron ceux-là

though (ðô^{ou}) conj bien que, encore que, quoique; adv pourtant

thought^1 (θoot) v (p, pp think)

thought^2 (θoot) n pensée f

thoughtful (θoot-feul) adj pensif; prévenant

thousand (θaou-zeunnd) num mille

thread (θrèd) *n* fil *m*; *v* enfiler

threadbare (θréd-bè^{eu}) *adj* usé

threat (θrèt) *n* menace *f*

threaten (θrè-teunn) *v* menacer; **threatening** menaçant

three (θrii) *num* trois

three-quarter (θrii-*kouoo*-teu) *adj* trois quarts

threshold (θrè-chô^{ou}ld) *n* seuil *m*

threw (θroû) *v* (p throw)

thrifty (θrif-ti) *adj* parcimonieux

throat (θrô^{ou}t) *n* gorge *f*

throne (θrô^{ou}n) *n* trône *m*

through (θroû) *prep* à travers

throughout (θroû-*aout*) *adv* partout

throw (θrô^{ou}) *n* lancement *m*

***throw** (θrô^{ou}) *v* jeter, lancer

thrush (θrach) *n* grive *f*

thumb (θamm) *n* pouce *m*

thumbtack (θamm-tæk) *nAm* punaise *f*

thump (θammp) *v* marteler

thunder (θann-deu) *n* tonnerre *m*; *v* tonner

thunderstorm (θann-deu-stoom) *n* orage *m*

thundery (θann-deu-ri) *adj* orageux

Thursday (θêûz-di) jeudi *m*

thus (ðass) *adv* ainsi

thyme (taïm) *n* thym *m*

tick (tik) *n* coche *f*; ~ **off** pointer

ticket (ti-kit) *n* billet *m*; contravention *f*; ~ **collector** contrôleur *m*; ~ **machine** distributeur de billets

tickle (ti-keul) *v* chatouiller

tide (taïd) *n* marée *f*; **high** ~ marée haute; **low** ~ marée basse

tidy (taï-di) *adj* ordonné; ~ **up** ranger

tie (taï) *v* nouer, attacher; *n* cravate *f*

tiger (taï-gheu) *n* tigre *m*

tight (taït) *adj* serré; étroit, juste; *adv* fortement

tighten (taï-teunn) *v* serrer; resserrer; se resserrer

tights (taïts) *pl* collants *mpl*

tile (taïl) *n* carreau *m*; tuile *f*

till (til) *prep* jusqu'à; *conj* jusqu'à ce que

timber (timm-beu) *n* bois d'œuvre

time (taïm) *n* temps *m*; fois *f*; **all the** ~ continuellement; **in** ~ à temps; ~ **of arrival** heure d'arrivée; ~ **of departure** heure de départ

time-saving (taïm-séï-vinng) *adj* qui fait gagner du temps

timetable (taïm-téï-beul) *n* horaire *m*

timid (ti-mid) *adj* timide

timidity (ti-mi-deu-ti) *n* timidité *f*

tin (tinn) *n* étain *m*; boîte *f*; ~ **opener** ouvreboîte *m*; **tinned food** conserves *fpl*

tinfoil (tinn-foïl) *n* papier d'étain

tiny (taï-ni) *adj* minuscule

tip (tip) *n* bout *m*; pourboire *m*

tire¹ (taï^{eu}) *n* pneu *m*; ~ **pressure** pression des pneus

tire² (taï^{eu}) *v* fatiguer

tired (taï^{eu}d) *adj* fatigué; ~ **of** las de

tiring (taïeu-rinng) *adj* fatigant

tissue (ti-choû) *n* tissu *m*; mouchoir de papier

title (taï-teul) *n* titre *m*

to (toû) *prep* jusque; à, pour, chez; afin de

toad (tô^{ou}d) *n* crapaud *m*

toadstool (tôoud-stoûl) *n* champignon *m*

toast (tô^{ou}st) *n* toast *m*

tobacco (teu-*bæ*-kô^{ou}) *n* (pl ~s) tabac *m*; ~ **pouch** blague à tabac

tobacconist (teu-*bæ*-keu-nist) *n* débitant de tabac; **tobacconist's** bureau de tabac

today (teu-*déï*) *adv* aujourd'hui

toddler (tod-leu) *n* bambin *m*

toe (tô^{ou}) *n* orteil *m*

toffee (to-fi) *n* caramel *m*

together (teu-*ghè*-ðeu) *adv* ensemble

toilet (*toï*-leut) *n* toilettes *fpl*; ~ **case** nécessaire de toilette; ~ **paper** papier hygiénique

toiletry (*toï*-leu-tri) *n* articles de toilette

token (*tôou*-keunn) *n* signe *m*; jeton *m*

told (tôould) *v* (p, pp tell)

tolerable (*to*-leu-reu-beul) *adj* tolérable

toll (tôoul) *n* péage *m*

tomato (teu-*mââ*-tôou) *n* (pl ~es) tomate *f*

tomb (toûm) *n* tombe *f*

tombstone (*toûm*-stôoun) *n* pierre tombale

tomorrow (teu-*mo*-rôou) *adv* demain

ton (tann) *n* tonne *f*

tone (tôoun) *n* ton *m*; timbre *m*

tongs (tonngz) *pl* pince *f*

tongue (tanng) *n* langue *f*

tonic (*to*-nik) *n* tonique *m*

tonight (teu-*naït*) *adv* cette nuit, ce soir

tonsillitis (tonn-seu-*laï*-tiss) *n* amygdalite *f*

tonsils (*tonn*-seulz) *pl* amygdales *fpl*

too (toû) *adv* trop; aussi

took (touk) *v* (p take)

tool (toûl) *n* instrument *m*, outil *m*; ~ **kit** boîte à outils

toot (toût) *vAm* klaxonner

tooth (toûθ) *n* (pl teeth) dent *f*

toothache (*toû*-θéïk) *n* mal aux dents

toothbrush (*toûθ*-brach) *n* brosse à dents

toothpaste (*toûθ*-péïst) *n* pâte dentifrice

toothpick (*toûθ*-pik) *n* cure-dent *m*

toothpowder (*toûθ*-paou-deu) *n* poudre dentifrice

top (top) *n* sommet *m*; dessus *m*; couvercle *m*; supérieur; **on** ~ **of** au-dessus de; ~ **side** haut *m*

topic (*to*-pik) *n* sujet *m*

topical (*to*-pi-keul) *adj* actuel

torch (tootch) *n* torche *f*; lampe de poche

torment[1] (too-*mènt*) *v* tourmenter

torment[2] (*too*-mènt) *n* tourment *m*

torture (*too*-tcheu) *n* torture *f*; *v* torturer

toss (toss) *v* lancer

tot (tot) *n* bambin *m*

total (*tôou*-teul) *adj* total; complet, absolu; *n* total *m*

totalitarian (tôou-tæ-li-*tèeu*-ri-eunn) *adj* totalitaire

touch (tatch) *v* toucher; *n* contact *m*, attouchement *m*; toucher *m*

touching (*ta*-tchinng) *adj* touchant

tough (taf) *adj* coriace

tour (toueu) *n* excursion *f*

tourism (*toueu*-ri-zeumm) *n* tourisme *m*

tourist (*toueu*-rist) *n* touriste *m/f*; ~ **class** classe touriste; ~ **office** syndicat d'initiative

tournament (*toueu*-neu-meunnt) *n* tournoi *m*

tow (tôou) *v* remorquer

towards (teu-*ouoodz*) *prep* vers; envers

towel (taoueul) *n* serviette *f*

towel(l)ing (*taoueu*-linng) *n* tissu-éponge *m*

tower (taoueu) *n* tour *f*

town (taoun) *n* ville *f*; ~ **centre** centre de la ville; ~ **hall** hôtel de ville

townspeople (*taounz*-pii-peul) *pl* citadins *mpl*

toxic (tok-sik) *adj* toxique

toy (toï) *n* jouet *m*

toyshop (*toï*-chop) *n* magasin de jouets

trace (tréïss) *n* trace *f*; *v* tracer, retracer

track (træk) *n* voie *f*; piste *f*

tractor (*træk*-teu) *n* tracteur *m*

trade (tréïd) *n* commerce *m*; métier *m*;

v *faire du commerce; **~ union** syndicat *m*

trademark (*tréïd*-mââk) *n* marque de fabrique

trader (*tréï*-deu) *n* commerçant *m*, -e *f*

tradesman (*tréïdz*-meunn) *n* (pl -men) marchand *m*

tradition (treu-*di*-cheunn) *n* tradition *f*

traditional (treu-*di*-cheu-neul) *adj* traditionnel

traffic (*træ*-fik) *n* circulation *f*; **~ jam** embouteillage *m*; **~ light** feu de circulation

tragedy (*træ*-djeu-di) *n* tragédie *f*

tragic (*træ*-djik) *adj* tragique

trail (tréïl) *n* piste *f*, sentier *m*

trailer (*tréï*-leu) *n* remorque *f*; *nAm* caravane *f*

train (tréïn) *n* train *m*; *v* dresser, former; **slow ~** omnibus *m*; **through ~** train direct; **~ ferry** ferry-boat *m*

trainee (tréï-*nii*) *n* apprenti *m*, e *f*; stagiaire *m,f*

trainer (*tréï*-neu) *n* entraîneur *m*, entraîneuse *f*; dresseur *m*, dresseuse *f*

training (*tréï*-ninng) *n* entraînement *m*

trait (tréït) *n* trait *m*

traitor (*tréï*-teu) *n* traître *m*

tram (træm) *n* tram *m*

tramp (træmp) *n* chemineau *m*, vagabond *m*; *v* vagabonder

tranquil (*træng*-k^ou il) *adj* tranquille

tranquillizer (*træng*-k^ou i-laï-zeu) *n* calmant *m*

transaction (træn-*zæk*-cheunn) *n* transaction *f*

transatlantic (træn-zeut-*læn*-tik) *adj* transatlantique

transfer (træns-*feû*) *v* transférer

transform (træns-*foom*) *v* transformer

transformer (træns-*foo*-meu) *n* transformateur *m*

transition (træn-*si*-cheunn) *n* transition *f*

translate (træns-*léït*) *v* *traduire

translation (træns-*léï*-cheunn) *n* traduction *f*

translator (træns-*léï*-teu) *n* traducteur *m*, traductrice *f*

transmission (trænz-*mi*-cheunn) *n* émission *f*

transmit (trænz-*mit*) *v* *émettre

transmitter (trænz-*mi*-teu) *n* émetteur *m*

transparent (træn-*spèeu*-reunnt) *adj* transparent

transport[1] (*træn*-spoot) *n* transport *m*

transport[2] (træn-*spoot*) *v* transporter

transportation (træn-spoo-*téï*-cheunn) *n* transport *m*

trap (træp) *n* piège *m*

trash (træch) *n* ordures *fpl*; **~ can** *Am* boîte à ordures

travel (*træ*-veul) *v* voyager; **~ agency** bureau de voyages; **~ agent** agent de voyages; **~ insurance** assurance voyages *f*; **travelling expenses** frais de voyage

travel(l)er (*træ*-veu-leu) *n* voyageur *m*, voyageuse *f*; **traveler's check** *Am*, **traveller's cheque** chèque de voyage

tray (tréï) *n* plateau *m*

treason (*trii*-zeunn) *n* trahison *f*

treasure (*trè*-jeu) *n* trésor *m*

treasury (*trè*-jeu-ri) *n* Trésor

treat (triit) *v* traiter

treatment (*triit*-meunnt) *n* traitement *m*

treaty (*trii*-ti) *n* traité *m*

tree (trii) *n* arbre *m*

tremble (*trèm*-beul) *v* frissonner, trembler; vibrer

tremendous (tri-*mèn*-deuss) *adj* énorme

trendy (*trèn*-di) *adj* à la (dernière) mode, dernier cri; dans le vent

trespass (*trèss*-peuss) *v* empiéter

trespasser (*trèss*-peu-seu) *n* intrus *m*

trial (traï*eu*l) *n* procès *m*; essai *m*

triangle (traï-æng-gheul) *n* triangle *m*

triangular (traï-*æng*-ghyou-leu) *adj* triangulaire

tribe (traïb) *n* tribu *f*

tributary (*tri*-byou-teu-ri) *n* affluent *m*

tribute (*tri*-byoût) *n* hommage *m*

trick (trik) *n* truc *m*

trigger (*tri*-gheu) *n* gâchette *f*

trim (trimm) *v* tailler

trip (trip) *n* excursion *f*, voyage *m*

triumph (*traï*-eummf) *n* triomphe *m*; *v* triompher

triumphant (traï-*amm*-feunnt) *adj* triomphant

troops (troûps) *pl* troupes *fpl*

tropical (*tro*-pi-keul) *adj* tropical

tropics (*tro*-piks) *pl* tropiques *mpl*

trouble (*tra*-beul) *n* ennui *m*, peine *f*, dérangement *m*; *v* déranger

troublesome (*tra*-beul-seumm) *adj* gênant

trousers (*traou*-zeuz) *pl* pantalon *m*

trout (traout) *n* (pl ∼) truite *f*

truck (trak) *nAm* camion *m*

true (troû) *adj* vrai; réel; loyal, fidèle

trumpet (*tramm*-pit) *n* trompette *f*

trunk (tranngk) *n* malle *f*; tronc *m*; *nAm* coffre *m*; **trunks** *pl* slip de bain

trunk-call (*tranngk*-kool) *n* appel interurbain

trust (trast) *v* *faire confiance; *n* confiance *f*

trustworthy (*trast*-ᵒᵘeû-ði) *adj* digne de confiance

truth (troûθ) *n* vérité *f*

truthful (*troûθ*-feul) *adj* véridique

try (traï) *v* essayer; tenter, s'efforcer; *n* tentative *f*; ∼ **on** essayer

tube (tyoûb) *n* tuyau *m*, tube *m*

tuberculosis (tyoû-beû-kyou-*lôou*-siss) *n* tuberculose *f*

Tuesday (*tyoûz*-di) mardi *m*

tug (tagh) *v* remorquer; *n* remorqueur *m*; à-coup *m*

tuition (tyoû-*i*-cheunn) *n* enseignement *m*

tulip (*tyoû*-lip) *n* tulipe *f*

tumbler (*tamm*-bleu) *n* gobelet *m*

tumo(u)r (*tyoû*-meu) *n* tumeur *f*

tuna (*tyoû*-neu) *n* (pl ∼, ∼s) thon *m*

tune (tyoûn) *n* air *m*; *v* accorder

tuneful (*tyoûn*-feul) *adj* harmonieux

tunic (*tyoû*-nik) *n* tunique *f*

Tunisia (tyoû-*ni*-zi-eu) Tunisie *f*

Tunisian (tyoû-*ni*-zi-eunn) *adj* tunisien; *n* Tunisien *m*

tunnel (*ta*-neul) *n* tunnel *m*

turbine (*teû*-baïn) *n* turbine *f*

Turk (teûk) *n* Turc *m*

Turkey (*teû*-ki) Turquie *f*

turkey (*teû*-ki) *n* dinde *f*

Turkish (*teû*-kich) *adj* turc; ∼ **bath** bain turc

turn (teûnn) *v* tourner; retourner; virer; *n* revirement *m*, tour *m*; tournant *m*; ∼ **back** retourner; ∼ **down** rejeter; ∼ **into** changer en; ∼ **off** fermer; ∼ **on** allumer; *ouvrir; ∼ **over** retourner; ∼ **round** retourner; se retourner

turning (*teû*-ninng) *n* virage *m*; ∼ **point** tournant *m*

turnover (*teû*-nôᵒᵘ-veu) *n* chiffre d'affaires; ∼ **tax** impôt sur le chiffre d'affaires

turnpike (*teûnn*-païk) *nAm* route à péage

turpentine (*teû*-peunn-taïn) *n* térébenthine *f*

turtle (*teû*-teul) *n* tortue *f*

tutor (*tyoû*-teu) *n* tuteur *m*

tuxedo (tak-*sii*-dôᵒᵘ) *nAm* (pl ∼s, ∼es) smoking *m*

TV (tii-*vii*) *n* télévision *f*

tweed (tᵒᵘiid) *n* tweed *m*

tweezers (*touii*-zeuz) *pl* pince *f*
twelfth (t^{ou}èlfθ) *num* douzième
twelve (t^{ou}èlv) *num* douze
twentieth (*touèn*-ti-euθ) *num* vingtième
twenty (*touèn*-ti) *num* vingt
twice (t^{ou}aïss) *adv* deux fois
twig (t^{ou}igh) *n* rameau *m*; branche *f*
twilight (*touaï*-laït) *n* crépuscule *m*
twine (t^{ou}aïn) *n* ficelle *f*
twins (t^{ou}innz) *pl* jumeaux *mpl*; **twin beds** lits jumeaux
twist (t^{ou}ist) *v* tordre; *n* torsion *f*

two (toû) *num* deux
two-piece (toû-*piiss*) *adj* deux-pièces *m*
type (taïp) *v* taper à la machine, dactylographier; *n* type *m*
typewriter (*taïp*-raï-teu) *n* machine à écrire
typhoid (*taï*-foïd) *n* typhoïde *f*
typical (*ti*-pi-keul) *adj* caractéristique, typique
typist (*taï*-pist) *n* dactylo *f*
tyre (taï^{eu}) *n* pneu *m*; **~ pressure** pression des pneus

U

ugly (*a*-ghli) *adj* laid
ulcer (*al*-seu) *n* ulcère *m*
ultimate (*al*-ti-meut) *adj* ultime
ultraviolet (al-treu-*vaïeu*-leut) *adj* ultra-violet
umbrella (amm-*brè*-leu) *n* parapluie *m*
umpire (*amm*-paï^{eu}) *n* arbitre *m*
unable (a-*néï*-beul) *adj* incapable
unacceptable (a-neuk-*sèp*-teu-beul) *adj* inacceptable
unaccountable (a-neu-*kaoun*-teu-beul) *adj* inexplicable
unaccustomed (a-neu-*ka*-steummd) *adj* inhabitué
unanimous (yoû-*næ*-ni-meuss) *adj* unanime
unanswered (a-*nâân*-seud) *adj* sans réponse
unauthorized (a-*noo*-θeu-raïzd) *adj* illicite
unavoidable (a-neu-*voï*-deu-beul) *adj* inévitable
unaware (a-neu-*ouèeu*) *adj* inconscient

unbearable (ann-*bèeu*-reu-beul) *adj* insupportable
unbreakable (ann-*bréï*-keu-beul) *adj* incassable
unbroken (ann-*brôou*-keunn) *adj* intact
unbutton (ann-*ba*-teunn) *v* déboutonner
uncertain (ann-*seû*-teunn) *adj* incertain
uncle (*anng*-keul) *n* oncle *m*
unclean (ann-*kliin*) *adj* malpropre
uncomfortable (ann-*kamm*-feu-teu-beul) *adj* inconfortable
uncommon (ann-*ko*-meunn) *adj* inhabituel, rare
unconditional (ann-keunn-*di*-cheu-neul) *adj* inconditionnel
unconscious (ann-*konn*-cheuss) *adj* inconscient
uncork (ann-*kook*) *v* déboucher
uncover (ann-*ka*-veu) *v* *découvrir
uncultivated (ann-*kal*-ti-véï-tid) *adj* inculte
under (*ann*-deu) *prep* en bas de, sous

undercurrent (*ann*-deu-ka-reunnt) *n* courant *m*

underestimate (ann-deu-rè-sti-méït) *v* sous-estimer

underground (*ann*-deu-ghraound) *adj* souterrain; *n* métro *m*

underline (ann-deu-*laïn*) *v* souligner

underneath (ann-deu-*niiθ*) *adv* dessous

underpants (*ann*-deu-pænts) *plAm* caleçon *m*

undershirt (*ann*-deu-cheût) *n* tricot de corps

***understand** (ann-deu-*stænd*) *v* *comprendre

understanding (ann-deu-*stæn*-dinng) *n* compréhension *f*

understatement (ann-deu-*stéït*-meunnt) *n* affirmation *f* qui reste au-dessous de la vérité; amoindrissement *m*

***undertake** (ann-deu-*téïk*) *v* *entreprendre

undertaking (ann-deu-*téï*-kinng) *n* entreprise *f*

underwater (*ann*-deu-ᵒᵘoo-teu) *adj* sous-marin

underwear (*ann*-deu-ᵒᵘèᵉᵘ) *n* sous-vêtements *mpl*

undesirable (ann-di-*zaïeu*-reu-beul) *adj* indésirable

***undo** (ann-*doû*) *v* *défaire

undoubtedly (ann-*daou*-tid-li) *adv* sans aucun doute

undress (ann-*drèss*) *v* se déshabiller

unearned (a-*neûnnd*) *adj* immérité

uneasy (a-*nii*-zi) *adj* mal à l'aise

uneducated (a-*nè*-dyou-kéï-tid) *adj* ignorant

unemployed (a-nimm-*ploïd*) *adj* en chômage

unemployment (a-nimm-*ploï*-meunnt) *n* chômage *m*

unequal (a-*nii*-kᵒᵘeul) *adj* inégal

uneven (a-*nii*-veunn) *adj* inégal, accidenté; irrégulier

unexpected (a-nik-*spèk*-tid) *adj* imprévu, inattendu

unfair (ann-*fèeu*) *adj* inéquitable, injuste

unfaithful (ann-*féïθ*-feul) *adj* infidèle

unfamiliar (ann-feu-*mil*-yeu) *adj* inconnu

unfasten (ann-*fââ*-seunn) *v* détacher

unfavo(u)rable (ann-*féï*-veu-reu-beul) *adj* défavorable

unfit (ann-*fit*) *adj* impropre

unfold (ann-*fôould*) *v* déplier

unfortunate (ann-*foo*-tcheu-neut) *adj* malheureux

unfortunately (ann-*foo*-tcheu-neut-li) *adv* hélas, malheureusement

unfriendly (ann-*frènd*-li) *adj* froid; hostile

ungrateful (ann-*ghréït*-feul) *adj* ingrat

unhappy (ann-*hæ*-pi) *adj* malheureux

unhealthy (ann-*hèl*-θi) *adj* malsain

unhurt (ann-*heût*) *adj* indemne

uniform (*yoû*-ni-foom) *n* uniforme *m*; *adj* uniforme

unimportant (a-nimm-*poo*-teunnt) *adj* insignifiant

uninhabitable (a-ninn-*hæ*-bi-teu-beul) *adj* inhabitable

uninhabited (a-ninn-*hæ*-bi-tid) *adj* inhabité

unintentional (a-ninn-*tèn*-cheu-neul) *adj* involontaire

union (*yoû*-nyeunn) *n* union *f*; ligue *f*

unique (yoû-*niik*) *adj* unique

unit (*yoû*-nit) *n* unité *f*

unite (yoû-*naït*) *v* unir

United States (yoû-*naï*-tid stéïts) Etats-Unis

unity (*yoû*-neu-ti) *n* unité *f*

universal (yoû-ni-*veû*-seul) *adj* général, universel

universe (*yoû*-ni-veûss) *n* univers *m*

university (yoû-ni-*veû*-seu-ti) *n* université *f*

unjust (ann-*djast*) *adj* injuste

unkind (ann-*kaïnd*) *adj* désagréable, peu aimable

unknown (ann-*nôoun*) *adj* inconnu

unlawful (ann-*loo*-feul) *adj* illicite

unleaded (ann-*lèd*-id) *adj* sans plomb

unlearn (ann-*leûnn*) *v* *désapprendre

unless (eunn-*lèss*) *conj* à moins que

unlike (ann-*laïk*) *adj* dissemblable, différent

unlikely (ann-*laï*-kli) *adj* improbable

unlimited (ann-*li*-mi-tid) *adj* illimité

unload (ann-*lôoud*) *v* décharger

unlock (ann-*lok*) *v* *ouvrir

unlucky (ann-*la*-ki) *adj* infortuné

unnecessary (ann-*nè*-seu-seu-ri) *adj* superflu

unoccupied (a-*no*-kyou-païd) *adj* vacant

unpack (ann-*pæk*) *v* déballer

unpleasant (ann-*plè*-zeunnt) *adj* ennuyeux, déplaisant; désagréable, antipathique

unpopular (ann-*po*-pyou-leu) *adj* peu aimé, impopulaire

unprotected (ann-preu-*tèk*-tid) *adj* non protégé

unqualified (ann-*kouo*-li-faïd) *adj* incompétent

unreal (ann-*rieul*) *adj* irréel

unreasonable (ann-*rii*-zeu-neu-beul) *adj* déraisonnable

unreliable (ann-ri-*laï*-eu-beul) *adj* douteux

unrest (ann-*rèst*) *n* agitation *f*; inquiétude *f*

unsafe (ann-*séïf*) *adj* dangereux

unsatisfactory (ann-sæ-tiss-*fæk*-teu-ri) *adj* insatisfaisant

unscrew (ann-*skroû*) *v* dévisser

unselfish (ann-*sèl*-fich) *adj* désintéressé

unskilled (ann-*skild*) *adj* non qualifié

unsound (ann-*saound*) *adj* malsain

unstable (ann-*stéï*-beul) *adj* instable

unsteady (ann-*stè*-di) *adj* branlant, instable

unsuccessful (ann-seuk-*sèss*-feul) *adj* infructueux

unsuitable (ann-*soû*-teu-beul) *adj* inadéquat

unsurpassed (ann-seu-*pââst*) *adj* sans pareil

untidy (ann-*taï*-di) *adj* désordonné

untie (ann-*taï*) *v* dénouer

until (eunn-*til*) *prep* jusqu'à

untrue (ann-*troû*) *adj* faux

untrustworthy (ann-*trast*-ᵒᵘeû-ði) *adj* sujet à caution

unusual (ann-*yoû*-jou-eul) *adj* inhabituel, insolite

unwell (ann-*ouèl*) *adj* indisposé

unwillingly (ann-*oui*-linng-li) *adv* à contrecœur

unwise (ann-*ouaïz*) *adj* imprudent

unwrap (ann-*ræp*) *v* déballer

up (ap) *adv* vers le haut, en haut

upholster (ap-*hôoul*-steu) *v* capitonner

upkeep (*ap*-kiip) *n* entretien *m*

uplands (*ap*-leunndz) *pl* hautes terres

upon (eu-*ponn*) *prep* sur

upper (*a*-peu) *adj* supérieur

upright (*ap*-raït) *adj* droit; *adv* droit

upset (ap-*sèt*) *v* déranger; *adj* bouleversé

upside-down (ap-saïd-*daoun*) *adv* sens dessus dessous

upstairs (ap-*stèeuz*) *adv* en haut

upstream (ap-*striim*) *adv* en amont

upwards (ap-ᵒᵘeudz) *adv* vers le haut

urban (*eû*-beunn) *adj* urbain

urge (eûdj) *v* exhorter; *n* impulsion *f*

urgency (*eû*-djeunn-si) *n* urgence *f*

urgent (*eû*-djeunnt) *adj* urgent

urine (*youeu*-rinn) *n* urine *f*

Uruguay (*youeu*-reu-gh^(ou)aï) Uruguay *m*

Uruguayan (you^(eu)-reu-*ghouaï*-eunn) *adj* uruguayen; *n* Uruguayen *m*

us (ass) *pron* nous

usable (*yoû*-zeu-beul) *adj* utilisable

usage (*yoû*-zidj) *n* usage *m*

use[1] (youz) *v* employer; ***be used to** *être habitué à; **~ up** user

use[2] (youss) *n* emploi *m*; utilité *f*; ***be of ~** *servir

useful (*youss*-feul) *adj* utile

useless (*youss*-leuss) *adj* inutile

user (*yoû*-zeu) *n* usager *m*

usher (*a*-cheu) *n* ouvreur *m*

usherette (a-cheu-*rèt*) *n* ouvreuse *f*

usual (*yoû*-jou-eul) *adj* ordinaire

usually (*yoû*-jou-eu-li) *adv* habituellement

utensil (yoû-*tèn*-seul) *n* outil *m*, ustensile *m*

utility (yoû-*ti*-leu-ti) *n* utilité *f*

utilize (*yoû*-ti-laïz) *v* utiliser

utmost (*at*-mô^(ou)st) *adj* extrême

utter (*a*-teu) *adj* complet, total; *v* *émettre

V

vacancy (*véï*-keunn-si) *n* vacance *f*

vacant (*véï*-keunnt) *adj* vacant

vacate (veu-*kéït*) *v* quitter

vacation (veu-*kéï*-cheunn) *n* congé *m*

vaccinate (*væk*-si-néït) *v* vacciner

vaccination (væk-si-*néï*-cheunn) *n* vaccination *f*

vacuum (*væ*-kyou-eumm) *n* vide *m*; *vAm* passer l'aspirateur; **~ cleaner** aspirateur *m*; **~ flask** thermos *m*

vague (véïgh) *adj* vague

vain (véïn) *adj* vaniteux; vain; **in ~** inutilement, en vain

valid (*væ*-lid) *adj* valable

valley (*væ*-li) *n* vallée *f*

valuable (*væ*-lyou-beul) *adj* de valeur, précieux; **valuables** *pl* objets de valeur

value (*væ*-lyoû) *n* valeur *f*; *v* estimer

valve (vælv) *n* soupape *f*

van (væn) *n* fourgon *m*

vanilla (veu-*ni*-leu) *n* vanille *f*

vanish (*væ*-nich) *v* *disparaître

vapo(u)r (*véï*-peu) *n* vapeur *f*

variable (*vèeu*-ri-eu-beul) *adj* variable

variation (vè^(eu)-ri-*éï*-cheunn) *n* variation *f*; changement *m*

varied (*vèeu*-rid) *adj* varié

variety (veu-*raï*-eu-ti) *n* variété *f*; **~ show** spectacle de variétés; **~ theatre** (*Am* theater) théâtre de variétés

various (*vèeu*-ri-euss) *adj* divers

varnish (*vââ*-nich) *n* laque *f*, vernis *m*; *v* vernir

vary (*vèeu*-ri) *v* varier; changer; différer

vase (vââz) *n* vase *m*

vaseline (*væ*-seu-liin) *n* vaseline *f*

vast (vââst) *adj* immense, vaste

vault (voolt) *n* voûte *f*; chambre forte

veal (viil) *n* veau *m*

vegetable (*vè*-djeu-teu-beul) *n* légume *m*; **~ merchant** marchand de légumes

vegetarian (vè-dji-*tèeu*-ri-eunn) *n* végétarien *m*, végétarienne *f*

vegetation (vè-dji-*téï*-cheunn) *n* végétation *f*

vehicle (*vii*-eu-keul) *n* véhicule *m*

veil (véïl) *n* voile *m*

vein (véïn) *n* veine *f*; **varicose ~** varice *f*

velvet (vèl-vit) *n* velours *m*

velveteen (vèl-vi-tiin) *n* velvet *m*

venerable (vè-neu-reu-beul) *adj* vénérable

venereal disease (vi-nieu-ri-eul diziiz) maladie vénérienne

Venezuela (vè-ni-zouéï-leu) Venezuela *m*

Venezuelan (vè-ni-zouéï-leunn) *adj* vénézuélien; *n* Vénézuélien *m*

ventilate (vèn-ti-léït) *v* ventiler; aérer

ventilation (vèn-ti-léï-cheunn) *n* ventilation *f*; aération *f*

ventilator (vèn-ti-léï-teu) *n* ventilateur *m*

venture (vèn-tcheu) *v* risquer

veranda (veu-ræn-deu) *n* véranda *f*

verb (veûb) *n* verbe *m*

verbal (veû-beul) *adj* verbal

verdict (veû-dikt) *n* sentence *f*, verdict *m*

verge (veûdj) *n* bord *m*

verify (vè-ri-faï) *v* vérifier

verse (veûss) *n* vers *m*

version (veû-cheunn) *n* version *f*

versus (veû-seuss) *prep* contre

vertical (veû-ti-keul) *adj* vertical

very (vè-ri) *adv* très; *adj* même, justement; tout

vessel (vè-seul) *n* vaisseau *m*; récipient *m*

vest (vèst) *n* chemise *f*; *nAm* gilet *m*

veterinary surgeon (vè-tri-neu-ri seûdjeunn) vétérinaire *m/f*

via (vaïᵉᵘ) *prep* via

vibrate (vaï-bréït) *v* vibrer

vibration (vaï-bréï-cheunn) *n* vibration *f*

vicar (vi-keu) *n* vicaire *m*

vice president (vaïss-prè-zi-deunnt) *n* vice-président *m*

vicinity (vi-si-neu-ti) *n* alentours *mpl*,

voisinage *m*

vicious (vi-cheuss) *adj* vicieux

victim (vik-timm) *n* victime *f*; dupe *f*

victory (vik-teu-ri) *n* victoire *f*

video camera (vi-di-ôᵒᵘ kæ-meu-reu) *n* caméra vidéo *f*

video recorder (vi-di-ôᵒᵘ ri-koo-deu) *n* magnétoscope *m*

view (vyoû) *n* vue *f*; point de vue, opinion *f*; *v* contempler

viewfinder (vyoû-faïn-deu) *n* viseur *m*

vigilant (vi-dji-leunnt) *adj* vigilant

villa (vi-leu) *n* villa *f*

village (vi-lidj) *n* village *m*

vine (vaïn) *n* vigne *f*

vinegar (vi-ni-gheu) *n* vinaigre *m*

vineyard (vinn-yeud) *n* vignoble *m*

vintage (vinn-tidj) *n* vendange *f*

violation (vaïᵉᵘ-léï-cheunn) *n* violation *f*

violence (vaïᵉᵘ-leunns) *n* violence *f*

violent (vaïᵉᵘ-leunnt) *adj* violent

violet (vaïᵉᵘ-leut) *n* violette *f*; *adj* violet

violin (vaïᵉᵘ-linn) *n* violon *m*

VIP (vii-aï-pii) *n* V.I.P. *m*

virgin (veû-djinn) *n* vierge *f*

virtue (veû-tchoû) *n* vertu *f*

visa (vii-zeu) *n* visa *m*

visibility (vi-zeu-bi-leu-ti) *n* visibilité *f*

visible (vi-zeu-beul) *adj* visible

vision (vi-jeunn) *n* vision *f*

visit (vi-zit) *v* visiter; *n* visite *f*; **visiting card** carte de visite; **visiting hours** heures de visite

visitor (vi-zi-teu) *n* visiteur *m*, -euse *f*, invité *m*, -e *f*

vital (vaï-teul) *adj* vital

vitamin (vi-teu-minn) *n* vitamine *f*

vivid (vi-vid) *adj* vif

vocabulary (veu-kæ-byou-leu-ri) *n* vocabulaire *m*

vocal (vôou-keul) *adj* vocal

vocalist (vôou-keu-list) *n* chanteur *m*

voice (voïss) *n* voix *f*

void (voïd) *adj* nul

volcano (vol-*kéï*-nô^{ou}) *n* (pl ~es, ~s) volcan *m*

volt (vô^{ou}lt) *n* volt *m*

voltage (*vôoul*-tidj) *n* voltage *m*

volume (vo-lyoum) *n* volume *m*; tome *m*

voluntary (*vo*-leunn-teu-ri) *adj* volontaire

volunteer (vo-leunn-*tieu*) *n* volontaire *m*

vomit (*vo*-mit) *v* vomir

vote (vô^{ou}t) *v* voter; *n* vote *m*

voter (*vôou*-teu) *n* votant *m*, votante *f*; électeur *m*, électrice *f*

voucher (*vaou*-tcheu) *n* reçu *m*, bon *m*

vow (vaou) *n* vœu *m*, serment *m*; *v* jurer

vowel (vaou^{eu}l) *n* voyelle *f*

voyage (*voï*-idj) *n* voyage *m*

vulgar (*val*-gheu) *adj* vulgaire, grossier

vulnerable (*val*-neu-reu-beul) *adj* vulnérable

vulture (*val*-tcheu) *n* vautour *m*

W

wade (^{ou}éïd) *v* patauger

wafer (*ouéï*-feu) *n* gaufrette *f*

waffle (*ouo*-feul) *n* gaufre *f*

wages (*ouéï*-djiz) *pl* gages *mpl*

wag(g)on (*ouæ*-gheunn) *n* wagon *m*

waist (^{ou}éïst) *n* taille *f*

waistcoat (*ouéïss*-kô^{ou}t) *n* gilet *m*

wait (^{ou}éït) *v* attendre; ~ **on** *servir

waiter (*ouéï*-teu) *n* garçon *m*

waiting (*ouéï*-tinng) *n* attente *f*; ~ **room** salle d'attente

waitress (*ouéï*-triss) *n* serveuse *f*

*****wake** (^{ou}éïk) *v* réveiller; ~ **up** s'éveiller, se réveiller

walk (^{ou}ook) *v* marcher; se promener; *n* promenade *f*; démarche *f*; **walking** à pied

walker (*ouoo*-keu) *n* promeneur *m*

walking stick (*ouoo*-kinng-stik) *n* canne *f*

wall (^{ou}ool) *n* mur *m*; cloison *f*

wallet (*ouo*-lit) *n* portefeuille *m*

wallpaper (*ouool*-péï-peu) *n* papier peint

walnut (*ouool*-nat) *n* noix *f*

waltz (^{ou}ools) *n* valse *f*

wander (*ouonn*-deu) *v* errer

want (^{ou}onnt) *v* *vouloir; désirer; *n* besoin *m*; carence *f*, manque *m*

war (^{ou}oo) *n* guerre *f*

warden (*ouoo*-deunn) *n* surveillant *m*, gardien *m*

wardrobe (*ouoo*-drô^{ou}b) *n* garde-robe *f*

warehouse (*ouèeu*-haouss) *n* magasin *m*, dépôt *m*

wares (^{ou}è^{eu}z) *pl* marchandise *f*

warm (^{ou}oom) *adj* chaud; *v* chauffer

warmth (^{ou}oomθ) *n* chaleur *f*

warn (^{ou}oon) *v* *prévenir, avertir

warning (*ouoo*-ninng) *n* avertissement *m*

wary (*ouèeu*-ri) *adj* prudent

was (^{ou}oz) *v* (p be)

wash (^{ou}och) *v* laver; ~ **and wear** sans repassage; ~ **up** *faire la vaisselle

washable (*ouo*-cheu-beul) *adj* lavable

washbasin (*ouoch*-béï-seunn) *n*

lavabo m

washing (ouo-chinng) n lavage m; lessive f; ~ **machine** machine à laver; ~ **powder** lessive

washroom (ouoch-roûm) nAm toilettes fpl

wasp (ouosp) n guêpe f

waste (ouéïst) v gaspiller; n gaspillage m; adj en friche

wasteful (ouéïst-feul) adj gaspilleur

wastepaper basket (ouéïst-péï-peu-bââ-skit) n corbeille à papier

watch (ouotch) v regarder, observer; surveiller; n montre f; ~ **for** guetter; ~ **out** *prendre garde

watchmaker (ouotch-méï-keu) n horloger m, horlogère f

watchstrap (ouotch-stræp) n bracelet pour montre

water (ouoo-teu) n eau f; **iced** ~ eau glacée; **running** ~ eau courante; ~ **pump** pompe à eau; ~ **ski** ski nautique; ~ **softener** adoucisseur d'eau

watercolo(u)r (ouoo-teu-ka-leu) n couleur à l'eau; aquarelle f

watercress (ouoo-teu-krèss) n cresson m

waterfall (ouoo-teu-fool) n cascade f

watermelon (ouoo-teu-mè-leunn) n pastèque f

waterproof (ouoo-teu-proûf) adj imperméable

waterway (ouoo-teu-ouéï) n voie d'eau

watt (ouot) n watt m

wave (ouéïv) n ondulation f, vague f; v *faire signe

wavelength (ouéïv-lèngθ) n longueur d'onde

wavy (ouéï-vi) adj ondulé

wax (ouæks) n cire f

waxworks (ouæks-ouêûks) pl musée des figures de cire

way (ouéï) n manière f, façon f; voie f;

côté m, direction f; distance f; **by the** ~ à propos; **one-way traffic** sens unique; **out of the** ~ écarté; **the other** ~ **round** en sens inverse; ~ **back** chemin du retour; ~ **in** entrée f; ~ **out** sortie f

wayside (ouéï-saïd) n bord de la route

we (ouii) pron nous

weak (ouiik) adj faible; léger

weakness (ouiik-neuss) n faiblesse f

wealth (ouèlθ) n richesse f

wealthy (ouèl-θi) adj riche

weapon (ouè-peunn) n arme f

***wear** (ouèeu) v porter; ~ **out** user

weary (ouieu-ri) adj las, fatigué

weather (ouè-ðeu) n temps m; ~ **forecast** bulletin météorologique

***weave** (ouiiv) v tisser

wedding (ouè-dinng) n mariage m; ~ **ring** alliance f

web (ouèb) n tissu m; toile f; **the Web** le Web, la Toile

wedge (ouèdj) n cale f

Wednesday (ouènz-di) mercredi m

weed (ouiid) n mauvaise herbe

week (ouiik) n semaine f

weekday (ouiik-déï) n jour de la semaine

weekly (ouii-kli) adj hebdomadaire

***weep** (ouiip) v pleurer

weigh (ouéï) v peser

weighing machine (ouéï-inng-meu-chiin) n bascule f

weight (ouéït) n poids m

welcome (ouèl-keumm) adj bienvenu; n accueil m; v *accueillir

weld (ouèld) v souder

welfare (ouèl-fèeu) n bien-être m

well[1] (ouèl) adv bien; adj sain; **as** ~ également, aussi bien; **as** ~ **as** aussi bien que; **well!** bien!

well[2] (ouèl) n source f, puits m

well-founded (ouèl-faoun-did) adj bien fondé

well-known (*ouèl*-nôᵒᵘn) *adj* connu

well-to-do (ᵒᵘèl-teu-*doû*) *adj* aisé

went (ᵒᵘènt) *v* (p go)

were (ᵒᵘeû) *v* (p be)

west (ᵒᵘèst) *n* occident *m*, ouest *m*

westerly (*ouè*-steu-li) *adj* occidental

western (*ouè*-steunn) *adj* occidental

wet (ᵒᵘèt) *adj* mouillé; humide

whale (ᵒᵘéïl) *n* baleine *f*

wharf (ᵒᵘoof) *n* (pl ⁓s, wharves) quai *m*

what (ᵒᵘot) *pron* quoi; ce que; ⁓ **for** pourquoi

whatever (ᵒᵘo-*tè*-veu) *pron* tout ce que

wheat (ᵒᵘiit) *n* blé *m*

wheel (ᵒᵘiil) *n* roue *f*

wheelbarrow (*ouiil*-bæ-rôᵒᵘ) *n* brouette *f*

wheelchair (*ouiil*-tchèᵉᵘ) *n* fauteuil roulant

when (ᵒᵘèn) *adv* quand; *conj* quand, lorsque

whenever (ᵒᵘè-*nè*-veu) *conj* n'importe quand

where (ᵒᵘèᵉᵘ) *adv* où; *conj* où

wherever (ᵒᵘèᵉᵘ-*rè*-veu) *conj* partout où

whether (*ouè*-ðeu) *conj* si; **whether .... or** si ... ou

which (ᵒᵘitch) *pron* quel; qui

whichever (ᵒᵘi-*tchè*-veu) *adj* n'importe quel

while (ᵒᵘaïl) *conj* tandis que; *n* moment *m*

whilst (ᵒᵘaïlst) *conj* tandis que

whim (ᵒᵘimm) *n* lubie *f*, caprice *m*

whip (ᵒᵘip) *n* fouet *m*; *v* fouetter

whiskers (*oui*-skeuz) *pl* favoris

whisper (*oui*-speu) *v* chuchoter; *n* chuchotement *m*

whistle (*oui*-seul) *v* siffler; *n* sifflet *m*

white (ᵒᵘaït) *adj* blanc

whiting (*ouaï*-tinng) *n* (pl ⁓) merlan *m*

Whitsun (*ouit*-seunn) Pentecôte *f*

who (hoû) *pron* qui

whole (hôᵒᵘl) *adj* complet, entier; intact; *n* ensemble *m*

wholesale (*hôoul*-séïl) *n* vente en gros; ⁓ **dealer** grossiste *m*

wholesome (*hôoul*-seumm) *adj* sain

wholly (*hôoul*-li) *adv* entièrement

whom (hoûm) *pron* à qui

whore (hoo) *n* putain *f*

whose (hoûz) *pron* dont; de qui

why (ᵒᵘaï) *adv* pourquoi

wicked (*oui*-kid) *adj* mauvais

wide (ᵒᵘaïd) *adj* vaste, large

widen (*ouaï*-deunn) *v* élargir

widow (*oui*-dôᵒᵘ) *n* veuve *f*

widower (*oui*-dôᵒᵘ-eu) *n* veuf *m*

width (ᵒᵘidθ) *n* largeur *f*

wife (ᵒᵘaïf) *n* (pl wives) épouse *f*, femme *f*

wig (ᵒᵘigh) *n* perruque *f*

wild (ᵒᵘaïld) *adj* sauvage; féroce

will (ᵒᵘil) *n* volonté *f*; testament *m*

*****will** (ᵒᵘil) *v* *vouloir

willing (*oui*-linng) *adj* disposé

willingly (*oui*-linng-li) *adv* volontiers

willpower (*ouil*-paouᵉᵘ) *n* volonté *f*

*****win** (ᵒᵘinn) *v* gagner

wind (ᵒᵘinnd) *n* vent *m*

*****wind** (ᵒᵘaïnd) *v* serpenter; enrouler; ⁓ **up** remonter

winding (*ouaïn*-dinng) *adj* serpentant

windmill (*ouinnd*-mil) *n* moulin à vent

window (*ouinn*-dôᵒᵘ) *n* fenêtre *f*

windowsill (*ouinn*-dôᵒᵘ-sil) *n* rebord de fenêtre

windscreen (*ouinnd*-skriin) *n* parebrise *m*; ⁓ **wiper** essuie-glace *m*

windshield (*ouinnd*-chiild) *n*Am parebrise *m*; ⁓ **wiper** *Am* essuie-glace *m*

windy (*ouinn*-di) *adj* venteux

wine (ᵒᵘaïn) *n* vin *m*; ⁓ **cellar** cave *f*; ⁓ **list** carte des vins; ⁓ **merchant** négociant en vins

wine-waiter (ouaïn-^{ou}éï-teu) n sommelier m

wing (^{ou}inng) n aile f

winkle (ouïnng-keul) n bigorneau m

winner (oui-neu) n vainqueur m

winning (oui-ninng) adj gagnant; **winnings** pl gains

winter (ouinn-teu) n hiver m; ~ **sports** sports d'hiver

wipe (^{ou}aïp) v ôter, essuyer

wire (^{ou}aï^{ch}) n fil m; fil de fer

wireless (ouaïeu-leuss) n radio f

wisdom (ouiz-deumm) n sagesse f

wise (^{ou}aïz) adj sage

wish (^{ou}ich) v désirer, souhaiter; n désir m, souhait m

witch (^{ou}itch) n sorcière f

with (^{ou}ið) prep avec; chez; de

***withdraw** (^{ou}ið-droo) v retirer

within (^{ou}i-ðinn) prep dans; adv à l'intérieur

without (^{ou}i-ðaout) prep sans

witness (ouit-neuss) n témoin m

wit (^{ou}it) n esprit m; intelligence f

wits (^{ou}its) pl raison f

witty (oui-ti) adj spirituel

wolf (^{ou}oulf) n (pl wolves) loup m

woman (ouou-meunn) n (pl women) femme f

won (^{ou}ann) v (p, pp win)

wonder (ouann-deu) n miracle m; étonnement m; v se demander

wonderful (ouann-deu-feul) adj splendide, merveilleux; délicieux

wood (^{ou}oud) n bois m

wooded (ouou-did) adj boisé

wooden (ouou-deunn) adj en bois; ~ **shoe** sabot m

woodland (ououd-leunnd) n pays boisé

wool (^{ou}oul) n laine f; **darning** ~ laine à repriser

wool(l)en (ouou-leunn) adj en laine

word (^{ou}eûd) n mot m

wore (^{ou}oo) v (p wear)

work (^{ou}eûk) n travail m; activité f; v travailler; fonctionner; **working day** jour ouvrable; ~ **of art** œuvre d'art; ~ **permit** permis de travail

worker (oueû-keu) n ouvrier m, ouvrière f

working (oueû-kinng) n fonctionnement m

workman (oueûk-meunn) n (pl -men) ouvrier m

works (^{ou}eûks) pl usine f

workshop (oueûk-chop) n atelier m

world (^{ou}eûld) n monde m; ~ **war** guerre mondiale

world-famous (^{ou}eûld-féï-meuss) adj de renommée mondiale

world-wide (oueûld-^{ou}aïd) adj mondial

worm (^{ou}eûmm) n ver m

worn (^{ou}oon) adj (pp wear) usé

worn-out (^{ou}oon-aout) adj usé

worried (oua-rid) adj soucieux

worry (oua-ri) v s'inquiéter; n souci m, inquiétude f

worse (^{ou}eûss) adj pire; adv pire

worship (oueû-chip) v adorer; n culte m

worst (^{ou}eûst) adj le plus mauvais; adv le pire

worth (^{ou}eûθ) n valeur f; ***be** ~ *valoir; ***be worth-while** *valoir la peine

worthless (oueûθ-leuss) adj sans valeur

worthy of (oueû-ði euv) digne de

would (^{ou}oud) v (p will) *avoir l'habitude de

wound¹ (^{ou}oûnd) n blessure f; v offenser, blesser

wound² (^{ou}aound) v (p, pp wind)

wrap (ræp) v envelopper

wreck (rèk) n épave f; v *détruire

wrench (rèntch) n clé f; mouvement m violent de torsion; v tordre

wrinkle (*rinng*-keul) *n* ride *f*
wrist (rist) *n* poignet *m*
wristwatch (*rist*-^{ou}otch) *n* braceletmontre *m*
*write (raït) *v* *écrire; **in writing** par écrit; **~ down** noter
writer (*raï*-teu) *n* écrivain *m*
writing pad (*raï*-tinng-pæd) *n* blocnotes *m*

writing paper (*raï*-tinng-péï-peu) *n* papier à lettres
written (*ri*-teunn) *adj* (pp write) par écrit
wrong (ronng) *adj* impropre, incorrect; *n* tort *m*; *v* *faire tort à; ***be ~** *avoir tort
wrote (rô^{ou}t) *v* (p write)

X

Xmas (*kriss*-meuss) Noël
X-ray (*èks*-réï) *n* radiographie *f*; *v*
radiographier

Y

yacht (yot) *n* yacht *m*; **~ club** yacht-club *m*
yachting (*yo*-tinng) *n* yachting *m*
yard (yââd) *n* cour *f*
yarn (yâân) *n* fil *m*
yawn (yoon) *v* bâiller
year (yi^{eu}) *n* année *f*
yearly (*yieu*-li) *adj* annuel
yeast (yiist) *n* levure *f*
yell (yèl) *v* hurler; *n* cri *m*
yellow (*yè*-lô^{ou}) *adj* jaune
yes (yèss) oui
yesterday (*yè*-steu-di) *adv* hier
yet (yèt) *adv* encore; *conj* pourtant, cependant

yield (yiild) *v* rendre; céder
yoke (yô^{ou}k) *n* joug *m*
yolk (yô^{ou}k) *n* jaune d'œuf
you (yoû) *pron* tu; te; vous
young (yanng) *adj* jeune
your (yoo) *adj* votre; ton; vos
yours (yooz) le tien, la tienne, les tiens, les tiennes; à toi; le (la) vôtre, les vôtres; à vous
yourself (yoo-*sèlf*) *pron* te; toi-même; vous-même
yourselves (yoo-*sèlvz*) *pron* vous; vous-mêmes
youth (yoûθ) *n* jeunesse *f*; **~ hostel** auberge de jeunesse

Z

zap (zæp) *colloquial v* zapper;
  agresser; assommer; détruire, filer (à
  toute allure); *n* vigueur *f*, énergie *f*,
  entrain *m*

zeal (ziil) *n* zèle *m*

zealous (zè-leuss) *adj* zélé

zebra (*zii*-breu) *n* zèbre *m*

zenith (*zè*-niθ) *n* zénith *m*; apogée *m*

zero (*zieu*-rô^{ou}) *n* (pl ~s) zéro *m*

zest (zèst) *n* entrain *m*

zinc (zinngk) *n* zinc *m*

zip (zip) *n* fermeture éclair; ~ **code**
  Am code postal

zipper (*zi*-peu) *n* fermeture éclair

zodiac (*zô*ou-di-æk) *n* zodiaque *m*

zone (zô^{ou}n) *n* zone *f*; région *f*

zoo (zoû) *n* (pl ~s) zoo *m*

Lexique gastronomique

Mets

almond amande

anchovy anchois

angel food cake gâteau aux blancs d'œufs

angels on horseback huîtres enrobées de lard, grillées et servies sur toast

appetizer amuse-gueule

apple pomme

~ **dumpling** sorte de chausson aux pommes

~ **sauce** compote de pommes

Arbroath smoky églefin fumé

artichoke artichaut

asparagus asperge

~ **tip** pointe d'asperge

assorted varié

avocado (pear) avocat

bacon lard à griller

~ **and eggs** œufs au lard

bagel petit pain en forme de couronne

baked au four

~ **Alaska** omelette norvégienne

~ **beans** haricots blancs dans une sauce tomate

~ **potato** pomme de terre en robe des champs cuite au four

Bakewell tart gâteau aux amandes et à la confiture

banana banane

~ **split** banane coupée en tranches, servie avec de la glace et des noix, arrosée de sirop ou de crème au chocolat

barbecue 1) hachis de bœuf dans une sauce relevée aux tomates, servi dans un petit pain 2) repas en plein air

~ **sauce** sauce aux tomates très relevée

barbecued grillé au charbon de bois

basil basilic

bass bar

bean haricot, fève

beef bœuf

~ **olive** paupiette de bœuf

beefburger bifteck haché, grillé et servi dans un petit pain

beet, beetroot betterave rouge

bilberry myrtille

bill addition

~ **of fare** carte des mets, menu

biscuit 1) petit gâteau sec, biscuit (GB) 2) biscuit sec (US)

black pudding boudin noir

blackberry mûre

blackcurrant cassis

bloater hareng saur

blood sausage boudin noir

blueberry myrtille

boiled bouilli

Bologna (sausage) sorte de mortadelle

boloney sorte de mortadelle

bone os

boned désossé

Boston baked beans haricots blancs au lard et à la mélasse dans une sauce tomate

Boston cream pie tourte à la crème en couches superposées, glacée au chocolat

brains cervelle

braised braisé

bramble pudding pudding aux mûres (souvent servi avec des pommes)

braunschweiger saucisson au foie fumé

bread pain

breaded pané

breakfast petit déjeuner

bream brème (poisson)

breast poitrine, blanc de volaille

brisket poitrine de bœuf

broad bean grosse fève

broth bouillon

brown Betty sorte de charlotte aux pommes et aux épices recouverte de chapelure

brunch repas qui tient lieu de petit déjeuner et de déjeuner

Brussels sprouts choux de Bruxelles

bubble and squeak sorte de galette de pommes de terre et choux, parfois accompagnés de morceaux de bœuf

bun 1) petit pain au lait avec des fruits secs 2) sorte de petit pain (US)

butter beurre

buttered beurré

cabbage chou

Caesar salad salade verte, ail, anchois, croûtons et fromage râpé

cake gâteau

cakes pâtisseries

calf veau

Canadian bacon carré de porc fumé, coupé en fines tranches

caper câpre

capercaillie, capercailzie grand coq de bruyère

carp carpe

carrot carotte

cashew noix de cajou

casserole en cocotte

catfish poisson-chat

catsup ketchup

cauliflower chou-fleur

celery céleri

cereal céréale, cornflakes

hot ~ porridge

check addition

Cheddar (cheese) fromage à pâte dure au goût légèrement acide

cheese fromage

~ **board** plateau de fromages

~ **cake** gâteau au fromage double crème

cheeseburger bifteck haché, grillé avec une tranche de fromage, servi dans un petit pain

chef's salad salade de jambon, poulet, œufs durs, tomates, laitue et fromage

cherry cerise

chestnut marron

chicken poulet

chicory 1) endive (GB) 2) (e)scarole, chicorée (US)

chili con carne hachis de bœuf aux haricots rouges et aux piments rouges

chili pepper piment rouge

chips 1) pommes frites (GB) 2) pommes chips (US)

chitt(er)lings tripes de porc

chive ciboulette

chocolate chocolat

choice premier choix

chop côtelette

~ **suey** émincé de porc ou de poulet, de riz et de légumes

chopped émincé, haché

chowder bisque

Christmas pudding cake anglais aux fruits secs, parfois flambé; très nourrissant et servi à Noël

chutney condiment indien épicé à saveur aigre-douce

cinnamon cannelle

clam palourde

club sandwich double sandwich au *bacon*, poulet, tomate, salade et mayonnaise

cobbler tourte aux fruits

cock-a-leekie soup crème de volaille et de poireaux

coconut noix de coco

cod cabillaud

Colchester oyster huître anglaise très

renommée

cold cuts/meat assiette anglaise, viandes froides

coleslaw salade de chou cru

cooked cuit

cookie biscuit

corn 1) blé (GB) 2) maïs (US)
~ **on the cob** épi de maïs

cornflakes flocons de maïs

cottage cheese fromage blanc égoutté

cottage pie hachis de viande aux oignons recouvert de purée de pommes de terre

course plat

cover charge prix du couvert

crab crabe

cracker biscuit salé, craquelin

cranberry canneberge
~ **sauce** sauce à la canneberge

crawfish, crayfish 1) écrevisse 2) langouste (GB) 3) langoustine (US)

cream 1) crème 2) velouté (potage) 3) crème (dessert)
~ **cheese** fromage double crème
~ **puff** chou à la crème

creamed potatoes pommes de terre coupées en dés dans une sauce béchamel

creole mets très relevé, préparé avec des tomates, des poivrons et des oignons, servi avec du riz blanc

cress cresson

crisps pommes chips

crumpet petite crêpe épaisse servie chaude et beurrée

cucumber concombre

Cumberland ham jambon fumé très réputé

Cumberland sauce sauce aigredouce; vin, jus d'orange, zeste de citron, épices et gelée de groseilles

cupcake petit gâteau

cured salé et parfois fumé

currant 1) raisin de Corinthe 2) groseille

curried au curry

custard crème anglaise, flan

cutlet sorte d'escalope, fine tranche de viande, côtelette

dab limande

Danish pastry pâtisserie ou gâteau riche en levure

date datte

Derby cheese fromage à pâte molle et au goût piquant, de couleur jaune pâle

devilled à la diable; assaisonnement très relevé

devil's food cake tourte au chocolat

devils on horseback pruneaux cuits dans du vin rouge et farcis d'amandes et d'anchois, enrobés de lard et grillés

Devonshire cream double crème, très épaisse

diced coupé en dés

diet food aliment diététique

dill aneth

dinner dîner, repas du soir

dish plat, assiette, mets

donut, doughnut beignet en forme d'anneau

double cream double crème, crème entière

Dover sole sole de Douvres, très réputée

dressing 1) sauce à salade 2) farce pour la volaille (US)

Dublin Bay prawn langoustine

duck canard

duckling caneton

dumpling boulette de pâte

Dutch apple pie tarte aux pommes saupoudrée de cassonade ou nappée de mélasse

eel anguille

egg œuf
boiled ~ à la coque

fried ~ au plat
hard-boiled ~ dur
poached ~ poché
scrambled ~ brouillé
soft-boiled ~ mollet
eggplant aubergine
endive 1) (e)scarole, chicorée (GB) 2) endive (US)
entrée 1) entrée (GB) 2) plat principal (US)
fennel fenouil
fig figue
fillet filet de viande ou de poisson
finnan haddock églefin fumé
fish poisson
  ~ **and chips** filets de poisson frits et pommes frites
  ~ **cake** galette de poisson et de pommes de terre
flan tarte
flapjack matefaim, crêpe épaisse
flounder flet, plie
forcemeat farce, hachis
fowl volaille
frankfurter saucisse de Francfort
French bean haricot vert
French bread baguette
French dressing 1) vinaigrette (GB) 2) sauce à salade crémeuse assaisonnée de ketchup (US)
French fries pommes frites
French toast croûte dorée
fresh frais
fried frit, grillé
fritter beignet
frogs' legs cuisses de grenouilles
frosting glaçage
fry friture
game gibier
gammon jambon fumé
garfish aiguille de mer
garlic ail
garnish garniture
gherkin cornichon

giblets abats, abattis
ginger gingembre
goose oie
  ~**berry** groseille à maquereau
grape raisin
  ~**fruit** pamplemousse
grated râpé
gravy jus de viande épaissi
grayling omble
green bean haricot vert
green pepper poivron vert
green salad laitue, salade verte
greens garniture de légumes verts
grilled grillé
grilse saumoneau
grouse petit coq de bruyère
gumbo 1) gombo (légume d'origine africaine) 2) plat créole à base d'*okra*, de viande, de poisson ou de fruits de mer et de légumes
haddock églefin
haggis panse de mouton farcie aux flocons d'avoine
hake colin
half moitié, demi
halibut flétan
ham jambon
  ~ **and eggs** œufs au jambon
hare lièvre
haricot bean haricot blanc
hash 1) émincé 2) hachis de bœuf recouvert de pommes de terre
hazelnut noisette
heart cœur
herb herbe aromatique
herring hareng
home-made fait maison
hominy grits bouillie de maïs, sorte de polenta
honey miel
  ~**dew melon** variété de melon très doux à la chair vert-jaune
horse-radish raifort
hot 1) chaud 2) épicé

~ **cross bun** brioche aux raisins (se mange pendant le Carême)

~ **dog** hot-dog, saucisse chaude dans un petit pain

huckleberry myrtille

hush puppy beignet de farine de maïs

ice-cream glace

iced glacé

icing glaçage

Idaho baked potato pomme de terre en robe des champs cuite au four

Irish stew ragoût de mouton aux oignons et aux pommes de terre

Italian dressing vinaigrette

jam confiture

jellied en gelée

Jell-O dessert à la gélatine

jelly gelée de fruits

Jerusalem artichoke topinambour

John Dory Saint-Pierre (poisson)

jugged hare civet de lièvre

juice jus

juniper berry baie de genièvre

junket lait caillé sucré

kale chou frisé

kedgeree miettes depoisson au riz, aux œufs et au beurre

kidney rognon

kipper hareng fumé

lamb agneau

Lancashire hot pot ragoût de côtelettes, de rognons d'agneau, de pommes de terre et d'oignons

larded lardé

lean maigre

leek poireau

leg gigot, cuisse

lemon citron

~ **sole** limande-sole

lentil lentille

lettuce laitue, salade verte

lima bean fève

lime lime, citron vert

liver foie

loaf pain, miche

lobster homard

loin filet, carré

Long Island duck canard de Long Island, très réputé

low-calorie pauvre en calories

lox saumon fumé

lunch déjeuner, repas de midi

macaroon macaron

mackerel maquereau

maize maïs

mandarin mandarine

maple syrup sirop d'érable

marinated mariné

marjoram marjolaine

marmalade confiture d'orange ou d'autres agrumes, marmelade

marrow moelle

~ **bone** os à moelle

marshmallow bonbon à la guimauve

marzipan pâte d'amandes

mashed potatoes purée de pommes de terre

meal repas

meat viande

~ **ball** boulette de viande

~ **loaf** rôti haché

medium (done) à point

melted fondu

Melton Mowbray pie croustade de viande

milk lait

mince hachis

~ **pie** tartelette aux fruits confits et aux épices

minced haché

~ **meat** viande hachée

mint menthe

mixed mélangé, panaché

~ **grill** assortiment de grillades

molasses mélasse

morel morille

mulberry mûre

mullet mulet

mulligatawny soup potage au poulet, très épicé, d'origine indienne

mushroom champignon

muskmelon sorte de melon

mussel moule

mustard moutarde

mutton mouton

noodle nouille

nut noix

oatmeal (porridge) porridge, bouillie d'avoine

oil huile

okra pousse de *gumbo* généralement utilisée pour lier les potages et les ragoûts

omelet omelette

onion oignon

ox tongue langue de bœuf

oyster huître

pancake crêpe

parsley persil

parsnip panais (racine comestible)

partridge perdrix

pastry pâtisserie

pasty pâté, chausson, rissole

pea petit pois

peach pêche

peanut cacahuète

~ **butter** beurre de cacahuètes

pear poire

pearl barley orge perlé

pepper poivre

peppermint menthe (poivrée)

perch perche

persimmon kaki

pheasant faisan

pickerel brocheton (poisson)

pickle 1) légume ou fruit au vinaigre 2) cornichon (US)

pickled en saumure, au vinaigre

pie tarte, recouverte le plus souvent d'une couche de pâte, farcie ou garnie de viande, de légumes, de fruits ou de crème anglaise

pig porc

pike brochet

pineapple ananas

plaice plie, carrelet

plain nature

plate plat, assiette

plum 1) prune 2) pruneau 3) raisin sec

~ **pudding** cake anglais aux fruits secs, parfois flambé; très nourrissant et servi à Noël

poached poché

popcorn grains de maïs éclatés

popover petit pain au lait

pork porc

porterhouse steak épaisse tranche de filet de bœuf

pot roast bœuf braisé aux légumes

potato pomme de terre

~ **chips** 1) pommes frites (GB) 2) pommes chips (US)

~ **in its jacket** pomme de terre en robe des champs

potted shrimps crevettes au beurre épicé (fondu et refroidi)

poultry volaille

prawn grosse crevette rose

prune pruneau

ptarmigan perdrix des neiges

pudding pudding (mou ou consistant) à base de farine, garni de viande, de poisson, de légumes ou de fruits

pumpernickel pain de seigle complet

pumpkin potiron, courge

quail caille

quince coing

rabbit lapin

radish radis

rainbow trout truite arc-en-ciel

raisin raisin sec

rare saignant

raspberry framboise

raw cru

red mullet rouget

red (sweet) pepper poivron rouge

redcurrant groseille rouge

relish condiment fait de légumes émincés au vinaigre

rhubarb rhubarbe

rib (of beef) côte (de bœuf)

rib-eye steak entrecôte

rice riz

rissole croquette de viande ou de poisson

river trout truite de rivière

roast(ed) rôti(e)

Rock Cornish hen variété de poulet de grain

roe œufs de poisson

roll petit pain

rollmop herring filet de hareng mariné au vin blanc, enroulé sur un cornichon

round steak quasi de bœuf

Rubens sandwich corned-beef sur toast, avec choucroute, emmenthal et sauce à salade, servi chaud

rumpsteak rumsteak

rusk biscotte

rye bread pain de seigle

saddle selle

saffron safran

sage sauge

salad salade

  ~ bar choix de salades

  ~ cream sauce à salade crémeuse, légèrement sucrée

  ~ dressing sauce pour salade

salmon saumon

  ~ trout truite saumonée

salt sel

salted salé

sauerkraut choucroute

sausage saucisse, saucisson

sauté(ed) sauté

scallop 1) peigne (coquille Saint-Jacques 2) escalope de veau

scone petit pain tendre à base de farine de blé ou d'orge

Scotch broth soupe à base d'agneau ou de bœuf et de légumes

Scotch woodcock toast avec œufs brouillés et beurre d'anchois

sea bass loup de mer

sea kale chou marin

seafood poissons et fruits de mer

(in) season (en) saison

seasoning assaisonnement

service charge montant à payer pour le service

service (not) included service (non) compris

set menu menu fixe

shad alose (sorte de sardine)

shallot échalote

shellfish crustacé

sherbet sorbet

shoulder épaule

shredded wheat croquettes de froment (servies au petit déjeuner)

shrimp crevette

silverside (of beef) gîte (de bœuf)

sirloin steak steak d'aloyau

skewer brochette

slice tranche

sliced coupé en tranches

sloppy Joe hachis de bœuf dans une sauce relevée aux tomates, servi dans un petit pain

smelt éperlan

smoked fumé

snack casse-croûte

soup potage, soupe

sour aigre

soused herring hareng au vinaigre et aux épices

spare rib côte de porc grillée

spice épice

spinach épinard

spiny lobster langouste

(on a) spit (à la) broche

sponge cake gâteau mousseline

sprat harenguet

squash courge

starter hors-d'œuvre

steak and kidney pie croustade de viande de bœuf et de rognons

steamed cuit à la vapeur

stew ragoût

Stilton (cheese) fromage anglais réputé (blanc ou à moisissures bleues)

strawberry fraise

string bean haricot vert

stuffed farci, fourré

stuffing farce

suck(l)ing pig cochon de lait

sugar sucre

sugarless sans sucre

sundae coupe de glace aux fruits, noix, crème Chantilly et parfois sirop

supper souper, léger repas du soir

swede rutabaga

sweet 1) doux 2) dessert

~ corn maïs jaune

~ potato patate douce

sweetbread ris de veau

Swiss cheese emmenthal

Swiss roll biscuit roulé à la confiture

Swiss steak tranche de bœuf braisée avec des légumes et des épices

T-bone steak morceau de contrefilet et de filet séparés par un os en forme de T

table d'hôte repas à prix fixe

tangerine mandarine

tarragon estragon

tart tarte (généralement aux fruits)

tenderloin filet (de viande)

Thousand Island dressing mayonnaise aux piments ou au ketchup, avec des poivrons, des olives et des œufs durs

thyme thym

toad-in-the-hole morceaux de viande ou de saucisse briochés

toasted grillé

~ cheese toast au fromage

tomato tomate

tongue langue

treacle mélasse

trifle sorte de charlotte russe à l'eau-de-vie avec amandes, confiture, crème Chantilly et crème anglaise

trout truite

truffle truffe

tuna, tunny thon

turkey dinde

turnip navet

turnover chausson

turtle tortue

underdone saignant

vanilla vanille

veal veau

~ bird paupiette de veau

vegetable légume

~ marrow courge

venison gros gibier

vichyssoise soupe froide aux poireaux, pommes de terre et crème

vinegar vinaigre

Virginia baked ham jambon cuit au four, piqué de clous de girofles, garni de tranches d'ananas, de cerises et glacé avec le jus des fruits

wafer gaufrette

waffle sorte de gaufre, chaude

walnut noix

water ice sorbet

watercress cresson de fontaine

watermelon pastèque

well-done bien cuit

Welsh rabbit/rarebit croûte au fromage

whelk buccin (mollusque)

whipped cream crème Chantilly

whitebait blanchaille

Wiener Schnitzel escalope viennoise

wine list carte des vins

woodcock bécasse

Worcestershire sauce condiment

liquide piquant, à base de vinaigre, de soja et d'ail

yoghurt yaourt

York ham jambon (fumé) d'York

Yorkshire pudding sorte de pâte à choux cuite et servie avec le rosbif

zucchini courgette

zwieback biscotte

Boissons

ale bière brune, légèrement sucrée, fermentée à haute température

bitter ~ brune, amère et plutôt lourde

brown ~ brune en bouteille, légèrement sucrée

light ~ blonde en bouteille

mild ~ brune à la pression, au goût prononcé

pale ~ blonde en bouteille

angostura essence aromatique amère ajoutée aux cocktails

applejack eau-de-vie de pomme

Athol Brose boisson écossaise composée de whisky, de miel, d'eau et parfois de flocons d'avoine

Bacardi cocktail cocktail au rhum avec du gin, du sirop de grenadine et du jus de lime (citron vert)

barley water boisson rafraîchissante à base d'orge et aromatisée de citron

barley wine bière brune très alcoolisée

beer bière

bottled ~ en bouteille

draft, draught ~ à la pression

bitters apéritifs et digestifs à base de racines, d'écorces ou d'herbes

black velvet champagne additionné de *stout* (accompagne souvent les huîtres)

bloody Mary vodka, jus de tomate et épices

bourbon whisky américain, à base de maïs

brandy 1) appellation générique désignant les eaux-de-vie de vin ou de fruit 2) cognac

~ Alexander mélange d'eau-de-vie, de crème de cacao et de crème fraîche

British wines vins «anglais» faits de raisins (ou de jus de raisin) importés en Grande-Bretagne

cherry brandy liqueur de cerise

chocolate chocolat

cider cidre

~ cup mélange de cidre, d'épices, de sucre et de glace

claret vin rouge de Bordeaux

cobbler *long drink* glacé à base de fruits, auquel on ajoute du vin ou une liqueur

coffee café

~ with cream crème

black ~ noir

caffeine-free ~ décaféiné

white ~ au lait

cordial liqueur

cream crème

cup boisson rafraîchissante composée de vin glacé, d'eau gazeuse, d'un spiritueux et décorée d'une tranche d'orange, de citron ou de concombre

daiquiri cocktail au rhum, au jus de lime et d'ananas

double double dose

Drambuie liqueur à base de whisky et de miel

dry martini 1) vermouth sec (GB) 2) cocktail au gin avec un peu de vermouth sec (US)

egg-nog boisson faite de rhum ou d'un autre alcool fort avec des jaunes d'œufs battus et du sucre

gin and it mélange de gin et de vermouth italien

gin-fizz gin avec jus de citron, sucre et soda

ginger ale boisson sans alcool, parfumée à l'essence de gingembre

ginger beer boisson légèrement alcoolisée, à base de gingembre et de sucre

grasshopper mélange de crème de menthe, de crème de cacao et de crème fraîche

Guinness (stout) bière brune légèrement sucrée, au goût très prononcé et à forte teneur en malt et houblon

half pint environ 3 décilitres

highball eau-de-vie ou whisky allongé d'eau gazeuse ou de *ginger ale*

iced glacé

Irish coffee café sucré, arrosé de whisky irlandais et nappé de crème Chantilly

Irish Mist liqueur irlandaise à base de whisky et de miel

Irish whiskey whisky irlandais, moins âpre que le *scotch*; outre l'orge, il contient du seigle, de l'avoine et du blé

juice jus

lager bière blonde légère, servie très fraîche

lemon squash citronnade

lemonade limonade

lime juice jus de lime (citron vert)

liquor spiritueux

long drink alcool allongé d'eau ou d'une boisson gazeuse, avec des glaçons

madeira madère

Manhattan whisky américain, vermouth et *angostura*

milk lait

~ shake frappé

mineral water eau minérale

mulled wine vin chaud aux épices

neat sans glace et sans eau, sec, pur

old-fashioned whisky, *angostura*, cerises au marasquin et sucre

on the rocks avec des glaçons

Ovaltine Ovomaltine

Pimm's cup(s) boisson alcoolisée mélangée à du jus de fruit ou du soda

~ No. 1 à base de gin

~ No. 2 à base de whisky

~ No. 3 à base de rhum

~ No. 4 à base d'eau-de-vie

pink champagne champagne rosé

pink lady mélange de blanc d'œuf, de Calvados, de jus de citron, de grenadine et de gin

pint environ 6 décilitres

port (wine) porto

porter bière brune et amère

quart 1,14 litre (US 0,95 litre)

root beer boisson gazeuse sucrée, aromatisée d'herbes et de racines

rum rhum

rye (whiskey) whisky de seigle, plus lourd et plus âpre que le *bourbon*

scotch (whisky) whisky écossais, généralement fait d'une combinaison de whisky d'orge et de whisky de blé

screwdriver vodka et jus d'orange

shandy *bitter ale* mélangée à une limonade ou une *ginger beer*

sherry xérès

short drink tout alcool non dilué

shot dose de spiritueux

sloe gin-fizz liqueur de prunelle avec soda et jus de citron

soda water eau de Seltz

soft drink boisson sans alcool
spirits spiritueux
stinger cognac et crème de menthe
stout bière brune fortement
houblonnée et alcoolisée
straight alcool bu sec, pur
tea thé
toddy grog
Tom Collins gin, jus de citron, sucre,
eau gazeuse
tonic (water) eau gazéifiée,
aromatisée de quinine
water eau
whisky sour whisky, jus de citron,
sucre et soda
wine vin
  dry ~ sec
  red ~ rouge
  sparkling ~ mousseux
  sweet ~ doux (de dessert) **white ~**
  blanc

Mini-grammaire anglaise

L'article

L'article défini (le, la, les) a une seule forme: *the*.

the room, the rooms   la chambre, les chambres

L'article indéfini (un, une, des) a deux formes: *a* s'emploie devant une consonne, *an* devant une voyelle ou un «h» muet.

a coat	un manteau
an umbrella	un parapluie
an hour	une heure

Some indique une quantité ou un nombre indéfini.

I'd like some water, please.   Je voudrais de l'eau, s.v.p.

Any s'emploie dans les phrases négatives et différents types d'interrogatives.

There isn't any soap.	Il n'y a pas de savon.
Do you have any stamps?	Avez-vous des timbres?

Le nom

Le pluriel de la plupart des noms se forme par l'addition de *-(e)s* au singulier.

cup – cups (tasse – tasses)   **dress – dresses** (robe – robes)

Note: Si un nom se termine par *-y* précédé d'une consonne, le pluriel se termine par *-ies*; si le *-y* est précédé d'une voyelle, il n'y a pas de changement.

lady – ladies (dame – dames)   **key – keys** (clef – clefs)

Quelques pluriels irréguliers:

man – men (homme – hommes)	**foot – feet** (pied – pieds)
woman – women (femme – femmes)	**tooth – teeth** (dent – dents)
child – children (enfant – enfants)	**mouse – mice** (souris – souris)

Le complément du nom (génitif)

1. Le possesseur est une personne: si le nom ne se termine pas par *-s*, on ajoute *'s*.

the boy's room	la chambre du garçon
the children's clothes	les vêtements des enfants

Si le nom se termine par *s*, on ajoute l'apostrophe (').

the boys' room   la chambre des garçons

2. Le possesseur n'est pas une personne: on utilise la préposition *of*:

the key of the door   la clef de la porte

L'adjectif

Les adjectifs se placent normalement avant le nom.

a large brown suitcase   une grande valise brune

Il y a deux façons de former le comparatif et le superlatif des adjectifs:

1. Les adjectifs d'une syllabe et de nombreux adjectifs de deux syllabes prennent la terminaison -(e)r et -(e)st.

small (petit) – **smaller** – **smallest**   pretty (joli) – **prettier** – **prettiest***

2. Les adjectifs de trois syllabes et plus, et certains de deux (en particulier ceux qui se terminent par -ful et -less) forment leurs comparatifs et superlatifs avec more et most.

expensive (cher) – **more expensive** – **most expensive**

Le pronom

		Sujet	Complément (dir./indir.)	Possessif 1	2
Singulier					
1ʳᵉ personne		**I**	**me**	**my**	**mine**
2ᵉ personne		**you**	**you**	**your**	**yours**
3ᵉ personne	(m)	**he**	**him**	**his**	**his**
	(f)	**she**	**her**	**her**	**hers**
	(n)	**it**	**it**	**its**	–
Pluriel					
1ʳᵉ personne		**we**	**us**	**our**	**ours**
2ᵉ personne		**you**	**you**	**your**	**yours**
3ᵉ personne		**they**	**them**	**their**	**their**

Note: L'anglais ignore le tutoiement. La forme *you* signifie donc «tu» et «vous».

Le cas complément s'emploie aussi après les prépositions.

Give it to me.   Donnez-le-moi.

La forme 1 du possessif correspond à «mon», «ton», etc., la forme 2 à «le mien», «le tien», etc.

Where's my key? Où est ma clef? **That's not mine.** Ce n'est pas la mienne.

---

* L'«y» se change en «i» lorsqu'il est précédé d'une consonne.

Verbes auxiliaires

a. **to be** (être)

	Forme contractée	Négatif – formes contractées	
I am	I'm		I'm not
you are	you're	you're not	ou you aren't
he is	he's	he's not	he isn't
she is	she's	she's not	she isn't
it is	it's	it's not	it isn't
we are	we're	we're not	we aren't
they are	they're	they're not	they aren't

Interrogatif: **Am I? Are you? Is he?** etc.

b. **to have** (avoir)

	Contraction		Contraction
I have	I've	we have	we've
you have	you've	you have	you've
he/she/it has	he/she/it's	they have	they've

Négation: **I have not (I haven't)**
Interrogation: **Have you? – Has he?**

c. **to do** (faire)

	Négatif contracté		Négatif contracté
I do	I don't	we do	we don't
you do	you don't	you do	you don't
he/she/it does	he/she/it doesn't	they do	they don't

Interrogation: **Do you? Does he/she/it?**

Autres verbes

L'infinitif est utilisé pour toutes les personnes du présent; on ajoute simplement
-(e)s à la 3ᵉ personne du singulier.

	(to) love (aimer)	**(to) come** (venir)	**(to) go** (aller)
I	love	come	go
you	love	come	go
he/she/it	loves	comes	goes
we	love	come	go
they	love	come	go

La négation se forme au moyen de l'auxiliaire *do/does* + *not* + infinitif du verbe.

We do not (don't) like this hotel.   Nous n'aimons pas cet hôtel.

L'interrogation se forme aussi avec l'auxiliaire *do* + sujet + infinitif.

Do you like her?   L'aimez-vous?

Verbes irréguliers

L'imparfait et le participe passé des verbes réguliers se forment en ajoutant -(e)d à l'infinitif. La liste suivante vous donne les verbes irréguliers anglais. Les verbes composés ou précédés d'un préfixe se conjuguent comme les verbes principaux: p.ex. *withdraw* se conjugue comme *draw* et *mistake* comme *take*.

Infinitif	Imparfait	Participe passé	
arise	arose	arisen	*(se) lever*
awake	awoke	awoken	*(se) réveiller*
be	was	been	*être*
bear	bore	borne	*porter*
beat	beat	beaten	*battre*
become	became	become	*devenir*
begin	began	begun	*commencer*
bend	bent	bent	*plier*
bet	bet	bet	*parier*
bid	bade/bid	bidden/bid	*ordonner*
bind	bound	bound	*attacher*
bite	bit	bitten	*mordre*
bleed	bled	bled	*saigner*
blow	blew	blown	*souffler*
break	broke	broken	*briser*
breed	bred	bred	*élever*
bring	brought	brought	*apporter*
build	built	built	*bâtir*
burn	burnt/burned	burnt/burned	*brler*
burst	burst	burst	*éclater*
buy	bought	bought	*acheter*
can*	could	–	*pouvoir*
cast	cast	cast	*jeter*
catch	caught	caught	*attraper*
choose	chose	chosen	*choisir*
cling	clung	clung	*se cramponner*
clothe	clothed/clad	clothed/clad	*vêtir*
come	came	come	*venir*
cost	cost	cost	*coter*
creep	crept	crept	*ramper*
cut	cut	cut	*couper*
deal	dealt	dealt	*conclure (marché)*
dig	dug	dug	*creuser*
do (he does)	did	done	*faire*

---

* présent de l'indicatif

draw	drew	drawn	*dessiner*
dream	dreamt/dreamed	dreamt/dreamed	*rêver*
drink	drank	drunk	*boire*
drive	drove	driven	*conduire (auto)*
dwell	dwelt	dwelt	*habiter*
eat	ate	eaten	*manger*
fall	fell	fallen	*tomber*
feed	fed	fed	*nourrir*
feel	felt	felt	*ressentir*
fight	fought	fought	*combattre*
find	found	found	*trouver*
flee	fled	fled	*fuir*
fling	flung	flung	*lancer*
fly	flew	flown	*voler*
forsake	forsook	forsaken	*abandonner*
freeze	froze	frozen	*geler*
get	got	got	*obtenir*
give	gave	given	*donner*
go	went	gone	*aller*
grind	ground	ground	*moudre*
grow	grew	grown	*croître*
hang	hung	hung	*pendre*
have	had	had	*avoir*
hear	heard	heard	*entendre*
hew	hewed	hewed/hewn	*couper*
hide	hid	hidden	*cacher*
hit	hit	hit	*frapper*
hold	held	held	*tenir*
hurt	hurt	hurt	*blesser*
keep	kept	kept	*garder*
kneel	knelt	knelt	*s'agenouiller*
knit	knitted/knit	knitted/knit	*tricoter/unir*
know	knew	known	*savoir*
lay	laid	laid	*étendre, placer*
lead	led	led	*guider*
lean	leant/leaned	leant/leaned	*s'appuyer*
leap	leapt/leaped	leapt/leaped	*sauter*
learn	learnt/learned	learnt/learned	*apprendre*
leave	left	left	*quitter*
lend	lent	lent	*prêter*
let	let	let	*permettre*
lie	lay	lain	*être couché*
light	lit/lighted	lit/lighted	*allumer*
lose	lost	lost	*perdre*

make	made	made	*faire*
may*	might	–	*pouvoir*
mean	meant	meant	*signifier*
meet	met	met	*rencontrer*
mow	mowed	mowed/mown	*faucher*
must*	–	–	*falloir*
ought (to)*	–	–	*devoir*
pay	paid	paid	*payer*
put	put	put	*mettre*
read	read	read	*lire*
rid	rid	rid	*débarrasser*
ride	rode	ridden	*monter (à cheval)*
ring	rang	rung	*sonner*
rise	rose	risen	*se lever*
run	ran	run	*courir*
saw	sawed	sawn	*scier*
say	said	said	*dire*
see	saw	seen	*voir*
seek	sought	sought	*chercher*
sell	sold	sold	*vendre*
send	sent	sent	*envoyer*
set	set	set	*poser*
sew	sewed	sewed/sewn	*coudre*
shake	shook	shaken	*secouer*
shall*	should	–	*devoir*
shed	shed	shed	*verser*
shine	shone	shone	*briller*
shoot	shot	shot	*tirer*
show	showed	shown	*montrer*
shrink	shrank	shrunk	*rétrécir*
shut	shut	shut	*fermer*
sing	sang	sung	*chanter*
sink	sank	sunk	*couler*
sit	sat	sat	*s'asseoir*
sleep	slept	slept	*dormir*
slide	slid	slid	*glisser*
sling	slung	slung	*jeter*
slink	slunk	slunk	*s'esquiver*
slit	slit	slit	*fendre*
smell	smelled/smelt	smelled/smelt	*sentir (odeur)*
sow	sowed	sown/sowed	*semer*
speak	spoke	spoken	*parler*

* présent de l'indicatif

speed	sped/speeded	sped/speeded	*accélérer*
spell	spelt/spelled	spelt/spelled	*épeler*
spend	spent	spent	*dépenser*
spill	spilt/spilled	spilt/spilled	*renverser*
spin	spun	spun	*filer*
spit	spat	spat	*cracher*
split	split	split	*fendre, séparer*
spoil	spoilt/spoiled	spoilt/spoiled	*gâter*
spread	spread	spread	*répandre, enduire*
spring	sprang	sprung	*jaillir*
stand	stood	stood	*se tenir debout*
steal	stole	stolen	*dérober*
stick	stuck	stuck	*coller*
sting	stung	stung	*piquer*
stink	stank/stunk	stunk	*empester*
strew	strewed	strewed/strewn	*joncher*
stride	strode	stridden	*marcher à grands pas*
strike	struck	struck/stricken	*frapper*
string	strung	strung	*ficeler*
strive	strove	striven	*s'efforcer*
swear	swore	sworn	*jurer*
sweep	swept	swept	*balayer*
swell	swelled	swollen	*enfler*
swim	swam	swum	*nager*
swing	swung	swung	*se balancer*
take	took	taken	*prendre*
teach	taught	taught	*enseigner*
tear	tore	torn	*déchirer*
tell	told	told	*dire*
think	thought	thought	*penser*
throw	threw	thrown	*jeter*
thrust	thrust	thrust	*pousser*
tread	trod	trodden	*piétiner*
wake	woke/waked	woken/waked	*(se) réveiller*
wear	wore	worn	*porter (habit)*
weave	wove	woven	*tisser*
weep	wept	wept	*pleurer*
will*	would	–	*vouloir*
win	won	won	*gagner*
wind	wound	wound	*enrouler*
wring	wrung	wrung	*tordre*
write	wrote	written	*écrire*

* présent de l'indicatif

Abréviations anglaises

AA	*Automobile Association*	Automobile Club de Grande-Bretagne
AAA	*American Automobile Association*	Automobile Club des Etats-Unis
ABC	*Amercican Broadcasting Company*	société privée de radio-diffusion et de télévision (US)
A.D.	*anno Domini*	apr. J.-C.
AIDS	*acquired immune deficiency syndrome*	SIDA
Am.	*America; American*	Amérique; américain
a.m.	*ante meridiem (before noon)*	du matin (de minuit à midi)
Amtrak	*American railroad corporation*	société privée des chemins de fer américains
AT & T	*American Telephone and Telegraph Company*	compagnie privée des télé-phones et télégraphes (US)
Ave.	*avenue*	avenue
BBC	*British Broadcasting Corporation*	société britannique de radio-diffusion et de télévision
B.C.	*before Christ*	av. J.-C.
bldg.	*building*	immeuble
Blvd.	*boulevard*	boulevard
B.R.	*British Rail*	chemins de fer britanniques
Brit.	*Britain; British*	Grande-Bretagne; britannique
Bros.	*brothers*	frères
¢	*cent*	1/100 de dollar
Can.	*Canada; Canadian*	Canada; canadien
CBS	*Columbia Broadcasting System*	société privée de radiodiffu-sion et de télévision (US)
CID	*Criminal Investigation Department*	police judiciaire (GB)
CNN	*Cable News Network*	société privée de télévision
CNR	*Canadian National Railway*	société nationale des chemins de fer canadiens
c/o	*(in) care of*	p.a., aux bons soins de
Co.	*company*	compagnie
Corp.	*corporation*	type de société
CPR	*Canadian Pacific Railways*	société privée des chemins de fer canadiens
D.C.	*District of Columbia*	District de Columbia (Washington, D.C.)

DDS	*Doctor of Dental Science*	dentiste
dept.	*department*	département
e.g.	*for instance*	par exemple
Eng.	*England; English*	Angleterre; anglais
EU	*European Union*	UE
excl.	*excluding; exclusive*	non compris, exclu
ft.	*foot/feet*	pied/pieds (30,5 cm)
GB	*Great Britain*	Grande-Bretagne
H.E.	*His/Her Excellency;*	Son Excellence;
	His Eminence	Son Eminence
H.H.	*His Holiness*	Sa Sainteté
H.M.	*His/Her Majesty*	Sa Mejesté
H.M.S.	*Her Majesty's ship*	bâtiment de la marine royale
		de Grande-Bretagne
hp	*horsepower*	chevaux-vapeur
i.e.	*that is to say*	c'est-à-dire
in.	*inch*	pouce (2,54 cm)
Inc.	*incorporated*	type de société anonyme
		américaine
incl.	*including, inclusive*	compris, inclus
£	*pound sterling*	livre sterling
L.A.	*Los Angeles*	Los Angeles
Ltd.	*limited*	type de société anonyme
		britannique
M.D.	*Doctor of Medicine*	médecin
M.P.	*Member of Parliament*	membre du Parlement
		britannique
mph	*miles per hour*	miles à l'heure
Mr	*Mister*	Monsieur
Mrs	*Missis*	Madame
Ms	*Missis/Miss*	Madame/Mademoiselle
nat.	*national*	national
NBC	*National Broadcasting*	société privée de radiodiffu-
	Company	sion et de télévision (US)
No.	*number*	numéro
N.Y.C.	*New York City*	ville de New York
O.B.E.	*Officer (of the Order)*	Officier de l'Ordre de l'Empire
	of the British Empire	britannique
p.	*page; penny/pence*	page; 1/100 de livre sterling
p.a.	*per annum*	par an, annuel
Ph.D.	*Doctor of Philosophy*	docteur en philosophie
p.m.	*post meridiem*	de l'après-midi/du soir
	(after noon)	(de midi à minuit)
PO	*Post Office*	bureau de poste

P.T.O.	*please turn over*	tournez, s'il vous plaît
RAC	*Royal Automobile Club*	Automobile Club de Grande-Bretagne
RCMP	*Royal Canadian Mounted Police*	police royale montée canadienne
Rd.	*road*	route, rue
ref.	*reference*	voir, comparer
Rev.	*reverend*	pasteur dans l'Eglise anglicane
RFD	*rural free delivery*	distribution du courrier à la campagne
RR	*railroad*	chemin de fer
RSVP	*please reply*	répondez, s'il vous plaît
$	*dollar*	dollar
soc.	*society*	société
St.	*saint; street*	saint; rue
STD	*Subscriber Trunk Dialling*	téléphone automatique
UK	*United Kingdom*	Royaume-Uni
UN	*United Nations*	Nations Unies
UPS	*United Parcel Service*	service d'expédition de colis (US)
US	*United States*	Etats-Unis
USS	*United States Ship*	bâtiment de la marine de guerre américaine
VAT	*value added tax*	TVA
VIP	*very important person*	personne jouissant de privilèges particuliers
Xmas	*Christmas*	Noël
yd.	*yard*	yard (91,44 cm)
YMCA	*Young Men's Christian Association*	Union Chrétienne de Jeunes Gens
YWCA	*Young Women's Christian Association*	Union Chrétienne de Jeunes Filles
ZIP	*ZIP code*	code postal

Nombres

Nombres cardinaux

0	zero
1	one
2	two
3	three
4	four
5	five
6	six
7	seven
8	eight
9	nine
10	ten
11	eleven
12	twelve
13	thirteen
14	fourteen
15	fifteen
16	sixteen
17	seventeen
18	eighteen
19	nineteen
20	twenty
21	twenty-one
22	twenty-two
23	twenty-three
24	twenty-four
25	twenty-five
30	thirty
40	forty
50	fifty
60	sixty
70	seventy
80	eighty
90	ninety
100	a/one hundred
230	two hundred and thirty
500	five hundred
1,000	a/one thousand
10,000	ten thousand
100,000	a/one hundred thousand
1,000,000	a/one million

Nombres ordinaux

1st	first
2nd	second
3rd	third
4th	fourth
5th	fifth
6th	sixth
7th	seventh
8th	eighth
9th	ninth
10th	tenth
11th	eleventh
12th	twelfth
13th	thirteenth
14th	fourteenth
15th	fifteenth
16th	sixteenth
17th	seventeenth
18th	eighteenth
19th	nineteenth
20th	twentieth
21st	twenty-first
22nd	twenty-second
23rd	twenty-third
24th	twenty-fourth
25th	twenty-fifth
26th	twenty-sixth
27th	twenty-seventh
28th	twenty-eighth
29th	twenty-ninth
30th	thirtieth
40th	fortieth
50th	fiftieth
60th	sixtieth
70th	seventieth
80th	eightieth
90th	ninetieth
100th	hundredth
230th	two hundred and thirtieth
500th	five hundredth
1,000th	thousandth

L'heure

Les Britanniques et les Américains utilisent le système des douze heures. L'expression *a.m.* (*ante meridiem*) désigne les heures précédant midi, *p.m.* (*post meridiem*) celles de l'après-midi et du soir (jusqu'à minuit).
Toutefois, en Grande-Bretagne, les horaires sont progressivement libellés sur le modèle continental.

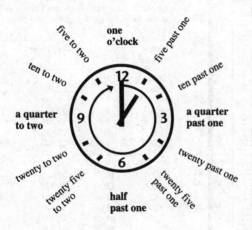

I'll come at seven a.m.	Je viendrai à 7 h. du matin.
I'll come at one p.m.	Je viendrai à 1 h. de l'après-midi.
I'll come at eight p.m.	Je viendrai à 8 h. du soir.

Les jours de la semaine

Sunday	dimanche	*Thursday*	jeudi
Monday	lundi	*Friday*	vendredi
Tuesday	mardi	*Saturday*	samedi
Wednesday	mercredi		

Conversion tables/
Tables de conversion

Metres and feet

The figure in the middle stands for both metres and feet, e.g. 1 metre = 3.281 ft. and 1 foot = 0.30 m.

Mètres et pieds

Le chiffre du milieu représente à la fois des mètres et des pieds. Par ex.: 1 mètre = 3,281 pieds et 1 pied = 0,30 m.

Metres/ Mètres		Feet/Pieds
0.30	**1**	3.281
0.61	**2**	6.563
0.91	**3**	9.843
1.22	**4**	13.124
1.52	**5**	16.403
1.83	**6**	19.686
2.13	**7**	22.967
2.44	**8**	26.248
2.74	**9**	29.529
3.05	**10**	32.810
3.66	**12**	39.372
4.27	**14**	45.934
6.10	**20**	65.620
7.62	**25**	82.023
15.24	**50**	164.046
22.86	**75**	246.069
30.48	**100**	328.092

Temperature

To convert Centigrade to Fahrenheit, multiply by 1.8 and add 32.
To convert Fahrenheit to Centigrade, subtract 32 from Fahrenheit and divide by 1.8.

Température

Pour convertir les degrés centigrades en degrés Fahrenheit, multipliez les premiers par 1,8 et ajoutez 32 au total obtenu.